Read this first!

Here's how to find the incredible wedding and special event information in *Here Comes The Guide:*

- **Event Venues**

    Sites are organized by region and city, with illustrated descriptions and details about capacities, fees and services. To find a specific site, see the index starting on page 575.

- **CERTIFIED BY THE GUIDE Event Services**

    We feature some of Southern California's best event professionals. To review the ones in this book, see pages 554–571. To see all of the caterers, coordinators, photographers, florists, DJs, etc. we've certified, go to HereComesTheGuide.com. And to find out how our vendors qualified to be in Here Comes The Guide, read page 549.

- **Useful Questions to Ask Venues & Event Professionals**

    Not sure what to ask a potential event location, photographer, caterer, etc.? Our lists of questions on pages 19–40 will make it easier for you to interview them and help you decide who to hire.

Don't forget to check out HereComesTheGuide.com!

HereComesTheGuide.com has the most up-to-date information on event venues, services and bridal fairs—as well as lots of photos and virtual tours. And if you have a certain type of location or event professional in mind, you'll really appreciate our amazingly useful search engine. We make it easy to find exactly what you're looking for.

Our Cover Photographer

Elizabeth Messina Photography

We confess to having a geeked-out gushing fan moment when the amazing, award-winning Elizabeth Messina let us use one of her photos on the front of our current book. We've always swooned over her lush images, which have graced the covers and lavish editorial spreads of just about every wedding publication out there. Now it's our turn!

With all the admiration she receives, Elizabeth is surprisingly humble—no diva attitude here! Her personal story has no doubt shaped her down-to-earth temperament. Elizabeth's love affair with photography was sparked at age 12, with her mother's gift of a Nikon FE2. Raised in California, she attended the San Francisco Art Institute where she began to develop her photographic signature.

After graduating with honors, she took her camera on an eye-opening cross-country bicycle trek. She then worked as a photographer for an East Coast newspaper until an apartment fire destroyed everything she owned. The only possession she still had was her camera. That rock-bottom moment profoundly influenced Elizabeth's artistry and deepened her commitment to photography. It also crystalized her strength and tenacious spirit. "The secret is to never give up, no matter what comes your way."

Today, she's at the top of her field. Elizabeth prefers to create images with film, because it has such latitude and gracefully captures light and tone variations. Her eye is instinctively drawn to the luminous quality inherent in shapes, textures and composition: Through her lens, the drape of a gown…the gentle play of sunshine through lace…the soft pastels of a bouquet… are like elements in an impressionist painting.

Yet perhaps Elizabeth's most consistent inspiration is relationships. "As a woman and an artist, I'm intrigued by the nuances of love." Her own emotional receptivity has also been enhanced by her craft. "The language of photography opened my heart," she acknowledges. And while her heart is open, so is her mind—she has long been a supporter of marriage equality and ethnic and religious diversity: "Love is love is love is love is beautiful …"

A happily married mother of three, Elizabeth excels at capturing the unspoken interplay between lovers. Her intimate compositions evoke Romance with a capital "R"—not only as a sentiment, but also as an appreciation of nature, authenticity and individuality. "Every couple is unique and special, so at each and every wedding I'm able to witness touching and poignant moments."

Often, those moments have a sweet playfulness about them, as in our cover image. The newlyweds' mirrored expressions and "we've got a secret" smiles can't help but charm the viewer. To us, their entwined bodies leaning into each other suggested a heart as the perfect emblem.

While there are no certainties on your wedding day, there's one thing we know for sure: Elizabeth Messina Photography = Guaranteed Gorgeous.

You can learn more about Elizabeth Messina in her book, The Luminous Portrait; *on ElizabethMessina.com; on her blog, "Kiss the Groom;" on Instagram @elizabethmessina; and on twitter @kissthegroom.*

Back cover photos also provided by Elizabeth Messina Photography.

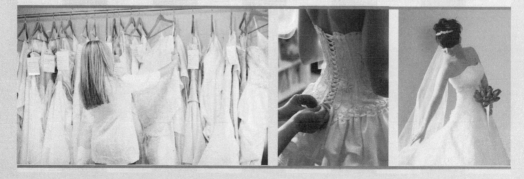

www.BridalShowplace.net
(562) 381-2865

Bridal Showplace
2014-2015 Bridal Shows

Meet some of Southern California's most distinguished wedding professionals offering everything you need to turn your Dream Wedding into a reality!

⟡

Taste cakes, hors d'oeuvres & chocolate delicacies.

⟡

Listen to the Entertainment Showcase and Bride & Groom 101 Seminar.

⟡

Enjoy a beauty makeover and have your photo taken at the photo booths.

⟡

Door prizes worth $1,000s including Luxurious Honeymoons.

⟡

Special prizes for the first 50 grooms in attendance.

⟡

First 50 brides in line receive an awesome SWAG Bag!

⟡

Bridal Showplace...
bringing Brides and Wedding Industry Professionals together for 19 years!

**Visit our website
for a current list of show dates.**

The Queen Mary
Long Beach

Knott's Resort Hotel
Buena Park

Sportsmen's Lodge
Studio City

Hyatt Regency
Long Beach

Hyatt Regency Resort
Huntington Beach

Marriott Hotel
Burbank

Marriott Hotel
Long Beach

Hilton Hotel
Pasadena

What Makes Us Different?

We do most of your homework for you.

1. **We actually visit the venues in *Here Comes The Guide*.**

   We check out 95% of our event sites in person before we include them in *The Guide*.

2. **We write every venue description with you in mind.**

   Each site description is based on our personal experience, so it's informative, accurate and often entertaining.

3. **We provide real pricing for venues, along with nitty-gritty details about each site's capacity, services and amenities.**

   This makes it easy to create a list of your top contenders, and by the time you call or visit a location you're totally informed!

4. **We prescreen all of our event professionals, which gives you a great head start on finding topnotch vendors.**

   All of the vendors in our Service Directory have been CERTIFIED BY THE GUIDE. That means we've thoroughly checked them out, and we're honored to represent them.

5. **We save you a ton of time.**

   By putting so much comprehensive information all in one place, we save you hours…days…maybe months of searching for event locations and professionals. And, you can actually do most of your planning without leaving home!

HereComesTheGuide.com has it ALL:

- ## Virtual Tours

  Most of the event sites we feature on **HereComesTheGuide.com** have virtual tours! It's *the* way to explore wedding locations on your own time (and in your pajamas).

- ## Photos of Hundreds of Wedding Venues and Services

  Each location and event professional has their own photo gallery.

- ## Fee Info for Every Venue

  HereComesTheGuide.com provides pricing for facility rental, catering and other costs.

- ## CERTIFIED BY THE GUIDE Event Services

  We don't just feature any old caterer or DJ. We've carefully checked out each event professional.

- ## Local Bridal Shows

  Find out what events are happening near you, like fab food tastings and fashion shows. Did you have something better to do this weekend?

- ## Wedding Dress Trunk Shows and Samples Sales Calendar

  Want to browse an entire collection of the latest designer wedding dresses? How about a discount on an in-stock bridal gown? This is the place to find special designer and sales events.

- ## MyGuide

  Log in to organize your **HereComesTheGuide.com** search results. You can save and share your favorite locations and event services.

- ## Guest Accommodations and Honeymoon Locations

  Need to book a block of rooms for your out-of-town guests? Looking for the perfect honeymoon spot? HereComesTheGuide.com is a great resource for both.

Our website also includes many venues and services that are so new they aren't even in this book!

What People Say

"This is a wonderful website, with all the details that a bride looks for when she's searching for a reception location. It's well organized and incredibly useful. I wish there were more sites like this one. THANK YOU!!!"
—*Amy, Bride*

"I have finally found a website that has it all! I'm planning my wedding from out of state and your event locations search is the best! I've been looking for a website that has all the information in one place. Thank you!!!"
—*Sarah, Bride*

"I'm in the process of helping my daughter research sites for her wedding reception and your website has been hugely helpful! The location information is thorough and consistent, making comparing the different locations so easy. We have found places to check out that we never would have thought of on our own. Thanks so much for all the work you must have done to put all this information together!"
—*Gail C., Mother of the Bride*

"I went out and spent the money on your book without hesitation. I'm so glad I did! I've gotten some great ideas and was able to create an outline for my budget. Not only did I find great reception locations in your book, but I think I found my rehearsal dinner place as well. It was a gold mine!"
—*Liz Davis, Bride*

"I got married in August and cannot stress how much help **Here Comes The Guide** was to me. I was often able to receive more information from your site than from my contacts with the actual locations and vendors! Especially since I was planning a Northern California wedding from Southern California, you saved me A TON of legwork."
—*Jamie Juster, Bride*

"I just had to let you know how WONDERFUL your website is. I was amazed to finally find a website with REAL information. Other wedding websites just gave me names and phone numbers, and I still had to do all the research on my own. Yours gave me all the nitty-gritty stuff I needed to know to find locations and vendors. With only two sessions at your website, my wedding was planned. Amazing!"
—*Christina R., Bride*

About Here Comes The Guide

"I have to tell you, I was blown away by your website. It's so beautiful and professionally done. The detail you provide is just enough so that the browser doesn't get bogged down in minutiae. Your site is such a great resource that I've started telling everybody about it. I've seen tons of wedding sites, so I know that you've come up with something that's really different."

—*Kimberly P., Bride*

"I went to about ten locations that are in your book and found that the site descriptions were pretty accurate. I'm amazed at how well you were able to capture the feeling of a place and put it into words."

—*Stephanie Stevensen, Bride*

"Having recently gotten married, I have a special appreciation for *Here Comes The Guide.* It was extremely helpful during my time of planning. The quick descriptions painted a beautiful picture of each and every venue, and were very helpful in narrowing down the search by budget, criteria and location. I feel this is a very important tool for every busy bride and still recommend it to all my engaged friends."

—*A Southern California Bride*

"I completely love your website and look forward to the book. This is the only resource that is so detailed on California sites, and it makes it so much easier to plan from a long distance. *Here Comes The Guide* is the best source of information."

—*Jocelyn, Bride*

"I absolutely love your new website. It's warm, feminine and has what one might call 'simple elegance.' Great job! I refer friends to your website all the time—for weddings, showers and of course, birthdays. Keep up the fabulous work."

—*Maria, Bride*

"I love your site! Most other sites that I visited seemed to have a hidden agenda to steer me towards only what benefited them. This site is non-biased and easy to use. Thank you!"

—*Elisa Parra, Bride*

"Thanks for providing this invaluable resource! I'll be using the site for corporate event planning—I don't know what I did without it!"

—*Mary, Corporate Planner*

We Need Your Help

- **Tell venues and event professionals that you're using _Here Comes The Guide_.**

  When you call the places and services we feature, let them know that you heard about them through _The Guide_.

- **Help us keep our information current.**

  We'd appreciate it if you'd contact us with your comments, corrections, suggestions and complaints. Your feedback helps us maintain the accuracy of our information.

- **Let us know if you discover a great venue or event professional that's not featured in _Here Comes The Guide_.**

  Please call or email us if you find an event site or vendor you think we should include in our book and on our website.

Hopscotch Press, Inc.

930 Carleton Street, Berkeley CA 94710

510/548-0400   fax 510/548-0144

info@HereComesTheGuide.com
www.HereComesTheGuide.com

Information Is Always Changing

Everything changes: pricing, services, décor, landscaping and even ownership.

We've tried to make the information in this book completely accurate, but it's not possible. Locations give us incorrect facts and figures, change ownership or management, revamp their pricing and policies and sometimes go out of business. Truth is, things in the event industry can turn upside down overnight.

So how can you make sure that you're getting correct information? It's simple:

- When you tour venues, bring your book with you or use your smart phone or tablet to quickly refer to each location's page on **HereComesTheGuide.com** for the most up-to-date info.

- When you contact a location, show or read the information in *Here Comes The Guide* to the facility's representative to verify that it's still current.

- Get everything that's been agreed on in writing, and review it carefully before you sign any contract!

Here Comes The Guide

Thirteenth Edition

Copyright © 2014–2015
Published by Hopscotch Press, Inc.
Printed in the U.S.A.

Here Comes The Guide, Southern California®

Thirteenth Edition

Jan Brenner, Co-Author/Editor-in-Chief
Jolene Rae Harrington, Co-Author/Editor

Meredith Monday Schwartz, Chief Operating Officer
Sharon Carl, Production Director
Jennifer Ahearn, Online Media Director
Denise Martinez, Director of Vendor Sales
Jenna Miller, Vendor Sales Manager
Angela Mullan, Regional Sales Manager
Maggie Munki, Production Specialist
Lisa Shields, Regional Sales Manager
Morgan Lambert, Regional Sales Manager
Stephanie Petersen, Regional Sales Manager

Lynn Broadwell, Publisher

Inside Illustrations: *Jon Dalton and Michael Tse*

Library of Congress Control Number: 2013950112
ISBN 9781885355-218

Here Comes The Guide®

Thirteenth Edition

Acknowledgments

Our deepest appreciation goes to our writers, Jolene Rae Harrington (also an invaluable editor) and Laurie Turner. Without them none of our books would ever get written.

Our artist, Jon Dalton, penned all the new illustrations for this edition of *Here Comes The Guide*. Using both computer graphics and fine art skills, he transformed photographs of the facilities into the distinctive line drawings that give *The Guide* its unique style.

And as always, we are eternally grateful to our clients and our readers. Your support year in and year out keeps *Here Comes The Guide* a popular resource.

Table of Contents

Our Cover Photographer ii

Information Is Always Changing xiii

Acknowledgments xvi

Preface xxiii

Really Really Important Information

Introduction 3

Understanding Our Information 5

Key to Services and Amenities 7

Key to Restrictions 8

Valuable Tips 9

Selecting an Event Venue 9

Tips for Previewing a Venue 14

Working with a Venue 15

Insurance Considerations 16

Recycling: Doing Your Part 18

Questions To Ask

The Guide Bride's Wedding Checklist 21

Questions to Ask

    Event Venues 24

    Wedding Photographers 26

        Photography Style Glossary 27

    Wedding Planners 28

    Caterers 30

    Floral Designers 32

    Cake Designers 34

        Wedding Cake Glossary 35

    DJ or Live Entertainment 36

    Invitations 38

        Invitations Glossary 40

Part One: Event Venues

Southern California Regional Map 45

Regional Areas and Cities

Eastern Sierras

Regional Map...47
June Lake 48
Mammoth Lakes 50

Central Coast

Regional Map...53
Cambria.. 54
Paso Robles 56

Santa Barbara Area

Regional Map...61
Carpinteria 62
Santa Barbara.. 64
Santa Ynez... 74

Ventura County

Regional Map... 77
Camarillo.. 78
Moorpark 86
Ojai.. 92
Piru.. 94
Santa Paula 96
Simi Valley 100
Somis...102
Thousand Oaks 104
Ventura..108
Westlake Village 114

San Fernando Valley

Regional Map...119
Agoura 120
Burbank 122
Calabasas 126
Granada Hills...132
Lake View Terrace...134

North Hollywood 136
Porter Ranch 138
Santa Susana 140
Studio City 142
Tarzana 144
Universal City 146
Woodland Hills 148

Santa Catalina Island

Regional Map..151
Avalon 152

Los Angeles Area

Regional Map..157
Beverly Hills 158
Hollywood 160
Los Angeles..164
Malibu 194
Marina del Rey...206
Pacific Palisades 210
Santa Monica 212
Whittier 222

San Gabriel Valley

Regional Map..225
Altadena 226
Azusa...228
La Cañada Flintridge 230
Pasadena 234
San Dimas...248

South Bay

Regional Map..253
Lakewood 254
Long Beach..256
Manhattan Beach...272
Palos Verdes Estates 278
Palos Verdes Peninsula 282
Rancho Palos Verdes...284
Redondo Beach 290
San Pedro..300
Torrance..302

Orange County

Regional Map... 305

Aliso Viejo..306

Anaheim...310

Anaheim Hills 314

Buena Park 316

Corona del Mar..318

Costa Mesa...320

Coto de Caza 326

Cypress..328

Dana Point 330

Dove Canyon...336

Fullerton..338

Huntington Beach 348

Irvine...356

La Mirada 360

Laguna Beach 362

Laguna Hills 372

Newport Beach..376

Newport Coast...394

San Clemente...396

San Juan Capistrano 398

Santa Ana...404

Seal Beach 408

Silverado 410

Mountain Lakes Area

Regional Map...413

Lake Arrowhead 414

Riverside/Inland Empire

Regional Map...419

Chino Hills 420

Claremont 424

Corona 428

Diamond Bar 436

Menifee 440

Oak Glen 442

Pomona..444

Rancho Cucamonga 446

Redlands 450

Riverside 452

Temecula..458
Upland..464
Victorville...466

San Diego Area

Regional Map..469
Bonita..470
Escondido..472
Fallbrook...476
La Jolla..480
Oceanside..490
Rancho Santa Fe..492
San Diego..494
Solana Beach...510
Vista...512

Greater Palm Springs

Regional Map..515
Indian Wells..516
Indio...520
Palm Desert...522
Palm Springs...530
Rancho Mirage...540

Maps

Southern California Regions 45
Eastern Sierras 47
Central Coast 53
Santa Barbara Area.. 61
Ventura Area 77
San Fernando Valley 119
Santa Catalina Island..151
Los Angeles Area..157
San Gabriel Valley 225
South Bay...253
Orange County 305
Mountain Lakes Area...413
Riverside/Inland Empire 419
San Diego Area..469
Greater Palm Springs 515

Part Two: Event Services

Certified By The Guide 549

Working with Event Professionals...550

Event Services by Category...553

Event Services by Company 593

Indexes

Event Venues by Name..575

Event Venues by Region 583

Event Services by Name..593

Preface

When I graduated from college, I thought I'd never have to do another endless research project again. Boy, was I wrong. Compared to looking for a place to get married, term papers were a piece of cake. I began my quest optimistically enough, but after a couple of days of frantic and fruitless networking (my wedding date was a mere three months down the road!), the enormity of my task started to sink in. It had taken me 33 years to find the right guy, and it was beginning to look like it might take an equally long time to find the right place.

Going into high gear, I reached out and touched just about everyone I knew, along with quite a few total strangers. Friends and friends of friends didn't have any recommendations that suited our particular needs, and although wedding consultants had information, they were reluctant to part with their lists of sites unless I hired them to plan my wedding. I even called some caterers, florists and cake makers, but they were usually too busy to give me in-depth descriptions of places over the phone. Some chambers of commerce had organized wedding location lists ready to mail out; others had nothing and knew nothing.

After days of phoning, all I had was a patchwork quilt of information. I still hadn't found *the* place, and finally had to face the painful truth: there was no central resource or comprehensive, detailed list. I became anxious. With a full-time job I was hardly free to conduct an exhaustive search, and I realized that I would never be able to find out about the vast majority of interesting or unusual wedding sites, let alone thoroughly evaluate them! My frustration was exacerbated by the fact that it was August and the wedding date in October was drawing closer with each passing day.

As luck would have it, my sister mentioned that her hairdresser had gotten married on a yacht in San Francisco Bay. Hallelujah! That's it! I cried. What a great idea! I'd never even thought about a floating wedding and had no idea you could do such a thing.

We got married on a hot, sunny day behind Angel Island in San Francisco Bay. The captain performed the ceremony on the bow, and afterwards the yacht tooted its horn, the crew let loose multicolored balloons, and a "Just Married" sign was thrown over the stern. As we swept past Alcatraz Island, Sausalito and the Golden Gate and Bay Bridges, our guests relaxed in the sun, enjoying drinks and hors d'oeuvres. What a wonderful day! Even my parents' friends had a great time, and wrote us after the wedding to let us know how much they'd loved their outing on the water.

Serendipity was largely responsible for making my wedding memorable, but you don't have to rely on luck. I created *Here Comes The Guide* so that others wouldn't have to experience what I went through, and I hope it makes your search for the perfect location easy and painless.

Lynn Broadwell
Publisher

Really Really Important Information

Introduction

Little did we know when we wrote *Here Comes The Guide, Northern California* in 1989 that we would receive such an overwhelming response from our readers. The first edition sold out in less than a year, and as public demand grew we launched our Southern California edition. Thanks to our enthusiastic readership of engaged couples, savvy party hostesses and event planners, *The Guide* continues to be a bestseller!

So what makes this book so popular?

We've done most of your homework for you.

We present comprehensive, solid information: a full description and illustration of each location, plus details about fees, capacities and services. Our wide selection of facilities includes delightful places that you might not have found on your own.

This book cuts your search time by 90%.

Instead of having to call dozens of facilities and ask the same questions over and over again, you can look up many of the answers in *The Guide*. Once you've narrowed down your list of potential sites, you can contact them to schedule an in-person visit. Not only does *The Guide* save you time, it often saves you money by letting you comparison shop!

We screen our venues.

We personally evaluate almost every property in *Here Comes The Guide*, sending a professional writer to 95% of our sites to make sure they meet our criteria. (Yes, we actually turn down locations that don't satisfy our requirements.)

All our service professionals are *Certified By The Guide*.

Our goal is to represent only the best event professionals in the industry. In order to achieve this, we thoroughly screen all of the service providers in *Here Comes The Guide*. That means you don't have to take a chance on some anonymous photographer or caterer. Every one of our vendors has been carefully checked out and *Certified By The Guide*.

Our rigorous certification process requires each vendor to submit up to 30 references, half wedding industry professionals and half recent brides. Then we contact each person and get their honest feedback. Only if the company gets a rave review do we accept them as a client.

(Even though we've checked out all of our professionals very carefully, we can't guarantee their performance. Here Comes The Guide is not responsible for the contract you ultimately sign with them, or for how your event goes. Our best advice is to be thorough, careful consumers and get every single thing in writing. This is what we tell our sisters and best friends, so this is what we're telling you.)

We're experienced.

We've been writing and publishing *Here Comes The Guide* since 1989. We're proud that our publication has become the essential resource for weddings—and just about any kind of event in California.

If you can't find the perfect venue or service in *Here Comes The Guide,* check out our website at HereComesTheGuide.com.

You'll have access to all the information in the *Here Comes The Guide* book online and a lot more:

- **More Southern California venues,** along with photo gallery slideshows and virtual tours. You'll be able to tour hundreds of sites in your pajamas.

- **Even more venues** in other regions of the U.S., like Northern California, New England, Chicago and Hawaii, just to name a few.

- **More services,** with lots of photos of floral designs, cakes, makeup and hair, you name it!

- **Trunk Shows & Sample Sales Calendar** for the latest styles and savings.

- **Bridal Fair Calendar** with deets about upcoming extravaganzas and wedding showcases.

- **Guest accommodations/room block options** plus photos and details.

- **Honeymoon destinations,** including romantic images and practical info.

Navigation is a snap, and our searchable database lets you find event sites by city, type, capacity, view, etc., and event professionals by company name, region or service category. A special *MyGuide* feature lets you save your favorites and share them with friends and family.

And check back often—we regularly update our website with event locations and services that are not featured in the book!

Understanding Our Information

Explanation of Main Headings

Each venue description in *Here Comes The Guide* follows the same format. To help you understand the information presented, we've provided an explanation of the main headings in the same order as they appear.

Description
Once you've selected a geographical area and you're clear about your needs, then thoroughly review all the sites listed in your area of preference. The descriptions are written to give you a sense of what places are like, from ambiance to physical layout. However, before reading the descriptions, you may want to check the *Capacity* and *Fees & Deposits* sections to determine which places seem to be a good fit from a size and budget perspective. If a facility is still a viable option after you've read the entire two-page editorial, flag it for easy reference when planning to contact and visit sites later on. You can also go to HereComesTheGuide.com and log in to MyGuide to save and share your favorites.

Ceremony Capacity
Standing and seated capacities are included for ceremonies since these numbers may be totally different than the corresponding numbers for receptions.

Reception Capacity
By now you should have a rough idea of how many people will be attending. If not, its time to zero in on the number, since many facilities want a deposit based on an estimated head count. Look at the capacity figures for each event location. Seated or sit-down capacity refers to guests seated at tables. Standing capacity refers to a function where the majority of guests are not seated, such as a champagne/hors d'oeuvres reception. Keep track of those facilities that are compatible with your guest count, or ad them to your MyGuide favorites. If you're planning well in advance and don't have your guest list whittled down yet, then you'll just have to estimate and refine the count as the date draws near. There is a world of difference in cost and planning effort between an intimate party of 60 and a large wedding with over 200 guests, so pin down your numbers as soon as you can.

Meeting Capacity
In general, the seated capacity for meetings is listed as a range or a maximum. Sometimes, specific spaces are named along with their individual capacities. Occasionally, seating configurations are also provided: *theater-style* (auditorium row seating with chairs arranged closely together), *classroom-style* (an organized table-and-chair arrangement, usually in rows) and *conference-style* (seating around tables).

Fees and Deposits
We've tried to make the information regarding costs as accurate as possible. However, keep in mind that we can't list the fees for all of the services a venue offers. Also, while packages tend to be more inclusive, they may not cover the full cost of your event—especially when you add in extras like appetizers or rentals. It's important to find out as soon as possible exactly what is—and isn't—included with any service or package you're considering in order to accurately assess how your venue choice will impact your budget.

It's a good idea to confirm pricing with the facility you're calling. If you're planning far in advance, anticipate price increases by the time you contract with a venue. Once you're definite about your location, you should lock in your fees in a contract, protecting yourself from possible rate increases later. Make sure you ask about every service provided and are clear about all of the extras that can really add up. Facilities may charge you for tables, chairs, linens, plateware and silverware, glassware and additional hours. Don't be surprised to see tax and service charges in fixed amounts applied to the total bill if the facility provides restaurant or catering services. Although it may seem redundant to include the phrase "tax, alcohol and service charge are additional" in each entry, we find that most people forget (or just don't want to accept the painful reality) that 23–33% will be applied to the food and beverage total.

> **Look at the information regarding fees and deposits and remember that these figures change regularly and usually in one direction—up!**

Sometimes a deposit is nonrefundable—a fact you'll definitely want to know if the deposit is a large percentage of the total bill. And even if it's refundable, you still need to read the cancellation policy thoroughly. Make sure you understand the policies that will ensure you get your cleaning and security deposit returned in full and, again, get everything in writing.

Food costs vary considerably. Carefully plan your menu with the caterer, event consultant or chef. Depending on the style of service and the type of food being served, the total food bill can vary dramatically—even if you're getting quotes from the same caterer. If, for example, you're having a multi-course seated meal, expect it to be the most expensive part of your event.

Alcohol is expensive, too, and you may be restricted in what you can serve and who can serve it. Some venues don't allow you to bring your own alcoholic beverages, and even if they do permit it you may be limited to beer, wine or champagne. Many places discourage you from bringing your own (BYO) by charging an exorbitant corkage fee to remove the cork and pour. Other places have limited permits that don't allow them to serve alcohol or restrict them from serving certain kinds; some will let you or the caterer serve alcohol, others require someone with a license. Make sure you know what's allowed. Decide what your budget is for alcohol and determine what types you're able to provide. And keep in mind that the catering fees you are quoted rarely include the cost of alcohol. If you provide the alcohol, make sure you keep your purchase receipts so you can return any unopened bottles.

So how much will your event cost? Hopefully not more than you can afford! There are a lot of variables involved in coming up with an estimated total for your event. Just make sure you've included them all in your calculations and read all the fine print before you sign any contract.

Availability

Some facilities are available 7am to 2am; others offer very limited "windows." If you'd like to save some money, consider a weekday or weeknight reception, or think about having your event in the off-season (often November, or January through March, but varies depending on the region). Even the most sought-after places have openings midweek and during non-peak months—and at reduced costs. Facilities want your business and are more likely to negotiate terms and prices if they have nothing else scheduled. Again, read all the fine print carefully and mark those facilities that have time slots that meet your needs. If the date you have in mind is already booked, it doesn't hurt to ask if someone actually confirmed that date by paying a deposit or signing a contract. If they haven't, you may be in luck.

Services/Amenities and Restrictions

Most facilities provide something in the way of services and many have limitations that may affect your function. For instance, they may not allow you to have amplified music outdoors or bring your own caterer.

We've attempted to give you a brief description of what each venue has to offer and what is restricted. Because of space limitations, we've shortened words and developed a key to help you follow our abbreviated notations. Once you're familiar with our shorthand, you'll be able to read through all the data outlined at the bottom of each entry and flag each facility that meets your requirements.

Services/Amenities Key

CATERING

- **in-house:** the facility provides catering (for a fee)
- **in-house, no BYO:** the facility provides catering; you cannot bring in your own
- **preferred list:** you must select your caterer from the facility's approved list
- **in-house or BYO:** the facility will provide catering or you can select an outside caterer of your own
- **BYO, licensed:** arrange for your own licensed caterer

KITCHEN FACILITIES

- **ample** or **fully equipped:** large and well-equipped with major appliances
- **moderate:** medium-sized and utilitarian
- **minimal:** small with limited equipment; may not have all the basic appliances
- **setup** or **prep only:** room for setup and food prep, but not enough space or utilities to cook food
- **n/a:** not applicable because facility provides catering or doesn't allow food

TABLES & CHAIRS

- **some provided** or **provided:** facility provides some or all of the tables and chairs
- **BYO:** make arrangements to bring your own

LINENS, SILVER, ETC.

- same as above

RESTROOMS

- **wheelchair accessible** or
- **not wheelchair accessible**

DANCE FLOOR

- **yes:** an area for dancing (hardwood floor, cement terrace, patio) is available
- **CBA, extra charge:** you can arrange for a dance floor to be brought in for a fee

BRIDE'S & GROOM'S DRESSING AREA

- **yes:** there is an area for changing
- **no:** there's no area for changing
- **limited:** smaller space, not fully equipped as changing room
- **CBA:** can be arranged

PARKING

- **CBA:** can be arranged
  other descriptions are self explanatory

ACCOMMODATIONS

If overnight accommodations are available on site, the number of guest rooms is listed.

- **CBA:** the facility will arrange accommodations for you

TELEPHONE

- **restricted:** calls made on the house phone must be local, collect or charged to a credit card
- **guest phones:** private phones in guest rooms
- **house phone:** central phone used by all guests
- **emergency use only:** self-explanatory

OUTDOOR NIGHT LIGHTING

- **yes:** there is adequate light to conduct your event outdoors after dark

OUTDOOR NIGHT LIGHTING (continued)

- **access only** or **limited:** lighting is sufficient for access only

OUTDOOR COOKING FACILITIES

- **BBQ:** the facility has a barbecue on the premises
- **BBQ, CBA:** a barbecue can be arranged through the facility
- **BYO BBQ:** make arrangements for your own barbecue
- **n/a:** not applicable

CLEANUP

- **provided:** facility takes care of cleanup
- **caterer:** your caterer is responsible
- **caterer or renter:** both you and/or your caterer are responsible for cleanup

MEETING EQUIPMENT

- **full range:** facility has a full range of audiovisual equipment, including projectors, overhead screens, etc.
- **no:** no equipment is available
- **BYO:** bring your own meeting equipment
- **CBA:** equipment can be arranged
- **CBA, extra fee:** equipment can be arranged for an extra fee

VIEW

We've described what type of view is available for each facility.

- **no:** the facility has no views to speak of

OTHER

Description of any service or amenity that is not included in above list.

Restrictions Key

ALCOHOL

- **provided, no BYO:** the facility provides alcoholic beverages (for a fee) and does not permit you to bring your own
- **BYO:** you can bring your own alcohol
- **corkage, $/bottle:** if you bring your own alcohol, the facility charges a fee per bottle to remove the cork and pour
- **WCB only:** *(or any combination of these three letters)* only wine, champagne and beer are permitted
- **licensed server:** the server of alcohol must be licensed

SMOKING

- **allowed:** smoking is permitted throughout the facility
- **outside only:** smoking is not permitted inside the facility
- **not allowed:** smoking is not permitted anywhere on the premises
- **designated areas:** specific areas for smoking have been designated

MUSIC

Almost every facility allows acoustic music unless stated otherwise. Essentially, restrictions refer to amplified music.

- **amplified OK:** amplified music is acceptable without restriction
- **outside only:** no amplified music allowed inside

- **inside only:** no amplified music permitted outside
- **amplified OK with limits or restrictions:** amplified music is allowed, but there are limits on volume, hours of play, type of instruments, etc.

WHEELCHAIR ACCESS

Accessibility is based on whether the event areas (not necessarily the restrooms) of a facility are wheelchair accessible or not.

- **yes:** the facility is accessible
- **limited:** the facility is accessible but with difficulty (there may be a step at the entrance, for example, but all of the rooms are accessible)
- **no:** the facility is not accessible

INSURANCE

Many facilities require that you purchase and show proof of some insurance coverage. The type and amount of insurance varies with the facility, and some facilities offer insurance for a minimal charge.

- **liability required, certificate required** or **proof of insurance required:** additional insurance is required
- **not required:** no additional insurance is required
- **may be required:** sometimes additional insurance is required

Valuable Tips

Selecting an Event Venue

Before you jump into the venue descriptions in *Here Comes The Guide,* identify what kind of celebration you want and establish selection criteria early. Here are some basics:

Your Venue's Geographical Location

For many couples, it's important that the location they select is easy for the majority of their guests to get to. However, whether you're hosting your event close to home or planning a destination wedding in another city, state or country, you need to think about the logistics of getting everyone to your event site.

Special Considerations in Southern California

Guests may be traveling a considerable distance by car to get to your party destination. Sure, they can use Google Maps or some other navigation tool to get directions to your venue, but those resources aren't always 100% reliable. Given the Southern California freeway system and traffic congestion, you'll save your guests lots of time and trouble if you provide, along with the invitation, specific directions on a separate map drawn to scale. Include symbols indicating directions (north, south, etc.) and the names of the appropriate off-ramps. If you're not sure about exits, landmarks or street names, take a dry run of the route to make sure everything on your map is accurate and easy to follow. If your function occurs after dark, do the test drive at night so you can note well-lit landmarks that will prevent your guests from getting lost—both coming to your event and going home.

If you're having a Friday evening event, take commuters into account, especially if your event site is in an area that gets bumper-to-bumper traffic. One solution is to schedule your get-together after 7pm when freeways are less congested.

Even if you have few constraints when picking a location, it's still worth considering the total driving time to and from your destination. When it's over two hours, an overnight stay may be necessary, and you may be limited to a Saturday night event, since your nearest and dearest won't be able to spend hours on the road during the week. If you're going to need lodging for some of your guests during your celebration, be sure to check out the "Guest Accommodations/Room Blocks" section on HereComesTheGuide.com for suggestions and info. If you have guests arriving by plane, it's certainly helpful if there's an airport nearby, and if your co-workers, friends or family enjoy drinking try to house them close to the event site.

There's no reason why you can't contemplate a special event in the San Diego mountains or in a wine cave in Santa Ynez. Just remember that if you're planning a wedding that's not local, a venue's on-site coordinator or a wedding planner can really help: Many are experienced in handling destination events and can be a great asset.

Budget

Many couples aren't very experienced with event budgeting and don't know how to estimate what locations, products and services will ultimately cost. If you're not sure what you can realistically afford, we recommend talking to a professional event planner or wedding coordinator early in the planning stages. You don't have to make a big financial or time commitment to use a professional; many will assist you on an hourly basis for a nuts-and-bolts session to determine priorities and to assign costs to items on your wish list.

Part of being realistic involves some simple arithmetic. Catering costs, for example, are usually calculated on a per-person basis. The couple who has $10,000 and wants to invite 250 guests should know that $40 per guest actually won't go very far. Tax and gratuity combined usually consume 23–33% of the food and beverage budget. If you subtract that 30% from $40, you have $28 left. If you also serve alcohol at $10/person, you're down to $18/person for food. That's usually not enough for appetizers and a seated meal, let alone location rental fees, entertainment, flowers, printed invitations, photography, etc.

Before you make any major decisions or commit any of your funds for specific items, take a serious look at your total budget, make sure it can cover all your anticipated expenses, and leave a little cushion for last minute items. If your budget doesn't cover everything, it's time for some hard decisions. If you have a very large guest list and a small pocketbook, you may need to shorten the list or cut back on some of

> **The important point is that if you know what kind of event you want and are clear about your budget, your search will be faster and easier.**

the amenities you want to include. No matter who foots the bill, be advised that doing the homework here really counts. Pin down your costs at the beginning of the planning stage and get all estimates in writing.

Style

Do you know what kind of event you want? Will it be formal or informal? A traditional wedding or an innovative party? Will it be held at night or during the day? Indoors or outdoors? Is having a garden ceremony or gourmet food a deal breaker? By identifying the geographical area and the most important elements of your dream wedding before you start looking for a venue, you can really narrow down your search.

Guest Count

How many people are anticipated? Many facilities request a rough estimate 60–90 days in advance of your function—and they'll want a deposit based on the figure you give them. A confirmed guest count or guarantee is usually required 72 hours prior to the event. It's important to come up with a solid estimate of your guest list early on in order to plan your budget and select the right ceremony or reception spot.

It's also important to ensure that the guest count you give the facility *before* your event doesn't change *during* your event. Believe it or not, it's possible to have more people at your reception than you expected. How? Some folks who did not bother to RSVP may decide to show up anyway. In one case we know of, the parents of the bride got an additional bill for $1,200 on the event day because there were 30 "surprise" guests beyond the guest count guarantee who were wined and dined. To prevent this from happening to you—especially if you're having a large reception where it's hard to keep track of all the guests—it's a good idea to contact everyone who did *not* RSVP. Let them know as politely as possible that you will need to have their response by a given date to finalize food and beverage totals.

Seasonal Differences

Southern California, for all its (pardon the expression) faults, has got some great advantages weather-wise. Outdoor special events, ceremonies and receptions can take place throughout most of the year, and from September to November you can anticipate sunny skies and warm temperatures. However, when the mercury rises in inland areas, watch out. A canopy or tables with umbrellas are essential for screening the sun. In fact, you should ask each facility manager about the sun's direction and intensity with respect to the time of day and month your event will take place. Guests will be uncomfortable facing into the sun during a ceremony, and white walls and enclosed areas bounce light around and can hold in heat. If your event is scheduled for midday in July, for example, include a note on your location map to bring sunglasses, hat and sunscreen. If you also mention words like "poolside," "yacht deck" or "lawn seating" on the map, it will help guests know how to dress. In summer, you might want to consider an evening rather than a midday celebration. Not only is the air cooler, but you may also get an extra bonus—a glorious sunset.

If you're arranging an outdoor party November through April, or in the foothills or mountain areas, expect cooler weather and prepare a contingency plan. Despite our region's favorable Mediterranean climate, it has rained in May, June and July, so consider access to an inside space or a tent.

Special Requirements

Sometimes, places have strict rules and regulations. If most of your guests smoke, then pick a location that doesn't restrict smoking. If alcohol is going to be consumed, make sure it's allowed and find out if bar service needs to be licensed. If dancing and a big band are critical, then limit yourself to those locations that can accommodate them and the accompanying decibels. Do you have children, seniors or disabled guests, vegetarians or folks who want kosher food on your list? If so, you need to plan for them, too. It's essential that you identify the special factors that are important for your event before you sign a contract.

Locking in Your Event Date

Let's say it's the first day of your hunt for the perfect spot, and the second place you see is an enchanting garden that happens to be available on the date you want. You really like it but, since you've only seen two locations, you're not 100% sure that this is *the* place. No problem. You decide to keep your options open by making a tentative reservation. The site coordinator dutifully pencils your name into her schedule book and says congratulations. You say thanks, we have a few more places (like 25) to check out, but this one looks terrific. Then off you go, secure in the knowledge that if none of the other sites you visit pans out, you still have this lovely garden waiting for you.

The nightmare begins a couple of weeks, or perhaps months, down the road when you've finished comparison-shopping and call back the first place you liked to finalize the details. So sorry, the coordinator says. We gave away your date because a) oops, one of the other gals who works here erased your name by mistake (after all, it was only *penciled* in), b) we didn't hear back from you soon enough, or c) you never confirmed your reservation with a deposit.

For the tiniest instant you picture yourself inflicting bodily harm on the coordinator or at least slapping the facility with a lawsuit, but alas, there's really not much you can do. Whether a genuine mistake was made or the facility purposely gave your date to another, perhaps more lucrative party (this happens sometimes with hotels who'd rather book a big convention on your date than a little wedding), you're out of luck. To avoid the pain (and ensuing panic) of getting bumped, here's what we suggest: Instead of just being penciled in, ask if you can write a refundable $100–250 check to hold the date for a limited time. If the person in charge is willing to do this but wants the full deposit up front (usually nonrefundable), then you'll need to decide whether you can afford to lose the entire amount if you find a more appealing location later on. Once the coordinator or sales person takes your money, you're automatically harder to bump. Make sure you get a receipt that has the event date, year, time and space(s) reserved written on it, as well as the date your tentative reservation runs out. Then, just to be on the safe side, check in with the facility weekly while you're considering other sites to prevent any possible "mistakes" from being made. When you finally do commit to a place, get a signed contract or at least a confirmation letter. If you don't receive written confirmation within a week, hound the coordinator until you get it, even if you have to drive to the sales office and stand there until they hand it over to you. And even after you've plunked down your money and have a letter and/or contract securing

> **If you try to pick a venue before you've made basic decisions, selection will be a struggle and it will take longer to find a spot that will make you happy.**

your date, call the coordinator every other month to reconfirm your reservation. It pays to stay on top of this, no matter how locked in you think you are.

Parking

Parking is seldom a critical factor if you get married outside an urban area, but make sure you know how it's going to be handled if you're planning a party in a parking-challenged place like downtown Los Angeles, Pasadena or Santa Monica.

A map is a handy supplement to any invitation, and there's usually enough room on it to indicate how and where vehicles should be parked. Depending on the location, you may want to add a note suggesting carpooling or mention that a shuttle service or valet parking is provided. If there's a fee for parking, identify the anticipated cost per car and where the entry points are to the nearest parking lots. The last thing you want are surprised and disgruntled guests who can't find a place to stash their car, or who are shocked at the $20–40 parking tab.

Professional Help

If you're a busy person with limited time to plan and execute a party, pick a facility that offers complete coordination services, from catering and flowers to decorations and music. Or better yet, hire a professional event or wedding coordinator. Either way, you'll make your life much easier by having someone else handle the details. And often the relationships these professionals have with vendors can end up saving you money, too.

Food and Alcohol Quality

Food and alcohol account for the greatest portion of an event's budget; consequently, food and beverage selections are a big deal. Given the amount of money you will spend on this category alone, you should be concerned about the type, quantity and quality of what you eat and drink. If in-house catering is provided, we suggest you sample different menu options prior to paying a facility deposit. If you'd like to see how a facility handles food setup and presentation, ask the caterer to arrange a visit to someone else's party about a half hour before it starts. It's wise to taste wines and beers in advance, and be very specific about hard alcohol selections.

Hidden Costs

This may come as a surprise, but not all services and event equipment are covered in the rental fee, and some facilities hide the true cost of renting their space by having a low rental fee. It's possible to get nickeled and dimed for all the extras: tables, chairs, linens, dance floor, cake cutting, valet service and so forth. You can also end up paying more than you expected for security and cleanup. All these additional charges can really add up, so save yourself a big headache by understanding exactly what's included in the rental fee and what's not before you sign any contract.

Bonus Info

If you're not sure what to ask potential venues and event professionals, check out our "QUESTIONS TO ASK" section starting on page 19. We've put together lists of questions that come in very handy when you're interviewing potential event locations, photographers, caterers, etc.

Tips for Previewing a Venue

Make Appointments.

If you liked what you read about a venue in *The Guide,* then we recommend you make an appointment to see that location rather than just driving by. Sometimes an unremarkable-looking building will surprise you with a secluded garden or hidden courtyard. And sometimes the opposite is true—you'll love the stunning façade, but the interior isn't your style.

Incidentally, we've withheld the addresses of privately owned properties. Should you happen to know where any of these facilities is located, we urge you to respect the owner's or manager's privacy and make an appointment instead of stopping by.

When you do call for an appointment, don't forget to ask for specific directions, including cross streets. You can also look up the location on *HereComesTheGuide.com* and print out a detailed street map. Try to cluster your visits so that you can easily drive from one place to another without backtracking. Schedule at least an hour per facility and leave ample driving time. You want to be efficient, but don't over-schedule yourself. It's best to view places when you're fresh and your judgment isn't clouded by fatigue.

Bring along *The Guide* or use your phone or tablet to access our website.

We've listed the street address for each site, and our illustrations in the book often make it easier to identify the venues you're planning to see. And if you bring the book or use your smart phone or tablet to look up venues on HereComesTheGuide.com, you can double-check our information with the site representative.

Bring a notebook—paper or digital!

You can make notes in your copy of *Here Comes The Guide,* but have a small notebook or digital device handy, too. Keep track of the date, time and name of the person providing the information, and then read back the info to the site representative to confirm that what you heard is correct. Remember to have your notes with you when you review your contract, and go over in detail what you were told versus what's in the contract before you sign anything.

Take pictures.

Video is particularly useful for narrating your likes, dislikes and any other observations while you're shooting a venue. However, if you're just taking still photos, make sure you have a system for matching shots to their respective locations. You'd be surprised how easy it is to confuse photos. And bring extra batteries and whatever else you need to make your gear work properly.

File everything.

Many facilities will hand you pamphlets, menus, rate charts and other materials. Develop a system for sorting and storing the information that keeps your notes, photos and handouts together, clearly labeled and easily accessible.

Bring a checkbook or credit card.

Some of the more attractive venues book a year to 18 months in advance. If you actually fall in love with a location and your date is available, plunk down a deposit to hold the date.

Working With a Venue

Confirm All the Details

When you make the initial phone call or email, confirm that the information presented in *Here Comes The Guide* is still valid. Show or read the information in our book to the site's representative, and have him or her inform you of any changes. If there have been significant increases in fees or new restrictions that you can't live with, cross the place off your list and move on. If the facility is still a contender, request a tour.

Once you've determined that the physical elements of the place suit you, it's time to discuss details. Ask about services and amenities or fees that may not be listed in the book and make a note of them. Outline your plans to the representative and make sure that the facility can accommodate your particular needs. If you don't want to handle all the details yourself, find out what the facility is willing and able to do, and if there will be an additional cost for their assistance. Venues often provide planning services for little or no extra charge. If other in-house services are offered, such as flowers or wedding cakes, inquire about the quality of each service provider and whether or not substitutions can be made. If you want to use your own vendors, find out if the facility will charge you an extra fee. For more help with working with a location, see our "Questions to Ask an Event Venue" on page 24.

The Importance of Rapport

Another factor to consider is your rapport with the person(s) you're working with. Are you comfortable with them? Do they listen well and respond to your questions directly? Do they inspire trust and confidence? Are they warm and enthusiastic or cold and aloof? If you have doubts, you need to resolve them before embarking on a working relationship with these folks—no matter how wonderful the facility itself is. Discuss your feelings with them, and if you're still not completely satisfied, get references and call them. If at the end of this process you still have lingering concerns, you may want to eliminate the facility from your list even though it seems perfect in every other way.

On the other hand, don't let your rapport with a banquet coordinator or site rep sway you to book a venue you aren't in love with—there's a lot of turnover in the hospitality industry, and you may call Brittany one day only to—surprise!—be referred to Brian. So if Brittany was your main reason for choosing this place, you could be in for a big disappointment if you and Brian don't hit it off and suddenly the venue's shortcomings really stand out.

Signing a Contract

It's easy to get emotionally attached to a location, but remember that it's not a done deal until you sign a contract. Now's the time to be businesslike and put your emotions aside. If you can't do that, get a non-emotional partner, friend or relative to help you review the small print and negotiate changes before you sign. Remember all those notes you took when you first visited the site? Compare them with what's actually written in the contract. No matter what someone told you about the availability of a dance floor, the price of pastel linens, or the ceremony arch, you can't hold the facility to it until the contract is signed. Places revise their prices and policies all the time, so assume that things may have changed since you originally saw the site or talked to a site representative.

If you're not happy with the contract, prepare to negotiate. Before your appointment with whoever has the power to alter the contract, make an itemized list, in order of importance, of the changes you want. Decide what you're willing to give up, and what you can't live without. If in the end the most important things on your list cannot be addressed to your satisfaction, this is probably not the right place for you. It's better to find another location than to stay with a facility that isn't willing to work with you.

Insurance Considerations

Nowadays, if someone gets injured at an event or something is damaged at or near the event site, it's likely that someone will be sued.

In order to protect themselves and spread the risk among all parties involved, facilities often require additional insurance and/or proof of insurance from service professionals and their clients.

Event sites and service professionals (such as caterers) are very aware of their potential liability and all have coverage of one kind or another. Many of the properties we represent will also require you, the renter, to get extra insurance.

What's funny (or not so funny) is that as more and more event sites require extra liability and/or a certificate of insurance, fewer insurance companies are willing to issue either one—even if you're covered under a homeowner's policy. At this point, insurance carriers don't want to attach extra clauses to your policy to increase coverage for a single event, and most, if not all, companies are unwilling to add the event site's name to your existing policy as an additional insured.

Don't despair. Even though it's hard to come by, you can get extra insurance for a specified period of time, and it's relatively inexpensive.

Obtaining Extra Insurance

- **The first thing to do is read your rental contract carefully.** Make sure you understand exactly *what's* required and *when* it's required. Most facilities want $1,000,000–2,000,000 in extra liability coverage. If you don't pay attention to the insurance clauses early in the game, you'll have to play catch-up at the last moment, frantically trying to locate a carrier who will issue you additional insurance. And, if you don't supply the certificate to the facility *on time,* you may run the risk of forfeiting your event site altogether.

- **The second thing is to ask your event site's representative if the site has an insurance policy through which you can purchase the required extra coverage.** If the answer is yes, then consider purchasing it—that's the easiest route (but not necessarily the best!). The facility's extra insurance coverage may not be the least expensive and it may not provide you with the best coverage. What you need to ask is: "If one of my guests or one of the professionals working at my event causes some damage to the premises or its contents, will this extra insurance cover it?" If the answer if yes, get it in writing.

- **The third thing, if the answer is no, is to find your own coverage.** We suggest you avoid random searches online and call one of these two insurance providers:

    1) WedSafe at 877/723-3933. This company insures weddings and private events. You can reach them at their toll-free number or online at wedsafe.com. They offer coverage for wedding cancellation and/or liability.

2) R.V. Nuccio & Associates, Inc. at 800/567-2685 or www.rvnuccio.com. They specialize in insuring special events, and can send you a brochure detailing what's offered.

Coverage starts at $95 for a wedding; the total cost will depend on what you want. Rob Nuccio's coverage is underwritten by Fireman's Fund.

Here are some of the items a typical policy might cover:

- Cancellation or postponement due to: weather, damage to the facility, sickness, failure to show of the caterer or officiant, financial reasons—even limited change-of-heart circumstances!

- Photography or videography: failure of the professional to appear, loss of original negatives, etc.

- Lost, stolen or damaged gifts

- Lost, stolen or damaged equipment rentals

- Lost, stolen or damaged bridal gown or other special attire

- Lost, stolen or damaged jewelry

- Personal liability and additional coverage

- Medical payments for injuries incurred during the event

If you use this service, call or email to let us know whether you're happy with them. We'd love to get your feedback.

It Can't Happen To Me

Don't be lulled into the notion that an event disaster can't happen to you. It could rain when you least expect it. Or your well-intentioned aunt might melt your wedding dress while ironing out a few wrinkles. Wouldn't it be nice to know that your dress, wedding photos, equipment rentals and gifts are covered? Naturally, a New Year's Eve party or a high school prom night is riskier than a wedding, but we could tell you stories of upscale parties where something did happen and a lawsuit resulted.

So even if extra insurance is not required, you may still want to consider additional coverage, especially if alcohol is being served. *You are the best predictor of your guests' behavior.* If you plan on having a wild, wonderful event, a little additional insurance could be a good thing.

Recycling

Do Your Part!

If you're wondering why we're including a brief item about recycling in a book like *Here Comes The Guide*, it's because parties and special events often generate recyclable materials and leftover food that the newlyweds don't want to take home. Nowadays, you and the caterer can feel good by donating the excess, and recycling plastic bottles, glass, metal and paper. An added benefit is that food donations are tax deductible for either you or the caterer. And if you recycle, the cost for extra garbage containers (bins) can be eliminated or reduced. To recycle, call your local recycling center to arrange a pickup.

Food donations are distributed to teenage drop-in centers, youth shelters, alcoholic treatment centers, AIDS hospices, senior centers and refugee centers throughout the region.

IMPORTANT: There are regulations that apply to the kinds of foods that can be donated and how they need to be packaged. If you plan to donate your leftovers, it's best to talk to your caterer about it or call your local food bank prior to your event to find out what their requirements for preparation and drop-off are.

We've provided a list of some well-known Southern California food banks, but you can also look online to find others that may be more convenient for you.

For more valuable tips about going green, read our article "It's A Nice Day for a Green Wedding." You'll find it in the "Green Weddings" category on the Wedding Checklist page on HereComesTheGuide.com!

Donation Organizations

- **Los Angeles Regional Food Bank**
  L.A. County   323/234-3030
  www.lafightshunger.org

- **Food Bank of SB County**
  Santa Barbara   805/967-5741
  www.foodbanksbc.org

- **Food Bank of Southern California**
  Long Beach   562/435-3577
  www.foodbankofsocal.org

- **Food Share, Inc.**
  Oxnard/Ventura   805/983-7100
  www.foodshare.com

- **Orange County Food Bank**
  Garden Grove   714/897-6670
  www.ocfoodbank.org

- **San Diego Food Bank**
  San Diego   866/350-3663
  www.sandiegofoodbank.org

- **Second Harvest Food Bank**
  Orange County   949/653-2900
  www.feedoc.org

- **Second Harvest**
  San Bernardino &
  Riverside Counties   951/359-4757
  www.secondharvest.us

Questions To Ask
Venues and Event Professionals

(including The Guide Bride's Wedding Checklist)

The Guide Bride's Wedding Checklist

10–12 Months To Go...

☑ Visit HereComesTheGuide.com and start planning your wedding!

☐ Work out your budget and establish your top priorities—where to save/where to splurge.

☐ Find ideas. Start browsing bridal blogs and magazines (or visit Pinterest.com/HCTG) to identify your wedding style and color palette.

☐ Compile your preliminary guest list (you'll need that guest count!).

☐ Choose your wedding party—who do you want by your side at the altar?

☐ Find a venue for your ceremony and reception, and reserve your date.

☐ Now that you have a date, tell everyone to save it! For destination weddings or weddings around a holiday, consider sending out Save-the-Date cards or emails. Or create your own wedding website, and let your invitees know about it.

☐ Find a dress and begin assembling the perfect accessories. Need inspiration? Visit a bridal fair.

☐ Already feeling overwhelmed? Consider hiring a Wedding Coordinator.

☐ Assemble an all-star vendor team. We'd start with:
  • Caterer
  • Photographer/Videographer
  • Officiant

When you hire a vendor, get all the details in writing!

☐ Another way to minimize stress: Start dreaming up your honeymoon…and check out our "Plan A Honeymoon" section on HereComesTheGuide.com.

6–9 Months To Go...

☐ Continue researching, interviewing and booking vendors. And don't forget, when you hire one make sure to put everything in writing!
  • Decide on arrangements with your Floral Designer.

  • Do a tasting and choose your wedding cake with your Cake Designer.
  • Hire the DJ/Entertainment for your ceremony, cocktail hour and reception.
  • Discuss the style and wording of your wedding invitations with a Stationer.

☐ Create your gift registry (and don't forget to update your wedding website!).

☐ Arrange hotel room blocks for out-of-town guests and book your own suite for the wedding night. See HereComesTheGuide.com for room block options.

☐ Shop for bridesmaid/flower girl dresses and give your attendants clear instructions on how to place their orders.

☐ Arrange and book any necessary transportation.

☐ Go over bridal shower/bachelorette details and the guest list with the person(s) hosting your party.

3–5 Months To Go...

☐ Book the rehearsal and rehearsal dinner location(s). If you're including entertainment or specialty details like a groom's cake, now's the time to lock in these elements.

☐ Put together your rehearsal dinner guest list.

☐ Make childcare arrangements for your guests' kids.

☐ Reserve all necessary party rentals and linens.

☐ Order wedding favors for your guests.

☐ Shop for and reserve men's formalwear.

☐ Concentrate on finalizing the:
  • Guest list. Get everyone's mailing address.
  • Invitation wording. Confirm your invitation text with the Stationer, and consider additional stationery (programs, menu cards, place cards, thank-you cards, etc.). Schedule a pickup date for your invites.
  • Ceremony readings and vows.
  • Menu, beverage and catering details.
  • Timeline of the reception formalities.

☐ Do a Makeup & Hair trial and book your stylists. While you're at it, come up with your own beauty and fitness regimen to be camera-ready for the big day.

☐ Shop for and purchase your wedding rings.

☐ Finalize honeymoon plans and obtain all necessary documents (are you sure your passports are up to date?).

6–8 Weeks To Go...

☐ You're getting close...mail out those invitations! Have a game plan for recording the RSVPs and meal choices.

☐ Touch base with your vendors to confirm date, deposits and details.

☐ Start researching marriage license requirements and name-change paperwork.

☐ Begin your dress fittings. Be sure to buy the appropriate undergarments beforehand.

☐ So you think you *can't* dance? Consider taking a dance lesson with your fiancé—a good way to break in your bridal shoes!

☐ Give the wedding party a nudge—make sure they've ordered all necessary attire.

☐ Write thank-you cards for shower gifts and any early wedding gifts received.

3–5 Weeks To Go...

☐ Send out rehearsal dinner invitations. If your get-together will be informal, feel free to send an Evite.

☐ Finalize and confirm:
- Wedding vows and readings with your Officiant.
- Shot list with your Photographer/ Videographer.
- Song list for ceremony, cocktail hour and reception with your DJ and/or Band/ Musicians.
- Timeline for the reception and who's giving the toasts.
- Wedding night and honeymoon accommodations.

☐ Obtain marriage license and complete name-change documents, if applicable.

☐ Pick up your wedding rings and proofread any engraving!

☐ If you're the traditional type, do you have something old, new, borrowed and blue?

☐ Purchase your guest book, toasting flutes, cake servers, unity candle, and all that good stuff.

☐ Buy gifts (optional) for the wedding party and parents of the bride and groom.

☐ Have your final dress fitting. Bring your shoes and accessories for the full impact.

☐ Sigh. Hunt down whoever hasn't RSVP'd yet.

1–2 Weeks To Go...

☐ Give your caterer/venue the final guest count.

☐ Arrange seating and create the seating chart and/or place cards.

☐ Pick up your gown. Swoon.

☐ Confirm arrival times and finalize the wedding timeline with vendors and the wedding party—make sure your MOH has a copy, too.

☐ Put together your own Bridal Emergency Kit.

☐ Speaking of emergencies: Check the weather report, and if things look iffy contact your venue to make sure a contingency plan is in place.

☐ Start packing for your honeymoon. (See "weather report" above.)

☐ In desperate need of a facial or massage? Now's the time to squeeze one in.

The Day Before...

☐ Make sure all wedding-day items are packed/ laid out and ready to go! (Don't forget the rings and marriage license!)

☐ Figure out tips and final payments for vendors. Put them in clearly marked envelopes and give them to the Best Man or another person you trust to hand out at the reception.

☐ Assign someone to pack up your gifts/ belongings after the reception (don't forget the top tier of your cake!).

☐ Thank your BFF for agreeing to return your groom's tux and other rental items the day after the wedding.

☐ Enjoy a mani-pedi.

☐ Attend the rehearsal and dinner. Now's the time to give out wedding party gifts.

☐ Try to go to bed early…you need your beauty sleep tonight.

Here Comes The Guide Bride!

☐ Allow plenty of time for the bride beautification process.

☐ Do the rounds at your wedding—greet everyone and thank them for coming.

☐ Take a deep breath. Stop to appreciate your new spouse and the day that you spent so much time planning!

After the Honeymoon/Back to Reality...

☐ Write and send thank-you cards. (Don't procrastinate!)

☐ Complete your registry and exchange any unwanted or duplicate gifts.

☐ Have your wedding dress cleaned and preserved by a reputable company.

☐ Keep in touch with your Photographer/ Videographer to work on albums, DVDs, etc.

☐ Enjoy wedded bliss…

Questions to Ask an Event Venue

Here Comes The Guide is a fantastic resource to help you find the location to host your wedding, rehearsal dinner or company party. Even with all the info we provide, though, you'll need to address your specific needs with each venue you visit to come up with a winner.

The following list of questions and tips will help you navigate through your location search (for a printable version, go to HereComesThe Guide.com). Use them as a guide while you're talking with a site contact or reviewing a site information packet. Feel free to add questions that relate to your particular event (e.g. "Can my dog be the ring bearer in my ceremony?") Make sure to get everything in writing in your final contract! **Don't forget to have a notebook or your planning binder handy so that you can record answers to all these questions.**

1. What dates are available in the month I'm considering?

2. How many people can this location accommodate?

3. What is the rental fee and what is included in that price? Is there a discount for booking an off-season date or Sunday through Friday?

4. How much is the deposit, when is it due, and is it refundable? What's the payment plan for the entire bill?

5. Can I hold my ceremony here, too? Is there an additional charge? Is the ceremony site close to the reception site? Is there a bride's changing area? How much time is allocated for the rehearsal?

6. Is the site handicap accessible? (To be asked if you have guests with mobility issues.)

7. What's the cancellation policy? *NOTE: Some places will refund most of your deposit if you cancel far enough in advance (often 60 days), since there's still a chance they can rent the space. After a certain date, though, you may not be able to get a refund—at least not a full one.*

8. What's your weather contingency plan for outdoor spaces?

9. How long will I have use of the event space(s) I reserve? Is there an overtime fee if I stay longer? Is there a minimum or maximum rental time?

10. Can I move things around and decorate to suit my purposes, or do I have to leave everything as is? Are there decoration guidelines/restrictions? Can I use real candles? *TIP: Keep the existing décor in mind when planning your own decorations so that they won't clash. If your event is in December, ask what the venue's holiday décor will be.*

11. What time can my vendors start setting up on the day of the wedding? Is it possible to start the setup the day before? How early can deliveries be made? How much time will I have for décor setup? Does the venue provide assistance getting gifts or décor back to a designated car, hotel room, etc. after the event has concluded?

12. Do you provide a coat check service (especially important for winter weddings)? If not, is there an area that can be used and staffed for that purpose?

13. Is there an outdoor space where my guests can mingle, and can it be heated and/or protected from the elements if necessary? Is there a separate indoor "socializing" space?

14. Do you have an in-house caterer or a list of "preferred" caterers, or do I need to provide my own? Even if there is an in-house caterer, do I have the option of using an outside caterer instead?

15. If I hire my own caterer, are kitchen facilities available for them? *NOTE: Caterers charge extra if they have to haul in refrigerators and stoves.*

16. Are tables, linens, chairs, plates, silverware and glassware provided, or will I have to rent them myself or get them through my caterer?

17. What is the food and beverage cost on a per/person basis? What is the service charge?

18. Can we do a food tasting prior to finalizing our menu selection? If so, is there an additional charge?

19. Can I bring in a cake from an outside cake maker or must I use a cake made on the premises? Is there a cake-cutting fee? If I use a cake made on site is the fee waived? Do you provide special cake-cutting utensils?

20. Can I bring my own wine, beer or champagne, and is there a corkage fee if I do? Can I bring in other alcohol?

21. Are you licensed to provide alcohol service? If so, is alcohol priced per person? By consumption? Are there additional charges for bar staff? Is there a bar minimum that must be met before the conclusion of the event? What is the average bar tab for the number of people attending my event? *NOTE: Some facilities (private estates and wineries in particular) aren't licensed to serve hard alcohol. You may need to get permission from the location to bring in an outside beverage catering company.*

22. Are there restrictions on what kind of music I can play, or a time by which the music must end? Can the venue accommodate a DJ or live band? *TIP: Check where the outlets are located in your event space, because that will help you figure out where the band can set up and where other vendors can hook up their equipment. You don't want the head table to block the only outlet in the room.*

23. Is there parking on site? If so, is it complimentary? Do you offer valet parking, and what is the charge? If there is no parking on site, where will my guests park? Are cabs easily accessible from the venue?? If a shuttle service is needed, can you assist with setting it up? *TIP: You should have the venue keep track of the number of cars parked for your event and add the total valet gratuity to your final bill so that your guests won't have to tip.*

24. How many restrooms are there? *TIP: You should have at least 4 restrooms per 100 people.*

25. Do you offer on-site coordination? If so, what services are included and is there an additional charge for them? Will the coordinator supervise day-of? How much assistance can I get with the setup/décor?

26. What security services do you offer? Do I need to hire my own security guards, or does the site hire them or have them on staff? *TIP: In general, you should have 2 security guards for the first 100 guests and 1 more for every additional 100 guests.*

27. Does the venue have liability insurance? *NOTE: If someone gets injured during the party, you don't want to be held responsible—if the site doesn't have insurance, you'll need to get your own. For info on insurance go to www.rvnuccio.com.*

28. Can I hire my own vendors (caterer, coordinator, DJ, etc.), or must I select from a preferred vendor list? If I can bring my own, do you have a list of recommended vendors? *TIP: Check out the prescreened vendors featured in this book and on HereComesTheGuide.com. They're all top event professionals who have passed our extensive reference check and been Certified By The Guide.*

29. What overnight accommodations do you provide? Do you offer a discount for booking multiple rooms? Do you provide a complimentary room or upgrade for the newlyweds? What are the nearest hotels to the venue? *TIP: Some venues have partnerships with local hotels that offer a discount if you book a block of rooms.*

30. Do you have signage or other aids to direct guests to my event?

31. Do you have a recycling policy?

More Tips:

- If you really love the site, ask the venue representative to put together a proposal with all the pricing and policies—including the tax and service charge—so you have an idea of the basic cost.

- Bring a digital or video camera with you when you visit locations. You can mention each location and its event spaces as you video a site; if you're using a digital camera you'll need to organize the photos by location name when you get home. After seeing a series of places it's easy to confuse them. Having a photographic record will help you remember what was special about each site.

- Pay attention to the venue as a whole: Check out everything, including the restrooms, the foyer, the dressing rooms, the outdoor lighting and even the kitchen. You want to be sure your vision can be realized at this location. If possible, make arrangements with the site representative to visit the venue when it's set up for a wedding.

- GET EVERYTHING IN WRITING. Your date is not officially reserved until you sign a contract and, in many cases, give a deposit—even if a site contact says you don't need to worry about it. Once you've found THE PLACE, make sure you ask what is required to get your booking locked in and then follow through on satisfying those requirements. And don't assume that just because the site coordinator said you can have 4 votive candles per table you'll get them. Before you sign a contract, read the fine print and make sure it includes everything you and the site contact agreed on. As new things are added or changed in your contract, have the updated version printed out and signed by you and the site representative. Also, document all your conversations in emails and keep your correspondence.

For PDF versions of these QUESTIONS TO ASK, visit www.HereComesTheGuide.com

Questions to Ask a Wedding Photographer

You've put so much time and effort into planning your wedding you'll want every special moment captured for your photo album. But how do you know which photographer is right for you? Whether you're considering any of our *Certified By The Guide* wedding photographers or another professional, you need to do your homework.

Here are the questions you should ask those photographers who've made your short list, to ensure that the one you ultimately choose is a good fit for you and your wedding.

The Basics

1. Do you have my date available? *NOTE: Obviously, if the answer is NO and you're not willing or able to change your date, don't bother asking the rest of these questions.*

2. How far in advance do I need to book with you?

3. How long have you been in business?

4. How many weddings have you shot? Have you done many that were similar to mine in size and style?

5. How would you describe your photography style (e.g. traditional, photojournalistic, creative)? *NOTE: It's helpful to know the differences between wedding photography styles so that you can discuss your preferences with your photographer. For descriptions of the various styles, see the next page.*

6. How would you describe your working style? *NOTE: The answer should help you determine whether this is a photographer who blends into the background and shoots what unfolds naturally, or creates a more visible presence by taking charge and choreographing shots.*

7. What do you think distinguishes your work from that of other photographers?

8. Do you have a portfolio I can review? Are all of the images yours, and is the work recent?

9. What type of equipment do you use?

10. Are you shooting in digital or film format or both? *NOTE: The general consensus seems to be that either format yields excellent photos in the hands of an experienced professional, and that most people can't tell the difference between film and digital images anyway. However, film takes longer to process than digital.*

11. Do you shoot in color and black & white? Infrared? *NOTE: Photographers who shoot in a digital format can make black & white or sepia versions of color photos.*

12. Can I give you a list of specific shots we would like?

13. Can you put together a slideshow of the engagement session (along with other photos the couple provides) and show it during the cocktail hour? What about an "instant" slideshow of the ceremony?

14. What information do you need from me before the wedding day?

15. Have you ever worked with my florist? DJ? Coordinator, etc.? *NOTE: Great working relationships between vendors can make things go more smoothly. It's especially helpful if your videographer and photographer work well together.*

16. May I have a list of references? *NOTE: The photographer should not hesitate to provide this.*

The Shoot

17. Are you the photographer who will shoot my wedding? If so, will you have any assistants with you on that day? If not, who will be taking the pictures and can I meet them before my wedding? *NOTE: You should ask the questions on this list of whoever is going to be the primary photographer at your event, and that photographer's name should be on your contract.*

18. Do you have backup equipment? What about a backup plan if you (or my scheduled photographer) are unable to shoot my wedding for some reason?

19. If my wedding site is out of your area, do you charge a travel fee and what does that cover?

20. Are you photographing other events on the same day as mine?

21. How will you (and your assistants) be dressed? *NOTE: The photographer and his/her staff should look professional and fit in with the style of your event.*

22. Is it okay if other people take photos while you're taking photos?

23. Have you ever worked at my wedding site before? If not, do you plan to check it out in advance? *NOTE: Photographers who familiarize themselves with a location ahead of time will be prepared for any lighting issues or restrictions, and will know how best to incorporate the site's architectural elements into the photos.*

24. What time will you arrive at the site and for how long will you shoot?

25. If my event lasts longer than expected, will you stay? Is there an additional charge?

Packages, Proofs and Prints

26. What packages do you offer?

27. Can I customize a package based on my needs?

28. Do you include engagement photos in your packages?

29. What type of album designs do you offer? Do you provide any assistance in creating an album?

30. Do you provide retouching, color adjustment or other corrective services?

31. How long after the wedding will I get the proofs? Will they be viewable online? On a CD?

32. What is the ordering process?

33. How long after I order my photos/album will I get them?

34. Will you give me the negatives or the digital images, and is there a fee for that?

Contracts and Policies

35. When will I receive a written contract? *TIP: Don't book a photographer—or any vendor—who won't provide a written contract.*

36. How much of a deposit do you require and when is it due? Do you offer a payment plan?

37. What is your refund/cancellation policy?

38. Do you have liability insurance?

Questions to Ask Yourself:

1. Do I feel a connection with this photographer as well as his/her photos? Are our personalities a good match?

2. Am I comfortable with this person's work and communication style?

3. Has this photographer listened well and addressed all my concerns?

Check references. *Ask the photographer for at least 5 references, preferably of couples whose weddings were similar to yours in size and/or style. Getting feedback from several people who have actually hired the photographer in question can really help you decide if that person is right for you. Be sure to check out the photographers in this book and on HereComesTheGuide. com. They're some of the best in the business and have all been Certified By The Guide.*

Photography Style Glossary

Though there are no standard "dictionary definitions" of photographic styles, it's still a good idea to have an understanding of the following approaches before you interview photographers:

Traditional, Classic: The main idea behind this time-less style is to produce posed photographs for display in a portrait album. The photographer works from a "shot list," ensuring he or she covers all the elements the bride and groom have requested. To make sure every detail of the shots is perfect, the photographer and her assistants not only adjust their equipment, but also the background, the subject's body alignment, and even the attire.

Photojournalism: Originally favored by the news media, this informal, reality-based approach is the current rage in wedding photography. Rather than posing your pictures, the photographer follows you and your guests throughout the wedding day, capturing events as they unfold in order to tell the story of your wedding. The photographer has to be able to fade into the background and become "invisible" to the crowd in order to get these candid or unposed shots. Since the photojournalist does not give direction, he'll need a keen eye and a willingness to "do what it takes to get the shot."

Illustrative Photography: This style, which is often used for engagement photos, is a pleasing blend of traditional and photojournalistic, with an emphasis on composition, lighting and background. The photographer places subjects together in an interesting environment and encourages them to relax and interact. Illustrative captures some of the spontaneity of candids, while offering the technical control of posed shots.

Portraiture: Traditional photographers generally excel at the precision required in portraiture—formal, posed pictures that emphasize one or more people. Couples interested in a more edgy result may prefer Fine Art Portraiture, with its dramatic lighting, unique angles and European flavor.

High Fashion: Commercial photographers excel at creating striking, simple photographs that dramatize the subject—and, of course, her clothes! Though not a style generally included in wedding photography, you may want to choose a photographer with high fashion experience if looking artsy and glamorous while showing off your dress is important to you.

Natural Light: Rather than using a camera flash, photographers use the natural light found in a setting, usually daylight. The look is warm and, well, natural—yet the photographer must be skilled to deal with shadows and other lighting challenges.

Questions to Ask a Wedding Planner

In the first flush of joy after your engagement, you'll probably begin browsing magazines and wedding websites…and soon feel buried by a blizzard of checklists and a daunting array of decisions. That's when you and your fiancé might want to think about hiring a professional wedding planner.

Good idea. Depending on your budget and needs, you can contract:

- a full-service planner to arrange every detail

- someone to assist you only in choosing your wedding location and vendors

- a day-of coordinator (which really means 30 days before your wedding)

NOTE: Many locations have in-house coordinators, but make sure you're clear on exactly what level of service they provide. Venue coordinators usually just handle day-of issues and offer a list of their preferred vendors, so having your own planner may still be a great help.

Even though hiring a planner is an added cost, they often end up saving you money in the long run. And no doubt about it—the right wedding planner can definitely save you time and stress (priceless!).

Before interviewing potential wedding planners, you and your fiancé should have an idea of:

- How much money you have in your budget

- How many people you would like to invite

- Your preferred wedding date

- Your vision for your wedding *(NOTE: If you aren't sure yet don't worry—getting help with this is one of the reasons why you're hiring a wedding planner!)*

After each interview is complete, ask yourselves:

- Did we feel heard?

- Does the planner understand our vision?

- Did we get a strong sense he/she will work with our budget?

- Was there a good connection and did our personalities mesh well?

Listen to your gut. If an interview doesn't feel right, then maybe that person just isn't a good fit for you. Your wedding planner is the vendor you'll be spending the most time with, so it's important to pick someone who's compatible with you and your fiancé.

Now, here are THE QUESTIONS!

Getting to Know a Planner

1. Do you have our wedding date open? If so, do you anticipate any issues with the date such as weather, travel for our guests, difficulty booking a venue, etc.?

2. What made you want to be a wedding planner?

3. Describe the most challenging wedding you planned and how you handled the problems that came up.

4. How would you rate your problem-solving skills?

5. How would you rate your communication skills?

6. Are you a certified wedding planner? If so, where did you get certified? What is your educational background?

7. Are you a member of any wedding association(s)? If so, does your association require you to satisfy yearly education requirements?

8. How long have you been in business? Do you have a business license?

9. How many full-scale weddings have you planned? When was your last one?

10. How many wedding clients do you take on in a year? How many do you expect to have during the month of our wedding?

11. Is wedding planning your full-time job? If it's part-time, what is your other job?

Working With the Venue

12. Have you ever worked at the venue we've chosen?

13. If our event is outdoors, what contingency plan would you have for bad weather? (Describe an event where you had weather issues and how you resolved them.)

Hiring Other Vendors

14. Are we required to book only the vendors you recommend or do we have the freedom to hire someone even if you haven't worked with them before?

15. Do you take a commission or discount from any of the vendors you would refer us to?

16. Will you be present at all of the vendor meetings and will you assist us in reviewing all of the vendor contracts and making sure everything is in order?

17. Will you invoice us for all the vendor fees or will we need to pay each one of them ourselves?

18. For the vendors who will be on site the day of our wedding, can I provide you with checks for final payment that you will distribute to them?

19. If issues arise with the vendors before, during or after our wedding, will you handle them or are we responsible for this?

Scope of Work

20. What kind planning do you offer? Logistical only (i.e. organizational—handling things like the timeline and floor plan) or Design and Logistical (i.e. bringing a client's vision to life as well as taking care of all the organizational aspects of the wedding)?

21. If you just do logistical planning, can you refer us to a vendor who can assist us with event design? (NOTE: Floral designers often do full event design, as do vendors who specialize in design.)

22. Will you handle every aspect of the planning or can we do some things on our own? In other words, what parts of the planning will we be responsible for?

23. Will you be the person on site the day of our wedding or will it be another planner? How many assistants will you have?

24. In case of an emergency that prevents you from being at our wedding, who will be the backup planner? What are their qualifications?

25. What time will you arrive and depart on the day of our wedding?

26. Will you stay on site after our wedding to make sure everything has been broken down and all vendors have left the location?

27. Will you provide us with a timeline of the wedding and a floor plan of the wedding venue?

28. Do you offer different package options or is everything customized based on what we're looking for?

29. How many meetings and phone calls are included in our package?

30. Is the wedding day rehearsal included in your services?

31. Do any of your packages include planning the rehearsal dinner and/or post-wedding brunch? If not, would you provide that service and what would be the extra cost to include it in our contract?

32. Do any of your packages include honeymoon planning? If not, would you provide that service and what would be the extra cost to include it in our contract?

33. Do any of your packages include assistance with finding my wedding dress and wedding party attire? If not, would you provide that service and what would be the extra cost to include it in our contract?

Getting Down to Business

34. Once we book with you, how quickly can we expect to receive the contract?

35. After we give you our budget, will you provide us with a breakdown of how the money is going to be allocated?

36. As changes are made to our plans, will you update us with a revised estimate and updated contract?

37. How do you charge for your services? Hourly, percentage of the wedding cost, or flat rate?

38. Can you provide a detailed list of all the items included in your fee?

39. What is your payment policy? Do you accept credit cards?

40. How much of a deposit is required to book your services? When is the final payment due?

41. Are there any fees that won't be included in your proposal that we should be aware of?

42. What is your refund or cancellation policy?

43. Can you provide a list of references? NOTE: Any experienced coordinator should be able to give you plenty of references. For a list of Coordinators/ Wedding Planners you can trust, see the ones we've featured in this book and on HereComesTheGuide. com. They've all passed our difficult certification process with flying colors! Brides told us how much they loved working with them, so we wanted to recommend them to you.

44. Can you provide us with a portfolio and/or video of weddings you have done?

Questions to Ask a Caterer

Besides your location, the food and drink for your wedding bash will probably consume the largest portion of your wedding budget. Catering costs are usually presented as "per-person" charges, sometimes abbreviated in wedding brochures as "pp" after the amount. But be aware—the per-person charge often doesn't include everything: Tax and the gratuity (sometimes called the "service charge") might be extra, and there may also be separate per-person charges for the meal, drinks, hors d'oeuvres, and even setup. So your actual per-person charge might end up being considerably more than you expect. Bring your calculator along when meeting with potential caterers to help you arrive at the real bottom line.

There's more to consider. Nowadays, many caterers offer a range of services in addition to catering. Some are actual "event producers," providing props, special effects, décor—in other words, complete event design. They might also be able to assist in finding a location, coordinating your affair, or lining up vendors. One thing a caterer can't do, however, is cook up a 5-course Beef Wellington dinner for $20 per person. When planning your menu, be realistic about what you can serve given your budget and the size of your guest list.

A lot of factors come into play when selecting a caterer, so don't be afraid to ask as many questions as you need to. You can refer to the following list, whether your potential caterer works at your event facility or you're hiring them independently.

The Basics

1. Do you have my date open?

2. How many weddings do you do per year, and how long have you been in business?

3. Have you done events at my location? *TIP: If you haven't chosen your location yet, ask the caterer if they can help you select one.*

4. Are you licensed by the state of California? Are you licensed to serve alcohol?

5. Will I need any permits for my event? If so, will you handle obtaining them?

6. Will you provide a banquet manager to coordinate the meal service or an on-site coordinator who will run the entire event?

7. Can you assist with other aspects of the wedding like selecting other vendors, event design (e.g. specialty lighting, elaborate décor, theme events, etc.)?

Food & Presentation

8. Given my budget, guest count and event style, what food choices would you recommend? Do you specialize in certain cuisines?

9. Do we have to work off a preset menu or can you create a custom menu for our event? If I have a special dish I'd like served, would you accommodate that?

10. Do you offer event packages or is everything à la carte? What exactly do your packages include?

11. Do you use all fresh produce, meat, fish, etc.? Can you source organic or sustainably farmed ingredients?

12. Can you accommodate dietary restrictions, such as kosher, vegan, etc.?

13. What décor do you provide for appetizer stations or buffet tables?

14. Do you offer package upgrades such as chocolate fountains, ice sculptures, cappuccino machines or specialty displays?

15. Can you do theme menus (e.g. barbecue, luau, etc.)? Would you also provide the décor?

16. What's the difference in cost between passed appetizers and appetizer stations? What's the price difference between a buffet and a sit-down meal? If we have a buffet, are there any stations that cost extra, like a carving station? *NOTE: Don't automatically assume that a buffet is going to be the less expensive option. Ask your caterer which type of service is more affordable for you, given the menu you're planning.*

17. How much do you charge for children's meals?

18. How much do you charge for vendor meals?

19. Do you do wedding cakes? If so, is this included in the per-person meal price or is it extra?

20. Can you show me photos of cakes you've done in the past?

21. If I decide not to serve cake, can you provide a dessert display instead?

22. If we use an outside cake designer, do you charge a cake-cutting fee?

23. Do you do food tastings and is there an extra charge for this?

24. Do you handle rental equipment such as tables, chairs, etc.?

25. What types of linens, glassware, plates and flatware do you provide? *NOTE: Some low-budget caterers have basic packages that use disposable dinnerware instead of the real thing, so make sure you know exactly what you'll be getting.*

26. Can you provide presentation upgrades such as chair covers, lounge furniture, Chiavari chairs, etc.? What would be the additional fees?

27. What is your policy on cleanup? *TIP: Be very clear about what "cleanup" means and who's responsible for handling it—and be sure to get it in writing. We've heard many tales about caterers that left dirty dishes, trash and uneaten food behind. In most cases, when you rent a location it will be YOUR responsibility to leave the place in acceptable condition. You want to spend your wedding night with your honey, not picking up empty bottles from the lawn!*

28. If there is leftover food from my event, can we have it wrapped up for guests to take home or have it delivered to a local shelter?

Drink

29. Do you provide alcoholic beverages and bartenders? Can you accommodate specialty cocktails?

30. What brands of alcohol will be served?

31. Can we provide the alcohol and you provide the bar labor?

32. Do you charge a corkage fee if we provide our own wine or champagne?

33. How do you charge for alcoholic and non-alcoholic beverages? Per consumption or per person? Which is more cost-effective?

34. Is the champagne toast after the ceremony included in your meal packages or is it extra?

35. Will your staff serve the wine with dinner?

36. How long will alcohol be served?

37. Is coffee and tea service included with the per-person meal charge? What brands of each do you offer and do they include decaf and herbal tea options?

Business Matters

38. What is the ratio of servers to guests?

39. How will the servers be dressed?

40. How is your pricing broken down (e.g. food, bar, cake-cutting, tax, gratuity)? *NOTE: Usually tax and a service charge are tacked on to your final cost. The service charge, which can range 18–23%, is used to tip the staff. And in many states, the service charge itself is taxable.*

41. How much time do you require for setting up and breaking down my event, and are there extra fees for this?

42. If my event runs longer than contracted, what are your overtime fees?

43. What is the last date by which I can give you a final guaranteed guest count?

44. What is your payment policy? Do you accept credit cards?

45. How much of a deposit is required to hold my date? When is the final payment due?

46. Are there any fees that won't be included in the proposal that we should be aware of?

47. Once we book with you, how quickly can we expect a contract? And if we make changes to menu choices or other items, will you update us with a revised estimate and contract?

48. What is your refund or cancellation policy?

49. Can you provide a list of recent references? *TIP: See the caterers we feature in this book and on HereComesTheGuide.com. These pre-screened companies provide great food and service, and they all passed our rigorous certification process with flying colors.*

Questions to Ask a Floral Designer

Floral designers do much more than just supply the bouquet! They help create the look and mood for your wedding ceremony, as well as centerpieces and other table decorations for the reception. They add the floral flourishes for the wedding party (don't forget that corsage for Grandma!), and some may even work with your cake designer to provide embellishments.

Before sitting down with a floral designer, you should already have reserved your ceremony and reception venue. That way you'll be able to discuss how much additional floral décor will be needed to either achieve a specific look at your site or complement an existing garden and/or room aesthetic.

Another must: Don't design the wedding bouquet until you've ordered your wedding dress. Since that task will hopefully be completed at least 6 months before your wedding date (hint, hint!), you should have plenty of time to work out the details of both your accessories and floral décor.

So where to start? Do a little research prior to interviewing floral artists by visiting the websites or shops of vendors you're considering. You want to know that whomever you hire can create bouquets and arrangements that suit your style.

Once you've compiled your short list of contenders, use these questions to zero in on your final choice:

The Basics

1. Do you have my date open?

2. Have you done events at my ceremony and reception location(s) before? If not, are you familiar with the sites?

3. How long have you been in business?

4. How many weddings have you done?

5. Where did you receive your training?

6. How many other weddings or events will you schedule on the same day?

7. Will you be doing my arrangements yourself or would it be another floral designer?

8. What design styles (e.g. ikebana, traditional, modern, trendy, European, Oriental) do you work in?

9. Can you work with my budget?

10. What recommendations can you give me to maximize my budget?

11. Do you offer specific packages or is everything customized?

12. Can you provide me with 3–4 recent brides that I can contact for references?

The Flowers

13. What flowers are in season for the month I am getting married?

14. Based on my color scheme and budget, what flowers do you recommend?

15. Is there a difference in price if I use one type of flower vs. a mixed arrangement or bouquet?

16. If I request it, can you provide any organic, pesiticide-free or sustainably grown varieties? *TIP: Organic roses cost more, but last so much longer!*

17. What are the different kinds of wraps (called "collars" in florist-speak) you can do for my bouquet?

18. What about coordinating boutonnières, bridesmaid flowers, and centerpieces? Can you suggest anything special to coordinate with the theme/venue/season of my event?

19. What other décor can you provide (aisle runner, candelabras, trees, arches, votives, mirrors, etc.)? How will these items affect the overall cost?

20. If I give you a picture of a bouquet and/or arrangement that I like, can you recreate it?

21. Do you have photos or live examples of florals designed in the style I want?

22. Can you do sketches or mockups of the arrangements you've described before I sign the contract? If so, is there an additional fee for this?

23. Will you work with my cake designer if I decide to add flowers to my wedding cake? If so, is there an additional setup fee for this?

24. How far in advance of the wedding will you create the bouquets and arrangements, and how are they stored?

25. Can you assist me in the preservation of my bouquet after the wedding? If not, can you recommend someone?

The Costs

26. Do you charge a delivery fee?

27. Do you have an extra charge for the setup and breakdown of the floral décor?

28. Is there an extra fee if I need you to stay through-out the ceremony to move arrangements to the reception site?

29. Are there any additional fees that have not already been taken into account?

The Contract

30. How far in advance do I need to secure your services? What is the deposit required to secure my date?

31. Will you provide me with an itemized list of all the elements we've discussed, along with prices?

32. When can I expect to receive my contract from you?

33. What is your refund policy if for some reason I need to cancel my order?

Useful Tips:

- Prior to meeting with potential floral designers: have your color scheme finalized; create a list of the kinds of flowers you like; and have some examples (pictures from magazines, the web, etc.) of the kind of bouquets and arrangements that appeal to you.

- After you've met with each floral designer ask yourself, "Did the florist answer all my questions to my satisfaction?" "Do I feel like the florist really listened and understood my vision?" "Am I comfortable with this person?"

- Once you've booked your floral designer you'll want to provide them with a picture of your dress and swatches or photos of the bridesmaids dresses and the linens you'll be using.

Don't forget to browse our Floral Designers in this book and on HereComesTheGuide.com! They all got rave reviews during our rigorous certification process, and received the Certified By The Guide seal of approval.

For PDF versions of these QUESTIONS TO ASK, visit www.HereComesTheGuide.com

Questions to Ask a Cake Designer

Next to your dress, the cake is probably a wedding's most important icon. And whether you want a traditional multitiered confection, a miniature Statue of Liberty (hey, that's where he proposed!) or a cupcake tower, your wedding cake should reflect your personality. Use the following questions as a guide when evaluating a potential cake designer. If you're not familiar with cake terms, please see the cake glossary on page 35.

Business Matters

1. Do you have my wedding date open?

2. How many wedding cakes do you schedule on the same day? *NOTE: You want to feel comfortable that your designer is sufficiently staffed to handle the number of cakes they've scheduled to deliver and set up on your date.*

3. How do you price your cakes? By the slice? Does the cost vary depending on the design and flavors I choose?

4. What is your minimum per-person cake cost?

5. What recommendations can you give me to maximize my budget?

6. Do you have a "menu" of cakes and prices that I can take with me?

7. What are the fees for delivery and setup of the cake? Do you decorate the cake table, too?

8. What do you do if the cake gets damaged in transit to or at my reception site?

9. Do you provide or rent cake toppers, a cake-cutting knife, cake stands, etc.? What are the fees?

10. How far in advance should I order my cake?

11. How much is the deposit and when is it due?

12. When is the final payment due?

13. Are there any additional fees that I should be aware of?

14. What is your refund policy if for some reason I need to cancel my order? What if I'm not happy with the cake?

15. When can I expect to receive my contract from you?

Background Check

16. How long have you been in business? Are you licensed and insured?

17. How many weddings have you done?

18. Where did you receive your training?

19. Can you provide me with 3–4 recent brides that I can contact for references? *TIP: Check out the cake vendors featured in this book and on*

HereComesTheGuide.com. They're some of the best cake designers in Northern California and they've all been Certified By The Guide.

The Cake

20. Do you have a portfolio of your work I can view, and did you make all the cakes in it?

21. What are your specialties?

22. Can you design a custom cake to match my theme, dress or color scheme, or do I select from set designs?

23. If I provide you with a picture of what I'd like, can you recreate it? Does it cost extra for a custom design?

24. I have an old family cake recipe. Can you adapt it for my wedding cake design?

25. If I don't have a clear vision of what I would like, can you offer some design ideas based on my theme and budget?

26. What flavors and fillings do you offer?

27. What are the different ingredients you typically use? Do you offer all organic or vegan options? *TIP: Quality ingredients cost more, but the investment is worth it—the cake will taste better.*

28. Do you have cake tastings? Is there a charge?

29. Do you do both fondant and buttercream icing?

30. Are there any other icing options I should consider? Which do you recommend for my cake design?

31. Can you create sugar paste, gum paste or chocolate flowers? If I decide to have fresh flowers on my cake will you work with my florist or will you obtain and arrange the flowers yourself?

32. Will you preserve the top tier of my cake for my first wedding anniversary or do you provide a special cake for the occasion?

33. Can you make a groom's cake? Is this priced the same as my wedding cake?

34. How much in advance of the wedding is the cake actually made? Do you freeze your cakes? *NOTE: Wedding cakes usually take at least a couple of days to make.*

Useful Tips:

- Arrange a consultation with your potential cake designer in person, and do a tasting before you sign a contract. *NOTE: Not all cake tastings are complimentary.*

- Make sure your cake designer specializes in wedding cakes. A wedding cake is generally much more elaborate than a birthday cake from your local bakery. Your cake professional should have special training in constructing this type of cake.

- In general, you should order your cake 6–8 months prior to your wedding.

- You might be able to save money by choosing one overall flavor for your cake, or by having a small cake for display and the cake cutting accompanied by a sheet cake to serve to your guests.

Wedding Cake Glossary

Icings

Buttercream: It's rich and creamy, is easily colored or flavored, and is used for fancy decorations like shells, swags, basketweaves, icing flowers, etc. Since it's made almost entirely of butter (hence the name), buttercream has a tendency to melt in extreme heat, so it's not recommended for outdoor weddings.

Fondant: Martha Stewart's favorite. This icing looks smooth and stiff and is made with gelatin and corn syrup to give it its helmet-like appearance (it's really very cool looking). It looks best when decorated with marzipan fruits, gum paste flowers, or a simple ribbon, like Martha likes to do. Although not as tasty as buttercream or ganache, fondant does not need refrigeration so it's the perfect icing to serve at your beach wedding.

Royal Icing: A mix of confectioner's sugar and milk or egg whites, royal icing is what the faces of gingerbread men are decorated with. It's white, shiny and hard, and does not need to be refrigerated. It's used for decorations like dots and latticework.

Ganache: This chocolate and heavy cream combination is very dark, and has the consistency of store-bought chocolate icing. It can be poured over cakes for a glass-like chocolate finish or used as filling (it stands up wonderfully between cake layers). Due to the ingredients, however, it's unstable—don't use it in hot or humid weather or the icing will slide right off the cake.

Whipped Cream: Delicious, but by far the most volatile, fresh whipped cream is usually not recommended for wedding cakes because they have to be out of the fridge for so long. If you really want to use it (it looks extremely white and fresh, which goes beautifully with real flowers) just keep it in the fridge until the very last second.

Decorations

Marzipan: An Italian paste made of almonds, sugar and egg whites that is molded into flowers and fruits to decorate the cake. They're usually brightly colored and very sugary. Marzipan can also be used as icing.

Gum Paste: This paste, made from gelatin, cornstarch, and sugar, produces the world's most realistic, edible fruit and flower decorations. Famous cake designers like Sylvia Weinstock are huge fans of gum paste. One nice benefit: these decorations last for centuries in storage.

Piping: Piping is ideal for icing decorations like dotted Swiss, basketweave, latticework, and shells. It comes out of a pastry bag fitted with different tips to create these different looks, which can range from simple polka dots to a layered weave that you'd swear is a wicker basket.

Pulled Sugar: If you boil sugar, water, and corn syrup it becomes malleable and the most beautiful designs can be created. Roses and bows that have been made from pulled sugar look like silk or satin—they're so smooth and shiny.

Dragees: These hard little sugar balls are painted with edible gold or silver paint, and they look truly stunning on a big ol' wedding cake.

Questions to Ask a DJ or Live Entertainment

Too often choosing the entertainment is left to the end of your overwhelming "Wedding To Do List"—but it shouldn't be. Not only does music set the appropriate mood, but a skilled Master or Mistress of Ceremonies will gracefully guide your guests from one spotlight moment to another. And practically speaking, the best performers are often booked well in advance—so shake your groove thing, or you may be stuck doing the chicken dance with Uncle Edgar.

To get you started, we've put together this list of questions that will help you evaluate a DJ, band, or other entertainer. Note that rather than interviewing a specific performer or DJ yourself, you might be dealing with an entertainment agency rep.

The Basics

1. Do you have my date open?

2. Have you done events at my ceremony and/or reception location before? If not, are you familiar with them?

3. How long have you been in business? *NOTE: If you are interviewing a live band, you'll want to ask how long the musicians have played together. However, if you work with a reputable agency, instead of booking a specific band you'll most likely be getting seasoned professionals brought together for your event. Even though all the band members may not have played together before, they're professional musicians who are able to work together and sound fantastic anyway. The key is to make sure you book the specific singer and/or bandleader that you liked in the demo. The players will take their cues from them.*

4. How many weddings have you done? How many do you do in an average weekend?

5. What sets you apart from your competition?

6. Are there any other services that you provide, such as lighting design?

7. How far in advance do I need to secure your services?

8. Can you provide me with 3–4 recent brides that I can contact for references?

Pricing and Other Business Details

9. What is your pricing? Does this include setup and breakdown between ceremony and reception locations?

10. How much is the deposit and when is it due? When is the final payment due?

11. If the event lasts longer than scheduled, what are the overtime charges?

12. What is the continuous music charge? *NOTE: For bands, bookings traditionally run for 4 hours divided into 4 sets, each lasting 45 minutes with a 15-minute break. If you want "continuous music," i.e. with band members trading breaks, there is usually an additional charge.*

13. When can I expect to receive my contract from you?

14. Are there any additional fees that could accrue that I am not taking into account, like travel expenses or charges for special musical requests? (One performer was asked to prepare an entire set of songs from *Phantom of the Opera!* Yes, he charged extra.)

15. What is your refund policy if for some reason I need to cancel or alter my date?

16. Do you carry liability insurance? *NOTE: This usually only applies to production companies that also supply lighting, effects, etc.*

17. If I hire musicians for the ceremony and want them to play at the wedding rehearsal, what is the extra charge?

The Music

18. Do you have a DVD of your music or a video from a prior wedding where you performed?

19. Can you assist me in choosing the music for my processional, recessional, father-daughter dance, etc.?

20. How extensive is your music library or song list? What genres can you cover? Can I give you a specific list of songs I want or don't want played?

21. Are we guaranteed to have the performer(s) of our choice at our event? *SEE NUMBER 3 ABOVE. As mentioned, many bands hired by an agency are made up of members who may not play together regularly. Even set bands often have substitute players. If there are specific performers (singer, harpist, guitarist, etc.) that you want, make sure that your contract includes them. Of course, illness or other circumstances may still preclude their being able to perform at your event.*

22. If the DJ or one of the band members scheduled for my event is unable to perform for some reason, do you have a backup replacement ready to go?

23. Can you provide wireless mics for the ceremony?

24. Does any of your equipment require special electrical outlets that I need to inform my wedding site about?

25. Do you bring backup equipment?

26. What kind of space or stage do you require for the DJ or band? If my site doesn't provide what you need, will you make arrangements for the stage or am I responsible for renting it? *NOTE: A band will require a specific amount of square feet per band member.*

27. How much time will you need for setup, sound check and breakdown on the day of the event?

28. What music will be provided during the breaks? *NOTE: If you have a preference, make it known. If you want them to play your home-burned CD mix, be sure to test it on their equipment first because not all CDs will play on every system.*

29. How many people will you staff for my event?

Useful Tips:

- Discuss with your site manager any restrictions that might affect your event, like noise limits, a music curfew and availability/load of electrical circuits. Also check with your facility and caterer about where and what to feed the performers.

- All professional entertainers have access to formalwear (if they don't, that's your first clue they're not professionals!) However, it is YOUR responsibility to be specific about how you expect your performers to be dressed. Any extraordinary requests (period costumes, all-white tuxes, etc.) are normally paid for by the client.

- Make notes of your general music preferences before you meet with your DJ, bandleader, etc. For example: "Classical for the ceremony, Rat Pack-era for the cocktail hour and a set of Motown during the reception." Not only will this help you determine which entertainment professionals are a good match for you, it will guide them in preparing your set list. *TIP: The DJs and Entertainers in this book and on HereComesTheGuide. com are first-rate. They all got great reviews during our certification process, and we're happy to recommend them.*

Questions to Ask When Ordering Your Wedding Invitations

Letterpress, thermography, engraved, matte, jacquard, glassine… ordering invites will mean learning a few new vocabulary words (see page 40). You'll also need to learn about all the components that you might want to include in your invitation, as well as what other printed materials could be part of your wedding scenario. With so many details to consider, you'll depend on a creative wedding invitation professional to clue you in on the jargon, and guide you in choosing invites that reflect your wedding style. After all, nothing sets the tone for an event like an impeccably designed wedding invitation.

Bring this list of must-ask questions to the stationery boutique or graphic designer you're considering to ensure that no detail is left unaddressed (no pun intended).

Getting To Know Your Invitation Professional

1. How long have you been in business?

2. What is your design background? *NOTE: This may or may not involve formal training. Remember, "good taste" isn't necessarily something that can be taught!*

3. What types of printing processes do you offer and which do you specialize in? Which do you recommend for my budget and style?

4. Is your printing done in-house or do you outsource it? *NOTE: Printing is usually less expensive if it's outsourced. However, a possible benefit of in-house printing is a quicker turnaround time, which could come in especially handy if any reprinting (say, due to an error) is required.*

5. Do you offer custom invitations as well as templated styles? Is there a fee if I want to order a sample of either an existing invitation style or a custom design? If so, how much?

6. If I choose a custom wedding invitation, what are my options for color, paper type, ink and fonts? What is the word limit for the text?

7. Can I also order my table numbers, place cards, escort cards, ceremony programs, menus, etc. from you?

8. Do you offer a package or a discounted price if I order all of the invitation components at the same time? (For a complete list of what might be included, see the next page.)

9. If I want to include a picture or graphic on my save-the-date card or invitation, can you accommodate that? If so, does the image need to be saved in a specific format? Do you have photo retouching available, and if so, what is the price range? Can your photo specialist also convert color images to black & white or sepia? Is there an additional cost?

10. Are there any new styles, trends and color combinations I might consider? Which are the most popular? What kinds of handmade or artisanal paper do you offer? *NOTE: The answers to these questions will give you a sense of how creative and up-to-the-minute your invitation professional is.*

11. Can my invitations be printed on recycled paper and/or with soy-based ink?

12. Based on the paper I select and the number of pieces involved, what would it cost to mail my wedding invitation? *NOTE: If you use a non-standard sized envelope, postage may be more expensive.*

Getting Down To Business

13. Once I place my order, how long will it take to have the completed invitations delivered? Do you have rush-order available and what are the extra fees? If you are ordering from an online company, ask: What are the shipping methods available to me, and their respective costs?

14. If the invitation involves multiple pieces, can you assemble them? If so, is there an additional fee? How will the assembly affect my delivery date?

15. Do you offer an invitation addressing service? If so, what is the charge for this? What lettering style options are available? Will the lettering push back my delivery date?

16. When is payment due?

17. I will have an opportunity to sign off on my invitation proof before you send my order to print, right?

18. Once I've signed off on the proof, I expect the printed invitations to match the approved sample. If they don't (i.e. an error was made after I signed off on the proof), will my invitations be corrected and reprinted at no additional cost? How much additional time will it take to redo my order if there is a problem with it?

19. What is your refund policy if for some reason I need to cancel my order?

20. When can I expect to receive my contract from you?

21. Can you provide me with the contact information of 3–4 recent brides who I can call or email for references?

Possible Printed Invitation Components

(Don't panic… most of the extra elements are OPTIONAL!!)

- Save-the-Date Cards

- Wedding Announcement

- Wedding Invitation Components:
  - Outer Envelope
  - Optional Inner Envelope
  Optional Belly Band
  - Invitation
  - Reception Card, if held at a different location than the ceremony
  - Directions/Map
  - Response Card & SASE (self-addressed stamped envelope)

- Thank-You Cards

- Shower Thank-You Cards

- Other Invites:
  - Engagement Party
  - Shower
  - Bachelor/Bacherlorette Party
  - Rehearsal Dinner
  - After Party

- Wedding Program

- Pew Cards

- Place Cards

- Table Cards

- Menus

- Napkins, Matchbooks or Labels for favors

Useful Tips:

- Ordering your invitations over the phone increases the possibility of mistakes, so order in person if possible. If you order your invitations from an online company, make sure your contract states that they will correct mistakes they make for free.

- Insist on getting a proof. Have at least two other people review all your proofs before you sign off on them—it's amazing what a fresh pair of eyes will see!

- If ordering online, remember that color resolution can vary drastically between computers. The best way to guarantee the exact color you want is to ask that a sample be snail mailed to you.

- Order 20–30 extra save-the-dates and/or invitations with envelopes in case you have to add to the guest list or you make a mistake when assembling or addressing the envelopes.

- Save-the-date cards should be sent out 6–9 months prior to your wedding.

- Invitations should be sent out 6–9 weeks prior to your wedding.

- Consider working with one stationer or graphic designer for all of your printed materials. She'll guide you in making sure all of the components convey a consistent design concept. Not that they have to be identical, but as Joyce Scardina Becker observes in *Countdown to Your Perfect Wedding,* "It's like making a fashion statement: All of the accessories in your wardrobe should coordinate and fit together nicely."

- To Evite or not to Evite? For the main event, even we progressives at *Here Comes The Guide* come down on the side of tradition and say go with real paper and snail mail—even if your budget determines that you have to DIY. However, if your overall wedding style is relaxed and casual, then we think Evites are fine for the supporting events, such as your Bachelorette Party. We like Evite's built-in RSVP system and creative style options.

Invitations Glossary

A glossary of common printing terms.

Printing Terms

Letterpress: Letterpress printing dates back to the 14th century, and involves inking the raised surface of metal type or custom-engraved plates and then applying the inked surface against paper with a press. When used with the right paper (thick, softer paper results in a deeper impression), typefaces and colors, letterpress creates an elegant product with a stamped, tactile quality. This process offers lots of options, but can cost more than other methods. Also, photographs and metallic inks generally don't work well with letterpress.

Embossing: Using a metal die, letters and images are pressed into the paper from behind, creating a raised "relief" surface, imparting added dimension to the invitation design. Usually used for large initials or borders. Ink or foil may be applied to the front of the paper so that the raised letters and images are colored.

Blind embossing: No ink or foil is applied, so the embossed (raised) image is the same color as the paper.

Thermography: This popular printing method uses heat to fuse ink and resinous powder, producing raised lettering. Though it looks almost exactly like engraved printing, thermography is much less expensive. This process will not reproduce detail as sharply as engraving will. The powder is added after the ink is applied, generally with an offset press, so the use of paper or metal offset plates affects quality here, too.

Engraving: Engraving is generally the most formal and expensive printing option. The image is etched into a metal plate, and the ink held in the etched grooves is applied to the paper with a press. The resulting raised image is comprised entirely of ink sitting on the surface of the paper. The ink applied is opaque, making it possible to print a lighter colored ink on a darker colored paper. Engraving is not the best printing choice if you have a photo or illustration that requires a screen.

Offset printing: Most printing these days is offset, which means the original image is transferred from a plate to a drum before it is applied to the paper. This process produces print that sits flat on the surface. There are many levels of quality with this method: If your printer uses paper printing plates, the job will cost less but the result may be fuzzy, inconsistent lettering. Metal plates yield much sharper, crisper type.

Digital printing: In this method the computer is linked to the printing press and the image is applied to paper or another material directly from a digital file rather than using film and/or plates. Digital is best for short-run, quick jobs. This can also be a good option if you want to use full color.

Foil stamping: Foil is applied to the front side of the paper, stamped on with a metal die. Foils can be metallic or colored, shiny or dull. They are usually very opaque, and this is a great way to print white on a dark colored paper.

Calligraphy: This is the perfected art of writing by hand. Often associated with fancy, curlicue script, calligraphy can be done in several genres and styles.

Paper Terms

Matte: A paper coating that's flat and non-reflective (no gloss).

Jacquard: Screen-printed paper that creates an illusion of layering; for example, paper that looks like it's overlaid with a swatch of lace.

Parchment paper: This paper is somewhat translucent and often a bit mottled to mimic the appearance of ancient, historical documents made out of animal skin. It's excellent for calligraphy.

Linen finish: Paper with a surface that actually mimics linen fabric. If you look closely, you see lines of texture going both horizontally and vertically on the surface.

Rice paper: Not actually made of rice, this paper is extremely thin and elegant.

Glassine: A very thin, waxy paper. Thinner than vellum (see below), its surface is slick and shiny, whereas vellum is more translucent. Glassine is best suited for envelope use, while vellum is sturdy enough to be printed on directly for invitation use.

Vellum: A heavier, finely textured, translucent paper made from wood fiber. Similar to parchment, it was originally made from the skin of a calf, lamb or baby goat and used for writing and painting during the pre-printing age.

www.HereComesTheGuide.com

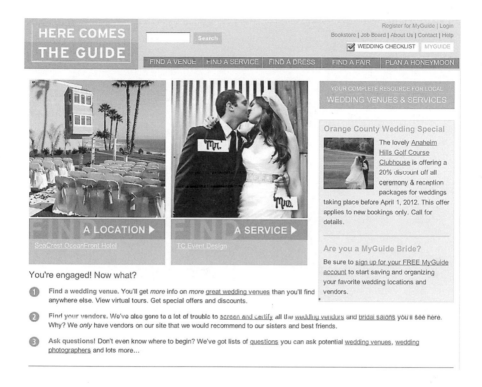

You've gotta visit our website!
Here's what you'll find:

- A fast and easy way to search for the perfect venues and services.

- Information about new venues that aren't in the book!

- More great wedding and special event services!

- Direct links to the event venues and services we feature.

- Tons of photos and videos. Real Wedding galleries, too!

- Virtual tours of most venues.

- Information about bridal fairs.

- Wedding dress trunk shows and sample sales calendar.

Part One: Event Venues

Southern California

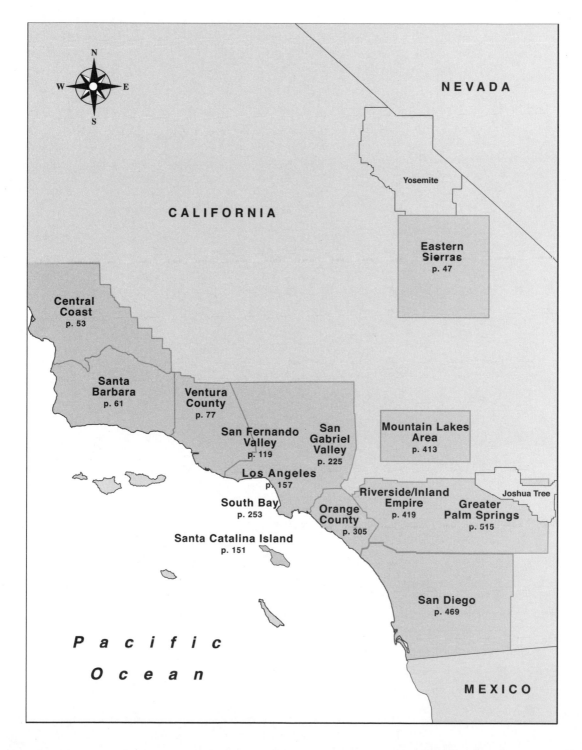

NEVADA

CALIFORNIA

Yosemite

Eastern
Sierras
p. 47

Central
Coast
p. 53

Santa
Barbara
p. 61

Ventura
County
p. 77

San Fernando
Valley
p. 119

San
Gabriel
Valley
p. 225

Mountain Lakes
Area
p. 413

Los Angeles
p. 157

South Bay
p. 253

Orange
County
p. 305

Riverside/Inland
Empire
p. 419

Joshua Tree

Greater
Palm Springs
p. 515

Santa Catalina Island
p. 151

San Diego
p. 469

Pacific

Ocean

MEXICO

Eastern Sierras

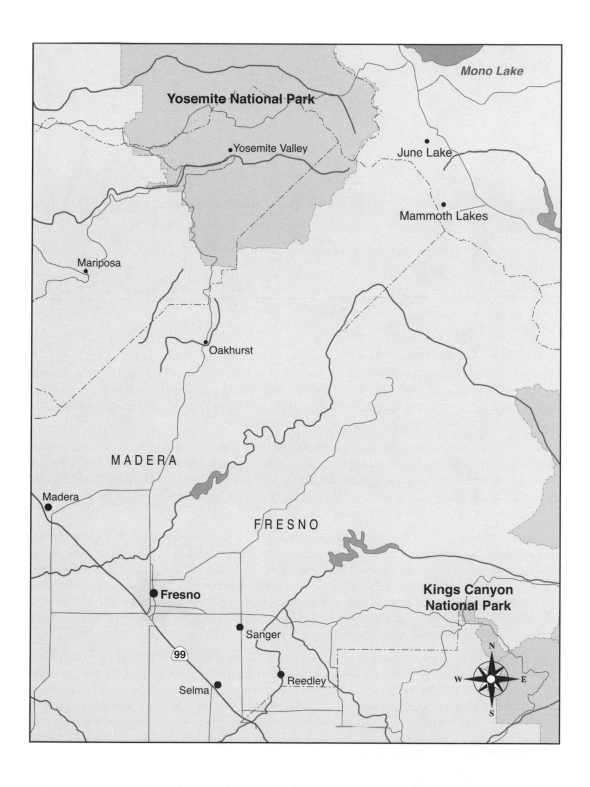

June Mountain Resort

Mountain Resort

3819 Highway 158, June Lake

760/648-7733

www.junemountain.com
weddings@junemountain.com

- Rehearsal Dinners
- Ceremonies
- Wedding Receptions
- Private Parties
- Corporate Events
- Meetings
- Film Shoots
- Accommodations

Why just look at a mountain when you can buy one … at least for a day! June Mountain, a majestic alpine setting more than 8,000 feet above sea level, not only comes with shimmering glacier lakes and the kind of "big sky" 360-degree views that take your breath away, it's also an affordable venue that will be exclusively yours when you host your wedding here.*

This pristine, laid-back "sister" to Mammoth Mountain is a favorite with locals and ski aficionados alike for its relaxed, friendly atmosphere and soul-stirring connection to the natural splendor around it. But it's not just popular in winter. From hiking and biking to fishing and boating, the mountain dazzles year-round, as does its changing tableau of snowcapped peaks, bursts of colorful wildflowers, and blazing golden aspens.

If "getting there is half the fun," then your guests are in for something special. Once they arrive, they'll board the chairlift for a picturesque, 10-minute ride that offers a spectacular peek at the varied landscape of the property's 500 acres and the small, lakeside town in the valley below. (For those who prefer to keep their feet on the ground, other transportation to the top is available.) As they disembark, they'll be greeted with refreshments before gathering on the Scenic Overlook, a large patio where ceremonies take place against unparalleled vistas of Carson Peak, Reverse Peak and the stunning Horsetail Falls in the distance.

With a view like that, you're going to want a dramatic entrance and you'll get one. As your guests look on with anticipation, your bridal party will step off the chairlift one by one, leaving the bride and her father on the final chair to walk down the aisle together. After exchanging vows, take a moment to linger and savor the grandeur of the incredible skies and the aquamarine hues of Gull, June and Mono Lakes, shining like gems on the valley floor. Then, while you pose for photos in front of this awe-inspiring backdrop, friends and family can head to the adjacent June Meadows Chalet to continue the celebration indoors.

Warmly inviting and casually comfortable, this mountain lodge has several spaces that can be used in any combination to accommodate the size and flow of your event. You may want to start with cocktails in the Great Room, featuring a high ceiling with open rafters, wood paneling and a wall of windows. A huge stone fireplace dominates one end and a nearby wooden staircase leads to a mezzanine that can be used as a lounge area. Buffet dinners are often enjoyed in the View Room, which runs the length of the building and is literally lined with windows that frame the rustic beauty outside. Then it's dancing in the Main Room, where you can also show home movies on the dropdown screens. Or, move the music to the Chalet's Sundeck for a romantic dance under the stars, while the village lights twinkle below.

When the party inevitably draws to a close, there's still one more mountain high—that exhilarating ride (or drive) back down. However, many of your nearest and dearest won't be ready to go home quite yet, so let June Mountain Vacation's staff arrange a few extra days of accommodations and activities for your guests, turning your big day into a destination getaway.

*Exclusivity applies only to non-winter weddings from April to December.

CEREMONY, EVENT/RECEPTION & MEETING CAPACITY: The resort holds 225 seated or standing guests indoors, and 500 seated or 1,000 standing outdoors.

FEES & DEPOSITS: A $2,000 deposit is required to reserve your date. This deposit is also your rental fee. There is a $2,000 food and beverage minimum due 60 days prior, and the balance of the total estimated event cost is due 30 days prior to the event. Meals range $24–33/person. Bar service is included. Tax and a 20% service charge are additional.

AVAILABILITY: Daily. Winter: Christmas–Easter, 5pm–midnight; Summer: June–September, 8am–midnight.

SERVICES/AMENITIES:

Catering: in-house
Kitchen Facilities: n/a
Tables & Chairs: provided
Linens, Silver, etc.: provided
Restrooms: not wheelchair accessible
Dance Floor: CBA, extra fee
Bride's & Groom's Dressing Area: yes
Meeting Equipment: provided
Other: spa services, picnic area, AV equipment on-site event coordinator

Parking: complimentary large lot
Accommodations: CBA through June Mountian Vacation, 888-JuneMtn (586-3686)
Telephone: house phone
Outdoor Night Lighting: yes
Outdoor Cooking Facilities: BBQ on site
Cleanup: provided
View: courtyard; panorama of mountains, forest, valley, hills and lakes

RESTRICTIONS:

Alcohol: in-house
Smoking: outside only
Music: amplified OK with restrictions

Wheelchair Access: limited
Insurance: not required

This is important! Tell venues you're reading HERE COMES THE GUIDE and ask if our information is still current.

49

Mammoth Mountain Resort

Mountain Resort

1 Minaret Road, Mammoth Lakes
888/400-MTNS (6867), 760/934-2571 X2220

www.weddingsatmammoth.com
weddings@mammoth-mtn.com

- Rehearsal Dinners
- Ceremonies
- Wedding Receptions
- Private Parties
- Corporate Events
- Meetings
- Film Shoots
- Accommodations

Mammoth Mountain isn't just for skiers anymore. In fact, leisure-seekers come to this Eastern Sierra oasis year-round for golf, fishing, and hiking—or to just kick back in the serene alpine environment. Still others, enticed by the dramatic terrain and the deluxe amenities, come here to wed.

Though the whole town of Mammoth Lakes is only four miles from end to end, the resort encompasses a vast assortment of lodges and event venues, each with its own distinctive appeal. The resort's knowledgeable staff will assist couples in customizing their Mammoth experience to suit their personal style.

For an experience as exhilarating as falling in love, adventurous couples say "I do" atop Mammoth's 11,000-foot summit—one of the highest peaks in California. In keeping with this wild wedding scenario, newlyweds can ski down the mountain, wedding veil trailing behind like a flurry of snowflakes. Or treat everyone to a champagne gondola ride for an authentic bird's-eye view of the town below. Disembark mid-mountain at Parallax, an elegant restaurant with soaring windows on two sides.

On Mammoth's northwest fringe, rustic romance flourishes at Tamarack Lodge and Resort, whose cabins overlook the crystalline shores of Twin Lakes. Boasting high-beamed ceilings and the warm patina of the past, Tamarack's wood-frame cabins are spread throughout the forest where chipmunks and mule deer meander among lodgepole pines and songbirds croon from fir trees. Here, you can bask in the ever-changing hues of the seasonal foliage, particularly breathtaking in early fall when golden autumnal light accentuates the orange-red of the aspens. Spring introduces its own palette, with deep blue lupine and the burnished reds and golds of Indian paintbrush in colorful clusters around the base of trees. In winter, everything is covered in pristine white. After an invigorating day on the slopes, cozy up in front of the fireplace with your sweetheart as a light snow falls outside. Views from Tamarack stretch across the lakes, and from summer through fall you can cross the footbridge that leads to a tiny islet holding the Forest Chapel. Have an intimate ceremony beneath a log trellis, then celebrate your union at one of Mammoth's many great reception sites.

The sky's the limit in the Eastern Sierra. Whether you're looking for a sophisticated soirée or a thrilling adventure, Mammoth Resort has an option that's perfect for you. The range of ceremony and reception sites, combined with Mammoth Catering's outstanding service, will ensure you have the wedding you envision.

CEREMONY, EVENT/RECEPTION & MEETING CAPACITY: Event spaces hold from 20 to 250 guests, seated or standing.

FEES & DEPOSITS: For special events, a nonrefundable deposit is required when booking a site. Rental fees range $250–2,700 depending on the guest count and the space rented. Wedding packages start at $50/person. Tax, alcohol and a 20% service charge are additional.

AVAILABILITY: Year-round, daily.

SERVICES/AMENITIES:

Catering: in-house, no BYO

Kitchen Facilities: n/a

Tables & Chairs: provided

Linens, Silver, etc.: provided

Restrooms: wheelchair accessible

Dance Floor: CBA, extra fee

Bride's & Groom's Dressing Area: no

Meeting Equipment: CBA, extra fee

Parking: ample, complimentary

Accommodations: 625 guest rooms and cabins

Telephone: pay phones

Outdoor Night Lighting: no

Outdoor Cooking Facilities: BBQ CBA

Cleanup: provided

View: mountains, lakes, pine trees, meadows

Other: on-site coordinator

RESTRICTIONS:

Alcohol: in-house, or BYO with corkage fee

Smoking: outside only

Music: amplified OK

Wheelchair Access: yes

Insurance: not required

Central Coast

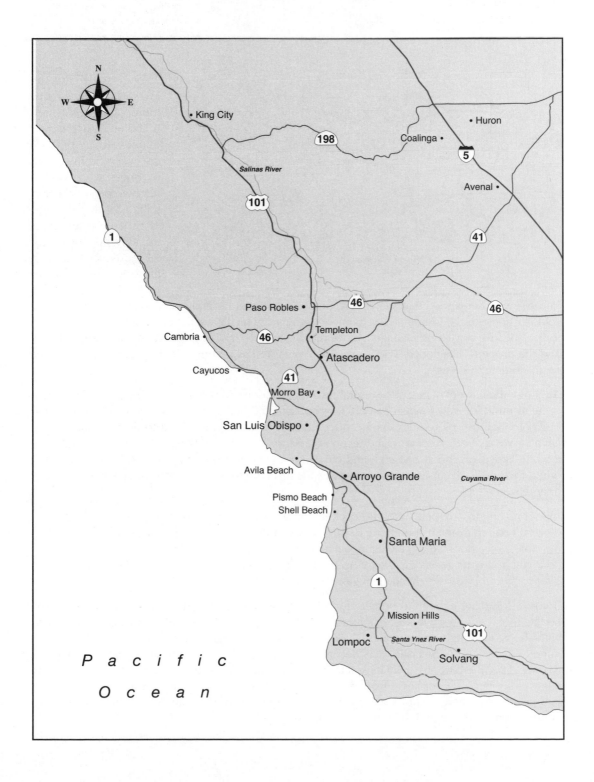

Cambria Pines Lodge

Historic Lodge

2905 Burton Drive, Cambria
805/927-6114 x2202

www.cambriapineslodge.com
rebeccar@moonstonehotels.com

- Rehearsal Dinners
- Ceremonies
- Wedding Receptions
- Private Parties
- Corporate Events
- Meetings
- Film Shoots
- Accommodations

As you settle into the relaxed setting of this hilltop lodge, it's hard to believe that it was established in 1927 for an eccentric European baroness who wanted her own personal resort within visiting distance of Hearst Castle. Unfortunately, her plans for an opulent American lifestyle were cut short by her husband back in Europe, who demanded that she choose between him and her lodge. She chose the baron, and sold her home to the Cambria Development Company, which used the lodge as a gathering place for prospective buyers of local land. Since that time, the Main Lodge building has been replaced, and the property has added world-class gardens as well as accommodations ranging from rustic rooms to deluxe suites.

Although the current Main Lodge resembles a huge, modern-day log cabin, the grounds behind it bring to mind a lovely English garden. Rows of sculpted hedges separated by paths, bushes and beds of vibrantly colored flowers meander among Monterey pines. Next to the garden, a broad lawn serves as both ceremony and reception site for outdoor weddings. Couples get married in a white lattice gazebo at one end, and dance on a patio in front of a covered bandstand at the other; the entire expanse of grass in between is turned into an al fresco dining room filled with linen-covered tables.

Indoor receptions are held in the Peacock Room. With wall coverings of rosy beige, it derives additional warmth from an abundance of pine wainscoting and trim. Other pluses are a high ceiling, movable dance floor, adjustable lighting and a built-in, granite-topped pine bar. After the celebration, you and your guests can chat it up in the Lounge, where a fire blazes in the floor-to-ceiling river rock fireplace, and chandeliers glow overhead.

If you're fortunate enough to be here for a few days, there's a world of things to do outside the Lodge, too. Cambria itself is a quaint village, noted for its local artists and craftspeople and filled with shops, galleries and boutiques. Hearst Castle is a mere eight miles to the north, the beach is minutes away, and wine tasting has become a popular pastime in surrounding San Luis Obispo County. Alas, the baroness may have left the country so quickly that she never had time to truly enjoy either her lodge or her surroundings. We suggest you don't make the same mistake: When you get married here, plan to stay long enough to take full advantage of all that this friendly, family-oriented venue and the Central Coast have to offer.

CEREMONY CAPACITY: The garden/gazebo area holds 250 seated.

EVENT/RECEPTION CAPACITY: The garden/gazebo area holds 200 seated. Indoors, the Peacock Room (which can be divided into 2 sections) accommodates up to 250 with a dance floor. Each half of the room can hold 90 seated with a dance floor.

MEETING CAPACITY: Several spaces are available that seat 40–400 guests.

FEES & DEPOSITS: To hold your date, the entire site rental fee is due at booking: $900–1,700 for the garden, Peacock Room, or half of the Peacock Room. A guest count guarantee is due 11 days prior to the event, and the food and beverage balance is payable at the event's conclusion. Cambria Pines Lodge offers a varied menu, with luncheons ranging $21–31/person and dinners $24–39/person; alcohol, tax and a 20% service charge are additional. An $850 ceremony charge covers the use of the gazebo, chairs, setup/takedown service and rehearsal.

For meetings, the Sycamore, Treetop and Peacock rooms are available. Please call for pricing.

AVAILABILITY: Indoor events, year-round, daily. Outdoor events, year-round, optimally mid-April to late October. For an outdoor reception and ceremony, 11am–4pm. For indoor functions, 11:30am–4pm or 6:30pm–11pm. Other times may be arranged; call for more information.

SERVICES/AMENITIES:

Catering: in-house, no BYO
Kitchen Facilities: n/a
Tables & Chairs: provided
Linens, Silver, etc.: provided
Restrooms: wheelchair accessible
Dance Floor: outdoor patio or indoor portable provided
Bride's Dressing Area: CBA, extra charge
Meeting Equipment: full range

Parking: large lots
Accommodations: 152 guest rooms and suites
Telephone: in guest rooms
Outdoor Night Lighting: no
Outdoor Cooking Facilities: BBQs CBA
Cleanup: provided
View: gardens, woods and hills

RESTRICTIONS:

Alcohol: in-house, or corkage $10/bottle
Smoking: outdoors only, not in the gardens
Music: amplified OK with volume restrictions

Wheelchair Access: yes
Insurance: not required
Other: no rice, birdseed, glitter or confetti; flames restricted

Cellar360 Paso Robles

Winery & Vineyard

7000 Highway 46 East, Paso Robles
877/774-9463
www.cellar360.com
cs_cellar360@cellar360.com

- Rehearsal Dinners
- Ceremonies
- Wedding Receptions
- Private Parties
- Corporate Events
- Meetings
- Film Shoots
- Accommodations

The distinctive labels that grace Cellar360 Paso Robles' wine bottles are vibrant interpretations of the Central Coast's geographic blessings: fertile meadows and oak-clad mountains, coastal breezes and sunny days. These natural charms, coupled with Cellar360's creative, stress-free hospitality, are luring brides to this scenic location in Paso Robles' burgeoning wine country.

Visitors enter via a leisurely driveway that gently climbs past an expansive frieze of grapevines. Up ahead stands the Tasting Room and its patio, shaded by 200-year-old blue oaks, luxuriant foliage and crape myrtle kissed with deep raspberry blooms. The natural stone building harmonizes with the tranquil surroundings, and arched doors trimmed in trumpet vines add rustic character. The patio and its adjoining lawn is a congenial place to stage your social hour. Lounging at bistro tables, guests enjoy appetizers and wine tasting at their ease. Nearby is another sensory treat: a fragrant native garden. Wine glass in hand, guests stroll the meandering paths where lemon verbena, French lavender and autumn sage present an aromatic bouquet, and ornamental plants like feathery ruby grass and berry-tipped manzanita reveal nuances of color and form.

Around the corner from the Tasting Room patio, Cellar360's sprawling Main Event Lawn and adjacent areas offer equally enticing locales. At one of our favorite ceremony sites, the bridal couple exchanges vows in front of a layered backdrop of oak boughs, wild roses, a pond and rows of grapevines against a blue horizon. A beguiling option for an intimate gathering is the Rose Garden, a horseshoe-shaped lawn edged with chiffon-petaled tree roses. From anywhere on the grounds, guests are regaled with phenomenal views of the painterly landscape burnished by the setting sun.

Indoor soirées take on an earthy glamour in the Barrel Chai, a high-ceilinged hall lined with oaken wine casks. A sensual aroma pervades this novel room, and when it's decorated with icicle lights, floral arrangements and candelabras, the ambiance is simply enchanting. There's space for 150 guests plus a dance floor, and a double-staircase at one end lets the new Mr. and Mrs. make a formal entrance.

Event hostesses, here's another benefit: discounts on the vineyard's exclusive, limited-release wines, which are only available on site. These easy-drinking vintages have been championed by *Wine Spectator & Wine Enthusiast* as best buys, and Cellar360's staff will work with you to create delicious wine pairings. In fact, the staff will lavish you with attention, as yours will be the only event for the entire weekend! They'll also provide an extensive list of local vendors who can help you put all the elements together.

Cellar360 Paso Robles captures what we love most about this region—a fresh, uncomplicated attitude; a breathtaking setting; and friendly, service-oriented professionals. Whether you're a connoisseur of wines or of the wine-country lifestyle, you'll take pleasure in the beauty and welcoming atmosphere of this estate vineyard.

CEREMONY & EVENT/RECEPTION CAPACITY: The site holds 175 seated or standing guests indoors, and 500 seated or standing outdoors.

MEETING CAPACITY: Meeting spaces hold 180 seated guests.

FEES & DEPOSITS: 25% of the site rental fee is required to reserve your date. The balance is due 10 days prior to the event. Rental fees range $2,000–8,000 depending on the space rented.

AVAILABILITY: Year-round, daily, 5:30pm–11pm.

SERVICES/AMENITIES:

Catering: select from list
Kitchen Facilities: limited
Tables & Chairs: BYO
Linens, Silver, etc.: BYO
Restrooms: wheelchair accessible
Dance Floor: BYO
Bride's Dressing Area: yes
Meeting Equipment: CBA
Other: picnic area

Parking: large lot
Accommodations: no guest rooms
Telephone: emergency use only
Outdoor Night Lighting: access only
Outdoor Cooking Facilities: BBQ CBA
Cleanup: renter or caterer
View: fountain, garden, lagoon, landscaped grounds; panorama of mountains, meadows and vineyards

RESTRICTIONS:

Alcohol: in-house
Smoking: designated areas outdoors only
Music: amplified OK with restrictions

Wheelchair Access: yes
Insurance: liability required

The Historic Park Ballroom and Park Place

Ballroom

1232 Park Street, Paso Robles
805/238-5042
www.parkballroom.com
debbie@acorneventmgt.com

- Rehearsal Dinners
- Ceremonies
- Wedding Receptions
- Private Parties
- Corporate Events
- Meetings
- Film Shoots
- Accommodations

Paso Robles' historic downtown combines everything you love about wine country communities: Friendly folks, a lively mix of shops and restaurants, and plenty of tasting rooms. And while wine has always been important to the region, Paso's original prime attractions were its fine weather and healing hot springs. During the 1920s, Paso became a fashionable destination for movie stars, famous athletes and even President Theodore Roosevelt. Today, the town's legacy of upscale hospitality has been rekindled in a luxurious two-for-one banquet facility: The Historic Park Ballroom and Park Place, where discerning couples are invited to celebrate in high style.

These chic venues are housed in neighboring landmark structures. The Ballroom occupies the entire second floor of the handsome bricked IOFF building, which dates to 1912 and has recently been spectacularly renovated. The newly launched Park Place resides in the iconic Acorn Building, known for its acorn-topped clock tower. Originally constructed in 1892, the Acorn was completely rebuilt in 2006, though its brick façade and ornate tower still retain their original turn-of-the-century character.

Just steps away is a lovely bonus: City Park, a photogenic greenscape with a water court and quaint gazebo, perfect for an al fresco ceremony. Afterward, while the bridal party lingers for scenic portraits, guests stroll to the Ballroom for cocktails.

The Ballroom is also well suited for indoor ceremonies. Friends and family make their way up to the smartly outfitted foyer, where a wet bar serves up welcome refreshments. Inside the Ballroom, chairs are arranged facing a proscenium stage. Couples exchange vows on the apron in front of light alderwood doors that run across the curtain line. After the first kiss, the doors dramatically slide open to reveal the maple-floored stage, already set with a bar and appetizers.

Guests mingle both on and off stage, taking in the sophisticated yet warm setting. A row of arched windows lets in natural light, casting a soft glow on the pale butter-hued walls and alderwood wainscoting. The rich carpeting is patterned with oak leaves, a unifying motif that's subtly woven into the décor throughout this dual venue. Crown moldings and antique-style fixtures recall the heady days of Prohibition, when the Ballroom is rumored to have hosted wild parties into the night.

When it's time for your own party, everyone gathers a few doors down at Park Place. Guests enter a formal mezzanine before descending to this glamorous, underground reception space.

Park Place's Deco-inspired aesthetic captures the cool sophistication of a Jazz Age supper club. A dynamic trio of adjoining salons begins with the Lounge, which boasts a long granite-topped bar and cozy sitting area. Next comes the Dining Room, whose swanky stylings include wrought-iron chandeliers and stamped metal embellishments. A grand piano stands at the ready, and on one wall, three framed flat-screen TVs display your customized visuals. After dinner, kick the festivities up a notch in the corner Club, where your DJ or band rocks the house from a raised hi-tech stage as revelers let loose on the adjacent dance floor.

For weddings, rehearsal dinners or any special occasion, Historic Park Ballroom and Park Place offer flexibility and vintage elegance, all in one neat package.

CEREMONY, EVENT/RECEPTION & MEETING CAPACITY: The site holds 250 seated or 300 standing guests indoors.

FEES & DEPOSITS: 50% of the total event cost is required to reserve your date, and the balance is due 14 days prior to the event. The rental fee ranges $2,500–5,500 depending on your guest count, and includes tables, chairs, place settings, 1 security guard and 1 bartender. Ceremonies are an additional $1,500. Special weekday and nonprofit rates are available; please contact for details.

AVAILABILITY: Year-round, daily, 7am–midnight.

SERVICES/AMENITIES:

Catering: BYO with approval
Kitchen Facilities: professional kitchen, fully equipped
Tables & Chairs: provided
Linens, Silver, etc.: CBA
Restrooms: wheelchair accessible
Dance Area: provided
Bride's Dressing Area: CBA
Meeting Equipment: some provided

Parking: on street
Accommodations: no guest rooms
Telephone: house and office phone
Outdoor Night Lighting: CBA
Outdoor Cooking Facilities: none
Cleanup: renter or caterer
View: cityscape, park
Other: AV equipment, stage, event coordination available, extra fee

RESTRICTIONS:

Alcohol: BYO
Smoking: outdoors only
Music: amplified OK

Wheelchair Access: yes
Insurance: liability required

Overwhelmed? Use the search criteria on www.HereComesTheGuide.com to narrow down your choices.

Santa Barbara Area

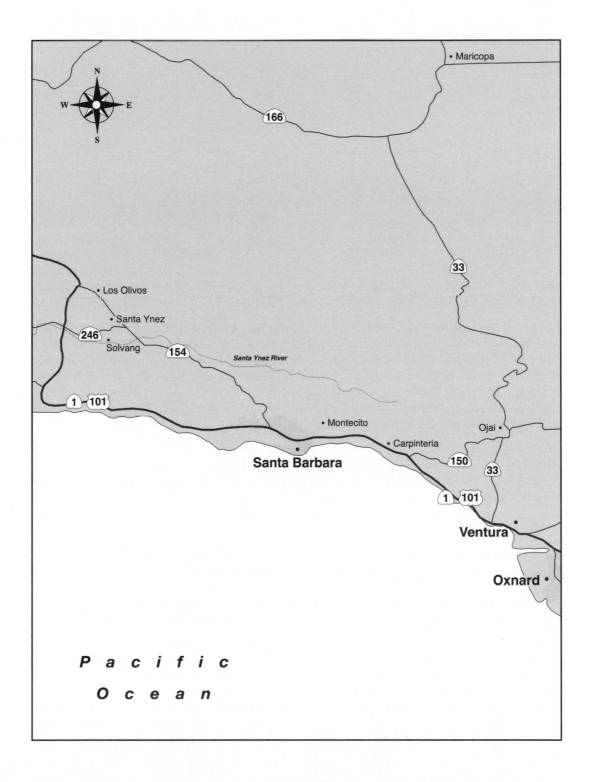

Rincon Beach Club

Waterfront Event Facility

3805 Santa Claus Lane, Carpinteria

805/566-9933

www.rinconbeachclub.com
caitlin@rinconcatering.com
carol@rinconcatering.com

- Rehearsal Dinners
- Ceremonies
- Wedding Receptions
- Private Parties
- Corporate Events
- Meetings
- Film Shoots
- Accommodations

The Rincon Beach Club, located in the seaside community of Carpinteria just south of Santa Barbara, is bound to make you smile as soon as you arrive: The club resides on "Santa Claus Lane" amid a quaint row of colorful shops and cafés along a bluff above the Pacific Ocean. We're pretty sure smiles will continue throughout your time at Rincon, a gracious, private setting with mountain vistas and an easy, coastal sophistication.

The Beach Club has two main event areas: the Dining Room, which exudes a quiet elegance; and the Wedding Garden, a leafy courtyard awash in sunlight during the late afternoon. Enclosed by dense green foliage, the garden is finished with grass-fringed flagstone. At one end, a wooden pergola laced with white roses tops an elevated deck, a pretty spot for ceremonies. A flowering shade tree leans in from one side as if listening closely, while the bridal party, dressed to impress, poses on the stairs. As the couple exchanges vows, loved ones watching from below are close enough to feel an intimate connection with the proceedings.

Guests enjoy the cocktail hour on the West Patio, which wraps around the exterior of the Dining Room. In one section, a mahogany bar, couches and chairs are a comfortable improvisation of an al fresco lounge; just around the corner, café tables form a cozy enclave next to a trickling fountain. As dusk descends, the sweet scent of star jasmine mingles with refreshing sea breezes, and antique-style heat lamps keep everyone toasty. Twinkle lights add their glow beneath a star-filled night sky.

For a formal reception, invite guests into the Dining Room, where French doors on two sides let in the garden view. The room's clean, uncluttered palette is a refined backdrop for personalized décor. The Club has a collection of furniture, props and other accoutrements to create whatever atmosphere you envision. Unique banquet chairs with a faux-pewter finish and classy up-lighting enhance the aura of refinement, while a skylit foyer showcases the buffet.

At Rincon Beach Club, you get much more than a picturesque venue: Expert planning, event production and palate-pleasing cuisine are also part of the package. This full-service approach is not only a time- and money-saver—it also results in a more cohesive expression of your vision. Rincon's experienced professionals know how to craft a celebration that reflects your style and taste. This is especially evident when it comes to your menu, which they'll customize from aperitif to dessert. If you want to honor your heritage, choose from among Rincon's many global-inspired delicacies: blinis with caviar, Beef Copenhagen, Greek Mousaka—not even escargot intimidates these culinary artists! More contemporary dishes include favorites like Seared Ahi on Sugar Cane with Wasabi Cream Sauce or Apricot Spiced Ginger Chicken Wontons.

Minutes from Santa Barbara, yet "miles from conventional," Rincon Beach Club and Catering's impressive presentation and devotion to details really sets them apart. As one satisfied bride put it: "I was so relaxed—I just showed up and had fun!"

CEREMONY CAPACITY: The site holds 350 seated guests outdoors.

EVENT/RECEPTION CAPACITY: The club can accommodate 130 seated or 350 standing guests indoors, and 300 seated or 350 standing outdoors.

MEETING CAPACITY: The club can accommodate up to 350 guests.

FEES & DEPOSITS: A deposit is required to reserve your date. Deposits range $3,100–5,750 depending on the day of the week rented. 50% is due 4 months prior, and the balance is due 2 weeks prior to the event. Rental fees range $350–5,750 depending on the day of the week of the event. Meals range $41–75/person. Tax, gratuity and beverages are additional, but included in a complete estimate.

AVAILABILITY: Year-round, daily, anytime.

SERVICES/AMENITIES:

Catering: in-house
Kitchen Facilities: n/a
Tables & Chairs: provided
Linens, Silver, etc.: provided
Restrooms: wheelchair accessible
Dance Floor: portable provided
Bride's & Groom's Dressing Area: yes
Meeting Equipment: some provided, CBA
Other: in-house wedding cake, AV equipment, groom's lounge, event coordination, day-of and full-service wedding planning

Parking: on street
Accommodations: no guest rooms
Telephone: office phone
Outdoor Night Lighting: provided
Outdoor Cooking Facilities: BBQ on site
Cleanup: provided
View: coastline, fountain, garden, landscaped grounds, mountains, ocean

RESTRICTIONS:

Alcohol: full in-house bar
Smoking: allowed on patio only
Music: amplified OK

Wheelchair Access: yes
Insurance: liability required

Canary Hotel Santa Barbara

Resort & Spa

31 West Carrillo Street, Santa Barbara
805/879-9144
www.canarysantabarbara.com
catering@canarysantabarbara.com

- Rehearsal Dinners
- Ceremonies
- Wedding Receptions
- Private Parties
- Corporate Events
- Meetings
- Film Shoots
- Accommodations

Santa Barbara, one of the most beautiful towns in the world, welcomes a gorgeous new venue: Canary Hotel, an upscale boutique hostelry that reigns from the historic city center, between the sparkling-blue Pacific and the tree-studded Santa Ynez foothills. This strategic location puts you steps from what the New York Times dubbed "shopping Nirvana," as well as theaters, galleries, and the exciting nightlife of State Street. Like the balmy tropical islands the Canary is named after, Santa Barbara boasts miles of sun-kissed beaches, as well as an artistic spirit and a convivial, laid-back attitude—qualities that are embodied by this very sophisticated hotel.

Canopied walkways lead inside this urban oasis, where lush native plantings blend with the indigenous sounds of exotic birds, tree frogs, lizards and crickets from the Canary Islands. This sultry ambiance is also reflected in the décor. Exotic North African textures combine with luxurious Spanish-Colonial style for a fashionably fun, yet plush, interior. Wainscoted walls, hand-carved woods and wrought-iron details complement carpets, upholstery and tile in rich shades evocative of fine Madeira. The hotel's restaurant and bar, Finch & Fork, is a popular Santa Barbara gathering spot. There's a lovely private dining room for rehearsal dinners, and all your event dining is catered by the accomplished culinary team, who specialize in New American cuisine paired with wonderful wines from around the world.

The hotel's most unique event locale is found atop its five stories: an exclusive rooftop pool and terrace. Already it's "a scene" for Hollywood types and celebs drawn to the phenomenal 360-degree view, which encompasses the red-tiled roofs of the "American Riviera" and spectacular sunsets over the ocean. The terrace is also attracting couples with weddings on their minds. Wicker resort furniture outfitted with comfy cushions and a Mission-style hearth transform the area into a spacious outdoor room. A profusion of greenery and terracotta pots brimming with flowers create a pretty garden milieu for ceremonies and open-air gatherings. A short staircase inlaid with Spanish tiles holds court between the terrace and the pool, making it a natural focal point for tying the knot. A pair of pergolas flanks the upper landing, where the cocktail hour flourishes around a swimming pool that mirrors the blue of the Pacific beyond.

Formal soirées take place in one of five banquet rooms that surround an elegant foyer on the hotel's lower level. They all have a warm, inviting character, including the largest venue, the Riviera Ballroom.

Your "after-party for two" unfolds in your cozy, yet refined, guest suite. With a CD of Spanish guitar music playing and ultra-soft robes to slip into, you'll feel as if you're indulging in a romantic Mediterranean honeymoon. While your friends and family hop the beach shuttle or hit the gym next door, you order in-room spa treatments or snuggle between deluxe linens. Go ahead and extend your siesta as long as you want—after all, in this delightful haven, room service is available 24 hours a day!

CEREMONY CAPACITY: The Terrace holds 130 seated guests, indoor spaces up to 130 seated guests.

EVENT/RECEPTION CAPACITY: Indoors, the site holds up to 130 seated or 200 standing guests; outdoors 130 seated or 175 standing guests. Several combinations of indoor and outdoor seating are available; call for details.

MEETING CAPACITY: Several spaces are available that accommodate up to 130 seated guests.

FEES & DEPOSITS: A $2,000 deposit is required to reserve your date. The balance is due 30 days prior to the event. Rental fees range $300–2,500 depending on space rented and guest count. Meals range $35–175/person. Tax, alcohol and a 22% service charge are additional.

AVAILABILITY: Year-round, daily, anytime.

SERVICES/AMENITIES:

Catering: in-house, no BYO
Kitchen Facilities: n/a
Tables & Chairs: provided
Linens, Silver, etc.: provided
Restrooms: wheelchair accessible
Dance Floor: provided
Bride's Dressing Area: yes
Meeting Equipment: CBA, extra charge

Parking: valet and adjacent public garage
Accommodations: 97 guest rooms
Telephone: office phones
Outdoor Night Lighting: yes
Outdoor Cooking Facilities: no
Cleanup: provided
View: ocean, mountains, cityscape
Other: coordination, spa services, AV equipment

RESTRICTIONS:

Alcohol: in-house, no BYO
Smoking: outside only
Music: amplified OK indoors with restrictions

Wheelchair Access: yes
Insurance: not required

Elings Park

1298 Las Positas Road, Santa Barbara
805/569-5611
www.elingspark.org
cfranquet@elingspark.org

Park

- Rehearsal Dinners
- Ceremonies
- Wedding Receptions
- Private Parties
- Corporate Events
- Meetings
- Film Shoots
- Accommodations

Located in beautiful Santa Barbara, Elings Park is a 230-acre nonprofit park blessed with incredible city, mountain and ocean views. This recreational paradise encompasses sports fields, picnic grounds, tennis courts, a hang-gliding hill, a sculpture garden, a Veteran's Memorial Walk—plus hiking and biking trails galore. However, Elings also has two lovely sites for romantic wedding celebrations.

To reach the first, take a short curvy drive up to Godric Grove, an estate-like venue at the park's summit. You're only 400 feet above sea level here, but the multifaceted perspective makes you feel like you're on top of the world: From one direction, the grove surveys velvety-green park meadows; from another, the Santa Barbara cityscape unfolds against the silhouette of the Santa Ynez Mountains—and whichever way you face, a ribbon of ocean winks in the distance.

Wedding ceremonies make the most of this dynamic vista at the Grove's stone amphitheater, gently terraced into the hillside overlooking a forest of oaks. The amphitheater is completely secluded, blissfully quiet (save for the occasional birdcall or rustle of leaves), and harmonizes with the surrounding landscape. The adjacent reception area is just as pleasing. A large free-form redwood deck is spread out along the rim of a plateau. Gnarled oak trees grow up right through the deck and around its perimeter, providing dappled shade for your cocktail hour and reception. Next to the deck there's a sizable patio with built-in barbecues that's just right for a buffet or dancing. A cozy, treelined lawn nearby also has event possibilities. From spring to summer, cheery matilija poppies are in bloom around the lawn, while in the autumn the liquid amber trees put on a colorful show.

The second site, Singleton Pavilion, provides a more expansive setting with its own special charms. The centerpiece of Singleton is a sweep of lawn that can easily accommodate both your ceremony and reception seating. At one end, a copse of trees on a slight rise makes a leafy milieu for exchanging vows; or say "I do" in front of a handsome gazebo at the opposite end. A path partly encircles the lawn and culminates in a stone terrace poised at the edge of the hillside. Here a petite grove of saplings creates a magical atmosphere for intimate dining or a novel cocktail hour. And one more (wonderful) thing about Singleton: It also boasts serene city and mountain vistas, as well as peeks of the Pacific Ocean.

Both Godric Grove and Singleton Pavilion can accommodate large canopies, and site rental includes dedicated parking along with a Park Host. You can also reserve time on one of the playing fields for friendly competitions among families—think a genial round of croquet or softball. The Events Director will help with ideas and finding quality local vendors.

This spectacular, unspoiled setting can be styled as elegantly as you please, but you really don't need to add a single flower, plant or ribbon because Nature has provided all the decoration.

CEREMONY, EVENT/RECEPTION & MEETING CAPACITY: The site holds up to 325 guests outdoors.

FEES & DEPOSITS: 50% of the rental fee is due as a security deposit and the full fee is required to reserve your date. The balance is due upon signing of the contract. Rental fees range $1,400–4,500 depending on the season and the space selected.

AVAILABILITY: Year-round, daily starting at 8am. All events must end by 10pm with cleanup completed by 11pm, with extended cleanup available until midnight upon request.

SERVICES/AMENITIES:

Catering: BYO
Kitchen Facilities: none
Tables & Chairs: CBA, through caterer or BYO
Linens, Silver, etc.: through caterer or BYO
Restrooms: wheelchair accessible
Dance Floor: BYO
Bride's Dressing Area: none
Meeting Equipment: BYO
Other: picnic area

Parking: large lot
Accommodations: no guest rooms
Telephone: none
Outdoor Night Lighting: BYO
Outdoor Cooking Facilities: BBQ on site
Cleanup: renter
View: panorama of ocean, mountains and cityscape; park, garden, landscaped grounds

RESTRICTIONS:

Alcohol: BYO
Smoking: in designated areas only
Music: amplified OK outdoors with minor restrictions

Wheelchair Access: yes
Insurance: liability required

Hyatt Santa Barbara

1111 E. Cabrillo Boulevard, Santa Barbara
805/879-1320

www.santabarbara.hyatt.com
beckie.bruffey@hyatt.com

- Rehearsal Dinners
- Ceremonies
- Wedding Receptions
- Private Parties
- Corporate Events
- Meetings
- Film Shoots
- Accommodations

Santa Barbara embodies the perfect balance of small-town charm and big-city attractions, and its irresistible mix of sun, surf and sand has earned it the nickname "The American Riviera." If a beautiful oceanview venue on the coast tops your wedding wish list, then consider Hyatt Santa Barbara your fairy godmother.

The historic hotel first opened its doors in 1931, and its Spanish Colonial architecture and décor, including antique tilework and wrought-iron embellishments, all add up to classic Santa Barbara style. Although a recent makeover combines sleek, contemporary refinement with the latest amenities, the Hyatt Santa Barbara's enviable location is timeless—three landscaped acres commanding a prime spot across from East Beach, bordered by a treelined park.

It's just a short stroll from the hotel to the breathtaking ceremony site, right on the soft sand. Your event manager has thoughtfully arranged all the details: A refreshment station greets your guests, who will be seated on white wooden chairs accented with starfish. The wedding aisle is lined with seashells and a white trellis frames you and your fiancé against a backdrop of gentle waves—everything you need for a dreamy beach wedding! But if you have your heart set on tying the knot at one of the town's other scenic parks or gardens, then Hyatt's event pros are happy to take your ceremony there.

The cocktail hour is simply sublime back at Hyatt's wraparound Vista Terrace, which, as its name implies, treats everyone to picture-postcard scenery. French doors open to the Vista Ballroom, a smartly decorated space in pleasing earth tones with windows that look out to the ocean on one side and to the hills on the other. An adjoining alcove can hold a buffet, gift table or photo booth. Leave the doors open to the evening sea breezes and wander outside with your sweetheart for some romantic stargazing.

Yes, it all sounds divine, but there's another glamorous ballroom to consider. From its second story vantage, Cabrillo's panoramas are even more sweeping and dynamic. One wall showcases the Pacific and another overlooks a park towards the hills. The Gazebo, a curved, windowed annex, is a novel setting for an intimate indoor ceremony or cocktails.

The smallest of the hotel's three banquet spaces, La Cantina, also boasts the most Old World character, thanks to hand-stenciled ceiling beams, dark wood trim and huge candelabra chandeliers. Arched windows capture swaying palms and a ribbon of ocean, while a soaring cut-stone fireplace just begs for a cozy winter wedding or rehearsal dinner.

The Hyatt's enticing banquet menus are fully customizable and their wedding packages feature lots of extras, including a complimentary oceanview room for the newlyweds. Of course, staying here is half the fun: The beach-facing pool deck with fire pit, as well as the bistro, bar and spa, make relaxing a snap; the plush guest rooms provide plenty of creature comforts; and a waterfront shuttle offers easy access to the area's many activities. Invite your friends and family to a destination wedding at this luxurious venue and they'll experience the best of Santa Barbara along with your memorable celebration.

CEREMONY CAPACITY: The facility holds 250 seated guests indoors or outdoors.

EVENT/RECEPTION: Indoors, the hotel can accommodate 250 seated or 320 standing guests; outdoors 60 seated or 150 standing.

MEETING CAPACITY: The site holds 250 seated guests.

FEES & DEPOSITS: A $1,000 deposit is required to reserve your date and the balance is due 1 month prior to the event. Rental fees range $0–10,000 depending on the day of the event, guest count and the space rented. Meal packages range $59–109/person. Tax, alcohol and a 21% service charge are additional.

AVAILABILITY: Year-round, daily, 8am–11pm.

SERVICES/AMENITIES:

Catering: in-house
Kitchen Facilities: n/a
Tables & Chairs: provided
Linens, Silver, etc.: provided
Restrooms: wheelchair accessible
Dance Floor: portable provided
Bride's Dressing Area: yes
Meeting Equipment: some provided
Other: spa services, centerpieces, complimentary room for the bride & groom, event coordination

Parking: large lot, on street, valet required
Accommodations: 171 guest rooms
Telephone: house phone
Outdoor Night Lighting: CBA
Outdoor Cooking Facilities: BBQ CBA
Cleanup: provided
View: pool area, park; panorama of ocean, coastline and mountains

RESTRICTIONS:

Alcohol: full in-house bar
Smoking: outdoors only
Music: amplified OK with restrictions

Wheelchair Access: yes
Insurance: not required

The professionals in the back of this book are the best in the business. How do we know? Read page 549.

Santa Barbara Zoological Gardens

Waterfront Zoological Gardens

500 Ninos Drive, Santa Barbara
805/845-1296
www.sbzoo.org
angie@rinconcatering.com

- Rehearsal Dinners
- Ceremonies
- Wedding Receptions
- Private Parties
- Corporate Events
- Meetings
- Film Shoots
- Accommodations

Sure, plenty of zoos have the requisite elephant or lion...but the Santa Barbara Zoo has something more: 30 acres of lush gardens laced with majestic ocean views. This isn't your typical wedding venue, and this isn't a typical zoo, either. For one thing, the meticulously maintained park rests between the beach and a bird sanctuary. For another, it's got a surprisingly pleasant aroma, a mixture of roses, jasmine and the sea. This zoo also has experienced event pros who are particularly attentive and enthusiastic about helping make your day special. Oh, and one more huge plus—privacy! When the public leaves at 5pm, the entire place becomes your exclusive wedding playground.

Arriving wedding guests are escorted along a landscaped path to Palm Garden, a stunning ceremony site tucked away in a sunken, grassy courtyard. Surrounded by palm trees, agapanthus and leafy green thickets, it has the exotic air of a tame jungle hideaway. Couples tie the knot in front of a cluster of palms, sometimes adding a *chuppah* or bamboo arch, with a hint of ocean in the distance.

Next, while you and your wedding party pose for photos in the park's scenic gardens, your guests take refreshments on nearby Lower Hilltop, a broad grassy "porch" set with cocktail tables and a bar. To make this time even more memorable, you might arrange some novel entertainment: Invite a penguin to join the party; hire the zoo train to take everyone on a tour (cocktails welcome); or have guests take turns feeding Audrey and Betty Lou, Masai giraffes who unfurl long purple tongues as they gently accept their food. Now that's something most wedding guests don't get to experience!

When it's time to serve your friends and family *their* dinner, a short flight of stone steps leads to Upper Hilltop, a circular expanse of lawn gorgeously arrayed for the reception. Since the field is so spacious, the event staff creates "outdoor rooms" to lend a feeling of intimacy, using a variety of optional amenities—a dance floor, tenting, chandeliers, market lights, heat lamps, specialty linens, lounge furniture and props. They stage the festivities either overlooking Lower Hilltop, which offers glimpses of the Pacific through the palm fronds in one direction and the Santa Ynez Mountains in the other; or on the interior section, which enjoys two different Pacific vistas plus a pergola and splashing fountain. The event team will personalize your wedding, whether you prefer traditionally elegant styling or something imaginative. (One couple recently had an Alice in Wonderland-themed gala!) Pretty much anything you can dream up, the zoo staff will help you pull off.

The same is true of the cuisine. *Zoo Catering Services by Rincon (ZCS)* boasts "Wild Flavors with Civilized Service," and they're equally adept at delivering a relaxed barbecue or a sophisticated candlelit affair, global fusion or the freshest California cuisine. You're in good hands with these culinary superstars!

The Santa Barbara Zoological Gardens is a private, nonprofit organization, which is perfect for green weddings—your special event fees help support the zoo's conservation and education efforts. With its picturesque setting and impeccable service, this unique location is a "natural" for out-of-the-ordinary celebrations.

CEREMONY CAPACITY: The facility holds up to 250 seated guests outdoors.

EVENT/RECEPTION CAPACITY: The site can accommodate 500 seated or standing outdoors.

MEETING CAPACITY: Meetings do not take place at this facility.

FEES & DEPOSITS: 50% of the site fee plus a $300 security deposit is required to reserve your date and the balance is due 60 days prior to the event. Rental fees range $550–4,000 depending on the day and time of the event. Meals range $16–40/person. Tax, alcohol and an 18% service charge are additional.

AVAILABILITY: Year-round.

SERVICES/AMENITIES:

Catering: in-house
Kitchen Facilities: n/a
Tables & Chairs: some provided, CBA
Linens, Silver, etc.: some provided, CBA
Restrooms: wheelchair accessible
Dance Floor: provided
Bride's Dressing Area: yes
Meeting Equipment: provided
Other: spa services, picnic area, AV equipment, event coordination

Parking: large lot
Accommodations: no guest rooms
Telephone: house or guest phone
Outdoor Night Lighting: yes
Outdoor Cooking Facilities: BBQ on site
Cleanup: provided
View: fountain, garden, courtyard, landscaped grounds; panorama of hills, mountains, ocean and coastline

RESTRICTIONS:

Alcohol: in-house, or BYO
Smoking: designated areas only
Music: amplified OK

Wheelchair Access: yes
Insurance: liability required

Unitarian Society of Santa Barbara

Historic Church & Event Facility

1535 Santa Barbara Street, Santa Barbara
805/965-4583 x223
www.ussb.org
facilities@ussb.org

● Rehearsal Dinners	● Corporate Events
● Ceremonies	● Meetings
● Wedding Receptions	● Film Shoots
● Private Parties	Accommodations

Directly across from the blossom-filled Alice Keck Park Memorial Garden is the Unitarian Society of Santa Barbara, a historic, nondenominational church with a long tradition as a wonderful wedding location. Their beautiful Sanctuary evokes a peaceful sense of divine mystery, and the congregation's inclusive philosophy makes this venue a congenial gathering place, perfectly suited for life's celebrations. Unitarian Universalists support one another on their various spiritual paths, and are nonjudgmental, compassionate and socially conscious. As you and your soul mate begin your own lifelong journey together, consider letting the tranquil surroundings of the Unitarian Society provide you with a memorable send-off.

The Unitarian Society campus includes the Sanctuary, a Reception hall, a Terrace and two Gardened Courtyards. Designed more than 75 years ago in the city's signature Spanish-Revival style, the Sanctuary's rustic glamour is enhanced by antique architectural elements: Vintage lantern-style light fixtures are suspended from the vaulted ceiling's open beams. The original wooden pews are flanked by lofty, rectangular stained-glass panels in subdued shades of pale blue and honey, each inscribed with the name of a famous Unitarian freethinker like essayist Ralph Waldo Emerson. At the front of the Sanctuary, the chancel is softly illuminated by a breathtaking stained-glass rose window in radiant jewel tones; a smaller rose window looks out over balcony seating at the rear. The Sanctuary conveys a momentous yet joyful ambiance, and its quality acoustics make music sound even more dramatic. Hire one of their recommended musicians, and walk down the aisle to the impressive sound of the Sanctuary's genuine 1,500-pipe organ or Steinway concert piano. Couples of any faith or sexual orientation are invited to pledge their love in this glorious space (a welcome solution for interfaith marriages and same-sex unions).

Following the ceremony, guests often enjoy an open-air social hour in the pretty Jefferson Courtyard. A brick patio flanked by twin lawns crowned with olive saplings is a delightful spot to toast the newlyweds; then, while refreshments are served, bridal parties can sneak across the street for photos in the park. A second-story terrace lets guests survey the festivities below. Tucked in one corner of the courtyard, a semiprivate enclave with a labyrinth and small amphitheater invites intimate conversations.

Outdoor receptions are usually held in the Parish Courtyard at the front of the facility. Lovely and serene, this bricked garden plaza is suffused with the soothing sound of splashing water, thanks to a tiled fountain at the center. Well-placed foliage provides filtered shade, and at the right time of year a grand magnolia tree shows off delicately fragrant flowers. A triple-arched breezeway is a perfect place for the bar and, once the sun sets, garden lights provide a romantic luster to the idyllic setting.

Through the breezeway lies the newly refurbished Parish Hall, an attractive banquet room with high ceilings. Earth-toned walls bring out the room's Mission-style flavor and complement a large stained-glass window (similar to the Sanctuary panels). The hardwood floor is great for dancing, and a proscenium stage puts the entertainment on display. Recent upgrades include an audiovisual system, and behind the scenes your caterer cooks up a feast in a professional kitchen.

Flexible, welcoming and aesthetically pleasing, the Unitarian Society continues its legacy as host to unforgettable events.

CEREMONY CAPACITY: The Sanctuary holds 285 seated guests; the courtyard 150 seated guests.

EVENT/RECEPTION CAPACITY: Indoors, the site holds up to 100 seated or 220 standing guests; outdoors 150 seated or 220 standing guests.

MEETING CAPACITY: Spaces are available that accommodate 150 seated guests.

FEES & DEPOSITS: A $500 deposit is required to reserve your date. The balance is due 6–9 months prior to the event. Rental fees range $1,650–4,800 depending on space and hours rented. For meetings or memorial services, please call for quote. To visit this facility, call or email ahead for special assistance.

AVAILABILITY: Year-round, daily. Monday–Saturday 9am–10pm; Sunday 3pm–10pm.

SERVICES/AMENITIES:

Catering: select from list or BYO
Kitchen Facilities: new commercial kitchen
Tables & Chairs: CBA
Linens, Silver, etc.: BYO
Restrooms: wheelchair accessible
Dance Floor: provided indoors
Bride's Dressing Area: yes
Meeting Equipment: some provided

Parking: on street and valet CBA
Accommodations: no guest rooms
Telephone: emergency use only
Outdoor Night Lighting: CBA
Outdoor Cooking Facilities: BBQ CBA
Cleanup: CBA
View: gardens, park, mountains
Other: grand piano; vocalists and organist CBA

RESTRICTIONS:

Alcohol: BYO, licensed server only
Smoking: not allowed
Music: amplified OK with restrictions

Wheelchair Access: yes
Insurance: one-day liability policy required

Gainey Vineyard

3950 East Highway 246, Santa Ynez
805/688-0558

www.gaineyvineyard.com
events@gaineyvineyard.com

Winery

- Rehearsal Dinners
- Ceremonies
- Wedding Receptions
- Private Parties
- Corporate Events
- Meetings
- Film Shoots
- Accommodations

Although its setting in the rolling, oak-studded hills of Santa Barbara's wine country is a picturesque one, Gainey Vineyard has earned a reputation for something other than its native good looks. With its year-round program of tastings, tours and concerts, the winery has become a purveyor of both fine wine and culture. The combination has met with success: All of Gainey's varietal wines have won coveted gold medals, while big names like Randy Newman, Count Basie, Emmylou Harris, Diana Krall, Lucinda Williams and Al Jarreau have been among the acts providing the music. Gainey Vineyard has over 25 years of experience hosting special events and weddings. The site's natural beauty can't help but attract couples from miles around, and when they get here, the bride and groom will find a supportive and energetic staff.

As you approach the winery, you get your first glimpse of its visual appeal. Over 90 acres of premium grapevines spread out on either side of the long entry drive, which ends in a sweep around a circular courtyard in front of the hacienda-style winery building. The Tasting Room inside is a handsome space for intimate gatherings. Spanish tile floors, dramatic lighting and a grand-scale fireplace give it a country-casual ambiance. Adjacent to the Tasting Room is the Wine Cellar, a long room whose walls are stacked with floor-to-ceiling bottles of aging wine. Add tables outfitted with linens, candelabras and bowls of fruit for a glowing Tuscan-style reception, or follow your own vision. The spacious Barrel Room, lined with casks of aging wine, is another option for a warm, elegant dinner.

Receptions also take place right outside on the Patio, a grassy open-air courtyard bordered on one side by a grapevine-covered trellis. At the end of the trellis, a barbecue and kitchen prep area make outdoor catering easy. Leafy rows of Sauvignon Blanc and Merlot grapes frame the Patio's uphill side, where two stately heritage oaks create a majestic focal point.

The Vineyard View Picnic Area, with its two massive oaks and commanding vistas, is the facility's most popular site for ceremonies. Couples say their vows on a raised knoll beneath one of the oaks, while their guests enjoy not only the moment but the view: acres of vineyards and the Santa Ynez Mountains in the distance.

Gainey's oldest event site is The Old Homestead, built in the 1890s. Located a half mile from the winery, this rustic barn is a terrific spot for dancing, and the expansive area around it makes a wonderful setting for either a western-style celebration or an upscale casual affair. Rolling hills, a nearby creek and shady oaks provide the scenery.

If Gainey Vineyard sounds like the kind of place where you'd like to get married or throw a party, come by for a wine tasting and take in a concert. After you've sampled its wine, song and pastoral surroundings, Gainey is sure to rank high on your list.

CEREMONY CAPACITY: The Vineyard View Picnic Area holds up to 300 seated guests; the Patio accommodates up to 200 seated.

EVENT/RECEPTION CAPACITY: The Courtyard holds up to 400 seated or standing guests; the Tasting Room 50; the Patio up to 200 seated; the Wine Cellar 50 seated and the Barrel Room 125 seated. The Barn grounds accommodate up to 500 guests.

MEETING CAPACITY: The Conference Room adjacent to the Patio holds 10 seated.

FEES & DEPOSITS: For weddings, a $5,000 nonrefundable deposit is required to book the site. The site rental fee for a BBQ wedding is $2,500 Monday–Thursday, $4,500 on Friday and $5,500 on Saturday and Sunday. For a catered wedding the site rental fee is $3,000 Monday–Thursday, $5,000 on Friday and $6,000 on Saturday and Sunday. The Barn rental fee is $3,000, which includes use of the Barn and grounds. The Conference Room rental fee is $200/day.

Sophisticated barbecues start at $38/person and include tableware, linens, tables and chairs. If you don't use the in-house caterer, you'll have to supply all event rentals. The event balance is payable 2 weeks prior to the function. With prior arrangement, the sophisticated kitchen may be used.

AVAILABILITY: Year-round, daily except major holidays, 10am–10pm. The Tasting Room, Wine Cellar and Barrel Room are available 5pm–10pm only.

SERVICES/AMENITIES:
Catering: in-house or BYO
Kitchen Facilities: fully equipped
Tables & Chairs: provided or BYO
Linens, Silver, etc.: provided or BYO
Restrooms: wheelchair accessible
Dance Floor: BYO
Bride's Dressing Room: lounge available
Meeting Equipment: BYO

Parking: large lot, valet required
Accommodations: no guest rooms
Telephone: CBA, local calls only
Outdoor Night Lighting: yes
Outdoor Cooking Facilities: BBQ
Cleanup: provided or caterer
View: vineyards, rolling hills
Other: coordination, extra fee

RESTRICTIONS:
Alcohol: Gainey Vineyard wines only; beer also available
Smoking: outside only
Music: amplified OK

Wheelchair Access: yes
Insurance: certificate required
Other: no rice or confetti

Ventura County

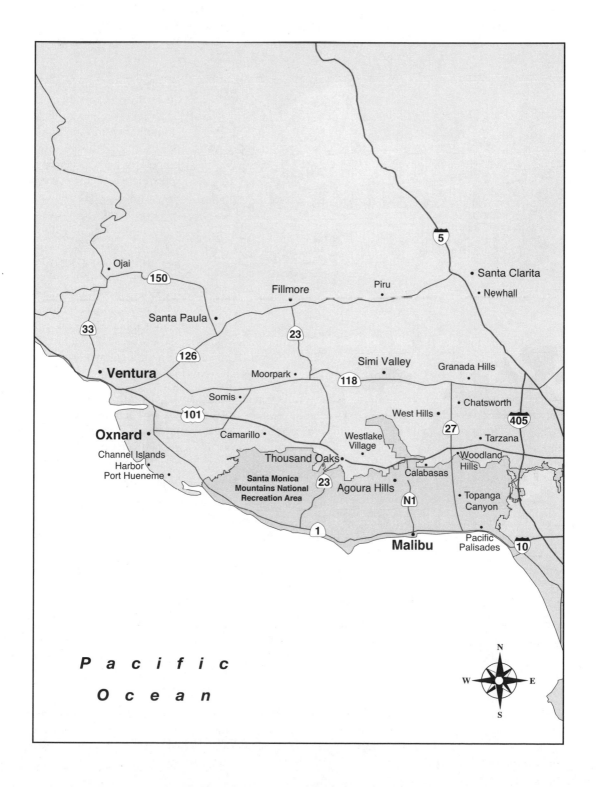

McCormick Home Ranch

Private Ranch

2034 East Fifth Street, Camarillo
805/482-1549
www.mccormickhomeranch.com
mccormickhomeranch@verizon.net

Rehearsal Dinners	● Corporate Events
● Ceremonies	● Meetings
● Wedding Receptions	● Film Shoots
● Private Parties	Accommodations

If only a real country wedding will do for you, then get on over to the McCormick Home Ranch in Camarillo. Built in 1918, this historic home is set on 11 verdant acres, eight of them devoted to avocado trees. The Ranch is surrounded by miles of farmland, where everything from strawberries to onions grows almost effortlessly in a fertile plain at the base of the Conejo foothills. That's what prompted Irish immigrant Thomas McCormick to settle in Camarillo back in 1888, and McCormick Home Ranch has been the scene of family weddings and parties for four generations. Now Sally McCormick, the current matriarch, invites you to experience a little bit o' country charm by staging your special event on the picturesque grounds.

Trees, flowers, and greenery of all kinds make this venue cheery and welcoming. Guests drive onto the property and park in an ample lot behind some shrubs to the side. Then it's just a short walk to the front of the main house, a white wood-frame Colonial with a trio of dormer windows and a broad brick veranda edged in fragrant star jasmine. A portico extends from one side of the house, and on the other side of it is where Sally's old wooden wagon holds your wedding gifts, and her vintage white iron stand supports your guest book.

The gravel driveway in front of the house encircles a large lawn, where receptions are held. There's plenty of room for a bar, buffet area, or even a band or DJ. A portable dance floor fits on the gravel drive in front of the veranda, so guests can two-step to their heart's content. Flowers are everywhere—some in pots, some growing wild like a delicate dusting of confetti. Guests are seated in rows of chairs facing a group of colorful jacarandas, palms, pine trees and more, but when the bride makes her entrance, all heads turn around to watch her walk down the aisle. At night, Tivoli lights twinkle through the jasmine, and Japanese lanterns glow softly like candlelight.

Another pretty spot for a ceremony is the Garden, reached by a small flagstone path next to the house. A brick patio bordered by trees faces the side of the house, which has a charmingly countrified feel thanks to trails of trumpet vine hugging its windows. At the center of the Garden a bed of lacy blooms encircles a stone birdbath, and the fluttering of sparrow wings and the occasional butterfly make it seem like spring here no matter what the time of year.

Behind the house, yet one more garden and veranda is available for your ceremony or small reception. An arbor laced with vines and nestled amongst the lush landscaping is an inviting spot to say your vows. Quaint garden furniture, birdhouses, and a swing with room enough for two make everyone feel right at home.

Delightful discoveries, like distressed watering cans tucked in garden nooks and a genuine cistern pump, contribute to the old-fashioned mood.

McCormick Home Ranch recaptures the rustic appeal of bygone days, and is bound to make your wedding a historic event.

CEREMONY, EVENT/RECEPTION & MEETING CAPACITY: The site accommodates up to 250 guests.

FEES & DEPOSITS: Half of the rental fee is a nonrefundable deposit required to reserve your date. The balance is due 2 weeks prior to the event. Rental fees range $3,000–3,700. A $300 refundable cleaning and security deposit is additional.

AVAILABILITY: Spring–Fall, daily, 11am–11pm.

SERVICES/AMENITIES:

Catering: BYO, licensed caterer
Kitchen Facilities: no
Tables & Chairs: provided
Linens, Silver, etc.: linens provided;
BYO tableware
Restrooms: wheelchair accessible, portable
Dance Floor: provided
Bride's & Groom's Dressing Area: yes
Meeting Equipment: BYO

Parking: large lighted lot
Accommodations: no guest rooms
Telephone: emergency use only
Outdoor Night Lighting: yes
Outdoor Cooking Facilities: no
Cleanup: caterer or renter
View: trees, garden

RESTRICTIONS:

Alcohol: BYO
Smoking: allowed
Music: amplified OK, curfew 10:30pm

Wheelchair Access: yes
Insurance: required

Want to know WHAT TO ASK a potential location or vendor? Check out our Questions to Ask starting on page 19.

79

Serra Center

Event Center

5205 Upland Road, Camarillo
805/482-6417 x356

www.serra-center.org
kay@padreserra.org

- Rehearsal Dinners
- Corporate Events
- Ceremonies
- Meetings
- Wedding Receptions
- Film Shoots
- Private Parties
- Accommodations

How would you like to host your wedding reception in a contemporary venue that's warmed by rustic touches, loaded with the latest amenities and large enough to accommodate the gala you envision? What if it overlooked an outdoor plaza in a secluded park-like setting—yet was only five minutes from a major freeway? And just for fun, we'll throw in high-quality catering and a reasonable price tag. Interested? We thought so.

Say hello to Serra Center, an attractive and welcoming 14,000-square-foot venue in the peaceful foothills of Camarillo. The center conveys a clean, modern aesthetic enhanced by Mission-era details. Pale peach and apricot-hued buildings are trimmed with turquoise and Catalina-blue tiles. Towering palm trees and large terracotta planters lining the curb pay a nod to California's heritage. Around the grounds, mini-courtyards offer pleasant respites where olive saplings hold lush promise and flowering herbs flavor the air with their piquant aroma. A favorite spot for photos is a circle of lawn edged by palms, roses and Early California-style wooden benches.

Arriving guests pass a garden of native foliage before ascending a broad staircase to the center's main entrance. A bright and airy lobby, with a sand-colored travertine tile floor and intricate wrought-iron chandeliers, is an elegant place to showcase your gift table. Handsome, dark oak double doors open into the spacious event hall with its lofty ceiling. Along two sides, tall windows are inset with corner squares of ruby stained glass for Deco-inspired flair. From on high, clerestory windows bathe your daytime reception in natural light—but should you wish to darken the room for your video montage, window shades and a huge viewing screen descend at the flip of a switch. (The center's state-of-the-art audiovisual capabilities really are quite impressive.) A stage and generous dance floor provide additional event elements to work with.

The hall can be divided into two sections, and there are several annexes should you need another room to entertain children or serve a buffet. The adjoining professional kitchen means food can be prepared, fresh and hot, right on site. Adjacent to the hall, a serene plaza and lawn lend themselves to an al fresco cocktail hour.

Serra Center's handpicked caterer, *Command Performance*, is known for their delectable cuisine, ethnic menus and creative styling. As customization specialists, they'll assist with staging, finding a ceremony site and personalizing your menu. They're an integral part of what makes the versatile Serra Center a "made to order" event location.

CEREMONY CAPACITY: Call to inquire about ceremonies.

EVENT/RECEPTION CAPACITY: The Center accommodates 500 seated or 600 standing guests indoors and 600 standing outdoors for cocktail receptions.

MEETING CAPACITY: Meeting spaces seat 600 guests indoors.

FEES & DEPOSITS: A deposit of $1,000 is required to reserve your date and the balance is due 90 days prior to the event. Rental fees range $2,900–5,000 depending on the number of guests and the area rented. Meals range $25–45/person. Tax, alcohol and a 15% service charge are additional.

AVAILABILITY: Year-round, daily until midnight.

SERVICES/AMENITIES:

Catering: provided by *Command Performance*
Kitchen Facilities: n/a
Tables & Chairs: provided
Linens, Silver, etc.: through caterer
Restrooms: wheelchair accessible
Dance Floor: portable provided
Bride's Dressing Area: no
Meeting Equipment: provided
Other: AV equipment, on-site representative included

Parking: large lot
Accommodations: no guest rooms
Telephone: house phone
Outdoor Night Lighting: yes
Outdoor Cooking Facilities: no
Cleanup: provided
View: garden, park, fountain, landscaped grounds

RESTRICTIONS:

Alcohol: BYO
Smoking: outdoors only
Music: amplified OK

Wheelchair Access: yes
Insurance: liability required
Other: Security guards required when alcohol is present

Tropical Paradise Camarillo

Garden Oasis

10350 Santa Rosa Road, Camarillo
805/377-2240

www.tropicalparadisecamarillo.com
facebook.com/tropicalparadisecamarillo
info@tropicalparadisecamarillo.com

● Rehearsal Dinners	● Corporate Events
● Ceremonies	● Meetings
● Wedding Receptions	● Film Shoots
● Private Parties	Accommodations

Welcome to Tropical Paradise, an oasis set on a private ranch in the tranquil countryside of Santa Rosa Valley. This special event venue was designed specifically for wedding celebrations, and is laid out to complement the natural flow of your big day.

It starts when guests drive through the gated entrance into the spacious (free!) parking lot, lined with palm trees, bamboo and agapanthus. The scenery becomes even more lush as they walk beneath a canopy of palm fronds and through a bamboo arch, and are greeted by a rock waterfall splashing into two ponds. The enchanting water feature is adorned with gladioli, birds of paradise, roses and candy-hued impatiens, a striking floral motif that's abundantly used throughout the grounds. The sound of flowing water, the soft music playing from the discreet sound system, and the melody of songbirds weave a harmonious, uplifting spell.

In front of the waterfall, three adjoining event areas are set off by white organza panels attached to tree trunks and billowing in the warm breeze. Straight ahead lies the Ceremony Lawn, lined with—what else?—palm trees, encircled with seasonal blooms. Down the center of the grass, a bridal aisle is dressed with a white runner and strewn with flower petals. Wedding vows are exchanged atop a broad demilune stage flanked by twin palms, in front of a carpet of white iceberg roses. A breathtaking mountain silhouette in the background is close enough to touch.

After the ceremony, you and your wedding party pose for photos, while guests gather in the adjacent Outdoor Lounge for drinks and appetizers. Picturesque and festive, this area makes use of the signature palms in a novel way: Cocktail tables are actually built around the tree trunks, with the fronds serving as natural umbrellas!

As sunset paints the horizon, guests stroll to the Reception Garden on the other side of the Ceremony Lawn. This is the time when the scene is transformed into a magical fairyland, with landscape lighting, spotlights on the waterfall, market lights strung across the lawns, and twinkle lights wrapped around palm trunks. There's a huge built-in dance floor, and a white wooden stage that's perfect for showcasing the cake cutting. Overhead, moonlight and a brilliant starscape illuminate the evening sky, creating the ultimate romantic ambiance.

Thoughtful touches abound here, like the elegantly outfitted Bride's Room, hidden away in one corner of the property, where you and your entourage can prepare in style. Considerable thought goes into the service and catering, too. Your site manager will be with you every step of the way, as will *DJs California Catering*. Not only are they superb with food, but they're also experienced event producers. Want to tent the reception area? Not a problem. Specialty menu items? As you wish. So accomplished is *DJs* that they've been the *Ventura County Star* "Reader's Choice Winner for Best Caterer" in 2009, 2010, 2011 and 2012.

Whether you plan on hosting a fun, casual wedding or a sophisticated open-air gala, this exciting new venue will put you in a lighthearted, tropical state of mind.

CEREMONY, EVENT/RECEPTION & MEETING CAPACITY: The site holds 400 seated or standing guests outdoors.

FEES & DEPOSITS: A $1,000 deposit is required to reserve your date and the balance is due 30 days prior to the event. Rental fees range $3,000–3,500 depending on the day of the event. There is a $500 refundable security deposit. Meals range $59–81/person. Tax, alcohol and a 15% service charge are additional.

AVAILABILITY: Year-round, daily, 9am–10pm.

SERVICES/AMENITIES:

Catering: in-house
Kitchen Facilities: n/a
Tables & Chairs: provided
Linens, Silver, etc.: provided
Restrooms: not wheelchair accessible
Dance Floor: provided
Bride's Dressing Area: yes
Meeting Equipment: provided
Other: sweetheart stage, complimentary event coordination

Parking: large lot, overflow parking available
Accommodations: no guest rooms
Telephone: emergency use only
Outdoor Night Lighting: provided
Outdoor Cooking Facilities: no
Cleanup: caterer
View: tropical gardens, fountain, waterfalls, landscaped grounds; panorama of meadow, mountains and hills

RESTRICTIONS:

Alcohol: in-house
Smoking: designated areas only
Music: amplified OK outdoors with restrictions

Wheelchair Access: yes
Insurance: liability required

Wedgewood Sterling Hills

901 Sterling Hills Drive, Camarillo
866/966-3009
www.wedgewoodbanquet.com/sterling-hills
sales@wedgewoodbanquet.com

Special Events Facility

● Rehearsal Dinners ● Corporate Events
● Ceremonies ● Meetings
● Wedding Receptions ● Film Shoots
● Private Parties   Accommodations

Camarillo lies at the heart of Pleasant Valley, cradled by the richly forested Las Posas Mountains. With arguably the best weather in the country, it's become one of the most desirable areas for living out the Southern California lifestyle. Wedgewood Sterling Hills perfectly reflects Camarillo's congenial attitude and idyllic surroundings.

The country road up to Sterling Hills winds past strawberry fields and orange groves and, as you crest the first rise, the handsome Sterling Hills clubhouse suddenly makes its appearance. The building is a sleek example of Mediterranean chic, with a red-tile roof and a double-arched portico supported by classical columns. Crowning the circular driveway is a grand stone fountain flanked by young palm trees. The glass-and-mahogany front door opens into a dramatic vaulted rotunda. Sunlight peeks through lofty arched windows, and an elaborate wrought-iron chandelier suspended from the cupola adds a nighttime glow. Further on is the banquet room and lounge, distinguished by an air of attractive refinement and an open floor plan. A working fireplace keeps things cozy, while a long row of windows treats guests to a vision of the emerald fairways of Sterling Hills Golf Course and picturesque countryside.

The outdoor wedding site is lovely, with the bridal couple silhouetted against the gently rolling greens. As the pink gauze of sunset veils the horizon, feathery clouds hover over the slopes along the valley's eastern edge, completing the romantic picture.

Cocktails are poured at the mahogany bar in the lounge, but guests usually wander outside to enjoy the central fountain terrace, set with the hors d'oeuvres display. A delicious dinner is served back in the banquet room and, as the evening progresses, guests spill out onto the south terrace facing the ninth hole. Here, lanky marsh grass and a thicket of reeds surround a small pond, from which a chorus of frogs often serenades the guests. For more traditional entertainment, place your band and dance floor on the south terrace and sway cheek-to-cheek under the stars.

Like the rest of Wedgewood's popular banquet centers, this one at Sterling Hills is not only beautiful, but convenient as well. Their thoughtful and comprehensive wedding packages are a terrific value, and make it easy for you to put your event details together.

Whether your wedding is a formal affair or a casual get-together of family and friends, the personalized service, appealing amenities and sophisticated country club setting of Wedgewood Sterling Hills will make you and your guests feel utterly indulged.

CEREMONY CAPACITY: The lawn holds 225 seated guests.

EVENT/RECEPTION CAPACITY: The site accommodates up to 225 seated or standing indoors.

MEETING CAPACITY: The dining room holds 225 seated theater style.

FEES & DEPOSITS: 25% of the estimated total event cost is required to reserve your date. An additonal 25% is due 120 days prior to the event and the balance (based on your final guest count) is due 10 days prior. All payments are credited towards your final balance and are nonrefundable and nontransferable. All-inclusive, completely customizable wedding packages start at $33/person. Tax, alcohol and a 21–22% service charge are additional.

AVAILABILITY: Year-round, daily, 10am–1am.

SERVICES/AMENITIES:

Catering: in-house
Kitchen Facilities: n/a
Tables & Chairs: provided
Linens, Silver, etc.: provided
Restrooms: wheelchair accessible
Dance Floor: provided
Bride's & Groom's Dressing Area: yes

Parking: large lot
Accommodations: no guest rooms
Telephone: pay phones
Outdoor Night Lighting: CBA
Outdoor Cooking Facilities: provided
Cleanup: provided
View: fairways, Santa Paula Mtns., orchards

RESTRICTIONS:

Alcohol: provided
Smoking: outdoors only
Music: amplified OK indoors

Wheelchair Access: yes
Insurance: not required
Other: no confetti or water balloons, open flames limited

Eden Gardens Weddings

Garden

Address withheld to ensure privacy. Moorpark
805/208-3098

www.edengardensweddings.com
edengardensweddings@gmail.com

- ● Rehearsal Dinners
- ● Ceremonies
- ● Wedding Receptions
- ● Private Parties
- ● Corporate Events
- ● Meetings
- ● Film Shoots
- Accommodations

Wanted: True Romantics to wed in fragrant garden paradise. Must love the sounds of flowing water and birdsong. Desire for unique celebration with family and friends a definite plus!

Equal parts enchanted forest and tropical oasis with a large helping of event-friendly amenities, Eden Gardens is two acres of "wow" from your first step inside the private gates. An arched entryway beckons you deep into fairyland. Lush, meandering paths canopied in greenery yield surprises at every turn: a waterfall that feeds a running brook…vintage birdcages aglow with luminarias…urns brimming with blooms…a covey of wedding-white peacocks. Down one walkway, you'll find yourself among a series of fantastical aviaries alive with sound and color. Vivid parrots engage in friendly chatter (Arturo se habla espanol!), while lovebirds and rosy-cheeked cockatiels trill a sweet serenade. A clearing serves as a pre-event welcome station, where guests quaff lemonade amid the fluttering of doves' wings. And you haven't even arrived at the Ceremonial Garden yet!

A series of twinkle-lit archways entwined with blush-pink Eden roses leads to a breathtaking vision: a picturesque pond dotted with blooming lily pads and fountain sprays. Spread along the bank, a pair of manicured lawns flanks a spacious stage which is elevated to allow views of the bridal couple from every angle. Behind them, an uplit waterfall cascades around a classical statue; in front of them, the sunset's reflection turns the pond into a scintillating waterscape. "Dreamy" doesn't begin to describe this storybook setting.

The myriad of photogenic backdrops lures the wedding party away during the social hour, but guests won't mind—they're busy exploring the several pondside terraces set with cocktail tables. As evening descends, your gathering moves on to the open-air Amphitheater, a swathe of grass with a low, colorfully lit waterfall along the perimeter. Overhead, market lights merge with the starscape for maximum magic. A raised demilune stage that looks as if it was made of alabaster is perfect for showcasing the sweetheart table and wedding cake or your entertainment.

Down a nearby path, the lofty whitewashed Pavilion, adorned with flower baskets, has the feel of an open-sided barn. A dollhouse porch off to one side is a fun spot to serve late-night snacks or the wedding cake.

With so many delights competing for your attention, it's easy to overlook Eden Gardens' practical enhancements. For example, an abundance of specialty lighting accentuates the nighttime glamour of each fountain and event area, and many of the tree trunks are wrapped with twinkle lights. Your choice of music fills the air, thanks to a sound system discreetly wired throughout the grounds.

Eden Gardens' chosen caterer, *Command Performance*, is experienced and caring with an expert staff: The company boasts a knowledgeable catering coordinator as well as chefs who specialize in exciting food station receptions and theme menus. Their wedding packages offer both convenience and flexibility, and customization is welcome.

For true romantics, Eden Gardens will be love at first sight, but anyone who appreciates natural beauty and exceptional services will fall under its spell.

CEREMONY CAPACITY: The site holds 300 seated guests outdoors.

EVENT/RECEPTION CAPACITY: The site accommodates 300 seated or 400 standing guests outdoors.

MEETING CAPACITY: Meeting spaces seat 400 guests outdoors.

FEES & DEPOSITS: A $1,750 deposit is required to reserve your date, and the balance is due 14 days prior to the event. Rental fees for use of the ceremony and reception area are $3,450 for Friday and $4,450 for Saturday or Sunday. There is an additional charge of $5/person for all Saturday events. Guest count minimums vary depending on the day of the week, and holiday rates may apply on certain dates. Valet, security and special event insurance are required.

Catering packages are available through *Command Performance Catering* and start at $72/person. A $1,000 deposit is required. Tax and a 20% service charge are extra. Alcohol is not included in catering packages; contact the catering coordinator for details.

Rental and catering fees are subject to change.

AVAILABILITY: Year round, daily, 8am–11pm.

SERVICES/AMENITIES:
Catering: in-house
Kitchen Facilities: n/a
Tables & Chairs: CBA
Linens, Silver, etc.: CBA
Restrooms: wheelchair accessible
Dance Area: provided
Bride's Dressing Area: yes
Meeting Equipment: CBA
Other: event coordination

Parking: large lot
Accommodations: no guest rooms
Telephone: guest phone
Outdoor Night Lighting: CBA
Outdoor Cooking Facilities: none
Cleanup: provided
View: creek, fountain, garden, lagoon, landscaped grounds and waterfall

RESTRICTIONS:
Alcohol: BYO
Smoking: designated areas only
Music: amplified OK outdoors

Wheelchair Access: yes
Insurance: liability required

Want to find more venues and services? Check out our informative website, www.HereComesTheGuide.com.

87

Rancho de las Palmas

3566 Sunset Valley Road, Moorpark
805/529-6699

www.ranchodelaspalmas.com
ranchodelaspalmas@yahoo.com

Private Estate

- Rehearsal Dinners
- Ceremonies
- Wedding Receptions
- Private Parties
- Corporate Events
- Meetings
- Film Shoots
- Accommodations

In describing an event facility, the word "oasis" gets thrown around pretty loosely, but Rancho de las Palmas, with its spring-fed lagoon, thousands of palm trees and 15 fountains, comes as close as we've ever seen to fitting the literal definition. Personally designed and executed over 18 years by the Cassar family, this unique private estate spread over 420 acres is also a registered turtle sanctuary, botanical garden and antiquities museum. Everything here is handmade and an outpouring of the family's seemingly unlimited creative energy. Fortunately, they've been kind enough to open their magnificent hideaway to us.

The focal point of Rancho de Las Palmas is the huge lagoon, with its three sparkling fountains and a marvelous island, where a bridge leads from the shore to the island. Weeping willows and stalwart palm trees make for a tropical setting on the shore, and a spacious serpentine deck, any part of which can be set up for entertaining, borders the lagoon. This is a great place to sip a mai tai with friends and enjoy the view.

Couples often get married in front of the double-tier waterfall, or on the short flight of brick stairs leading to the deck. The stairs have an overhead arch and side railings in ornate wrought iron, perfect for twining with flowers. From here, it's only a few steps to the Pavilion for the reception. The Pavilion is quite charming as is, but for a more formal wedding, organza can be draped from the center post to soften the look. Nighttime celebrations are especially glamorous here, since virtually every structure (the deck, island, and Pavilion) is strung with twinkle lights.

If you're planning a large ceremony, you'll be thoroughly delighted by the estate's newest wedding site. Here, the bride walks down a 100-foot-long aisle and through a series of five ornate archways, all of which can be festooned with flowers and tulle. Vows are exchanged beneath the last arch against a backdrop of tropical foliage.

One of the greatest pleasures of being at Rancho de las Palmas is taking a stroll around the grounds. As you do, notice the unique architectural details. On the deck, wood railings change to wrought iron, and pathways that start out brick turn to cobblestone, then to concrete poured in imaginative designs. Classical fountains rub shoulders with abstract stone structures made of river rock and brick, some decorated with leaping dolphins. However, if you think this sounds like an artistic hodgepodge, you're in for a treat. It all harmonizes beautifully—the manmade structures seem to have grown as naturally as the palms, pepper trees and flowers that surround them. And if children are included in your celebration, they'll be enchanted (and occupied!) by a Swiss Family Robinson-style tree house, complete with slide and swings.

Incidentally, the Rancho only holds one event per day, so you're welcome to start setting up in the morning, and spend a little time relaxing before the festivities. In addition to weddings, Rancho de las Palmas has hosted numerous movie shoots, luaus, casino nights and auctions. If you can't stand the thought of renting a stuffy ballroom or crowded banquet hall for your event, try Rancho de Las Palmas—it's as refreshing as an oasis in the desert!

CEREMONY CAPACITY: Ceremony areas hold 230 seated guests.

EVENT/RECEPTION & MEETING CAPACITY: The covered Pavilion can accommodate up to 230 seated guests. For corporate events, the site holds up to 230 guests.

FEES & DEPOSITS: For weddings, a $3,000 nonrefundable deposit is payable when reservations are confirmed; the balance is due 2 weeks prior to the event. The rental fee is $3,000 on Saturday, $2,000 on Sunday and $1,500 on Friday evening. Wedding packages start at $59/person, and include use of the property, a buffet or dinner, hors d'oeuvres, unlimited social bar and champagne toast, chairs, tables and tableware. Tax and a 17% service charge are additional.

For corporate events a nonrefundable deposit totaling 50% of the estimated event total is payable when reservations are confirmed; the balance is due 2 weeks prior to the event. The rental fee varies depending on guest count, day of week and event type; call for more information.

AVAILABILITY: Year-round, daily including holidays, 9am–10pm.

SERVICES/AMENITIES:

Catering: in-house, no BYO
Kitchen Facilities: n/a
Tables & Chairs: provided
Linens, Silver, etc.: provided
Restrooms: wheelchair accessible
Dance Floor: rental available
Bride's Dressing Area: yes
Meeting Equipment: BYO

Parking: large, lighted lot
Accommodations: no guest rooms
Telephone: emergency use only
Outdoor Night Lighting: yes
Outdoor Cooking Facilities: through caterer
Cleanup: caterer
View: tropical botanical gardens, freshwater lake, turtle rescue sanctuary, palm trees, fountains

RESTRICTIONS:

Alcohol: in-house, or BYO
Smoking: designated areas
Music: amplified OK outdoors

Wheelchair Access: mostly yes
Insurance: extra insurance CBA
Other: no rice or confetti

The Walnut Grove at Tierra Rejada Farms

Ranch

3370 Sunset Valley Road, Moorpark
805/558-8279
www.walnutgroveweddings.com
info@walnutgroveweddings.com

● Rehearsal Dinners	● Corporate Events
● Ceremonies	● Meetings
● Wedding Receptions	● Film Shoots
● Private Parties	Accommodations

It takes practically no time at all for Walnut Grove at Tierra Rejada Farms to rejuvenate the flagging spirit of anyone beleaguered by city stresses. The road into the 120-acre spread follows along a creek, past a majestic stand of eucalyptus and row upon row of walnut trees. In springtime, you're treated to a breathtaking view of the surrounding hills covered with the green felt of new grass, and apricot trees exploding in a cloud of white blossoms; in summer and autumn, oranges, avocados and harvest vegetables grow on nearby fields and hillsides. By the time you've reached the wedding site, the fragrant air and pervasive calm have already begun to smooth your rough edges.

The main celebration area is a clearing in the midst of a 50-year-old walnut grove, where a brick path in a feathery green meadow makes a fetching wedding aisle. Couples say their vows while above them tree branches intertwine forming a dense leafy canopy.

Not far from the grove, a brick patio sweeps around a huge polished dance floor at the foot of a cut-stone stage. Fashioned in three side-by-side half-moon sections, the stage inspires imaginative flourishes: Put your DJ in one section, lounge furniture in another and the wedding cake or the sweetheart table in the center for maximum effect. The steps leading up to center stage are inset with path lights, while along the back of the stage a low stone wall culminates in a flagstone fireplace. A wooden pergola overhead looks enchanting strung with fairy lights, floral garlands or strings of crystals to catch the sun or moonlight. Meanwhile, guests dine at tables set on the patio. At night, the starry sky is echoed by a galaxy of twinkling lights in the tree branches.

Originally founded in 1935, historic Tierra Rejada is still a working farm that gives visitors a glimpse into the simple life and traditions of bygone days. Yet the bucolic setting can also be dressed to impress. With the fine cuisine and event styling of *Command Performance Catering,* weddings at this beautiful locale can run the gamut from chic soirée to family-friendly barbecue. Exciting presentations, such as elaborate food station receptions or theme weddings, are a *Command Performance* specialty. And the superb chefs love to customize menus, so don't hesitate to ask!

Whether you choose to have a formal affair in the Walnut Grove or something much more relaxed, you're bound to be smitten by this wedding venue's country charm.

CEREMONY & EVENT/RECEPTION CAPACITY: The Walnut Grove and the Lawn each hold approximately 300 seated guests.

MEETING CAPACITY: Outdoor meetings can be held in the areas above; no indoor meeting facilities are available.

FEES & DEPOSITS: For weddings, a $1,500 nonrefundable security deposit is payable when reservations are confirmed; the facility balance is due 14 days prior to the event along with a $200 security/cleanup deposit that will be refunded after the event, less any expenses. The catering balance is due 3 days before the event.

For 2013, the rental fee for the Walnut Grove starts at $3,750 for up to 250 persons. Additional guests are billed at $10 each. There is an additional $5 per person charge to all events booked for Saturday. Catering packages range $59–85/person. Tax, alcohol and a 15% service charge are additional. There is a 125-person minimum for Saturday events and a 75-person minimum for Friday and Sunday events. For groups that are less than the minimums, call for special pricing.

For business functions, meetings and other special events, fees vary depending on guest count and day of the week; call for more details.

AVAILABILITY: April–mid-October, daily, 10am–10pm.

SERVICES/AMENITIES:

Catering: provided by
Command Performance Catering
Kitchen Facilities: no
Tables & Chairs: provided
Linens, Silver, etc.: provided
Restrooms: wheelchair accessible
Dance Floor: yes
Bride's Dressing Area: yes
Meeting Equipment: CBA

Parking: large lot
Accommodations: CBA
Telephone: emergency use only
Outdoor Night Lighting: yes
Outdoor Cooking Facilities: CBA
Cleanup: caterer and renter
View: fields, walnut orchards, 100-foot eucalyptus trees, creek, mountains

RESTRICTIONS:

Alcohol: BYO or CBA
Smoking: allowed
Music: amplified OK with volume limits

Wheelchair Access: yes
Insurance: certificate required

The Ranch House

Restaurant & Garden

500 South Lomita Avenue, Ojai
805/646-2360
www.theranchhouse.com
ojairanchh@aol.com

● Rehearsal Dinners	● Corporate Events
● Ceremonies	● Meetings
● Wedding Receptions	● Film Shoots
● Private Parties	Accommodations

A picturesque 20-minute drive into the hills east of Ventura leads to Ojai, a quaint art colony and resort village. With its mystical heritage as a Chumash sacred site and a mecca for spiritual seekers of the early 20th century, it's no wonder Ojai has a reputation as a magical place. Most everyone around here agrees that magic certainly happens at the Ranch House, the venue of choice for both local weddings and destination celebrations. Tucked against a hillside on a cul-de-sac at the edge of town, this gourmet restaurant combines the laid-back friendliness for which Ojai is famous with award-winning cuisine and an enchanting garden setting.

As you walk through the Ranch House gate, the lush, peaceful environs are instantly soothing. To the left of the entrance, there's a circular brick patio where event guests can sample hors d'oeuvres or dance. It's completely enclosed by greenery and sheltered by a large market umbrella. To the right, along the edge of the property, is an elevated redwood terrace shaded by oaks growing right up through it and bordered by eucalyptus trees and an ivy-covered hillside. There's enough room for a band, and it's also a lovely area for sipping a glass of wine. From the deck, a brick path winds through thick stands of bamboo past a koi pond filled with flashing orange, black and white fish. A petite footbridge, an Oriental Tea House and the occasional arbor or statue encourage you to stop and savor the bucolic surroundings, which are particularly romantic as evening falls and ambient lighting creates a scattered glow.

Most wedding ceremonies take place in the rose garden on a sunny expanse of lawn at the far end of the restaurant. Guests are seated on the grass or on the adjoining dining room terrace, where they have an "opera box" vantage of the proceedings just below. Everywhere you look there are boldly-hued flowers, banana palms and hanging ferns. Over 100 varieties of herbs, many of which find their way into the restaurant's dishes, scent the balmy breeze with their earthy aroma. In the spring, a trellis laden with wisteria creates a stunning lavender canopy over those lucky enough to be dining or dancing beneath it.

Indoors, multilevel dining spaces showcase the pretty panorama. A refreshing, island-elegant ambiance is enhanced by plantation palms, whimsical mobiles and a green-and-white decorative palette. What really makes the dining rooms special, however, is that they are entirely glassed in, giving the illusion of being part of the outdoors. For a more immediate al fresco experience, doors open onto the terrace, where heaters dispel any evening chill, and the soothing sound of rippling water comes from a tiny stream that runs through the grounds. It doesn't take long before the fragrant calm has you bewitched, and you realize that this restaurant would have an uplifting effect on you even if you never ate a single bite here.

But you'll want to make sure you DO eat here. The fresh bread from their own bakery, an extensive wine list and an innovative menu have made devotees out of many a patron, including actor Paul Newman who declared, "Cuisine is cuisine, but the Ranch House is original."

Owner David Skaggs is also devoted to the place, having begun his career here as a dishwasher at age 15. He and his banquet staff will work with you to make your celebration a memorable one in this small corner of paradise.

CEREMONY, EVENT/RECEPTION & MEETING CAPACITY: The site holds 120 seated or standing guests outdoors and 100 seated indoors.

FEES & DEPOSITS: A $500 deposit is required to reserve your date. The balance is due 6 weeks prior. Food and beverage minimums range $4,900–8,900 depending on the day and time. Meals range $38–63/person. Tax, alcohol and an 18% service charge are additional.

AVAILABILITY: Year-round, daily, 10am–10pm.

SERVICES/AMENITIES:

Catering: in-house
Kitchen Facilities: n/a
Tables & Chairs: provided
Linens, Silver, etc.: provided
Restrooms: wheelchair accessible
Dance Floor: portable provided
Bride's & Groom's Dressing Area: CBA
Meeting Equipment: some provided

Parking: large lot
Accommodations: no guest rooms
Telephone: house phone
Outdoor Night Lighting: provided
Outdoor Cooking Facilities: no
Cleanup: provided
View: fountain, garden, lagoon, landscaped grounds, mountains, waterfall

RESTRICTIONS:

Alcohol: in-house
Smoking: not allowed
Music: amplified OK with restrictions

Wheelchair Access: yes
Insurance: liability required

Newhall Mansion

829 Park Street, Piru

805/398-5042

www.newhallmansion.com
guestrelations@newhallmansion.com

Historic Mansion & Garden

- Rehearsal Dinners
- Ceremonies
- Wedding Receptions
- Private Parties
- Corporate Events
- Meetings
- Film Shoots
- Accommodations

Despite its decades-long popularity as a location for film and TV shoots, you've probably never heard of Piru before. Yet the quiet agricultural community on the Eastern fringe of scenic Heritage Valley is a mere 10 minutes from Valencia's Magic Mountain. The town is emerging from its relative obscurity, however, thanks to the spectacular renovation of its crown jewel, Newhall Mansion. This enchanting Queen Anne-style hilltop residence, set on nine landscaped acres, was originally built in 1890 by Piru's founder, publishing magnate David C. Cook, as a gift for his wife. The ensuing years saw a series of owners, a fire and two earthquakes, until at last the mansion was rescued in 2013. The current proprietors have completely transformed the Ventura County landmark, adding modern amenities, lush gardens and exquisite décor that accentuates its vintage glamour.

Passing through the mansion's imposing wrought-iron gates, you're greeted by a citrus grove flanking a long, rose-lined promenade. Next comes the Park, a lovely hedged lawn in front of the mansion with a splashing fountain and panoramic mountain view. The estate's fairy-tale façade, featuring wraparound verandas, intricate scrollwork and a stone tower, makes a grand backdrop for exchanging vows.

A stroll to the backyard reveals a tiled Courtyard that's a delightful locale for dining and dancing under the stars. Extras include a fire pit, a swimming pool with white cabanas, and an old-fashioned pagoda to showcase the wedding cake, sweetheart table or bar. Specialty lighting throughout the grounds adds to the evening's magic. The terraced gardens and rolling lawns that overlook the Courtyard hold more wedding options. An illuminated stairway makes a dramatic wedding aisle, and the couple exchanges vows in front of a twinkle-lit arch. Groves of olive, pomegranate, apricot and fig trees form a leafy background, a legacy of David Cook's "Second Garden of Eden." In the tranquil twilight, the romantic milieu does seem a lot like paradise.

The best way to indulge in all the mansion's luxuries is to spend the weekend, which also lets you expand your event into the breathtaking 12,000-square-foot interior. Each room is lavished with period details, antiques and artistic restorations. The Ballroom's magnificent stained-glass transom frames a glorious view, and is a favorite spot for bridal portraits. The Dining Room, with its stunning coffered ceiling, and the stately fire-lit Library offer classic Victorian elegance. Scheduled for a 2014 debut, the Bridal Hospitality Suite will provide 3,000 square feet of seclusion and queenly comforts.

The mansion's most imaginative entertainment option is the Tavern, an underground man-cave whose circular stone entryway recalls a Gothic castle. A series of brick-walled salons radiate an aura of mystery, and a giant flat-screen TV, custom redwood bar and cool stylings make the Tavern a novel setting for a cocktail reception, bachelor party or rehearsal dinner. A hidden bedroom will have you feeling like characters in a romance novel. Seven sumptuous bedrooms in the main house boast a collective assortment of deluxe treats: a fireplace, an extravagant stone shower with carved mermaids, a wooden Jacuzzi and a huge stained-glass oriel window.

Newhall Mansion welcomes you to celebrate in complete privacy amid nostalgic opulence, all while surrounded by nature. Not only has this historic charmer put Piru on the map—it's also a treasure of a wedding venue.

CEREMONY & EVENT/RECEPTION CAPACITY: The facility can accommodate 100 seated or standing guests indoors and 300 seated or standing outdoors.

MEETING CAPACITY: Meetings do not take place at this facility.

FEES & DEPOSITS: 25% of the total event cost is required to reserve your date. 25% is due 180 days prior to the event, another 25% 90 days prior, and the remaining 25% is due 10 days prior. Rates start at $7,000, and prices vary depending on customizable options such as interior access and overnight accommodations. Indoor usage is only available when overnight accommodations are booked. Please contact the site for your personalized quote.

AVAILABILITY: Year-round, daily, 10am–11pm.

SERVICES/AMENITIES:

Catering: BYO with approval
Kitchen Facilities: limited
Tables & Chairs: provided
Linens, Silver, etc.: through caterer or BYO
Restrooms: wheelchair accessible
Dance Area: provided
Bride's Dressing Area: yes
Meeting Equipment: n/a
Other: picnic area, AV equipment

Parking: large complimentary lot
Accommodations: 7 guest rooms
Telephone: house phone
Outdoor Night Lighting: provided
Outdoor Cooking Facilities: BBQ on site
Cleanup: caterer or renter
View: canyon, forest, fountain, garden, landscaped grounds, pool, vineyards

RESTRICTIONS:

Alcohol: BYO
Smoking: designated areas only
Music: amplified OK with restrictions

Wheelchair Access: yes
Insurance: liability required

This is important! Tell venues you're reading HERE COMES THE GUIDE and ask if our information is still current.

95

Limoneira Ranch

Historic Ranch & Garden

1141 Cummings Road, Santa Paula
805/525-5736
www.limoneira.com/shopping/venues.html
jasoncollis@yahoo.com

- Rehearsal Dinners
- Ceremonies
- Wedding Receptions
- Private Parties
- Corporate Events
- Meetings
- Film Shoots
- Accommodations

The historic township of Santa Paula in Heritage Valley presents a refreshing contrast to the urban bustle just an hour away. Visitors warm to its slower pace and small-town charms, which include vintage homes, antique airplanes and a train depot that dates to 1887. Acres upon acres of fruit groves in this "Citrus Capital of the World" are hugged by oak-studded hillsides and rugged mountain peaks. A center of silent film production in the 1920s, the picturesque region still attracts Hollywood filmmakers ... and lately, engaged couples who've discovered an authentic venue for staging their own wedding masterpiece.

Limoneira Ranch perfectly embodies the valley's rich legacy. Founded in 1893, the 7,300-acre spread remains the county's largest producer of oranges, avocados, and, of course, lemons. Limoneira may have one foot in the past, but the other is firmly set in a very green future—innovations like their solar orchard demonstrate their commitment to a sustainable natural lifestyle. *(Tip: Their new fruit-based skincare products make fab bridesmaid gifts!)*

Entering the property between rows of fir trees, you inhale the pleasing aroma of ripening fruit and sweet lemon blossoms. To your right stands the handsome Craftsman-style Ranch Lobby building; on your left, the original Sunkist lemon packinghouse—an architectural award-winner—conveys a timeless allure. Between their two striking facades, Limoneira's event team creates a festive setting with an open-sided tent, market lights, floral displays, tables and lounge seating, food stations, and whatever else it takes to realize your reception vision.

The Ranch Lobby interior is a graceful gathering place in its own right, with lustrous hardwood floors, 20-foot-high oak-beam ceilings and antique furnishings. A floor-to-ceiling river rock fireplace makes a stunning backdrop for winter ceremonies. Soaring picture windows overlook a flower-dappled lawn, and in the many sunny months, guests can take their drinks out onto the two adjacent garden breezeways.

Next to the packinghouse, the Visitor's Center is an endearingly offbeat and party-friendly option. Formerly the Limoneira Company Store, the high-ceilinged room features quirky farm relics and photos of Limoneira's bygone days. A covered deck and adjoining saloon make great social hour hubs, while just outside, retro-chic couples take pictures by a pair of old-fashioned gasoline pumps.

Limoneira's lush grounds offer several appealing ceremony spots, but for an all-in-one wedding locale, the North Lawn can't be beat. Set against the backdrop of fragrant lemon groves traced by mountain silhouettes, the Lawn's approach holds 12 bocce ball courts (a terrific ice-breaker activity for cocktail hours or rehearsal dinners). Crowning the scene, steps lead to a broad landing, a dramatic place to exchange vows. Just above, a grassy expanse provides plenty of room for a lavish reception, including dancing under an explosion of stars. Novel rehearsal dinners or candlelit get-togethers are magical on Hilltop Orchard. Guests are shuttled up a steep, winding road to a petite plateau, and rewarded with a spectacular valley panorama stretching to the sea.

With so much to arrange, couples can count on the ranch's experienced event coordinator, Jason Collis of *Plated Events*. They're lucky: Not only is Jason a chef extraordinaire, he's also passionate about helping them make the most of the ranch's many attributes.

Steeped in nostalgia, this green wedding venue brings together Nature's splendor and heartwarming family celebrations. After over 100 years, Limoneira is still keeping it real.

CEREMONY, EVENT/RECEPTION & MEETING CAPACITY: The site holds 200 seated or 500 standing guests indoors and 1,000 seated or 3,000 standing outdoors.

FEES & DEPOSITS: A $300 deposit is required to reserve your date and the balance is due 30 days prior to the event. Rental fees range $500–2,000 depending on the day of the event and the space rented. Meals range $20–125/person. Tax, alcohol and a 20% service charge are additional.

AVAILABILITY: Year-round, daily, until midnight.

SERVICES/AMENITIES:

Catering: in-house

Kitchen Facilities: n/a

Tables & Chairs: through caterer

Linens, Silver, etc.: through caterer

Restrooms: wheelchair accessible

Dance Floor: provided

Bride's Dressing Area: yes

Meeting Equipment: provided

Other: picnic area, AV equipment, trolley service, hot-air balloons, event coordination

Parking: large lot, valet required

Accommodations: no guest rooms

Telephone: house phone

Outdoor Night Lighting: CBA

Outdoor Cooking Facilities: BBQ CBA

Cleanup: provided

View: fountain, garden, creek, landscaped grounds, waterfall; panorama of mountains, ocean, and valley

RESTRICTIONS:

Alcohol: in-house

Smoking: designated areas only

Music: amplified OK

Wheelchair Access: yes

Insurance: liability required

Vintage Weddings
at the Ventura County Agriculture Museum

Museum

926 Railroad Avenue, Santa Paula

805/525-5736

www.venturamuseum.org/rent-the-agriculture-museum
jason@platedevents.com

- Rehearsal Dinners
- Ceremonies
- Wedding Receptions
- Private Parties
- Corporate Events
- Meetings
- Film Shoots
- Accommodations

Surrounded by tree-cloaked hills, mountain peaks and sunswept orchards, Santa Paula's historic downtown boasts an award-winning theater company, fine art murals, old-fashioned airplanes, and a real haunted house. Another of the quaint community's treasures is the Ventura County Agriculture Museum, which—lucky you! —also offers a unique Vintage Weddings Package.

The museum is housed in a barn-red country charmer, the Mill Building, which dates back to 1888. Right next door is Railroad Plaza Park and a 19th-century train depot, adding more nostalgic flair to the setting. Alongside the vast (and free!) parking area, a footbridge spans a dry creek bed bordered by river rocks, lavender and native grasses. A pair of trees marks the entrance to a bricked courtyard, where guests take their seats for the wedding ceremony. Couples wishing to amp up the retro theme can opt for a dramatic arrival by either horse and carriage or the antique Fillmore & Western railcar, complete with train whistle. Vows are exchanged on the steps of the museum's broad front porch, framed by a peaked white portico. It's a scene straight out of olden times, with all the heartwarming appeal of a classic love story.

Afterwards, the wedding party explores various photogenic backdrops—a nearby rose garden, the railroad yard's original gazebo, and the train tracks themselves. Meanwhile, friends and family stroll through a treelined breezeway into Calavo Hall for an interactive social hour. Calavo is spacious and airy, thanks to whitewashed walls and a lofty open-beam ceiling inset with skylights; the original hardwood floor enhances the building's aura of authenticity. The hall is filled with intriguing exhibits that serve as instant ice-breakers among your guests: One corner holds a buggy pulled by a lifelike replica of a horse—clamber on up and take the reins. In another corner, young'uns try on the costumes of yesteryear. Tucked into an alcove, an active bee colony makes honeycomb to the delight of partygoers. All this, and hors d'oeuvres and cocktails, too!

One-of-a-kind receptions are held among the rustic memorabilia on display in Limoneira Hall. Elegantly dressed dining tables are spread out in the center of the room so that each guest has an up-close view of the Americana lining the perimeter: A wine press, a bright red bean planter and a fully outfitted smithy spark visions of bygone days. Amid rusted backhoes and pitchforks, a weathered steamer trunk packed with paper luggage tags invites your loved ones to write their well-wishes for the newlyweds, then hang them on a Western stile. But the museum's pride and joy is their collection of antique tractors, whose distressed Crayola-colored finishes enliven the festivities. In both halls, quilted panels, artistic landscapes and black-and-white prints bring the county's farming and ranching traditions to life. Should you wish to put on your own historical retrospective, the museum has full AV capabilities.

The Ag Museum (as locals call it) is flexible, fascinating and enormously fun. Its Vintage Weddings option is available exclusively through *Plated Events by Chef Jason,* a catering company that serves up customized menus with panache, and will help you bring together all the elements to turn your special celebration into a true original.

CEREMONY CAPACITY: The museum holds 200 seated guests indoors and 300 seated outdoors.

EVENT/RECEPTION CAPACITY: The site can accommodate 250 seated or 500 standing indoors and 1,000 seated or standing outdoors.

MEETING CAPACITY: Meeting spaces seat 150 guests.

FEES & DEPOSITS: A $500 deposit is required to reserve your date and the balance is due 7 days prior to the event. Event space rental fees range $350–2,000 depending on the day of the week. Meals range $30–129/person. Tax, alcohol and a 20% service charge are additional. Catering includes basic rentals. Upgrades are available upon request.

AVAILABILITY: Year-round, daily, 9am–11pm.

SERVICES/AMENITIES:

Catering: in-house, outside ethnic caterers permitted with approval
Kitchen Facilities: n/a
Tables & Chairs: some provided, more CBA
Linens, Silver, etc.: CBA
Restrooms: wheelchair accessible
Dance Floor: CBA
Bride's Dressing Area: yes
Meeting Equipment: provided

Parking: large lot
Accommodations: no guest rooms
Telephone: office phone
Outdoor Night Lighting: CBA
Outdoor Cooking Facilities: none
Cleanup: provided
View: cityscape, garden patio, park, landscaped grounds; panorama of hills and mountains
Other: event coordination, AV equipment

RESTRICTIONS:

Alcohol: full in-house bar
Smoking: designated areas only
Music: amplified OK

Wheelchair Access: yes
Insurance: liability required

Wood Ranch Golf Club

Golf Club

301 Wood Ranch Parkway, Simi Valley
888/998-6396

www.countryclubreceptions.com
www.woodranchgc.com
lbemiller@americangolf.com

● Rehearsal Dinners   ● Corporate Events
● Ceremonies   ● Meetings
● Wedding Receptions   ● Film Shoots
● Private Parties   Accommodations

Framed by the rugged Santa Susanna Mountains, the upscale Simi Valley community of Wood Ranch, located a stone's throw from the Reagan Library, is prized for its quiet lifestyle, wide boulevards and manicured lawns. At its center lie the verdant greens of the exclusive Wood Ranch Golf Club and its striking contemporary clubhouse, reminiscent of Frank Lloyd Wright.

Masterfully marrying nature and architecture, the building's exterior incorporates elements of Wright's enduring designs, such as cast cement bricks, wood beams and strong, clean lines softened by feathery ferns and colorful blooms. Step under the porte-cochère and you'll feel like you're visiting a sleek, private lodge. That feeling is enhanced when a greeter welcomes your guests and directs them down the walkway to the left, which takes them to a scenic knoll for your ceremony. Shaded from the afternoon sun by a tall stand of trees and brightened by an ever-changing landscape of flowering plants, the site's large lawn and gazebo overlook a glistening lake below.

Once vows have been exchanged, it's time to move inside to the beautifully appointed clubhouse. The foyer's cool slate floor and the enormous barrel-shaped skylight overhead set the tone for the Arts and Crafts touches throughout each room. The Main Lobby, where cocktails are served, makes generous use of luxury materials for an understated elegance: The slate and marble fireplace, for example, is adorned with a large metallic artwork and contributes a modern focal point to the room. Mahogany accents not only add richness to the space, but also mirror the warm wood of the grand piano. A massive chandelier hangs from the high ceiling and reflects the best of Craftsman style in burnished copper, which is picked up again in the room's distinctive copper-and-glass-enclosed wine cellar to your right. The entire room is flooded with light filtering in from the Grand Ballroom, just beyond the tall silk drapes that separate the two spaces (but allow your guests a peek at what's in store for them during the reception).

The Ballroom's most arresting feature is its wall of floor-to-ceiling windows. Over 20 feet tall, they provide a panorama of the golf course below, fringed by the mountains beyond it. For smaller groups, there's the Lakeview Room to the left, which has an outdoor terrace overlooking the gazebo, lawns and lakes of the signature 18th hole.

Wood Ranch Golf Club's seamless combination of timeless design, modern sensibilities, and first-class service creates a beautiful setting for a most memorable wedding celebration.

CEREMONY CAPACITY: The Gazebo Lawn holds up to 350 seated guests; the Ballroom up to 300 seated.

EVENT/RECEPTION & MEETING CAPACITY: The Club holds up to 300 seated or 400 standing guests indoors or outdoors.

FEES & DEPOSITS: A nonrefundable deposit, which is applied to your food and beverage total, is required to reserve your date. The amount of the deposit varies, depending on how far in advance you book. Payment terms for the balance also vary, and may be arranged on an individual basis. Food and beverage minimums will apply. Wedding packages start at $55/person. Tax, alcohol and service charge are additional. Menus and packages can be customized to fit your needs and budget. Call for details.

AVAILABILITY: Year-round, daily, anytime. Closed on Christmas Day.

SERVICES/AMENITIES:

Catering: in-house
Kitchen Facilities: n/a
Tables & Chairs: provided
Linens, Silver, etc.: provided
Restrooms: wheelchair accessible
Dance Floor: provided
Bride's Dressing Area: provided
Meeting Equipment: some provided
Other: grand piano, secluded gazebo, reception lawn

Parking: large lot, valet optional
Accommodations: no guest rooms
Telephone: house phone
Outdoor Night Lighting: access only
Outdoor Cooking Facilities: BBQ
Cleanup: provided
View: fairways, hills, lakes, landscaped grounds

RESTRICTIONS:

Alcohol: in-house
Smoking: outside only
Music: amplified OK

Wheelchair Access: yes
Insurance: not required

Hartley Botanica

4465 Balcom Canyon Road, Somis
805/532-1997
www.hartleybotanica.com
barbara@hartleybotanica.com

Botanical Gardens

- Rehearsal Dinners
- Ceremonies
- Wedding Receptions
- Private Parties
- Corporate Events
- Meetings
- Film Shoots
- Accommodations

Just beyond the hills of Camarillo in the peaceful Las Posas Valley you'll find the small hamlet of Somis, home to generations of family farmers. Somis has so far managed to escape the pressure of development, and boasts one post office, one store, and the oldest wooden gas station in California. It's the kind of place that makes you want to slow down for a while, stop and smile at a stranger, and breathe in the fresh country air that seems to make all that grows here flourish.

At Hartley Botanica, not only do the plants and flowers thrive, they also end up in beautiful shapes and clever arrangements. That's because this Somis nursery doubles as a landscaping company, and throughout the property you'll discover artistic examples of garden design. Nowhere is this more impressive than in the wedding area, a spectacular garden oasis that owes its creation to a proud father's love.

It all started when owner Barbara Goodrich took over the place in 1995. Her interest in landscaping came from her parents, creative types whose 30 years of experience include such notable clients as Janet Jackson and Michael Landon. When Barbara got engaged, Mom offered to make her a fabulous wedding gown. Not to be outdone, Dad took advantage of the nursery's natural beauty to create a dream ceremony and reception site for his daughter's wedding. Now Barbara wants to share her fantasy garden with you for your own wedding or special event.

Party guests are free to explore the nursery's novelties, like its rock waterfall with grotto, peacocks, and sculptured rose garden. Yet the celebration grounds themselves are shielded from the public by custom-designed metal gates. The bride has her own changing room to prepare for the walk down the aisle—and you've never seen an aisle quite like this one!

A dramatic, sweeping promenade winds around an expanse of verdant lawn. Along the way you pass under no fewer than 18 vine-covered archways set in bases of flowering stone urns. The rose-colored walkway is embellished with real leaves pressed into the concrete, and caged songbirds add to the magical effect. To the left, a pond featuring an aquatic garden and a cascading waterfall accompany you until you reach the final stretch of the aisle. Then a delicate canopy of tree branches laden with honeysuckle leads to your groom, standing at the center of an enormous daisy permanently etched right into the aisle. (A smaller daisy just beyond can hold an accompanist.) Your guests enjoy the spectacle from the lawn, with the rolling hills as a picturesque backdrop.

A row of shrubs marks the rear of the Ceremony Garden, and on the other side lies the reception area, an even larger swath of lawn dotted with trees, decorative statuary, and pots overflowing with colorful flowers. A stand of Chinese pistachio trees shelters a long bar fashioned of smooth stones; its countertop, embedded with leaves, is the ideal spot to serve drinks and a buffet. Each botanical treatment features built-in seating areas, and some offer intriguing surprises: In the center of the lawn, for example, a lush forest environment of eucalyptus trees serves as a natural aviary for cockatiels and doves.

After a short time at the Gardens, your cares seem to float away on a gentle rose-scented breeze. Everything here is fresh, green and blossoming—an enchanting environment for a celebration of new beginnings.

CEREMONY CAPACITY: The Wedding Area holds 375 guests.

EVENT/RECEPTION CAPACITY: The Reception Area holds 375 guests.

MEETING CAPACITY: Several spaces accommodate up to 375 guests.

FEES & DEPOSITS: A $3,000 nonrefundable deposit is required to secure your date; the event balance is payable 60 days prior to the event along with a refundable security/cleanup deposit. Wedding packages start at $65/person and include use of the property, valet parking, catering, 4½ hours of beverage service, catering staff and bartender, linens, tableware and event coordination. Tax and a 15% service charge are additional.

AVAILABILITY: Year-round, Saturday or Sunday, 8am–2:30pm or 3:30pm–midnight.

SERVICES/AMENITIES:

Catering: in-house
Kitchen Facilities: n/a
Tables & Chairs: provided
Linens, Silver, etc.: provided
Restrooms: wheelchair accessible
Dance Floor: provided
Bride's Dressing Area: yes
Meeting Equipment: BYO

Parking: valet parking
Accommodations: no guest rooms
Telephone: house phone
Outdoor Night Lighting: yes
Outdoor Cooking Facilities: no
Cleanup: caterer or renter
View: gardens, waterfalls, foothills, pond
Other: DJ, florist, cake

RESTRICTIONS:

Alcohol: BYO, no corkage fees
Smoking: designated areas
Music: amplified OK outdoors

Wheelchair Access: yes
Insurance: liability required
Other: no rice, birdseed or confetti

Overwhelmed? Use the search criteria on www.HereComesTheGuide.com to narrow down your choices.

103

Palm Garden Hotel

Hotel

495 North Ventu Park Road, Thousand Oaks
805/716-4200
www.palmgardenhotel.com
brandi@palmgardenhotel.com

- Rehearsal Dinners
- Ceremonies
- Wedding Receptions
- Private Parties
- Corporate Events
- Meetings
- Film Shoots
- Accommodations

First-time visitors to Palm Garden Hotel are always pleasantly surprised to discover this suburban oasis tucked amidst a busy commercial district a mere minute from the 101. The hustle and bustle instantly melts away once you step inside the marble-clad lobby, where you're greeted by an electronic grand piano playing familiar tunes. This is your first taste of Palm Garden's arts and music motif: Veteran Big Band leader Harry Selvin purchased the boutique hotel in 2012, and began a loving transformation that has all the hallmarks of pride of ownership. From grounds to guest rooms, the jazzy décor reflects an Old Hollywood vibe that's both jaunty and elegant.

The hotel is built around a sun-washed garden courtyard that encircles a sparkling swimming pool and spa, with plush loungers and cabanas beckoning from the pool deck. Landscaped pathways pass a whimsical bronze statue of a trio of child musicians that's sure to bring a smile. Continue on to two hospitality suites that serve as basecamp for your wedding weekend. The guys gather in the Hollywood Suite, where a legendary pool table once belonging to late comedian George Burns holds court in the front room. Framed black & white photos of Burns' celebrity billiard buddies line one wall, a testament to their having played on—and autographed—this very table. Two flatscreen TVs, a bar, kitchen and bedroom enhance the suite's fun factor, as does the putting green just outside.

Meanwhile, the bride and her attendants prepare in the lovely Garden Suite, which includes a comfortably furnished living room, kitchen, and garden-view bedroom (where the newlyweds spend their wedding night). Brides especially appreciate the roomy walk-in closet and makeup area, as well as the window that lets them watch the guests taking their seats for the ceremony on the Garden Lawn. This lush setting, sheltered by greenery, palm trees and trellises entwined with bougainvillea and fragrant jasmine, is pure romance. A built-in wedding aisle ends at a spacious white wood gazebo. Trimmed with fairy lights and white roses, it's a picturesque backdrop for exchanging vows.

Afterwards, guests stroll over to the Garden Room and Patio for cocktails. The bar is usually set inside the cheerful, airy space, which is also a popular choice for bridal showers and rehearsal dinners. Keep the French doors open and the party flows out onto the patio, where cushioned seating clustered around copper-lined fire pits invites conversation.

Receptions are held in the Palm Ballroom, outfitted with whitewashed shutters, potted palms and abstract chrome fixtures, all of which create a breezy sophistication. Catering is provided by the hotel's on-site restaurant, Brendan's Irish Pub, known for its fine food. Their chefs can whip up delicious dishes in a range of culinary styles—just ask! Brendan's semi-private dining room, featuring rich dark woods and folksy Irish décor, is another rehearsal dinner option.

Palm Garden Hotel makes it easy to gather loved ones (and their pets!) under one roof for an extended celebration, from welcome cocktails to day-after brunch. And with all the freebies—WiFi, banquet equipment, AV, full hot breakfast, parking and more—it's a great value, too. Add its convenient location and effortless charm, and the new Palm Garden seems destined to become a classic.

CEREMONY, EVENT/RECEPTION AND MEETING CAPACITY: The facility holds 200 seated guests indoors or outdoors.

FEES & DEPOSITS: A $250 deposit is required to reserve your date and the balance is due on the day of the event. Event space rental fees start at $250 and vary depending on the space rented. Meals range $11–75/person. Tax, alcohol and a 19% service charge are additional.

AVAILABILITY: Year-round, daily, anytime.

SERVICES/AMENITIES:

Catering: in-house
Kitchen Facilities: n/a
Tables & Chairs: provided
Linens, Silver, etc.: provided
Restrooms: wheelchair accessible
Dance Floor: portable provided
Bride's Dressing Area: yes
Meeting Equipment: provided

Parking: large lot
Accommodations: 150 guest rooms
Telephone: guest phone
Outdoor Night Lighting: provided
Outdoor Cooking Facilities: none
Cleanup: provided
View: garden, landscaped grounds, mountains, pool area

RESTRICTIONS:

Alcohol: full in-house bar
Smoking: outdoors only
Music: amplified OK

Wheelchair Access: yes
Insurance: not required

Sunset Hills Country Club

Country Club

4155 Erbes Road North, Thousand Oaks
888/998-6386
www.countryclubreceptions.com
lbemiller@americangolf.com

● Rehearsal Dinners	● Corporate Events
● Ceremonies	● Meetings
● Wedding Receptions	● Film Shoots
● Private Parties	Accommodations

Nestled in the rolling hills of Thousand Oaks, Sunset Hills Country Club is just outside Los Angeles but feels like it's worlds away. The club is spread over 85 lush acres, whose gently rolling hills are dotted with majestic oaks, mature elms, and a wealth of other trees. In addition to a clubhouse and golf shop, the property features an 18-hole golf course and an Olympic-sized swimming pool.

Situated on three separate levels with interconnecting stairways, the two clubhouse buildings and Pro Shop are arranged in a horseshoe around the sparkling pool. With their arched façades and red-tile roofs, these one-story stuccos reflect a contemporary melding of California and Spanish architecture.

Sunset Hills welcomes events of all kinds—weddings, birthday parties, and golf tournaments to name a few. If marriage is on your mind, two sites are available for ceremonies. For a big wedding, the best place to tie the knot is in a flat green valley surrounded by stately oaks that affords ample room for theater-style seating. More intimate ceremonies take place at the crest of a little hill beneath overarching alder branches.

After saying "I do" outdoors, bring your festivities inside the Sunset Hills Ballroom, located on the clubhouse's upper level. This spacious, L-shaped venue comes with a parquet dance floor and features an arching, adobe-style brick fireplace. Wrought-iron chandeliers and sconces illuminate earth-tone walls adorned with Tuscan-style artwork, imparting a tasteful elegance. If your event calls for more space, a movable wall rolls easily aside, allowing the ballroom and the lounge to combine into a single large room overlooking the patio and pool.

Sunset Hills offers a variety of wedding packages, all of which can be customized. Their executive chef is happy to personalize your menu, and the on-site coordinator and catering manager will work with you and/or your wedding planner to choreograph your affair from start to finish.

The team at Sunset Hills Country Club is experienced at hosting all types of celebrations. Their expertise and marvelous *esprit de corps* will ensure that yours will be a resounding success.

CEREMONY CAPACITY: The lawn area holds 200 seated guests.

EVENT/RECEPTION CAPACITY: The Ballroom accommodates 200 seated with dance floor.

MEETING CAPACITY: The Ballroom holds 200 guests seated theater-style.

FEES & DEPOSITS: A nonrefundable deposit, which is applied to your food and beverage total, is required to reserve your date. The amount of the deposit varies, depending on how far in advance you book. Payment terms for the balance also vary, and may be arranged on an individual basis. Luncheons start at $15/person, dinners at $25/person. Tax, alcohol and service charge are additional. Menus and packages can be customized to fit your needs and budget. Call for details.

For business meetings, rates vary depending on the services required; call for details.

AVAILABILITY: Year-round, daily, 6pm–midnight. Earlier events can be arranged.

SERVICES/AMENITIES:

Catering: in-house
Kitchen Facilities: n/a
Tables & Chairs: provided
Linens, Silver, etc.: provided
Restrooms: wheelchair accessible
Dance Floor: yes
Bride's Dressing Area: yes
Meeting Equipment: CBA, extra fee

Parking: ample, large lots
Accommodations: no guest rooms
Telephone: available
Outdoor Night Lighting: yes
Outdoor Cooking Facilities: none
Cleanup: provided
View: pool

RESTRICTIONS:

Alcohol: in-house or BYO with corkage fee
Smoking: outside only
Music: amplified OK indoors, outdoors with restrictions

Wheelchair Access: yes
Insurance: not required

Crowne Plaza Ventura Beach Hotel

Hotel

450 East Harbor Boulevard, Ventura
805/652-5108
www.cpventura.com
Jwagner@cpventura.com

- Rehearsal Dinners
- Ceremonies
- Wedding Receptions
- Private Parties
- Corporate Events
- Meetings
- Film Shoots
- Accommodations

Living is easy in Ventura, California, a laid-back coastal town midway between the hectic Los Angeles scene and pricey Santa Barbara resorts. Ventura's beaches are picturesque even when the morning fog swirls above the breakers; on its many sunny days, beachcombers can spy the Channel Islands—a necklace of atolls—etched on the horizon.

As the only beachfront hotel in Ventura, this Crowne Plaza provides everything you need for a beach wedding ceremony right on the powdery sand. Their event team will arrange white folding chairs beside the aisle, and set a ceremonial arch in front of the surf so that you can exchange vows just steps from the shore—a microphone and speaker are included, too. Afterwards, your photographer captures shots of the two of you walking off into a glorious sunset, while friends and family begin the party on the Lanai Patio, a private terrace that faces the sea. As twilight descends, everyone moves indoors for your reception.

The versatile San Miguel Ballroom is conveniently located right on the first floor, and can accommodate a party of 200 or be sectioned off for more intimate gatherings. Alternatively, take the elevator 12 stories up to the most spectacular ballroom in the county. The circular Top of the Harbor Ballroom looks out on a captivating panorama through floor-to-ceiling glass: the Ventura hills in one direction and the sinuous shoreline in the other. At twilight, wisps of mist play along the crashing waves; as night descends, the city lights and the illuminated Ventura pier vie with a star-filled indigo sky in a contest of sparkle. The ballroom's contemporary styling, like the rest of the hotel, is both relaxed and confident and suits the soothing surroundings.

The venue's catering packages include many amenities that enhance your celebration at a very good value, such as custom floral centerpieces, table linens, chair covers, wine with dinner, custom wedding cake and an oceanview bridal suite. If you want to pamper your guests even more, consider adding hand-rolled cigars, an espresso cart or a decadent chocolate fountain—or save these treats for your rehearsal dinner or post-wedding brunch.

The executive chef of their on-site restaurant, C-Street, also handles the event catering and that's a plus for bridal couples. His California-inspired cuisine showcases fresh, local ingredients complemented by an outstanding wine list. We were delighted with the meal we sampled, and bet your guests will be, too. (And yes, the chef is happy to customize your menu!)

At evening's end, overnight guests retire to their oceanview accommodations, which feature the Crowne's "Seven Layers of Comfort" bed. As the newlyweds, you get to sleep in and then enjoy room service delivery of your complimentary breakfast. Eventually, though, you'll want to venture forth and explore the area's attractions. The hotel is walking distance to downtown, and you can also take an easy stroll along the promenade and watch the surfers ply the waves. Other diversions include kayaking around the Channel Islands (adventurous) or renting an on-site bicycle (fun), visiting the hotel's art gallery (cultured), or simply lounging by the oceanfront swimming pool (sublime!).

Every step of the way, the Crowne Plaza Ventura Beach will contribute to a scenic and stress-free wedding weekend.

CEREMONY CAPACITY: The hotel holds 400 seated guests, indoors or out.

EVENT/RECEPTION CAPACITY: The hotel accommodates 300 seated or 400 standing guests indoors and 100 seated or 200 standing outdoors.

MEETING CAPACITY: Meeting spaces seat 400 guests indoors.

FEES & DEPOSITS: 15% of the food and beverage minimum is required to reserve your date and the balance is due 10 days prior to the event. Rental fees range $2,500–20,000 depending on the day and time of the event and the space rented. Meals range $45–120/person. Tax, alcohol and a 22% service charge are additional.

AVAILABILITY: Year-round, daily, hours vary depending on event.

SERVICES/AMENITIES:

Catering: in-house
Kitchen Facilities: fully equipped
Tables & Chairs: provided
Linens, Silver, etc.: provided
Restrooms: wheelchair accessible
Dance Floor: provided
Bride's Dressing Area: yes
Meeting Equipment: provided
Other: AV equipment, beach ceremonies

Parking: large lot, covered garage
Accommodations: 258 guest rooms
Telephone: house or guest phone
Outdoor Night Lighting: yes
Outdoor Cooking Facilities: BBQ
Cleanup: provided
View: pool area, cityscape and panorama of the ocean, coastline and mountains

RESTRICTIONS:

Alcohol: in-house
Smoking: outdoors only
Music: amplified OK

Wheelchair Access: yes
Insurance: required for vendors only

Serra Cross Park

Oceanview Park

Brakey Road, Ventura
805/223-5505
www.serracrosspark.org
amber@amberweir.com

Rehearsal Dinners	Corporate Events
● Ceremonies	Meetings
● Wedding Receptions	● Film Shoots
● Private Parties	Accommodations

What California bride doesn't fantasize about getting married in a beautiful, natural setting with a sweeping ocean view? Yet for some couples, it seems that the right to gaze out to sea during their most important celebration is reserved for those with a lavish budget. Don't despair! You'll feel like you've landed on Easy Street when you learn about our latest discovery: Serra Cross Park, a hilltop aerie with a breathtaking coastal panorama, a modest pricetag, and a rich history.

It all started back in 1782. Shortly after Father Junipero Serra founded the San Buenaventura Mission, a large wooden cross was placed on a neighboring hillside as a guidepost for travelers. Over the years, the original cross and a series of replacements were lost to the elements, but locals never gave up. The current cross has stood atop its circular stone pedestal since 1941, and today the Serra Cross Conservancy and community volunteers are committed to maintaining and improving the park for everyone's enjoyment. Serra Cross Park also has a romantic legacy—throughout the years, countless couples have been married here, making this a particularly cherished piece of local heritage.

From a side street behind Ventura's handsome City Hall, the short but sinuous drive to the park begins. Once you and your guests reach the top, expect wide eyes and open mouths as the awe-inspiring view unfolds. In one direction, a curve of beach embraces the crashing surf; in another, the Channel Islands are etched against a billowing stretch of blue; behind you are the multilayered contours of chaparral-cloaked hills. Taking it all in from your exalted perch, you're filled with a sense of humility and wonder—even reverence. For many, these powerful feelings are symbolized by the simple wooden cross, poised atop its stone platform.

It's on this small stage that you'll exchange your vows, with a filigree of olive trees and the watery vista in the background. Champagne toasts follow, and if you want to continue the party, you'll be treated to a magnificent sunset. As evening falls, the moon, the stars and the city lights set the horizon aglow. Reserve the park in the month of August, and you'll get the best seat in the house for a stunning fireworks display, courtesy of the Ventura County Fair! It's hard to imagine a more exhilarating finale than this exuberant, multicolored spectacle.

With its dramatic vantage, friendly pricing and enduring tradition, Serra Cross Park just might be the answer to your wedding prayers.

CEREMONY & EVENT/RECEPTION CAPACITY: The site holds 300 seated or 450 standing outdoors.

MEETING CAPACITY: Meetings do not take place at this location.

FEES & DEPOSITS: The rental fee is required to reserve your date. Site rental fees range $450–1,500 and vary depending on hours rented and type of event.

AVAILABILITY: Year-round, daily, 10am–10pm in set blocks of time.

SERVICES/AMENITIES:

Catering: BYO, recommendations available
Kitchen Facilities: n/a
Tables & Chairs: through caterer
Linens, Silver, etc.: through caterer
Restrooms: not wheelchair accessible
Dance Floor: CBA
Bride's & Groom's Dressing Area: no
Meeting Equipment: n/a
Other: site coordination

Parking: large lot
Accommodations: no guest rooms
Telephone: emergency use only
Outdoor Night Lighting: access only, additional through caterer
Outdoor Cooking Facilities: BBQ CBA
Cleanup: through caterer
View: garden, landscaped grounds; panorama of coastline, hills, canyon and mountains

RESTRICTIONS:

Alcohol: through caterers
Smoking: not allowed
Music: amplified OK outdoors with restrictions

Wheelchair Access: limited
Insurance: $1 million liability policy required for catered events
Other: security required for large events

Wedgewood Buenaventura

5880 Olivas Park Drive, Ventura
866/966-3009
www.wedgewoodbanquet.com/buenaventura
sales@wedgewoodbanquet.com

Special Events Facility

● Rehearsal Dinners	● Corporate Events
● Ceremonies	● Meetings
● Wedding Receptions	● Film Shoots
● Private Parties	Accommodations

Between Ventura's sandy beaches and wooded hillsides lie acres of farmland, where everything from strawberries to snapdragons flourishes in the pleasant climate. Such an appealing locale has naturally attracted many golf courses to the area, and the first public course in the county is the San Buenaventura, whose manicured greens, billowing treetops and small-town friendliness have been courting customers for decades. Sound like a picture-perfect setting for a special event? It is, and Wedgewood Buenaventura, which shares the scenic grounds with the golf course, not only ensures your celebration will unfold effortlessly, they'll do it all for a reasonable price.

The banquet center is perched on a gentle rise overlooking the sweeping fairways and the Ceremony Rose Garden just below. In the garden, palm trees encircle a splash of lawn, and star jasmine and rose blossoms adorn the air with their sweet perfume. The bride begins her entrance by descending the stairway from the center's banquet room. Then she glides along the wedding aisle to her groom, who waits in front of an arched wooden pergola. You can add embellishments like tulle and flowers, but with the rolling greens and the pretty landscaping little else is needed.

The same is true of the banquet room itself, designed with sophisticated touches that contribute to a sense of classic comfort and ease. Just inside the room, a blazing fireplace provides warmth. Guests have a birds-eye view of the golf greens, thanks to windows that run the length of the banquet room. There's nothing like a serene vista to help folks unwind, except maybe a champagne toast in the Lounge next to the foyer. Here an old-fashioned built-in bar makes your cocktail hour a breeze. Then, when it's time to dine, guests adjourn to tables set in the center of the banquet room. Opposite the windows, a raised level boasts a row of dark-green leather booths where the wedding party is properly displayed.

A built-in dance floor separates diners from a stage area, a prime spot for a formal head table or to showcase the band. However, most of Wedgewood's patrons prefer the services of their dynamic DJs, who hold court from a state-of-the-art sound booth, discreetly styled to blend in with the rest of the room. These outgoing songsters expertly MC your reception, and entertain with a customized song list. And here's the kicker—this service is included as part of your wedding package, along with a choice of wedding invitations, floral centerpieces and engraved champagne flutes.

With a variety of packages to fit most budgets and tastes, Wedgewood seems to have thought of everything (so you won't have to!). The popular Gold Package, for example, offers extra goodies like personalized cocktail napkins, a deluxe wedding cake selected from a premier local bakery and a wedding night hotel room for the bridal couple. Upgrade to the Millennium Package, and treat your guests to custom uplighting, petit fours and a real-time photo booth!

Wedgewood Buenaventura has one more specialty offering: They'll arrange your wedding ceremony right on the beach. Their chosen spot is just 10 minutes away on a stretch of coastline adjacent to Ventura Harbor. The staff will arrange chairs for your guests right on the sand, facing a wooden arch with the rolling waves as the backdrop. Follow up with a cocktail hour among tiki torches and admire the sunset before heading back to the banquet center; or if you have your heart set on a beach wedding reception, they'll arrange that for you, too. Wedgewood Buenaventura is clearly user friendly, and the staff truly accommodating—all you have to do is sit back and enjoy the day.

CEREMONY CAPACITY: The Ceremony Rose Garden holds 350 seated guests. Indoors, the site can also seat 350. A Wedgewood Buenaventura beach wedding ceremony can accommodate 350 guests.

EVENT/RECEPTION & MEETING CAPACITY: The Banquet Room accommodates 350 seated or standing guests.

FEES & DEPOSITS: 25% of the estimated total event cost is required to reserve your date. An additonal 25% is due 120 days prior to the event and the balance (based on your final guest count) is due 10 days prior. All payments are credited towards your final balance and are nonrefundable and nontransferable. All-inclusive, completely customizable wedding packages start at $33/person. Tax, alcohol and a 21–22% service charge are additional.

AVAILABILITY: Year-round, daily, 6am–1am.

SERVICES/AMENITIES:

Catering: in-house
Kitchen Facilities: n/a
Tables & Chairs: provided
Linens, Silver, etc.: provided
Restrooms: wheelchair accessible
Dance Floor: provided
Bride's Dressing Area: yes
Meeting Equipment: screen, overhead projector, TV/VCR, more CBA

Parking: ample parking
Accommodations: no guest rooms
Telephone: emergency only
Outdoor Night Lighting: access only
Outdoor Cooking Facilities: no
Cleanup: provided
View: fairways, landscaped grounds

RESTRICTIONS:

Alcohol: in-house
Smoking: outdoors only
Music: amplified OK

Wheelchair Access: yes
Insurance: not required
Other: no birdseed, confetti or rice

Want to know WHAT TO ASK a potential location or vendor? Check out our Questions to Ask starting on page 19.

Hyatt Westlake Plaza in Thousand Oaks

Hotel

880 South Westlake Boulevard, Westlake Village

805/557-4650

www.hyattwestlake.com
briana.wellman@hyatt.com

- Rehearsal Dinners
- Ceremonies
- Wedding Receptions
- Private Parties
- Corporate Events
- Meetings
- Film Shoots
- Accommodations

The Hyatt Westlake Plaza feels like a secluded world of European opulence and serenity, thanks to lush landscaping and a captivating ambiance.

The design of the ivory stucco hotel reflects Westlake's Spanish heritage, as well as a dash of contemporary Mediterranean elegance. Its open architecture features a spectacular skylit atrium, with indoor verandas curving around a central plaza. Everywhere you turn, intriguing elements catch your eye: a rustic wall sconce, chandeliers that appear hand-wrought, fresh floral arrangements, a limestone fountain. Most arresting are the colorful murals flanking the foyer from lobby to ballroom.

Fourteen different meeting spaces, all comfortable and tastefully appointed, are available for luncheons, seminars or company gatherings, including the brand new Vista Ballroom. This versatile, attractive space is lined with windows that bring in natural light for daytime events while capturing views of the hotel gardens.

In fact, if you've always fantasized about a garden wedding, then Hyatt Westlake can make your dreams a reality. Picture your guests gathered on a swath of lawn, basking in the warm California sunshine while they await your appearance. At last, you begin the walk down the aisle alongside a waterfall cascading over rocks into a placid pond. You join your groom at an ivy-covered gazebo under the protective shade of lofty evergreens. What a perfect place for exchanging vows or taking romantic photos! Cocktails and even receptions can be enjoyed right in the garden, too.

Or retire indoors to the Grand Ballroom, which reflects the same attention to detail as the rest of the Hyatt. Large beveled mirrors, framed in oak overlaid with an ornate iron design, and a coordinating cornice around the Ballroom's perimeter lend the room an air of distinction. Alabaster dome-shaped lighting fixtures with faux candles hang from the recessed ceiling, and vibrant shades of blue and gold in the carpet add to the room's inviting atmosphere. Air walls allow you to divide the room in half or quarters. The Grand Ballroom Foyer, with one wall of windows, is a light and airy spot to host a cocktail reception.

The Hyatt offers exceptional gourmet fare, and any of their menus can be customized. Friends and family spending the night will appreciate Hyatt Westlake's comfortable guest rooms, decorated with rich, warm tones, sumptuous fabrics, and every amenity for an enjoyable stay. The hotel is also TAG Approved®, and proud to welcome LGBT events.

For a full-service venue with all the grace and tranquility of a Mediterranean villa, consider the Hyatt Westlake Plaza for your most special event.

CEREMONY CAPACITY: The Grand Ballroom holds up to 800 seated guests; the garden area up to 350.

EVENT/RECEPTION & MEETING CAPACITY: The Grand Ballroom accommodates up to 450 seated or 900 standing guests; the garden up to 300 seated or 650 standing.

FEES & DEPOSITS: 25% of the estimated event total is required to reserve your date with the remaining balance due 10 days prior to your event. Wedding packages include 4 passed hors d'oeuvres, choice of meal, wine with dinner, champagne toast, cake cutting and a complimentary guest room for the bride and groom. Package prices start at $70/person. All charges are exclusive of tax and service charge.

Other options for your event include, but are not limited to, hosted bar, chair covers, chargers, audiovisiual and lighting. Call for details.

AVAILABILITY: Year-round, daily, 6am–midnight indoors, 8am–10pm outdoors.

SERVICES/AMENITIES:

Catering: in-house or select from approved ethnic caterers
Kitchen Facilities: fully equipped
Tables & Chairs: provided
Linens, Silver, etc.: provided
Restrooms: wheelchair accessible
Dance Floor: portable provided
Bride's Dressing Area: yes
Meeting Equipment: full range
Other: grand piano, spa services, AV equipment

Parking: large lot, self-parking and valet are available
Accommodations: 262 guest rooms
Telephone: pay and house phones
Outdoor Night Lighting: yes
Outdoor Cooking Facilities: no
Cleanup: provided
View: pool, garden, hills, manicured grounds, cascading waterfalls

RESTRICTIONS:

Alcohol: in-house
Smoking: outside in designated areas
Music: amplified OK with restrictions

Wheelchair Access: yes
Insurance: required for vendors such as caterers and entertainment

Westlake Village Inn

Inn

31943 Agoura Road, Westlake Village
818/889-0230

www.westlakevillageinn.com
catering@wvinn.com

●	Rehearsal Dinners	●	Corporate Events
●	Ceremonies	●	Meetings
●	Wedding Receptions	●	Film Shoots
●	Private Parties	●	Accommodations

Just a half hour north of Los Angeles at the base of the Santa Monica Mountains, you'll find an idyllic retreat—the Westlake Village Inn. Encompassing over 17 lush acres spread around a lake and vineyard, the inn feels more like a European private estate than a hotel.

The main areas include beautiful guest rooms and suites nestled throughout the manicured grounds; Mediterraneo, their chic, on-site bistro with al fresco dining; Bogie's, a lively nightclub; Stonehaus, an Italian-inspired coffeehaus & wine bar with its own vineyard; and the Provence building, an opulent, view-filled reception facility for special events. Everything is connected by picturesque stone walkways, and each turn reveals a fresh surprise. One moment you amble down a cobbled path under a magnificent rose arbor, and the next you find yourself strolling lakeside, feeding the resident ducks. A Mediterranean flair is reflected in details like floral-laced trellises, European statuary and trickling fountains. Flourishing gardens fill the air with the fragrance of jasmine.

For your ceremony, you may choose from among several enchanting outdoor locales, each individualized in theme. The inn's traditional setting is the Lakeside Gazebo, whose charming footbridge and white-wooden railing capture a nostalgic ambiance, perfumed by heritage roses and Provençal herbs. The classic Mediterranean Gazebo has sleek Romanesque columns, and overlooks the lake and gardens. Or walk down the aisle beneath an arbor entwined with flowering vines in the Tuscan Garden, and wed alongside an iron filigree cupola and a splashing fountain. A third option is next to a dramatic waterfall, which cascades over an expanse of polished rocks into two streams and is surrounded by swaths of lawn and tropical foliage. The inn's newest gathering place is Stonehaus, a unique venue unto itself: This stylish tasting room serves up gourmet coffee, casual eats, and a lavish wine list. Outside, a stone courtyard and private vineyard patio with a waterfall and outdoor fireplace are perfect for an intimate ceremony and social hour.

After vows are exchanged, your guests take an easy stroll to the Provence building. The Provence Patio, with its covered outdoor bar and heat lamps, is a congenial and refreshing place to serve pre-party cocktails. One of the most popular spaces for receptions is the bi-level Provence Room, with crystal chandeliers suspended from an open-beam ceiling. Floor-to-ceiling windows treat diners to a lake and waterfall vista. Adjacent to the Provence Room are two stylishly decorated banquet spaces for more formal events. The second-story Fairway Room features generous views of both the neighboring golf course and the sparkling lake. On the lower story, the Lakeside Room and its adjoining patio let you dine at the water's edge and sip champagne under the stars. The wine cellar and Vintage Room and patio are also great options for smaller get-togethers.

The Westlake Village Inn also offers genuine European-style hospitality for your out-of-town guests, who'll appreciate the chance to spend more time at the inn. Accommodations include sumptuous Italian bedding, Jacuzzi tubs, fireplaces and a private patio or balcony.

If you long for a venue that combines grace and refinement with the most luxurious modern amenities, then come to the Westlake Village Inn. You'll find exactly what you were looking for.

CEREMONY CAPACITY: There are 5 outdoor locations that seat up to 250 guests each.

EVENT/RECEPTION CAPACITY: Event spaces accommodate seated guests as follows: Provence Room, 230; Vintage Room, 60; Stonehaus Tasting Room, 40; Fairway Room, 120; Lakeside Room and patio, 150; Wine Cellar, 70. All capacities are without a dance floor.

MEETING CAPACITY: 6 meeting spaces accommodate 10–230 guests.

FEES & DEPOSITS: 25% of the estimated event total or $3,000 (whichever is greater) is the deposit required to reserve your date. 50% of the balance is due 90 days prior to the event, the final payment 2 weeks prior. Receptions average $70–90/person and include hors d'oeuvres, 2 entrées, glass of wine, champagne toast, nonalcoholic beverage and cake cutting. Custom menus and special rates on hotel rooms are available. Ceremony and reception events receive one complimentary standard hotel room for an overnight stay.

AVAILABILITY: Year-round, daily 8am–midnight.

SERVICES/AMENITIES:

Catering: in-house, no BYO
Kitchen Facilities: n/a
Tables & Chairs: provided
Linens, Silver, etc.: provided
Restrooms: wheelchair accessible
Dance Floor: yes
Bride's Dressing Area: CBA
Meeting Equipment: full range, additional fee
Other: ice carving, chocolate fountain

Parking: large lot, free self-parking, valet available for an extra fee
Accommodations: 141 guest rooms
Telephone: guest phones
Outdoor Night Lighting: yes
Outdoor Cooking Facilities: yes
Cleanup: provided
View: lake, fairways, garden and vineyard

RESTRICTIONS:

Alcohol: in-house
Smoking: outside only
Music: amplified OK

Wheelchair Access: yes
Insurance: not required
Other: no rice or birdseed

San Fernando Valley

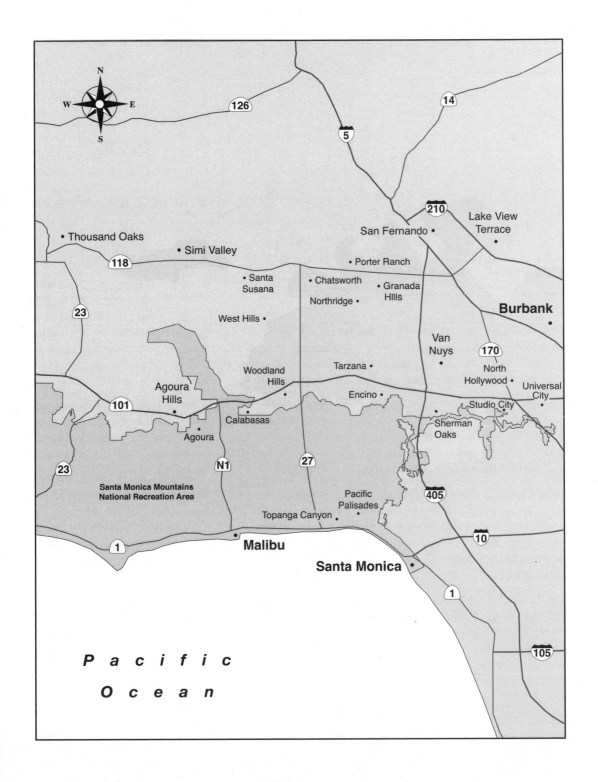

Malibou Lake Mountain Club

Private Lakeside Club

29033 Lake Vista Drive, Agoura
818/753-6772

www.maliboulakeclub.com
www.trulyyourscatering.com
laura@trulyyourscatering.com

- Rehearsal Dinners
- Ceremonies
- Wedding Receptions
- Private Parties
- Corporate Events
- Meetings
- Film Shoots
- Accommodations

Two natural rock pillars frame the entryway to the Malibou Lake Mountain Club, a private club nestled in the Santa Monica Mountains. A rustic colonial façade with a wide front veranda leads you into the clubhouse, and once inside the spacious main room, it's easy to envision a terrific event here. Wood walls are finished in a whitewashed gray with white trim, providing a neutral backdrop for any color scheme. The warm glow from a fireplace adds a homey touch. On the right side of the room a huge bay window flanked by French doors overlooks a gently sloping lawn, bordered by eucalyptus and pine trees. The stage in front of the window can be used for a band, making toasts or even an indoor ceremony.

Given its neutral décor, you can have a field day decorating the club. One group had an elegant black-and-white affair, with guests garbed in tuxedos and snazzy dresses; another staged a western-theme party, with bales of hay, white foam horses on the tables and a barbecue reception on the lawn. Still a third hosted a renaissance gala, complete with period costumes, wandering minstrels and rounds of croquet and bocce ball.

Most weddings take place at the far end of the lawn, overlooking the lake. Feel free to customize your ceremony too, by adding an arch, gazebo, tent or any other element you choose. Afterwards, your guests can mingle on the grass and admire the view of the sparkling lake with the Santa Monica mountains in the distance. The lawn also lends itself to lively company picnics, reunions or anniversary parties—there's plenty of room for all kinds of interactive games, sports or carnival activities.

The beauty of this place—aside from its country setting—is that you have carte blanche (within reason) to design whatever celebration you desire. No two parties are alike here, so if you want plenty of control over your event, come to the Malibou Lake Mountain Club and have the creative time of your life.

CEREMONY CAPACITY: The lawn holds up to 400 guests.

EVENT/RECEPTION CAPACITY: Indoors, the facility holds up to 200 seated. A smaller room is available for 10–50 guests.

MEETING CAPACITY: The facility can accommodate 175 seated theater-style or 200 conference-style.

FEES & DEPOSITS: A $2,000 nonrefundable deposit and signed contract are required to secure your date. 20% of the food and beverage cost is due within 90 days of booking, and the balance is due 12 days before the event. The rental fees for 2014 are as follows: Monday–Thursday, $250/hour with a 4-hour minimum; Friday, $2,800; Saturday, $4,800; and Sunday, $2,800. The rental fees for 2015 are: Monday–Thursday, $275/hour with a 4-hour minimum; Friday, $3,000; Saturday, $5,000; and Sunday, $3,000. Wedding packages start at $41/person and include food, beverage and some rentals.

AVAILABILITY: Year-round, Sun–Thurs until 10pm, Fri–Sat until 11pm.

SERVICES/AMENITIES:

Catering: provided by *Truly Yours Gourmet Foods and Catering*
Kitchen Facilities: n/a
Tables & Chairs: provided through caterer
Restrooms: wheelchair accessible
Linens, Silver, etc.: provided through caterer
Dance Floor: wood floor provided
Bride's & Groom's Dressing Area: yes
Meeting Equipment: BYO

Parking: 2 large lots
Accommodations: no guest rooms
Telephone: pay phone
Outdoor Night Lighting: twinkle lights in trees
Outdoor Cooking Facilities: provided through caterer
Cleanup: caterer or renter
View: lake, an island and mountains
Other: event coordination, outdoor lounge-style furniture, and draping

RESTRICTIONS:

Alcohol: BYO or through caterer
Smoking: outdoors only
Music: amplified OK indoors, Sun–Thurs until 10pm, Fri–Sat until 11pm; acoustic only outdoors

Wheelchair Access: yes
Insurance: required for DJ or live band

Calamigos Equestrian

Equestrian Center

480 Riverside Drive, Burbank
818/972-5940

www.calamigosequestrian.com
info@calamigosequestrian.com

Rehearsal Dinners	● Corporate Events
● Ceremonies	● Meetings
● Wedding Receptions	● Film Shoots
● Private Parties	Accommodations

Set against the scenic backdrop of the Santa Monica Mountains on 75 beautifully landscaped acres, the L.A. Equestrian Center has hosted everything from celebrity-studded polo matches to Elizabeth Taylor's perfume launch, and has been used for filming hit movies like *Pretty Woman.*

What you'll find here are charming ceremony locations for bridal couples, and an appealing variety of upscale event spaces for celebrants of all kinds—even those with only a passing interest in horses. As an added bonus, the event producers of Calamigos Ranch (best known for hosting decades of special events at their facility in Malibu) have recently brought their experience to this unique locale. So relax and let them coordinate your entire celebration!

One of the favorite sites is the Little White House and Garden Courtyard in the middle of Hunt Field, a vast expanse of lawn enclosed by a traditional white picket fence. From the parking lot, guests stroll along a path that winds through majestic sycamore trees. Some couples like to say their vows under the trees' graceful boughs, and the entire field can be set up for cocktails for up to a thousand guests. The Little White House, which provides a private dressing room for the bride, is a quaint cottage with French doors that open to the Garden Courtyard, bordered by fragrant rose bushes.

Another option for tying the knot is the raised demi-gazebo at the far end of the Courtyard, where the soothing strains of songbirds accompany a cascading waterfall. And for added romance, many couples opt to come through the Courtyard gates on an old-fashioned horse-drawn carriage! After the ceremony, guests amble back across Hunt Field to one of the Center's private rooms for a formal reception.

Beautiful wrought-iron gates invite you into the Equestrian Ballroom, a sophisticated space with chandeliers and a large bar. Panel doors swivel open to the Equestrian terrace, a lovely spot for post-reception mingling or a garden ceremony among California pines. The garden atmosphere is enhanced by a jasmine-covered trellis, rock waterfall, and views of Griffith Park and the distant mountains. For a different feel, the Grand Prix Room offers a more formal setting with rich red and gold carpeting, spectacular chandeliers and an impressive wood-burning fireplace.

The Polo Room has a comfortable bar and lounge separate from its casually elegant dining room. French doors open onto a veranda, enabling guests to enjoy cocktails outdoors or wander off to observe the equestrian competitions. The horses and the grounds are all impeccably maintained, so everything will be fresh and clean for your event.

Calamigos has prepared an array of tempting event packages that include plenty of extras, and their in-house caterers will happily customize your menu with delicious offerings. All this, and horses too!

CEREMONY CAPACITY: The Little White House holds up to 350 seated, Hunt Field Lawn up to 1,000 guests and the Equestrian Terrace up to 250 seated guests.

EVENT/RECEPTION CAPACITY: The facility has a variety of areas that accommodate up to 550 seated or 1,200 standing indoors, and 250 to 5,000 seated outdoors.

MEETING CAPACITY: The Equestrian Ballroom (divisible into 4 sections) holds 120–800 guests. The Grand Prix Room (divisible into 3 sections) holds 800 guests. The Little White House can accommodate up to 500 guests, seated theater-style.

FEES & DEPOSITS: A $1,500 nonrefundable deposit is required to reserve your date. 50% of the estimated event total is due 6 months prior to the event; the balance is payable 10 days prior. Wedding packages range $59–101/person and include a half-hour wedding rehearsal, a seated or buffet meal, room rental fees, cake-cutting and a 3-hour hosted champagne, wine and beer package. Tax and a 20% service charge are extra. For other kinds of special events, prices range $50–85/person. Tax, alcohol and a 20% service charge are additional. Meetings start at $55/person and include continental breakfast, lunch, room rental fees and 2 breaks with beverages and snacks.

AVAILABILITY: Year-round, daily, 7am 1am.

SERVICES/AMENITIES:

Catering: in-house, no BYO
Kitchen Facilities: n/a
Tables & Chairs: Chiavari chairs provided
Linens, Silver, etc.: provided
Restrooms: wheelchair accessible
Dance Floor: provided
Bride's Dressing Area: yes
Meeting Equipment: some provided, extra CBA
Other: coordination, horse-drawn carriage

Parking: ample lot
Accommodations: no guest rooms
Telephone: pay phone
Outdoor Night Lighting: yes
Outdoor Cooking Facilities: CBA
Cleanup: provided
View: mountains, horse arena, landscaped grounds

RESTRICTIONS:

Alcohol: in-house
Smoking: outdoors only
Music: amplified OK indoors, outdoors with restrictions

Wheelchair Access: yes
Insurance: liability required for vendors

Want to find more venues and services? Check out our informative website, www.HereComesTheGuide.com.

123

Pickwick Gardens

Garden

1001 Riverside Drive, Burbank
818/845-5300 X171

www.pickwickgardensconferencecenter.com
info@pickwickgardens.com

- Rehearsal Dinners
- Ceremonies
- Wedding Receptions
- Private Parties
- Corporate Events
- Meetings
- Film Shoots
- Accommodations

For anyone who only knows Pickwick Gardens from their sign on Riverside Drive, walking through the wrought-iron gate in the back will be a revelation, because this has to be one of the most idyllic outdoor wedding spots in the San Fernando Valley.

This area was once the bustling aquatic section of a public recreation complex, but today it's an expansive, two-and-half-acre, woodland oasis that's at the very heart of any event at Pickwick Gardens. Paved walkways lit by old-fashioned street lamps meander through the lawns. The varied landscape of this bucolic retreat combines towering pines, graceful jacarandas, spiky palms and majestic oak trees. Old stone fountains serve as multitiered planters, and colorful flowerbeds punctuated with rose bushes and seasonal blooms line the walkways. At the center of the garden is a huge tented pavilion with overhead fans. A raised stage at one end is anchored by a curving, river rock wall that would make a beautiful altar backdrop for your ceremony…or you can exchange vows on a lawn, shaded by trees. Afterwards, serve cocktails under the pavilion as the late afternoon and evening breezes come off the Santa Monica Mountains in nearby Griffith Park.

Bordering the gardens are several banquet rooms, each with a private bridal room where you and your attendants can get ready. Most have full-on, outdoor views and awning-covered patios. The very popular Garden Room features a unique rotunda and circular parquet dance floor set against tall windows, while the charming, newly renovated Terrace Room is bright with a white, wood-beamed ceiling, white wainscoting and golden candelabra chandeliers. Just outside the Terrace Room windows sits a bubbling fountain in its own private mini-garden, separated from the main gardens by a low wall of natural stone.

If your guest list truly includes *all* your nearest and dearest, there's the 8,500-square-foot Royal Crest Ballroom, which can comfortably accommodate 550 guests for a sit-down dinner and dancing. Decorated in rich tones of garnet and gold paisley, its regal ambiance is further established by windows draped with swags and valances, and huge chandeliers dripping with crystals.

Whether you desire a formal dinner, a buffet with ethnic specialties or more casual fare for a bridal shower or rehearsal dinner, an executive chef is on site to help you customize your menu. And if you feel like arranging a fairy-tale entrance on horseback or by horse-drawn carriage from the neighboring Equestrian Center, a full-time wedding planner can assist you in tailoring your event to make it suit you perfectly.

CEREMONY CAPACITY: The site holds 1,000 seated guests indoors and 1,200 seated outdoors.

EVENT/RECEPTION CAPACITY: The site accommodates 550 seated or 1,000 standing guests indoors and 1,200 seated or 2,000 standing outdoors.

MEETING CAPACITY: Meeting spaces hold 1,000 seated guests.

FEES & DEPOSITS: A $500–2,500 deposit is required to reserve your date and the balance is due 45 days prior to the event. Rental fees range $1,500–8,500 depending on the guest count. Meals range $30–90/person. Tax, alcohol and a 19% service charge are additional.

AVAILABILITY: Year-round, daily, 7am–1am.

SERVICES/AMENITIES:

Catering: in-house
Kitchen Facilities: n/a
Tables & Chairs: provided
Linens, Silver, etc.: provided
Restrooms: wheelchair accessible
Dance Floor: provided
Bride's Dressing Area: yes
Meeting Equipment: provided
Other: picnic area, AV equipment, ceremony coordinator, meeting planner

Parking: large lot
Accommodations: no guest rooms
Telephone: house phone
Outdoor Night Lighting: yes
Outdoor Cooking Facilities: BBQ
Cleanup: provided
View: garden, mountains, fountain, landscaped grounds

RESTRICTIONS:

Alcohol: in-house
Smoking: in designated areas only
Music: amplified OK with restrictions

Wheelchair Access: yes
Insurance: liability required

Agoura Hills/Calabasas Community Center

Community Center

27040 Malibu Hills Road, Calabasas
818/880-2993
www.ahccc.org
jenna@ahccc.org

- Rehearsal Dinners
- Ceremonies
- Wedding Receptions
- Private Parties
- Corporate Events
- Meetings
- Film Shoots
- Accommodations

Nestled in the Santa Monica foothills, the family-friendly towns of Calabasas and Agoura Hills are among the most desirable places to live in Southern California. Some long-time residents were lured here by the wide-open spaces that welcomed their horses, while many newcomers fled the confines of the city for exclusive, creekside neighborhoods. It's quiet here, but not too quiet, with plenty of upscale shopping and trendy dining to content erstwhile urbanites. Now this pleasant enclave has one more enviable feature: a Community Center that's part health club, part "activities central," and part special event facility. Lucky for you, you don't have to be a resident to enjoy what the Center has to offer.

During normal business hours, both the young and the young-at-heart indulge in a potpourri of fun at the Center, including Swing Salsa lessons, youth camps, belly dancing classes, rock-climbing lessons, and annual events like the St. Patrick's Day Community Barbecue. However, on most weekends you can hold a private celebration here.

Set back against the hills and surrounded by attractive landscaping, the Center is housed in a contemporary building boasting a huge, avant-garde arch over the entryway. The lobby is bright and airy, thanks to the double-tall windows and a vaulted atrium that let in the sunshine, nourishing the potted plantation ferns. Everything here is "quality"—even the vending machine serves fresh-ground Starbuck's cappuccinos! Party planners and brides find this space so welcoming they often use it for their cocktail hour.

On the outdoor patio, which runs the length of the Community Room, banks of African violets, French lavender and native grasses border one side, and several faux brick planters hold graceful saplings. Guests can enjoy their champagne and hors d'oeuvres while lounging on teak garden furniture, and when it's time for the reception they simply walk through a set of doors that open right into the Community Room.

The Community Room holds up to 300, but can be divided into three sections for smaller groups. The high, barrel-vaulted ceiling—made of open beams and wooden planking—coordinates with the floor, polished to a gleam. A row of accent tiles marks the floor's perimeter, but other than that, neutral earth tones keep the look light and accessible. If you're planning a gala-sized affair, the 10,000-square-foot Gymnasium accommodates 800 guests with ease.

With two generous spaces you can decorate nearly any way you like, you're free to design a thoroughly original event. One bride enlisted a local nursery to transform the Community Room into an enchanted forest with potted trees, garlands of greenery, and hanging floral baskets. Another inspired client hung draping from the ceiling to separate five themed areas inside the Gymnasium.

The folks at the Center encourage your creativity, and there are no limitations on catering, so they say YES! to specialty cuisine. You'll appreciate their friendly, helpful attitude, and the way they make you feel like part of the community, even if you visit from afar.

CEREMONY CAPACITY: The Community Room holds 308 seated guests.

EVENT/RECEPTION & MEETING CAPACITY: The Community Room holds 308 seated or standing guests and can be divided into 3 smaller sections. The Patio holds up to 50 guests.

FEES & DEPOSITS: A deposit ranging $175–500 is required to reserve your date; the balance is due 30 days prior to the event. Community room rental fees range $55–255/hour. A security guard is required, whether alcohol is served or not, at an additional charge.

AVAILABILITY: Year-round, daily, 6am–2am.

SERVICES/AMENITIES:
Catering: BYO
Kitchen Facilities: large warming kitchen
Tables & Chairs: provided
Linens, Silver, etc.: BYO
Restrooms: wheelchair accessible
Dance Floor: wood floor
Bride's Dressing Area: no
Meeting Equipment: wireless internet, projector, PA system, microphones

Parking: large lot
Accommodations: no guest rooms
Telephone: emergency only
Outdoor Night Lighting: yes
Outdoor Cooking Facilities: BYO BBQ
Cleanup: provided or through renter
View: mountains and hills
Other: limited event coordination

RESTRICTIONS:
Alcohol: BYO
Smoking: not allowed
Music: amplified OK indoors

Wheelchair Access: yes
Insurance: liability required
Other: no rice, glitter, confetti or birdseed, no duct tape or anything that mars walls

Calabasas Country Club

Golf Club

4515 Park Entrada, Calabasas
818/222-8111

www.calabasasgolf.com
info@calabasasgolf.com

- Rehearsal Dinners
- Ceremonies
- Wedding Receptions
- Private Parties
- Corporate Events
- Meetings
- Film Shoots
- Accommodations

Wouldn't it be nice if you could invite your friends and family to a wedding at your own private club—even if you're not actually a member? At the Calabasas Country Club you can, because the entire clubhouse, inside and out, is yours to enjoy for the duration of your celebration—*totally yours*.

This picturesque venue in the hills of the west San Fernando Valley has an interesting history and a place in the hearts of classic cinema buffs. Once part of the Warner Ranch Group, it served as a rugged backlot for the production of such notable films as *National Velvet, Carousel, Robin Hood, The Good Earth, Giant* and *Showboat*. In honor of that heritage, when the country club was built each of the 18 holes of its verdant golf course was named after one of the famous films. Today, since the club is mainly open for special events in the evening after the golfers have gone home, you and your groom will get top billing in your own "love story" production here.

For your ceremony, your guests are first ushered to an expansive patio, landscaped with islands of roses and magnolia trees. On one side is a shady pergola covered in cascading greenery; on the other is the golf course with the 18th hole in the foreground. You can opt for a cocktail reception outdoors, or take advantage of the Cocktail Lounge/Dining Room in the main building. This upstairs location has a high, peaked ceiling and wraparound picture windows so celebrants can enjoy a bird's-eye view of the newlyweds posing for photogenic shots beside the lovely waterfalls, bridges and old oaks on the golf course below. The bar area is dominated by a curved cherrywood-and-marble bar, while the modern dining area is punctuated with colorful floral paintings. But since the room faces southwest, the best visual show might be the spectacular sunsets over the 130-acre property.

The main reception takes place in the Calabash Room, decorated in deep, rich burgundy and gold tones. Floor-to-ceiling windows look out onto the golf course, and dramatic, angular crystal chandeliers hang from the coffered ceiling, creating a romantic glow over the tables and ample dance floor. An outer Foyer can be used as a kids' party room, a retreat for quiet conversation or a buffet setup. Whether you dine buffet-style or opt for a more formal seated dinner, it should be noted that the executive chef has over 30 years' experience working coast to coast in a range of venues, from noteworthy bistros to a 5-star resort. Although he specializes in California cuisine, his dishes reflect many regional and ethnic influences, and he's happy to accommodate special menu requests.

And because this is a private club—*your* private club for the night—the large, outside Terrace offers guests not only a quiet retreat for a nightcap, but also one of the few places in Calabasas where you may even see a few meandering deer.

CEREMONY & EVENT/RECEPTION CAPACITY: The facility holds 250 seated or 300 standing guests indoors and out.

MEETING CAPACITY: Meeting spaces seat 300 guests indoors.

FEES & DEPOSITS: A $2,000 deposit is required to reserve your date and the balance is due 30 days prior to the event based on your contract agreement. Rental fees range $250–5,000 depending on the day of the event and the space rented. Meals range $25–75/person. Tax, alcohol and a 20% service charge are additional.

AVAILABILITY: Year-round, daily, 6am–midnight.

SERVICES/AMENITIES:
Catering: in-house or BYO
Kitchen Facilities: fully equipped
Tables & Chairs: provided
Linens, Silver, etc.: provided
Restrooms: wheelchair accessible
Dance Floor: portable provided
Bride's Dressing Area: yes
Meeting Equipment: some provided, more CBA
Other: event coordination

Parking: complimentary
Accommodations: no guest rooms
Telephone: house or office phone
Outdoor Night Lighting: CBA
Outdoor Cooking Facilities: BBQ CBA
Cleanup: provided
View: garden, lake, fountain, landscaped grounds, waterfall, fairways, creek; panorama of mountains, forest and hills

RESTRICTIONS:
Alcohol: in-house or BYO wine with corkage fee
Smoking: designated areas only
Music: amplified OK with restrictions

Wheelchair Access: yes
Insurance: liability required

Saddle Peak Lodge

Restaurant

419 Cold Canyon Road, Calabasas
818/222-3888

www.saddlepeaklodge.com
taylor@saddlepeaklodge.com

● Rehearsal Dinners   ● Corporate Events
● Ceremonies   ● Meetings
● Wedding Receptions   ● Film Shoots
● Private Parties   Accommodations

Saddle Peak Lodge is one of the more intriguing event sites we've ever seen. Steeped in California history, this turn-of-the-century hunting lodge began over 100 years ago as a small one-room cabin where cowboys, miners, fishermen and oil riggers imbibed the local "Hillbilly Punch" and swapped tall stories. Later the lodge carved a new identity, first as a way-stop and general store and then as a summer resort. In the '30s and '40s, Saddle Peak became the in-vogue hangout for movie stars such as Errol Flynn, Clark Gable and Charlie Chaplin. Today it prospers as a restaurant specializing in exotic game, and is renowned as an extraordinary place to host any special occasion.

As you enter the lodge, the antler door pulls and three-hoofed lamp in the foyer signal that you're in for a unique dining experience. The provocative aroma of roasting elk, venison, buffalo and mesquite lingers in the air—so tantalizing it gives you pangs of hunger in anticipation.

With its rough-hewn, tall-timbered interior, Saddle Peak is warm and elegantly rustic in its décor. An antique pistol collection gleams in a display case, while old western saddles and riding tack are slung casually over large beams. Populating the wood walls is an amusing mix of mounted trophy heads—deer, moose, pronghorn, eland—as well as authentic saloon paintings from the 1800s.

Saddle Peak's log-cabin ambiance lends itself beautifully to weddings: With hurricane lamps glowing on white tablecloths and a fire crackling in the Main Dining Room's massive rock hearth, the lodge is a wildly romantic setting.

Most weddings are celebrated on the lodge's picturesque and secluded Far Patio, just a short walk from the Main Dining Room. Couples exchange vows on a circular, two-tiered slate rock area that overlooks a spectacular view of Santa Monica Mountains' rolling hills and canyons. Note that as an added perk when you buy out the lodge, the third-floor Loft is transformed into a bridal suite where the bride can get ready for her walk down the aisle.

Post ceremony, guests sip wine under the shade of pine and eucalyptus trees, or relax fireside in the dining room in handsome, handmade willow chairs. Small parties may want to savor hors d'oeuvres in the upstairs Den or Library—cozy pine-paneled rooms lined with windows and eclectically decorated with collectibles, antique books, and relics of the Old West. Dinner and dancing take place in the Main Dining Room, or al fresco on the Main Patio under a canopy of trees with the natural sounds of the nearby waterfall in the background.

The restaurant's extensive menu includes seafood, poultry, lamb and beef in addition to game, and they're perfectly happy to prepare vegetarian entrées as well. Not only is the food award winning (earning "best-of" honors from the *Los Angeles Times* and *Conde Nast Traveler*, as well as the highest ratings from ZAGAT, DiRoNA and Four Diamond AAA), but the lodge also boasts an award-winning domestic wine collection. Plus the staff are incredibly friendly and accommodating, making you feel like you're part of the Saddle Peak family.

From their distinctive cuisine and impeccable service to the incredible vistas, Saddle Peak Lodge earns rave reviews.

CEREMONY & EVENT/RECEPTION CAPACITY: The facility holds 150 seated or 175 standing guests indoors and 150 seated or 200 standing outdoors.

MEETING CAPACITY: Meeting spaces seat 80 guests indoors.

FEES & DEPOSITS: A $200–750 deposit is required to reserve your date. Rental fees range $200–750 depending on the space needed and day of the week. Food and beverage minimums vary, also depending on space needed and day of the week. Meals range $35–75/person. Tax, beverages and a 20% service charge are additional.

AVAILABILITY: Year-round. Daytime and evening events available.

SERVICES/AMENITIES:

Catering: in-house
Kitchen Facilities: n/a
Tables & Chairs: provided
Linens, Silver, etc.: provided
Restrooms: wheelchair accessible
Dance Floor: provided, CBA
Bride's Dressing Area: yes
Meeting Equipment: CBA
Other: in-house florals, AV equipment

Parking: large lot, valet only
Accommodations: no guest rooms
Telephone: office phone
Outdoor Night Lighting: provided
Outdoor Cooking Facilities: no
Cleanup: provided
View: canyon, fountain, garden, landscaped grounds; panorama of mountains, forest and hills

RESTRICTIONS:

Alcohol: full in-house bar
Smoking: designated areas only
Music: amplified OK with restrictions

Wheelchair Access: yes
Insurance: not required

This is important! Tell venues you're reading HERE COMES THE GUIDE and ask if our information is still current.

Knollwood Golf Course

Country Club

12024 Balboa Boulevard, Granada Hills
888/991-5042
www.countryclubreceptions.com
privateeventdirector@knowllwoodgc.com

- Rehearsal Dinners
- Ceremonies
- Wedding Receptions
- Private Parties
- Corporate Events
- Meetings
- Film Shoots
- Accommodations

When Granada Hills was founded in 1927, town members chose the name "Granada" after its sister city Granada, Spain. Although separated by thousands of miles, the two communities have similarities: Both are in the foothills of mountain ranges, and both have temperate climates—a quality making them prime candidates for outdoor weddings.

One of this city's best-known wedding locations is Knollwood Golf Course, an affordable public golf course and clubhouse with a friendly attitude. Ceremonies are held outside on a trim lawn backed by pine trees and the rolling fairways. You can say your vows under the open sky beneath a metal arch that can be ornamented with flowers, tulle or even pine boughs. And, speaking of pines, there are so many around here you can almost imagine you're getting married in a quiet mountain meadow.

After the ceremony, guests walk over to the clubhouse, an unpretentious fieldstone-faced building with three event spaces. Here, they sip cocktails in the private bar area while you and your new spouse have your pictures taken under the trees. The reception follows in the spacious Granada Room. With its unadorned white walls, this room easily adapts to your event theme and color scheme. Light streams in through floor-to-ceiling windows during the day, while faux-candle fixtures hanging from the high ceiling provide illumination at night. The Granada Room also has its own large built-in dance floor with a mirrored ball overhead.

If your event is more intimate or you need additional space, there are two other smaller banquet rooms: the Gallery and the Fairway. Both are neutral-toned with floor-to-ceiling windows; the larger Gallery Room also has a fieldstone wall and its own bar.

Next to the relaxed golf-club setting, it's the ease of planning an event here that draws couples to Knollwood. Wedding packages include your choice of linens, tray-passed hors d'oeuvres, and the cake (with cutting). Choose the Platinum Package, and you'll also receive an open bar and assorted pastries! Although Knollwood provides a wide selection of packages, the catering staff is happy to customize one to meet your specific needs.

Knollwood offers another perk that's especially popular with the men in your group: You can integrate a little golf into your event! Grooms frequently schedule a morning tee time to loosen up with family and friends on the wedding day.

Granada Hills is known as the "Valley's Most Neighborly Town," and you might say that Knollwood is its most neighborly wedding site. You don't have to be a member—or even a golfer—to get married here, and they take such good care of you, you may end up feeling that you've definitely hit a wedding hole in one.

CEREMONY CAPACITY: The lawn holds 250 seated guests; the indoor areas hold 300 seated.

EVENT/RECEPTION & MEETING CAPACITY: The clubhouse accommodates 300 seated or 400 standing guests.

FEES & DEPOSITS: A nonrefundable deposit, which is applied to your food and beverage total, is required to reserve your date. The amount of the deposit varies, depending on how far in advance you book. Payment terms for the balance also vary, and may be arranged on an individual basis. Inclusive packages start at $47/person. Tax, alcohol and service charge are additional. Menus and packages can be customized to fit your needs and budget. Call for details.

AVAILABILITY: Year-round, daily.

SERVICES/AMENITIES:

Catering: in-house
Kitchen Facilities: n/a
Tables & Chairs: provided
Linens, Silver, etc.: provided
Restrooms: wheelchair accessible
Dance Floor: provided
Bride's Dressing Area: yes
Meeting Equipment: some provided

Parking: large complimentary lot
Accommodations: no guest rooms
Telephone: emergency use only
Outdoor Night Lighting: CBA
Outdoor Cooking Facilities: no
Cleanup: provided
View: fairways, mountains, garden
Other: event coordination

RESTRICTIONS:

Alcohol: in-house
Smoking: outside only
Music: amplified OK, subject to management approval

Wheelchair Access: yes
Insurance: not required

Middle Ranch

Country Club

11700 Little Tujunga Canyon Road, Lake View Terrace
818/897-4029
www.middleranch.com
middle.ranch@hotmail.com

- Rehearsal Dinners
- Ceremonies
- Wedding Receptions
- Private Parties
- Corporate Events
- Meetings
- Film Shoots
- Accommodations

Surrounded by the San Gabriel Mountains and bordered by the Angeles National Forest on three sides, Middle Ranch's civilized lawns and attractive buildings are a pleasant surprise in the midst of this rugged landscape.

The 650-acre property, known primarily as an exclusive equestrian country club, is also a spectacular place for a wedding. Ceremonies are held on the expansive front lawn with a backdrop of trees and mountains. The venue's main building, the award-winning Lodge, harmonizes nicely with its surroundings and has been recognized for its architectural style. Beneath its Spanish tile roof you'll find a large "living room" that's ideal for socializing over cocktails and hors d'oeuvres. The ambiance here is very relaxed, with a lofty, open-beamed ceiling, an abundance of warm natural wood, terracotta-tile floors and a handsome, two-sided fieldstone fireplace. Leather couches and chairs, along with antique Oriental carpets, complete the décor.

French doors open out to a lovely and spacious garden patio. Partly shaded by fragrant eucalyptus trees, it's an intimate spot for an al fresco reception. A few steps uphill, there's a pool with a large deck backed by an untamed hillside. You and your guests can sit by the water enjoying cocktails, or dine at tables set up on the patio.

The contrast between the wild, natural setting and the effortless elegance of the venue itself makes Middle Ranch a very special—and distinctly Californian—place to celebrate.

CEREMONY CAPACITY: The grass field can accommodate up to 225 seated guests. The Patio holds up to 100 seated, 150 standing.

EVENT/RECEPTION CAPACITY: The Lodge accommodates 150 seated, 175 standing; the Patio holds 225 seated or 225 standing guests. From late fall through early spring there is a 150 guest maximum.

MEETING CAPACITY: The Lodge holds 150 seated, the conference room up to 30 seated.

FEES & DEPOSITS: A $1,000 nonrefundable deposit is required to reserve your date. 50% of the total estimated event cost is due 180 days prior to the event; the balance is payable 14 days prior. The facility rental fee is $25/person (minimum $2,000) and includes tables, chairs, linens and choice of linen color, place settings, facility personnel, and 6 hours of facility rental time. The ceremony fee is $700 and includes an additional half hour of rental time, your choice of oakwood or white chairs, white wedding arch, bridal dressing room, and rehearsal time.

AVAILABILITY: Year-round, daily, until midnight.

SERVICES/AMENITIES:

Catering: select from approved list
Kitchen Facilities: fully equipped
Tables & Chairs: provided
Linens, Silver, etc.: linens, silver and china provided
Restrooms: wheelchair accessible
Dance Floor: CBA, extra fee
Bride's & Groom's Dressing Area: yes
Meeting Equipment: limited in-house, or BYO
Other: can arrange horse-drawn carriages

Parking: large lot
Accommodations: no guest rooms
Telephone: CBA
Outdoor Night Lighting: yes
Outdoor Cooking Facilities: n/a
Cleanup: provided
View: landscaped patio and pool area; Angeles Forest

RESTRICTIONS:

Alcohol: in-house, no BYO
Smoking: outdoors only
Music: amplified OK

Wheelchair Access: yes
Insurance: not required for social functions; required for business functions

Ca' Del Sole Ristorante

Italian Restaurant

4100 Cahuenga Boulevard, North Hollywood
818/753-8889
www.cadelsole.com
cadelsole@aol.com

● Rehearsal Dinners	● Corporate Events	
● Ceremonies	● Meetings	
● Wedding Receptions	● Film Shoots	
● Private Parties	Accommodations	

Welcome to Ca' Del Sole—"House of the Sun"—where life is good, the food even better, and the setting sublime. When you visit this updated version of an authentic trattoria, the tantalizing aroma of fresh roasted garlic and herbs mingled with an infectious mood of contentment will make you want to linger as long as possible.

Ca' Del Sole was fashioned after a Venetian country inn. Details like dark wooden beams and the double-sided fireplace in the main dining rooms recall an Old World village where strangers are wined and dined, and even the most trivial milestone is cause for celebration.

However, a recent remodel brings contemporary chic to the rustic décor, artfully realized in the two adjoining private banquet rooms: the Gondolier and the Venetian. A new floor has a walnut patina that may make you think of a renovated Tuscan farmhouse, and a distressed white hutch displaying vintage ceramics lends a handcrafted touch. Italian Mod lounge furniture in tomato-red and marine-blue adds a colorful contrast to accents like oversized rough-hewn bowls adorning dove-gray walls. The eclectic blend all comes together beautifully, and provides a clean and classy canvas for your own event stylings.

At the far end of the Venetian, French doors lead you onto an L-shaped, brick terrace enclosed by smooth plaster walls. Vibrant bougainvillea spills from the top of a slanted wooden awning, while leafy trees, espaliered jasmine and creamy-white urns brimming with flowers transport you to a balmy Mediterranean garden. In the corner of the terrace, water cascades from a triple-tiered stone fountain, a refreshing backdrop for you and your fiancé to exchange wedding vows. An al fresco cocktail hour and reception are also divine out here, with cafe umbrellas for shade or heat lamps to ward off any chill.

An extra "wow factor" comes courtesy of the striped olive-and-white curtained cabanas along one wall, each sporting a stunning glass chandelier. These glamorous tents are ripe with event possibilities: You can showcase your wedding cake in one, your sweetheart table in the other, and a distinctive head table in the spacious center cabana. Next to the terrace, Ca' Del Sole's new bar patio is so cool that it's already a local hotspot. Also cool: There are no room charges at Ca' Del Sole, so feel free to use the event spaces for everything from your bridal shower to the most lavish gala.

Whatever type of gathering you host here, count on a chorus of satisfied "oohs" and "aahs" from your guests after their first bite of the tantalizing cuisine. The light Northern Italian fare lets classic Mediterranean flavors shine through—garlic and capers, parmesan and polenta—each dish is a feast for the senses. The fresh, imaginative creations taste like the ingredients were plucked from the sun-kissed hills of Veneto. And if there's any special food you require, just ask.

The ristorante's approach is extremely professional, yet guests are able to relax amid a joyous atmosphere. "We at Ca' Del Sole want to make everyone feel comfortable," assures co-owner Signor Costella. Your event at the "House of the Sun" will have guests so comfortable that they won't want to leave!

CEREMONY CAPACITY: The patio holds up to 15 seated guests.

EVENT/RECEPTION CAPACITY: The restaurant holds up to 150 guests seated both inside in the private dining rooms and outside on the private patio. The private patio alone accommodates 120 seated.

MEETING CAPACITY: The Gondolier Room holds up to 30 and Venetian Room holds up to 40. Combined, these rooms accommodate up to 80 seated guests.

FEES & DEPOSITS: For weddings, a $500 deposit is required to reserve your date. 50% of the estimated event total is due 2 weeks prior to the event; the balance is payable 3 days prior. Meals range $35–55/person; alcohol, tax and service charges are additional. A $300 ceremony setup fee is additional, as is a $1.50/person cake-cutting fee.

For other kinds of functions, a $300 deposit is required to reserve the date, and full payment is due on the day of the event.

AVAILABILITY: Year-round, daily, 11am–midnight.

SERVICES/AMENITIES:

Catering: in-house, no BYO
Kitchen Facilities: n/a
Tables & Chairs: provided
Linens, Silver, etc.: provided
Restrooms: wheelchair accessible
Dance Floor: provided, extra charge
Bride's & Groom's Dressing Area: no
Meeting Equipment: CBA or BYO

Parking: valet or self-parking on street
Accommodations: no guest rooms
Telephone: emergency use only
Outdoor Night Lighting: yes
Outdoor Cooking Facilities: CBA
Cleanup: provided
View: garden setting with fountain
Other: event coordination

RESTRICTIONS:

Alcohol: in-house, no BYO
Smoking: outdoors only
Music: amplified music OK indoors with volume restrictions, outdoors acoustic only

Wheelchair Access: yes
Insurance: not required

Porter Valley Country Club

Country Club

19216 Singing Hills Drive, Porter Ranch
818/360-1071 x231/232

www.portervalley.com
contactus@portervalley.com

● Rehearsal Dinners	● Corporate Events
● Ceremonies	● Meetings
● Wedding Receptions	● Film Shoots
● Private Parties	Accommodations

Nestled in the foothills of the Santa Susana Mountains, Porter Valley Country Club is a lushly land-scaped private club surrounded by green rolling hills. As you survey the property, an abundance of trees, flowers, lawns, and water features makes you feel like you're in paradise.

Weddings take place at your choice of two locations: The first is the rose garden at the west end of the clubhouse. Here, most couples exchange vows under an arbor adorned with flowers, tim-ing the ceremony to coincide with a beautiful sunset. Seating on the lawn and Clubhouse Ter-race affords guests an excellent view of the fairways as well as the nearby lake with its sparkling fountain. The second ceremony site is on the first tee overlooking the lake. This option gives the bride a more dramatic entrance, as all eyes are on her as she walks from the clubhouse down a path and up a long aisle to the elevated tee.

After the ceremony the bride and groom are welcome to pose for photographs on the greens or alongside the club's impressive arched portico with the lake in the background. At the same time, guests can get ready for the reception in the Pinehurst Room, a setting that's both classic and elegant. Painted in pale cream hues and with a wall of west-facing windows, it opens directly onto the Terrace through glass doors. English country chandeliers and handsome wooden pillars buttressing a coffered ceiling lend an air of quiet dignity. Large enough for a 36-piece band and dance floor, this room is suitable for small to midsize gatherings. Need more space? Simply pull back the Pinehurst's retractable wall and expand into the equally appealing Homestead Room, which has swimming pool and golf course views.

Porter Valley's expertise is definitely proven. Their staff has a reputation for being warm and welcoming, and they're especially adept at hosting large events. They've orchestrated hundreds of weddings, corporate functions, private parties and, of course, golf tournaments, so you know you'll be in skilled hands.

CEREMONY CAPACITY: The outdoor Terrace holds up to 300 seated guests; the Homestead Room holds 150 seated.

EVENT/RECEPTION CAPACITY: Outdoors, the Pool Area holds up to 150 seated guests. Indoors, several spaces hold 25–300 seated guests.

MEETING CAPACITY: There are 3 areas which accommodate 20–300 seated guests.

FEES & DEPOSITS: For weddings, a $2,000 nonrefundable deposit is required to secure your date. 50% of the estimated total is due 60 days prior to the event, and the balance and final guest count are due 2 weeks prior. Several wedding packages can include: hors d'oeuvres, wine and beverages, bar service, champagne toast, cake, 2-course meal, and coffee or tea. Tax and a 20% service charge are additional. Luncheon packages start at $60/person, dinner packages at $64/person; à la carte luncheons start at $27/person and dinners start at $29/person. For business functions or meetings, room rental fees vary depending on the time frame. Food and beverage services are provided; call for more specific information.

AVAILABILITY: Year-round, daily. Luncheons 11am–4pm, 11:30am–4:30pm or noon–5pm; dinners 6:30pm–11:30pm or 7pm–midnight. Additional hours are available for a nominal fee. Business functions or meetings can take place anytime; private golf tournaments can be held on Mondays.

SERVICES/AMENITIES:

Catering: in-house, no BYO
Kitchen Facilities: n/a
Tables & Chairs: Chiavari chairs provided for reception
Linens, Silver, etc.: provided
Restrooms: wheelchair accessible
Dance Floor: provided
Bride's Dressing Area: CBA
Meeting Equipment: LCD screen, VCR, TVs, flip charts, microphone, podium
Other: photo booth, coordination, flowers, vendor referrals

Parking: complimentary large lot, valet CBA, security provided
Accommodations: no guest rooms, hotels nearby
Telephone: complimentary local calls
Outdoor Night Lighting: yes
Outdoor Cooking Facilities: BBQ
Cleanup: provided
View: fairways, lake with wildlife, Santa Susana Mountains

RESTRICTIONS:

Alcohol: in-house
Smoking: outside only
Music: amplified OK with volume limits

Wheelchair Access: yes, elevator
Insurance: not required
Other: no rice, confetti, glitter, or birdseed; votive candles OK, decorations must be approved

Overwhelmed? Use the search criteria on www.HereComesTheGuide.com to narrow down your choices.

139

Hummingbird Nest

2940 Kuehner Drive, Santa Susana
805/579-8000

www.hummingbirdnestranch.com
info@hummingbirdnestranch.com

Private Estate & Garden

- Rehearsal Dinners
- Ceremonies
- Wedding Receptions
- Private Parties
- Corporate Events
- Meetings
- Film Shoots
- Accommodations

Far from the hustle and bustle of city life, the Hummingbird Nest ranch is an oasis of tranquility and beauty. Extending over 140 acres, the estate's landscape transitions from the earth tones of the Santa Susana Mountains that surround it to the vibrantly colored blooms of the native plants lining its curving roadways and lush green pastures.

There are so many things here that please the eye and inspire the soul, among them bubbling fountains, meandering pathways, hidden gazebos and spectacular mountain vistas. This is truly an extraordinary location for events ranging from weddings and formal dinners to awards ceremonies and charity balls. Corporations also find that Hummingbird's serene environment is conducive to successful meetings and seminars.

Presiding over the property at the top of a hill is the sprawling, 17,000-square-foot Spanish Colonial-style villa. Arched entryways, curved columns, tiled staircases and the prodigious use of fancy ironwork add grace and drama to the crisp white façade. At the front of the building, the main circular court with its central fountain has such a lovely view that it's often used during the ceremony as a backdrop to the bride's dramatic entrance down the front steps of the villa.

Just to the left of the main entrance, there's a wrought-iron gate that leads to a garden, complete with a natural stone waterfall and a Spanish-tiled gazebo—another favorite ceremony backdrop. To the right, a multilevel patio with fountains, iron lanterns and an array of palms offers enormous flexibility for receptions, whether large scale or more intimate. From this vantage, you can look down over the sweeping acreage to the vast Grand Prix Lawn below, which can be tented and is perfect for very large weddings, music festivals and other grand events. Hummingbird Nest's newest area is the expansive Lake Lawn. Bordering a tranquil lake, it makes a beautiful area for celebrations as well as an excellent backdrop for bridal photos.

Yet, there are still more tempting options to explore on the park-like grounds. At a recent wedding, guests had cocktails on the patio, then strolled along a paved pathway to a large open field that can easily accommodate 1,000. The bride and groom, in keeping with the pastoral surroundings, arrived by horse-drawn carriage.

For a very romantic setting that draws upon the history of the property, there's the secluded original 1920s ranch house, known as "Sitting Bull." Utterly charming, the brick-and-adobe building is shaded by century-old eucalyptus and olive trees. It features a cobblestone courtyard (where you can add a dance floor), a sizeable garden, and a sparkling pool area.

To complete the experience, extend your stay in one of several fully equipped three- to four-bedroom cottages. Hummingbird Nest Ranch takes you away from your daily routine, providing a place to relax, laugh and just let go. By the time you leave, you'll feel enriched, refreshed and looking forward to returning for future events.

CEREMONY, EVENT/RECEPTION & MEETING CAPACITY: Various locations accommodate 100–5,000 seated or standing guests outdoors.

FEES & DEPOSITS: 50% of the estimated event total is required to reserve your date and the balance is due 30 days prior to the event. Site fees start at $5,500 and the price varies depending on the date, guest count and the space rented. Security and valet parking are required. All service providers must be insured to perform services on the property.

AVAILABILITY: Year-round. The site is shown by appointment only.

SERVICES/AMENITIES:

Catering: BYO with approval
Kitchen Facilities: commercial, rented with approval
Tables & Chairs: BYO
Linens, Silver, etc.: BYO
Restrooms: wheelchair accessible in some areas
Dance Floor: BYO
Bride's & Groom's Dressing Area: yes
Meeting Equipment: BYO

Parking: valet required, extra fee
Accommodations: various guest houses have a total of 21 bedrooms
Telephone: guest phones
Outdoor Night Lighting: limited
Outdoor Cooking Facilities: no
Cleanup: caterer and renter
View: cityscape, fountain, garden, hills, lake, landscaped grounds, meadows, mountains, pool area, valley

RESTRICTIONS:

Alcohol: BYO, licensed server only
Smoking: designated outside areas only
Music: amplified OK

Wheelchair Access: limited
Insurance: liability required

Sportsmen's Lodge Events Center

Event Center

12833 Ventura Boulevard, Studio City
818/755-5000
www.sportsmenslodge.com
weddings@sportsmenslodge.com

● Rehearsal Dinners	● Corporate Events
● Ceremonies	● Meetings
● Wedding Receptions	● Film Shoots
● Private Parties	● Accommodations

The fantastic renovation of the iconic Sportsmen's Lodge Events Center, an artful blending of historic charm and updated flair, proves that the classics never go out of style.

This unique property, once a rustic playground for Hollywood's most famous players, like John Wayne, Clark Gable, Bogey & Bacall and Tracy & Hepburn, was never your typical Tinseltown watering hole. Water, however, was definitely part of its appeal. Long before the movie industry even began, travelers making the journey on dirt roads through rural San Fernando Valley would stop at this oasis, catch their own trout in the spring-fed lake and have the chef cook it up for dinner. As the valley grew and the pace quickened along Ventura Boulevard, countless visitors continued to embrace this landmark where they'd often celebrate life's memorable moments.

Devoted exclusively to special events now, the popular center is like a world unto itself. Spread out over eight acres, this enchanting retreat combines century-old trees, bucolic gardens, romantic bridges, outdoor patios and elegant interior venues with views of the legendary ponds and waterways. The sprawling Events Center building retains its familiar mid-century lodge architecture, but has been completely refreshed in sparkling white, from the large porte-cochère to the welcoming front lobby, outfitted with chic white leather seating and antique mirrored sconces.

There are two heavenly outdoor ceremony sites. The Waterfall Gazebo overlooks the south pond and provides a picture-perfect moment as the bride crosses a wrought-iron bridge to join her groom and exchange vows against a woodsy backdrop of towering eucalyptus, redwoods and Monterey pines. The expansive Garden Gazebo at the back of the property is a huge plaza, lushly landscaped on both sides. A center aisle runs between two rows of mature trees for a very dramatic entry by the bridal party. Both sites include ample room for post-ceremony toasting—especially the Garden Gazebo, where the bar faces a delightful scene of a blooming island in the nearby pond.

Options abound when it comes to reception areas. There are ten of them, ranging from a cozy fireplace room for an intimate affair to spectacular, flowing spaces, several of which can be combined. The Cascade-Starlight-Waterfalls combination is the most requested and it's easy to see why. Floor-to-ceiling windows frame a soothing tableau of fountains, a footbridge arching over a rose garden and water cascading over natural stone and moss. (Nature's white, cream and soft green tones are often repeated in the interiors.) The Starlight Ballroom adds a touch of pizzazz with a raised stage and a step-down dance floor encircled by an ornate iron railing.

If you dream of full-out glamour, then you'll love the Empire-Regency Ballroom's regal proportions, dazzling crystal-drop chandeliers, crown molding, curtained stage and built-in bar. The luxe atmosphere carries over into the adjacent Rear Lobby, an impressive grand foyer with a gracious, curving, two-story staircase—an absolute "must" for some great wedding photos.

For more than a hundred years, Sportsmen's Lodge has held a special place for generations of Angelenos. Now, updated and better than ever, its legacy continues—along with the tradition followed by many newlyweds of coming back to celebrate future anniversaries, too.

CEREMONY CAPACITY: The site features two outdoor decks in garden settings with two gazebos. The South Garden seats 150 and the North Garden seats 600.

EVENT/RECEPTION CAPACITY: The center can accommodate 800 seated indoors and 600 seated outdoors.

MEETING CAPACITY: Meeting spaces hold 1,000 seated guests.

FEES & DEPOSITS: 25% of the total event cost is required to reserve your date and the balance is due 14 days prior to the event. Wedding packages range $55–95/person. Tax and a 20% service charge are additional. They have kosher catering capabilities, and welcome outside ethnic caterers upon approval.

AVAILABILITY: Year-round, daily, 6am–midnight

SERVICES/AMENITIES:

Catering: in-house
Kitchen Facilities: n/a
Tables & Chairs: provided
Linens, Silver, etc.: provided
Restrooms: wheelchair accessible
Dance Floor: portable provided
Bride's Dressing Area: yes
Meeting Equipment: some provided
Other: spa services, AV equipment, garden ceremonies, complimentary event coordination

Parking: large lot, complimentary self-parking, valet $7/car
Accommodations: 191 guest rooms
Telephone: house phone
Outdoor Night Lighting: yes
Outdoor Cooking Facilities: no
Cleanup: provided
View: fountain, garden, lagoon, landscaped grounds, waterfall

RESTRICTIONS:

Alcohol: in-house
Smoking: outdoors only
Music: amplified OK

Wheelchair Access: yes
Insurance: required for vendors

Braemar Country Club

Country Club

4001 Reseda Boulevard, Tarzana
818/345-6520
www.braemarclub.com
contactus@braemarclub.com

● Rehearsal Dinners		● Corporate Events	
● Ceremonies		● Meetings	
● Wedding Receptions		● Film Shoots	
● Private Parties		Accommodations	

Nestled in the canyons and arroyos along the northern slopes of the Santa Monica Mountains, Braemar Country Club offers an oasis of peace away from the hustle and bustle of the city. The beautifully designed clubhouse is an elegant, modern setting for all types of events. One walks on cool, creamy marble through an open floor plan flooded with natural light. There are graceful columns along every hallway, lots of French doors, and a tiled deck that wraps around the entire structure. The pleasing architectural elements are perfectly complemented by the natural colors of the carpeting and comfortable furniture.

The venue's newest addition is the Cypress Lawn, a serene outdoor ceremony site just a short walk from the clubhouse. This secluded spot is sheltered on one side by a stand of tall cypress trees and on the other by a tree-covered hillside. Guests seated on the grass enjoy watching you exchange vows against a lovely backdrop of the rolling hills in the distance.

Open-air ceremonies are also held on the brick terrace, which works well for receptions, too. This space offers a breathtaking panoramic view of the Masters Course and San Fernando Valley. During evening celebrations, city lights glitter in the distance, and for more sparkle you may want to add candles and twinkle lights. Customized cocktail bars and buffet stations can be set up on the terrace, making it the perfect place for guests to mingle on a balmy night. The terrace is also a popular spot for al fresco rehearsal dinners. Other dining options are inside the clubhouse's Main Dining Room or poolside.

The best location for an indoor ceremony is a versatile suite of three rooms, each of which overlooks the same spectacular view available from the terrace: the emerald hills of the golf course in the foreground, the Santa Susana and San Gabriel mountains in the background. Laid out in an L-shape with floor-to-ceiling windows, the rooms can be opened up to allow for very large parties or partitioned into five separate spaces that collectively serve as ceremony site, cocktail area, and banquet hall with dance floor.

Flexibility is the name of the game here, and no matter how you orchestrate your celebration nature is always within reach.

CEREMONY CAPACITY: The Club holds 50–300 seated guests outdoors, and 50–250 seated indoors.

EVENT/RECEPTION CAPACITY: The Main Dining Room holds 200 seated or 300 standing. The entire Clubhouse holds 300 seated or 500 standing.

MEETING CAPACITY: 3 areas accommodate 10–250 seated guests.

FEES & DEPOSITS: For weddings, 25% of the estimated event total (nonrefundable) is required to hold your date. 50% is payable 60 days prior to the event; the balance and a guest count guarantee are due 10 days prior. Reception luncheons run approximately $19–30/person, dinners $35–53/person, luncheon buffets $31–34/person and dinner buffets $45/person. Hors d'oeuvres, alcohol, tax and a 20% service charge are additional. Wedding receptions are held in 5-hour blocks; overtime is $250/hour. Pricing includes the ceremony, dance floor, room rental, linens and cake cutting fee. The ceremony includes rehearsal, white folding chairs, wired microphone, and speakers.

For business functions or meetings, a nonrefundable deposit is required to hold your date. All-day meeting packages, including breakfast, lunch and afternoon snack, start at $19/person. A $50–800 cleanup/setup fee, depending on room and menu, is extra.

AVAILABILITY: Year-round, daily, in 5-hour blocks.

SERVICES/AMENITIES:

Catering: in-house, outside caterers may be permitted
Kitchen Facilities: n/a
Tables & Chairs: provided
Linens, Silver, etc.: provided
Restrooms: wheelchair accessible
Dance Floor: provided
Bride's & Groom's Dressing Area: yes
Meeting Equipment: full range

Parking: valet or self-parking
Accommodations: no guest rooms
Telephone: emergency use only
Outdoor Night Lighting: yes
Outdoor Cooking Facilities: BBQs CBA
Cleanup: provided
View: golf course, valley and distant mountains
Other: full event planning and coordination

RESTRICTIONS:

Alcohol: in-house, no BYO
Smoking: outdoors only
Music: amplified OK

Wheelchair Access: yes
Insurance: not required
Other: no rice or birdseed outdoors

Sheraton Universal

Hotel

333 Universal Hollywood Drive, Universal City
818/509-2726 Catering Department

www.sheratonuniversal.com
sciccarelli@sheratonuniversal.com

- Rehearsal Dinners
- Ceremonies
- Wedding Receptions
- Private Parties
- Corporate Events
- Meetings
- Film Shoots
- Accommodations

A gleaming tower that rises up from the back lot of famed Universal Studios Hollywood, the Sheraton Universal has provided a swank place to stay for an impressive roster of actors and actresses. Celebrity patrons have earned it the nickname "The Hotel of the Stars," and a similar moniker could be applied to its most spectacular wedding spot—the Starview Room on the 21st floor. In this case, however, "The Wedding Site of the Stars" derives its sparkle not from Hollywood's brightest, but from the heavenly bodies glittering in the night sky.

A botanical haven, the Starview Room is a glassed-in aerie with wraparound views of the Hollywood Hills and the San Fernando Valley as far as the eye can see. At night, twinkling lights in the ceiling compete with the great L.A. Basin light show.

If a sky-high perch isn't what you had in mind, the first floor offers a series of handsome banquet facilities, starting with the Grand Ballroom. It features rich woodwork, beveled mirrors, sparkling chandeliers, and carpeting in subdued shades of taupe and ocean blue. The Ballroom's foyer—aptly named the Great Hall—is a terrific prefunction space, with six crystal chandeliers and floor-to-ceiling windows framed in flowing, sheer white fabric. They overlook a garden ringed with magnolia trees. You can tie the knot in the Grand Ballroom, although some couples prefer to have their ceremony outside in the garden.

There are several other spacious banquet rooms, all with a similarly refined décor. And for a small wedding, you might want to reserve the Terrace Room, which opens onto a terracotta patio next to the pool.

The Sheraton Universal offers a full range of gourmet menus that can be customized for each client—and it's one of the few event sites in L.A. that can provide glatt kosher catering. As we discovered, there's a great deal of choice and flexibility here, and this is one place where the sky is, quite literally, the limit.

CEREMONY CAPACITY: The Starview Room seats 300 guests indoors and the Ballroom Garden seats 500 outdoors.

EVENT/RECEPTION CAPACITY: Indoor spaces accomodate 150–850 seated or 250–1,200 standing. Outdoors, the site holds up to 500 seated or 600 standing.

MEETING CAPACITY: 3 areas accommodate 150–1,200 seated guests.

FEES & DEPOSITS: For weddings, a $4,500 nonrefundable deposit is payable within 10 days of your receipt of the contract. The guest count guarantee and the balance of all estimated charges are due 4 days before the event. Each event is customized; reception luncheons start at $35/person, dinners at $45/person. For functions in the Starview Room, an additional $3/person charge is added to meal prices; $5/person is added for Saturday evening affairs. Alcohol, tax and a 21% service charge are additional. For ceremonies, there is a $1,000 charge.

For business functions and meetings, rental fees vary depending on room(s) and services selected, guest count and time frame; call for more specific information.

AVAILABILITY: Year-round, daily. Meetings take place 8am–5pm; weddings are held noon–4pm or 6:30pm–12:30am.

SERVICES/AMENITIES:

Catering: in-house, no BYO
Kitchen Facilities: n/a
Tables & Chairs: provided
Linens, Silver, etc.: provided
Restrooms: wheelchair accessible
Dance Floor: provided
Bride's & Groom's Dressing Area: yes
Meeting Equipment: full range, in-house audiovisual company
Other: event coordination

Parking: self-parking or valet, extra charge
Accommodations: 442 guest rooms
Telephone: none
Outdoor Night Lighting: yes
Outdoor Cooking Facilities: no
Cleanup: provided
View: city view from Starview Room, San Fernando Valley skyline, Hollywood Hills skyline
Kosher: glatt kosher kitchen

RESTRICTIONS:

Alcohol: in-house, no BYO
Smoking: outside only
Music: amplified OK indoors

Wheelchair Access: yes
Insurance: liability required

The professionals in the back of this book are the best in the business. How do we know? Read page 549.

147

Woodland Hills Country Club

Golf Course

21150 Dumetz Road, Woodland Hills
818/347-1511
www.woodlandhillscc.org
rebecca@woodlandhillscc.org

● Rehearsal Dinners	● Corporate Events
● Ceremonies	● Meetings
● Wedding Receptions	● Film Shoots
● Private Parties	Accommodations

In the early 1920s, Victor Girard saw the hills and open land of the west San Fernando Valley and decided to develop his dream city there. A showman to the core, he wanted something extra to lure homeowners so he imported 120,000 trees and built a golf course and clubhouse. Although his grand city vision was never realized, the trees and clubhouse remain: The former shade the streets of what is now Woodland Hills, and the latter has evolved into the Woodland Hills Country Club, a beautiful wedding site offering some of the best panoramic views in the valley.

Drive through the iron gates and up the long curved road and you'll immediately see Girard's legacy: towering, mature Eucalyptus trees giving way to tantalizing peeks of the golf course. At the top of the hill sits the clubhouse (rebuilt three times since the 1920s) with a prominent porte-cochère covered in climbing vines and surrounded by flowering shrubs. There are flowers and greenery everywhere, and since all plants throughout the property are replaced seasonally, there will always be fresh, colorful blooms to greet you.

Directly across from the clubhouse is the peaceful Ceremony Garden. Its expansive lawn overlooking the 18th green features a magnificent wrought-iron gazebo, as well as a raised concrete area that's perfect for a small musical ensemble or whatever you choose to personalize and enhance your event. A grove of oak, pepper and eucalyptus trees runs the length of the garden, providing shade from the afternoon sun. If you'd like, you can hold an al fresco cocktail reception for 300 people here, or move inside to one of several venues.

The Main Lobby and adjoining Trophy Hall, displaying 80 years of the club's history, can be staged with chairs and couches for a cocktail lounge effect. Afterwards, your guests will be welcomed to the Terrace Ballroom for your main reception. This spacious banquet area has a built-in dance floor and raised stage for your band, DJ or cake table display. Decorated in muted, neutral tones, the room boasts a marble-topped bar where friends and family can mingle for conversation, as well as a small back patio with red roses, overlooking the putting green and surrounding hills.

If you're planning a more intimate affair, the Sunset Room on the opposite side of the clubhouse is a little gem. A warmly inviting spot with a wall of natural stone and floor-to-ceiling windows, it's ideal for a rehearsal dinner. It can also be used as a cocktail and/or dance area for the larger, adjacent Oak Room, replete with oak-beamed ceilings and breathtaking views. Just outside is the wraparound Back Terrace, a very popular location for enjoying those fabulous vistas that extend all the way to Warner Center.

Myriad photo opportunities take advantage of the views and scenic backdrops from the terraces, or you can arrange to pose beside picturesque sites on the fairways, like a stone bridge, waterfall or pond floated with lily pads.

There are many options available in planning your celebration here, and the staff takes pride in helping each bride determine her ideal wedding—and stay within her budget. After all, this was a location built on dreams.

CEREMONY CAPACITY: The site holds 160 seated guests indoors and 300 seated outdoors.

EVENT/RECEPTION CAPACITY: The facility accommodates 250 seated or 325 standing guests indoors and 300 seated or 400 standing outdoors.

MEETING CAPACITY: Meeting spaces hold up to 325 seated guests.

FEES & DEPOSITS: A deposit of $2,000 is required to reserve your date and the balance is due 7 days prior to the event. Wedding packages range $45–114/person, and may include the room rental, meals, liquor and linen (depending on which package is chosen). Tax and a service charge are additional.

AVAILABILITY: Year-round, daily.

SERVICES/AMENITIES:

Catering: in-house
Kitchen Facilities: n/a
Tables & Chairs: provided
Linens, Silver, etc.: provided
Restrooms: wheelchair accessible
Dance Floor: provided
Bride's Dressing Area: yes
Meeting Equipment: some provided, more CBA
Other: coordination, grand piano, in-house florals, AV equipment

Parking: large lot
Accommodations: no guest rooms
Telephone: house phone
Outdoor Night Lighting: CBA
Outdoor Cooking Facilities: BBQ CBA
Cleanup: provided
View: garden patio; panorama of mountains, valley, cityscape, hills and fairways; fountain, landscaped grounds

RESTRICTIONS:

Alcohol: in-house
Smoking: outdoors only
Music: amplified OK

Wheelchair Access: yes
Insurance: not required

Santa Catalina Island

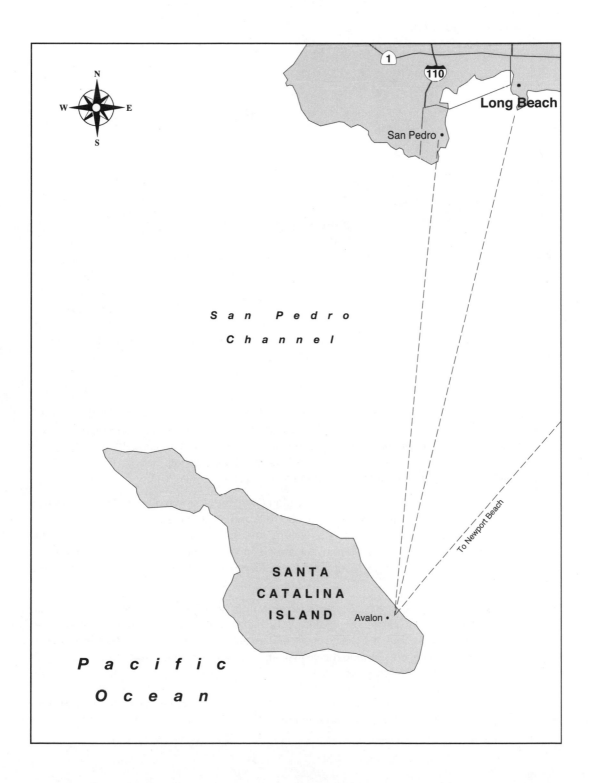

Casino Ballroom
A Santa Catalina Island Company Wedding Venue

1 Casino Way, Avalon
310/510-7400 x1208 Sales

www.visitcatalinaisland.com
dstevenson@scico.com

Waterfront Ballroom

- Rehearsal Dinners
- Ceremonies
- Wedding Receptions
- Private Parties
- Corporate Events
- Meetings
- Film Shoots
- Accommodations

"…Twenty-six miles across the sea, Santa Catalina is waitin' for me…"

This once exclusive isle still beckons those in search of "fun in the sun" in a tranquil setting free of pollution, skyscrapers, and yes, cars (golf carts are the vehicle of choice here). Make your destination wedding an extended vacation by inviting your friends and family to celebrate amidst this island paradise, just over an hour from the mainland by express boat. The staff at the fabulous Santa Catalina Island Company will gladly help you arrange everything, including transportation, tours, golf, accommodations, dining and, of course, all the event details. They'll even help you select the wedding site that's right for you!

Catalina Island's most famous venue is the Casino Ballroom, a grand, Art Deco landmark built in 1929. The Casino Ballroom wasn't actually a gambling house, but rather a spectacular dance pavilion that attracted thousands of well-dressed socialites from the mainland. Today the aura of elegance still lingers around this historic treasure, and its glamorous legacy is carried on by 21st-century event hosts seeking the maximum amount of panache.

Located on a rocky harbor break at the edge of Avalon Cove, the Casino is a huge, 12-story circular building. The forum-like structure boasts a red-tile roof and an impressive triple-arched portico. Above the entryway a tiled mural portrays a fetching underwater sea sylph who welcomes light-hearted revelers inside. Downstairs, flamboyant murals in vibrant hues decorate the walls of the Casino's sumptuous movie theater, where visitors can still enjoy nightly cinematic diversions while relaxing in red-velvet seats.

However, you and your guests are headed up to the top floor, to a simply enormous ballroom that is the Casino's crowning glory. Recently repainted, the ballroom retains its original style—a lavish medley of rose-hued walls, black Art Deco reliefs, and an arching 50-foot ceiling. No less than five resplendent Tiffany chandeliers illumine the crowd, and curving windows capture postcard views of the aqua sea. The ballroom is so spacious that you can set up an altar and theater-style seating for a wedding ceremony in one area, then host a sit-down reception on raised seating areas that surround the dance floor. A vintage full-service bar in the back serves up refreshments, and an elevated stage is just the spot for the entertainment.

An outdoor veranda encircles the ballroom and overlooks the protected coves of Avalon Bay; from here the fabulous view of the mainland sometimes stretches all the way from Ventura to San Diego. In the twilight it's still possible to see seals, dolphins and brightly colored fish splashing about in the clear waters of the cove. At night the scenery takes on an air of dreamy mystery, with an endless starscape sparkling in the surf.

The Santa Catalina Island Company has two more outstanding and very different event venues: The Descanso Beach Club is great for a casual outdoor party or relaxed rehearsal dinner, while the Catalina Country Club exudes Old World charm and sophistication. For more details on all three locations, please visit the Santa Catalina Island Company website.

CEREMONY CAPACITY: The Ballroom accommodates up to 250 seated guests.

EVENT/RECEPTION & MEETING CAPACITY: The Ballroom holds up to 650 seated or 1,200 standing guests; the balcony up to 25 seated or 100 standing guests.

FEES & DEPOSITS: Venue rental is required to reserve your date. The balance is due 1 month prior to the event. Rental fees range $3,000–5,000 depending on the space rented and guest count. Meals range $45–75/person. Tax, alcohol and a 20% service charge are additional.

AVAILABILITY: Year-round, daily, anytime.

SERVICES/AMENITIES:

Catering: in-house, no BYO
Kitchen Facilities: n/a
Tables & Chairs: provided
Linens, Silver, etc.: some provided
Restrooms: wheelchair accessible
Dance Floor: provided
Bride's Dressing Area: CBA
Meeting Equipment: some provided
Other: AV equipment

Parking: on street, limited
Accommodations: 2 Santa Catalina Island Company hotels and other local options
Telephone: pay phone
Outdoor Night Lighting: access only
Outdoor Cooking Facilities: no
Cleanup: provided
View: Pacific Ocean, bay, coast, hills

RESTRICTIONS:

Alcohol: in-house or BYO with corkage fee
Smoking: outside only
Music: amplified OK indoors with restrictions

Wheelchair Access: yes
Insurance: liability required

Descanso Beach Club
A Santa Catalina Island Company Wedding Venue

1 Descanso Canyon Road, Avalon
310/510-7400 X1208 Sales

www.visitcatalinaisland.com
dstevenson@scico.com

Beach Club

● Rehearsal Dinners	● Corporate Events
● Ceremonies	● Meetings
● Wedding Receptions	● Film Shoots
● Private Parties	Accommodations

If your wedding fantasy involves sipping mai tais on the beach under the California sun, then come to the Descanso Beach Club, a little slice of paradise on Catalina Island. This idyllic haven is less than an hour from the mainland by ferry or private boat; visitors disembark in Avalon, which is more laid-back beach town than tourist metropolis—there are no cars, no malls, and not one single billboard! A scenic ten-minute stroll along the shore takes you past the historic Catalina Casino and on to Descanso Beach, a peaceful curve of shoreline that the club calls home.

With such a sublime locale, it's no surprise that this venue is a favorite of locals and tourists alike. Beachfront weddings are popular on the club's Terraced Lawn, a series of four spacious grass plateaus sloping down towards the water's edge. Ceremonies are held on the lower terrace: Tiki torches and ribbons mark the aisle, and couples say their vows against the backdrop of the azure ocean. Receptions take place on the upper terraces, which offer the same wonderful view of the beach and the sea, complete with yachts bobbing on the water and the landmark Catalina Casino just up the coastline.

Though weddings are traditionally evening events, luncheon receptions take best advantage of the club's views and refreshing atmosphere. Sailboats lean into the wind, sea birds feed in the ebbing tide, and the balmy weather ensures sunny dispositions. You're surrounded by lush greenery and slender palms, whose languorous fronds sway in the warm breeze. With the boundless Pacific Ocean stretching out in front of you, the urban hustle and bustle feels a million miles away. Some people liken the setting to the picturesque coves of the French Riviera, while for others it's reminiscent of the Big Island. Why not let your imagination run wild, and enhance the natural elements with your own creative touches? Decorate the stage with exotic potted plants and sheer, jewel-toned panels; or string Chinese lanterns across the stage, and give each guest a mutlicolored parasol. Tables topped with linen umbrellas provide a crisp café-style look; or dress the tables with upscale linens and luminarias for a sophisticated soirée.

Whatever you envision, the club's event pros are eager to help; they've got the scoop on local vendors, as well as lodging and transportation. They've also got you covered when it comes to culinary matters, offering a variety of banquet menus created by their in-house, world-class chefs. And if you don't see what you want, just ask! The most requested bill of fare is the Descanso Luau Buffet, with such tropical taste treats as "Kahlua Pig Smoked in Hawaiian Ti Leaves" and "Macadamia-Crusted Mahi Mahi with Coconut-Scented Rice."

One more benefit of a destination wedding on Catalina: You and your family and friends are in such close proximity for the weekend that you end up spending quality time with each other … and since everyone is in a vacation state of mind, the mood is relaxed and lighthearted. By celebrating at the Descanso Beach Club, you're inviting your guests to share a true Catalina experience.

CEREMONY CAPACITY: The Terraced Lawn area holds 120 seated guests.

EVENT/RECEPTION CAPACITY: The Terraced Lawn area holds 200 seated or 300 standing guests.

MEETING CAPACITY: Meeting spaces seat up to 120 guests.

FEES & DEPOSITS: The venue rental fee is required to reserve your date. The balance is due 1 month prior to the event. Rental fees start at $3,000 and vary depending on the season and the space rented. Meals range $45–75/person. Tax, alcohol and a 20% service charge are additional.

AVAILABILITY: May–October, daily, noon–11pm.

SERVICES/AMENITIES:

Catering: in-house, no BYO
Kitchen Facilities: n/a
Tables & Chairs: provided
Linens, Silver, etc.: provided
Restrooms: wheelchair accessible
Dance Floor: provided
Bride's Dressing Area: CBA
Meeting Equipment: no
Other: AV equipment

Parking: large lot
Accommodations: 2 Santa Catalina Island Company hotels and other local options
Telephone: pay phone
Outdoor Night Lighting: CBA
Outdoor Cooking Facilities: BBQ
Cleanup: provided
View: panoramic view of ocean and coastline

RESTRICTIONS:

Alcohol: in-house or BYO with corkage fee
Smoking: outdoors only
Music: amplified OK outdoors with restrictions

Wheelchair Access: limited
Insurance: liability required

Los Angeles Area

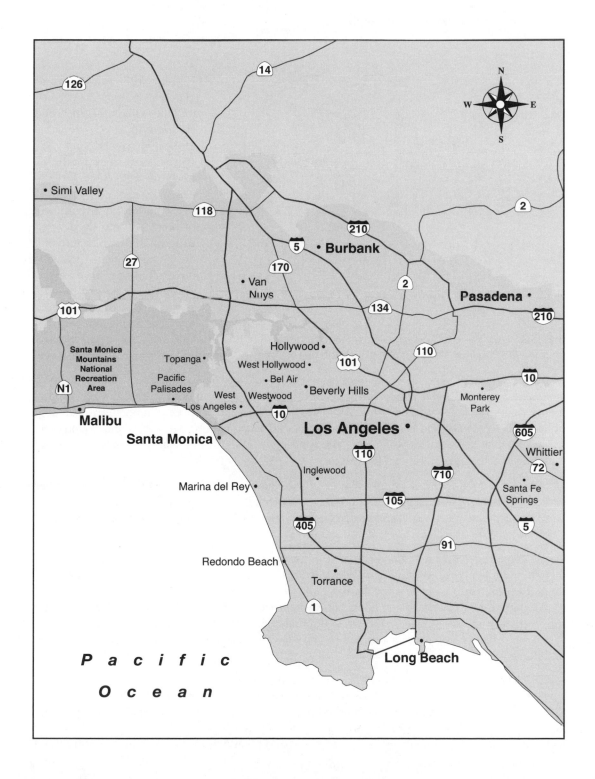

Lawry's The Prime Rib

Restaurant

100 N. La Cienega Boulevard, Beverly Hills
310/360-6281 x4
www.lawrysonline.com/lawrys-primerib/beverly-hills
efremaux@lawrysonline.com

- Rehearsal Dinners
- Ceremonies
- Wedding Receptions
- Private Parties
- Corporate Events
- Meetings
- Film Shoots
- Accommodations

Not far from the glitz and glamour of Hollywood you'll find the other red carpet: one steeped in seven decades of Los Angeles history, rich British/American culinary tradition and Beverly Hills elegance. Lawry's The Prime Rib combines the comforts of home—if you lived in an expansive English estate along the Thames—with a sumptuous dining experience executed flawlessly by professional servers who treat you like royalty. And if you're worried that this venue's famed Restaurant Row location or opulent English Edwardian décor puts it out of your league, don't be—Lawry's The Prime Rib provides classic sophistication with Old World prices.

Step inside the foyer and the contemporary world fades away into a timeless, softly lit realm of amenable luxury. Tasteful period furniture in the cocktail room and adjacent bar area complements wainscoted, jewel-toned walls. Antique chandeliers and sconces illuminate eye-catching polished silver pieces and gold-framed paintings of English nobles, dignitaries and countryside scenes. Despite its formal accoutrements, the atmosphere is warm and relaxed—perfect for guests mingling over hors d'oeuvres while awaiting your arrival.

Double doors open to reveal a step-down into the brilliant, emerald-colored Oak Room, a popular choice for smaller celebrations. Here, a bust of the Duke of Wellington and a bas-relief of William Shakespeare adorn the fireplace mantel, while the mixed-shade parquet flooring highlights a colorful coat of arms.

Larger ceremonies and receptions are held in the spacious main dining room, where a pair of majestic wooden lions evocative of regal courtyards presides over your grand entrance. An uplit, domed ceiling casts a subtle glow on the dark wooden columns and beveled glass, lending a festive nighttime ambiance at any hour. The sweetheart table is housed in the "garden," a central space that features a sweeping hand-painted mural overhead. The adjacent Vintage Room, a private wine cellar, can be used as a bride's room or for rehearsal dinners and post-reception family traditions, including tea ceremonies.

Lawry's The Prime Rib's reputation for great food has stood the test of time. One of the oldest single-family-owned restaurants in Los Angeles, it has served its signature British-style dinner of slow-roasted Midwestern prime beef, mashed potatoes and Yorkshire pudding alongside flavorful gravy, horseradish, and its original seasoning salt since 1938. The almost-theatrical tableside service includes spinning salad prepared on a bed of ice and a carving of the roast from a 500-pound silver cart inspired by London's famous Simpsons-in-the-Strand restaurant. The meal finishes with a selection of traditional British and American desserts, including an ice cream sundae made with C.C. Brown's hot fudge sauce, a secret recipe bought by the Lawry family from Hollywood's most legendary but now-defunct ice cream parlor.

From their family to yours, Lawry's The Prime Rib serves up the most authentic Anglo-British (and award-winning) culinary experience this side of the pond, lending its cherished traditions to your celebration.

CEREMONY CAPACITY: The restaurant can accommodate 250 seated guests indoors.

EVENT/RECEPTION & MEETING CAPACITY: The restaurant holds 450 seated or standing guests indoors.

FEES & DEPOSITS: 20% of the total event cost is required to reserve your date and the balance is due the day of the event. There is a ceremony fee of $350. Meals range $47–62/person. Tax, alcohol and a 20% service charge are additional.

AVAILABILITY: Year-round, daily, 4pm–11pm, except Christmas. Luncheon hours are Monday–Friday 7am–4pm, Saturday 7am–3:30pm and Sunday 7am–3pm. Off-Site Catering: any hours except December 25th.

SERVICES/AMENITIES:

Catering: in-house
Kitchen Facilities: n/a
Tables & Chairs: provided
Linens, Silver, etc.: provided
Restrooms: wheelchair accessible
Dance Floor: provided
Bride's Dressing Area: yes
Meeting Equipment: provided

Parking: large lot, valet required
Accommodations: no guest rooms
Telephone: emergency use only
Outdoor Night Lighting: CBA
Outdoor Cooking Facilities: no
Cleanup: provided
View: no
Other: clergy on staff, AV equipment, event coordination

RESTRICTIONS:

Alcohol: in-house
Smoking: not allowed
Music: amplified OK indoors

Wheelchair Access: yes
Insurance: not required

Want to know WHAT TO ASK a potential location or vendor? Check out our Questions to Ask starting on page 19.

Hollywood Hotel®

Hotel

1160 North Vermont Avenue, Hollywood
310/701-8828

www.hollywoodhotel.net
mandy@hollywoodhotel.net

- Rehearsal Dinners
- Ceremonies
- Wedding Receptions
- Private Parties
- Corporate Events
- Meetings
- Film Shoots
- Accommodations

For decades untold numbers of people have been flocking to Hollywood to make their dreams come true. Today, as old Tinseltown glamour mixes with an *au courant* edge, the city that's always reinventing itself is experiencing a renaissance. And the Hollywood Hotel, undergoing its own metamorphosis after a $2 million renovation, offers a quiet haven at the nexus of trendy Los Feliz and pricey Beachwood Canyon.

From Vermont Avenue, a main thoroughfare buzzing with hip energy and restoration activity, enter the hotel's cool pink-and-peach lobby with its decorative Art Deco fountain.

The hotel is built around a central courtyard, which serves as the site for wedding ceremonies held here. While you and your bridal party get ready in your complimentary wedding night suite (equipped with Jacuzzi), your guests will be shown to the rectangular open-air space. A large stone fountain greets them as they find their seats on either side of the long aisle. Towards the front of the courtyard, a three-tiered flagstone platform forms a natural altar where you and your groom will exchange vows. (Don't be surprised if you have more admiring well-wishers than you expected, since this space is surrounded by the iron-railed balconies of the guest rooms above.)

Once you've tied the knot, you and your guests will be ushered back inside where you can take the lobby elevator down one level to the newly refurbished restaurant and event facility. Soft lighting, rich cherrywood and opaque glass sconces set a tone of Italianesque luxury. This feeling is enhanced by the marble floors and Venetian glass chandeliers, elements that reveal the care that went into the hotel's redesign. Your cocktail reception can be set up in the foyer on your right, with its artfully inlaid marble floor bordered with custom mosaics. Pinkish peach faux-finish walls enhance the décor.

Curved archways lead down a wainscoted hall with several sets of double doors opening into the Main Ballroom. Lush green and gold carpeting is the perfect counterpoint to the unique and dramatic ceiling design, a series of white shadowboxes that resemble wooden window frames. Peeking through from above are hand-painted clouds against a blue background, designed by the very same artist who did The Venetian Hotel in Las Vegas. As your eye is drawn upward, it's as if you're looking at the sky, which gives the room a nice, airy ambiance. Once the music starts, however, you'll probably be looking down, since the illuminated wooden dance floor has lights that flicker and pulse to the beat of each song.

The hotel, which hosts wedding celebrations for virtually every ethnic group in Los Angeles, handles all catering, but will allow you to bring in your own ethnic specialty foods to make your guests feel at home. And to make them feel even more comfortable, they offer a special price that includes a complimentary breakfast with overnight accommodations. The Hollywood Hotel can't make your dreams of movie stardom come true, but it can certainly set the stage for a terrific wedding day.

CEREMONY CAPACITY: The Courtyard holds 150 seated guests, the Main Ballroom 250.

EVENT/RECEPTION CAPACITY: Indoors, Main Ballroom accommodates up to 250 guests, seated or standing without a dance floor. The Courtyard holds 100 seated or 200 standing guests.

MEETING CAPACITY: Spaces hold up to 250 guests seated theater-style.

FEES & DEPOSITS: A $1,000 minimum deposit is required to reserve your date. The balance is due 30 days prior to the event. Rental fees range $500–10,000 depending on space rented, the day and time of the event and guest count. If you use the on-site caterer, meals range $20–200/person. Tax, alcohol, and a 19% service charge are additional.

AVAILABILITY: Year-round, daily, anytime.

SERVICES/AMENITIES:

Catering: in-house, select from list or BYO
Kitchen Facilities: fully equipped
Tables & Chairs: provided
Linens, Silver, etc.: provided
Restrooms: wheelchair accessible
Dance Floor: provided
Bride's Dressing Area: yes
Meeting Equipment: some provided, more CBA

Parking: large lot, valet required
Accommodations: 127 guest rooms
Telephone: pay, house and office phones
Outdoor Night Lighting: yes
Outdoor Cooking Facilities: CBA
Cleanup: provided
View: garden patio
Other: event coordination, grand piano, AV equipment

RESTRICTIONS:

Alcohol: in-house or BYO with corkage fee
Smoking: outside only
Music: amplified OK indoors and outdoors with restrictions

Wheelchair Access: yes
Insurance: liability required if using off-site caterer

Taglyan Cultural Complex

Cultural Center

1201 North Vine Street, Hollywood
323/978-0005
www.taglyancomplex.com
info@taglyancomplex.com

● Rehearsal Dinners	● Corporate Events
● Ceremonies	● Meetings
● Wedding Receptions	● Film Shoots
● Private Parties	Accommodations

Opened to great fanfare in 2008, the Taglyan Arts and Cultural Complex offers a dazzling combination of Old World opulence and cutting-edge audiovisual technology. Located mere blocks from the world-famous intersection of Hollywood and Vine, this venue may be new to the event scene, but with its stately limestone façade it looks like it's been part of the neighborhood for years.

As soon as you enter the massive iron gates on a quiet side street, you feel like you've been transported to a European villa. Italian cypress, magnolia and olive trees, along with vintage-look streetlamps, dot the property. Immediately on your right is the formal brick courtyard, anchored by the kind of huge two-tiered fountain you might find in an Italian piazza, complete with figural fish and turtles spouting water. A formal garden containing white roses encircles the fountain, creating a very romantic spot for wedding ceremonies. As an added enhancement, the historic French Normandy-style building across the street acts as a charming backdrop. Taglyan's upper patio, which could serve as an alternate ceremony site or for cocktails, overlooks the courtyard and has its own cherub fountain with two small gardens and marble pillars.

Inside the building itself, it's obvious that no expense has been spared in workmanship or materials. The dramatic Grand Foyer is a feast for the eyes, highlighted by an Italian marble floor inlaid with various patterns—the first one symbolizing eternity, which seems rather fitting for couples who've just exchanged vows. This palatial-sized space has natural light streaming in through tall windows draped in rich green velvet, as well as filtering in through stained-glass inserts in the high, coffered ceiling. Along one wall you can set up couches in front of faux fireplaces, creating a cozy area for small-group mingling. Another option for intimate conversation is the outdoor flagstone patio, which makes a perfect bar and lounge setting.

But the *pièce de résistance* is the Main Ballroom—truly a "grand" ballroom. Set off by green marble pillars and elaborate, cascading crystal chandeliers, its 5,000-square-foot, circular stained-glass ceiling is flat-out, jaw-droppingly beautiful. And as if its artistry alone wasn't mesmerizing enough, it can even be programmed to shift colors with an elaborate lighting system. In fact, the entire facility incorporates state-of-the-art audiovisual equipment, including scrims and projectors with screens that descend around the room so you can screen personal movies, then take it up a notch by bathing the stage and dance floor in sound and light.

Taglyan Complex has devoted just as much attention to every detail behind the scenes as well, from its two top-of-the-line kitchens to the ample underground parking and luxurious bridal room (and large groom's room). Their exclusive in-house caterer, *Divine Food & Catering,* will customize your menu whether you desire a multicultural meal, Continental fare, or something in between. When you're here, all you have to do is relax, revel in your surroundings and get ready for a very memorable event.

CEREMONY CAPACITY: The Complex holds 300 seated guests indoors and 200 seated outdoors.

EVENT/RECEPTION CAPACITY: The site accommodates 600 seated or 1,000 standing guests indoors and 150 seated or 400 standing outdoors.

MEETING CAPACITY: Meeting rooms hold up to 25 seated guests.

FEES & DEPOSITS: A $5,000 minimum deposit is required to reserve your date. The balance is due 7 days prior to the event. Packages that include venue rental, furniture, linens, and in-house catering start at $115/person. Tax, alcohol and an 18% service charge are additional. A $25,000 minimum is required for a Friday or Sunday event, and a $40,000 minimum for a Saturday event.

AVAILABILITY: Year-round, daily, Sunday–Thursday 9am–5pm and 5pm–11pm; Friday and Saturday 9am–3pm and 6pm–midnight.

SERVICES/AMENITIES:
Catering: in-house or BYO
Kitchen Facilities: fully equipped
Tables & Chairs: provided
Linens, Silver, etc.: provided
Restrooms: wheelchair accessible
Dance Floor: portable provided
Bride's Dressing Area: yes
Meeting Equipment: provided

Parking: large lot, valet required
Accommodations: no guest rooms
Telephone: house phone
Outdoor Night Lighting: yes
Outdoor Cooking Facilities: BBQ CBA
Cleanup: provided
View: garden courtyard, landscaped grounds
Other: coordination, in-house wedding cake and florals, clergy on staff, AV equipment

RESTRICTIONS:
Alcohol: BYO
Smoking: in designated areas only
Music: amplified OK with restrictions

Wheelchair Access: yes
Insurance: not required

Chester Washington Golf Course

Golf Club

1930 West 120th Street, Los Angeles
888/227-5795
www.countryclubreceptions.com
privateeventmanager@chesterwashingtongc.com

- Rehearsal Dinners
- Ceremonies
- Wedding Receptions
- Private Parties
- Corporate Events
- Meetings
- Film Shoots
- Accommodations

Chester Washington Golf Course offers amenities you won't find at most big L.A. hotels: a beautiful outdoor ceremony site, a banquet room with verdant views and plenty of natural light, great rates and ample free parking.

Ceremonies take place in the gazebo, against a backdrop of rolling green hills and mature trees. Afterwards, cocktails and hors d'oeuvres are served on the clubhouse patio, just off the bar/lounge. The congenial lounge is a far cry from the stuffy, dark bars you find at some golf clubs. There's an oak bar and tall, floor-to-ceiling windows inset with doors that open to the patio, permitting your event to flow seamlessly indoors and out.

You also have exclusive use of the foyer when you celebrate here. This space connects to both the bar and the banquet room, so in addition to being a handy location for place card and gift tables it can host your cocktail reception if the weather doesn't cooperate.

The banquet room's recent remodel accentuates its natural assets: a high ceiling and tall windows on three sides, all of which create a light and airy ambiance. On one side, floor-to-ceiling windows and sliding glass doors form a long curved wall overlooking manicured lawns, lofty eucalyptus trees, and pines. Cream-colored walls, amber wood wainscoting, chandeliers with diminutive silk shades, and a built-in parquet dance floor make the space even more inviting. Since nothing about the décor is heavy handed, you can dress it up any way you want. With its clean, crisp look, this room is handsome enough that you don't need to be a set designer to make it look good.

In addition to its appealing event spaces, the venue has a rich history. Back in 1928 when it was built, this part of L.A. was just fields of corn and beans. Later this facility would become one of the most important courses available to African-American golfers in the United States. Not only did a number of the great African-American golf players of the era make this course their home base, other famous African-Americans could be found swinging their clubs here too, like heavyweight champion Joe Louis and baseball great Jackie Robinson.

In 1982, the course was renamed to honor one of its habitués: award-winning African-American journalist Chester Washington. Today the players at Chester Washington Golf Course are as ethnically diverse as the surrounding neighborhoods. Golf lovers and history buffs may have a special connection to this place, but you don't have to be either to appreciate this lovely spot, which scores high in our book.

CEREMONY CAPACITY: The ceremony site holds up to 300 seated guests, indoors or outdoors.

EVENT/RECEPTION & MEETING CAPACITY: Indoor spaces hold up to 300 seated or 350 standing guests.

FEES & DEPOSITS: A nonrefundable deposit, which is applied to your food and beverage total, is required to reserve your date. The amount of the deposit varies, depending on how far in advance you book. Payment terms for the balance also vary, and may be arranged on an individual basis. Meals start at $25/person. Tax, alcohol and service charge are additional. Menus and packages can be customized to fit your needs and budget. Call for details.

AVAILABILITY: Year-round, daily, 8am–1am.

SERVICES/AMENITIES:

Catering: in-house, no BYO

Kitchen Facilities: n/a

Tables & Chairs: provided

Linens, Silver, etc.: provided

Restrooms: wheelchair accessible

Dance Floor: yes

Bride's Dressing Area: CBA

Meeting Equipment: CBA, extra charge

Parking: large lot

Accommodations: no guest rooms

Telephone: emergency use only

Outdoor Night Lighting: CBA

Outdoor Cooking Facilities: no

Cleanup: provided

View: fairways, garden, landscaped grounds

RESTRICTIONS:

Alcohol: in-house

Smoking: outside only

Music: amplified OK

Wheelchair Access: yes

Insurance: not required

City Club Los Angeles

Private Club

555 Flower Street, 51st Floor, Los Angeles
213/620-9662

www.cityclubla.com
contactus@icityclubla.com

- Rehearsal Dinners
- Ceremonies
- Wedding Receptions
- Private Parties

- Corporate Events
- Meetings

Film Shoots

Accommodations

One look is worth a thousand words, so if you're planning a wedding or special event in Los Angeles you definitely want to check out this stylish, new 51st-floor venue that delivers jaw-dropping views of city and coastline.

After 25 years on Bunker Hill and a multimillion-dollar reinvention, the City Club Los Angeles has relocated to the Gold LEED Certified City National Plaza Tower situated in the heart of L.A.'s thriving central business district. Your guests will love exploring this area, which is home to the fabulous Staples Center and the L.A. Live entertainment complex with its glamorous theaters, restaurants and hotels.

Step into the City Club itself and you enter a world of privacy and exclusivity—one where all of the spaces reflect a unique interpretation of Los Angeles' diverse districts. Elevators whisk guests up to the dramatic lobby, whose chic furnishings, art, and 3-D jewel-toned wall convey the spirit of the Jewelry District.

The spectacular Angeles Ballroom is truly a room with a view: 280 degrees of top-of-the-world vistas through its floor-to-ceiling windows. Chandeliers that look like delicate clusters of stars drop from the beautiful white, coffered ceiling. The room's brilliant mélange of posh and trendsetting touches, no doubt inspired by the nearby Fashion District, includes luxurious champagne and icy-blue colorations, as well as striking wall and carpet designs whose intersecting lines and angles suggest the freeway system that crisscrosses L.A.

If you use the entire ballroom, its vast dimensions make it ideal for ultra-grand functions with multiple bars, stages, dining areas and dance floors, but it also breaks into three more intimate chambers, each overlooking the tower's picturesque surround. The Santa Monica Room, Harbor Room and Hollywood Ballroom can be used individually or in combination to create varying environments for your function. You might start by exchanging vows in the Harbor Room with its Pacific or sunset views, and then progress to the Hollywood Ballroom and Santa Monica Room for cocktails and/or dining enhanced by the gorgeous nighttime cityscape glittering all around you. State-of-the-art lighting and audiovisual systems let you fine-tune each room's ambiance at the touch of a button (think colored LED and GOBO lights).

If you're planning a weekend extravaganza, there are additional entertainment areas you can add to the mix. The club's vibrant Anytime Lounge, outfitted with "spotlight" chandeliers, a bar top that resembles a grand piano, and a lush red wall framing a giant TV screen, brings to mind the Theater District. In the Private Dining Room, which looks out on the Hollywood sign, walls "blooming" with faux orchids evoke the Flower District. Even the hallway leading to the lounge showcases art from the private collections of L.A. residents—a nod to the city's Art Walk.

And don't forget, City Club Los Angeles has 25 years of experience in superior service and fine dining. You can sample your proposed menu's mouthwatering selections at a private tasting.

What more can you ask for? Oh, yes, a great time before, during, and after your party! Whether you and your guests are locals or out-of-towners, we guarantee you'll find plenty of terrific places to stay and loads of fun things to do in this club's one-of-a-kind setting.

CEREMONY CAPACITY: The Angeles Room holds 380 seated guests. The Harbor Room accommodates up to 250 for a ceremony. The Hollywood Ballroom accomodates up to 400 for a ceremony.

EVENT/RECEPTION CAPACITY: The Santa Monica, Hollywood and Harbor Rooms combined hold up to 360 guests seated with a dance floor or 600 for a cocktail recepetion. They can also be broken out to accommodate a smaller more intimate wedding.

MEETING CAPACITY: 11 rooms can accommodate 5–600, including a screening room that seats 15.

FEES & DEPOSITS: For weddings and special events, a $2,000 nonrefundable and nontransferable deposit is required to secure your date; 50% is due 60 days prior to the event and the balance is payable 10 working days prior. Menus can be customized. Wedding receptions start at $100/person; alcohol/beverages, tax and service charges are additional. For all events, there is a food and beverage minimum, not including tax and service charge.

AVAILABILITY: Year-round, daily including holidays, 7am–2am.

SERVICES/AMENITIES:

Catering: in-house, no BYO
Kitchen Facilities: n/a
Tables & Chairs: provided
Linens, Silver, etc.: provided
Restrooms: wheelchair accessible
Dance Floor: available
Bride's & Groom's Dressing Area: yes
Meeting Equipment: full range plus AV
Other: full event coordination, private screening room

Parking: in-house garage, valet on weekdays, self-park on weekends
Accommodations: no guest rooms, hotels nearby
Telephone: house phones
Outdoor Night Lighting: n/a
Outdoor Cooking Facilities: n/a
Cleanup: provided
View: panorama of Los Angeles

RESTRICTIONS:

Alcohol: in-house
Smoking: not allowed
Music: amplified OK

Wheelchair Access: yes
Insurance: required for vendors only

Want to find more venues and services? Check out our informative website, www.HereComesTheGuide.com.

167

DoubleTree by Hilton Los Angeles Downtown

Hotel

120 South Los Angeles Street, Los Angeles

213/253-9200

www.losangelesdowntown.doubletree.com
gloria.guiles@hilton.com

- Rehearsal Dinners
- Ceremonies
- Wedding Receptions
- Private Parties
- Corporate Events
- Meetings
- Film Shoots
- Accommodations

For the bride who's always envisioned a tranquil garden wedding, but also wants the chic energy of a downtown hotel, DoubleTree by Hilton Los Angeles Downtown offers both. Conveniently located at the edge of Little Tokyo, near Chinatown and mere minutes from the art district's world-class museums, theaters and concert venues, this newly updated, 21-story, luxury hotel has a modern, cosmopolitan air. But it's the hotel's re-creation of an ancient treasure that truly sets it apart.

Tucked away on the third floor is a half-acre, miniature scale version of a 400-year-old, historic Tokyo garden. Replete with cascading waterfalls, pebble-lined ponds and a wooden bridge, the dual-level garden offers a variety of beautiful ceremony and reception backdrops. While you get ready in a complimentary guest room, your friends and family will be escorted to this urban anomaly, an outdoor haven that celebrates the serenity of its pastoral design while reveling in its city surroundings. Particularly appealing is the upper lawn, landscaped with azalea shrubs and mature trees. Here, a Zen-like, meandering waterway contrasts cleverly with skyline views of some of L.A.'s most recognizable landmarks. To add even more drama, you can make your entrance by seeming to float across the water on a pathway of flat rocks. After the ceremony, you can head to the lower garden and terrace for cocktails, or usher your guests inside the hotel for champagne and hors d'oeuvres.

After cocktails, dinner and dancing take place in your choice of two ballrooms. The Thousand Cranes Ballroom on the Garden level features floor-to-ceiling windows overlooking the large waterfall and stone pond. One level below is the Golden State Ballroom, which is larger and offers a 15-foot ceiling along with a series of modern chandeliers that run the length of the room. Smaller, less formal weddings or even rehearsal dinners work beautifully in any of the hotel's more intimate dining options, from the private Orchid Room to the light, bright Azalea Restaurant that boasts a domed ceiling, lower-level dance floor and views of City Hall. There's even a tree-fringed patio that connects you to the city outside while still providing privacy.

With all the dining options comes a plethora of menu choices, because the hotel's chefs are adept at virtually every type of cuisine, from Continental and California-American to Asian and other ethnic specialties. In fact, the entire hotel and event staff's multicultural savoir-faire means they can—and will—accommodate almost any unique request: They've set aside a nearby room for a Korean bride's multiple costume changes; customized menus to incorporate religious, ceremonial or "taste of home" foods; even arranged an Indian groom's arrival via decorated horse at the hotel's front entrance. If they can pull that off, you can be certain they'll help you bring your own wish list to life.

CEREMONY CAPACITY: The site holds 300 seated guests indoors or 200 seated outdoors.

EVENT/RECEPTION CAPACITY: The hotel accommodates 300 seated or 400 standing guests indoors and 100 seated or 300 standing outdoors.

MEETING CAPACITY: The hotel accommodates up to 500 seated guests.

FEES & DEPOSITS: 25% of the estimated event total is required to reserve your date. The balance is due 14 days prior to the event. Wedding ceremony and reception packages start at $98/person. Brunch or reception-only packages start at $75/person. Tax and a 21% service charge are additional.

AVAILABILITY: Year-round, daily, anytime. Contact for details.

SERVICES/AMENITIES:
Catering: in-house
Kitchen Facilities: n/a
Tables & Chairs: provided
Linens, Silver, etc.: provided
Restrooms: wheelchair accessible
Dance Floor: portable provided
Bride's Dressing Area: provided
Meeting Equipment: some provided
Other: grand piano, AV equipment, complimentary event coordination

Parking: valet and self-parking available
Accommodations: 434 guest rooms, 20 suites
Telephone: house phone
Outdoor Night Lighting: yes
Outdoor Cooking Facilities: BBQ CBA
Cleanup: provided
View: panorama of cityscape; garden patio, waterfall, fountain, landscaped grounds

RESTRICTIONS:
Alcohol: in-house, no BYO
Smoking: designated areas only
Music: amplified OK

Wheelchair Access: yes
Insurance: not required

The Ebell of Los Angeles

Historic Landmark

4400 Wilshire Boulevard, Los Angeles
323/931-1277
www.ebelloflosangeles.com
inquiry@ebelloflosangeles.com

Rehearsal Dinners	● Corporate Events
● Ceremonies	● Meetings
● Wedding Receptions	● Film Shoots
● Private Parties	Accommodations

A visual delight, The Ebell of Los Angeles was built in the late 1920s to house the nation's most prestigious women's club. Arched doorways, including an intricately crafted wrought-iron main entrance, lead into sunny galleries and lofty salons, all of which have their own intriguing details.

The large, pleasant Main Dining Room features a series of carved columns with arches supporting its high ceiling, and a bank of tall French doors opens onto the adjacent courtyard, flooding the room with light.

Enclosed by picturesque arcades, flowering shrubs and trees, it's no surprise that this serene courtyard garden is the preferred spot for ceremonies. Exchange vows in front of a fountain topped with an appealing bronze statue or under the tall arched doorway of the Art Salon. This unique room, with its dramatic draped archways, is hung with original paintings by local artists. It serves as a foyer for the larger Lounge, a magnificent space with a striking carved Italian ceiling, wrought-iron chandeliers, antique couches and chairs, a grand piano, plus a mezzanine from which to look down on it all!

Both elegance and functionality were important to the leading society women who designed this extraordinary social center, and The Ebell bears the marks of their good judgment and distinguished taste in every detail.

CEREMONY CAPACITY: The Garden holds approximately 150 seated guests, and up to 400 standing. Indoors, the Lounge can seat 260 in rows, and for a wedding in-the-round can accommodate 150.

EVENT/RECEPTION & MEETING CAPACITY: Indoor spaces hold 100–250 seated with dance floor; the garden accommodates up to 150 seated or 400 standing guests.

FEES & DEPOSITS: A refundable $2,000 security deposit is required to book the event date. Estimated balance will be divided into three separate payments. Final payment is due ten business days prior to the event. Average price for all-inclusive Ebell services ranges $185–250/person. This includes menus, beverages, personnel, setup fee, room rental fee, tasting, security, lighting, linens, place settings, in-house tables and banquet chairs. Sales tax and a 21% service charge are additional.

AVAILABILITY: Year-round, anytime until midnight.

SERVICES/AMENITIES:

Catering: in-house

Kitchen Facilities: fully equipped

Tables & Chairs: provided

Linens, Silver, etc.: provided

Restrooms: wheelchair accessible

Dance Floor: hardwood floors

Bride's Dressing Area: yes

Meeting Equipment: some provided

Parking: ample

Accommodations: no guest rooms

Telephone: emergency only

Outdoor Night Lighting: limited

Outdoor Cooking Facilities: no

Cleanup: provided

View: no

RESTRICTIONS:

Alcohol: in-house, or wine corkage $15/bottle, $20/magnum

Smoking: outside only

Music: amplified OK; time restrictions on patio

Wheelchair Access: yes

Insurance: certificate required

Other: no rice, birdseed, glitter or confetti

Hilton Los Angeles Airport

Hotel

5711 West Century Boulevard, Los Angeles
310/410-4000

www.losangelesairport.hilton.com
elena.morales@hilton.com

- Rehearsal Dinners
- Ceremonies
- Wedding Receptions
- Private Parties
- Corporate Events
- Meetings
- Film Shoots
- Accommodations

Standing at the gateway to California's largest and arguably most diverse city, the Hilton Los Angeles Airport is grand in scale, combining a soothing elegance with artistic flourishes. Located just a quarter mile outside of LAX and within an easy drive to downtown, the beaches or Beverly Hills, it's an excellent locale to gather your far-flung friends and relatives for an upscale wedding celebration.

This world-class hotel, while managed by the Hilton organization, is privately owned and much of the décor has been handpicked by the owners. That attention to detail is evident as soon as you enter the lobby, which balances its three-story-high proportions with lots of human-scaled conversation areas. Gleaming marble floors and granite consoles are softened with richly patterned rugs and velvet armchairs, all layered in a neutral palette of cream, gold and honey. At the far end of the lobby an impressive center staircase, all glass and gold railings, makes a stellar backdrop for wedding photos.

Just beyond the staircase are two of the hotel's premier banquet rooms, which are often used together for a seamless affair. If you have your ceremony on site, you may want to hold it in the International Ballroom, a palatial-sized space that has ample room for a traditional or ethnic ceremony even when divided in two. This formal ballroom is decorated in tones of peach and cream, with silk fabric adding a touch of luxury to the walls. A series of mirrors around the room accentuates the dramatic impact of the enormous, rectangular, icicle-crystal chandeliers suspended from the high, coffered ceiling.

After you've said "I do," invite everyone across the foyer to the similarly themed (same colors, same chandeliers) but smaller Pacific Ballroom, a somewhat more intimate setting for mingling over cocktails. Then it's back to the International Ballroom for a sumptuous dinner and dancing, taking advantage of the venue's full 11,000 square feet of splendor. (Although the hotel has an extensive catering menu, you're free to bring in ethnic or specialty foods from an outside caterer.)

For something quite different, head up to the La Jolla Room and Foyer on the mezzanine level. Along the way, take a moment to enjoy the aerial views of the lobby below, then check out the display of dazzling accoutrements that you pass en route to the event spaces: a framed golden brocade, Asian tapestries and gorgeous geodes of amethyst and crystal—all arranged using the principles of Feng Shui. Cocktails and hors d'oeuvres are served in the warmly inviting La Jolla

Foyer, followed by dinner in the La Jolla Room, which is adorned with unusual chandeliers that look like flower petals descending from the ceiling, and mirrored French doors along the back wall.

There are several other options for weddings of 50 or fewer guests, and the staff will happily work with you to design an event that suits your style and budget. Your out-of-town guests can relax at the hotel (there's a pool, sports bar, fitness center and restaurants) or they can visit many of the local attractions. And when their stay at the Hilton is over, it's just a quick trip back to the airport.

CEREMONY CAPACITY: The site holds 450 seated guests, indoors or outdoors.

EVENT/RECEPTION CAPACITY: The facility can accommodate 800 seated or standing guests indoors, and 375 or 600 standing outdoors.

MEETING CAPACITY: Meeting spaces hold up to 1,000 seated guests.

FEES & DEPOSITS: 20% of the total event cost is required to reserve your date and the balance is due 72 hours prior to the event. Rental fees range $800–5,000 depending on the space rented. Meals range $40–100/person. Tax, alcohol and a facility charge are additional.

AVAILABILITY: Year-round, daily.

SERVICES/AMENITIES:

Catering: in-house, or BYO
Kitchen Facilities: limited
Tables & Chairs: provided
Linens, Silver, etc.: provided
Restrooms: wheelchair accessible
Dance Floor: portable provided
Bride's Dressing Area: CBA
Meeting Equipment: provided

Parking: large lot, self park or valet available
Accommodations: 1,234 guest rooms
Telephone: pay, house, office or guest phones
Outdoor Night Lighting: yes
Outdoor Cooking Facilities: no
Cleanup: provided
View: no
Other: AV equipment

RESTRICTIONS:

Alcohol: in-house, or BYO with corkage fee
Smoking: outdoors only
Music: amplified OK indoors

Wheelchair Access: yes
Insurance: liability required

InterContinental Los Angeles Century City

Hotel

2151 Avenue of the Stars, Los Angeles
310/284-6512
www.intercontinentallosangeles.com
lasales@ihg.com

- Rehearsal Dinners
- Ceremonies
- Wedding Receptions
- Private Parties
- Corporate Events
- Meetings
- Film Shoots
- Accommodations

The best way to ensure a flawless wedding celebration is to go with a name you know and respect. The InterContinental Los Angeles Century City not only comes with the sterling reputation of the InterContinental Hotel Group, it features an enchanting garden, food that's (almost!) too extraordinary to eat, and impeccable service.

Ideally situated on Avenue of the Stars, the hotel overlooks the Fox studios, and is just minutes away from the lively Westfield Century City Shopping Plaza and Beverly Hills' famous Rodeo Drive. (The hotel has a complimentary Mercedes limousine to ferry you to these and other local destinations.) Once you enter the large circular drive, verdantly landscaped with trees and flowering shrubs, you're welcomed to the InterContinental's luxurious atmosphere by the soothing sounds of a waterfall in the motor court.

The lobby is a study in understated elegance, with its judicious use of inlaid marble, crackle-glass sconces and gracefully fluted tables set with tall vases of flowers. Three tiers of expansive skylights bathe the area in natural light during the day; large opaque glass chandeliers give it a soft glow in the evening. Straight ahead is the sophisticated Lobby Lounge, with the California-cuisine Park Grill Restaurant behind it.

In planning your wedding celebration, why not include a day at the sumptuous Spa InterContinental? With its hushed atmosphere and private outdoor terrace, it's an excellent prelude to the big event for you and your wedding party. Once thoroughly pampered and relaxed, you'll be able to fully appreciate the hotel's lush garden for your wedding ceremony. The large lawn, bordered by flowers and trees, has a center stone pathway for your walk down the aisle to a raised natural altar that's ringed with flagstone. This south-facing bit of Eden (guests don't have to squint into the sun) can comfortably accommodate 300 guests. Once you've exchanged vows, the festivities begin with a cocktail reception on the surrounding shaded patio. Heaters are available in case there's a chill, or if you prefer cocktails indoors, bring your guests to the Grand Foyer, located to the right of the main lobby.

With only one wedding scheduled at a time, you and your guests will enjoy this entire wing of the hotel, moving easily from the gold-toned Foyer to the Grand Salon for dinner and dancing. Here the décor is French influenced, with large crystal-and-brass chandeliers suspended from high ceilings, and fabric-covered walls embroidered with gold foliage. The service you'll receive at your reception—like the service provided throughout the hotel—prides itself on anticipating your every need.

In addition to your exquisitely appointed, complimentary Bridal Room, the hotel offers special rates on rooms for your out-of-town guests. And, having picked a location whose name is synonymous with quality and service, you know they'll be in good hands even after you've left for your honeymoon.

CEREMONY CAPACITY: The site holds 300 seated guests, indoors or outdoors.

EVENT/RECEPTION CAPACITY: Outdoors, the lawn holds 300 seated or 400 standing guests; indoors, the Grand Salon up to 300 seated or 400 standing.

MEETING CAPACITY: The hotel accommodates up to 400 guests seated theater-style.

FEES & DEPOSITS: 25% of the total event cost is required to reserve your date. Flexible payment terms are available for remaining balance. Packages range $140–200/person. Tax, alcohol and service charge are extra. Additional fees range $500–1,500 depending on the day of the event and guest count.

AVAILABILITY: Year-round, daily, 10am–1am.

SERVICES/AMENITIES:

Catering: in-house, select from list or BYO w/approval
Kitchen Facilities: no
Tables & Chairs: provided
Linens, Silver, etc.: provided
Restrooms: wheelchair accessible
Dance Floor: provided
Bride's Dressing Area: provided
Meeting Equipment: full range

Parking: valet only
Accommodations: 361 guest rooms
Telephone: house phone
Outdoor Night Lighting: yes
Outdoor Cooking Facilities: yes
Cleanup: provided
View: cityscape, garden patio

RESTRICTIONS:

Alcohol: in-house, no BYO
Smoking: designated areas only
Music: amplified OK

Wheelchair Access: yes
Insurance: liability required

This is important! Tell venues you're reading HERE COMES THE GUIDE and ask if our information is still current.

175

The Legendary Park Plaza

Landmark Building

607 South Park View Street, Los Angeles
213/381-6300 x103
www.parkplazala.com
trisha@parkplazala.com

- Rehearsal Dinners
- Ceremonies
- Wedding Receptions
- Private Parties
- Corporate Events
- Meetings
- Film Shoots
- Accommodations

An architectural tour de force, the opulent Park Plaza embodies the rich and decadent boomtown times of Los Angeles before the 1929 stock market crash. Built in 1925 (it was originally an Elks Lodge), the Hotel languished into a lamentable state of disrepair during the 80s and 90s. Fortunately, it's been rescued from ruin by the same folks who refurbished the Oviatt. Finishing touches on the extensive facelift were completed in October of '99.

Don't expect to hold a shy and demure event here. The sheer scale and splendor of the building calls for affairs on the grander end of the spectrum. Big weddings, band premieres and corporate Christmas parties are equal to the Park Plaza's sensibility.

Hold onto your hat when exploring this location, because much of your time will be spent with head tipped back, ogling its many wonders. Occupying almost an entire city block, the building's façade is embellished by a series of arches, pilasters, cornices and majestic friezes featuring intriguing statuary of Roman women. This neoclassical motif is carried over to the inside as well. Enchanting you from the moment you step across the transom is the Park Plaza Lobby, a cathedral-like space with a Romanesque vaulted ceiling at least three stories high. Sunlight streams through the immense Palladian glass doorway and fanlight, burnishing the Tennessee-rose granite floor.

The Park Plaza offers a plethora of exhilarating event sites. On the ground floor is the Gold Ballroom, the Park's most intimate space. Just right for cocktails or small seated dinners, this space boasts dark wood wainscoting, tasseled antique chandeliers and Corinthian pilasters whose tops are crowned in gleaming gold leaf. Equally gorgeous is the Bronze Ballroom, featuring burgundy wall-to-wall carpeting, a mammoth Art Deco bar, hand-stenciled ceiling beams and fantastic columns gilded in copper leaf. On the room's south side, glass doors open out onto the Tuscan Garden. This private open-air courtyard, filled with greenery and flower planters, is a beautiful setting for exchanging vows.

Take the magnificent stairway up from the Lobby, turn left and you'll encounter our favorite event site—the Grand Ballroom. It is, in a word, spectacular. On either side of the room twin colonnades create a linear dynamism, drawing the eye along the length of the room. The meticulously restored beamed ceilings showcase hand-painted floral designs, patterned after a palace ceiling in Florence. Chandeliers suspended from the beams spotlight these amazing works of art. Not to be outdone is the Terrace Room, the hotel's most capacious ballroom. Art Deco in motif, and featuring elaborate wall sconces and a ceiling of dizzying height, this vast multilevel space can accommodate almost any kind of pageantry you can dream up.

One of Los Angeles' best kept secrets, the Park Plaza has become the place for film shoots, record launchings, wrap parties and Hollywood bashes. In fact, at a birthday party for a "recently arrived" star, the hotel was packed with glitterati. And even these jaded, been-everywhere-done-everything luminaries could be overheard exclaiming, "I never knew this place existed; it's SO beautiful!"

The secret is out … .

CEREMONY CAPACITY: The Gold Ballroom holds 90, the Bronze Ballroom 250, the Grand Ballroom 270, the Terrace Ballroom 475, and the Tuscan Garden 350 seated guests.

EVENT/RECEPTION CAPACITY: Indoor spaces accommodate 90–490 seated or 145–750 standing. Outdoors, the garden holds 275 seated or 450 standing guests.

MEETING CAPACITY: Several spaces hold 145–750 seated guests.

FEES & DEPOSITS: A signed contract plus a nonfundable deposit equal to 15% of the estimated event total are required to secure your date. 65% of the event total is due 90 days prior to the event, and the balance is due 30 days prior. A 10% refundable security deposit is due 14 days prior. Catering packages are available, and range $115–210/person including staff and rentals.

AVAILABILITY: Year-round, daily, until 2am.

SERVICES/AMENITIES:

Catering: in-house or BYO
Kitchen Facilities: fully equipped, kosher kitchen CBA
Tables & Chairs: provided, or BYO
Linens, Silver, etc.: provided, or BYO
Restrooms: wheelchair accessible
Dance Floor: provided
Bride's & Groom's Dressing Area: yes
Meeting Equipment: CBA, extra fee
Other: event coordination

Parking: valet parking or nearby public lots
Accommodations: no guest rooms
Telephone: guest phones
Outdoor Night Lighting: yes
Outdoor Cooking Facilities: yes
Cleanup: provided, extra fee
View: downtown cityscape and park
Kosher: provides kosher catering, or BYO

RESTRICTIONS:

Alcohol: in-house, no BYO
Smoking: outdoors only
Music: amplified OK indoors; outdoors OK with volume limits

Wheelchair Access: yes
Insurance: liability required for social functions
Other: some decorations require approval

The Los Angeles Athletic Club

431 West Seventh Street, Los Angeles
213/630-5287
www.laac.com
laac.catering@laac.net

Private Social & Athletic Club

- Rehearsal Dinners
- Ceremonies
- Wedding Receptions
- Private Parties
- Corporate Events
- Meetings
- Film Shoots
- Accommodations

The moment you step into the Los Angeles Athletic Club's first-floor lobby, its elegant, wall-to-wall wood interior and restored original marble floor makes it obvious that you've arrived at a very classy place.

An L.A. landmark for over a century, the LACC was founded in 1880 by a small group of businessmen destined to become some of the city's most influential citizens. In 1912 its members financed the construction of the present-day building that houses the club's recreational and special event facilities as well as 72 guest rooms. Many remarkable people have since passed through its doors—Rudolph Valentino practiced boxing here, Charlie Chaplin considered it his home base, and Johnny Weissmuller trained for the Olympics in the 7th-floor swimming pool (the first suspended pool in Los Angeles).

The club's 12th-story rooftop terrace is a spectacular setting for a one-of-a-kind wedding. From this urban aerie, guests seated for the ceremony are treated to a sweeping panorama, while towering skyscrapers nearby seem like abstract sculptures of steel and glass poised against a pale blue skyline. As nighttime descends, city lights and a panoply of stars illuminate the horizon, forming a dramatic backdrop to your reception.

If you'd prefer to take the party indoors, start by hosting your cocktail hour in the re-imagined Invention Bar & Lounge, a spacious and upscale mixology bar on the third floor designed like a swanky gentleman's club. An abundance of rich mahogany paneling and custom leather and suede furniture create a warm, inviting atmosphere. Classic items like a grandfather clock and antique racquets arranged on a wall coexist harmoniously with modern elements like the avant-garde "molecule" lighting fixtures overhead. For a truly unique experience, upgrade your wedding package to include a world-famous mixologist who's an expert in whipping up custom drinks as well as signature cocktails invented over the last 200+ years. While you and your guests are sampling vintage libations such as the Fish House Punch (1732), the Dark N Stormy (early 1900s), and The Last Word (1937), your mixologist can regale you with each cocktail's interesting history.

Dinner is served just steps away in the beautifully remodeled Centennial Ballroom, where the décor evokes the Great Gatsby era of the 1920s. The original wall-to wall woodwork now has an added luster, and multiple upgrades have made the space more event-friendly than ever. Glittering crystal chandeliers on dimmers let you control the mood, while sconces on the pillars cast a soft light. At one end, a faux fireplace comes to life thanks to its illuminated interior and mantel. Even the ceiling has been enhanced with elaborately embossed white wood panels. In short, the ballroom is simply gorgeous.

The Athletic Club's friendly, attentive staff will tailor your wedding package to your specific needs. They offer a food tasting and are happy to customize your menu, providing dozens of hors d'oeuvre, entrée and cake options to choose from. A champagne toast, wine with dinner and the wedding cake are all included, along with a well-appointed overnight suite that awaits you at evening's end.

CEREMONY CAPACITY: The Olympian Lounge holds 220 seated or 400 standing guests. The site can accommodate up to 250 seated guests indoors and 150 seated outdoors.

EVENT/RECEPTION CAPACITY: The Centennial Ballroom holds up to 350 seated or 500 standing guests; the Empire Room, 120 seated or 200 standing; the President's Lounge, 50 seated or 75 standing; the John R. Wooden Award Court, 450 seated or 800 standing; the Olympian Lounge, 200 standing; Invention Bar, 200 standing.

MEETING CAPACITY: 9 rooms can accommodate 10–300 seated guests; the reception rooms listed above are used for larger groups.

FEES & DEPOSITS: A $2,500 nonrefundable deposit is required to reserve your date; the balance is due 1 week prior to the date. For ceremonies, there is a $1,500 indoor ceremony charge and a $2,500 rooftop charge. Wedding packages start at $110/person, including hors d'oeuvres, tray-passed wine and champagne during cocktail hour, champagne toast, 3-course meal, wine with dinner, cake, dance floor and complimentary suite for bride and groom.

There is no room rental fee for weddings or social functions if the food and beverage minimum is met. Luncheons range $30–50/person and dinners range $40–60/person. Buffets and cocktail receptions start at $30/person; alcohol, tax and a 20% service charge are additional.

For business functions or meetings, per-person meal prices are: breakfast $16–32, luncheon $24–50, and dinner $30–60. Rental fees for meeting rooms range $80–1,300 and may be waived depending on food and beverage totals.

AVAILABILITY: Year-round, daily including holidays, 7am–midnight in 5-hour blocks; additional hours are negotiable.

SERVICES/AMENITIES:

Catering: in-house
Kitchen Facilities: fully equipped
Tables & Chairs: provided
Linens, Silver, etc.: provided
Restrooms: wheelchair accessible
Dance Floor: provided
Bride's & Groom's Dressing Area: suite
Meeting Equipment: full range
Other: coordination, wedding cakes, grand piano

Parking: secured, underground garage, $4.50/car
Accommodations: 63 guest rooms, 9 newly renovated suites
Telephone: pay phones
Outdoor Night Lighting: access lighting only
Outdoor Cooking Facilities: no
Cleanup: provided
View: cityscape of downtown L.A.

RESTRICTIONS:

Alcohol: in-house, or corkage $15/bottle
Smoking: designated areas
Music: amplified OK indoors, and rooftop before 10pm

Wheelchair Access: yes
Insurance: not required
Other: no rice, birdseed, confetti or glitter

Los Angeles Union Station

Landmark Railway Station & Event Facility

800 North Alameda Street, Ste 100, Los Angeles
213/617-0111
www.hollywoodlocations.com
jcooper@hollywoodlocations.com

- Rehearsal Dinners
- Ceremonies
- Wedding Receptions
- Private Parties
- Corporate Events
- Meetings
- Film Shoots
- Accommodations

Ever notice how train travel always looks so romantic in old movies, with lovers joyfully greeting or tearfully saying goodbye as a train whistle blows? Perhaps it's those grand old railway stations that set the stage for drama, with few as grand as Union Station, a paradigm of Art Deco artistry.

Arguably L.A.'s most recognizable landmark, it positively exudes a sense of excitement. Completed in 1939, this Spanish Revival masterpiece has ceilings that can soar to 50 feet and decorative touches that tempt even the most harried modern commuter to stop for a moment and admire them. Even better, some of the station's most amazing sites are reserved exclusively for weddings, events and film shoots.

The main terminal, marked by its distinctive tower, opens onto a concourse with various waiting rooms stretching out in front of you. But directly to your left is the original Main Ticketing Concourse, blocked off to the general public these days. Majestic in feel, this great room has a Moorish influence with tall windows lining one wall and magnificent ironwork chandeliers suspended from the crossbeam ceiling, painted in green and black and rising more than five stories. Opposite the windows, there's an antique wooden ticket counter, which runs the length of the room and can double as a bar or cocktail area. Hidden behind the counter are several spacious back rooms where the bride and groom can get ready. This palatial-sized space can easily seat 500 with a dance floor or accommodate 1,000 for cocktails in an unforgettable setting.

Outside and to the right of the main terminal is the South Patio, a formal garden set back from the street for a courtyard feel. Flanked by white concrete pillars and planted with flowerbeds in a circular design, this is a favorite ceremony site.

On the other side of the patio is the phenomenal Fred Harvey Restaurant, once part of an upscale chain sponsored by the railroads. Immortalized in the Judy Garland movie *The Harvey Girls,* most of the restaurants closed in the late 60s. Fortunately, this vibrant gem has been maintained as a showstopper event venue. Brass-and-glass doors open to a huge main room with a knockout tile floor patterned after a Navajo rug. The design theme is Native American-meets-Art Deco and the combination works beautifully, at once very retro and very hip. Raised circular booths covered in leather line the sides, and a large horseshoe-shaped bar in the center of the room can be set up for a buffet or cake-cutting ceremony. A brass-railed balcony is a perfect spot for your band or DJ, and there's a fabulous art moderne cocktail lounge off the main room that boasts a copper bar and mirrors with "encapsulated" bubbles.

This has to be one of the coolest and most unique spots in L.A…a memorable treat for your awestruck guests who otherwise wouldn't have a chance to see it.

CEREMONY CAPACITY: The site holds 600 seated guests indoors and 550 seated outdoors.

EVENT/RECEPTION CAPACITY: The facility can accommodate 500 seated or 1,000 standing guests indoors, and 350 seated or 1,000 standing outdoors.

MEETING CAPACITY: Meeting spaces hold 600 seated guests.

FEES & DEPOSITS: 50% of the rental fee is required to reserve your date. The balance is due 30 days prior to the event. Rental fees range $6,000–10,000 depending on the space rented.

AVAILABILITY: Year-round, daily; call for details.

SERVICES/AMENITIES:

Catering: BYO
Kitchen Facilities: no
Tables & Chairs: BYO
Linens, Silver, etc.: BYO
Restrooms: wheelchair accessible
Dance Floor: provided
Bride's & Groom's Dressing Area: CBA
Meeting Equipment: BYO

Parking: limited, valet available, garage nearby
Accommodations: no guest rooms
Telephone: pay phone
Outdoor Night Lighting: provided
Outdoor Cooking Facilities: BBQ CBA
Cleanup: provided
View: cityscape, garden patio, landscaped grounds

RESTRICTIONS:

Alcohol: BYO
Smoking: not allowed
Music: amplified OK with restrictions

Wheelchair Access: yes
Insurance: liability required

Luxe Sunset Boulevard Hotel

Hotel

11461 Sunset Boulevard, Los Angeles
310/691-7510 Special Events

www.luxesunset.com
specialevents@luxehotels.com

- Rehearsal Dinners
- Ceremonies
- Wedding Receptions
- Private Parties
- Corporate Events
- Meetings
- Film Shoots
- Accommodations

It's not always easy to find tranquility in Los Angeles, but the Luxe Sunset Boulevard Hotel will make you feel like you've gotten away from it all. Occupying seven hilltop acres, this boutique property is a secluded oasis that happens to be a stone's throw from the Getty Center and a short drive to other favorite L.A. sites like Santa Monica Beach, UCLA, and the Skirball Cultural Center.

When you have your wedding here, your event is the only one taking place at that time so it receives top priority. The hotel also has some of the most appealing event spaces in West Los Angeles, most notably the elegant Luxe Sunset Ballroom. Designed like a home away from home, it's sophisticated, yet inviting. The neutral color scheme—shades of taupe, cream and bronze—compliments almost any decoration, and the room is dramatically lit with modern chandeliers, recessed lighting and wall sconces. If you have a particular ambiance in mind, state-of-the-art audiovisual equipment is available to help you create just the right mood.

For a *plein air* ceremony or cocktails under the stars, the adjacent patio is a true urban garden. Olive trees shade conversational seating areas, while fountains lend a pleasing background sound. A unique feature of the garden is the Luxe Sunset Terrace. As you walk down the central aisle of this intimate courtyard, lacy elm trees provide a natural canopy and frame views of the "fountain wall" backdrop. An upper patio makes a lovely spot for mingling and casual drinks.

Your out-of-town guests will find the hotel an extremely comfortable, enjoyable place to stay. All of its superior and deluxe rooms, as well as most of their suites, have windows or doors that open to the outside, and they're decorated in warm, natural shades, with custom-made furniture. Additional amenities include free WiFi and high-speed internet, designer bedding, and a Keurig Single Cup Brewer with complimentary coffee and tea. In-room dining is available 24 hours a day, and Luxe also offers daily turndown service and plush cotton robes.

Far from the madding crowd, the Luxe Hotel is a stylish L.A. getaway. Have your celebration here, or come for a weekend "vacation." Stroll through the gardens, go for a swim, and luxuriate in the full-service spa. After you unpack your bags, the soothing setting and accommodating staff will quickly help you relax and unwind.

CEREMONY & EVENT/RECEPTION CAPACITY: The Luxe Sunset Ballroom holds 300 seated guests and the Luxe Terrace holds 250 seated guests.

MEETING CAPACITY: Three rooms hold 12–300 seated guests.

FEES & DEPOSITS: A nonrefundable deposit of $5,000 is required when the space is booked. Half the anticipated total is due 90 days prior to the event; the final payment is due 72 hours prior. There are 3 wedding packages ranging $110–175/person for lunch and $125–200/person for dinner. Tax and a 20% gratuity are additional.

AVAILABILITY: Year-round, daily, 6am–midnight.

SERVICES/AMENITIES:

Catering: in-house, no BYO
Kitchen Facilities: n/a
Tables & Chairs: provided
Linens, Silver, etc.: provided
Restrooms: wheelchair accessible
Dance Floor: CBA, $600 fee
Bride's & Groom's Dressing Area: yes
Meeting Equipment: full range, extra fee
Kosher: provides kosher catering and has kosher kitchen

Parking: valet only, $8/car
Accommodations: 162 guest rooms
Telephone: pay phones, guest phones
Outdoor Night Lighting: yes
Outdoor Cooking Facilities: n/a
Cleanup: provided
View: garden
Other: also provide off-site catering

RESTRICTIONS:

Alcohol: in-house, or wine corkage $25/bottle
Smoking: outside only
Music: amplified OK indoors, until 10pm outdoors

Wheelchair Access: yes
Insurance: liability required
Other: no rice or birdseed

Overwhelmed? Use the search criteria on www.HereComesTheGuide.com to narrow down your choices.

183

Matteo's Restaurant

2321 Westwood Boulevard, Los Angeles
310/475-4521
www.matteosla.com
events@matteosla.com

Restaurant

●	Rehearsal Dinners	●	Corporate Events
●	Ceremonies	●	Meetings
●	Wedding Receptions	●	Film Shoots
●	Private Parties		Accommodations

Since it first came onto the scene in 1963, Matteo's in West L.A. has been the epitome of cool. Maybe it was because Frank Sinatra—an old pal of Matty "Matteo" Jordan's from back home in Hoboken—often came to dinner along with his rat pack crowd. Maybe it was the great Italian food, served in an upscale supper club atmosphere. Or maybe it was just because no matter who you were, you were greeted like a friend as you enjoyed your dinner next to a Who's Who of Hollywood movers and shakers. What's amazing is that more than 50 years and a whole new generation later, the restaurant, recently renovated, still has that winning combination of homey and hip.

Their unique wedding spot, dubbed The Townhouse, gives you that same feeling in a city sophisticated way. Head up the private stairs and it's as if you've arrived at a chic New York brownstone. The first thing that greets your guests is a smart little lounge, complete with its own bar, where they can check in. The entire upstairs is yours to enjoy, so you can create whatever flow works best for you. Perhaps you'd like to start by inviting everyone out to the rooftop terrace for an open-air ceremony or cocktail reception. The tile floor and textured plaster walls embellished with green latticework panels give this cosmopolitan space a country charm. Huge planters with flowering shrubs and a weathered lion's head fountain set into a niche in the wall add to the sense of an in-town getaway.

When you're ready for dinner, the French doors will be opened to reveal the Townhouse Dining Room, decorated like a spacious penthouse drawing room. This lovely venue takes full advantage of both natural and reflected light: A pale blue, barrel ceiling features a skylight as well as drop chandeliers, and the mirror over a beautifully crafted antique hutch shimmers behind an array of flickering candles.

The Townhouse menu includes all the great Italian fare from the restaurant downstairs, and the chef is also quite open to whipping up innovative ethnic or cultural dishes on request. After dinner, continue your festivities with dancing al fresco under the stars as well as hundreds of twinkling lights strung overhead.

In addition to all its other assets, one of The Townhouse's greatest perks is that the resident event manager will work with you from your initial consultation to the end of your event, making sure the space fits your needs and your vision. Very cool.

CEREMONY CAPACITY: The banquet room holds 78 seated guests indoors and 28 seated outdoors.

EVENT/RECEPTION CAPACITY: Upstairs, the banquet room holds 78 seated or 100 standing indoors and the adjoining patio seats 28 outdoors. Downstairs, the restaurant can accommodate 145 seated or standing guests with a buyout.

MEETING CAPACITY: Meeting spaces hold up to 78 seated guests.

FEES & DEPOSITS: A $500–1,000 deposit is required to reserve your date and the balance is due on the date of the event. Rental fees are waived if the food and beverage minimums are met. Meals range $30–65/person. Tax, alcohol and a 20% service charge are additional.

AVAILABILITY: Year-round, daily, 6am–2am.

SERVICES/AMENITIES:

Catering: in-house
Kitchen Facilities: n/a
Tables & Chairs: provided
Linens, Silver, etc.: provided
Restrooms: wheelchair accessible
Dance Floor: provided
Bride's & Groom's Dressing Area: yes
Meeting Equipment: provided
Other: coordination, grand piano, AV equipment, in-house wedding cake and florals

Parking: on street, valet required, garage nearby
Accommodations: no guest rooms, hotel nearby
Telephone: office and guest phones
Outdoor Night Lighting: yes
Outdoor Cooking Facilities: BBQ CBA
Cleanup: provided
View: sky view from patio

RESTRICTIONS:

Alcohol: in-house
Smoking: outdoors only
Music: amplified OK indoors

Wheelchair Access: limited
Insurance: not required

MountainGate Country Club

Country Club

12445 Mountaingate Drive, Los Angeles
888/995-7937
www.countryclubreceptions.com
privateeventdirector@mtngatecc.com

● Rehearsal Dinners		● Corporate Events	
● Ceremonies		● Meetings	
● Wedding Receptions		● Film Shoots	
● Private Parties		Accommodations	

Situated at the top of a steep winding road at the gateway to Brentwood and Bel Air, MountainGate does not disappoint. The country club—the jewel of a private residential development—is a breath of fresh air for L.A. brides and grooms seeking panoramic views and a location that's convenient to both Beverly Hills and the Valley.

Fronted by a cobblestone entryway and a white porte-cochère with a red-tiled roof, the clubhouse is embraced by a grove of tall conifers and native trees. The building evokes Frank Lloyd Wright's aesthetic, with its geometric configuration and interior use of natural wood and glass. In contrast to the angular architectural lines, the slender entry walkway makes its way over a large, oval-shaped pond encircled by ferns, bougainvillea, azaleas, birds of paradise, and other tropical plants. It's a calming and inviting environment, and guests take time to appreciate it before stepping into the building's foyer. Needless to say, the pond and walkway are favorite backdrops for individual or group photos.

The best spot for outdoor ceremonies is a picturesque, perfectly manicured tee box at the edge of an expansive golf course that constitutes MountainGate's backyard. The ceremony site overlooks serene rolling hills and sits beneath a cluster of birch trees, which provide respite from the sun. It's backed by dozens of multicolored roses that lend a heavenly fragrance to the air during the early summer.

Wedding receptions are held in the club's dining room or, for larger parties, on the garden patio adjacent to the main dining room. A continuum of floor-to-ceiling windows along three sides let in plenty of light and showcase three tee-off greens, emerald fairways, and the Santa Monica Mountains in the distance. The rich warmth of the cherrywood ceiling and crown molding is enhanced at night by the romantic glow emanating from the rustic wrought-iron chandeliers and matching wall sconces. Walls are a creamy taupe imprinted with a subtle pattern, and an earth-tone carpet completes the décor.

Separating the main dining room from the bar is a double-sided fireplace, clad in slate tiles. Guests mingle and enjoy cocktails and hors d'oeuvres in the bar, and can then easily flow into the dining room for a seated reception. When the music starts and it's time to party, you can use a portable dance floor in the main dining room or dance the night away in the atrium, which affords a panoramic view.

In addition to the smart architecture and attractive landscaping, what really makes a MountainGate wedding so memorable is the hospitable attitude that prevails among staffers. Everyone goes out of his or her way to make your celebration feel special, and you get a lot of extra attention thanks to MountainGate's policy of hosting only one wedding at a time.

CEREMONY CAPACITY: The Main Dining Room seats up to 200 guests. The adjoining patio accommodates up to 330 seated.

EVENT/RECEPTION CAPACITY: The Main Dining Room holds 180 seated guests with a dance floor, 200 without, or 330 standing guests. The garden patio (which can be tented) accommodates 330 seated guests with a dance floor, and 400 without.

MEETING CAPACITY: The Main Dining Room can accommodate 100 guests classroom-style or 150 guests theater-style.

FEES & DEPOSITS: A nonrefundable deposit, which is applied to your food and beverage total, is required to reserve your date. The amount of the deposit varies, depending on how far in advance you book. Payment terms for the balance also vary, and may be arranged on an individual basis. Wedding packages start at $105/person. Tax, alcohol and service charge are additional. Menus and packages can be customized to fit your needs and budget. Call for details.

AVAILABILITY: Year-round, Tuesday, Friday and Saturday evenings in 6-hour blocks, with some exceptions. The first Sunday evening of the month is also available in a 6-hour block. There's a $750/hour fee to extend an event beyond a 6-hour block.

SERVICES/AMENITIES:

Catering: in-house or BYO
Kitchen Facilities: n/a
Tables & Chairs: provided
Linens, Silver, etc.: provided
Restrooms: wheelchair accessible
Dance Floor: provided
Bride's & Groom's Dressing Area: yes
Meeting Equipment: microphone, screen
Other: event coordination, wedding cakes

Parking: on site; valet included w/some packages
Accommodations: no guest rooms
Telephone: guest phones
Outdoor Night Lighting: yes
Outdoor Cooking Facilities: n/a
Cleanup: provided
View: hills, golf fairways and city skyline

RESTRICTIONS:

Alcohol: in-house
Smoking: outside only
Music: amplified OK until midnight

Wheelchair Access: yes
Insurance: not required
Other: no rice, glitter or birdseed

Oviatt Penthouse

Penthouse of Landmark, Art Deco Building

617 South Olive Street, Los Angeles
213/379-4172
www.oviatt.com
weddings@trulyyourscatering.com

- Rehearsal Dinners
- Ceremonies
- Wedding Receptions
- Private Parties
- Corporate Events
- Meetings
- Film Shoots
- Accommodations

Seldom does Old Hollywood meet New Hollywood as spectacularly as at the Oviatt Penthouse, an exclusive 13th-story aerie of Art Deco splendor. Once the private residence of James Oviatt, the dapper haberdasher behind the building of this 1927 landmark, the penthouse now lends its sophisticated elegance—and a 360-degree view of the downtown L.A. skyline—to weddings and other special events.

The moment you enter the building's lobby, you get a hint of what awaits you in the Penthouse. Many of the glass and metal features you see here—the windows, doors, pillars and ceiling—are the work of the famous Parisian glassmaker, René Lalique. His genius is also evident in the Penthouse's light fixtures and glasswork. The elevator that whisks you up to the 13th floor might as well be a time machine, because when the doors open and you step into the Penthouse foyer, you find yourself in another world, one that's a virtual time capsule from the 1930s.

As you and your guests wander among the Penthouse's seven rooms, notice the extraordinary details: the arched hallway ceiling, painted like a starry night sky and edged with Lalique light fixtures; the autographed photos of Mr. Oviatt's wonderfully dressed movie star clients; the Saddier et Fils Art Deco bar in the dining room; the living room's parquet floor fashioned from precious woods; and the bathroom, which has a sunken marble tub and glazed terracotta tiles etched with a palm-leaf design. The entire penthouse is incredibly sensual and tactile, tempting you to stroke the rose-colored, velvet-covered chairs and the cool surface of the marble fireplace. Even the powder room's commode and lavatory basin are veneered in burled maple and upholstered with cut velvet.

As though all this weren't enough, the splendor extends to the outdoors as well on the terrace. This breathtaking space has a slightly Moorish feel, with a colorful tiled fountain and arabesques of wrought iron adorning staircases and rooftops. A Spanish-tiled stairway leads you up to the Martini Lounge, a chic new area for up to 25 guests. Formerly just an observation deck that had been closed to the public for 15 years, it's now outfitted with lounge furniture, draperies and dramatic uplighting. This is *the* place to host an intimate private party on a warm summer night, with the glittering city spread out beneath you—especially if you enhance the space with gobos, twinkle lights or other mood lighting.

Truly Yours Catering, the company handling events at the Penthouse, has been working with the Los Angeles Conservancy to preserve the space, returning some of the original antiques, and repainting the interior. They've also built their own kitchen on site so that all their fabulous food arrives the way it was prepared: fresh and hot.

In addition to being a one-of-a-kind location for weddings, rehearsal dinners and brunches, the Penthouse has become a prime spot for bridal mixers (where brides meet each other over drinks and desserts and share ideas) and seminars (free events where brides can meet with wedding vendors). Check with *Truly Yours* to find out what's scheduled!

The Oviatt Penthouse is truly an extraordinary venue that makes an indelible impression on everyone who sees it, so no matter what event you host at this "castle in the air" it's bound to be unforgettable.

CEREMONY, EVENT/RECEPTION & MEETING CAPACITY: The site—indoor areas and terrace combined—holds 120 people, maximum. The terrace can seat 120.

FEES & DEPOSITS: A nonrefundable deposit of 100% of the total site fee is required to secure the date. The rental fee ranges $800–5,500 depending on the day of the week. For filming fees, please contact the venue. Wedding packages range $10,000–18,000 and include site, food, rentals and lighting.

AVAILABILITY: Year-round.

SERVICES/AMENITIES:
Catering: provided by *Truly Yours Catering*
Kitchen Facilities: n/a
Tables & Chairs: provided
Linens, Silver, etc.: through caterer
Restrooms: wheelchair accessible
Dance Floor: no
Bride's & Groom's Dressing Area: yes
Meeting Equipment: BYO
Other: stereo system provided indoors, outdoor heaters

Parking: valet CBA; adjacent fee lots
Accommodations: no guest rooms
Telephone: CBA
Outdoor Night Lighting: yes
Outdoor Cooking Facilities: yes
Cleanup: $250 fee per event
View: stunning 360-degree L.A. cityscape from terrace

RESTRICTIONS:
Alcohol: in-house or BYO
Smoking: terrace only
Music: amplified OK

Wheelchair Access: limited
Insurance: liability required

Petersen Automotive Museum
and Rooftop Penthouse

6060 Wilshire Boulevard at Fairfax, Los Angeles
323/964-6348
www.petersenevents.org
specialevents@petersen.org

Automotive Museum

- Rehearsal Dinners
- Ceremonies
- Wedding Receptions
- Private Parties
- Corporate Events
- Meetings
- Film Shoots
- Accommodations

Millions of dollars' worth of beautiful cars make an amazing backdrop for a glamorous reception, but the Petersen Automotive Museum also offers a unique setting that dazzles without cars: a private rooftop penthouse with a fabulous view.

Their fourth-floor "terrace in the sky" is an architecturally intriguing space: an all-glass venue surrounded by a smooth, slate patio. Many couples have their ceremony on one side of the patio and host a seated reception on the other, using the penthouse itself for cocktails and dancing. When you add lounge furniture, the "room" takes on the feeling of a nightclub. However, you're free to choreograph your celebration any way you like, and no matter where you are in this thoroughly modern aerie you'll be cooled by passing breezes and enjoy a vista that's pure L.A. The daytime panorama showcases the Hollywood Hills and Century City, with the sheer walls of nearby high-rises adding a special Miracle Mile thrill. At night, Los Angeles becomes a sea of glittering lights.

The seven galleries that make up the second floor are also available for corporate parties, conferences, product launches and other events. They showcase exhibits (two of them rotating) of a wide range of vehicles, from vintage, celebrity and race cars to hot rods and motorcycles. Cocktail receptions are especially popular in the Hollywood Gallery, which features cars that have starred in movies, the most famous of which is the Batmobile. From here guests move into the adjacent Grand Salon for dinner and dancing among a completely different set of impressive cars. If you have a very large group, reserve the Pavilion just off the second floor. With 18,000 square feet and room to seat up to 800, it's perfect for galas and fundraisers.

Even the exhibits on the first floor, which depict the history of the automobile, serve as a fun, interactive environment for cocktail receptions or informal gatherings. Lifelike dioramas and settings allow guests to experience the automobile as it relates to everyday life. You can also pose for photos next to some of the museum's celebrity cars.

Pay a visit to the Petersen Automotive Museum, and you'll see firsthand what a special place it is for events. One of the perks of having your wedding here is a 1-year museum membership for the bride and groom. It includes unlimited free admission, invitations to the members-only special events and a 10% discount in the museum store. Whether you party in the Penthouse or in one of the other galleries, your guests will be thanking you for introducing them to this gem of a location.

CEREMONY CAPACITY: The Penthouse/Terrace (fourth floor) holds 200 seated or 300 standing; the Grand Salon (2nd floor) holds 200 seated.

EVENT/RECEPTION CAPACITY: The Museum can accommodate 100 seated or 500 standing on the first floor, 400 seated or 800 standing on the second floor, 800 seated or 2,000 standing in the Pavilion, and 150 seated or 300 standing guests in the Penthouse/Terrace.

MEETING CAPACITY: The Penthouse holds 200 seated theater-style; the Founder's Lounge holds 50 seated theater-style or 20 seated conference-style.

FEES & DEPOSITS: 50% of the total event cost is required to reserve your date and the balance is due 21 days prior to the event. Rental fees range $3,500–15,000 depending on the space rented and the guest count.

AVAILABILITY: Year-round, daily; 6pm–2am for museum interior, 10am–2am for tent and roof-top spaces.

SERVICES/AMENITIES:

Catering: select from preferred list, or BYO
Kitchen Facilities: prep only
Tables & Chairs: provided
Linens, Silver, etc.: through caterer
Restrooms: wheelchair accessible
Dance Floor: CBA
Bride's Dressing Area: yes
Meeting Equipment: some provided

Parking: large lot
Accommodations: no guest rooms
Telephone: emergency use only
Outdoor Night Lighting: yes
Outdoor Cooking Facilities: BBQ CBA
Cleanup: provided
View: panoramic views of city
Other: AV equipment

RESTRICTIONS:

Alcohol: select from preferred provider list
Smoking: outside only
Music: amplified OK

Wheelchair Access: yes
Insurance: liability required
Other: no rice, birdseed or glitter

The professionals in the back of this book are the best in the business. How do we know? Read page 549.

Vibiana

214 South Main Street, Los Angeles
213/626-1507

www.vibiana.com
info@vibiana.com

Historic Ballroom & Garden

● Rehearsal Dinners	● Corporate Events
● Ceremonies	● Meetings
● Wedding Receptions	● Film Shoots
● Private Parties	Accommodations

They say there are no second acts in life, but the magnificent Vibiana has an exciting new focus under the direction of husband-and-wife restaurateurs Neal Fraser and Amy Knoll Fraser, along with partner Bill Chait. Neal has long been one of L.A.'s premier chefs, having worked with culinary luminaries such as Thomas Keller and Wolfgang Puck. He's also the first California chef to win the prestigious Iron Chef America TV show. Together, the Frasers bring their hand-crafted approach to food and event services to this full-service venue that's a star in its own right: Not only is Vibiana an architectural treasure, it's also a "take your breath away" setting for weddings, concerts and special occasions.

Designed in the Spanish Baroque style and patterned after San Miguel Del Mar in Barcelona, Vibiana (originally St. Vibiana's Cathedral) was built in 1876 as the Catholic Archdiocese in Los Angeles. Over the next century it flourished—until the 1994 Northridge earthquake, when it suffered some severe damage. Eventually, one of L.A.'s most respected developers began a long and expensive process to completely retrofit, redefine and revitalize Vibiana.

Mindful of maintaining the integrity of this landmark, the developer strengthened and secured the building while keeping its original beauty and appearance intact. At first glance, the limestone exterior may still resemble a church, but the site has been desanctified and its massive double doors thrown open to welcome celebrants of all backgrounds, faiths and persuasions. In short, it's now secular heaven.

The foyer entryway is dazzling with its gold embellished barrel ceilings and black-and-white marble floor. To your left are massive glass-and-iron doors that lead to a beautiful garden on the property's grounds at Main and Second. Surrounded by tall wrought-iron fencing and enough greenery to ensure privacy, it has a long center aisle that ends at a landscaped island, a natural spot for exchanging your vows. From this verdant vantage point, you can look up and see such notable buildings as City Hall and the historic L.A. Times Building, both of which light up at night making the cityscape come alive.

But it's Vibiana's interior and its truly grand proportions that make this a one-of-a-kind wedding location. It's an architectural marvel with soaring gilded ceilings, an abundance of white marble, and clerestory windows that let in natural light. Long rows of white columns on either side stand in contrast to the deeply burnished dark wood floors. At the far end, the old altar is now an impressive white marble stage with plenty of space to set up your sweetheart table, make toasts or bring in a band (the acoustics here are great). While the grandeur of the old cathedral can be seen in the scale of the venue, some features have been re-imagined in fun new ways, like the old confessionals, which can be turned into photo booths for your guests. Perhaps it's this combination of putting a modern spin on Old World beauty that's made Vibiana such a runaway success since the day it opened.

CEREMONY CAPACITY: The site holds 600 seated guests indoors and 300 seated outdoors.

EVENT/RECEPTION & MEETING CAPACITY: The facility can accommodate 600 seated or 789 standing guests indoors, and 300 seated or 500 standing outdoors.

FEES & DEPOSITS: 50% of the venue rental fee and a $2,500 food & beverage deposit are required to reserve your date. 50% of the estimated food & beverage total is due no later than 60 days after booking your event. The remaining balance is due 14 days prior to the event along with a $1,000 refundable damage deposit. Rental fees range $8,500–16,500 depending on the event date.

AVAILABILITY: Year-round, daily, 9am–2am.

SERVICES/AMENITIES:

Catering: in-house
Kitchen Facilities: n/a
Tables & Chairs: provided
Linens, Silver, etc.: provided
Restrooms: wheelchair accessible
Dance Floor: provided, extra fee
Bride's & Groom's Dressing Area: yes
Meeting Equipment: BYO

Parking: valet available
Accommodations: no guest rooms
Telephone: office phone
Outdoor Night Lighting: yes
Outdoor Cooking Facilities: BBQ CBA
Cleanup: provided
View: cityscape, garden

RESTRICTIONS:

Alcohol: in-house
Smoking: allowed outside in the garden
Music: amplified OK with restrictions

Wheelchair Access: yes
Insurance: liability required

Calamigos Ranch Malibu

327 South Latigo Canyon, Malibu
818/889-6280

www.calamigos.com
weddings@calamigos.com

Ranch and Conference Center

● Rehearsal Dinners	● Corporate Events
● Ceremonies	● Meetings
● Wedding Receptions	● Film Shoots
● Private Parties	Accommodations

Although Calamigos bills itself as a country ranch set amongst 130 acres of rolling hills, verdant meadows, lakes, ancient oaks, and its own vineyard, most of its event facilities are far from rustic.

There are four different outdoor ceremony options, each with its own reception site. The Garden Patio near the ranch's entrance is an expansive lawn with picturesque waterfalls at each end. Guests are seated on either side of a stone aisle, facing a redwood arbor adorned with flowers where the bride and groom exchange vows. Shaded by trees, it's a peaceful and private area. From here it's just a few steps to the Lodge, a delightful, sun-filled space thanks to light streaming in through "walls" of French doors. One of the room's remarkable features is the romantic "waterfall," a curtain of water that descends like a light rain just outside the glass doors.

The Oaks Deck is popular for intimate ceremonies. Rows of chairs are set up in front of a wood arbor with a rock waterfall directly behind it, and a backdrop of eucalyptus, pine and oak trees. Couples who get married here usually have their reception in the dining room nearby. Like the Lodge, it uses French doors to maximize light and views of the outdoors. Crisp white table linens contrast nicely with the warm pine ceiling beams and doorframes, and ferns and ficus trees provide indoor greenery. Buffets are often served on the adjoining redwood deck, which is partially shaded by oak branches.

A third option is the Cottage and Pavilion, a secluded little meadow ringed by trees and natural landscaping. Couples tie the knot on an earthen terrace beneath a majestic spreading oak, or in front of a clear pond at the base of a river rock waterfall. Afterwards, guests are invited to the reception under an elegant white tent draped with sheer fabric and twinkle lights.

Lastly, the Secret Garden is a charming venue designed for more intimate gatherings. Ceremonies unfold on a grassy field bordered by roses, plum trees and a large cascading waterfall. The reception can be held on the private, multilevel deck nearby. Surrounded by nature, including a couple of streams, this spot is beautiful and calm. Sunset and evening events are lovely here, especially when the thousands of twinkle lights lacing the trees add their sparkle.

And if you've come to the ranch for one of their legendary western-style celebrations (including Barn Mitzvahs!), check out The Barn. It's the real thing: The floor is covered with sawdust, bales of hay are scattered about, and it's painted—you guessed it—bright red.

We were pleasantly surprised by the ranch's reception facilities and the Calamigos staff, who are true professionals when it comes to helping you plan your wedding. They'll design your event to suit your special needs, and coordinate everything down to the last detail.

CEREMONY CAPACITY: Indoors, the ranch holds up to 400 seated guests; outdoors up to 800 seated guests.

EVENT/RECEPTION CAPACITY: Indoor areas accommodate 75–500 seated or 150–600 standing guests. The site has a 75-guest minimum.

MEETING CAPACITY: The site accommodates up to 35–500 guests for conferences.

FEES & DEPOSITS: For weddings, a $1,500 nonrefundable deposit is required to reserve your date and is applied to the final bill; the balance is payable 3 days prior to the event. A variety of wedding packages (including customized ones) are available, with prices ranging $97–117/person.

For day conferences, all-inclusive packages start at $55/person.

AVAILABILITY: Year-round, daily, including holidays. Conferences and other corporate events are by arrangement.

SERVICES/AMENITIES:

Catering: in-house, or BYO, buyout required
Kitchen Facilities: fully equipped
Tables & Chairs: provided
Linens, Silver, etc.: provided
Restrooms: wheelchair accessible
Dance Floor: provided
Bride's Dressing Area: yes; groom's CBA
Meeting Equipment: CBA, extra fee

Parking: large lot, free valet
Accommodations: no guest rooms
Telephone: emergency use only
Outdoor Night Lighting: yes
Outdoor Cooking Facilities: BBQs
Cleanup: provided
View: Santa Monica Mountains
Other: ceremony coordination & rehearsal

RESTRICTIONS:

Alcohol: in-house, BWC corkage $10/bottle
Smoking: outdoors only
Music: amplified OK until 11pm

Wheelchair Access: yes
Insurance: liability required
Other: no rice, confetti or sparklers

Cypress Sea Cove

Private Beachfront Estate

33572 Pacific Coast Highway, Malibu
310/589-3344
www.malibufilmlocations.com
richard.mark@usrecorp.com

● Rehearsal Dinners	● Corporate Events
● Ceremonies	● Meetings
● Wedding Receptions	● Film Shoots
● Private Parties	Accommodations

Poised on a flat bluff overlooking the wide blue backdrop of the Pacific, this two-acre, ocean-front private estate is an exceptionally dramatic locale for any occasion. Beauty greets you at every turn: Majestic Monterey cypress are silhouetted against the sky, an acre of velvety lawn spreads all the way to the end of the bluff, and on summer nights the cliff-edge gazebo is backlit by the setting sun. The nautical white Victorian home, reminiscent of the East Coast Hamptons, is generally not available for events, but the gorgeous grounds, festooned with roses and multicolored blooms, leave little to be desired.

Most celebrations are held on the bluff's expansive lawn. Here a large brick patio beneath towering cypress trees works perfectly for a buffet setup, and every table on the grass has an ocean view. The white gazebo, spacious enough for the bride and all her bridesmaids, also serves as a classic frame for wedding photos as well as displaying and cutting the cake.

For smaller receptions or seaside ceremonies, walk down through Palm Canyon to the secluded beach patio, where young Marilyn Monroe attended many luaus. As you descend, you'll see hundreds of phoenix, Mexican fantail and date palms, some of them over 150 feet tall! The tropical-style beach bar and patio, really a series of three lushly landscaped brick and adobe terraces that end on the sand, is an intimate and romantic spot to exchange vows. The couple stands with their backs to the crashing surf, while guests seated on the palm-shaded lawn have a view of the sea. The patio also boasts a delightful bamboo cabana. With canvas rollback windows and wired for sound, it's a sublime place to spend an evening listening to your favorite music, sipping mai tais and watching the moon drop into the sea.

Cypress Sea Cove hosts many types of events, including corporate barbecues and private parties, but the estate's owners have a particular fondness for weddings and provide a cottage just for the bride. In addition, the owners can suggest several experienced wedding and special event planning companies that will help make your event worry-free. A *New York Times* pick as one of the best wedding locations in the U.S., this stunning waterfront venue is truly a little piece of paradise found.

CEREMONY, RECEPTION & MEETING CAPACITY: The formal lawn holds up to 300 seated guests. The lower beach patio can accommodate up to 50 guests.

FEES & DEPOSITS: The rental fee ranges $8,000–20,000 depending on the season, date selected and group size. A cleaning fee may be additional.

AVAILABILITY: Year-round, daily, including holidays.

SERVICES/AMENITIES:

Catering: BYO
Kitchen Facilities: prep area for outdoor caterers
Tables & Chairs: BYO
Linens, Silver, etc.: BYO
Restrooms: wheelchair access CBA
Dance Floor: BYO
Bride's Dressing Area: Bridal Cottage with restroom
Meeting Equipment: BYO, wireless internet provided

Parking: shuttle or valet
Accommodations: no guest rooms
Telephone: CBA
Outdoor Night Lighting: yes
Outdoor Cooking Facilities: yes
Cleanup: caterer
View: 180° panorama of Pacific Ocean and beach; palm trees and sunsets

RESTRICTIONS:

Alcohol: BYO
Smoking: not restricted
Music: amplified OK with time & volume restrictions

Wheelchair Access: yes
Insurance: certificate required

Duke's Malibu

Oceanfront Restaurant

21150 Pacific Coast Highway, Malibu
310/317-6204
www.dukesmalibu.com
events@dukesmalibu.com

- Rehearsal Dinners
- Ceremonies
- Wedding Receptions
- Private Parties
- Corporate Events
- Meetings
- Film Shoots
- Accommodations

Duke's enviable waterfront location, fun-loving yet professional staff, and elegant event spaces will tempt you to celebrate right here on Malibu's famous shores. This supremely popular restaurant and its private banquet rooms enhance all types of occasions—wedding ceremonies, receptions, rehearsal dinners, day-after brunches, and more—with gracious hospitality and gorgeous Pacific panoramas. It's the perfect atmosphere for old friends and new families to come together.

Duke's Malibu was inspired by the memory of the legendary Duke Kahanamoku and the benevolent values that he personified. This extraordinary Olympic athlete set numerous swimming records and is credited with popularizing the sport of surfing. In his twilight years, Duke served as Hawaii's official "Ambassador of Aloha." He also had a profound impact on the beach culture of Southern California, so Malibu is an ideal site for a restaurant in his honor.

The "aloha" spirit embraces guests as they're welcomed through a private entrance and ushered into the Moana Room. This lovely space has two walls of beachfront windows that are just steps away from the splashing surf. The other walls, paneled in the rare and valuable Hawaiian koa wood, give off a rich luster. In addition, doors open onto a balcony situated over the sand where guests may enjoy a quiet moment away from the festivities—perhaps to take in one of Malibu's extraordinary sunsets. At Duke's Malibu, you can create a casual celebration or transform the room into a stylish affair limited only by your imagination.

For more intimate celebrations, like bridal and baby showers, Duke's Malibu can accommodate your group in its "Board" Room (as in surfboard). This private, oceanview room is located in the restaurant and seats 36. As with the Moana Room, mahogany Chiavari chairs, a choice of linens in various colors, and votive candles are provided for your event.

Just as satisfying as the view, Duke's coastal-inspired menus feature Hawaiian-influenced fresh fish and premium steaks, offered in both plated and buffet options.

When you desire to treat guests to an oceanfront experience, Duke's Malibu is the ideal spot for a truly unique and memorable gathering.

CEREMONY CAPACITY: The Moana Room holds 150 seated guests.

EVENT/RECEPTION CAPACITY: The Moana Room holds up to 250 seated or 400 standing guests.

MEETING CAPACITY: The Moana Room holds 250 seated, the Board Room 36 seated.

FEES & DEPOSITS: A $2,000 nonrefundable deposit for the Moana Room or $500 for the Board Room is required to guarantee a specified date, time and space for an event. Food and beverage minimums are required for certain times and dates. Luncheons start at $30/person, dinners at $40/person; alcohol, tax and a 20% service charge are additional.

AVAILABILITY: Year-round, daily, until midnight. Closed Christmas Day.

SERVICES/AMENITIES:

Catering: in-house, no BYO
Kitchen Facilities: n/a
Tables & Chairs: provided
Linens, Silver, etc.: provided
Restrooms: wheelchair accessible
Dance Floor: CBA, extra charge
Bride's Dressing Area: yes
Meeting Equipment: CBA or BYO

Parking: valet
Accommodations: no guest rooms
Telephone: emergency use only
Outdoor Night Lighting: access lighting only
Outdoor Cooking Facilities: n/a
Cleanup: provided
View: 180-degree panorama of Pacific Ocean and beach; palm trees and sunsets

RESTRICTIONS:

Alcohol: in-house; wine and champagne corkage $20/750 ml bottle, $35/1.5 l bottle
Smoking: designated area outdoors
Music: amplified OK indoors

Wheelchair Access: yes
Insurance: not required

Want to know WHAT TO ASK a potential location or vendor? Check out our Questions to Ask starting on page 19.

Malibu West Beach Club

Private Beach Club

30756 W. Pacific Coast Highway, Malibu
310/457-0195
www.malibuwestbeachclub.com
events@malibuwestbc.com

- Rehearsal Dinners
- Ceremonies
- Wedding Receptions
- Private Parties

- Corporate Events
- Meetings
- Film Shoots
- Accommodations

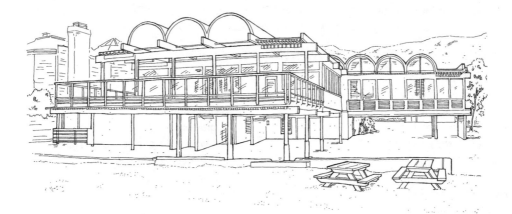

Standing at the edge of the ocean between Zuma State Beach and Broad Beach, the Malibu West Beach Club occupies one of the most desirable slices of real estate in Southern California. Glorious white sand stretches 200 yards from the clubhouse to the breaking surf, and from the facility's deck there's a 180-degree panorama of the vast Pacific and miles of Malibu coastline. When it's clear, you can even see all the way to Catalina Island and the Channel Islands! As an added treat, whales migrate close to shore in the winter months, and almost daily you'll spot dolphins leaping out of the water as they swim by.

This private club has provided beach access to countless families since it was built in 1962. The unassuming two-story structure is partially screened from the street behind some hot pink bougainvillea and evergreen trees; you'd never know it was there if you didn't go looking for it. The bright and airy event space, which is on the top floor, is essentially one large room with a high vaulted ceiling and an adjacent deck. It's clean, simple and unadorned as can be—a blank canvas on which to create your own decoration. Of course, the sunsets, visible through the club's glass façade, complement any décor.

Speaking of sunsets, that's when most ceremonies take place. Guests are seated facing the ocean on the tiled 50-foot-wide deck, while bride and groom tie the knot under a flower-covered arch or *chuppah*. Afterwards, the newlyweds go down to the beach for wedding photos. All the elements are there for fabulous pictures: sun, sand, ocean—there's even a Baywatch-style lifeguard tower on which everyone can pose for a group shot.

Generally, dinner and dancing are indoor activities, while sipping champagne, sampling hors d'oeuvres and lingering over a setting sun all take place on the deck. If you prefer, tables can be set up on the deck for an al fresco reception. From your ocean-front perch, you'll feel the cool breezes and taste the tang of sea salt in the air. At night, you can look up and see millions of stars.

In addition to the banquet room, Malibu West also offers a versatile bride's room. The club has outfitted it with thoughtful amenities to help the ladies primp and prepare—mirrors, vanities, dress racks—and there's even an ocean view! After the ceremony, it's also a quiet retreat where the bride and groom can have a moment alone together before the festivities begin; and during the reception this space can be set up as a kiddies' play area.

As if all this weren't enough, Malibu West also boasts a knowledgeable, friendly staff that will assist you in selecting vendors that match your vision and your budget. Given its beachfront location, genial ambiance and affordable prices, the Malibu West Beach Club is understandably in demand.

CEREMONY CAPACITY: The oceanview deck holds 150 seated guests.

EVENT/RECEPTION & MEETING CAPACITY: The site holds up to 200 seated or 250 standing guests. 150 or fewer is suggested for weddings, if you want everyone in the same room at the same time.

FEES & DEPOSITS: For events, 50% of the rental fee is a nonrefundable deposit required to reserve your date. The remaining balance and a $1,000 refundable security deposit are payable 60 days prior to the event. Weekend and holiday rental fees range $4,340–6,340 depending on guest count. An on-site representative is required for the duration of the event and is included in the rental fee. Midweek rates start at $2,340.

AVAILABILITY: Year-round, daily, 8am–1am, in 12-hour blocks.

SERVICES/AMENITIES:

Catering: BYO, bonded and licensed
Kitchen Facilities: most appliances
Tables & Chairs: provided, 150 chairs and tables for up to 200 guests
Linens, Silver, etc.: caterer or BYO
Restrooms: two are wheelchair accessible
Dance Floor: included
Bride's Dressing Area: yes
Meeting Equipment: BYO
Kosher: kosher kitchen CBA

Parking: on street, limited on site, valet service recommended
Accommodations: no guest rooms
Telephone: emergency use only
Outdoor Night Lighting: access lighting only
Outdoor Cooking Facilities: BYO
Cleanup: through caterer
View: panoramic ocean views and sunsets, Catalina and Channel Islands, Malibu coastline

RESTRICTIONS:

Alcohol: BYO; server bonded and licensed
Smoking: outdoors only
Music: amplified OK indoors until 10pm, volume reduced until midnight

Wheelchair Access: ramp
Insurance: required for caterers not on preferred list
Other: no rice, staples, nails, birdseed or confetti

Saddlerock Ranch and Vineyard

Ranch

Address withheld to ensure privacy. Malibu

818/889-0008 x22

www.malibufamilywines.com
weddings@malibufamilywines.com

● Rehearsal Dinners	● Corporate Events
● Ceremonies	● Meetings
● Wedding Receptions	● Film Shoots
● Private Parties	Accommodations

Touted as "one location, a million scenes," this thousand-acre privately owned estate in the hills of Malibu is a much sought-after film site. Which isn't surprising: Saddlerock Ranch and Vineyard has views of the Conejo Valley, and is itself a veritable cornucopia of visual delights, with fruit and avocado orchards, acres of vineyards and pastureland dotted with heritage oaks and grazing herds of horses, cattle and llamas. Craggy rocks—including a landmark outcropping shaped like a saddle—jut up from vineyard-covered slopes, and ribbons of white fences meander alongside fields and tree-shaded driveways. Look carefully, and you'll see a few peacocks or even a camel or zebra as you wind your way through the ranch.

Happily for you, all this scenic beauty is available for special events. Four separate areas lend themselves to wedding ceremonies: the rose garden adjacent to the estate's main house; under the cascading fronds of a willow tree next to the rose garden; beneath a willow tree that overlooks a bucolic horse pasture (imagine mares and foals frolicking in the sun as morning mist rises from the fields); and lastly, under the branches of a 250-year-old oak, centered in a large grassy clearing surrounded by thickets of trees. Twinkle lights in the oak and nearby trees make this a spectacular spot for evening affairs, although the natural grandeur of the ranch doesn't need much adornment.

Many couples like the convenience of having their reception on one of the expansive level lawns at each of the wedding sites, but there are numerous other possibilities. One couple covered the tennis courts near the oak tree with AstroTurf, decorated it with lights, and hosted a black-tie reception for 500. Another couple opted for a country western theme—they rode horses to their ceremony, and then celebrated with a barbecue.

Saddlerock's newest event site is Chateau Le Dome, located on a hilltop in the middle of the ranch's vineyards. The Chateau in this case is an octagonal stone house, set on a manicured lawn that's large enough for a ceremony and reception. From this elevated vantage, you have panoramic views of the surrounding vineyards, valleys and pastures. As the bride prepares inside the house, guests take their seats for a ceremony on one side of the lawn. In keeping with the natural setting, vows are exchanged beneath a fallen oak-tree arch, entwined with grapevines. Afterwards, as friends and family dine in the serenity of their secluded perch, they'll feel like they're on top of the world.

Another appealing gathering area is the Malibu Wines Tasting Room, an expansive and artfully landscaped outdoor venue. Instead of the usual cocktail hour, why not treat your guests to an array of savory local vintages? The Tasting Room's temperate hilltop climate and gorgeous views are the perfect accompaniments to a glass of Saddlerock Chardonnay or their award-winning Semler Merlot.

At Saddlerock Ranch you start with a breathtaking backdrop and add whatever props you like. Fill the sky with butterflies or doves, bring in an elephant, or wave goodbye to your guests from a helicopter or hot-air balloon. Virtually anything is possible here, where you get to be the star in a fantasy uniquely your own.

CEREMONY CAPACITY: There are several spots on the grounds surrounding the Main House; each can accommodate hundreds of guests.

EVENT/RECEPTION & MEETING CAPACITY: The site holds 10–2,500 guests.

FEES & DEPOSITS: Half of the rental fee is required upon booking; the balance plus a refundable $1,000 security deposit are due 10 days prior to the event. The rental fee for the Ranch starts at $12,000 for up to 400 guests, plus $25/person for each person over 400. The rental fee for Chateau Le Dome is $6,000 for up to 100 guests; the rental fee for the Oak Grove is $10,000 for up to 400 guests, plus $25/person for each additional guest. Security and valet parking are required; all service providers must be insured to perform services on the property.

AVAILABILITY: Year-round, daily, anytime.

SERVICES/AMENITIES:
Catering: select from preferred list or BYO
Kitchen Facilities: prep only
Tables & Chairs: through caterer or rental co.
Linens, Silver, etc.: through caterer or rental co.
Restrooms: wheelchair access CBA
Dance Floor: BYO
Bride's & Groom's Dressing Area: yes
Meeting Equipment: CBA, extra charge

Parking: valet required, extra fee
Accommodations: no guest rooms
Telephone: deposit required
Outdoor Night Lighting: access only
Outdoor Cooking Facilities: CBA
Cleanup: caterer and renter
View: mountains, orchards, lawns and pastures, rose garden, vineyards

RESTRICTIONS:
Alcohol: wines purchased through Saddlerock
Smoking: not allowed
Music: amplified OK

Wheelchair Access: yes
Insurance: liability required

The Sunset Restaurant

6800 Westward Beach Road, Malibu
310/589-2027

www.thesunsetrestaurant.com
eventscoordinator@thesunsetrestaurant.com

Waterfront Restaurant

● Rehearsal Dinners	● Corporate Events
● Ceremonies	● Meetings
● Wedding Receptions	● Film Shoots
● Private Parties	Accommodations

You can have it all—a romantic setting, delectable cuisine, and gracious service—at the Sunset Restaurant, tucked against the Malibu bluffs just steps from Zuma Beach. Housed in an updated version of a classic beach bungalow, the two-story restaurant breathes with space and light, thanks to the expanse of windows along the front wall. One of the many benefits of staging your wedding at the Sunset is the ease of having everything in one package. This venue is particularly event-friendly, with distinct areas that coordinate with each phase of a wedding celebration.

First, say your marriage vows right on the beach. For a fee that includes the city permit, the Sunset arranges a platform walkway, runner and a wood stage area with the blue Pacific as a vibrant backdrop. Other elements further enhance this idyllic place: Sailboats drift across the horizon … a pelican dives for its dinner … the sound of the waves is in soothing harmony with the music of your accompanist. As you walk down the aisle, a light breeze lifts your veil, which floats around you like sea foam. Your guests are entranced, and the fun is only beginning. (This writer knows from personal experience: She had her wedding here, and the guests are still raving!)

After the ceremony, your photographer captures dramatic photos of the bridal party during one of Malibu's jewel-toned sunsets. Meanwhile, your friends and family gather on the outdoor patio that adjoins the Event Room. Here they enjoy the cocktail hour and scrumptious hors d'oeuvres, while mingling around cocktail tables or relaxing on couches. You can add your own festive touches with colored paper lanterns, string lights or vibrant throw pillows.

When it's time for the reception, everyone moves into the Event Room. Simple, yet classy, its understated décor adapts easily to your own vision … but this room has a couple of tasteful features that add to your celebration: The white fabric lining the ceiling lends a wavy softness to the space, and a row of view-filled windows curves shoreward, like a long ripple in the nearby surf. At some point during your festivities, you might drift outside with your sweetheart to stroll on the sugary sand and soak up a bit of moonlight.

Two cozy upstairs venues, the North and South Rooms, prove that the views are even more spectacular from the second floor. Picture windows keep these spaces bathed in golden daylight, when the warm, cheery ambiance is perfect for wedding brunches or showers; at night, star-filled horizons and city-light vistas are sparkling additions to rehearsal dinners.

The Sunset Restaurant, which is open for weekend brunch and dinner every night, has a large number of regular (and often celebrity!) clientele and attracts more loyal fans every day. After paying a visit to this divine seaside locale, you're bound to become a regular, too.

CEREMONY CAPACITY: The beach holds up to 150 seated guests.

EVENT/RECEPTION & MEETING CAPACITY: Indoors, the restaurant holds 120 seated with a dance floor or 140 without, or 200 standing guests. Outdoors the parking lot may be tented for 200 guests or 300 standing.

FEES & DEPOSITS: 10% of the estimated event total (or $1,500) is required to reserve your date and another 50% is due 4 months prior to the event. Both deposits are nonrefundable. Rental fees range $500–10,000 depending on space and time rented and guest count. Meals range $45–110/person and there is a beverage minimum of $20/person. Tax, 20% service charge and mandatory valet charges are additional.

AVAILABILITY: Year-round.

SERVICES/AMENITIES:

Catering: in-house
Kitchen Facilities: n/a
Tables & Chairs: provided
Linens, Silver, etc.: provided
Restrooms: wheelchair accessible
Dance Floor: n/a
Bride's Dressing Area: n/a
Meeting Equipment: BYO

Parking: mandatory valet
Accommodations: no guest rooms
Telephone: emergency use only
Outdoor Night Lighting: CBA
Outdoor Cooking Facilities: no
Cleanup: provided
View: Malibu coastline, ocean
Other: beach ceremony

RESTRICTIONS:

Alcohol: in-house, no BYO
Smoking: outside only
Music: amplified OK

Wheelchair Access: yes
Insurance: not required

California Yacht Club

Yacht Club

4469 Admiralty Way, Marina del Rey
310/448-4771 Catering Department
www.clubweddings.com
cycater@calyachtclub.net

● Rehearsal Dinners	● Corporate Events
● Ceremonies	● Meetings
● Wedding Receptions	● Film Shoots
● Private Parties	Accommodations

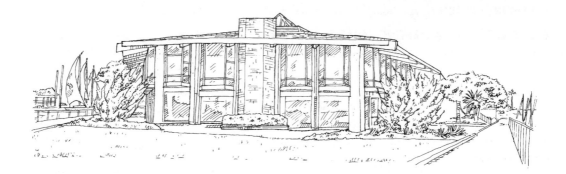

Cleverly designed in an octagonal shape with glass walls that showcase a panoramic view of the harbor, California Yacht Club is a great place for a waterside wedding.

Lovers of the sea will naturally want to get married as close to the ocean as possible, and the Club has a stellar site: a triangular expanse of lawn that advances from the building and tapers to a rounded point in front of the water's edge. Couples exchange vows here, while their guests enjoy the sea air, glittering Pacific and the colorful parade of boats that pass by just beyond the point. After the ceremony, everyone strolls over to the adjacent patio for cocktails and hors d'oeuvres.

The Yacht Club itself is a handsome, two-story building that devotes its entire first floor to celebrations. Receptions take place in the spacious Fireside Room, named for its beautiful brick fireplace, which is set into a wall of windows. Before the dining begins, all eyes are on the bride, who makes a dramatic entrance as she gracefully descends a sweeping atrium staircase. The room's décor is completely up to your imagination—anything from a Polynesian buffet with tiki torches, hula dancers and a fire show (held outdoors), to a formal Black & White Ball. No matter where you sit you're virtually on the water, and the 180-degree view allows every guest to watch the sun set over the ocean.

For very large events, a custom-ordered tent can seat up to 270 beneath a 40-foot ceiling. This expansive space is a blank slate: Hang swags of fabric, add colored gel lights, or bring in a stage for a show or a ten-piece band. And no matter how you design the interior, a view of the water is always available.

The accommodating staff will customize every detail, so you'll get the event that you want along with a lovely location. This is a place where water surrounds you, flocks of sea birds fly overhead, and ships slip quietly in and out of the harbor. Set sail together at California Yacht Club.

CEREMONY CAPACITY: The Club's outdoor lawn holds 250 seated; the indoor Fireside Room 170 seated guests.

EVENT/RECEPTION CAPACITY: The Fireside Room can accommodate 170 seated with a dance floor or 250 for a cocktail reception. The Tent can hold up to 400 guests for cocktail reception or 270 for dining and dancing.

MEETING CAPACITY: The Gallery Room holds up to 48 seated; the Fireside Room up to 200 seated guests.

FEES & DEPOSITS: A nonrefundable deposit equal to the facility fee plus a percentage of the food and beverage minimum is required to secure your date and is applied to the event balance. The balance is due 10 days prior to the event. Luncheons range $38–48/person, dinners or buffets $42–65/person; alcohol, tax and a 20% service charge are additional. A $1,250 ceremony setup fee includes white garden chairs, a 1-hour rehearsal, microphone and PA system, bridal changing room, and water station.

AVAILABILITY: Year-round, daily, 7am–12:30am. The Club is closed on Mondays and Tuesdays and is available for buyouts on those days.

SERVICES/AMENITIES:

Catering: in-house

Kitchen Facilities: yes

Tables & Chairs: provided

Linens, Silver, etc.: provided

Restrooms: wheelchair accessible

Dance Floor: portable provided, extra fee

Bride's & Groom's Dressing Area: yes

Meeting Equipment: CBA, extra fee

Parking: valet parking required for over 75 guests

Accommodations: no guest rooms

Telephone: emergency use only

Outdoor Night Lighting: access only

Outdoor Cooking Facilities: BBQs CBA

Cleanup: provided

View: marina, Pacific Ocean

RESTRICTIONS:

Alcohol: in-house, or corkage $15/bottle

Smoking: outdoors only

Music: amplified OK indoors until 12:30am, outdoors until 11:30pm

Wheelchair Access: yes

Insurance: required of all vendors

Other: no rice or birdseed

Want to find more venues and services? Check out our informative website, www.HereComesTheGuide.com.

207

Hornblower Cruises & Events

Yachts

13755 Fiji Way, Marina del Rey
310/301-6000

www.hornblower.com
mdr@hornblower.com

- Rehearsal Dinners
- Ceremonies
- Wedding Receptions
- Private Parties
- Corporate Events
- Meetings
- Film Shoots
- Accommodations

If boats could talk, what tales the Hornblower Cruises and Events fleet could tell! Collectively, the five Marina del Rey–based yachts have entertained movie stars, politicians, playboys, and proletariat alike.

Set foot on an Hornblower Cruises and Events yacht and you encounter a classy operation: Each vessel is meticulously maintained—it's as sleek and well-groomed as a thoroughbred. Mahogany and teak boiseries gleam; brass railings sparkle. Quality is the byword here. It defines all aspects of a Hornblower Cruises and Events event, from the gracious uniformed staff to the meals, which are exquisite in taste as well as presentation.

Weddings on board are exhilarating—exchange vows dockside or while the yacht's underway, plying the harbor's gentle waters. And if you want to take full advantage of the maritime motif, enlist the ship's captain to perform your ceremony.

Entertainer boasts two large, fully enclosed decks, each with a full bar and dance floor. With a full galley, high-quality sound system, and open-air lounge deck, she can accommodate 400 guests for seated dining or 550 for cocktails and a buffet. The aft deck provides a "back porch," additional deck space for guests who want to take in the sea air or dance under the stars!

Hornblower's nostalgic *Zumbrota* is a Roaring Twenties masterpiece rich in history: Mae West and Douglas Fairbanks both took their turns at ownership. The *Zumbrota* is a truly majestic vessel, showcasing walls paneled in Burmese teak, a bar with whimsical brass elephant-head fixtures and the wheelhouse's original compass.

Also available for events is the *Dream On*. This custom-built beauty, with a large main salon and comfortable bow area, provides all the modern features you might expect of a luxury liner. Guests can dine and dance on the roomy and fully enclosable upper deck, while taking in the spectacular view of the Marina del Rey harbor. Nice touches like wide staircases and a private "bride's cabin" right next to the ceremony area make having a wedding on board a breeze.

Hornblower Cruises and Events has other luxurious yachts in its fleet, so if none of these seems to fit your needs, let them match you up with just the right vessel for your celebration. Through the years, the seasoned Hornblower Cruises and Events staff has hosted more than 50,000 events!

And besides, what better way to begin life's journey together than with a buoyant send-off on a beautiful boat? It doesn't get much better than this.

CEREMONY & EVENT/RECEPTION CAPACITY: The yachts can accommodate 10–550 guests.

MEETING CAPACITY: The yachts can accommodate up to 350 seated guests.

FEES & DEPOSITS: A $1,000–8,000 deposit (depending on the vessel's size) is required to book a boat; the balance is payable 30 days prior to the event. Hornblower Cruises and Events offers wedding packages starting at $73/person that include boat rental, food, cake, non-alcoholic beverages and a ceremony by the captain. Hourly boat rental rates and à la carte services can also be arranged.

AVAILABILITY: Year-round, daily.

SERVICES/AMENITIES:

Catering: in-house, no BYO
Kitchen Facilities: n/a
Tables & Chairs: provided
Linens, Silver, etc.: provided
Restrooms: wheelchair access varies
Dance Floor: provided
Bride's & Groom's Dressing Area: some yachts
Meeting Equipment: provided

Parking: fee lots near dock
Accommodations: available on some yachts
Telephone: ship-to-shore
Outdoor Night Lighting: yes
Outdoor Cooking Facilities: no
Cleanup: provided
View: ocean, bay views
Other: event coordination

RESTRICTIONS:

Alcohol: in-house, no BYO
Smoking: outdoors only
Music: amplified OK

Wheelchair Access: limited
Insurance: not required

The Riviera Country Club

Private Country Club

1250 Capri Drive, Pacific Palisades
310/454-6591 x264
www.therivieracountryclub.com
khopkins@rccla.com

- Rehearsal Dinners
- Ceremonies
- Wedding Receptions
- Private Parties
- Corporate Events
- Meetings
- Film Shoots
- Accommodations

Tucked between the Santa Monica foothills and the ocean in upscale Pacific Palisades lies a hidden treasure: The Riviera Country Club, a historic venue with a long tradition of high-class entertaining. Since its opening in 1926, The Riviera's posh comforts and championship golf course have attracted dignitaries, movie stars and the "Rat Pack" who famously played and partied here—the picturesque grounds have even been featured in classic Hollywood films. Though exclusive and private, The Riviera welcomes nonmembers to celebrate at its storied property.

With its Mediterranean architecture and 1920s décor, the majestic clubhouse exudes nostalgic glamour. It also commands a sweeping view of the park-like course, with the Santa Monica Bay in the distance. For wedding ceremonies, guests take the stairs from the clubhouse down to the Vista Riviera, a gorgeous expanse of manicured lawn on a gentle rise overlooking the ocean. Crowning the scene is an ornate wrought-iron gazebo, especially stunning when embellished with garlands, flowers or other decorative touches. Couples say their vows against the breathtaking backdrop of tree-laced fairways, with the sea and sky melding together in two blue layers on the horizon. Just below them is the 18th hole, one of the most famous finishing holes in golf. If we were to name our Top 10 ceremony sites, the magical Vista Riviera would certainly make that list.

Cocktail hours are held on the clubhouse's broad tiled terrace. From this lofty vantage, guests enjoy spectacular sunsets and a glorious coastal panorama. Receptions unfold in your choice of two indoor spaces. The resplendent Crystal Ballroom is named for the original crystal chandeliers suspended from the dramatic, coved ceiling. A marble-manteled fireplace at one end complements the gleaming marble floor, perfect for dancing. Tall Deco-style French windows open to the terrace and ocean breezes. Larger galas are supremely elegant in the Grand Ballroom, whose Spanish Revival aesthetic is expressed in arched entryways and a high ceiling with dark wood beams. A light oak dance floor in the center of the room ensures everyone has a clear view of the revelers. From its private terrace, there's a superb view of the 1st fairway and neighboring Tennis Club.

The intimate George C. Thomas Room, with mahogany-paneled walls, crystal chandeliers and an antique fireplace, evokes a cozy, sophisticated ambiance that's just right for rehearsal dinners or wedding brunches. An expansive bay window frames views, and an adjoining veranda adds versatility.

This distinguished venue hosts only one event at a time, and is dedicated to providing "The Riviera Experience": personalization and customization of each event along with exceptional service. While The Riviera's acclaimed chef is known for his crowd-pleasing cuisine, you may also bring in kosher and other ethnic foods prepared by outside caterers.

And here's something else not often found at country clubs—overnight accommodations. Once known as the "Grand Hotel of Golf," The Riviera offers 27 guest rooms, including a complimentary bridal suite, that combine vintage finery with modern amenities. With an experienced, congenial staff at your service throughout your stay and an on-site restaurant cooking up three meals a day, there's no reason not to bask in The Riviera's gracious hospitality for as long as possible.

CEREMONY CAPACITY: The site holds 275 seated guests indoors and 500 seated outdoors.

EVENT/RECEPTION CAPACITY: The club can accommodate 250 seated or 350 standing guests indoors, and 250 seated or 500 standing outdoors.

MEETING CAPACITY: Meeting spaces hold up to 350 seated guests.

FEES & DEPOSITS: A deposit is required to reserve your date. Personalized event packages start at $225/person. The use of professional coordinators may be required for weddings and bar/bat mitzvahs.

AVAILABILITY: Year-round, daily, anytime.

SERVICES/AMENITIES:

Catering: in-house or select from preferred list
Kitchen Facilities: fully equipped
Tables & Chairs: provided
Linens, Silver, etc.: provided
Restrooms: wheelchair accessible
Dance Floor: provided
Bride's Dressing Area: yes
Meeting Equipment: provided

Parking: large lot, valet available
Accommodations: 30 guest rooms
Telephone: house or guest phones
Outdoor Night Lighting: yes
Outdoor Cooking Facilities: BBQ CBA
Cleanup: provided
View: landscaped grounds; panorama of hills, mountains, fairways, forest, ocean

RESTRICTIONS:

Alcohol: in-house
Smoking: designated areas only
Music: amplified OK with restrictions

Wheelchair Access: yes
Insurance: liability required

Casa del Mar

Oceanfront Hotel

1910 Ocean Way, Santa Monica
310/581-5533
www.hotelcasadelmar.com
tlent@hotelcasadelmar.com

● Rehearsal Dinners	● Corporate Events
● Ceremonies	● Meetings
● Wedding Receptions	● Film Shoots
● Private Parties	○ Accommodations

During the Roaring Twenties, Santa Monica was the heart of California's Gold Coast, the chic stretch of beach that became the personal playground of L.A.'s elite. Of the many lavish beach clubs that were built during this era, Club Casa Del Mar was the uncontested Grande Dame. The building's Renaissance Revival architecture fed designers' imaginations. Hand-painted ceilings, bronze statuary, and the poshest of furnishings gave the club an unrivaled elegance. The lively social scene, led by Hollywood celebrities and business magnates, tempted everyone who was anyone to take part in the excitement.

Casa del Mar survived the Depression, but World War II finally closed this stylish landmark. Now, a dedicated team of hotel developers has restored the Grande Dame to her former magnificence. This lavish restoration evokes the glamour and creative spirit of the hotel's glory days, while incorporating modern amenities that the discriminating guest has come to expect from a premier facility.

First, notice the brick-and-sandstone façade, decorative sculpted accents and the Mediterranean flair of a red-tile roof and iron balconies. The beautiful hotel is separated from the sand by palm trees and a promenade, but you enter streetside through an exquisite two-story door made of ornate stained glass. The foyer is a grand rotunda dominated by a wrought-iron chandelier and twin sweeping staircases inlaid with mosaic tiles. As you make your way up to the lobby, you hear the faint strains of a ragtime piano from a distant past as you're caught up in the magical ambiance. Your eyes take in the gorgeous rugs, intriguing Art Nouveau-inspired lighting fixtures and gold-inlaid ceilings before resting on the scintillating seascape visible through the tall windows lining the far wall. Design details throughout are an artful mix of the casual and the refined, ranging from Miami-style furnishings in the seaside restaurant to plush chairs and velvet sofas in the lobby living room. Warm fruitwood paneling and the soothing tones of peach, marine blue, and sage predominate. Comfort, a top priority here, is easy to come by: Enjoy a cocktail while lounging on the oceanside veranda, unwind in the full-service spa, or curl up by one of the many fireplaces.

If you've come for a celebration, let the good times roll in the Casa's stunning ballroom, the Colonnade. Two-tiered Venetian glass chandeliers suspended from the sculpted ceiling gently illuminate the pale walls. It's almost a shame to cover the sumptuous plum carpeting with a dance floor. Silk draperies in celadon and gold frame a wall of windows that reveal breathtaking Pacific sunsets. Open the French doors, step out onto the loggia, and let a refreshing ocean breeze caress your cheek. The Colonnade can easily be divided into smaller sections to suit the size of your event, and several other well-appointed spaces are available for intimate dinners, business meetings, or conferences.

The entire restoration blends quality craftsmanship with nostalgic elegance. For a special event as original as the setting, experience the romance of Hotel Casa Del Mar.

CEREMONY & EVENT/RECEPTION CAPACITY: The Oceanview Colonnade holds 320 seated (with dance floor) or 500 standing guests.

MEETING CAPACITY: The Boardroom holds up to 18 guests seated conference-style. The Crimson Room holds up to 50 seated guests.

FEES & DEPOSITS: For weddings, a nonrefundable deposit of 30% of your food and beverage minimum is due to reserve your date. 40% of the anticipated event total is due 60 days prior to the event; the remaining balance is due 10 working days prior. Wedding packages start at $190/person for lunch, and range $225–280/person for dinner; alcohol, tax and a 20% service charge are included. A wedding planner is required for all weddings, and must be chosen from the venue's preferred list.

For meetings or business functions, room rental fees vary depending on room and/or services selected, and may be waived with food and beverage minimums or overnight accommodation minimums. A conference coordinator and business center are available.

AVAILABILITY: Year-round, daily, anytime until 1am.

SERVICES/AMENITIES:
Catering: in-house, no BYO
Kitchen Facilities: n/a
Tables & Chairs: provided
Linens, Silver, etc.: provided
Restrooms: wheelchair accessible
Dance Floor: provided, wood floor
Bride's & Groom's Dressing Area: no
Meeting Equipment: full AV, additional charge

Parking: on-site valet, extra charge
Accommodations: 129 guest rooms
Telephone: pay phone, internal phones
Outdoor Night Lighting: yes
Outdoor Cooking Facilities: no
Cleanup: provided
View: Pacific Ocean, from Palos Verdes to Malibu

RESTRICTIONS:
Alcohol: in-house, no BYO
Smoking: nonsmoking hotel
Music: amplified OK indoors, acoustic only outdoors on the Ballroom Terrace

Wheelchair Access: yes
Insurance: hold harmless waiver required
Other: no rice

Loews Santa Monica Beach Hotel

Beachfront Hotel

1700 Ocean Avenue, Santa Monica
310/458-6700
www.loewshotels.com/santamonica
vbernardo@loewshotels.com

● Rehearsal Dinners	● Corporate Events
● Ceremonies	● Meetings
● Wedding Receptions	● Film Shoots
● Private Parties	● Accommodations

Mention Loews Santa Monica Beach Hotel to anyone who's recently stayed there, eaten there or attended an event there and they start to rave because, frankly, it's just that fabulous. From its coveted perch above the Pacific, this world-class luxury hotel, mere blocks from the Santa Monica Pier and lively Promenade, exudes a uniquely local ambiance. In this hip seaside town, that means unpretentious elegance in a waterfront setting.

This dynamic is evident as soon as you enter the stunning lobby, a four-story, light and airy atrium lined with 40-foot palm trees and interior balconies. Decorated in breezy blues and white, the effect is like walking into an *Architectural Digest* spread of the quintessential beach house done on a grand scale. The reception area to the left has a high-tech live video feed of the Santa Monica Beach and straight ahead, visible through walls of glass, is a breathtaking panorama of ocean and sand. Because this is a particularly wide swath of beach with long wooden walkways, there's an ever-changing tableau of activity for you to watch and enjoy.

Loews has a veritable treasure trove of picture-perfect wedding sites, and one of the best ways to start your event is at the Pool Area, where you can exchange vows with unobstructed views of the ocean and the Pier's historic Ferris wheel visible in the distance. If you prefer an indoor ceremony, there's the Ocean Atrium, a soaring three-story space with natural light streaming in through floor-to-ceiling windows. (You can even arrange a permit with the city for a ceremony on the beach.)

One of the hotel's most popular spots is the Venice Room, a secluded and sophisticated gem that faces the ocean. This multilevel locale encompasses a covered, outdoor patio and a two-tiered indoor reception area, affording views from every angle. Guests can mingle on the lower level, linger over cocktails on the patio, then walk up a staircase—sheathed with rippled glass panels echoing the waves outside—to a beautiful dining room boasting coffered ceilings and white columns.

But if you have your heart set on all-out glamour, nothing beats the Arcadia Grand Ballroom on the hotel's fifth floor. Begin with cocktails in the expansive Arcadia Foyer, overlooking the lobby atrium. Then, invite your guests into the exquisite Arcadia Ballroom featuring walls covered in rich ocean blue, green and gold silk, contemporary sand dollar chandeliers, and lush carpet swirled in tones of underwater blue.

While hotels are not generally singled out for their haute cuisine, Loews Santa Monica is an exception to the rule. Their gourmet, market-fresh menu is consistently lauded by critics and locals alike and can be savored in each of their private event rooms as well as their glowingly reviewed Ocean & Vine Restaurant, a great pick for a memorable dinner.

Loews is both a Four Diamond hotel and a beach resort, offering just the right balance of luxury and relaxation. With its impeccable service, spectacular views and fabulous food, this Santa Monica fixture can indeed be your dream wedding venue.

CEREMONY & EVENT/RECEPTION CAPACITY: The hotel holds 450 seated or standing guests, indoors and out.

MEETING CAPACITY: Meeting spaces seat up to 450 guests indoors.

FEES & DEPOSITS: A deposit is required to reserve your date and the balance of the estimated total is due before the event. Ceremony fees range $1,000–10,000 depending on the space selected. Wedding packages start at $200/person. Tax and a 22% service charge are additional.

AVAILABILITY: Year-round, daily, anytime. Call or email for details.

SERVICES/AMENITIES:

Catering: in-house
Kitchen Facilities: provided
Tables & Chairs: provided
Linens, Silver, etc.: provided
Restrooms: wheelchair accessible
Dance Floor: portable provided
Bride's Dressing Area: yes
Meeting Equipment: provided
Other: spa services, AV equipment

Parking: valet required
Accommodations: 342 guest rooms
Telephone: house phone
Outdoor Night Lighting: access only
Outdoor Cooking Facilities: BBQ CBA
Cleanup: provided
View: pool area; panorama of Pacific Ocean, Santa Monica Pier and Malibu

RESTRICTIONS:

Alcohol: in-house
Smoking: not allowed
Music: amplified OK

Wheelchair Access: yes
Insurance: not required

Le Méridien Delfina Santa Monica

Hotel

530 Pico Boulevard, Santa Monica
310/309-8020

www.lemeridiendelfina.com
kayli.yoong@lemeridiendelfina.com

- ● Rehearsal Dinners
- ● Ceremonies
- ● Wedding Receptions
- ● Private Parties
- ● Corporate Events
- ● Meetings
- ● Film Shoots
- ○ Accommodations

After an $11-million makeover, Le Méridien Delfina Santa Monica has a whole new look. The updated version of this hotel favorite may remind you of that friend you secretly envy, the cosmopolitan traveler who always seems to know about the hot gallery opening and latest dining craze ... a veritable design diva who throws together an eye-catching outfit at a moment's notice. Always chic, always confident, she's the most interesting guest at a dinner party.

Like your hip friend, Le Méridien Delfina Santa Monica is a paragon of cutting-edge style. Perched on a gentle rise, this urban sanctuary commands a spectacular view of bustling Santa Monica and the ocean just a few blocks away. Its double-tall lobby instantly sets a fashion-forward tone: The interiors are a triumph of eclectic artistry, combining textures, shapes and global influences into an intriguing style matrix that nevertheless breathes soothing simplicity.

Coastal soirées often gather around the hotel's beautiful swimming pool for drinks and finger food. A trio of cabanas is wonderful for showcasing dramatic presentations of culinary masterpieces or your favorite VIPs—or use one of them as a cozy enclave for intimate conversation.

For the ultimate Le Méridien Delfina Santa Monica experience, bring your guests up to the top floor, where the Delfina Ballroom & Penthouse Foyer are the toast of the town. Stepping into the Foyer, your eyes go first to a row of windows that take in the city stretched out below. Handpicked artworks dress up the walls. Tastefully understated, the space is equally suitable for a corporate meet-and-greet or a classy cocktail reception. The Foyer might also be used in conjunction with the adjoining Lucina Room; cocktails go down just fine here as well, and your guests still enjoy that sweeping view.

Then for the main event, open the doors to the Delfina Ballroom. The hotel's signature décor perfectly complements the astounding view: A tapestry of breathtaking coastline, ocean waves, and rugged mountains in the distance fills two long walls of windows. As twilight fades to a rainbow-hued sunset, the stars and the city lights begin to sparkle on the horizon, adding extra pizzazz to your festivities.

Le Méridien Delfina Santa Monica offers wedding packages that include an oceanview Honeymoon Suite, so you and your spouse can sleep late while your out-of-town guests explore Santa Monica's many attractions.

Remember your trendsetting friend? She's about to announce that she's having her next private party here. It sure will be fun to see the look on her face when she hears that you've already booked the luxurious Le Méridien Delfina Santa Monica for your own upcoming wedding celebration!

CEREMONY CAPACITY: The Lucina Room holds up to 120 guests. Outdoors, the garden accommodates 120 and the deck holds up to 150 seated guests.

EVENT/RECEPTION CAPACITY: The Delfina Ballroom holds up to 300 seated or 500 standing guests, the Lucina Room holds up to 100 seated or 130 standing.

MEETING CAPACITY: The venue accommodates up to 500 guests.

FEES & DEPOSITS: 25% of the estimated event total is required to reserve your date; the balance is due 14 calendar days prior to the event. Wedding packages start at $109/person and include food, beverage and cake-cutting fee. Tax and service charge are additional.

For meetings or business functions, meeting room costs are based on food, beverage and guest room requirements.

AVAILABILITY: Year-round, daily, 7am–midnight. Additional hours can be arranged.

SERVICES/AMENITIES:
Catering: in-house, or BYO with approval, extra fee
Kitchen Facilities: fully equipped
Tables & Chairs: provided
Linens, Silver, etc.: provided
Restrooms: wheelchair accessible
Dance Floor: provided
Bride's Dressing Area: yes
Meeting Equipment: CBA

Parking: valet parking
Accommodations: 310 guest rooms
Telephone: emergency use only
Outdoor Night Lighting: yes
Outdoor Cooking Facilities: no
Cleanup: provided
View: cityscape, mountains, ocean
Other: event coordination

RESTRICTIONS:
Alcohol: in-house, or wine and champagne only with corkage fee
Smoking: outdoors only
Music: amplified OK indoors with restrictions

Wheelchair Access: yes
Insurance: proof of insurance required for outside vendors

Shutters on the Beach

Oceanfront Hotel

1 Pico Boulevard, Santa Monica
310/458-0030
www.shuttersonthebeach.com
tlent@shuttersonthebeach.com

- Rehearsal Dinners
- Ceremonies
- Wedding Receptions
- Private Parties
- Corporate Events
- Meetings
- Film Shoots
- Accommodations

With an oceanfront address as stylish as its chic, unpretentious décor, Shutters outclasses most of the nearby hotel competition. Its crisp gray and white exterior, enlivened with flower-covered trellises and balconies, brings to mind an upscale version of the classic clapboard beach cottage. Inside, the attractive lobby gives guests their first experience of Shutters' snappy appeal. Original artwork, comfy sofas, and a stenciled ceiling contribute to an atmosphere that's both sophisticated and relaxed. A few steps from the lobby you'll find the pool, and one of the nicest outdoor terraces we've seen anywhere. Sunny, but sheltered, this spacious stone tiled deck commands a panoramic view of the ocean. Ceremonies are held here at day's end, just as the sun is setting and the sky is awash in color.

For receptions, Shutters offers function rooms of various sizes, all practical and attractively decorated in pale pastels with unique handcrafted light fixtures. The Grand Salon is the largest and most luxurious of the rooms, creating a refined ambiance for special celebrations. A floor-to-ceiling marble mantel holds a handsome fireplace, flanked by alternating panels of antiqued beveled mirrors and French moiré satin. The Grand Salon also boasts five spectacular Venetian chandeliers made of hand-blown glass "leaves."

The more intimate Promenade Room divides into three spaces, each of which opens onto an outdoor terrace. Another "room with a view" is the Beachside Room. Adjacent to Shutters' popular Coast Café & Bar, Beachside features hardwood flooring and wood millwork throughout, giving the space a warm and cozy feel with a spectacular view of the sea and sand. Rehearsal dinners, bridal and baby showers taking place in this room are unique and refreshing.

Shutters' many attractions include its resort-like accommodations. Rooms have sliding shuttered doors that open to a balmy Pacific breeze, and suites also include a fireplace lined with handmade tiles, and wood floors adorned with thick rugs. Marble baths with windows to the outside, and a host of thoughtful amenities make you feel like you're a guest in someone's exclusive beach house.

At the romantic Shutters, you can stage your entire wedding—from rehearsal dinner to honeymoon—right on one of the most beautiful beaches in the world.

CEREMONY CAPACITY: The Oceanview Pacific Terrace seats 220 for a ceremony; the Promenade Room and Terrace accommodate 140 seated or 200 standing.

EVENT/RECEPTION CAPACITY: The Grand Salon accommodates 220 seated (with dance floor) or 400 standing; the Pacific Terrace, 150 seated or 300 standing; the Promenade Room holds 140 seated or 200 standing. Beachside holds 90 seated or 150 standing guests.

MEETING CAPACITY: Several spaces hold 20–400 seated guests.

FEES & DEPOSITS: For weddings, a nonrefundable deposit of 30% of the food and beverage minimum is required to reserve your date; 40% of the estimated event total is due 60 days prior to the event and the remaining balance is due 10 working days prior. Wedding packages start at $190/person for lunch, and range $225–280/person for dinner. Alcohol, tax and a 20% service charge are included. A wedding planner is required for all weddings, and must be chosen from the venue's preferred list.

Room rental fees for business functions or meetings vary depending on room and/or services selected, and may be waived with food and beverage minimums or overnight accommodation minimums. Shutters has both a conference coordinator and a business center plus in-house audiovisual services.

AVAILABILITY: Year-round, daily, anytime until 1am.

SERVICES/AMENITIES:

Catering: in-house
Kitchen Facilities: n/a
Tables & Chairs: provided
Linens, Silver, etc.: provided
Restrooms: wheelchair accessible
Dance Floor: parquet floor
Bride's Dressing Area: no
Meeting Equipment: full range; AV in-house

Parking: on-site valet, extra charge
Accommodations: 198 guest rooms
Telephone: pay phone or internal with outside access
Outdoor Night Lighting: minimal provided
Outdoor Cooking Facilities: no
Cleanup: provided
View: Pacific Ocean, Santa Monica Mountains, Santa Monica Pier

RESTRICTIONS:

Alcohol: in-house, no BYO
Smoking: limited, outdoors only
Music: amplified OK indoors, acoustic outdoors

Wheelchair Access: yes
Insurance: hold harmless waiver required
Other: no rice or birdseed

The Victorian

2640 Main Street, Santa Monica
310/392-4956
www.thevictorian.com
info@thevictorian.com

● Rehearsal Dinners	● Corporate Events
● Ceremonies	● Meetings
● Wedding Receptions	● Film Shoots
● Private Parties	Accommodations

Santa Monica is famous for trendy boutiques and bistros, oceanview resorts and powder-sand beaches … it's probably the last place you would expect to find a historic Victorian home and garden. Yet tucked inside Heritage Square on Santa Monica's Main Street, a pale yellow shingled mansion lends a turn-of-the-century gentility to the lively seaside town. This unexpected juxtaposition of old-fashioned glamour in a contemporary coastal milieu makes The Victorian a delightfully intriguing venue for formal banquets, family get-togethers and all sorts of parties—bridal couples in particular are drawn to the home's heirloom look and storied elegance.

Originally built near the Hotel Miramar in 1892 as the residence of one the neighborhood's founding families, the two-story building was moved to its current location in 1973. Heritage Square is a prime pocket of nostalgic architecture, with the California Heritage Museum and its sprawling lawn on one side and The Victorian on the other. Completely and carefully renovated, The Victorian has had its main rooms enlarged and added a wine cellar for a total of 15,000 square feet of event space including the landscaped grounds.

A brick path leading to the front door (and lined with candles and twinkle lights at night) curves among oak trees, blooming flowers and outdoor seating. As you enter, you're greeted by a polished oak bar, a congenial spot for cocktails, as are the home's two patios. Throughout, the décor is characteristic of the late 19th century—a mixture of fine antique furnishings, classical artwork and candles.

Couples often exchange vows upstairs in a lovely room with a built-in bar for champagne toasts and a covered veranda for pre-ceremony mingling. Open-air ceremonies are held on the Heritage Museum lawn or even on the beach, a short walk from here.

There's plenty of room both indoors and out for a sit-down reception or elegant buffet. The intimate main dining room features an octagonal enclave framed by tall windows at one corner, perfect for the bride and groom's table or to showcase the wedding cake. A line of French doors opens to a terrace, where guests sit among trees that seem to grow right up from the wooden floor and through the latticework canopy. The terrace is enclosed for warmth and comfort, and guests are soothed by the sound of a nearby waterfall.

The Victorian boasts an experienced staff that will help you make the most of this unique property. They've even put together an inclusive wedding package that covers: meal service by their in-house caterer; beer, wine, champagne and soft bar; rental fee; on-site parking; a spacious dance floor; tables, linens and Chiavari chairs; and setup and breakdown—in other words, an easy and stress-free way to entertain.

The quaint home and its tranquil garden are awash in vintage charm, yet the salty tang in the air reminds visitors that the rolling waves are just one block away. With plenty of lodging options close by, your out-of-town guests will be thrilled with the opportunity to explore the local scene. Whether you fancy a cozy gathering or a lavish gala, the hospitality offered by The Victorian will lend your celebration the romantic sophistication of a bygone era.

CEREMONY CAPACITY: The Main Room holds 200 seated guests, the Museum Lawn up to 400, and the Upstairs Room up to 130 seated. A beach ceremony is also an option.

EVENT/RECEPTION CAPACITY: Indoors, the house accommodates 24–200 seated or 40–450 standing. Outdoors, the lawn holds 300 seated or 400 standing guests.

MEETING CAPACITY: Several spaces hold 30–200 seated guests.

FEES & DEPOSITS: A $1,500 nonrefundable deposit is required upon booking to secure your date. An additional $1,500 (also nonrefundable) is due 1 month from the initial deposit, 50% of the estimated event total is due 6 months prior and the the remaining 50% is due 2 months prior to the event. Holiday rates apply. Guaranteed guest count is due 14 days prior and final payment is due 10 days prior to the event.

Wedding packages run approximately $115/person depending on menu selected and guest count; the package price includes a sit-down dinner, dance floor, 3-hour bar service, candles, linens, coordination, service charge and parking. Other special events begin at approximately $40/person for seated meals or approximately $35/person for cocktail receptions; tax, alcohol and a 20% service fee are additional. An extra fee applies to events on Saturday nights (and there is a food and beverage minimum).

Full-day meeting packages start at approximately $55/person including breakfast buffet, lunch, afternoon snack and unlimited nonalcoholic beverage service.

AVAILABILITY: Year-round, daily, anytime.

SERVICES/AMENITIES:

Catering: in-house
Kitchen Facilities: n/a
Tables & Chairs: provided
Linens, Silver, etc.: provided
Restrooms: wheelchair accessible 1st floor only
Dance Floor: provided
Bride's Dressing Area: provided
Meeting Equipment: CBA
Kosher: outside kosher caterer with approval

Parking: 100-car lot with attendant, valet CBA
Accommodations: no guest rooms
Telephone: emergency use only
Outdoor Night Lighting: yes
Outdoor Cooking Facilities: no
Cleanup: provided
View: no
Other: event coordination

RESTRICTIONS:

Alcohol: available
Smoking: outdoors only
Music: amplified OK indoors until 2am

Wheelchair Access: main floor only
Insurance: liability required
Other: no rice or flower petals

Friendly Hills Country Club

Country Club

8500 South Villaverde Drive, Whittier
562/698-0331
www.friendlyhillscc.com
cabobadilla@friendlyhillscc.com

- Rehearsal Dinners
- Ceremonies
- Wedding Receptions
- Private Parties
- Corporate Events
- Meetings
- Film Shoots
- Accommodations

This green oasis on Whittier's north side is everything you expect in a traditional country club: A curving pine- and oleander-lined road whisks you up to its gate, and there's a sea of trees at the entrance and a feeling of leafy quiet once you arrive. When you do hear sounds, they're the happy shouts and squeals of children romping around the club pool while their moms and dads laze about chatting and laughing.

The clubhouse exterior is creamy white stucco with wide chocolate-colored wood beams and trim. Its look is one of simple sophistication, with Craftsman-style good proportions. But the focus here is on the outdoors, where all wedding ceremonies are held (yes, the weather is that good). They take place on a tiled terrace whose backdrop, the golf course's 1st and 18th holes, is easily the visual highlight of Friendly Hills. The fairways rise, side by side, up a commanding slope that disappears into the distance. Between them, a long cascade of water, with willows, firs and sycamores strung along its course, spills its way over large boulders to a small lake next to the terrace. The lake, populated with plump swans and ducks, can be reached via an elegant stone-faced bridge that makes a perfect photo-op site.

You can't help but constantly gaze at this combination of water, greenery and dramatic ascent, which is why few brides choose to wed under an arch here. The backdrop is all the decoration you need.

Friendly Hills has two excellent places to hold a post-ceremony party: a downstairs banquet room, and an upper reception area that can be used alone or in combination with an adjacent sleek bar. The downstairs space has a wall of tall windows facing the club's signature first and last holes, and a full-service bar at the far end of room. Flattering indirect lighting along with natural light from outside keeps the place wonderfully well lit. Glass doors lead to the terrace, which is dotted with canopies for sheltering guests.

The upper reception area, off the clubhouse's elegant lobby, has white truss ceilings and big windows looking onto the course. Just a few steps down from it is an elegant bar, finished in warm brown tones of leather and wood. Invitingly soft leather lounge seats are arranged beside a bank of ten-foot-high windows, offering perhaps the best view in the house. The bar—subdued, simple and classy—is a very agreeable place where guests can lift heartfelt toasts to the newlyweds.

Whoever designed Friendly Hills understood the dynamics of heat and light. Southern California's almost year-round equable climate and golden sun make this club a bright, exhilarating wedding venue. Yet, when the excitement of the day is done and cooling shadows creep over the terrace, your psyche is gently tugged into a restful, stress-free zone. You quietly chat with your guests, watching the sunset's light burnish the fairways, taking in a memorable moment and scene. Heavenly!!

CEREMONY, EVENT/RECEPTION & MEETING CAPACITY: The location holds 250 seated or 400 standing guests.

FEES & DEPOSITS: A $2,500 deposit is required to reserve your date. The balance is due 14 days prior to the event. Rental fees range $1,000–10,000 depending on space, day and time rented and guest count. Meals range $22–75/person. Tax, alcohol and a 20% service charge are additional.

AVAILABILITY: Year-round, daily.

SERVICES/AMENITIES:

Catering: in-house, no BYO
Kitchen Facilities: n/a
Tables & Chairs: provided
Linens, Silver, etc.: provided
Restrooms: wheelchair accessible
Dance Floor: provided
Bride's Dressing Area: yes
Meeting Equipment: some provided, more CBA

Parking: large lot
Accommodations: no guest rooms
Telephone: pay phone
Outdoor Night Lighting: yes
Outdoor Cooking Facilities: BBQ
Cleanup: provided
View: waterfall, lake, forest, fountain, hills
Other: event coordination, grand piano

RESTRICTIONS:

Alcohol: in-house, no BYO
Smoking: outside only
Music: amplified OK

Wheelchair Access: yes
Insurance: not required

Overwhelmed? Use the search criteria on www.HereComesTheGuide.com to narrow down your choices.

223

San Gabriel Valley

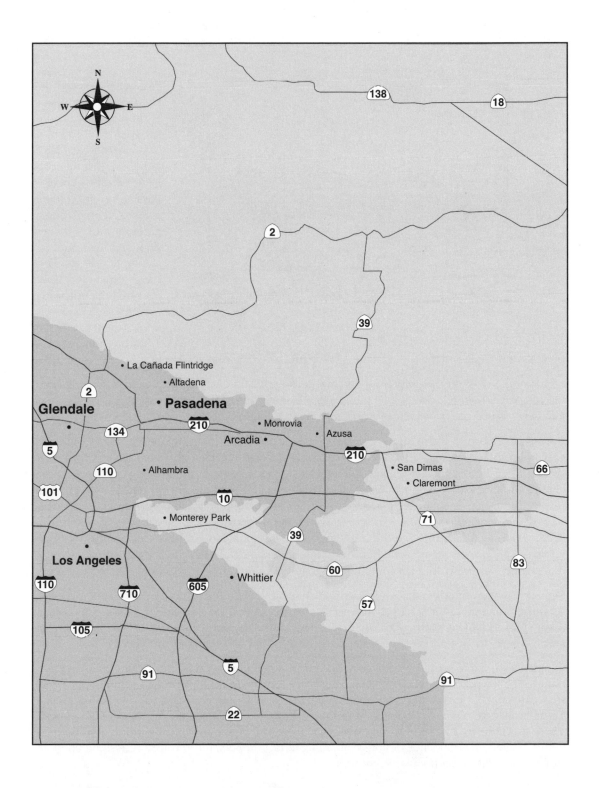

Altadena Town & Country Club

Country Club

2290 Country Club Drive, Altadena
626/794-7163
www.altaclub.com
sandy@altaclub.com

● Rehearsal Dinners	● Corporate Events
● Ceremonies	● Meetings
● Wedding Receptions	● Film Shoots
● Private Parties	Accommodations

Residing at the foot of the San Gabriel Mountains is the serenely beautiful Altadena Town & Country Club. It's hard to believe that this gorgeous estate—encompassing several verdant acres of tennis courts, gardens and a swimming pool—began as a simple, Craftsman-style bungalow. Built in 1910, the Altadena Country Club (as it was known then) weathered a stormy adolescence; floods, Santa Anas and the Great Depression nearly caused its ruin at several points along the way.

Fortunately, in 1946 community pride and ingenuity ended the club's run of bad luck. Rechristened the Altadena Town & Country Club, the facility matured into what it is today: a gracious, gabled multilevel structure that serves as a very stylish place to hold a celebration.

A handsome porte-cochère directs you through the club's front doors and into the Foyer. Here, it's easy to imagine guests sinking into the cozy armchairs and musing to the melodies of Cole Porter issuing from the black baby grand. Double doors on either side of the Foyer swing open to the club's ballrooms—the Mendocino and Victorian Rooms. Depending on your party's size, you can reserve these spaces either separately or in tandem. The Mendocino Room features a Craftsman-style wood-paneled ceiling and enormous windows that provide ample light as well as views of the San Gabriel Mountains and the club's expansive grounds. More sophisticated is the Victorian Room, distinguished by its blond hardwood floors, ornamental fireplace and charming bay window. Parties may also spill out from the Victorian Room onto the club's lovely covered veranda.

Right below the veranda is the South Lawn. Enclosed by tall trees, and bordered by stone benches, flowerbeds and an arbor, it's a private enclave that works well for a ceremony. Guests can mingle on the grass, enjoying views of the golf course as well as the garden setting. If you choose to get married here, it's just a few steps to the adjacent Victorian Room for your reception.

Couples also marry on the Wedding Court, a pristine patio shaded by a towering pine and surrounded by lawn, roses and crisp green hedges. A stairway descending from the club's upper level showcases the bride's entrance, while a trellis at the court's south end serves as an exquisite frame for the exchange of vows. One more reception area is also available here: the Terrace Room with a spacious balcony that shows off a panoramic view of the club grounds. Sporting green canvas umbrellas and an abundance of bright blooming terracotta pots, the Terrace's refreshing open-air atmosphere makes it a popular event spot.

The Altadena Town & Country Club has also been a favorite site for a number of film shoots. *Wonder Years, Speechless, Dirty Dancing* and *Starsky & Hutch* have all taken advantage of this classy backdrop. Why not follow their cue and reserve the club for your own production?

CEREMONY CAPACITY: The outdoor area holds 240 seated or standing; a variety of rooms inside the Clubhouse can accommodate 50–240 seated guests.

EVENT/RECEPTION CAPACITY: Several areas accommodate 100–240 seated guests.

MEETING CAPACITY: Several spaces available accommodating 20–240 seated guests.

FEES & DEPOSITS: For weddings, a $1,000–1,500 nonrefundable deposit per room is required to secure your date. The rental fee for the Wedding Court or South Lawn is $1,000. For other spaces, the setup charges run $5/person/room. Half of the estimated total is payable 90 days prior, an additional 25% is due 60 days prior, and the balance is due 30 days before the event.

Wedding packages range $70–85/person and include hors d'oeuvres, complete meal, wedding cake, champagne toast, wine with dinner, bartender and bar setup, room setup, parking security guard, a night's stay for the bride and groom at one of the participating hotels, service charges and tax. À la carte menus run $30–42/person plus alcohol, tax and a 20% service charge. For business functions or meetings, rates will vary depending on the rooms and services selected. Call for additional information.

AVAILABILITY: Year-round, daily. Ceremonies take place before sunset only. Closed on Christmas and New Year's Eve.

SERVICES & AMENITIES:

Catering: in-house, no BYO
Kitchen Facilities: n/a
Tables & Chairs: provided
Linens, Silver, etc.: provided
Restrooms: wheelchair accessible
Dance Floor: hardwood floors provided
Bride's & Groom's Dressing Area: yes
Meeting equipment: CBA, extra fee

Parking: large lots, valet
Accommodations: no guest rooms
Telephone: house phones
Outdoor night lighting: no
Outdoor cooking facilities: cba
Cleanup: provided
View: San Gabriel Mountains, golf course, landscaped grounds and pool area

RESTRICTIONS:

Alcohol: in-house, no BYO
Smoking: designated areas
Music: amplified ok with volume limits; acoustic music only on the south lawn

Wheelchair access: yes
Insurance: not required
Other: no rice or open flames

Lindley-Scott House and Gardens

Private Estate

710 & 720 East Foothill Boulevard, Azusa
626/334-5215
www.lindleyscotthouse.com
historicallindleyscotthouse@gmail.com

Rehearsal Dinners	● Corporate Events
● Ceremonies	● Meetings
● Wedding Receptions	● Film Shoots
● Private Parties	Accommodations

What is it that draws us to vintage houses? Maybe it's their grace and elegance, which reminds us of a bygone era when artisans had pride in their work and people took their time. One such place is the historic Lindley-Scott House and Gardens, a serene private estate in the San Gabriel foothills.

The Georgian-style home was built in 1911 by famed architect Robert D. Farquhar, and it's sheltered from the outside world by tall trees, green hedgerows and wrought-iron gates. A curving driveway climbs to the stately two-story home, painted a cheery yellow with green shutters and white trim. A garden setting surrounds the house, featuring a wide expanse of lawn with a majestic cypress, a California live oak and other lush foliage.

In keeping with the home's nostalgic feeling, some brides make their grand entrance in a horse-drawn carriage or an antique auto. But most often the bride and her attendants prepare upstairs in the Victorian-style dressing room. From here she descends the classic staircase in the Lindley-Scott foyer, then steps outside and follows a walkway between the trees to meet her groom at a storybook staging area—an arched arbor bordered by a pair of white picket fences with potted plants and flowers. Another romantic site for saying "I do" is near the Carriage House—it's a secluded white gazebo standing on a carpet of manicured grass ringed with hedges and trees.

After vows are exchanged, the bridal party makes use of the picturesque grounds for photos. One of the most photogenic spots is the Rose Garden, filled with fragrant blooms that serve as a natural—and colorful—backdrop. Guests enjoy coming here, too: There's a lawn bordered by Jacaranda trees where they can mingle … or simply stop to smell the roses!

Receptions take place in the magnificent Carriage House. Its white-columned portico welcomes family and friends into an elegant ballroom, where vintage-style chandeliers suspended from the lofty ceiling illuminate the dining and dancing. An abundance of natural light flows in through a wall of windows and French doors, which open to a cozy patio overlooking the beautifully landscaped grounds.

In contrast to events at many private estates, a celebration at Lindley-Scott House and Gardens is "one-stop shopping": Everything you'll need for a stylish reception is included in your wedding package, like a choice of wedding cakes and linen colors—even a keyboardist! All you'll have to do is thank your guests for coming and receive their enthusiastic compliments.

CEREMONY CAPACITY: The garden holds up to 200 seated.

EVENT/RECEPTION & MEETING CAPACITY: The facility accommodates 200 seated guests indoors in the Carriage House.

FEES & DEPOSITS: A 25% nonrefundable deposit is required to reserve your date. 50% of the total is due 90 days prior, and the balance is due 1 month prior to the event. Meals range $40–65/person; tax, alcohol and a 20% service charge are additional. There's also a $950 ceremony setup fee.

AVAILABILITY: Year-round, Friday, Saturday, Sunday, until midnight.

SERVICES/AMENITIES:

Catering: in-house
Kitchen Facilities: n/a
Tables & Chairs: provided
Linens, Silver, etc.: provided
Restrooms: wheelchair accessible
Dance Floor: oak parquet floor
Bride's Dressing Area: yes
Meeting Equipment: CBA, extra fee

Parking: on-site or street
Accommodations: no guest rooms
Telephone: use with approval
Outdoor Night Lighting: yes
Outdoor Cooking Facilities: CBA
Cleanup: provided
View: landscaped grounds, lawns and garden
Other: bar service, event coordination, organist for ceremonies, PA system

RESTRICTIONS:

Alcohol: in-house
Smoking: outside only, designated areas
Music: amplified OK

Wheelchair Access: yes
Insurance: not required
Other: no rice, birdseed, confetti or open flames

Descanso Gardens

1418 Descanso Drive, La Cañada Flintridge
818/949-4291

www.descansogardens.org
mvandeusen@descansogardens.org

Historic Home and Gardens

● Rehearsal Dinners	● Corporate Events
● Ceremonies	● Meetings
● Wedding Receptions	● Film Shoots
● Private Parties	Accommodations

As you drive down the quiet, oak-lined residential street that leads to the gardens, you get your first taste of this facility's peaceful seclusion. Living up to its name (*descanso* means "rest" in Spanish), Descanso Gardens is indeed a tranquil, verdant oasis at the foot of the arid San Gabriel Mountains.

Once a large private estate, the gardens occupy over 150 acres, offering a wide variety of enchanting sites for weddings. One favorite is a classic California setting—a broad, open lawn under widespreading coast live oaks that convey a rustic simplicity.

Another option is the Magnolia Lawn. A wall of lattice entwined with crabapple vines and ruby-red buds marks the entrance, and guests pass beneath a pretty archway before taking their seats facing a pair of mature magnolia trees. The trees serve as a natural altar for the bride and groom, while their creamy white flowers evoke a feminine grace. The surrounding greenery is punctuated by seasonal surprises—think cheery tulips in April and perfumed paperwhites in late autumn—enhance the picturesque environs.

If you're exchanging vows with a few family and friends looking on, then consider the serene Japanese gardens. Your guests cluster along the bank of a koi-filled stream as you share your first kiss in front of the Full Moon Tea House. A red footbridge and springtime show of pink cherry blossoms create a colorful, exotic milieu for photos.

And who can resist the romance of a rose garden? Descanso's five-acre International Rosarium boasts over 4,000 rosebushes. Couples can wed at the wrought-iron Rose Garden Gazebo, and continue their outdoor celebration in a timber-and-stone pavilion bordered by fragrant blooms.

Seated receptions can also be held in the cozy Boddy House, poised at the edge of the oak forest. Larger gatherings convene in Van De Kamp Hall, which is situated near the garden's main entrance. This Craftsman-style building boasts a lofty open-beamed ceiling and French windows that open onto a lovely and expansive tiled courtyard flanked by flowerbeds and a bubbling natural-rock fountain.

With its shade-dappled lawns, brilliant flowers, majestic camellia forests and secluded woodland clearings, Descanso Gardens has just the right wedding spot for any nature-loving couple. But whether you get married here or not, a visit to the gardens is a tonic to urban stresses and—dare we suggest it—frayed prenuptial nerves. You can breathe easy in this serene setting, or, as they say in Spanish, *aquí puede usted descansar.*

CEREMONY CAPACITY: Various outdoor locations hold 25–400 seated guests.

EVENT/RECEPTION CAPACITY: Van de Kamp Hall and the Courtyard hold 180 seated; the Rose Garden Pavilion holds 180 seated guests or 200 in conjunction with adjacent lawn areas (during July–September). The Boddy House seats 50 guests indoors or 90 guests outdoors.

MEETING CAPACITY: Van de Kamp Hall holds 250 seated theater-style or 220 conference-style; Classrooms Maple and Birch each hold 50 seated theater- or conference-style, Classroom Minka holds 20 seated.

FEES & DEPOSITS: The rental fee starts at $3,600 for a ceremony only, $4,100 for a reception only, or $5,700 for both. Discounted rates are available on Friday and Sunday.

For ceremonies or receptions, a nonrefundable $1,000 deposit is required when the date is booked. Half the rental fee is due 6 months prior to the event; the balance is payable 2 months prior. For other special events, a 50% deposit is required with a signed contract; the balance is due 30 days prior to the event. The site has an in-house caterer. Wedding packages start at $100/person. Tax and service charge are included, alcohol is additional.

For meetings, rental fees run $425–2,500, depending on room, guest count, day of week and time frame. Half of the estimated event total is required to reserve your date; the balance is payable 1 month prior to the event.

AVAILABILITY: Indoors year-round, daily, except Christmas. Business meetings, 8am–4pm or 5pm–10pm; wedding ceremonies 7am–9am or 5pm–7pm. Evening receptions, 5pm–10pm; at some reception venues, the time can be extended until 11pm for an additional fee.

SERVICES/AMENITIES:

Catering: in-house
Kitchen Facilities: n/a
Tables & Chairs: provided
Linens, Silver, etc.: provided
Restrooms: wheelchair accessible
Dance Floor: provided
Bride's Dressing Area: yes
Meeting Equipment: PA system, 2 microphones

Parking: two large complimentary lots
Accommodations: no guest rooms
Telephone: emergency use only
Outdoor Night Lighting: yes
Outdoor Cooking Facilities: n/a
Cleanup: provided
View: rose garden, stream and koi pond, lawns, woods, estate home

RESTRICTIONS:

Alcohol: in-house
Smoking: designated areas
Music: amplified OK

Wheelchair Access: yes
Insurance: liability required

La Cañada Flintridge Country Club

Country Club

5500 Godbey Drive, La Cañada Flintridge
818/790-0611

www.lcfcountryclub.com
catering@lcfcountryclub.com

● Rehearsal Dinners	● Corporate Events	
● Ceremonies	● Meetings	
● Wedding Receptions	● Film Shoots	
● Private Parties	Accommodations	

The drive up Angeles Crest Highway to La Cañada Flintridge Country Club provides such spectacular views of the valley below you'll probably be surprised no one thought of adding a scenic turnout for you to stop the car and admire it for a while. Don't worry; the view gets even better by the time you reach the clubhouse.

Located northeast of downtown Los Angeles, roughly halfway between Glendale and Pasadena, the affluent community of La Cañada Flintridge hugs the San Gabriel Mountains to the north. Beautiful homes, partially hidden by profuse vegetation, dot the hillsides and overlook the city below. Enjoying what must be one of the choicest spots in the area is the private La Cañada Flintridge Country Club, which—fortunately for nonmembers!—welcomes the public to use their event spaces.

For nearly 50 years, LCFCC and its extensive banquet facilities have been available for special occasions of every size and variety, from weddings and holiday parties to reunions, bar/bat mitzvahs and quinceañeras. The classic Jack Simison-designed mid-century clubhouse has seven banquet rooms to choose from, with magnificent vistas in every direction.

Guests enjoy a sweeping view of the Los Angeles skyline at the intimate, oak-accented Top O' The Club, just to the right of the lobby. Yes, there's a Top O' The Club bar as well, and it's another great setting for a cocktail reception, plus it's right next to the La Cañada Flintridge Room (aka the LCF Room). This lovely main reception area has wraparound windows and a shaded outdoor patio, from which you can appreciate the distinctive combination of palm trees and towering pines around the property. As the sun sets, the twinkling lights of the city appear in the distance, creating a new and equally appealing backdrop.

For larger or more formal weddings there's the Ballroom on the opposite side of the lobby. Floor-to-ceiling windows showcase the 18-hole golf course and the Angeles National Forest. A raised stage to the left of the built-in hardwood dance floor is a perfect spot for a DJ or band to entertain at your event.

If you choose to start your celebration by exchanging vows at La Cañada Flintridge Country Club, there's a large bride's room with its own TV and private patio. The pine-shaded gazebo ceremony site down the hill is bordered by colorful flowers and lush foliage. You may also tie the knot on the balcony of the LCF Room or the Pool Deck, both of which have inspiring mountain, forest and fairway views.

Before walking back uphill (golf carts are waiting for those who prefer to ride), take a moment to drink in that stupendous panorama of the valley below, which, coupled with the '60s panache of the clubhouse, makes this location a California classic.

CEREMONY CAPACITY: The outdoor ceremony site holds up to 300 seated guests.

EVENT/RECEPTION CAPACITY: The Clubhouse holds up to 300 seated or 500 standing guests.

MEETING CAPACITY: The Clubhouse accommodates up to 400 seated guests.

FEES & DEPOSITS: A minimum $1,000 deposit is required to reserve your date. Prices start at $48/person, and vary depending on day and time of the event. Tax and a 19% service charge are additional.

AVAILABILITY: Year-round, daily, 6am–1am.

SERVICES/AMENITIES:

Catering: in-house, no BYO

Kitchen Facilities: n/a

Tables & Chairs: provided

Linens, Silver, etc.: provided

Restrooms: wheelchair accessible

Dance Floor: provided

Bride's Dressing Area: yes

Meeting Equipment: CBA

Other: ceremony coordination, champagne toast, chair covers with sash

Parking: complimentary self-parking

Accommodations: no guest rooms

Telephone: pay phone

Outdoor Night Lighting: yes

Outdoor Cooking Facilities: BBQ

Cleanup: provided

View: panorama of San Gabriel Mountains and valley, downtown Los Angeles skyline and golf course

RESTRICTIONS:

Alcohol: in-house, no BYO

Smoking: outdoors only

Music: amplified OK

Wheelchair Access: limited

Insurance: not required

The professionals in the back of this book are the best in the business. How do we know? Read page 549.

233

Brookside Golf Club

Golf Club

1133 Rosemont Avenue, Pasadena
888/212-4652

www.countryclubreceptions.com
www.brooksidegc.com
privateevents@brooksidegc.com

● Rehearsal Dinners	● Corporate Events
● Ceremonies	● Meetings
● Wedding Receptions	● Film Shoots
● Private Parties	Accommodations

If you think golf clubs are haughty and pretentious, then you haven't been to Brookside. Nestled in the picturesque arroyo next to Pasadena's famed Rose Bowl, and surrounded by palm trees and two championship golf courses, this impeccably maintained golf club will enfold you in its warm hospitality. From its humble beginnings in 1920, Brookside has grown into one of Southern California's most popular golf courses.

When you plan a special event at the completely renovated club, you have several distinctive options to choose from. The largest is the Mediterranean Room. Combining a clean, contemporary feel with Spanish details, it works equally well for weddings, fundraisers and corporate events. Recessed antiqued-brass chandeliers provide nighttime illumination, while sunshine streams in through glass walls during the day. One "wall" looks directly out onto a verdant golf course; another faces the adjacent patio with its panorama of emerald fairways in the background. Many couples exchange vows beneath a flower-festooned pergola on the patio, and then bring their guests inside for a seated reception.

Adjoining the Mediterranean Room is an inviting suite for the bride, outfitted with a vanity, comfortable couches and floral accents. There's plenty of space for her entourage, and while they're all preparing for the ceremony they're fortified with champagne and hors d'oeuvres. This room also doubles as a lounge for guests who want a bit of private relaxation during the festivities.

Brookside Restaurant, in a separate location on the club's grounds, is also extremely popular for receptions, rehearsal dinners and parties. Its centerpiece is a floor-to-ceiling, double-sided river rock fireplace that warms the entire space. Arched picture windows along two walls frame views of the manicured greens as well as the San Gabriel Mountains in the distance. The adjoining covered patio lets guests dine al fresco while savoring the beautiful surroundings.

Several other spaces at the club are perfect for smaller events like rehearsal dinners, business meetings, wedding showers or luncheons. Each one offers a unique ambiance: The Arroyo Room reflects Pasadena's history with black & white photos from the turn of the century; the Madrid

Room features floor-to-ceiling windows with wonderful views of the Rosemont Avenue hills; and the Rose Room showcases classic paintings that depict great moments from the Tournament of Roses. All of these spaces can be outfitted with a full range of audiovisual equipment.

Whether you want a casual celebration right on the golf course or a five-course gourmet banquet, you can bet that the Brookside family will treat you like one of their own.

CEREMONY CAPACITY: Outdoors, the Mediterranean Patio accommodates up to 250 seated guests. Indoors, the Mediterranean Room holds 300 seated guests.

EVENT/RECEPTION & MEETING CAPACITY: The Mediterranean Room holds 300 seated for dining, 400 for stand-up receptions, and 200 seated classroom-style. Seated capacities for other spaces are: the Brookside Restaurant, 150; the Arroyo Room, 80; the Madrid Room, 50; and the Rose Room, 40.

FEES & DEPOSITS: A nonrefundable deposit, which is applied to your food and beverage total, is required to reserve your date. The amount of the deposit varies, depending on how far in advance you book. Payment terms for the balance also vary, and may be arranged on an individual basis. Wedding packages start at $48/person. Tax, alcohol and service charge are additional.

AVAILABILITY: Year-round, daily.

SERVICES/AMENITIES:

Catering: in-house, or BYO
Kitchen Facilities: n/a
Tables & Chairs: provided
Linens, Silver, etc.: provided
Restrooms: wheelchair accessible
Dance Floor: portable available, nominal charge
Bride's and Groom's Dressing Area: provided
Meeting Equipment: screens, podiums, large-screen TV, VCR, and microphones, nominal fee; all others CBA

Parking: lots, street, complimentary
Accommodations: no guest rooms
Telephone: emergency use only
Outdoor Night Lighting: yes
Outdoor Cooking Facilities: BBQ
Cleanup: provided
View: flower garden; overlooking golf course and Arroyo
Other: event coordination

RESTRICTIONS:

Alcohol: in-house, or BYO wine or champagne only with corkage fee
Music: amplified OK outdoors until 10pm and indoors until 1am.
Smoking: outdoors only, at least 20 feet away from the building

Wheelchair Access: yes
Insurance: required for vendors

Castle Green

Historic Landmark

99 South Raymond Avenue, Pasadena
626/793-0359
www.castlegreen.com
events@castlegreen.com

Rehearsal Dinners	● Corporate Events
● Ceremonies	● Meetings
● Wedding Receptions	● Film Shoots
● Private Parties	Accommodations

The ornate rooftops of this inviting Pasadena landmark soar high above Old Pasadena, advertising Castle Green as a unique place to hold a special event. Once a posh hotel, this grand 1898 building is designed in an unusual style called Moorish Colonial, an arresting mixture of European and Middle Eastern architectural elements. Several towers capped with red domes and wrought-iron balconies lend the castle its handsome and distinctive silhouette. Also of visual interest is a whimsical bridge that extends from the main façade and connects the two wings of the historic building.

If you get married here, your ceremony can be held in the Ballroom or in the surrounding garden, which is landscaped with tall, graceful palms and a tranquil fountain that trickles into a lily pool, evoking a feel of Old World romance.

Recently restored, the castle's interior displays a wealth of late Victorian splendor. A pair of massive oak doors invites guests into a lofty lobby with a sweeping marble staircase and crystal chandelier. To the left you'll find a cluster of impressive "sitting" rooms, including the spacious Main Salon and the circular Moorish Room. These now possess their original, turn-of-the-century colors of deep rose, soft green and ochre. The original antique furnishings, warm wood mouldings, and extraordinary fireplaces complete the lovely and singular décor.

A grand hallway takes you to the Ballroom, where silent movie stars Rudolph Valentino and Lilian Gish once danced the night away by the light of the moon, streaming in through a wall of arched windows. The room is in shades of cream, with a high ceiling, pale stone-tiled floors and majestic alabaster pillars—all providing an elegant and sophisticated backdrop. Further enhancing the entire main floor is lavish carpeting that replicates the beautiful colors and patterns of the 1898 original. Just imagine holding your reception in this magnificent space, or strolling its broad verandas and park-like grounds!

Weddings here enjoy exclusive access to this one-of-a-kind privately owned estate. However, Castle Green is also an intriguing venue for any type of event: corporate gala, fundraiser, family reunion, or retirement party. This historic treasure will captivate you with an abundance of visual delights, so arrange for a tour and see why it's one of Pasadena's favorite places to celebrate.

CEREMONY CAPACITY: The Ballroom holds 250 seated or standing guests. The Garden holds 300 seated guests.

EVENT/RECEPTION CAPACITY: The Ballroom holds 220 seated or 300 standing guests; the Garden/Veranda 300 seated or 400 standing. The Grand Salon accommodates up to 300 standing.

MEETING CAPACITY: Several areas accommodate 20–220 seated guests.

FEES & DEPOSITS: Half the facility rental fee and a $1,000 refundable damage deposit are required to secure your date. The remaining balance is due 60 days prior to the event. The rental fee is $5,200 on Friday and Sunday, $7,200 on Saturday, and $3,700 Monday through Thursday evenings. Weekend rental pricing includes: the use of up to twenty 60-inch roundtables; 200 gold Chiavari chairs; 2 portable bars; and a complimentary 1-hour rehearsal time.

AVAILABILITY: Year-round, daily. Weddings usually take place Fridays, Saturdays and Sundays. Weekday business meetings take place 10am–7pm. Only one major event is booked per day.

SERVICES/AMENITIES:

Catering: select from approved list; or BYO, extra fee
Kitchen Facilities: no
Tables & Chairs: provided indoors
Linens, Silver, etc.: through caterer
Restrooms: wheelchair accessible
Dance Floor: provided indoors, CBA outdoors
Bride's and Groom's Dressing Area: yes
Meeting Equipment: BYO
Other: fires in fireplace CBA, 3 grand pianos, newly installed air conditioning, 50″ screen TV, children's room

Parking: large lot nearby, $6/car; or guest-provided valet
Accommodations: no guest rooms, discounts at nearby hotels
Telephone: use with approval
Outdoor Night Lighting: limited to bridge & veranda
Outdoor Cooking Facilities: yes
Cleanup: caterer
View: garden

RESTRICTIONS:

Alcohol: BYO, but caterer must serve
Smoking: outdoors only, in designated areas
Music: amplified OK indoors with volume limits, outdoors with City of Pasadena rules

Wheelchair Access: limited
Insurance: liability required from caterer
Other: open-flame candles require permit, no rice or birdseed; decorations restricted; children must be supervised

The Grand Ballroom & Civic Auditorium
at the Pasadena Convention Center

Historic Theatre & Convention Center

300 East Green Street, Pasadena
626/395-0208

www.pasadenacenter.com
tmok@pasadenacenter.com

- Rehearsal Dinners
- Ceremonies
- Wedding Receptions
- Private Parties
- Corporate Events
- Meetings
- Film Shoots
- Accommodations

The Pasadena Convention Center is popular for gala celebrations, but it's also a spectacular boutique venue for weddings and special events. It has an amazing variety of event sites, so, brides, whatever type of wedding you imagine, you can have it here.

The Grand Ballroom is one of the center's most recent additions. At 25,000 square feet, it's the largest ballroom in the San Gabriel Valley, but it can be divided into 10 separate sections to comfortably accommodate a group as small as 100 or as large as 3,000. Its neutral, modern interior is a blank canvas on which you can paint your own event picture. At one gala, they hung oversized inflatable stars from the ceiling, creating a glittering night "sky." Metallic linens covered the tables, special colored lighting was projected on the walls, and the room was turned into a luminous vision. The ballroom is equipped with state-of-the-art audio and lighting systems and provides internet and WiFi access. It also opens to an 11,000-square-foot lobby, with a sparkling terrazzo floor and artistic, free-form chandeliers. This prefunction space is ideal for cocktails and hors d'oeuvres, and can be turned into a congenial lounge area with the simple addition of couches and chairs.

Weddings can be held on the building's lower level, which houses another chic, contemporary event space. Done in soft grays and off-white, it complements almost any color scheme. Hang swags of fabric from the ceiling for an element of softness and movement, or add a disco ball for sparkle. Brides enjoy tossing their bouquet over the sleek metal railing on the upper level.

The Civic Auditorium, crafted in the Italian Renaissance style, has always charmed visitors with its soaring archways and dramatic artistry. Exchange vows on the same stage where Pavarotti sang his arias and television stars attend award shows and TV specials. Or, with the theater's technical elements at your disposal, hold your very own "command performance" for an audience of friends and family. You can also give your guests the star treatment and host the reception right on stage! The auditorium's resplendent Gold Room, featuring a rosette ceiling and elaborate moldings, continues to attract smaller wedding ceremonies and receptions.

A 22,000-square-foot plaza runs in front of all three of the center's main event spaces. Its beautiful tiled surface is perfect for your ceremony or an al fresco cocktail reception, before moving inside for the main festivities.

The Pasadena Convention Center's in-house culinary professionals specialize in California cuisine using locally grown ingredients, and will customize your menu. The center has also implemented a host of "go green" initiatives, which should please environmentally conscious brides. And guests attending your event will have plenty to keep them happy, too: The facility is close to the Burbank and Los Angeles airports and just blocks from Old Pasadena, a historic area filled with shops, boutiques, restaurants and clubs. Museums, golf, and live theater are nearby as well.

CEREMONY CAPACITY: The Civic Auditorium holds 150 seated guests, and the Civic Terrace seats up to 1,000. The 25,000-square-foot Grand Ballroom, which can be divided into 10 sections, accommodates up to 3,120 seated; the Conference Center seats up to 1,100.

EVENT/RECEPTION CAPACITY: The Gold Room holds up to 200 seated guests. The historic Theater accommodates up to 2,900 seated guests. The Grand Ballroom accommodates up to 1,656 and the Conference Center can hold up to 588 seated banquet style.

MEETING CAPACITY: The Exhibit Hall seats 5,400 guests.

FEES & DEPOSITS: The site fee and 25% of the food and beverage minimum are required to secure your date. Wedding packages start at $85/person. A 21% service charge and tax are additional.

AVAILABILITY: Year-round, daily.

SERVICES/AMENITIES:

Catering: in-house, no BYO
Kitchen Facilities: n/a
Tables & Chairs: provided
Linens, Silver, etc.: provided, specialty linens available for additional fee
Restrooms: wheelchair accessible
Dance Floor: yes
Bride's & Groom's Dressing Area: yes
Meeting Equipment: CBA

Parking: large lot, valet CBA
Accommodations: no guest rooms, premium hotels nearby
Telephone: pay phone
Outdoor Night Lighting: yes
Outdoor Cooking Facilities: CBA
Cleanup: provided
View: cityscape, mountains
Other: event coordination

RESTRICTIONS:

Alcohol: in-house, no BYO
Smoking: outside, in designated areas only
Music: amplified OK

Wheelchair Access: yes
Insurance: liability required

Happy Trails Garden

207 South Fair Oaks Avenue, Pasadena
626/796-9526

www.happytrailscatering.com
events@happytrailscatering.com

Historic Garden

- Rehearsal Dinners
- Ceremonies
- Wedding Receptions
- Private Parties
- Corporate Events
- Meetings
- Film Shoots
- Accommodations

Who would ever guess that behind the _Happy Trails Catering Company's_ narrow storefront is one of the best-kept event location secrets in Pasadena? Well, we certainly didn't, and were pleasantly surprised when we left the sun-soaked main street and walked down a short driveway into the cool shade of an expansive, park-like courtyard.

Here you'll find soft grass underfoot, high ivy-covered walls, palm trees, bamboo stands and a formidable, century-old camphor tree that rises from the garden's center like an enormous protective umbrella. As you approach the tree you can't help but notice the boards and pipes embedded in its trunk. They're left over from a plumber's shop that occupied this spot a hundred years ago. Apparently the tree had grown right through the wall and roof of the shop, and when it was pulled down, the parts of the building that had been absorbed into the living flesh of the tree simply remained for posterity.

An elevated wooden deck has been built around the trunk of the tree, and some couples exchange vows here; others prefer to get married in front of a tall stand of bamboo against the back wall of the courtyard. Tables are set up on the grass for the reception, their white linens and colorful centerpieces contrasting beautifully with the green surroundings. Soft night lighting is provided by Craftsman-style lanterns hanging from the tree, and you can dance beneath them on the deck or on the patio next to the quaint brick building that houses the catering kitchen.

Happy Trails Catering is dedicated to fresh, exciting food. When they customize your menu they pull out all the stops: They'll incorporate family recipes, take the garlic (or other seasonings) out of dishes if you request it, or whip up a completely vegetarian meal if that's what you want. And being a full-service caterer, they'll coordinate all the details so that you'll have very little to do.

CEREMONY CAPACITY: The location holds up to 200 seated guests.

EVENT/RECEPTION CAPACITY: The garden holds 200 seated guests.

MEETING CAPACITY: The brick patio holds 50 seated theater-style, the lawn area holds 200 seated in a circular theater-style configuration, and the raised deck accommodates 30 with additional bench seating around the edge.

FEES & DEPOSITS: To reserve your date for a wedding, 50% of the event total and a completed contract are required; the final balance is due the day of the event. The rental fee is $3,000 for the entire day. Catering, which is provided, runs $100–150/person and includes a full menu, staff, most rentals (e.g. tables, chairs, linens, china, etc.), and gratuity.

AVAILABILITY: Weddings and special events, April 1st–November 30th, 9am–midnight, one function per day. Business meetings, weekdays, 9am–5pm.

SERVICES/AMENITIES:

Catering: in-house, no BYO

Kitchen Facilities: n/a

Tables & Chairs: provided

Linens, Silver, etc.: provided

Restrooms: wheelchair accessible

Dance Floor: on wood deck or brick patio

Bride's & Groom's Dressing Area: yes

Meeting Equipment: PA system, podiums, special lighting, heaters extra charge

Parking: on-street or valet service

Accommodations: no guest rooms

Telephone: pay phone

Outdoor Night Lighting: CBA, extra fee

Outdoor Cooking Facilities: BBQs CBA

Cleanup: provided

View: of enclosed garden

Other: some coordination

RESTRICTIONS:

Alcohol: in-house, or BYO with corkage fee

Smoking: allowed

Music: amplified OK

Wheelchair Access: mostly accessible

Insurance: not required

Want to know WHAT TO ASK a potential location or vendor? Check out our Questions to Ask starting on page 19.

Noor

Event Facility

260 East Colorado Boulevard, Pasadena
626/793-4518
www.noorevents.com/content/home
sales@noorevents.com

● Rehearsal Dinners	● Corporate Events	
● Ceremonies	● Meetings	
● Wedding Receptions	● Film Shoots	
● Private Parties	Accommodations	

Ah, Noor! This dramatic event venue in the historic heart of Old Pasadena seems to have the power to elevate any occasion and surround it in magic. Named *Pasadena Weekly's* "Best Wedding Location & Banquet Hall" for 2011 and 2012 and "Most Stylized Venue 2012" by *Pasadena Magazine,* this function-dedicated property features a collection of elegant spaces designed specifically with transcendent celebrations in mind.

Indoors, you'll find two stunning ballrooms with fabulous foyers. Outdoors, there's a room-sized second-story balcony overlooking views of City Hall and the San Gabriel Mountains, plus a spectacular terrace spacious enough for a grand open-air gala.

Heads will turn and eyes will widen when guests step into the Sofia Ballroom's lavish 1920s-inspired foyer. The long, burnished wood bar, high ceilings, and magnificent chandeliers will transport them to a world of glamour and gaiety. From here, your party can flow to the Sofia Ballroom, with its Art Nouveau styling and city and mountain views or onto the Sofia Balcony, a sophisticated al fresco lounge where you can practically reach out and touch the city skyline.

Like the Sofia Foyer and Ballroom complex, the Ella Foyer and Ballroom have their own fashionable entrance. Big black double doors welcome you from the patio out front into what feels like a very chic Hollywood club. Art Deco-imbued touches—the shiny black bar, Venetian plaster walls sculpted to look like tufted dove-gray leather, the wraparound black leather banquette, and the ethereal "ghost" chandeliers—enhance the luxurious vibe. It's a striking introduction to the Ella Ballroom. Not quite as vast as the Sofia, this room's more intimate "members only" atmosphere conjures up an era of opulence and prestige.

If you want to host a large event entirely outdoors, the Promenade—which seats up to 1,500!—is also available. You have a lot of options here, and the staff, who are experts in hospitality, will help you select the spaces, menu and services that best suit your vision. You'll see why politicians, celebrities, and individuals from all walks of life have enjoyed entertaining and being entertained at Noor. From relaxed to formal, traditional to the unexpected, Noor is committed to creating a personalized event that is both exquisite and uniquely yours.

CEREMONY CAPACITY: The Noor Terrace holds 250 seated guests outdoors.

EVENT/RECEPTION CAPACITY: The Ella Ballroom can accommodate 130 seated or 250 standing, the Sofia Ballroom 330 seated or 600 standing indoors, and the Noor Terrace 170 seated or 300 standing guests.

MEETING CAPACITY: Meeting spaces hold up to 320 seated guests.

FEES & DEPOSITS: 25% of the food and beverage minimum is required to reserve your date. 25% of the estimated event total is due 4 months prior to the event and the balance is due 10 days prior. Minimums vary depending on the spaces reserved, time of event and day of the week. For weekday evening events (Monday–Thursday, 5pm–12am) the food and beverage minimum is $2,800, for weekend events (Friday, Saturday and Sunday, 5pm–2am) it is $6,000. Luncheons start at $35/person and dinners start at $70/person. Tax, room rental, and service fee are included. Alcohol, AV, lighting, packages and valet service are additional.

AVAILABILITY: Year-round, daily.

SERVICES/AMENITIES:

Catering: in-house, or BYO with approval
Kitchen Facilities: fully equipped
Tables & Chairs: provided
Linens, Silver, etc.: provided
Restrooms: wheelchair accessible
Dance Area: provided
Bride's Dressing Area: yes
Meeting Equipment: provided

Parking: large lot, on-street, valet required
Accommodations: no guest rooms
Telephone: guest phone
Outdoor Night Lighting: provided
Outdoor Cooking Facilities: BBQ CBA
Cleanup: provided
View: cityscape, mountains
Other: in-house wedding cake and florals, AV equipment, photobooth, DJ services; day-of coordination available, extra fee

RESTRICTIONS:

Alcohol: full in-house bar
Smoking: designated areas only
Music: amplified OK

Wheelchair Access: limited
Insurance: not required

Sheraton Pasadena

Hotel

303 Cordova Street, Pasadena
626/449-4000
www.sheraton.com/pasadena
execoffice@sheratonpasadena.com

- Rehearsal Dinners
- Ceremonies
- Wedding Receptions
- Private Parties
- Corporate Events
- Meetings
- Film Shoots
- Accommodations

The Sheraton Pasadena, ideally located just blocks from Old Town, has been a magnet for out-of-towners and locals alike for more than 30 years. Gracing one end of a wide, treelined pedestrian plaza, with the new Convention Center on one side and the landmark 1930s Civic Auditorium on the other, the hotel offers almost 12,000 square feet of event and banquet space, including one of the most open, airy and utterly romantic places you could choose for a wedding.

The Piazza Ballroom is positively luminous. Natural light filters in through sheer-draped, glass doors topped with fan-shaped glass arches and a dramatic, peaked skylight that runs virtually the length of the room. This gorgeous interior venue actually feels like the courtyard of an elegant hacienda: Spanish tile floors, peach-toned walls and a soaring ceiling give the room a warm and beautiful glow, aided by huge ironwork chandeliers fitted with dozens of glass shades.

While there's ample space to have your ceremony *and* reception here, the Piazza is actually part of a multilevel private event area that gives you enormous flexibility in creating your dream celebration. For example, a raised mezzanine, set apart by a fancy scrollwork railing, provides another great spot for exchanging vows, making toasts or even placing the head table. But if you really want to expand the festivities, go for all out drama: After cocktails, open the mirrored, arched doors on the mezzanine to reveal Justine's, an elegant dining room with deep green carpeting and antiqued brass chandeliers. While your guests enjoy a beautifully presented sit-down dinner, the Piazza is turned into a dance floor with DJ or band setup on the mezzanine … or, as in one recent African-themed wedding, a stage for a Fire Dancer. Whether it's fire or ice (as in transforming the space into a winter wonderland for another wedding), the event staff will be happy to work with you to make your wedding unique. Want to go beyond a simple waltz as your first dance? They're open to helping you unleash your inner Michelle Kwan by arranging your first dance at the ice skating rink next door.

For smaller gatherings or for rehearsal dinners, there's Soleil, the hotel's restaurant. Done in muted shades of cream and cocoa, it has a cozy private room in the back with a terrace that overlooks the pool.

CEREMONY, EVENT/RECEPTION & MEETING CAPACITY: The hotel can accommodate 300 seated or 600 standing guests indoors and 300 seated or standing outdoors.

FEES & DEPOSITS: 25% of the total event cost is required to reserve your date. A portion is due 90 days prior to the event and the balance is due 72 hours prior. Meals range $18–87/person. Tax and a 21% service charge are additional.

AVAILABILITY: Year-round, daily, 6am–midnight.

SERVICES/AMENITIES:

Catering: in-house or BYO
Kitchen Facilities: fully equipped
Tables & Chairs: provided
Linens, Silver, etc.: provided
Restrooms: wheelchair accessible
Dance Floor: provided
Bride's Dressing Area: yes
Meeting Equipment: provided

Parking: garage
Accommodations: 311 guest rooms
Telephone: pay phone
Outdoor Night Lighting: CBA
Outdoor Cooking Facilities: no
Cleanup: provided
View: none
Other: coordination, in-house wedding cake, AV equipment

RESTRICTIONS:

Alcohol: in-house or BYO with corkage fee
Smoking: outdoors only
Music: amplified OK indoors

Wheelchair Access: yes
Insurance: not required

Westminster Presbyterian Church

Historic Church

1757 North Lake Avenue, Pasadena
626/794-7141
www.wpcpas.org
weddings@wpcpas.org

● Rehearsal Dinners	● Corporate Events
● Ceremonies	● Meetings
● Wedding Receptions	● Film Shoots
● Private Parties	Accommodations

Visible for miles, the magnificent Westminster Presbyterian Church rises above Pasadena like the mirage of a fantastic sand castle. Unlike the ephemeral sand castle, however, this awesomely graceful church has been a rock solid part of the community since 1928. Its enduring appeal as a wedding location is evident in the fact that the church has performed ceremonies for daughters and granddaughters of brides who've exchanged their vows here.

Stretching one square block on Lake Avenue, the church compels you to take a moment and admire its beauty and workmanship. Designed in the French Gothic style, it was patterned after the medieval cathedrals of Metz, Beauvais and Amiens. (Its 150-foot bell tower resembles that of the Église St. Maclou in Rouen.) Constructed of cement blocks with intricately carved adornments, the massive structure stands like a citadel on its corner.

Enter the church through three arches, connected by block pillars. From this shaded portico, three sets of dark wood-and-iron doors lead into the narthex, an impressive vestibule. With its beamed ceilings, filigree iron chandeliers and stone archways framing stained-glass windows, it lends the proper tone to your solemn, yet joyous, occasion.

The sanctuary itself is breathtaking. Dark mahogany pews and polished stone floors contrast with the soaring vaulted ceilings of deep azure and crimson. Rendered in the fresco style by master stone painter Julian Gurnsey, they depict a starry heaven, incorporating crosses and fleurs-de-lis. Several antique brass-and-glass chandeliers suspended from the joists create a golden glow throughout the church. Along both sides, six original 1920s stained-glass devotional windows by Judson Studios are accentuated by stone archways leading to the enormous triptych centerpiece up front. The church is laid out in the classic T-shaped cruciform with a long center aisle, and can accommodate 1,000 people. Gleaming pipes from the original (and well-maintained) Reuter Organ frame the chancel area, where additional pews are available for the choir, although many brides opt for a string quartet or soloist.

There's a charming bridal room, in shades of dusty rose, for you and your attendants to use downstairs, while upstairs, the groom's party has their own lounge. When you're ready, you'll make your dramatic entrance down that long aisle, which can be dressed with flowers or candles. In a lovely touch symbolizing the start of your new life together, you and your groom will be invited by the pastor to light a unity candle. Then, after you've pledged your troth and walked back down the aisle as husband and wife, you can re-enter through a side door to take pictures inside.

If you're hosting your reception here, too, Morrison Hall, a large wood-paneled room in the adjoining building, has a stage with velvet curtains and a service kitchen for your caterer. If you're continuing your celebration in one of the hotels or restaurants nearby, be sure to take full advantage of the church grounds for your wedding album photos. One day, they may inspire your own daughter to get married at this same venerable church and carry on the tradition.

The sanctuary has been featured extensively in film and on TV as well as in *People* and *US* magazines.

CEREMONY CAPACITY: The Sanctuary holds 500 seated guests on the main floor.

EVENT/RECEPTION & MEETING CAPACITY: Morrison Hall holds up to 300 seated guests.

FEES & DEPOSITS: A $500 nonrefundable deposit is required to reserve your date. The balance is due 30 days prior to the event. The total wedding fee is $2,200, including minister and premarital counseling. Co-officiation is common. The reception rental fee is $1,500.

AVAILABILITY: Saturdays and Sundays. Only Christmas-themed weddings are allowed from Thanksgiving through New Year's Day.

SERVICES/AMENITIES:

Catering: BYO
Kitchen Facilities: fully equipped
Tables & Chairs: provided
Linens, Silver, etc.: BYO
Restrooms: wheelchair accessible
Dance Floor: provided
Bride's Dressing Area: yes
Meeting Equipment: provided

Parking: lot and street parking
Accommodations: no guest rooms
Telephone: office phone
Outdoor Night Lighting: yes
Outdoor Cooking Facilities: no
Cleanup: provided
View: hills
Other: coordination, clergy available, grand piano

RESTRICTIONS:

Alcohol: BYO champagne and wine only
Smoking: outside only
Music: amplified OK indoors, no recorded music

Wheelchair Access: yes
Insurance: not required

Puddingstone Resort

1777 Campers View Road, San Dimas
909/592-2221
www.hottubsresort.com
info@hottubsresort.com

● Rehearsal Dinners	● Corporate Events
● Ceremonies	● Meetings
● Wedding Receptions	● Film Shoots
● Private Parties	Accommodations

We know how stressful wedding planning can be. That's why we've included this tranquil oasis—we challenge you to get stressed out here!

Although not a resort in the conventional sense (there are no overnight accommodations), Puddingstone is a great place to unwind. Stroll down brick paths that meander through stands of pines and eucalyptus. Listen to the trees rustling in the breeze. Fill your eyes with panoramic lake and valley vistas. You're feeling more relaxed already, right?

Now, imagine you're getting married here. With its impressive views of Puddingstone Lake and the San Gabriel Valley, the Gazebo Lawn is a fabulous site for a ceremony. There are two spots at the edge of the lawn to choose from, and at sunset either one will reward you with the grand backdrop of a rose-and-amber sky. From either aerie, you'll feel like you could simply take off and soar out over the shimmering lake below.

Some couples take advantage of Puddingstone's custom canopy-style tent, which spans the lawn and creates a chapel-like feeling: A series of peaked metal arches down the center of the tent create a corridor for the processional to walk to the gazebo.

After the ceremony, guests are directed to the multilevel canopied Hilltop Deck for hors d'oeuvres and cocktails. While everyone mingles, the lawn is reset with tables for dining. The DJ or band typically sets up on the bandstand and a dance floor can be placed anywhere on the grass.

Over the years, the resort has hosted Hawaiian luaus with fire dancers, Renaissance weddings and even a traditional African wedding where the bride was carried in on a carriage-like sedan chair on the shoulders of four men. And, in keeping with Puddingstone's goal to soothe all guests, the owners have recently renovated the bride's changing room, so that it's an especially cool and relaxing hideaway.

Puddingstone is also home to a secluded mountain-and-lakeview event site. Tucked away on a lush mountaintop mesa with unobscured views of Puddingstone Lake and the San Gabriel Valley, this tranquil setting is the perfect retreat for a couple looking for a private location. Create a distinctive and intimate atmosphere as you set your ceremony under a crisp white canopy with a sunset backdrop. A quaint room nearby allows the bride to calm her nerves before the walk down the aisle.

If all this isn't enough to put you at ease, tucked discreetly among the trees are plenty of three-sided cabanas with hot tubs overlooking the lake below. You and your honey can soak in private, while you contemplate your future together.

Historically, Puddingstone has been very good for relationships: Couples have gotten engaged in a hot tub, married at the resort, and even returned for an anniversary soak. "People come here for candlelight, starlight, and city lights," says owner Sandy Perkins. "This place is different from anything else in the valley. It's pure romance."

CEREMONY, EVENT/RECEPTION & MEETING CAPACITY: The Vista facility holds up to 250 seated guests, the Mesa facility up to 150.

FEES & DEPOSITS: A deposit ranging $300–1,500 is required to reserve the date. 30% of the rental fee is due 6 months prior to the event, 30% is due 3 months prior, and the remaining balance is due 30 days prior. Rental fees range $1,000–7,000 depending on space and time rented, guest count, and type of function.

AVAILABILITY: Year-round, daily, 6am–1am.

SERVICES/AMENITIES:

Catering: BYO, must be insured
Kitchen Facilities: no
Tables & Chairs: provided
Linens, Silver, etc.: provided, extra charge
Restrooms: wheelchair accessible
Dance Floor: yes
Bride's Dressing Area: yes
Meeting Equipment: CBA

Parking: large lot
Accommodations: no guest rooms
Telephone: pay phones
Outdoor Night Lighting: yes
Outdoor Cooking Facilities: BBQs
Cleanup: provided, extra charge or through renter
View: Puddingstone Lake, valley, cityscape

RESTRICTIONS:

Alcohol: BYO
Smoking: outdoor only
Music: amplified OK

Wheelchair Access: yes
Insurance: not required
Other: no rice, confetti or birdseed

Want to find more venues and services? Check out our informative website, www.HereComesTheGuide.com.

249

San Dimas Canyon Golf Course

Golf Club

2100 Terrebonne Avenue, San Dimas
888/998-6126

www.countryclubreceptions.com
privateeventdirector@sandimasgc.com

- Rehearsal Dinners
- Ceremonies
- Wedding Receptions
- Private Parties
- Corporate Events
- Meetings
- Film Shoots
- Accommodations

While some wedding venues have only one attribute that makes brides say "Yes!" right away, San Dimas Canyon Golf Course has several. For starters, it offers a beautiful location at the base of the San Gabriel Mountains, a tranquil ceremony area that's just steps away from the banquet room, and a seasoned private event staff.

But the thing that most endears brides to this place may well be the terrace adjoining the banquet facility. It's like a broad tropical veranda—open, airy and decorated with small fan palms. From here you have quite a view: a putting green along with the fairways, plus some of the grandest peaks of the San Gabriels. The tree-dotted golf course slopes gently down to a seasonal creek that descends from the mountains in winter. This is a lovely vista, both for its geology and its Inland Empire palette of greens, browns, golds and soft grays.

The recently refurbished banquet room features stylish chandeliers and sconces as well as custom uplighting, plus rich chocolate-colored carpets and molding that give the space an uptown feel. Renovated even more recently, the enclosed ceremony site has become a charming, private garden area. Guests are seated on a long lawn facing the new wedding "arch," a spacious, white pergola bordered by flowers, blooming bushes, and other greenery. A sweet, two-tiered fountain fills one corner of the garden, and there's another wonderful grace note: three handsome eucalyptus trees that soar like living sculptures over the far end of the lawn.

San Dimas has two lakes on site—perfect for wedding photos—but keep in mind that they're accessible only to the couple and their photographer. For shots involving larger groups and the rest of the wedding party, the favorite spot is under a pair of massive oaks standing a stone's throw from the banquet room. The wedding pavilion and ceremony lawn are also preferred and convenient places for posing.

If you're hoping for a free hand with decorations, you're in luck here. Aside from requesting that you refrain from using confetti or glitter to shower the newlyweds, they have very few restrictions. Besides the terrace and the views, brides who've had their wedding at San Dimas laud the staff's catering prowess and general helpfulness. Menus are varied, and choices range from simple to elaborate. The club can also recommend reliable, experienced vendors.

From the setting and décor to the service and amenities, you'll find that San Dimas really does provide many of the things that make a bride say "Yes!"

CEREMONY CAPACITY: Ceremony spaces hold 200 seated guests outdoors.

EVENT/RECEPTION CAPACITY: The site accommodates 200 seated or 250 standing guests indoors, and 120 seated or standing outdoors.

MEETING CAPACITY: Meeting spaces can seat up to 200 guests.

FEES & DEPOSITS: A nonrefundable deposit, which is applied to your food and beverage total, is required to reserve your date. The amount of the deposit varies, depending on how far in advance you book. Payment terms for the balance also vary, and may be arranged on an individual basis. Meals start at $25/person. Tax, alcohol and service charge are additional. Menus and packages can be customized to fit your needs and budget. Call for details.

AVAILABILITY: Year-round, daily.

SERVICES/AMENITIES:

Catering: in-house
Kitchen Facilities: n/a
Tables & Chairs: provided
Linens, Silver, etc.: provided
Restrooms: wheelchair accessible
Dance Floor: provided
Bride's & Groom's Dressing Area: yes
Meeting Equipment: some provided
Other: in-house wedding cake, event coordination

Parking: large lot
Accommodations: no guest rooms
Telephone: office phone
Outdoor Night Lighting: provided
Outdoor Cooking Facilities: no
Cleanup: provided
View: canyon, forest, garden, fairways, hills, landscaped grounds; panorama of mountains and valley

RESTRICTIONS:

Alcohol: in-house
Smoking: designated areas only
Music: amplified OK

Wheelchair Access: yes
Insurance: not required

South Bay

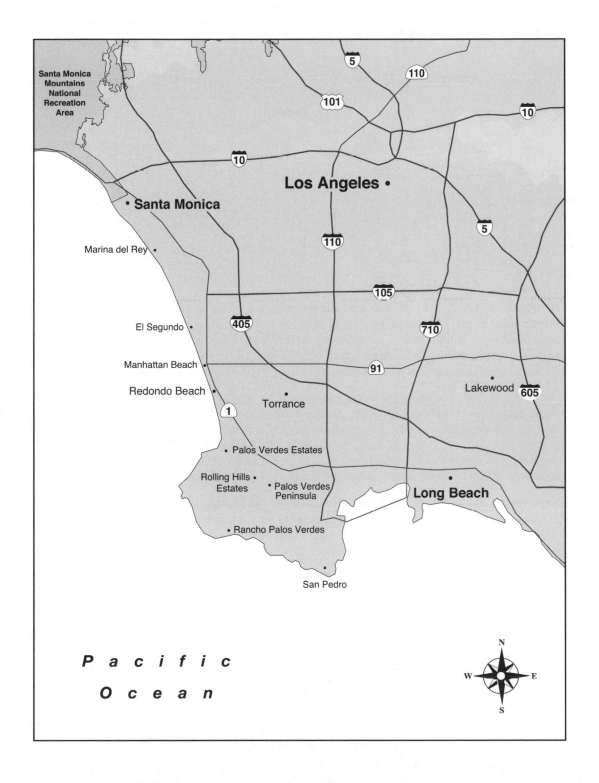

Lakewood Country Club

Country Club

3101 Carson Street, Lakewood
888/993-6396

www.countryclubreceptions.com
privateeventdirector@lakewoodgolf.net

- Rehearsal Dinners
- Ceremonies
- Wedding Receptions
- Private Parties
- Corporate Events
- Meetings
- Film Shoots
- Accommodations

Lakewood Country Club is both a delightful and convenient venue for gathering family and friends. Though mere minutes from a major airport, the club is tucked away on a quiet residential street, surrounded by 11 verdant acres of golf greens. Built in 1930 when golf was still an elite sport, the club now welcomes the public. Though hints remain throughout the property of its gracious past, Lakewood has been completely updated to accommodate the contemporary bride.

Lakewood's historic Spanish-style clubhouse adjoins a sprawling garden lawn encircled by lush foliage. Outdoor ceremonies are lovely on this manicured expanse, with flowering borders and trees providing natural adornment. A gazebo, archway, columns or the décor of your choice sets the stage for your walk down the aisle. You'll begin your grand entrance from the spacious bridal suite on the second floor of the clubhouse, where you've prepared in comfort and style. A musical cue is your signal to descend an exterior wrought-iron and stone staircase to the garden below.

Following the ceremony, you and your new spouse will be whisked away to pose for photos amid the beautiful lakes and greenery. Meanwhile, guests are invited inside the Saltillo-tiled foyer for cocktails and hors d'oeuvres. This vintage-influenced interior courtyard leads to three separate, and quite different, room options for your reception.

Host an impressive gala in the spacious Ballroom, where your nearest and dearest can celebrate beneath ornate brass chandeliers. Tall windows overlook the golf course, and the view of the emerald fairways is like an artfully rendered landscape painting. More modest affairs are held in the Hacienda Room, a wonderfully airy and light-filled space, thanks to an open-beamed cathedral ceiling. For something cozier, the marvelously intimate Fireside Room retains many details of the original building, including a decorative hearth—place flickering candles on it for a romantic glow. The angular lines of an interior roof, complete with eaves and Spanish tiles, add to this room's nostalgic atmosphere. Each of the banquet spaces also opens to an outdoor patio, where guests take in the treelined golf greens and rose-scented breeze.

With its pastoral setting, attention to detail, and competitively priced wedding packages, the Lakewood Country Club deftly answers the needs of today's brides.

CEREMONY, EVENT/RECEPTION & MEETING CAPACITY: The location holds up to 300 guests, indoors or outdoors.

FEES & DEPOSITS: A nonrefundable deposit, which is applied to your food and beverage total, is required to reserve your date. The amount of the deposit varies, depending on how far in advance you book. Payment terms for the balance also vary, and may be arranged on an individual basis. Wedding packages start at $37/person. Tax, alcohol and service charge are additional. Food and beverage minimums may apply. Menus and packages can be customized to fit your needs and budget. Call for details.

AVAILABILITY: Year-round, daily.

SERVICES/AMENITIES:

Catering: in-house
Kitchen Facilities: n/a
Tables & Chairs: provided
Linens, Silver, etc.: provided
Restrooms: wheelchair accessible
Dance Floor: provided
Bride's Dressing Area: yes
Meeting Equipment: CBA

Parking: large complimentary lot
Accommodations: no guest rooms
Telephone: emergency use only
Outdoor Night Lighting: yes
Outdoor Cooking Facilities: BBQ
Cleanup: provided
View: fairways, lake, landscaped grounds
Other: house centerpieces and wedding cake are included

RESTRICTIONS:

Alcohol: in-house
Smoking: outside only
Music: amplified OK

Wheelchair Access: yes
Insurance: not required

Aquarium of the Pacific

Aquarium and Event Facility

100 Aquarium Way, Long Beach
562/951-1663

www.aquariumofpacific.org/plan_your_event
arosen@savorsmglb.com

- Rehearsal Dinners
- Corporate Events
- Ceremonies
- Meetings
- Wedding Receptions
- Film Shoots
- Private Parties
- Accommodations

You're exchanging vows in a place like no other: Behind you slivers of light filter down through three stories of liquid turquoise, illuminating tall flowing sea plants and the iridescent sea creatures that are your audience. As your senses take in the enveloping hush and the gentle sway of the blue water, you feel at once serene and enlivened.

Such is the magical effect of the brilliant Blue Cavern, the ceremony site of choice at the Aquarium of the Pacific in Long Beach. Receptions can be held in this area as well, or in many other indoor and outdoor spaces at the facility. A particular favorite is the Terrace, where gorgeous sunsets are a regular occurrence. Here, the scent of salt water is carried on the breeze, as are the calls of exotic birds from nearby Lorikeet Forest, an outdoor aviary that mimics the lush coastal lowlands of Australia. Smaller parties, rehearsal dinners, and bridal showers often take place upstairs in Café Scuba or on its terrace overlooking the docks.

Larger events unfold in The Great Hall, a generous space that features multiple skylights and an enormous suspended blue whale that presides majestically over the festivities. A state-of-the-art sound and video system can be used to project the Aquarium's award-winning short films, a display of your wedding footage, or any imagery of your choice. Automated screens, which cover the skylights at the touch of a button, project images around the room for all to see.

The space can be "designed" to create whatever mood suits you, from low-key to theatrical. Have your reception bathed in dramatic blue and gold light, punctuated by dozens of golden stars projected onto the dance floor. This dazzling setup captures the essence of a starry night reflected on a dark blue sea. Or go with a more fanciful theme, like silhouettes of hammerhead sharks and penguins swimming by amidst blue and green swirling lights.

Depending on the arrangements you've made with the museum, guests can wander among aquarium exhibits and marvel at the wonders of the deep. Many remarkable habitats and ecosystems are represented here in engaging watery displays. Amber forests of giant swaying kelp beds, multihued tropical coral reefs, and translucent floating sea life grab your attention and ignite the imagination. Watch playful otters, sea lions and harbor seals…delight in the penguins that meet and mate for life. One is instantly immersed in the enchantment of the sea and its fascinating inhabitants.

Located adjacent to Rainbow Harbor in downtown Long Beach, the Aquarium is truly a one-of-a-kind event location with incredible marine views and spectacular exhibits. For ocean lovers or those just looking for a truly singular environment for their celebration, this is a magnificent place. Its sights and sounds will transport you and your guests to an underwater fantasy come to life.

CEREMONY CAPACITY: The site holds 300 seated guests indoors and outdoors.

EVENT/RECEPTION & MEETING CAPACITY: The site can accommodate 450 seated or 2,500 standing indoors, and 200 seated outdoors.

FEES & DEPOSITS: 25% of the event total is required to reserve your date. An additional 25% payment is due 90 days prior, and the balance is due 14 days prior to the event. Packages range $59–89/person. Tax, alcohol and a 22% service charge are additional.

AVAILABILITY: Year-round, daily. Picnic events take place 11am–3pm; evening events begin at 7pm.

SERVICES/AMENITIES:

Catering: in-house
Kitchen Facilities: n/a
Tables & Chairs: some provided, CBA
Linens, Silver, etc.: some provided, CBA
Restrooms: wheelchair accessible
Dance Floor: CBA
Bride's & Groom's Dressing Area: yes
Meeting Equipment: CBA

Parking: garage nearby
Accommodations: no guest rooms
Telephone: office phone
Outdoor Night Lighting: CBA
Outdoor Cooking Facilities: BBQ CBA
Cleanup: provided
View: cityscape, coastline, bay
Other: in-house florals, picnic area, AV equipment

RESTRICTIONS:

Alcohol: in-house
Smoking: not permitted
Music: amplified OK with restrictions

Wheelchair Access: yes
Insurance: liability required

Earl Burns Miller Japanese Garden
California State University, Long Beach

Japanese Garden

Earl Warren Drive, Long Beach
562/985-8889

www.csulb.edu/~jgarden
jgcoordinators@csulb.edu

- Rehearsal Dinners
- Ceremonies
- Wedding Receptions
- Private Parties
- Corporate Events
- Meetings
- Film Shoots
- Accommodations

Breathe deep, relax, and let yourself fall into the lush embrace of the Earl Burns Miller Japanese Garden. Situated in a tranquil enclave on the campus of Cal State Long Beach, the Miller Garden melts away any stress associated with hosting an important celebration. Not only are you instantly enveloped in beauty, you're relieved of any lingering concerns by your experienced in-house event coordinator.

The same careful attention is bestowed on the meticulously maintained garden. Rocks and plants are artistically transformed into poetic compositions of form and texture; living things play amidst a harmonious world of earth and water, light and shadow. This powerful place enhances your appreciation of subtle aesthetics, like the velvety lavender of bearded irises or the rustle of the breeze through the weeping willows. In this state of heightened awareness, the joy shared with your friends, family, and that "special someone" seems almost tangible.

Arriving guests gather in a rectangular courtyard outside the main garden. A row of lemon eucalyptus trees screens the courtyard from the outside world and flavors the air with a tangy aroma. Bonsai trees are grouped around the perimeter, and a wooden entry gate is flanked by stone "lion dogs." Lest they seem threatening, a cluster of bamboo bends gently towards the entrance and beckons you inside.

Spread before you is a vision of nature's nirvana: A pathway winds around a curvaceous pond rippling with the movement of over 200 brightly colored koi. Nearby, the graceful branches of a Chinese flame tree frame the wedding cake, dynamically showcased by a spotlight hidden within the leaves. Other decorative accents whisper rather than shout—stone lanterns peek out from lacy greenery; a three-tiered pagoda rests among rare black-stemmed bamboo; an ebony-pebbled beach glistens in the sunlight. Seasonal offerings include a springtime rhapsody of rainbow blooms, and a fall aria by the flame tree, bursting into scarlet song.

The garden's structural elements help define your celebration. At the far end of the pond a Moon Bridge arches across a waterfall that cascades down moss-covered rocks. Dressed with tulle and garlands, or unadorned against the watery backdrop, the Moon Bridge puts the bridal party on dramatic display. While the immediate family is seated at the base of the bridge, the rest of the guests have a view across the pond from the wooden Zig Zag Bridge alongside another waterfall. Feel free to add multicultural flourishes. For example, one bride had African-American "prayer dancers" parade through the crowd, and a Jewish *chuppah* is a standout on the Moon Bridge.

During the cocktail hour, guests adjourn to the courtyard while the garden is set up for the reception. When everyone reconvenes at the pond, guests are wined and dined around the water's edge, while the newlyweds snuggle at a sweetheart table on their own pondside platform. As dusk falls, the bridges and pathways come aglow with romantic lighting.

The garden invites creative adaptations to the usual wedding rituals: Whether or not you hail from the Land of the Rising Sun, you might get into the spirit at the Tea House (reached from a small side path), and greet your guests with a steaming cup of tea. The adjacent Zen Garden, featuring loose gravel in patterns resembling the sea, is a peaceful spot for a hired masseuse to give guests a few minutes of pampering. Rather than showering the newlyweds with rice, loved ones toss food to the *koi*, symbols of strength and longevity. The possibilities are virtually endless, and so are the memories created at this very special place.

CEREMONY CAPACITY: The Garden holds 200 seated guests.

EVENT/RECEPTION & MEETING CAPACITY: The Garden accommodates 160 seated or 200 standing guests.

FEES & DEPOSITS: For ceremonies, a $900 deposit is required to reserve your date; for receptions and other social functions, a $1,100 deposit is required. The balance is due 60 days prior to the event. Rental fees are $2,400 for a ceremony and $4,500 for a wedding and reception plus the cost of catering and equipment. Special rates are available on Friday and Sunday evenings and Saturday mornings. Meals by *Choura Venue Services* and *Jay's Catering* range $38–80/person. Tax, alcohol and a 20% service charge are additional.

AVAILABILITY: Ceremonies: mid-March through mid-December, Friday evenings, Saturdays and Sundays. Receptions: mid-April through mid-October, Friday, Saturday and Sunday evenings.

SERVICES/AMENITIES:

Catering: provided by *Choura Venue Services* and *Jay's Catering*

Kitchen Facilities: n/a

Tables & Chairs: available

Linens, Silver, etc.: through caterer

Restrooms: wheelchair accessible

Dance Floor: available

Bride's Dressing Area: yes

Meeting Equipment: available

Parking: ample, included in packages

Accommodations: no guest rooms

Telephone: no

Outdoor Night Lighting: yes

Outdoor Cooking Facilities: CBA

Cleanup: provided

View: garden, waterfall

Other: site coordinator

RESTRICTIONS:

Alcohol: provided by *Choura Venue Services* and *Jay's Catering*

Smoking: courtyard only

Music: amplified OK with volume restrictions

Wheelchair Access: yes

Insurance: included in packages

Other: no rice, birdseed, confetti or rose petals

This is important! Tell venues you're reading HERE COMES THE GUIDE and ask if our information is still current.

El Dorado Park Golf Course

Golf Course

2400 N. Studebaker Road, Long Beach
888/876-8247

www.countryclubreceptions.com
privateeventmanager@eldoradoparkgc.com

● Rehearsal Dinners	● Corporate Events
● Ceremonies	● Meetings
● Wedding Receptions	● Film Shoots
● Private Parties	Accommodations

Set in the quiet El Dorado Park neighborhood of Long Beach, this historic golf course—once the site of the Queen Mary Open and now home to the prestigious Long Beach Open—is a favorite event location for locals and visitors alike. The lovely public park that surrounds the landscaped course frames it with even more trees, pretty paths and picturesque waterways—all ideal for beautiful day-of-portraits of the bride and groom.

Couples can exchange vows outdoors on the Garden Ceremony Lawn overlooking the 18th green and gorgeous views of the course. Towering trees act as green "umbrellas," providing natural shade. There's also a "Winner's Board" here that often serves as a backdrop for a mini stage where wedding party photos can be taken.

Cocktail receptions and dinner dances are held just a few steps away in the airy, white Garden Pavilion, a dramatic tented venue. Set apart from the clubhouse, it features a private Garden Patio entrance and a high, peaked ceiling with elegant draping; at night, chandeliers and twinkle lights contribute to a magical, fairy-tale atmosphere.

The space is incredibly flexible, which helps explain its widespread appeal. In addition to wedding receptions, this affordable and immensely popular setting accommodates corporate events, bar and bat mitzvahs, quinceañeras, sweet sixteen parties, anniversary celebrations—even auctions, mini-festivals and tournaments! El Dorado will provide all of your tables, chairs, linens, glassware, flatware and more. However, you can also bring in lounge furniture, decorations, special uplighting and floral arrangements to personalize the environment and create an ambiance that suits your party style.

Require more space? Inside the recently renovated clubhouse, you'll find additional options. The handsome restaurant treats diners to floor-to-ceiling windows that showcase patio and golf course vistas, while the private dining room with coffered ceilings, mood lighting, and stained-glass accents is ideal for rehearsal dinners or smaller functions. When schedules permit, both can be used to expand and enhance your function.

El Dorado's on-site Private Event Manager and experienced staff will make sure your every expectation is met. Come see why those who have hosted their important celebrations here call their experiences "unforgettable."

CEREMONY CAPACITY: The facility holds 120 seated guests indoors and 600 seated outdoors.

EVENT/RECEPTION & MEETING CAPACITY: Indoors, the facility accommodates 120 seated or 250 standing guests. Outdoors, it accommodates 320 seated or 400 standing.

MEETING CAPACITY: Meeting spaces seat 320 guests.

FEES & DEPOSITS: A nonrefundable deposit, which is applied to your food and beverage total, is required to reserve your date. The amount of the deposit varies, depending on how far in advance you book. Payment terms for the balance also vary, and may be arranged on an individual basis. Meals start at $20/person. Tax, alcohol and service charge are additional. Menus and packages can be customized to fit your needs and budget. Call for details.

AVAILABILITY: Year-round, daily, anytime.

SERVICES/AMENITIES:

Catering: in-house
Kitchen Facilities: n/a
Tables & Chairs: provided
Linens, Silver, etc.: provided
Restrooms: wheelchair accessible
Dance Floor: portable provided
Bride's Dressing Area: CBA
Meeting Equipment: CBA
Other: AV equipment, event coordination

Parking: large lot, on-street
Accommodations: no guest rooms
Telephone: house phone
Outdoor Night Lighting: provided
Outdoor Cooking Facilities: BBQ CBA
Cleanup: provided
View: forest, garden; panorama of fairways and park

RESTRICTIONS:

Alcohol: full in-house bar
Smoking: designated areas only
Music: amplified OK with restrictions

Wheelchair Access: yes
Insurance: not required

Hyatt The Pike

285 Bay Street, Long Beach
562/432-1234 x105

thepikelongbeach.hyatt.com
hazel.urtis@hyatt.com

Waterfront Boutique Hotel

●	Rehearsal Dinners	●	Corporate Events
●	Ceremonies	●	Meetings
●	Wedding Receptions	●	Film Shoots
●	Private Parties	●	Accommodations

City sophistication meets easy, beachy cool at the relaxed and urbane Hyatt The Pike hotel in Long Beach. And, like a really good marriage, the hotel manages to blend these two very different personalities into one cohesive identity.

This sleek urban oasis is also a chic, seaside wedding and events venue situated in an area known as The Pike. Once a rowdy port stop where sailors cut loose, the neighborhood was razed to the ground in the '80s but has risen like a phoenix since then. Today, the hotel enjoys an enviable location just a few steps from the picturesque waterfront's park and attractions and a short stroll from Pine Avenue's pulsating local scene.

The lobby invites you in with a soothing color palette of muted blues and grays, accented by warm teakwood and butter-yellow sofas. A sculptural tree, "planted" in the mirrored floor, seems to rise up from the "water." Water is definitely a theme here, as evidenced in the Lounge, which offers a modern riff on a nautical motif with wood plank floors, white leather couches and navy blue rugs. Natural light streams in through floor-to-ceiling windows that look out to a charming "pocket park" across the street (great for photos).

Most weddings start in the Courtyard, an al fresco gem at the heart of the hotel. Nestled between the glass-walled lobby and the sandstone guest tower, the large wood-decked space is perfect for your ceremony, where you walk down the long center aisle to exchange vows against a backdrop of feathery bamboo. If you prefer to tie the knot indoors, try the private Gallery Room on the other side of the lobby. Either way, glass "nano" doors can slide back to give you access to cocktails in the lobby, Lounge or the courtyard-adjacent Club Room, which can also accommodate your band/DJ and dance floor.

Then, invite everyone back to the Courtyard for a sit-down reception under the stars, enhanced by twinkle lights wrapped around tall potted evergreen trees. And just for fun, why not project home movies starring the bride and groom directly on the courtyard wall?

There's a lot of flexibility in how you choreograph your event here, but one spot that is not to be missed is the Rooftop Pool Deck. The breathtaking, 360-degree panoramas from this 8th-floor vantage encompass the nearby Aquarium, *Queen Mary,* 1940s Ferris wheel, Long Beach port and downtown skyline. Combine a couple of cabanas for a posh, and truly spectacular, intimate reception or rehearsal dinner. And speaking of dinner, Hyatt The Pike's inventive chef enjoys putting interesting twists on old favorites, and will gladly work with you to customize your menu. In addition, the enthusiastic staff is happy to help your out-of-town guests turn their stay into a mini-vacation.

CEREMONY CAPACITY: The hotel accommodates 100 seated guests indoors or outdoors.

EVENT/RECEPTION CAPACITY: The hotel holds 60 seated with a dance floor, 80 seated without or 150 standing guests indoors and 125 seated or standing outdoors.

MEETING CAPACITY: Meeting spaces hold up to 70 seated guests, classroom-style, or 50 seated conference-style.

FEES & DEPOSITS: A $1,000 deposit is required to reserve your date and the balance is due 10 business days prior to the event. Rental fees range $500–1,000 depending on the spaces reserved, guest rooms and food & beverage totals. Meals start at $50/person. Tax, alcohol and a 22% service charge are additional.

AVAILABILITY: Year-round, daily.

SERVICES/AMENITIES:

Catering: in-house
Kitchen Facilities: n/a
Tables & Chairs: provided, CBA
Linens, Silver, etc.: provided, CBA
Restrooms: wheelchair accessible
Dance Floor: provided, CBA
Bride's Dressing Area: yes
Meeting Equipment: provided
Other: picnic area, AV equipment, event coordination

Parking: garage nearby
Accommodations: 138 guest rooms
Telephone: house phone
Outdoor Night Lighting: provided
Outdoor Cooking Facilities: BBQ CBA
Cleanup: provided
View: courtyard, landscaped grounds, pool; panorama of ocean, coastline and mountains

RESTRICTIONS:

Alcohol: in-house
Smoking: not allowed
Music: amplified OK with restrictions

Wheelchair Access: yes
Insurance: not required

Queen Mary

1126 Queens Highway, Long Beach

562/499-1749

www.queenmary.com
weddings@queenmary.com

Historic Ship & Wedding Chapel

●	Rehearsal Dinners	●	Corporate Events
●	Ceremonies	●	Meetings
●	Wedding Receptions	●	Film Shoots
●	Private Parties	●	Accommodations

Celebrate in a place that is like no other—aboard the *Queen Mary*. Permanently docked in Long Beach Harbor, this luxury ocean liner-turned-hotel/attraction offers the perfect venue for your wedding as well as breathtaking views.

The legendary *Queen Mary* set out on her maiden voyage from Southampton, England to New York City in 1936 and was considered the only way to travel for the world's rich and famous. As soon as you step onto the ship, you get a sense of the glamour of that bygone era. She's a treasure trove of Art Deco design, with event facilities guaranteed to wow your guests.

Fourteen recently renovated salons are available for your reception, and collectively feature a wealth of handcrafted touches including exquisite paneling, unique light fixtures, etched-glass doors, original murals and carved marble fireplaces. And while you and your guests are appreciating the splendid surroundings, the *Queen Mary's* full-service catering staff will take excellent care of everyone.

The *Queen Mary* also provides both outdoor and indoor options for your ceremony. To take advantage of the sunshine or sunset, get married on the bow or stern, under the Gazebo or on one of the decks. For a more traditional setting, the finely crafted Royal Wedding Chapel is a stunning choice.

An on-site wedding specialist can help you plan every detail of your wedding, from the rehearsal dinner through the ceremony, reception, and even the breakfast before your honeymoon.

When the festivities have ended and the moon has risen over the harbor, retire to one of the ship's original first-class staterooms for a romantic and peaceful night. It's no mystery why every year hundreds of couples have their wedding on this extraordinary landmark: The *Queen Mary* sets the stage for an unforgettable experience.

CEREMONY CAPACITY: The Royal Wedding Chapel holds 150 seated. The Sun Deck Gazebo holds 130 seated. The Verandah Deck holds 350 seated.

EVENT/RECEPTION CAPACITY: The ship has 14 rooms that can accommodate 20–1,500 seated guests. With a tent in the Queen Mary Park, receptions of up to 2,000 guests may be accommodated (a minimum of 800 is required for the tent, and additional rental fees and permits are required).

MEETING CAPACITY: There is 45,000 square feet of meeting space and 50,000 square feet of exhibit space. Up to 500 seated guests can be accommodated.

FEES & DEPOSITS: For weddings, a nonrefundable/nontransferable deposit is required to hold your date. The estimated event total is payable 30 days prior to the event date. Reception packages start at $59/person (ceremony cost is additional). Tax, beverages and a 22% service charge are additional.

AVAILABILITY: Year-round, daily, including holidays.

SERVICES/AMENITIES:

Catering: in-house

Kitchen Facilities: n/a

Tables & Chairs: provided

Linens, Silver, etc.: provided

Restrooms: wheelchair accessible

Dance Floor: provided

Bride's Dressing Area: in Chapel only

Meeting Equipment: full range, extra charge

Parking: hosted and non-hosted parking available

Accommodations: 346 guest rooms

Telephone: pay phone

Outdoor Night Lighting: CBA

Outdoor Cooking Facilities: no

Cleanup: provided

View: Long Beach Harbor and city skyline

Other: event coordination

RESTRICTIONS:

Alcohol: in-house, no BYO

Smoking: on deck only

Music: amplified OK

Wheelchair Access: limited (no wheelchair access to Verandah Deck)

Insurance: not required

Other: security optional

Recreation Park 18 Golf Course

Golf Club

5001 Deukmejian Drive, Long Beach
888/998-3560

www.countryclubreceptions.com
privateeventdirector@recreationparkgc.com

- Rehearsal Dinners
- Ceremonies
- Wedding Receptions
- Private Parties
- Corporate Events
- Meetings
- Film Shoots
- Accommodations

From its earliest days, Recreation Park 18 Golf Course has been *the* place for Long Beach residents to get away from it all. Back in 1909, as a beautiful-but-rugged country club, it attracted golfers who were willing to take a train from town and then hike to the course where the "greens" were actually made of slicked-down sand. Eventually the club approved a horse and buggy to shuttle the players, which vastly improved the golfers' experience and no doubt increased membership.

Today, even with a wide boulevard circling the grounds, you still get that sense of leaving the city behind once you enter this full-service park. As you drive in, you first notice the lawn bowlers enjoying their genteel pastime. Then you pass a long row of tennis courts and turn up a hill where the white Spanish Colonial clubhouse, with its columned portico and red-tile roof, basks in the peaceful views of the surrounding property. Built in 1926 by the Bixby family, this historic landmark was deeded to the city of Long Beach in 1980 for one dollar in what has to be one of the better real estate deals of the century.

Only one wedding is held in the clubhouse at a time, so you and your guests have free rein of the facilities. Begin your affair in the circular Rose Garden, a delightful ceremony spot featuring a 75-foot garden pathway leading you to a beautiful gazebo encircled by rosebushes. Afterwards, serve cocktails right there on the lawn or follow the short pathway to an intimate hedged patio festooned with twinkle lights. At the appointed time, three sets of French doors open to the grandly proportioned Main Ballroom.

Here, architectural details, such as the soaring ceiling and original dark wood crossbeams with period chandeliers, evoke the lifestyle of the wealthy in the 1920s. A gilded *trompe l'oeil* balcony accentuates the room's height and lends a European flavor. Above it, artisan stained-glass windows set off a subtle interplay of light, as the rays from the setting sun softly stream in while tiny runner lights begin to glitter just below the beams. A large built-in dance floor in front of a massive decorative fireplace provides ample room for a band or DJ.

Since the entire place is yours to enjoy, take advantage of the adjacent parlor for quiet conversation by a cozy hearth—it's perfect as a retreat for the bridal party or as a separate children's room. You can also step out onto the front portico to savor the night air. At the end of the evening, when your celebration has wound down and you drive back through the park's entrance, you'll find it hard to believe you were so close to the city all this time.

CEREMONY CAPACITY: The Rose Garden holds 250 seated guests; indoor spaces hold up to 200 seated guests.

EVENT/RECEPTION & MEETING CAPACITY: The Garden holds up to 300 seated or 350 standing guests; the Main Ballroom accommodates 180 seated or 200 standing guests.

FEES & DEPOSITS: A nonrefundable deposit, which is applied to your food and beverage total, is required to reserve your date. The amount of the deposit varies, depending on how far in advance you book. Payment terms for the balance also vary, and may be arranged on an individual basis. Meals start at $37/person. Tax, alcohol and service charge are additional. Menus and packages can be customized to fit your needs and budget. Call for details.

AVAILABILITY: Year-round, daily, 6am–midnight.

SERVICES/AMENITIES:

Catering: in-house

Kitchen Facilities: n/a

Tables & Chairs: provided

Linens, Silver, etc.: provided

Restrooms: wheelchair accessible

Dance Floor: provided

Bride's Dressing Area: yes

Meeting Equipment: microphone, WiFi, projection screens

Parking: large lot and on-street

Accommodations: no guest rooms

Telephone: pay phone

Outdoor Night Lighting: yes

Outdoor Cooking Facilities: BBQ CBA

Cleanup: provided

View: park, fairways, landscaped grounds

RESTRICTIONS:

Alcohol: in-house

Smoking: outside only

Music: amplified OK

Wheelchair Access: yes

Insurance: not required

Overwhelmed? Use the search criteria on www.HereComesTheGuide.com to narrow down your choices.

Renaissance Long Beach Hotel

Waterfront Hotel

111 E. Ocean Boulevard, Long Beach
562/437-5900
www.renaissancelongbeach.com
daryn.benton@renaissancehotels.com

- Rehearsal Dinners
- Ceremonies
- Wedding Receptions
- Private Parties
- Corporate Events
- Meetings
- Film Shoots
- Accommodations

The Renaissance Long Beach Hotel's vibrant look is a sensuous mix of casual island elegance and sleek sophistication. This seaside venue fits in beautifully with the trendy dining scene on Pine Avenue, just steps away, and it offers a range of appealing spaces for all types of events.

Walking into this premier hotel, you have the sense of being whisked away to Miami's color-drenched South Beach. And like Miami's hottest resorts, the style here is sublimely modern, but with a laid-back California twist. Scanning the interior, you're drawn to splashes of bold blues, oranges and greens, along with abstract ocean motifs. Orchids and colored-glass votives adorn countertops, and guests sit beneath palm trees in the lobby lounge, sipping drinks from frosted glasses. The warmth of the décor is further enhanced by the warmth of the staff, who greet you with smiles and the kind of savvy, attentive service that quickly wins you over.

Gowns and tuxedos are the perfect attire for the Renaissance Ballroom, whose 16-foot coffered ceiling and lavish crystal chandeliers impart a feeling of grandeur. For one Indian wedding, the room was scintillating with golden rattan chairs and beautifully embroidered fabrics. The adjoining foyer, which is often used for cocktail receptions, is filled with light flowing in through enormous windows. The more intimate Sicilian Ballroom also features classic décor, and affords a spectacular view of the marina from its cozy, horseshoe-shaped alcove.

The Pool Terrace up on the third floor is the prime spot for an al fresco party. Once the pool furniture is removed, it becomes a blank slate for your own decoration ideas. Dress it up with linen-covered cocktail tables and candles (feel free to float some in the pool), and set up a bar and seating areas. You can create the mood you want by adding special spot lighting, hurricane lamps and heaters.

The Naples Ballroom, tucked away on the lobby level, is completely separated from all the other event spaces. It affords the most seclusion, as well as a contemporary setting for your celebration. Additionally, it provides direct access to The Promenade, a wide walkway that not only leads to nearby clubs and boutique shops, but is also a unique open-air event site in its own right. Cordoned off for privacy, it's a fabulous option for parties of up to 1,000.

The Renaissance Long Beach is unquestionably a posh urban oasis—and a great destination for out-of-town guests. When they stay here they'll enjoy a plethora of room amenities (yes, the luxurious bedding includes 300-thread-count linens and a down comforter), as well as an extensive list of things to do. The hotel's central location puts Long Beach's arts and entertainment district within walking distance, and golf, hiking, swimming, and many other activities are easily accessible.

CEREMONY CAPACITY: The site holds 850 seated guests indoors and 400 seated outdoors.

EVENT/RECEPTION CAPACITY: The hotel can accommodate 540 seated or 800 standing guests indoors, and 350 seated or 500 standing outdoors.

MEETING CAPACITY: Meeting rooms hold up to 850 seated guests.

FEES & DEPOSITS: 25% of the estimated food and beverage total is required to reserve your date. A portion is due 60 days prior to the event. The balance is due 7 days prior to the event. Rental fees range $0–6,000 depending on the day and time of the event, space rented and guest count. Meals range $26–180/person. Tax, alcohol and a 15% service charge are additional.

AVAILABILITY: Year-round, daily, 6am–2am.

SERVICES/AMENITIES:

Catering: in-house or select from list
Kitchen Facilities: fully equipped
Tables & Chairs: provided
Linens, Silver, etc.: provided
Restrooms: wheelchair accessible
Dance Floor: portable provided
Bride's & Groom's Dressing Area: CBA
Meeting Equipment: provided

Parking: self or valet, garage nearby
Accommodations: 374 guest rooms
Telephone: house phone
Outdoor Night Lighting: CBA
Outdoor Cooking Facilities: BBQ CBA
Cleanup: provided
View: cityscape, coastline, ocean, pool area
Other: grand piano, spa services, in-house floral arrangements, in-house wedding cake, event coordination, AV equipment

RESTRICTIONS:

Alcohol: in-house, or BYO with corkage fee
Smoking: not allowed
Music: amplified OK with restrictions

Wheelchair Access: yes
Insurance: liability required

Skylinks at Long Beach

Golf Club

4800 East Wardlow Road, Long Beach
888/625-6682

www.countryclubreceptions.com
privateeventmanager@skylinksgc.com

- Rehearsal Dinners
- Ceremonies
- Wedding Receptions
- Private Parties
- Corporate Events
- Meetings
- Film Shoots
- Accommodations

The sky's the limit at Skylinks Golf Course when it comes to satisfying every wish, dream and special request for your wedding. You want doves released after the ceremony? No problem. Tents set up outside? No problem. Feel like having your ceremony on the fairway itself? Consider it done! In fact, it's hard to find a more accommodating staff than the one at Long Beach's premier public golf course.

While you're thinking up ways to let your creativity run wild, you'll be pleased to know that an extensive renovation has recently updated every area, from the clubhouse and banquet room to the golf course itself.

Their new ceremony site is a thing of beauty. Couples say "I do" beneath a white, trellised arch set against a striking backdrop: a free-form rock waterfall and cascading pools, surrounded by a lush landscape of palm trees, flowering bushes and other greenery. As vows are exchanged, guests look on from their lawn seating, arranged in rows on either side of a petal-strewn aisle.

Many couples opt to get married right on the golf course. Just before the ceremony, the bridal party is transported via golf carts to an area on the first fairway next to a lovely lake, where seating and any decorative elements have been set up. After the ceremony, a caravan of golf carts takes them back to the clubhouse for dinner.

No matter where you tie the knot, the reception is held in the expansive Sky Room, whose vaulted ceiling makes it feel even more spacious. A wall of windows overlooks the property's signature waterfall, which is dramatically lit up at night. Just outside the Sky Room, a comfortable patio is yours to enjoy as well, with the nearby greens and the glorious waterfall balancing nature and artistry.

However, if you happen to have a guest list of 200 or more, consider hosting your festivities in a custom-designed tent on the driving range. In most cases, you can still have your ceremony in front of the gorgeous waterfall just a few yards away. Tenting the grass is also popular for corporate parties and fundraisers.

Providing numerous choices and flexibility, the Skylinks banquet staff functions like an attentive concierge—diligently translating what you imagine into the wedding you've always wanted.

CEREMONY CAPACITY: The fairways hold up to 400 seated guests.

EVENT/RECEPTION CAPACITY: The Sky Room accommodates up to 200 seated guests. Outdoors, the site holds 500 seated.

MEETING CAPACITY: Several spaces seat up to 200 guests.

FEES & DEPOSITS: A nonrefundable deposit, which is applied to your food and beverage total, is required to reserve your date. The amount of the deposit varies, depending on how far in advance you book. Payment terms for the balance also vary, and may be arranged on an individual basis. Rental fees vary depending on the day of the event and guest count. Meals start at $15/person. Tax, alcohol and service charge are additional. Menus and packages can be customized to fit your needs and budget. Call for details.

AVAILABILITY: Year-round, daily, 6am–midnight.

SERVICES/AMENITIES:

Catering: in-house
Kitchen Facilities: n/a
Tables & Chairs: provided
Linens, Silver, etc.: provided
Restrooms: wheelchair accessible
Dance Floor: yes
Bride's Dressing Area: yes
Meeting Equipment: some provided, more CBA

Parking: large lot, on street
Accommodations: no guest rooms
Telephone: office phone
Outdoor Night Lighting: provided
Outdoor Cooking Facilities: CBA
Cleanup: provided
View: waterfall, garden, pond, fairways
Other: some coordination

RESTRICTIONS:

Alcohol: in-house
Smoking: outdoors only
Music: amplified OK

Wheelchair Access: yes
Insurance: not required

Manhattan Beach Marriott

Hotel

1400 Parkview Avenue, Manhattan Beach
310/939-1431
www.marriott.com
kristy.smith@marriott.com

- Rehearsal Dinners
- Ceremonies
- Wedding Receptions
- Private Parties
- Corporate Events
- Meetings
- Film Shoots
- Accommodations

Southern California's upscale coastal community of Manhattan Beach is cool … cool, as in trendy and hip, as in designer sunglasses, fashionable bistros, and miles of roller blade trails … cool, as in refreshing ocean breezes, bodysurfing, and the provocative fragrance of seashells … cool, as in the Manhattan Beach Marriott.

The interior of this contemporary resort hotel seems inspired by a modern sandcastle, like those found along the nearby shore. Crafted in marble and stone, the magnificent lobby boasts sleek columns and mottled marble floors that glisten in the diffused light from lofty windows and skylights. Tropical floral displays, exotic accents, and furnishings in lively hues add flashes of color to the polished space.

In the middle of the lobby, twin marble staircases descend, merging at a landing in front of a rock garden with abstract glass rods depicting the reeds along the ocean. From here the stairways continue downward until they reach the Garden Terrace Patio and the adjoining outdoor Garden Terrace where wedding ceremonies are held.

At the center of the cobbled Garden Terrace, a rectangular water feature flows out into a small lake below, and the wedding arch frames the couple against a picturesque backdrop. The hotel overlooks the Manhattan Beach Marriott golf course, so from the expansive terrace everyone is treated to the fairways' verdant panorama. Out on the greens, a pond with a petite footbridge and quaint grotto attracts the area's wildlife. This fresh, serene atmosphere feels more like an exclusive country club than a hotel—just one of the reasons weddings are so popular here.

For the reception, choose from several event spaces, each with its own distinctive attractions. The Terrace Ballroom and Foyer are right on the Garden Level, and windows look out to the terrace or the turquoise pool. "Casual Resort" is the theme of the Manhattan Ballroom. Plantation ferns brighten the corners, and plush carpeting in tropical colors adorns both the Ballroom and the adjacent Prefunction Area. This is a terrific space for the cocktail hour, with a row of floor-to-ceiling windows that overlook the Garden Terrace and golf course. For an intimate and utterly private affair, consider reserving the Parkview. Its foyer features greenery overflowing from long planters, and picture windows that showcase the rolling fairways. The room has hand-blown Murano glass chandeliers, attractive artwork, and a crisp, uncluttered look.

The Marriott's wedding planners have put together comprehensive packages that even include a made-to-order cake and those (usually hidden) tax and service charges. Ah, lucky you—starting at $127 per person, you can have a fabulous experience here, complete with all the amenities and exceptional service. And Manhattan Beach Marriott's very cool ambiance? Well, it's on the house.

CEREMONY CAPACITY: The Terrace holds up to 450 guests outdoors, the Manhattan Ballroom up to 450 seated indoors.

EVENT/RECEPTION CAPACITY: Several spaces seat 130–450 guests.

MEETING CAPACITY: Several spaces accommodate 20–900 guests seated theater-style.

FEES & DEPOSITS: 25% of the estimated event total is required to reserve your date; an additional 50% is due 90 days prior to the event and the balance is due 7 days prior. Wedding packages run $95–215/person and include the first hour of cocktails, hors d'oeuvres, a wedding cake, champagne toast, 4-course meal, choice of linens, and a complimentary suite for the bridal couple. Alcohol is additional. A $2,000 ceremony fee is additional.

For other types of events, lunches range $35–58/person, dinners $48–70/person. Room rental fees may apply, depending on food and beverage minimums.

AVAILABILITY: Year-round, daily, anytime.

SERVICES/AMENITIES:

Catering: in-house, or BYO ethnic and kosher catering only
Kitchen Facilities: n/a
Tables & Chairs: provided
Linens, Silver, etc.: provided
Restrooms: wheelchair accessible
Dance Floor: provided
Bride's & Groom's Dressing Area: yes
Meeting Equipment: CBA, extra charge

Parking: valet or self-parking
Accommodations: 385 guest rooms
Telephone: pay phones
Outdoor Night Lighting: no
Outdoor Cooking Facilities: CBA
Cleanup: provided
Kosher: can bring your own kosher caterer
View: golf course, pond
Other: event coordination

RESTRICTIONS:

Alcohol: in-house, or corkage $15+/bottle
Smoking: outdoors only
Music: amplified OK

Wheelchair Access: yes
Insurance: liability required
Other: no rice, birdseed or fog machines

Shade Hotel

Hotel

1221 North Valley Drive, Manhattan Beach
310/546-4995
www.shadehotel.com
jvought@shadehotel.com

- Rehearsal Dinners
- Ceremonies
- Wedding Receptions
- Private Parties
- Corporate Events
- Meetings
- Film Shoots
- Accommodations

If event sites were rated by their "cool" factor, Shade would be off the charts. This luxuriously hip, five-star boutique hotel perfectly captures the breezy, laid-back essence of its seaside community. Shade's super-convenient location at the edge of Metlox Plaza puts you just two blocks from the beach and steps away from a wide variety of shops and restaurants.

As you walk through the hotel, the trappings of "cool" are everywhere, from the flower-filled vases that seem to float like magic in front of the mirrored wall in the lounge to the eye-catching cyclone fireplaces in many of the guest rooms. Accents such as handmade sea urchin chandeliers and an artful display of sea ferns are visual links to the nearby ocean.

The setting is an inspired one for a destination wedding (not to mention a wrap party, corporate bash or product launch). Although you can reserve individual areas for your event, we recommend "The Ultimate Wedding" package: booking the entire hotel—including its 38 guest rooms—for the weekend. You'll not only have a fabulous home-to-die-for all to yourselves, you'll be free to choreograph your celebration exactly as you like, taking advantage of the dynamic flow between Shade's unique spaces.

You might want to kick things off with cocktails on the slate-tiled rooftop Skydeck, where your guests can mingle over martinis and mojitos while checking out the view of Manhattan Beach and the Pacific, spread out below. Then everyone gathers downstairs for your ceremony in the Courtyard, Shade's signature space. Enclosed on three sides by the hotel, this versatile open-air venue works well for daytime or evening events. Couples exchange vows on the tile-and-stone steps at the far end, with a striking 20-foot-high stone waterfall behind them. Walls of ivy framing the waterfall and planters sprouting bright green bamboo add natural bursts of color. Fabric banners or colored lighting can be strung overhead for a dramatic effect, and brides often use one of the second-story balconies facing the Courtyard for the bouquet toss.

Après-ceremony, the party moves into the Zinc Lounge for hors d'oeuvres and more drinks while the Courtyard is reset for the reception. The mix of warm cherrywood, cool steel, and soft lighting create a sultry atmosphere. Folding glass doors open to the Zinc Terrace, the perfect al fresco spot for nursing that sub-zero martini (in a glass made of ice) and people-watching in the plaza below.

Dinner is served back in the Courtyard, which has been transformed into as casual or elegant a scene as you wish. And if you need more space for that extra-long guest list, additional seating can be arranged in the Green Room upstairs. It overlooks the Courtyard, so celebrants on both floors will still feel connected.

The staff at Shade are finicky about everything, and they almost never say "no" to anything. They'll help you plan your dream wedding, including a customized menu based on the freshest, highest-quality products. They'll even replicate your grandmother's Swedish meatballs!

In the curious alchemy of perfection, all the elements at Shade—the fluid design, the exquisite details, the people and the very air—come together in a harmonious environment that, well, makes people happy. Very happy. So give yourself the most sublime wedding gift of all: a day—or three!—in the Shade.

CEREMONY & EVENT/RECEPTION CAPACITY: The hotel holds 150 seated or 200 standing guests indoors and outdoors.

MEETING CAPACITY: Meeting spaces seat 60 guests indoors.

FEES & DEPOSITS: 50% of the event minimum is required to reserve your date and the balance is due 10 days prior to the event. Minimums range $2,000–25,000 depending on the date and time of the event. Meals range $35–100/person. Tax, alcohol and a 22% service charge are additional.

AVAILABILITY: Year-round, daily, noon–midnight.

SERVICES/AMENITIES:

Catering: in-house
Kitchen Facilities: n/a
Tables & Chairs: provided
Linens, Silver, etc.: provided
Restrooms: wheelchair accessible
Dance Floor: CBA
Bride's Dressing Area: CBA
Meeting Equipment: some provided
Other: event coordination, AV equipment, custom décor, chair covers, ice carvings, lounge furniture, photo booth

Parking: valet available
Accommodations: 38 guest rooms
Telephone: emergency use only
Outdoor Night Lighting: yes
Outdoor Cooking Facilities: BBQ CBA
Cleanup: provided
View: garden, cityscape, coastline, pool area, fountain

RESTRICTIONS:

Alcohol: in-house or BYO with corkage fee
Smoking: outdoors only
Music: amplified OK with restrictions

Wheelchair Access: yes
Insurance: liability required

The professionals in the back of this book are the best in the business. How do we know? Read page 549.

275

Verandas Beach House

401 Rosecrans Avenue, Manhattan Beach
310/546-7805
www.verandasmb.com
info@verandasmb.com

Special Events Facility

- Rehearsal Dinners
- Ceremonies
- Wedding Receptions
- Private Parties
- Corporate Events
- Meetings
- Film Shoots
- Accommodations

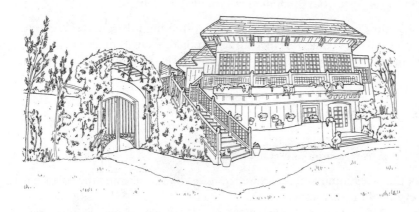

We love beach chic for a Southern California wedding, and that's exactly what this two-story, Cape Cod-style confection of a Manhattan Beach venue serves up—along with fabulous service and outstanding fare. Tucked away in a walled garden just a short walk from the sandy shore (where beach ceremonies are an option), the delightful Verandas Beach House will make you feel as if the honeymoon has already begun.

A black wrought-iron gate invites you behind the high white walls and into a fragrant little oasis, complete with well-groomed lawn and pathways, trellises, two petite waterfalls and a small but exquisite koi pond full of flowering water plants and jewel-bright fish. Sunlit and dazzling by day, trimmed in twinkling lights at night, it's an entrancing setting for a wedding ceremony or a garden party.

A grand staircase, ideal for dramatic entrances and group photos, leads from the garden to the patio lounge upstairs. Furnished casually in rattan, it's perfect for chilling and chatting outdoors. Then, when you set foot inside the house, you'll think you've been swept away to some faraway sun-drenched place: Design details like soft seashell colorations against crisp white contrasts, luxurious fabrics, and surprising textures suggest Mediterranean islands, hilltop villas, the sand and the sea.

Have a Champagne cocktail or some other specially concocted libation in the enticing white-wainscoted vestibule with its driftwood accents and black marble bar, then step into a capacious chamber with handsome French hardwood flooring, a gorgeous white fireplace, and a beautiful lounge area where billowing sheer white curtains drift on Pacific breezes around enormous windows that frame an ocean view. A divine environment for exchanging vows, a cocktail reception, dining or dancing, it will elevate any event and invest it with a fresh, easy elegance.

From here, another stunning staircase (there's an elevator as well) descends to more lovely spaces, but you might want to pause on the landing—which is large enough to seat a string quartet and a super spot for photos—to bask in the opulent atmosphere. Downstairs the "swept away" experience continues. The exquisitely appointed bride's room and restrooms have a gracious spa-like ambiance, but the real show-stopper is the large skylit banquet room in which flashes of white play against sophisticated neutral shades, sumptuous textures and Italianate details to create a rich yet contemporary tone.

The final element that makes this luxurious beach house an extraordinary event site is *New York Food Company,* renowned for their talented catering team and brilliantly presented cuisine. These creative professionals will have you and your guests believing, for an enchanted moment in time, that you're the very fortunate residents of your own seaside kingdom.

CEREMONY CAPACITY: Verandas holds up to 250 seated, indoors or outdoors.

EVENT/RECEPTION & MEETING CAPACITY: The entire facility can accommodate up to 250.

FEES & DEPOSITS: For weddings: A first payment of $4,000, which is applied toward the event total, is required to book the site. Half the estimated total is due 6 months prior to the event; the balance is due 9 days prior. Event pricing starts at $56/person. The venue rental fee, tax, alcohol and a 22% production fee are additional. For ceremonies, an additional $1,500 is charged. Menus are provided and the venue rental fees range $1,500–8,500 depending on day of week and time frame. All-inclusive midweek wedding packages start at $159/person. Off-season pricing is available between November and June, offering significant discounts on venue rental fees.

For business functions: Breakfast meetings start at $15/person, luncheon meetings at $18/person. A $1,250 room rental fee and an $850 food minimum apply for events taking place Monday–Thursday, 8am–5pm.

AVAILABILITY: For weddings: Year-round, daily, 11am–4pm or 6pm–11pm. Additional hours can be accommodated for an extra fee.

SERVICES/AMENITIES:

Catering: provided by *New York Food Company*
Kitchen Facilities: n/a
Tables & Chairs: provided
Linens, Silver, etc.: provided
Restrooms: wheelchair accessible
Dance Floor: provided
Bride's Dressing Area: yes
Meeting Equipment: CBA, extra fee

Parking: attended lot
Accommodations: no guest rooms
Telephone: restricted use
Outdoor Night Lighting: yes
Outdoor Cooking Facilities: provided
Cleanup: provided
View: ocean and garden
Other: event design and coordination; invitation maps; sound system

RESTRICTIONS:

Alcohol: in-house or BYO
Smoking: outside only
Music: amplified OK indoors

Wheelchair Access: yes
Insurance: required for all vendors

La Venta Inn

796 Via Del Monte, Palos Verdes Estates
310/373-0123
www.laventa.com
info@laventa.com

Banquet Facility with Garden

- Rehearsal Dinners
- Ceremonies
- Wedding Receptions
- Private Parties
- Corporate Events
- Meetings
- Film Shoots
- Accommodations

Early South Bay developers designed La Venta Inn as a place to entertain prospective land buyers, and it occupies a prime spot on a hill overlooking the sweep of the Palos Verdes Peninsula. Built in the 1920s, its Spanish-style architecture is set off by a distinctive tower, red-tiled roofs and, in front, a courtyard with a bubbling fountain enclosed by a bougainvillea-covered arbor. The building was at one time used as a private residence, and has all the warmth and convenience of a home.

Inside, the rooms are spacious, airy and bright, with wood floors and cream-colored walls providing a neutral backdrop for decorations. The large main ballroom has lofty open-beamed ceilings, antique wrought-iron chandeliers and a handsome fireplace with a carved stone mantelpiece. French doors open out onto a Palos Verdes stone patio that spans the length of the house, commanding stunning views of the entire L.A. Basin and Santa Monica Bay below. Two steps lead down onto a broad semicircle of lawn surrounded by flowering shrubs and palm trees. A simple white gazebo stands at the lawn's edge, with the sweep of the coastline as a dramatic backdrop. The developers chose this site well—it has a view that makes you want to stay here long after your celebration.

CEREMONY CAPACITY: La Venta can accommodate up to 250 guests.

EVENT/RECEPTION CAPACITY: La Venta holds 250 seated or standing guests.

MEETING CAPACITY: Up to 75 guests can be seated conference-style or up to 125 theater-style.

FEES & DEPOSITS: For weddings, a $4,000 deposit, which is applied toward the food and beverage total, is required to book the site. A second payment for half the estimated food and beverage total is due 6 months prior to the event; the balance and guaranteed guest count are due 9 days prior. For ceremonies, an additional $2,000 is charged. Menus are provided, and food and beverage minimums range $6,500–20,000 depending on the day of week and time frame. During the off-season (November 1st–June 30th), minimums range $5,000–15,000.

Event pricing starts at $122/person; a $14.50/person beverage charge, which is part of the food and beverage minimum, includes unlimited nonalcoholic beverages, portable bars, and professional bartenders. Clients can bring their own alcoholic beverages. Per-person prices include exclusive use of the property, a personal event designer and complimentary parking. Tax and a 22% production fee are additional. Off-season pricing (November 1st–June 30th) offers significant discounts from posted food and beverage minimums.

For business functions and meetings, fees vary depending on guest count and food service. Call for details.

AVAILABILITY: For weddings: Year-round, daily, 10am–3pm or 5pm–10pm. Functions are in 5-hour blocks, with 2 events per day. Additional hours and all-day events can be accommodated for an extra fee.

For business functions: Meeting space is available Monday–Thursday in blocks of 4, 6 or 8 hours.

SERVICES/AMENITIES:

Catering: provided by *New York Food Company*
Kitchen Facilities: n/a
Tables & Chairs: provided
Linens, Silver, etc.: provided
Restrooms: not wheelchair accessible
Dance Floor: provided
Bride's & Groom's Dressing Area: yes
Meeting Equipment: full range AV, extra fee
Other: invitation maps, microphone, event coordinator, state-of-the-art sound system

Parking: valet or attended parking provided
Accommodations: no guest rooms
Telephone: restricted use
Outdoor Night Lighting: yes
Outdoor Cooking Facilities: yes
Cleanup: provided
View: Santa Monica Bay, L.A. Basin and coastal vistas

RESTRICTIONS:

Alcohol: in-house, or BYO
Smoking: outdoors only
Music: vendors require approval

Wheelchair Access: limited access; call for details
Insurance: required for all vendors

Palos Verdes Golf Club

Country Club

3301 Via Campesina, Palos Verdes Estates
310/375-2533
www.pvgc.com
catering@pvgc.com

- Rehearsal Dinners
- Ceremonies
- Wedding Receptions
- Private Parties
- Corporate Events
- Meetings
- Film Shoots
- Accommodations

With its commanding ocean, city and mountain views, this location is a stunner. The rural surroundings also add a peaceful quality to the setting: picturesque stables nearby, horses walking down the street, and woods everywhere you look. Although the rambling Mediterranean Revival-style clubhouse has recently undergone an $11 million renovation, all of its rustic touches—wrought-iron gates and chandeliers, wood-beamed ceilings, and distressed furniture—have been preserved. The result? Palos Verdes Golf Club is more fabulous than ever for hosting an ultra-glam event.

When the club opened in 1924 it was an instant success, immediately attracting film stars and celebrities to the beautiful Palos Verdes Peninsula. Today, the venue specializes in weddings and other celebrations, offering a grand collection of handsomely appointed indoor and outdoor spaces for large or small extravaganzas.

The brilliant blue Southern California sky, the Spanish tile roof, the stately palms, and the bougainvillea-draped hillside will make your feel as if you have just stepped into a painting. Here, you're front and center for the best vista ever: breathtaking views of the Queen's Necklace—the sparkling curve of coastline between Rancho Palos Verdes and Malibu, visible from the event spaces as well as the outside areas. Have your ceremony against that backdrop in the broad Wedding Garden, followed by cocktails and hors d'oeuvres on the clubhouse's spacious Patio Terrace—your photographer's camera will definitely be clicking.

For an indoor variation on the picture-perfect theme, let guests head into the Lunada Bay Room. Elegantly furnished and large enough for banquet tables, food stations, a quartet, or strolling performers—there's even a grand piano—it looks out onto the Wedding Garden and can also serve as the Grand Ballroom foyer for super-large celebrations. The adjacent Grand Ballroom, with its high open-beam ceiling, floor-to-ceiling windows, and spectacular Patio Terrace, affords more golf course and seaside panoramas as well as plenty of room for dining and whirling around on a dance floor.

That's not all. For more intimate occasions like rehearsal dinners, the Monte Malaga Room, where unobstructed views, terrace access, mood lighting and great audio are *de rigueur,* is an excellent choice. And if you combine it with the adjacent Malaga Cove Dining Room, you nearly double its size. With a property of this magnitude there are additional areas that can be used alone or in combination, not to mention special spots like the Altamira Tower—a bride's retreat with an adorable Juliet balcony. The club's on-site specialists will be delighted to walk you through the many possibilities.

Naturally, Palos Verdes Golf Club also delivers flawless service and superb cuisine. Their talented chef—a member of the internationally renowned *Confrerie de la Chaine des Rotisseurs*—has prepared pages and pages of mouthwatering menu options. After decades of catering to high expectations, the event experts here know how to throw a phenomenal party—plus they love weddings and it shows. You and your guests will undoubtedly rave, like so many who have come before you, about your wonderful experience at this dazzling country club.

CEREMONY CAPACITY: The site holds 500 seated guests indoors and 300 seated outdoors.

EVENT/RECEPTION CAPACITY: The facility can accommodate 350 seated or 600 standing guests indoors and 125 seated or 300 standing outdoors.

MEETING CAPACITY: Meeting spaces hold up to 600 seated guests.

FEES & DEPOSITS: A deposit is required to reserve your date. Wedding packages start at $100/person. Personalized and à la carte menus are available.

AVAILABILITY: Year-round, daily, 6am–midnight.

SERVICES/AMENITIES:

Catering: in-house or BYO ethnic caterer with approval
Kitchen Facilities: fully equipped
Tables & Chairs: provided
Linens, Silver, etc.: provided
Restrooms: wheelchair accessible
Dance Floor: portable provided
Bride's & Groom's Dressing Area: yes
Meeting Equipment: provided
Other: grand piano, picnic area, AV equipment

Parking: large complimentary lot
Accommodations: no guest rooms
Telephone: house phone
Outdoor Night Lighting: CBA
Outdoor Cooking Facilities: BBQ on site
Cleanup: included
View: panorama of ocean, mountains, and coastline; cityscape, garden, landscaped grounds, fairways and lake

RESTRICTIONS:

Alcohol: full in-house bar
Smoking: outdoors only
Music: amplified OK

Wheelchair Access: yes
Insurance: not required

South Coast Botanic Garden

Garden

26300 Crenshaw Boulevard, Palos Verdes Peninsula
310/544-1948
www.southcoastbotanicgarden.org
events@southcoastbotanicgarden.org

● Rehearsal Dinners	● Corporate Events
● Ceremonies	● Meetings
● Wedding Receptions	● Film Shoots
● Private Parties	Accommodations

Gardenias, lilies, iris, honeysuckle and more than 1,600 rosebushes are only a tiny part of the spectacular floral display at South Coast Botanic Garden. And flowers are just one of the attractions here: With 87 acres of over 150,000 plants and trees—accompanied by arbors, ponds, fountains, meadows, and terraces of every shape and size—this horticultural wonderland is unquestionably one of the most scenic outdoor wedding sites in Los Angeles County.

Whatever the event, your guests will enjoy congregating in the trellised Cornish Courtyard, named after one of the early supporters of this flowering paradise. The small gift shop here is a great place to look for your botanically inspired party favors or for guests to select their own mementos of a celebration they won't want to forget.

From the courtyard, a cart path and walkways lead to a series of garden environments of surprising variety and dimension. The spacious upper meadow features two pergolas and broad lawns with sightlines that draw your attention to a lacy gazebo set like a gemstone in a flowery surround with sweeping views of the rest of the property. This area is roomy enough for any kind of large-scale entertaining—picnics to garden parties to swank nighttime affairs—tented or *en plein air*. The lower meadow, which can be used by itself or in tandem with the upper meadow, has another gazebo and a much more intimate feel.

But this is one location where there are no walls and every short walk takes you to extraordinary places... so why not explore more of the many possibilities? In the children's garden, set between the meadows, young and old will appreciate an enchanting oasis full of bowers and butterflies—it even has its own little bridge. Imagine treating your guests to the magic of a cactus garden at twilight, or watching them happily mingle in an award-winning rose garden full of fragrant paths and special gathering spots. If a stage is in order, consider using the amphitheater, where a border of star jasmine, flowering cherries, white camellias and angel's trumpets will frame any kind of production to perfection. Prefer a setting that's simple and serene? A petite patio complete with koi pond, stone lanterns, and plantings reminiscent of a Japanese garden might be exactly what you're looking for.

Of course there are nonstop photo ops throughout the grounds, but you'll also find lots of practical amenities like an assembly hall, prep kitchen for the caterers, classrooms, and plenty of parking.

This foundation- and county-run property is a testament to the power of community and a definite labor of love. With its endless array of bloom-filled event options, as well as a happy and supportive staff that aims to please, South Coast Botanic Garden is a venue that feels as good as it looks.

CEREMONY CAPACITY: The facility holds 350 seated guests indoors and 1,000 seated outdoors.

EVENT/RECEPTION CAPACITY: Several event spaces can accommodate 250 seated or 500 standing indoors and 1,000 seated or 2,000 standing outdoors.

MEETING CAPACITY: The facility holds 400 seated guests.

FEES & DEPOSITS: A $100–1,000 deposit (depending on the space reserved) is required to reserve your date and the balance is due 30 days prior to the event. Event space rental fees start at $150 and prices vary depending on the spaces reserved, day and time of the event, and the guest count.

AVAILABILITY: Year-round, daily, 8am–10pm.

SERVICES/AMENITIES:

Catering: BYO
Kitchen Facilities: prep only
Tables & Chairs: provided
Linens, Silver, etc.: some provided, more CBA
Restrooms: wheelchair accessible
Dance Floor: CBA
Bride's Dressing Area: yes
Meeting Equipment: some provided, more CBA
Other: picnic area, gazebo, event coordinator, extra fee

Parking: large lot
Accommodations: no guest rooms
Telephone: emergency use only
Outdoor Night Lighting: CBA
Outdoor Cooking Facilities: CBA
Cleanup: renter or caterer
View: garden, forest, fountain, courtyard, landscaped grounds, pond, meadow

RESTRICTIONS:

Alcohol: BYO
Smoking: designated areas only
Music: amplified OK with restrictions

Wheelchair Access: limited
Insurance: liability required

Want to know **WHAT TO ASK** a potential location or vendor? Check out our Questions to Ask starting on page 19.

Los Verdes Golf Course

Golf Club

7000 West Los Verdes Drive, Rancho Palos Verdes
888/995-4503
www.losverdesgc.com
privateeventdirector@losverdesgc.com

- Rehearsal Dinners
- Ceremonies
- Wedding Receptions
- Private Parties
- Corporate Events
- Meetings
- Film Shoots
- Accommodations

"The promise of paradise fulfilled" is how one author describes Rancho Palos Verdes, a chic community nestled on a picturesque peninsula. In this coastal Eden, dream homes built on rugged bluffs enjoy panoramas of lush hillsides, crashing surf and spectacular sunsets. Grazing cattle and family farms once inhabited this beautiful 13-square-mile neighborhood, but in 1913 banker Frank Vanderlip began transforming it into a "fashionable and exclusive residential colony." He envisioned an enclave in harmony with its natural surroundings, and during the few minutes it takes to drive through Rancho Palos Verdes you realize how well Vanderlip succeeded.

One of the most striking sites belongs to Los Verdes Golf Course, a private event venue perched on the crest of a gentle slope. If you fantasize about a wedding with the ocean as your backdrop, but are daunted by sky-high prices and attitudes to match, then meet the accommodating folks at Los Verdes—they call the regulars by name and welcome newcomers like they're old friends. On-site event experts offer advice, such as design tips for the reception or the most romantic spots for memorable photographs. They'll also match you up with the cream of the local vendors, who have worked together for years and also know their way around Los Verdes—all of which ensures that your event will come off without a hitch.

And as for getting hitched...Los Verdes has a truly inspiring spot for a wedding ceremony. A circular driveway leads to a pair of wrought-iron gates that open onto the Catalina Terrace, which is flanked by towering pines on one side and glass doors leading to the newly renovated Vista Ballroom on the other. Overlooking the golf greens, the Terrace will seduce your guests with a sweeping view of rolling fairways dotted with blossoms and evergreens, and the azure Pacific beyond. In fact, Los Verdes Golf Course boasts an ocean view from every hole, and couples can wed right on the scenic 10th or 11th tee. At any of the ceremony sites, wedding guests are treated to a captivating scene—stretching from Malibu to Catalina Island—of tranquil ocean, soaring seabirds, and graceful sailboats.

Amidst all this beauty, everyone will want to stay outdoors a little bit longer, so hors d'oeuvres can be set up under the shade of the Terrace's awning. When it's time for the reception, guests flow into the Vista Ballroom, where two walls of floor-to-ceiling windows keep that gorgeous view at hand. Adjoining the Vista is a smaller meeting space that can be sectioned off for restless kids and their toys.

If you're planning a corporate golf tournament or theme party, consider taking over the entire country club. Whatever your celebration requires, Los Verdes delivers with fine cuisine, reasonable prices, and lovely surroundings.

CEREMONY CAPACITY: The Ceremony Terrace seats 175; the 10th tee 350; and the 11th tee 150.

EVENT/RECEPTION CAPACITY: The Vista Ballroom holds 375 seated or 500 standing guests. The Catalina Terrace holds 90 seated or 250 standing guests.

MEETING CAPACITY: The Vista Ballroom holds 350 seated theater-style or 200 classroom-style.

FEES & DEPOSITS: A nonrefundable deposit, which is applied to your food and beverage total, is required to reserve your date. The amount of the deposit varies, depending on how far in advance you book. Payment terms for the balance also vary, and may be arranged on an individual basis. Wedding packages start at $66/person. Tax, alcohol and service charge are additional. Menus and packages can be customized to fit your needs and budget.

For corporate, golf-related or other special events, call for pricing details.

AVAILABILITY: Year-round, daily.

SERVICES/AMENITIES:

Catering: in-house or BYO
Kitchen Facilities: fully equipped
Tables & Chairs: provided
Linens, Silver, etc.: provided
Restrooms: wheelchair accessible
Dance Floor: provided
Bride's & Groom's Dressing Area: yes
Meeting Equipment: CBA, extra fee
Other: ceremony coordination

Parking: large lots, no fee
Accommodations: no guest rooms
Telephone: emergency use only
Outdoor Night Lighting: yes
Outdoor Cooking Facilities: CBA, extra fee
Cleanup: provided
View: panorama of ocean, Catalina Island and Malibu; golf fairways
Kosher: off-site kosher caterer allowed

RESTRICTIONS:

Alcohol: in-house or wine corkage $12/bottle
Smoking: outdoors only
Music: amplified OK indoors or outdoors

Wheelchair Access: yes
Insurance: not required
Other: no glitter, birdseed, rice or confetti

Trump National Golf Club, Los Angeles

Golf Club

One Trump National Drive, Rancho Palos Verdes
310/303-3220

www.trumpnationallosangeles.com
mwotherspoon@trumpnational.com

●	Rehearsal Dinners	●	Corporate Events
●	Ceremonies	●	Meetings
●	Wedding Receptions	●	Film Shoots
●	Private Parties		Accommodations

Billionaire businessman, consummate dealmaker, author, TV star and philanthropist, Donald Trump is the ultimate American success story. It seems that almost everything he touches turns to gold, and Trump National Golf Club is no exception.

To have your wedding here is to experience luxury and elegance—Trump style. A long serpentine driveway takes you to this exclusive bluff-top facility, where an impressive classical fountain at the entrance captures your attention. No sooner do you arrive beneath the grand porte-cochère, than a valet whisks your car away and your day at Trump National begins.

If you're hosting a rehearsal dinner or an intimate reception, Trump's Room will seduce you instantly. This room, reminiscent of Trump's ornate Mar-a-Lago estate in Palm Beach, is a study in opulence: The walls and angled ceiling are made up of mirrored panels trimmed in elaborately carved molding, completely overlaid with gleaming 24-carat gold. In the center of the ceiling a lavish chandelier drops from a pale blue *trompe l'oeil* sky full of whisper-soft clouds. Private niches along the back of the room, framed by sumptuous gold swagged drapes, are used for tabletop setups and displays. Along the front, floor-to-ceiling windows treat diners to spectacular fairway and Pacific Ocean vistas.

Café Pacific, the club's primary restaurant, has an elegantly relaxed appeal. Here, a French ambiance prevails, thanks to the vaulted ceiling with its colorful hand-painted frescoes, the old-fashioned glass-and-metal light fixtures and an enormous hand-carved limestone fireplace. Tall windows running the length of the restaurant showcase stunning views of the Pacific below.

The atmosphere changes once again in the Grand Ballroom, where gilded chairs and six Waterford crystal chandeliers—all hand-polished to a brilliant sparkle—shine against a background of pale taupe and cream walls. A 10-foot-high limestone fireplace presides at one end of the room, and a series of French doors open to the Loggia, a fabulous glass-enclosed balcony that runs along the entire ocean side of the clubhouse. From here the views are glorious, and sliding windows can be opened to the breeze in summer.

The Grand Ballroom has a private entrance, and the bride's dressing room—beautifully designed with arches, glittering chandeliers, comfortable furnishings, an abundance of mirrors and its own patio and rose garden—is only steps away.

Ceremonies are held outdoors on the Vista Terrace, an expansive lawn adjacent to the clubhouse. When vows are exchanged in this lovely secluded area, you're backed by a breathtaking panorama of emerald-green fairways, the endless ocean and technicolor sunsets.

As you would expect, the service and cuisine at Trump National match the inimitable surroundings. The food is considered some of the best in Los Angeles, and your menu—not to mention the rest of your event—can be fully customized. Mr. Trump says that a round of golf will never just be a round of golf at this course. And we'd have to say that a wedding here will never just be a wedding.

CEREMONY CAPACITY: The Vista Terrace accommodates 250 seated guests.

EVENT/RECEPTION & MEETING CAPACITY: The Grand Ballroom holds up to 300 seated or standing, and the Trump's Room can accommodate up to 100 guests.

FEES & DEPOSITS: A $5,000 deposit is required to reserve your date. 50% of the estimated total is due 3 months prior to the event; the balance is due 15 days prior. There is a $2,000 Ballroom fee and a $3,000 ceremony fee. Meals range $80–110/person. Tax, alcohol, setup fees and a 21% service charge are additional.

AVAILABILITY: Year-round, daily, 8am–midnight.

SERVICES/AMENITIES:

Catering: in-house, or BYO
Kitchen Facilities: fully equipped, extra fee
Tables & Chairs: provided
Linens, Silver, etc.: provided
Restrooms: wheelchair accessible
Dance Floor: provided
Bride's Dressing Area: yes
Meeting Equipment: some provided, more CBA

Parking: valet required
Accommodations: no guest rooms
Telephone: available upon request
Outdoor Night Lighting: yes
Outdoor Cooking Facilities: no
Cleanup: provided
View: panorama of ocean, coastline, fairways
Other: event coordination, wedding cake, AV equipment

RESTRICTIONS:

Alcohol: in-house, no BYO
Smoking: outdoors only
Music: amplified OK indoors or outdoors with restrictions

Wheelchair Access: yes
Insurance: liability required for vendors

Wayfarers Chapel

5755 Palos Verdes Drive South, Rancho Palos Verdes
310/377-1650
www.wayfarerschapel.org
joanm@wayfarerschapel.org

Chapel

Rehearsal Dinners	Corporate Events
● Ceremonies	Meetings
Wedding Receptions	Film Shoots
Private Parties	Accommodations

Panoramic ocean views and a spectacular "glass church" set high on a seaside bluff amidst redwood groves and landscaped gardens should be enough to entice you to this awe-inspiring wedding venue, but the Wayfarer's Chapel has so much more to offer.

Designed by noted landscape and structural architect Lloyd Wright, son of Frank Lloyd Wright, this exquisite glass chapel and its setting are known not just for their startling physical beauty, but for a spiritual grace that is every bit as compelling. For over 50 years this citadel of the Swedenborgian Church has welcomed individuals from all religious backgrounds and beliefs to celebrate their weddings, memorials, baptisms and other important life-affirming occasions in an elegant nature-inspired sanctuary.

Your experience begins as soon as you drive up the hill. The grounds themselves are stunning: Tranquil and serene, they consist of 3.5 meticulously landscaped acres. Arriving guests can congregate briefly in front of the recently constructed Visitors Center before taking the stone walkway from the parking lot past a meditation pond, gardens and stately pines to the chapel entrance. Some might want to linger on the way to chat beneath the trees in an adjacent glade or gaze out contemplatively over the glittering sea. From this high vantage, you can see Catalina Island on a clear day and watch dolphins leap through the waves or pelicans sweep over the ocean swells far below.

The church itself may be even more breathtaking than the grounds. Framed in timber and steel, but walled and roofed in glass, the many-faceted building gleams like a gem. The soaring walls and ceiling, whose panes are slanted at 30- and 60-degree angles, catch the light and illuminate every event, no matter what time of day, in a shower of sunshine, moonlight or candlelight. And there's no need for additional flowers: The interior of the church, like the outside, is garlanded in living greenery and furnished in wood and local Palos Verdes stone. Here the master artist is nature. For example, the massive circular window above the altar creates a living tableau of the surrounding trees and the ever-changing sky.

Within this transparent cloister every moment is picture-perfect, but comfort and ease are also a huge part of the property's attraction. The bride and groom each have quarters where they can

288

retire with their respective entourages and get ready for the ceremony. Just beyond these, a breezy colonnade with Pacific views is another gloriously situated spot where the bridal party and guests often relax for conversation and photos or listen for the carillon set in the crown of the chapel's handsome Hallelujah Tower. It rings after each and every celebration, sending its joyous message out over land and sea.

CEREMONY CAPACITY: The Chapel accommodates 100 seated guests.

EVENT/RECEPTION & MEETING CAPACITY: Receptions and meetings do not take place at this facility.

FEES & DEPOSITS: A $50 nonrefundable reservation fee is required to reserve your date and the balance is due 15 days after the reservation is made. Event space contributions range $1,500–3,400 depending on the day of the week and the time of day.

AVAILABILITY: Year-round.

SERVICES/AMENITIES:

Catering: no catering allowed

Kitchen Facilities: n/a

Tables & Chairs: n/a

Linens, Silver, etc.: n/a

Restrooms: wheelchair accessible

Dance Floor: no dancing allowed

Bride's & Groom's Dressing Area: yes

Meeting Equipment: n/a

Other: chapel musician, wedding director and minister provided

Parking: large lot

Accommodations: no guest rooms

Telephone: emergency use only

Outdoor Night Lighting: yes

Outdoor Cooking Facilities: no

Cleanup: n/a

View: fountain, garden, landscaped grounds; panorama of ocean and coastline

RESTRICTIONS:

Alcohol: no alcohol permitted

Smoking: designated areas only

Music: acoustic only

Wheelchair Access: yes

Insurance: not required

Bluewater Grill

Restaurant

665 North Harbor Drive, Redondo Beach
310/318-3474
www.bluewatergrill.com
vdye@bluewatergrill.com

- Rehearsal Dinners
- Ceremonies
- Wedding Receptions
- Private Parties
- Corporate Events
- Meetings
- Film Shoots
- Accommodations

Bluewater Grill isn't just a local favorite—it's also a hotspot for rehearsal dinners, wedding receptions and lots of private parties. The reason for its popularity is obvious to anyone who dines here: It offers a picturesque waterfront location and the kind of food that keeps people coming back again and again.

Sitting right at the edge of King Harbor, the restaurant overlooks the water. Guests seated inside or out on the deck are treated to a fantastic, up-close view of hundreds of colorful boats either passing by or bobbing at their moorings. The ambiance in the main dining room is comfortably casual, with vintage photos of fishermen and their prize catches adorning the walls, teak floors, and polished brass fixtures throughout. But if you're planning a special celebration, you'll want to reserve one of their two private dining rooms.

Both versatile rooms offer harbor vistas and can accommodate a wide range of events, from a birthday bash to a business meeting. The intimate Captain's Cabin is ideal for a rehearsal dinner or small reception. Its unique interior features an abundance of wood in the barrel ceiling and wainscoting, as well as floor-to-ceiling windows that let in lots of natural light along with a harbor view. On cool evenings, a fireplace at one end adds a warm glow. The room works equally well for an informal gathering or a sophisticated soirée.

The Avalon Room upstairs hosts larger groups, and this is where most wedding receptions take place. Wraparound windows and a high, peaked ceiling lend this space an open, airy quality. It's easy to transform this room into whatever style you have in mind: Go festive with vibrant table settings and balloons floating overhead, or host an elegant sit-down dinner with custom linens, covered chairs and stunning centerpieces. No matter what ambiance you create inside, you'll always be able to look out onto the harbor scene and, if you're lucky, a glorious sunset.

The on-site Event Coordinator will help you plan your celebration from start to finish. And although this eatery specializes in fresh, sustainable fish, their banquet menus offer a wide range of dishes that will satisfy everyone in your group.

Bluewater Grill is within walking distance of many Redondo Beach hotels and beaches, making it convenient not just for events but for a great lunch or dinner out while you and your guests are staying in town. Drop by, relax with an exotic martini, and enjoy a quintessential beach city experience at one of the area's best loved restaurants.

CEREMONY & MEETING CAPACITY: The restaurant can accommodate 100 seated guests.

EVENT/RECEPTION CAPACITY: The Captain's Cabin holds 60–70 seated or 80 standing guests, and the Avalon Room holds 100–120 seated or 150 standing.

FEES & DEPOSITS: A $2,000 deposit is required to reserve your date. A portion is due 90 days prior to the event and the balance is due at the end of the event. There are no separate rental fees, but food and beverage minimums may apply. Meals start at $30/person for luncheon and range $40–55/person for dinner. Tax, alcohol and a 20% service charge are additional.

AVAILABILITY: Year-round, daily, 11am–11pm.

SERVICES/AMENITIES:

Catering: in-house
Kitchen Facilities: n/a
Tables & Chairs: provided
Linens, Silver, etc.: provided
Restrooms: wheelchair accessible
Dance Floor: portable provided
Bride's Dressing Area: no
Meeting Equipment: some provided

Parking: large lot, valet required
Accommodations: no guest rooms
Telephone: emergency use only
Outdoor Night Lighting: yes
Outdoor Cooking Facilities: none
Cleanup: provided
View: ocean, marina, coastline
Other: wedding coordinator

RESTRICTIONS:

Alcohol: in-house
Smoking: outdoors only
Music: amplified OK indoors

Wheelchair Access: yes
Insurance: not required

Want to find more venues and services? Check out our informative website, www.HereComesTheGuide.com.

291

Chart House Redondo Beach

Oceanfront Restaurant

231 Yacht Club Way, Redondo Beach
310/798-7666
www.chart-house.com
ebrack@ldry.com

- Rehearsal Dinners
- Ceremonies
- Wedding Receptions
- Private Parties

- Corporate Events
- Meetings
- Film Shoots

Accommodations

This is a true story: The Chart House of Redondo Beach can trace its origins to a 1960s surf-safari. That's right—legendary longboarders Buzzy Bent and Joey Cabell surfed their way down the West Coast on an enviable twofold mission: to find the best surf in California and a stellar restaurant location. When the duo reached the Redondo Beach breakwaters, they knew they'd hit pay dirt—they had not only discovered a surfing paradise, but also a building with unsurpassed ocean views and beach access.

After an extensive remodel by the noted architect Kendrick Bangs Kellog, the Chart House opened in 1969 and has enjoyed renown as both an exceptional restaurant and event venue for over three decades.

Built on sturdy piers, the Chart House is a contemporary, low-profile, cream stucco building with a red-tile hipped roof. Huge beams and pillars define the restaurant's newly renovated, smartly dressed interior, while a ribbon of tinted windows around the perimeter heightens the sense of space and provides guests with a breathtaking seascape. Diners enjoy a rare 180-degree view of the Pacific Ocean from anywhere in the house. During winter's high tides, a window seat is a giddy ride, as the surf thunders and splashes against the glass. On chillier days, a fireplace in the restaurant's lounge area adds warmth and comfort.

If you're having a large event, reserve the entire restaurant so guests can mingle freely and enjoy the facility's amenities: an upscale circular bar with snazzy lighting fixtures, new furnishings with royal blue accents, and a wall hung with sepias of lifeguards, red cars and images of Redondo Beach in a more innocent era. We particularly liked the hand-blown glass art situated near the entry.

Smaller-scale parties can raise their glasses for a toast in the Sunset Room, a private space offering an expansive view of the north coast. This room can be completely separated from the rest of the dining area by simply closing its glass doors.

The Chart House is one of the only places in the South Bay where you can get married on the beach, and weddings here are conducted with ease. As you might imagine, sunset is often the preferred hour for ceremonies, with couples exchanging vows barefoot, right on the sand. It's a glorious tableau, with the sun's last shimmering light preserving the moment in a golden glow.

CEREMONY CAPACITY: Indoors, overlooking the ocean, the site seats up to 100 guests; outdoors, the beach holds up to 300 seated.

EVENT/RECEPTION & MEETING CAPACITY: For daytime receptions when the restaurant is closed, the venue can accommodate up to 225 seated indoors. Evening receptions are held in a private room that seats up to 90 guests (65 with a dance floor) or up to 100 for a rehearsal dinner or other nighttime special event.

FEES & DEPOSITS: A nonrefundable deposit is required at the time of booking to reserve your date. The reception package is $850. For an indoor ceremony, add $8/person. Beach ceremony packages range $1,700–2,000. Plated entrées range $39–80/person and buffets range $48–60/person. Tax, alcohol, and service charge are additional. Food and beverage minimums may apply to specific times, days and rooms.

AVAILABILITY: Year-round, daily, 11am–4pm, 5pm–10pm or 6pm–11pm.

SERVICES/AMENITIES:

Catering: in-house, no BYO
Kitchen Facilities: n/a
Tables & Chairs: provided
Linens, Silver, etc.: provided
Restrooms: wheelchair accessible
Dance Floor: provided, extra fee
Bride's Dressing Area: CBA
Meeting Equipment: CBA
Other: event coordination

Parking: included during the day; valet only at night, $3.50/car
Accommodations: no guest rooms
Telephone: emergency use only
Outdoor Night Lighting: yes
Outdoor Cooking Facilities: no
Cleanup: provided
View: 180-degree ocean view, coastline vistas, Redondo Beach Harbor and sailboats

RESTRICTIONS:

Alcohol: in-house, no BYO
Smoking: designated area only
Music: amplified OK

Wheelchair Access: yes
Insurance: not required

Crowne Plaza Redondo Beach
and Marina Hotel

Marina Hotel

300 North Harbor Drive, Redondo Beach
310/318-8888
www.cpsplash.com
sheree.deweese @ihg.com

- Rehearsal Dinners
- Ceremonies
- Wedding Receptions
- Private Parties
- Corporate Events
- Meetings
- Film Shoots
- Accommodations

Located in the heart of the Redondo Beach Marina, the Crowne Plaza is just a few steps away from the Redondo Beach Pier and within walking distance of many local attractions.

The hotel's proximity to the water makes it popular for weddings, and their second-floor Harbor Terrace is a stunning spot for an outdoor ceremony. This expansive area gives you a 180-degree panorama of the sailboats in the marina as well as the Pacific beyond, and on very clear days you can see Catalina Island. A refreshing sea breeze keeps things cool as you exchange vows, with the glittering ocean as a backdrop. And because you're so high up, a gorgeous sunset is practically guaranteed to add a romantic glow to the occasion.

Reception possibilities abound. Medium-sized events work well in the Seascape Ballroom and the adjacent Coral Foyer. We love the high planked-wood ceiling here, an unusual touch for a hotel ballroom. A wall of glass lets in natural light, and French doors open out onto a private patio. Large events are held in the Coral Ballroom, which features modern chandeliers and comes with its own foyer. Since this ballroom divides into three sections, it provides a lot of flexibility.

The completely private Promenade Room on the mezzanine level is an attractive choice for smaller weddings, vow renewals or rehearsal dinners. Serve cocktails in the private foyer, and then move into the room itself for dinner and dancing. Large windows on two sides overlook the ocean, and at night the view sparkles with lights from the boats in the marina.

Splash, the hotel's California/Mediterranean restaurant, offers a completely different ambiance for events. Its sophisticated private room (it has a high black ceiling and fireplace) can be used on its own or with an adjoining patio for your rehearsal dinner or farewell brunch. We also can't resist the fun of the Chef's Table, which seats 10 in the exhibition kitchen. After the staff has helped personalize your menu (they'll even create specific dishes just for you), you and your guests will have the pleasure of watching the chef cook dinner right before your eyes!

The hotel takes maximum advantage of its ocean exposure, so 85% of their stylish guest rooms have water views and private balconies, while special room packages and suite options give you amenities usually found only in boutique hotels. The on-site European day spa will tempt you with their couple's treatment room, and there's even a package for your entire bridal party. You won't have to worry about looking fantastic on the Big Day, either: Le Room Salon specializes in wedding-day hair and makeup. And if you're experiencing any pre-wedding jitters, you can work them out at the gym next door, complimentary to hotel guests.

The Crowne Plaza Redondo Beach staff take care of everything: Not only can they customize one of their all-inclusive wedding packages to fit your budget and style, an Event Manager will assist you from the planning stage through the end of your reception.

CEREMONY CAPACITY: Indoors up to 800 guests seated; outdoors up to 500 seated guests.

EVENT/RECEPTION & MEETING CAPACITY: Indoor spaces hold up to 500 seated or 1,000 standing guests, outdoors up to 400 seated or 800 standing.

FEES & DEPOSITS: A $1,000 nonrefundable deposit is required to reserve your date. A second deposit may be required. The balance is due 8 business days prior to the event. The ceremony site rental fee starts at $1,850. Wedding packages range $73–110/person. Tax, alcohol, and a service charge are additional.

AVAILABILITY: Year-round, daily, 6am–1am. Harbor Terrace (the outdoor venue) is available until 8pm with some acoustic music allowed. Call for details.

SERVICES/AMENITIES:

Catering: in-house or BYO ethnic caterer with approval
Kitchen Facilities: fully equipped
Tables & Chairs: provided
Linens, Silver, etc.: provided
Restrooms: wheelchair accessible
Dance Floor: provided
Bride's Dressing Area: CBA
Meeting Equipment: provided

Parking: valet & garage available, fees apply
Accommodations: 342 guest rooms and suites
Telephone: pay phone
Outdoor Night Lighting: no
Outdoor Cooking Facilities: BBQ CBA
Cleanup: provided
View: coastline, cityscape, marina, ocean, patio
Other: event coordination; spa services; hair/makeup salon and floral designer on site

RESTRICTIONS:

Alcohol: in-house or BYO wine with corkage fee
Smoking: outside only
Music: amplified OK with restrictions

Wheelchair Access: yes
Insurance: liability required

The Portofino Hotel & Marina

Hotel & Marina

260 Portofino Way, Redondo Beach
310/798-5874

www.hotelportofino.com
weddings@hotelportofino.com

- Rehearsal Dinners
- Ceremonies
- Wedding Receptions
- Private Parties
- Corporate Events
- Meetings
- Film Shoots
- Accommodations

If Redondo Beach, with its sunshine and balmy ocean breezes epitomizes the Southern California lifestyle, then the Portofino Hotel & Marina is the perfect place to enjoy it. Set on a lush private peninsula, it offers guests a chance to relax, let loose, and embrace the "endless summer" experience.

The venue has the unassuming intimacy of a boutique hotel, and its casual, nautical-chic ambiance makes you feel immediately at home. The inviting lobby is actually dubbed "the Living Room," although we don't know too many people who have a three-story atrium in their house—or such an astounding view! Tall, multipaned windows overlook the lagoon, where kayaks and yachts regularly make their way out to sea. There's no sign of land, only rippling sapphire-blue water, so you have the impression of floating on some elaborate houseboat. It's a remarkably soothing vision, and between the soft jazz playing on the sound system and the cocktail you're served from the bar tucked discreetly in one corner, you might want to lounge in the comfortable Living Room chairs indefinitely.

But there's a celebration afoot, beginning with a Seaside Lawn ceremony. It's surprising how many guests this intimate area can accommodate, but up to 200 of your friends and family can watch you exchange vows under an archway or gazebo with the water as the backdrop. The tropical garden atmosphere and the refreshing scent of sea spray provide natural adornments.

A short stroll from the hotel proper takes you to the Pavilion, a crisp contemporary building with two distinctive ballrooms for receptions. The sophisticated Bayside Ballroom has a 180-degree view of the ocean, and at night the twinkling stars and the lights of the Palos Verdes Peninsula cast a dreamy shimmer on the water. Next door, the Pacific Ballroom features floor-to-ceiling windows that take in the action of the lagoon and the cityscape beyond. Step out to the Pacific Terrace for cocktails or a whiff of sea air, and perhaps you'll spy dolphins cavorting in the ocean waves.

Your Portofino wedding package includes a room for your wedding night so that you can snuggle under the covers and savor your ocean view a while longer. With first-class service, a long list of amenities and a spectacular setting, it's no wonder The Portofino Hotel & Marina has become one of California's most desirable spots for weddings, vacations and romantic getaways.

CEREMONY CAPACITY: The Pacific or Bayside Ballrooms each hold 250 seated. Outdoors, the Seaside Lawn holds 200 seated guests.

EVENT/RECEPTION CAPACITY: The Bayside Ballroom holds 250 seated or 350 standing. The Pacific Ballroom holds 140 seated or 250 standing guests.

MEETING CAPACITY: The Pacific or Bayside Ballrooms hold 200–300 seated, depending on the seating configuration.

FEES & DEPOSITS: 40% of the estimated event total is required to reserve your date; partial payments are due 6 months and 4 business days prior to the event. Wedding packages run $120–190/person, and include a custom wedding cake and an oceanside room for the bridal couple. Tax and a 23% service charge are additional.

A $2,500 ceremony setup fee is extra, as is hosted valet or self-parking at $5/car. Special discounted room rates for overnight hotel accommodations are available.

AVAILABILITY: Year-round, daily, 11am–4pm and 6pm–midnight.

SERVICES/AMENITIES:

Catering: in-house
Kitchen Facilities: n/a
Tables & Chairs: provided
Linens, Silver, etc.: provided
Restrooms: wheelchair accessible
Dance Floor: provided
Bride's Dressing Area: provided
Meeting Equipment: full range AV, extra fee

Parking: large lots, $5/car valet or self-parking
Accommodations: 161 guest rooms
Telephone: house phones
Outdoor Night Lighting: access only
Outdoor Cooking Facilities: n/a
Cleanup: provided
View: ocean and coastline
Other: event coordination

RESTRICTIONS:

Alcohol: in-house
Smoking: outdoors only
Music: amplified indoors with restrictions

Wheelchair Access: yes
Insurance: not required
Other: no rice, birdseed or smoke/fog machines

The Redondo Beach Historic Library

Oceanfront Historic Library

309 Esplanade, Redondo Beach
310/937-6844
www.rbhistoriclibrary.com
info@rbhistoriclibrary.com

- Rehearsal Dinners
- Ceremonies
- Wedding Receptions
- Private Parties
- Corporate Events
- Meetings
- Film Shoots
- Accommodations

Book lovers that we are, it was a foregone conclusion that the Redondo Beach Historic Library would capture our hearts. Whether you're a bibliophile or not, however, the library is bound to appeal to you and all who walk through its impressive double wooden doors.

Local architect Lovell Pemberton built the library in 1930, positioning it to command a view of both the Pacific and the sprawling lawn of Veterans' Park.

Combining both Spanish and Dutch colonial styles, the library is a handsome three-story ivory stucco building with arched windows, a red-tile roof and straight-edged gables peaking on its north and south wings. Ornamental ironwork on the windows and Art Deco moldings on the front façade spice up the architectural mix still further. Shading the library is its gorgeous companion—a giant Moreton Bay Fig, itself a registered landmark.

Guests stepping out onto the library's main floor will undoubtedly be a little in awe of the expansive, illumined space that greets them. With windows set in almost every wall and skylights opening up the ceiling, the main floor is radiant in light—ideal for large celebrations. Cream-colored walls offset by a dusky burgundy-and-blue carpeting impart a simple elegance. Overhead, arches and dark wood beams echo the Spanish motif. Although renovated throughout, some of the library's original amenities remain, namely the circular brass lamps suspended from the ceiling and the wooden bookshelves bracketing three walls—an excellent showcase for memorabilia, pictures, votive candles or flowers.

Most couples say their vows during sunset's lavish light, in front of a quartet of ocean-facing windows on the main floor. Other possible ceremony sites include the long stretch of lawn directly behind the library or on the Veterans' Park concert green, situated on the building's north side. If it's a more intimate fête you're hosting—perhaps a communion or baby shower—then you'll want to reserve one of the library's smaller spaces: either the overflow room or the third floor mezzanine, which also affords a glorious ocean view.

Since its opening in 1996 as an event venue, the library has proved to be one of the most popular event facilities in Redondo Beach, booking almost every weekend. Call to make an appointment to visit this site, and chances are you'll sign their dance card too.

CEREMONY CAPACITY: The outdoor ceremony area holds 320 seated, the indoor ceremony area 150 seated guests.

EVENT/RECEPTION CAPACITY: The site holds up to 320 seated or standing guests indoors.

MEETING CAPACITY: The main room holds 320 seated. There are 3 smaller rooms that hold up to 50 guests each.

FEES & DEPOSITS: A $3,000 nonrefundable deposit is required to secure your date, 75% of your estimated total is due 6 months prior to your event. All balances and guest counts are due 10 business days prior to your event. Wedding inclusive packages start at $15,000. Customized events are always available. No additional service charges apply to any events with guest counts exceeding 100.

AVAILABILITY: Year-round, daily, anytime.

SERVICES/AMENITIES:

Catering: by *Spectrum Catering,* no BYO
Kitchen Facilities: n/a
Tables & Chairs: provided, including Chiavari chairs
Linens, Silver, etc.: provided
Restrooms: wheelchair accessible
Dance Floor: provided
Bride's Dressing Area: yes
Meeting Equipment: CBA, extra charge
Other: event coordination, theme events

Parking: valet included in package
Accommodations: no guest rooms
Telephone: emergency use only
Outdoor Night Lighting: access lighting only
Outdoor Cooking Facilities: CBA
Cleanup: provided
View: Pacific Ocean, Redondo Beach Pier, Palos Verdes Peninsula and nearby park

RESTRICTIONS:

Alcohol: in-house, no BYO
Smoking: outside only
Music: amplified OK

Wheelchair Access: yes
Insurance: not required
Other: no confetti or glitter

This is important! Tell venues you're reading HERE COMES THE GUIDE and ask if our information is still current.

299

Michael's Tuscany Room

Restaurant

470 West 7th Street, San Pedro
310/519-7100
www.michaelstuscanyroom.com
michaeltuscanyroom@att.net

- Rehearsal Dinners
- Ceremonies
- Wedding Receptions
- Private Parties
- Corporate Events
- Meetings
- Film Shoots
- Accommodations

Exciting things are happening in San Pedro these days. Thanks to a spruced up waterfront and a resurgent downtown, locals and tourists alike are flocking to this vibrant area where the First Thursday art walk brings a party atmosphere to the newly created cultural district. Right in the midst of this dynamic neighborhood, supporting unique mom-and-pop stores as well as hip art galleries, is Michael's Tuscany Room, a beautiful and very romantic wedding and event venue. Owner Michael Cutri has been an integral part of this burgeoning scene for more than a decade (he created the original Marcello's Restaurant), and his latest endeavor is one gorgeous setting.

Wrought-iron gates and slender trees in terracotta pots adorn the outside of the building, where three sets of French doors are topped with magnificent stained-glass windows. Step inside and you feel like you've been transported to an upscale, yet rustic, country home somewhere in Tuscany.

As you take in this soaring, 30-foot-high space, your eye is drawn up to the open-beamed ceiling with its pyramid-shaped skylights and mix of ornate Old World chandeliers. Once one of Mr. Cutri's warehouses, the room has been lovingly refashioned to capture the charms of his homeland. The walls are sandblasted weathered brick, punctuated with rows of French doors in a rich dark wood. There's a decorative balcony that runs the length of both sides of the room, creating the illusion of being in an outdoor courtyard. Faux windows and flower boxes brim with colorful blooms, and the fancy wrought-iron railing is laced with green, cascading vines.

Near the back of the room is a gracious, curving staircase that leads up to the mezzanine. Entwined with twinkle lights, it's perfect for the bride making her grand entrance for a ceremony at the base of the stairs.

Afterwards, guests mingle on the main floor and up on the mezzanine, as they raise a glass of bubbly and toast to *amore*. Dinner is served at tables set around the central dance floor. The mezzanine, which is decorated with a bucolic countryside mural and fireplace, can also be used for your band/DJ or set up as a lounge or even a photo booth area.

As captivating as this place is, it's not just a feast for the eyes. With an owner whose first love was the culinary arts (which he studied in Tuscany), you'd expect a lot of care to go into the cuisine and you won't be disappointed. A truly mouth-watering array of dishes—most with an Italian influence—is offered, but menus can also be customized for your particular event and budget.

CEREMONY CAPACITY: The site holds 150 seated guests indoors.

EVENT/RECEPTION CAPACITY: The facility can accommodate 250 seated or 300 standing guests indoors.

MEETING CAPACITY: Meeting spaces hold 300 seated guests.

FEES & DEPOSITS: A $10/person deposit is required to reserve your date. 50% of the event cost is due 30 days prior and the balance is due 1 week prior to the event. Rental fees range $0–500 depending on the time in excess of standard hours. Ceremony fee is additional. Luncheon starts at $20/person. Tax, alcohol and a 20% service charge are additional.

AVAILABILITY: Year-round, daily.

SERVICES/AMENITIES:

Catering: in-house
Kitchen Facilities: n/a
Tables & Chairs: provided
Linens, Silver, etc.: provided
Restrooms: wheelchair accessible
Dance Floor: provided
Bride's Dressing Area: CBA
Meeting Equipment: BYO

Parking: large lot, on street
Accommodations: no guest rooms
Telephone: emergency use only
Outdoor Night Lighting: access only
Outdoor Cooking Facilities: no
Cleanup: provided
View: no
Other: event coordination

RESTRICTIONS:

Alcohol: beer and liquor in-house, or BYO wine or champagne with corkage fee
Smoking: outdoors only
Music: amplified OK indoors with restrictions

Wheelchair Access: yes
Insurance: not required

Torrance Cultural Arts Center

Arts Center

3330 Civic Center Drive, Torrance
310/781-7150
www.tcac.torranceca.gov
tcac@torranceca.gov

●	Rehearsal Dinners	●	Corporate Events
●	Ceremonies	●	Meetings
●	Wedding Receptions	●	Film Shoots
●	Private Parties		Accommodations

Since its 1991 inauguration, the Torrance Cultural Arts Center has become a mecca for all types of events, including thousands of bridal showers, wedding receptions, parties and dinners. With its many different event venues, this unique complex easily sparks the imagination of many a bride or event planner. The spacious facilities spread out in a series of lofty buildings joined together by open spaces, such as a sweeping entry plaza, a large courtyard and a serene Japanese Garden.

The most popular reception room is the Toyota Meeting Hall. This room has high ceilings and a bright foyer for pre-dinner gatherings. An entire wall of glass doors opens onto the Torino Festival Plaza, an inner courtyard that accommodates tented seating or simply affords diners a place to mingle in the fresh air. A fully equipped professional kitchen is accessible to any licensed caterer.

The Ken Miller Recreation Center offers two event spaces with a shared kitchen connected by an open lobby. The Auditorium benefits from lots of natural light, and its stage will accommodate a DJ or small band with ease. The adjoining Assembly Room features hardwood floors and track lighting.

Couples getting married here often like to have their ceremony in the natural environment of the Pine Wind Japanese Garden, which contains two waterfalls, a small stream and a pond. As you enter this diminutive world (it holds approximately 60 people), you're greeted by the sound of rushing water. The wide modern fountain by the entrance releases a continuous sheet of falling water; the more romantic rock-lined waterfall in the garden's center serves as a beautiful backdrop for a ceremony or formal photo shoot. Guests may sit on redwood risers in the small amphitheater, or stand above the garden on an overlooking walkway. Afterward, they'll enjoy wandering along a circular pathway of stepping stones leading through a landscape of dainty bonsai, maple trees and bamboo.

Adjacent to the garden, the Garden Room provides a more intimate space for a bridal shower, or preparation for a wedding party holding their ceremony at the center. A custom wall divider and two separate entrances allow flexibility in the room setup, and guests will appreciate the view of the Pine Wind Japanese Garden through large picture windows.

With an easy, accessible location, free parking, competitive rental rates, and a professional staff, the Torrance Cultural Arts Center promises to make your event a success.

CEREMONY CAPACITY: The Pine Wind Japanese Garden holds 60 seated guests; the Toyota Meeting Hall can accommodate 250 seated; the outdoor Torino Festival Plaza 530 seated guests.

EVENT/RECEPTION CAPACITY: Indoors, the center holds up to 300 seated or 350 standing. Outdoors, the site accommodates 530 seated or 600 standing guests.

MEETING CAPACITY: Indoor facilities can accommodate up to 502 guests theater-style, 150 conference-style or classroom-style.

FEES & DEPOSITS: A $500 refundable deposit is required to secure your date. For events where alcohol is served, 2 Torrance police officers are required at an additional hourly fee, as is an additional $500 deposit and alcohol insurance. There's a small fee to use the Toyota Meeting Hall or Ken Miller Recreation Center kitchens. Liability insurance is required for all events. Rental fees for wedding functions range $36–186/hour depending on space and length of time rented. Setup and staff charges are additional. Please call for specific information.

AVAILABILITY: Year-round, daily, until midnight.

SERVICES/AMENITIES:

Catering: Toyota Meeting Hall requires licensed caterer; BYO for Ken Miller Recreation Center
Kitchen Facilities: 2 available
Tables & Chairs: provided
Linens, Silver, etc.: caterer or renter
Restrooms: wheelchair accessible
Dance Floor: varies per space
Bride's & Groom's Dressing Area: CBA
Meeting Equipment: full range

Parking: large lot, complimentary parking
Accommodations: no guest rooms
Telephone: pay phone
Outdoor Night Lighting: some, call for details
Outdoor Cooking Facilities: through caterer
Cleanup: caterer and renter
View: Torino Festival Plaza and Pine Wind Japanese Garden
Other: grand piano, PA system, video projector, free WiFi

RESTRICTIONS:

Alcohol: BYO BWC only; licensed and insured server required
Smoking: outside only
Music: amplified OK indoors, OK outdoors with restrictions

Wheelchair Access: yes
Insurance: liability required
Other: no birdseed, rice, glitter, confetti or open flames

Orange County

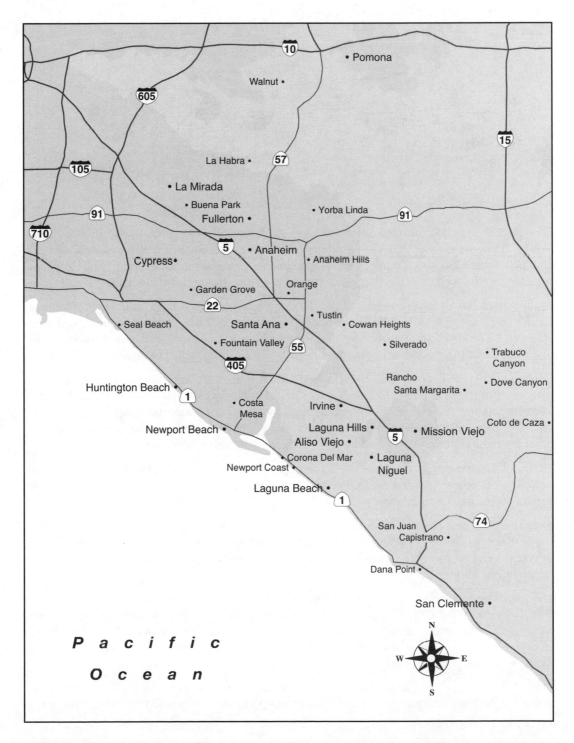

Pacific

Ocean

Aliso Viejo Conference Center

Conference Center

31 Santa Barbara Drive, Aliso Viejo
949/425-2555
www.alisoviejoconferencecenter.com
avevents@kempersports.com

● Rehearsal Dinners	● Corporate Events
● Ceremonies	● Meetings
● Wedding Receptions	● Film Shoots
● Private Parties	Accommodations

"The Place with Panoramic Views of the Saddleback Valley and a Gorgeous Golf Course" might be a more apt name for the Aliso Viejo Conference Center, peacefully perched above the valley and adjacent to the Aliso Viejo Country Club. Although its serene setting makes you feel like you're far from the city, the center is easily accessible from the freeway and other main thoroughfares.

A standout facility in South Orange County, the Conference Center is as appealing for weddings as it is for corporate events. With the neighboring golf course as a backdrop, the outdoor ceremony stage is set. The Mediterranean-style buildings and well-tended fairways provide a neutral landscape that complements any color scheme and style of wedding, from casual to opulent.

Bookended by the Country Club and the Conference Center, the ceremony lawn can be set up two ways: In the first, guests face the center's grand pillars, which serve as a readymade "arch," formally framing the couple as they exchange vows. In the second, the setup is reversed and guests face the fairways. While the latter option doesn't include a built-in arch, you may add one or let the natural beauty of the Saddleback Valley be your only decoration.

The pool fireside ceremony site is the center's newest addition and is available during the off-season. With private views of the golf course and a stone fireplace as the backdrop, it offers the perfect ambiance for an evening wedding.

After the photographer has captured the couple's post-ceremony smiles and husband-and-wife kisses, the celebration kicks off with the cocktail hour on the center's spacious patio. From here, the view could not be more picturesque: As guests toast the newlyweds, they gaze out past manicured greens into the valley.

The patio connects to the ballroom, allowing a smooth transition to the reception. Natural light flowing in through multiple glass doors and windows gives the room its open, airy feeling. The vaulted, wood-beamed ceiling and ivory walls lend considerable warmth to the space. There's plenty of room for dancing indoors, but on a balmy evening guests are more likely to head for the patio, where they can enjoy the starry night sky.

At the Conference Center, they've paid as much attention to the cuisine as they have to the facilities. Their culinary creations are one of the Center's main attractions and bear no comparison to "wedding food." Upscale yet relatable, tasty but not standoffish, the menu options include choices for the easiest-to-please and the pickiest palates.

Whether your event is simply elegant or elegantly simple, the center's professional Private Events staff will give it the attention it deserves.

CEREMONY CAPACITY: The Fireside site holds 250 seated guests and the Arbor site seats 200.

EVENT/RECEPTION CAPACITY: The Center accommodates 250 seated or 400 standing guests indoors and 150 seated or 250 standing outdoors.

MEETING CAPACITY: Meeting spaces seat 250 guests indoors.

FEES & DEPOSITS: A $2,000 deposit is required to reserve your date. 50% of the estimated total is due 3 months prior to the event, and the balance is due 14 days prior. Rental fees range $500–1,500 depending on the day and time of the event and the room rented. Meals range $30–65/person. Tax, alcohol and a 21% service charge are additional.

AVAILABILITY: Year-round, daily, 7am–midnight.

SERVICES/AMENITIES:

Catering: in-house
Kitchen Facilities: n/a
Tables & Chairs: provided
Linens, Silver, etc.: provided
Restrooms: wheelchair accessible
Dance Floor: portable provided
Bride's Dressing Area: yes
Meeting Equipment: provided
Other: coordination, AV equipment

Parking: large lot
Accommodations: no guest rooms
Telephone: office phone
Outdoor Night Lighting: CBA
Outdoor Cooking Facilities: none
Cleanup: provided
View: fairways; panorama of valley, hills and mountains

RESTRICTIONS:

Alcohol: in-house
Smoking: designated areas only
Music: amplified OK

Wheelchair Access: yes
Insurance: not required

Aliso Viejo Country Club

Golf Club

33 Santa Barbara Drive, Aliso Viejo
949/609-3305
www.alisogolf.com
contactus@alisogolf.com

- Rehearsal Dinners
- Ceremonies
- Wedding Receptions
- Private Parties
- Corporate Events
- Meetings
- Film Shoots
- Accommodations

Its gracious hacienda-like architecture hints at California's past, but in personality and performance this distinctive venue is stylishly contemporary. Located in the rolling hills overlooking the Saddle-back Valley, the Aliso Viejo Country Club is a warm and welcoming special event setting that serves up memorable celebrations of all kinds with panache.

One of Orange County's newest private country clubs (and boasting one of the only two Jack Nicklaus-designed golf courses in the region), its little lakes and woods are home to a plethora of small woodland creatures. Kingfishers, green herons, snowy egrets, and western meadowlarks are just a few of the many wonderful birds that can be seen around the waterways and well-tended fairways and greens. Fragrant herbs and colorful blooms fill the gardens. Balconies, bell towers and elegant French doors open onto the terraces and courtyards.

Ceremonies and receptions are often held on the Celebration Lawn, where both the handsome arbor framed by beds of white roses and the well-manicured course provide applause-worthy backdrops for any festivity. Whether your event is a wedding, a brunch, a baby shower, a corporate shindig, or an anniversary dinner, it will be well placed and beautifully served here.

Indoors, an elevator and a handsome wrought-iron staircase off the lobby take you up to an attractive second-story foyer, which adjoins a series of lovely salons where guests can unwind, sip cocktails and dine in private and unhurried bliss. The Bell Tower Room serves as an elegant lounge. In it, French doors open onto a small half-moon-shaped Juliet balcony in the clubhouse tower. Its arched, brick window openings looking out over the grounds create an ultra-romantic frame for photos of the bride and groom.

Also on this floor is a rustic living room with a Spanish-style fireplace and comfortable furnishings, plus a private dining room featuring a full granite bar; vaulted, beamed ceiling; two outdoor terraces suitable for dining and dancing; and panoramic views of the golf course and valley. After a dinner of the culinary team's delicious California fusion cuisine, you may want to gather in the adjacent wine room for the cake cutting. With its masculine décor—handsome mahogany floors and dark walnut wine lockers—and patio access, this space is perfect for cigar aficionados, too.

The spectacular spa-caliber ladies room is a bonus. Just the place for prepping and pampering, it has club chairs, leather ottomans, beamed ceilings, carpeted and tumbled travertine marble floors, and a four-station granite vanity with sinks. Rumor has it the gentlemen's locker room is equally plush.

And, of course, there's the golf course—a stunning location for those joyful wedding pictures. You're sure to be flushed with happiness and wearing big smiles because your wedding here is the best one…ever.

CEREMONY & EVENT/RECEPTION CAPACITY: The facility accommodates 150 seated or 200 standing guests indoors or outdoors.

MEETING CAPACITY: Meeting spaces seat 50 guests indoors.

FEES & DEPOSITS: 20% of the estimated event cost is required to reserve your date. 50% is due 60 days prior to the event and the balance is due 10 days prior. Rental fees start at $400 depending on the day and time of the event, guest count, and the space rented. Meals start at $35/person. Tax, alcohol and a 21% service charge are additional.

AVAILABILITY: Year-round, daily, 6am–midnight.

SERVICES/AMENITIES:

Catering: in-house
Kitchen Facilities: n/a
Tables & Chairs: provided
Linens, Silver, etc.: provided
Restrooms: wheelchair accessible
Dance Floor: provided
Bride's Dressing Area: yes
Meeting Equipment: CBA
Other: event coordination, AV equipment

Parking: large lot
Accommodations: no guest rooms
Telephone: house phone
Outdoor Night Lighting: CBA
Outdoor Cooking Facilities: BBQ CBA
Cleanup: provided
View: cityscape, courtyard, fairways, hills, mountains, landscaped grounds

RESTRICTIONS:

Alcohol: in-house
Smoking: designated areas only
Music: amplified OK with restrictions

Wheelchair Access: yes
Insurance: not required

Overwhelmed? Use the search criteria on www.HereComesTheGuide.com to narrow down your choices.

309

Hotel Ménage

1221 South Harbor Boulevard, Anaheim

949/315-2224

www.hotelmenage.com
events@casaresortsinc.com

Boutique Hotel

- Rehearsal Dinners
- Ceremonies
- Wedding Receptions
- Private Parties

- Corporate Events
- Meetings
- Film Shoots
- Accommodations

If you're in the market for an affordable, fun-packed wedding with a taste of the tropics in one of the planet's most popular destinations, you can stop looking. At Hotel Ménage, Anaheim's first boutique hotel, you'll find a playscape that will make any event exciting.

Just beyond the lobby is a wealth of paradisiacal outdoor pleasures: a sprawling complex of terraces, lawns, shady lounges, and a lushly landscaped pool cast an inviting spell. The festive spirit begins in the Palapa Bar & Lounge, where a traditional palm-covered palapa, tiki torches, and rattan-style furnishings make mingling easy. Follow the winding stone walkway past graceful palms and other tropical plantings to the Palm Court. Ideal for a ceremony, cocktail reception or seated dinner (highlighted by comfort food from the hotel's restaurant, American Tavern Eatery & Drink), its gently curving shape mirrors the footprint of the nearby pool and creates a sense of movement and flow. The sunny South Lounge nearby, also well-suited to both ceremonies and receptions, can be used in combination with other outdoor and indoor spaces to extend your party. The North Lounge on the opposite side of the spa and pool area is surrounded by towering palms, has a beautiful fountain, and offers still more room for your dining and dancing delight.

Indoors, the hotel's newest addition, the Ballroom Lounge, puts an innovative spin on the ballroom concept. The look is upscale and contemporary, with warm wood-paneled walls, modern lighting fixtures and a soothing earth-tone color scheme. There's a full bar at one end as well as a pair of white stone fireplaces; modern couches, chairs and coffee tables are arranged in cozy conversational groupings. Sliding glass doors open to the Palm Court, providing an indoor/outdoor experience. Designed with the utmost flexibility in mind, the "ballroom" can be configured in whatever way you like: as a lounge, a reception room with dance floor, or both.

A variety of smaller event spaces and meeting rooms are are also available for intimate cocktail receptions and private parties. Guest rooms are outfitted with luxurious touches like leather headboards, executive desks, and 42-inch high-def plasma TVs, but we have a feeling your guests won't spend much time in them. Disneyland, Knott's Berry Farm, Universal Studios and the seashore are close at hand, and at night there's magic by the pool where you can watch Disneyland's Fireworks Spectacular from the very best seats in the county.

CEREMONY CAPACITY: The hotel holds 200 seated guests indoors and 300 seated outdoors.

EVENT/RECEPTION CAPACITY: The hotel can accommodate 180 seated or 200 standing guests indoors, and 200 seated or 500 standing outdoors.

MEETING CAPACITY: Meeting spaces hold 200 seated guests.

FEES & DEPOSITS: 30% of the total event cost is required to reserve your date and the balance is due 72 hours prior to the event. Rental fees range $250–1,000 depending on the space rented. Meals range $39–59/person. Tax, alcohol and a 21% service charge are additional.

AVAILABILITY: Year-round, daily, 8am–11pm.

SERVICES/AMENITIES:

Catering: in-house
Kitchen Facilities: n/a
Tables & Chairs: provided
Linens, Silver, etc.: provided
Restrooms: wheelchair accessible
Dance Floor: CBA
Bride's Dressing Area: no
Meeting Equipment: provided

Parking: valet required
Accommodations: 244 guest rooms
Telephone: office phone
Outdoor Night Lighting: CBA
Outdoor Cooking Facilities: no
Cleanup: provided
View: landscaped grounds, pool area
Other: event coordination

RESTRICTIONS:

Alcohol: in-house
Smoking: outdoors only
Music: amplified OK with restrictions

Wheelchair Access: yes
Insurance: not required

Sheraton Anaheim Hotel

Hotel

900 South Disneyland Drive, Anaheim
714/778-1700

www.sheraton.com/anaheim
catering@sheratonanaheim.com

- Rehearsal Dinners
- Ceremonies
- Wedding Receptions
- Private Parties
- Corporate Events
- Meetings
- Film Shoots
- Accommodations

If you live in Southern California, you've probably passed the Tudor-style Sheraton Anaheim hundreds of times as you've made your way north or south along the I-5 Freeway. And if you stopped to check out the hotel, there's a good chance you were impressed by its stylish porte-cochère entryway, majestic fireplace, and charming outdoor courtyards. But if you haven't visited recently, you'll be delighted by all the enhancements at this centrally located landmark.

After passing through the attractive lobby, you arrive at a picturesque outdoor koi pond surrounded by giant ferns, with a bubbling waterfall as a focal point. This is a lovely spot for photographs after you've tied the knot!

Adjacent to the pond is the Pond Courtyard, a manicured enclave where couples exchange vows. Enclosed by the quaint façades of the hotel buildings, with their stone and brick turrets, and high- and low-pitched roofs, it's a peaceful, private space with an enchanting gazebo. And since the gazebo is located just off the bridal changing room, you won't have far to venture after the last hair is put in place.

More intimate ceremonies are hosted in the Rose Garden, where you can say "I do" under a rustic archway entwined with rose vines and festooned with fragrant blooms. A two-tier fountain adds a romantic element to the setting.

All the reception rooms are accented with cream-colored damask stripes, crown molding, dome-shaped chandeliers and wall sconces. No matter which area you select, you can count on fine cuisine and flawless service overseen by the Banquet Director and Executive Chef, who've been with the hotel for more than 40 years combined.

Convenient to airports and attractions in both Los Angeles and Orange counties, the Sheraton Anaheim caters to your out-of-town visitors' comfort. It boasts the largest guest rooms in town (typically more than 500 square feet), all outfitted with "Sheraton Sweet Sleeper Beds" and wood furnishings. And just so no one's bored after your big event, the hotel offers complimentary transportation and a concierge desk to assist with purchasing multiple-day passes to neighboring Disneyland Resort.

Oh yes, one more thing about being so close to the Magic Kingdom—if fireworks from the park happen to light up your celebration, no one need know they're not intended for you!

CEREMONY CAPACITY: The banquet rooms hold up to 600 seated guests, the courtyard up to 300.

EVENT/RECEPTION CAPACITY: The location accommodates up to 600 seated or 1,000 standing guests indoors and up to 250 seated or 350 standing outdoors.

MEETING CAPACITY: Spaces seat up to 1,000 guests.

FEES & DEPOSITS: A percentage of the estimated event total is required to reserve your date. The balance is due in 2 installments with the final payment being made 15 days prior to the event. Rental fees range $1,000–1,500 depending on space, day and time rented and guest count. Meals range $35–68/person. Tax, alcohol and a service charge are additional.

AVAILABILITY: Year-round, daily, anytime.

SERVICES/AMENITIES:

Catering: in house, no BYO
Kitchen Facilities: n/a
Tables & Chairs: provided
Linens, Silver, etc.: provided
Restrooms: wheelchair accessible
Dance Floor: provided
Bride's Dressing Area: yes
Meeting Equipment: full range

Parking: large lot
Accommodations: 489 oversized guest rooms
Telephone: house phone
Outdoor Night Lighting: yes
Outdoor Cooking Facilities: no
Cleanup: reception area by hotel; ceremony area by renter
View: fountain, garden, pond, pool, fireworks, landscaped grounds, garden courtyard

RESTRICTIONS:

Alcohol: in-house, no BYO
Smoking: outdoors only
Music: amplified OK with restrictions

Wheelchair Access: yes
Insurance: not required

Anaheim Hills Golf Course Clubhouse

Golf Club & Restaurant

6501 E. Nohl Ranch Road, Anaheim Hills
714/998-3041 X3
www.hillsclubhouse.com
clubhouse@earthlink.net

● Rehearsal Dinners	● Corporate Events
● Ceremonies	● Meetings
● Wedding Receptions	● Film Shoots
● Private Parties	Accommodations

With its clean-lined Spanish Mediterranean style and desert landscaping, the Anaheim Hills Golf Course Clubhouse could be a villa in Palm Springs or along Spain's Costa del Sol. Instead, it's in upscale Anaheim Hills, a city of rolling knolls, pastoral vistas and cool valleys in the bosom of central Orange County. A local favorite, this 30,000-square-foot facility is a top pick for brides seeking casual elegance in a contemporary setting.

Although built on City property, the facility is independently run and staffed by full-service wedding and special event coordinators. They'll assist you with everything from favors, linens and place cards to the wedding cake and décor—all in keeping with the style and colors of your celebration. In addition, they offer a long list of referrals for DJs, musicians, florists, photographers, videographers and even officiants, and are happy to help guide you in your selections.

Getting ready on the Big Day is a breeze, thanks to a spacious bridal dressing room with a quartet of mirrors and a private restroom. While you prepare to make your entrance, guests step through the arched entryway of the clubhouse into a gracious lobby with a high, beamed ceiling. Another set of arched double doors leads to the North Terrace, an expansive patio where umbrella-shaded tables and portable cocktail bars can be set up for your party.

Outdoor ceremonies are also held on the patio, which overlooks the course's rolling fairways, punctuated with stands of oaks and sycamores. A pair of columns provides a focal point, while a multitiered fountain adds Mediterranean flair. Before or after saying your vows, you can opt to take photos in a sheltered enclave of the course, shaded by tall greenery—your ivory gown will be beautifully highlighted against the emerald lawn.

The Grand Ballroom is an impressive space for a large wedding ceremony, reception or corporate affair. A high, coffered ceiling, ironwork chandeliers, tied-back draperies, and a Byzantine-motif carpet set a sophisticated tone. Light flows in through three walls of floor-to-ceiling arched windows that also afford panoramic views of the golf course.

The Anaheim Hills Golf Course is not just another golfing facility that does weddings. This is a venue that really knows how to host the 'Big Day,' from their expert staff and smartly designed clubhouse (the layout is perfect for events) to the topnotch food and abundant free parking. The Clubhouse gets great word-of-mouth from satisfied couples saying things like, "The Catering Manager and Wedding Day Coordinator were awesome—simply amazing at getting all the details ironed out and working with us on the pricing and menu," and "Wow! Great customer service still exists!" One bride summed up her experience this way: "If you choose this venue, you will not be disappointed."

CEREMONY & EVENT/RECEPTION CAPACITY: The clubhouse holds 350 seated with a dance floor, or 650 standing guests indoors. Outdoors the site can accommodate 250 seated or 650 standing.

MEETING CAPACITY: Meeting spaces hold 300 seated guests.

FEES & DEPOSITS: A deposit is required to reserve your date. 50% of the estimated event total is due 90 days prior to the event, the balance is due 7 days prior. Rental fees are waived with minimum food purchases. All-inclusive wedding packages range $49–111/person. Tax and a 19% service charge are additional.

AVAILABILITY: Year-round, daily, 10am–4pm or 6pm–midnight, except Sunday morning.

SERVICES/AMENITIES:

Catering: in-house or BYO

Kitchen Facilities: fully equipped

Tables & Chairs: provided

Linens, Silver, etc.: provided

Restrooms: wheelchair accessible

Dance Floor: portable provided

Bride's & Groom's Dressing Area: yes

Meeting Equipment: provided

Parking: large lot, free self-parking

Accommodations: no guest rooms, hotel nearby

Telephone: office phone

Outdoor Night Lighting: provided

Outdoor Cooking Facilities: CBA

Cleanup: yes

View: fairways, hills, landscaped grounds

Other: on-site coordination, wedding cake, chair covers, dropdown screen

RESTRICTIONS:

Alcohol: in-house

Smoking: allowed outdoors only

Music: amplified OK

Wheelchair Access: yes

Insurance: liability required with outside catering

Los Coyotes Country Club

Country Club

8888 Los Coyotes Drive, Buena Park
888/995-4188

www.countryclubreceptions.com
eventdirector@loscoyotescc.com

● Rehearsal Dinners	● Corporate Events
● Ceremonies	● Meetings
● Wedding Receptions	● Film Shoots
● Private Parties	Accommodations

The two things people ooh and aah the most about at Los Coyotes Country Club are the food and the facility's good looks. The Executive Chef, along with his culinary team, has given this site a reputation for consistently serving gourmet meals. And the club's Mission-style architecture—with its tiled roofs, arched colonnades and beautiful vantage atop a small hill—is a bragging point among regulars.

But there's a third thing to tout here, and it may be just as important as the other two: the golf course itself. It's probably best viewed from the grand flagstone-paved terrace along one side of the clubhouse. Here, you look out over a putting green and beyond toward three long verdant fairways, each separated from the others by lines of mature trees. And while you're gazing off at those fairways—even though you know there are millions of people and all the trappings of modern civilization within a few miles of where you stand—you'd swear the green earth goes on forever. The sense of being away from the Southland's pressure-cooker environment is both palpable and soothing.

The terrace, part of which is shaded under an archway, adjoins a spacious ballroom featuring an 18-foot-high ceiling, six-lamp chandeliers, and beautiful wall sconces. The terrace-facing side of the ballroom, as well as another side that looks out onto a small manmade lake, are lined with picture windows and French doors. The room can be divided into three sections, but most couples decide to reserve the entire space. They love this ballroom's drama—it looks impressive (because of its height) and inviting (thanks to its big, sun-loving windows) at the same time.

Los Coyotes' lush setting inspires many al fresco ceremonies and offers two options for exchanging vows: The lakeside site, bordered by a tranquil lake on one side and a large putting green on another, provides the quintessential golf course experience. The clubhouse terrace affords the convenience of saying "I do" and then stepping right into the ballroom for the reception. During those rare times when the weather is inclement, or for smaller parties seeking an indoor setting, the Cypress Palm Room, with its French door-framed view of the lake, is popular.

Located down the hall from the ballroom, the bride's dressing room is a posh extension of Los Coyotes' stylish décor. It's nicely appointed with an oversized oak-trimmed vanity mirror, a sink, a large closet and a wall mirror.

Even the drive up to Los Coyotes has appealing touches: The curving road sweeps through a well-landscaped neighborhood of large ranch-style houses, and the tall palms along the median strip evoke an almost resort-like feel. When you reach the club, the banquet room's dramatic porte-cochère entrance only reinforces that feeling of refinement. Ah, if a day can unfold so agreeably just getting to Los Coyotes, you can be confident it will continue that way long after you've arrived.

CEREMONY CAPACITY: The Lakeside site and the Terrace hold up to 300 seated guests. Indoors, the Cypress Palm Room accommodates up to 80 seated.

EVENT/RECEPTION & MEETING CAPACITY: The Ballroom holds 350 seated with a dance floor or 500 standing guests. It can be divided into two smaller sections, each accommodating up to 122 seated with a dance floor or 200 standing. Outdoors, the Terrace accommodates up to 150 seated or 450 standing.

FEES & DEPOSITS: A nonrefundable deposit, which is applied to your food and beverage total, is required to reserve your date. The amount of the deposit varies, depending on how far in advance you book. Payment terms for the balance also vary, and may be arranged on an individual basis. Wedding packages start at $40/person. Tax, alcohol and service charge are additional. Food and beverage minimums apply. Menus and packages can be customized to fit your needs and budget, call for details.

AVAILABILITY: Year-round, daily.

SERVICES/AMENITIES:

Catering: in-house
Kitchen Facilities: n/a
Tables & Chairs: provided
Linens, Silver, etc.: provided
Restrooms: wheelchair accessible
Dance Floor: provided
Bride's Dressing Area: yes
Meeting Equipment: CBA, extra charge

Parking: large lot, valet required for over 50 guests
Accommodations: no guest rooms
Telephone: emergency use only
Outdoor Night Lighting: yes
Outdoor Cooking Facilities: CBA
Cleanup: provided
View: fairways, trees, lake

RESTRICTIONS:

Alcohol: in-house, or BYO wine with corkage fee
Smoking: outdoors only
Music: amplified OK

Wheelchair Access: yes
Insurance: not required
Other: no open flames or confetti, no affixing anything to the walls or ceiling

The professionals in the back of this book are the best in the business. How do we know? Read page 549.

317

Five Crowns Restaurant

Restaurant & Garden

3801 East Coast Highway, Corona del Mar
949/760-1115 or 949/760-0331
www.thefivecrowns.com
arobbins@lawrysonline.com

● Rehearsal Dinners	● Corporate Events	
● Ceremonies	● Meetings	
● Wedding Receptions	● Film Shoots	
● Private Parties	Accommodations	

If you're familiar with Orange County's fine dining scene, chances are you've heard of Five Crowns. Established in 1965 in upscale Corona del Mar—one of Southern California's most idyllic coastal villages—the Tudor-style culinary landmark is a recreation of England's oldest country inn, Ye Olde Bell (est. 1135 A.D.). In this pocket of seaside affluence, it's also an icon of patrician respectability, award-winning cuisine, and premier vintages, owned by the Frank and Van De Kamp families of Lawry's Restaurants fame.

Known for serving up some of the best prime rib in town, as well as contemporary renditions of fresh seafood, roasted fowl, and succulent lamb, Five Crowns has hosted legions of discriminating local diners and such illustrious guests as Elizabeth Taylor and past President Richard Nixon.

What you may not know is that this revered dining establishment is also a classic setting for weddings, receptions, rehearsal dinners and other singular celebrations. With its rich wood paneling, ceiling beams, antique maritime memorabilia and cozy nooks, the venue exudes an Old World ambiance. Indeed, a bride might imagine herself part of a Shakespearean sonnet as she makes her way down from the upstairs dressing room to meet her groom. And while she primps with her bridesmaids, her husband-to-be and his groomsmen can enjoy male bonding in the SideDoor, a gastropub with a large fireplace and high-backed Tudor chairs.

The most popular area for saying your vows in this historic site is the herb gardens, off the restaurant's sunlit greenhouse. A traditional trellis, adorned with flowers and herbs, lends just the right amount of formality to the intimate setting. An awning and umbrellas provide shade for guests on sunny days, while a tent can shelter the entire outdoor area during inclement weather.

Depending on the size of your party, guests will enjoy pre- and post-ceremony hospitality in the fern-draped greenhouse and brick-lined patio, the main Nelson Crown Room, or The Brighton Room, named for the pleasure palace George IV of England built in 1782. In all of these areas, service is provided by a friendly and very professional staff. An outdoor staircase is the perfect spot for flinging a bouquet or for taking photographs of the wedding party in the garden. Alternatively, many couples opt to capture memories of the day at the front entrance of the restaurant, where an antique red British telephone booth is a recognizable landmark on the East Coast Highway.

Before and after the merrymaking, out-of-town guests can enjoy accommodations in many four- and five-star hotels along the coast, or at the newly restored Crystal Cove Cottages, just a mile down the road in the Crystal Cove State Park Historic District. You might consider a post-celebration treat of your own: a romantic moonlit walk with your new spouse along this stretch of pristine coastline.

CEREMONY CAPACITY: The capacity varies depending on the time of day and spaces used. For daytime ceremonies, the venue can accommodate up to 150 seated guests. In the evening, ceremonies are limited to 100 seated.

EVENT RECEPTION CAPACITY: The venue holds up to 150 seated for daytime receptions and 100 seated in the evening. If you buy out the restaurant, the seated capacity increases to 200. The maximum capacity for a standing reception day or night is 300.

MEETING CAPACITY: The restaurant holds 150 seated guests.

FEES & DEPOSITS: 20% of the food and beverage minimum is required to reserve your date. The balance is due 14 days prior to the event date. Ceremony fee is $1,000 if their chairs are used. Meals range $25–63/person. Tax, alcohol and a 20% service charge are additional.

AVAILABILITY: Year-round, daily, anytime.

SERVICES/AMENITIES:

Catering: in-house or select from list
Kitchen Facilities: fully equipped
Tables & Chairs: provided
Linens, Silver, etc.: provided
Restrooms: wheelchair accessible
Dance Floor: CBA
Bride's & Groom's Dressing Area: yes
Meeting Equipment: CBA

Parking: valet required
Accommodations: no guest rooms
Telephone: pay phone
Outdoor Night Lighting: provided
Outdoor Cooking Facilities: BBQ CBA
Cleanup: provided
View: garden courtyard
Other: AV equipment, event coordination

RESTRICTIONS:

Alcohol: in-house
Smoking: not allowed
Music: amplified OK with restrictions

Wheelchair Access: yes
Insurance: not required

Ayres Hotel & Suites Costa Mesa/Newport Beach   *Hotel*

325 Bristol Street, Costa Mesa
714/429-9372 x448, 800/322-9992
www.ayreshotels.com
jmckee@ayreshotels.com

- Rehearsal Dinners
- Ceremonies
- Wedding Receptions
- Private Parties
- Corporate Events
- Meetings
- Film Shoots
- Accommodations

Imagine a cobblestone piazza dotted with marble tables. Sparrows flit in and out of ficus trees, and terracotta planters ring an elegant, three-tiered fountain set in a turquoise-tiled pool. You're sipping wine with your beloved and a summery breeze carries the smell of roasting herbs and garlic. Paris you ask? Perugia? Rome? No, far from it…you're in Costa Mesa at the Ayres Hotel & Suites, a modern hotel with a decidedly old-world sensibility that Zagat's Survey rated as "the best bargain hotel in California."

Despite its size (the hotel has 284 rooms), the Ayres Hotel & Suites retains a homespun, friendly atmosphere. Your guests will immediately feel at ease as they walk through the hotel's lobby to the wedding site, pausing to admire antiques from around the world—Ching Dynasty elephant sculptures, rare model ships and life-size cloisonné lambs.

The Garden Courtyard, with its cultured and international ambiance, is the hotel's most popular ceremony site. Couples usually say their vows in front of the fountain, positioning the bridesmaids and groomsmen on either side along its steps. Come evening, the incandescent street lamps and the glittering necklace of fountain lights add a touch of magic to the courtyard. From the wedding site it's just a short walk to the reception and pool area on the lower level of the main hotel. You can host your reception in one of four rooms, each decorated with warm wood wainscoting, oil paintings, and custom wall treatments. All banquet rooms open onto a large, inviting pool patio. The Living Room can accommodate a buffet or a small sit-down dinner, while the Camberley, Essex or Breton Rooms are more spacious areas—big enough for a crowd and a dance floor. Tables can also be set up around the pool.

When the day's celebration is over, the bride and groom have the luxury of retiring to their hotel suite, compliments of the Hotel. Awaiting them will be a bottle of chilled champagne, just one of the many fine and caring touches you are sure to encounter when you hold your event at the Ayres Hotel & Suites.

CEREMONY CAPACITY: Outdoors, the Garden Courtyard holds up to 200 guests.

EVENT/RECEPTION CAPACITY: Indoor spaces accommodate up to 120 seated or 75–160 standing. The Camberley Room holds up to 120 seated, and up to 220 can be seated poolside.

MEETING CAPACITY: The total indoor meeting space is 11,000 square feet, which can accommodate 10–150 seated guests.

FEES & DEPOSITS: For weddings, a nonrefundable deposit is required to confirm your date. The estimated total is payable 3 months in advance. A guest count guarantee is due 72 hours prior; any remaining charges are to be paid at the conclusion of the event. There are two wedding packages, for lunch or dinner which include the following: a 3-course meal, hors d'oeuvres, wedding cake, champagne toast, dance floor, banquet room or event space, and a complimentary wedding suite for the bride and groom. Tax and service charge are additional. Wedding packages start at $40/person. Any menu package can be customized. For ceremonies only the setup fee is $1,000, with a reception the fee is $500. Receptions occur in 4-hour time blocks, receptions with ceremonies in 5-hour blocks. Shuttle service and special rates for overnight wedding guests are available.

AVAILABILITY: Year-round, daily.

SERVICES/AMENITIES:

Catering: in-house, no BYO
Kitchen Facilities: n/a
Tables & Chairs: provided
Linens, Silver, etc.: provided
Restrooms: wheelchair accessible
Dance Floor: provided with package
Bride's Dressing Area: yes
Meeting Equipment: full range AV, extra charge

Parking: large complimentary lot
Accommodations: 284 guest rooms and suites
Telephone: pay phone
Outdoor Night Lighting: yes
Outdoor Cooking Facilities: no
Cleanup: provided
View: courtyard and pool area
Other: wedding cakes, complimentary suite

RESTRICTIONS:

Alcohol: in-house, or corkage $10/bottle
Smoking: outside only
Music: amplified OK indoors only until 11pm

Wheelchair Access: yes
Insurance: not required

Center Club

Private Club

650 Town Center Drive, Costa Mesa
714/438-3860 Catering
www.center-club.com
chris.hartley@ourclub.com

● Rehearsal Dinners	● Corporate Events
● Ceremonies	● Meetings
● Wedding Receptions	● Film Shoots
● Private Parties	Accommodations

If you want your wedding or special event to take center stage, then definitely consider the Center Club. Talk about centrally located! This prestigious member of the ClubCorp family is located in the center of Orange County, in the center of South Coast Metro at the base of the award-winning Center Tower adjacent to the glamorous Segerstrom Center for the Arts. Occupying the garden level of a performing arts complex, the swank business club has been an in-demand event site for more than 25 years, and it's now going to attract even more fans thanks to its brand new look.

A recent $3.1 million renovation has taken the Center Club from elegantly traditional to magnificently contemporary. Grand social and professional affairs will be right at home here, in a place that's chic, sophisticated and ultra-upscale.

From the moment you step into the pleasingly posh lobby, you'll be swept away by an arts-inspired setting. Waltz down the lustrous, handsomely appointed hall—there's a musical score subtly worked into its walls—toward the Symphony Ballroom. No ordinary rectangular box, this stunning space has an architectural splendor that allows for intimacy without sacrificing scale. That "far corner of the room" syndrome does not exist here. Three adjoining chambers create the ballroom's dynamic arrowhead shape, and when they're all used together they offer sightlines from the central "prow" that make the whole room visible and enticingly accessible in spite of its lavish dimensions. In addition, the three chambers can function independently as the Mozart, Chopin and Beethoven Rooms—each totally alluring in its own right.

The Chopin Room, for example, has a spacious outdoor terrace that's perfect for ceremonies or cocktails. It features sculptural details like the "green wall" planted with ferns, the Four Lines Oblique Gyratory-Square IV structure by George Rickey, and towering eucalyptus trees for a look that's sleek and streamlined, yet serene. The Mozart and Beethoven Rooms, like the Chopin, have floor-to-ceiling windows, although these look out onto a palatial water garden (designed by leading Modernist movement landscape architect, Peter Walker) that radiates tranquility and a grand museum feel. All three rooms are decorated in tasteful shades of pewter, bronze and dove-gray that allow their beautiful bones—high ceilings, crown moldings and impressive soffits—to shine. Nothing has been overlooked—even the furnishings are works of art, sculpted and finished to echo and enhance a design perspective that bespeaks luxury and taste.

Of course, as you'd expect from a world-class event venue like this one, a variety of other options is also available for your partying pleasure: The traditional Zen, and high-tech Earth, Wind, and

Fire rooms provide private boardroom and dining opportunities. If more space is required, the sumptuous Encore Lounge with its clubby leather and hardwood accents; the VIP Lounge; and a spectacular Founders Room further expand your choices. Top it off with Center Club's impeccable service, culinary expertise and unparalleled farm-to-table cuisine, and you'll have a recipe for smashing success.

CEREMONY CAPACITY: The Mozart Room seats 130, and the Symphony Ballroom Patio seats 200 guests.

EVENT/RECEPTION & MEETING CAPACITY: The Symphony Ballroom holds 250 seated or 350 standing, the Beethoven Room holds 130 seated or 200 standing, the Mozart Room holds 60 seated or 100 standing, and the Chopin Room holds 20 seated or 30 standing.

FEES & DEPOSITS: A $2,500 nonrefundable deposit is required to secure your date. Half of the estimated event total is due 90 days prior to the event; the balance is payable 2 weeks prior. Any menu can be customized: luncheons start at $45/person, dinners at $55/person. Alcohol, tax and a 22% service charge are additional. For ceremonies there is a $1,200 charge which includes setup, chairs, runner, rehearsal, and sound system. On Fridays, Saturdays and Sundays, food and beverage minimums may apply.

AVAILABILITY: Year-round, daily, 7am–2am in 5-hour blocks. Additional hours are available for a fee.

SERVICES/AMENITIES:

Catering: in-house or BYO
Kitchen Facilities: n/a
Tables & Chairs: provided
Linens, Silver, etc.: provided
Restrooms: wheelchair accessible
Dance Floor: provided, extra charge
Bride's & Groom's Dressing Area: yes
Meeting Equipment: yes
Other: chocolate fountain, ice sculptures

Parking: valet $4.50/person
Accommodations: no guest rooms
Telephone: guest phones
Outdoor Night Lighting: yes
Outdoor Cooking Facilities: n/a
Cleanup: provided
View: water and sculpture gardens

RESTRICTIONS:

Alcohol: in-house, no BYO
Smoking: outside only
Music: amplified OK

Wheelchair Access: yes
Insurance: not required

Westin South Coast Plaza

Hotel

686 Anton Boulevard, Costa Mesa
714/662-6637

www.westinsouthcoastplaza.com
martha.hsu@westin.com

● Rehearsal Dinners	● Corporate Events	
● Ceremonies	Meetings	
● Wedding Receptions	● Film Shoots	
● Private Parties	● Accommodations	

An oasis of tranquility in Orange County's sophisticated cultural Mecca, the Westin South Coast Plaza resonates with discreet style and a Zen-like calm following its baseboards-to-ballrooms redesign in 2008. And with its new look and feel, it offers a cosmopolitan backdrop for an elegant reception or destination wedding.

Entering the airy lobby of what has long been a premier hotel in the area for business and pleasure travelers, you're welcomed by a soothing ambiance. Luxuriant floral accents and white tea aromatic accents simultaneously arouse the senses and quiet the nerves. The minimalist style and palette of warm grays, translucent greens and soft purples inspire a feeling of unhurried peace. Abundant natural light and a view of flowing water beyond further draw you into the space.

Before the festivities begin, you and your bridal party might pose for wedding album pictures at the beautiful Waterfall Terrace, or head next door to the Orange County Performing Arts Center where more photo opportunities abound.

You may also want to exchange vows on the Waterfall Terrace, beneath a scalloped shade canopy in a California-tropical setting lush with ferns, climbing vines and blooming impatiens. Against a cascading stream, you and your groom will kiss for the first time as husband and wife.

The adjacent Lido Ballroom provides the stage for a casually chic reception. This light-filled venue opens onto its own terrace, encouraging an easy indoor-outdoor flow throughout your event and giving celebrants lots of room to mingle.

If your guest list is long, tie the knot under the Terrace Gazebo. Presiding over the 4,000-square-foot Terrace Pavilion, it's a grand, curtained structure whose sheer drapes can be customized to suit your color scheme. As a string quartet plays in concert with the sound of the tumbling waterfall below, guests can relax on comfy couches before taking their seats for your outdoor ceremony. Afterwards, they'll enjoy appetizers and champagne under the stars, enclosed by long planters filled with stately palms and birds of paradise.

Formal receptions are held in the Plaza Ballroom, illuminated by seven crystal chandeliers. With its neutral décor, it's easily tailored to any bride's design wishes, and its smaller-than-typical size makes it more intimate than most grand ballrooms.

After you've thrown the bouquet and danced your last dance, retire to your luxurious bridal suite, where you'll sleep ever-so-soundly on Westin's patented Heavenly Bed®. When you wake up the next day, you can look forward to plenty of wonderful options: Walk arm-in-arm across the pedestrian bridge leading to South Coast Plaza and its world-class shops and restaurants. Pay a visit to one or more of the nearby museums or attend a performance at the adjacent Orange County Performing Arts Center. Why not take a day trip to Catalina Island, Disneyland or the Aquarium of the Pacific?—they're all less than 30 minutes away. With so much to do and see here, you and your very happy out-of-town guests will be able to turn your destination wedding into a true vacation.

CEREMONY CAPACITY: The hotel accommodates 600 seated guests indoors or out.

EVENT/RECEPTION CAPACITY: The hotel holds 650 seated or 1,000 standing guests indoors and 400 seated or 600 standing outdoors.

MEETING CAPACITY: Meeting spaces seat 600 guests indoors.

FEES & DEPOSITS: 25% of the total estimated event cost is required to reserve your date and the balance is due 14 business days prior to the event. Rental fees are waived when food and beverage minimums are met. Wedding packages start at $64/person. Tax, alcohol and a 22% service charge are additional.

AVAILABILITY: Year-round, daily.

SERVICES/AMENITIES:

Catering: in-house
Kitchen Facilities: n/a
Tables & Chairs: provided
Linens, Silver, etc.: provided
Restrooms: wheelchair accessible
Dance Floor: portable provided
Bride's Dressing Area: yes
Meeting Equipment: provided
Other: AV lighting services

Parking: valet or self-parking, garage nearby
Accommodations: 393 guest rooms
Telephone: office phone
Outdoor Night Lighting: CBA
Outdoor Cooking Facilities: BBQ CBA
Cleanup: provided
View: garden, waterfall, pool area, landscaped grounds

RESTRICTIONS:

Alcohol: in-house
Smoking: not allowed
Music: amplified OK with restrictions

Wheelchair Access: yes
Insurance: liability required

Want to know WHAT TO ASK a potential location or vendor? Check out our Questions to Ask starting on page 19.

Coto de Caza Golf & Racquet Club

Country Club

25291 Vista del Verde, Coto de Caza

949/858-4100

www.coto-de-caza.com
contactus@coto-de-caza.com

- Rehearsal Dinners
- Ceremonies
- Wedding Receptions
- Private Parties
- Corporate Events
- Meetings
- Film Shoots
- Accommodations

The exclusive community of Coto de Caza has always been a secluded universe unto itself—a peaceful microcosm set securely behind a stone entry, and laced with hiking and horseback riding trails. At the pinnacle of its 4,000 verdant acres, capped by a tower that's visible from almost anywhere inside Coto's wrought-iron gates, is a chic world within a world: the Coto de Caza Golf & Racquet Club, one of only three private 36-hole country clubs in metropolitan Southern California.

With Craftsman-style architecture that reflects a Frank Lloyd Wright penchant for 90-degree turns and angles, the club's 44,000-square-foot clubhouse is a theatrical venue for tying the knot. At its entrance a graceful bridge stretches over a pond fed by trickling streams and cascading waterfalls that create a Zen-like calm. After walking up the wide staircase fronting its expansive stone and glass façade, guests step into a lobby filled with rich woods, Mission-style furnishings and light streaming in through floor-to-ceiling windows. While they chat and sip lemonade, you'll relax and prepare for the day's festivities in the Ladies Lounge, outfitted with a large closet, TV and cushy sofas.

When your ceremony is about to begin, friends and family will take their seats on the lower outdoor patio, near the flower-ringed half circle looking out over the club's velvety fairways. As strains of "Here Comes the Bride" begin, they'll turn and see you appear at the apex of the club's dramatic stairway, ready to descend the long aisle to meet your groom. With the rolling hills of the Trabuco Canyon as a backdrop, you'll exchange your vows.

Reception options abound here. For larger gatherings the outdoor pavilion, Paraiso, overlooks the greens and comes alive in the evening, with twinkling lights on lacy trees surrounding the adjacent rock waterfall. Count on comfort in all seasons, as the expansive space is equipped with ceiling fans, heat lamps and roll-down sides for wind protection. The club's Serra Bela Room and attached outdoor terrace, with views of the golf course and canyon, is a more intimate setting for post-ceremony cocktails and dinner. Another alternative is the homey A Nossa Room, with its built-in bar and interior fireplace.

No matter where in the facility you choose to celebrate, your coordinator at the club can arrange for many special touches. Opt for a chocolate-dipped strawberry bar with an attendant to infuse the plump fruits with guests' choice of liqueur; have your new initials scrolled in chocolate on your cake plate; or heat up the party with a flambé dessert station. If you can't make it to the tropics for a honeymoon escape, create your own singular world at the club: Follow the example of one bride who brought the spirit of aloha to the mainland by importing tiki torches, leis and flowers from the islands for a colorful luau, Coto-style. This private country club is sure to fulfill your wedding dreams and impress your guests.

CEREMONY CAPACITY: The Ceremony Circle seats up to 250 guests. Indoors, the Main Dining Room holds up to 120 seated guests.

EVENT/RECEPTION CAPACITY: Indoor spaces hold up to 120 seated or 200 standing guests; outdoor spaces up to 250 seated or 350 standing guests.

MEETING CAPACITY: The Main Dining Room holds up to 120 seated guests.

FEES & DEPOSITS: A $3,500 nonrefundable deposit is required to reserve your date. The balance is due in advance of the event. The Sunday inclusive wedding package is $10,000 for 100 guests, and the Saturday package is $15,000 for 120 guests. Packages include ceremony, cocktail hour, champagne toast, plated meal, linens, valet parking, tax and service charge.

AVAILABILITY: Year-round, daily with flexible hours. Call for details.

SERVICES/AMENITIES:

Catering: in-house, no BYO
Kitchen Facilities: n/a
Tables & Chairs: provided
Linens, Silver, etc.: provided
Restrooms: wheelchair accessible
Dance Floor: provided
Bride's Dressing Area: yes
Meeting Equipment: CBA
Other: event coordination, spa services, AV equipment, athletic center, golf

Parking: large lot, valet included
Accommodations: no guest rooms
Telephone: house phone
Outdoor Night Lighting: yes
Outdoor Cooking Facilities: no
Cleanup: provided
View: canyon, garden patio, fairways, hills, waterfall

RESTRICTIONS:

Alcohol: in-house, no BYO
Smoking: outside only
Music: amplified OK with restrictions

Wheelchair Access: yes
Insurance: not required

Eagle's Nest Restaurant & Banquets

Restaurant

5660 Orangewood Avenue, Cypress

714/889-1453

www.eaglesnestclubhouse.com
info@eaglesnestclubhouse.com

- Rehearsal Dinners
- Ceremonies
- Wedding Receptions
- Private Parties

- Corporate Events
- Meetings
- Film Shoots
- Accommodations

For years, Eagle's Nest Restaurant & Banquets has verged on being a military secret, but now that word is out about this venue it's good news for brides. Tucked into a quiet, residential neighborhood convenient to both Orange and Los Angeles Counties, Eagle's Nest offers a picturesque setting on the sprawling greens of the Cypress Navy Golf Course. A second locale run by the same folks is available on a private beach at the Seal Beach Weapons Station off Pacific Coast Highway, 10 minutes away by car. The tranquil grounds of both facilities provide numerous options for ceremonies and receptions of any size.

With its distinctive California Mission architecture, Mediterranean-inspired furnishings and comfortable lounge, the Eagle's Nest clubhouse offers a relaxed ambiance for guests to mix and mingle. Before they arrive, prepare for your big day in a spacious bride's room, where you and your bridesmaids can sip champagne and nibble on fresh strawberries. Grooms have their own private space, too.

Larger ceremonies are held outdoors in the Pavilion, a wood-beamed, open-air structure overlooking the golf course. Decorated with flowers, fabric or left au naturel, it's a dramatic al fresco shelter. A brick walkway, often strewn with rose petals, leads to the raised area where you and your groom will exchange vows. Alternatively, you can tie the knot under a white Victorian gazebo on the neighboring lawn against a backdrop of leafy trees.

If you've always dreamed of a beach wedding, get married at Eagle's Nest's private beach, just five miles away. Have your reception right on the sand with a stately battleship in the background, or dine back at the clubhouse.

Eagle's Nest's banquet rooms all offer views of the golf course, and a variety of wedding packages allow you to make your chosen room look exactly the way you want. Decorating options include swagging, customized lighting, chair covers, and more. The ballroom is equipped with state-of-the-art audiovisual equipment, and an on-site DVD player or projector and big screen are at your disposal for a memorable slideshow.

Your reception meal will be prepared by Eagle's Nest's professional culinary staff. They're the exclusive caterers for the adjacent naval base, and they're known for using the freshest ingredients in classically elegant dishes.

Photographic opportunities abound throughout the clubhouse, as well as on the golf course—a favorite spot is in front of a fountain on the fairways. If you and your wedding party are golf aficionados, you can arrange for a pre-wedding game, or capture post-wedding moments while posing on golf carts.

A lovely way to spend some post-wedding time with your guests (especially those staying for the weekend) is to invite them onto the fairways for a congenial round of golf. As you relax with friends and family, you'll be able to relive all the wonderful moments of your wedding, and fully appreciate how seamlessly it was orchestrated by your attentive Eagle's Nest pros.

CEREMONY CAPACITY: The restaurant holds 500 seated guests indoors and 1,000 seated outdoors.

EVENT/RECEPTION CAPACITY: The restaurant accommodates 400 seated or 700 standing guests indoors and 1,000 seated or 1,500 standing outdoors.

MEETING CAPACITY: Meeting spaces seat 600 guests indoors.

FEES & DEPOSITS: A deposit of $1,000 is required to reserve your date and the balance is due 14 days prior to the event. Meals range $10–30/person. Tax, alcohol and a 20% service charge are additional.

AVAILABILITY: Year-round, daily, 6am–midnight.

SERVICES/AMENITIES:

Catering: in-house
Kitchen Facilities: n/a
Tables & Chairs: provided
Linens, Silver, etc.: provided
Restrooms: wheelchair accessible
Dance Floor: provided
Bride's Dressing Area: yes
Meeting Equipment: provided
Other: coordination, in-house wedding cake and florals, picnic area, AV equipment, outdoor area for up to 2,000

Parking: large lot
Accommodations: no guest rooms
Telephone: emergency use only
Outdoor Night Lighting: yes
Outdoor Cooking Facilities: BBQ CBA
Cleanup: provided
View: fairways, lake, fountain, landscaped grounds, garden

RESTRICTIONS:

Alcohol: in-house
Smoking: outdoors only
Music: amplified OK

Wheelchair Access: yes
Insurance: not required

Chart House Dana Point

Waterfront Restaurant

34442 Green Lantern Street, Dana Point
949/460-6071

www.chart-house.com
chdp@ldry.com

● Rehearsal Dinners	● Corporate Events
● Ceremonies	● Meetings
● Wedding Receptions	● Film Shoots
● Private Parties	Accommodations

If ever there was a "Wait, there's more!" venue in *Here Comes The Guide,* Dana Point's Chart House has to be one of them. Start with the restaurant's show-stopping vista, a sensational hillside view of Dana Point Harbor, its long breakwater and the Pacific beyond. High palisades rise to the east, topped with luxurious homes, then drop down to an inviting, leafy shoreside park. Boats of all kinds are constantly arriving and departing, and two sleek twin-masted sailing ships moor at the bottom of the hill. This is easily one of the best sea views in Orange County. So naturally the long, carefully manicured ceremony lawn that overlooks it is one of the most dramatic wedding sites in all of the Southland.

With a panorama this incredible, it would be a shame to limit the lawn to ceremonies. Fortunately, it doubles as a spot for "California luau" dinners, which feature Hawaiian music, tiki torches and buffet food. News about the appealingly informal parties has gotten around—some nearby upscale resorts often send wedding parties here for their rehearsal dinners. They know that casual dining overlooking a great view is just the thing to soothe pre-wedding jitters.

There's more! Chart House, a modernistic building of three interconnected circular spaces called "pods," is the design of architect Kendrick Bangs Kellogg, a student of the great Frank Lloyd Wright. Completed in the late 1970s, the building beautifully melds rough-textured concrete, redwood, steel and glass into a memorable configuration. It's very much in the style of Wright, with its creative use of curves and materials, as well as its exterior palette of rust-red wood and light blue steel.

Inside, a harmonious medley of light gray concrete, 62 miles of bent redwood formed into concentric circles on the ceilings, and seeming acres of windows create a striking interior. Almost every seat in the house has a view. All of the booths in the restaurant's three pods have plush leather cushions and backrests with subdued, but playful, abstract patterns. Pod 1 has a built-in dance floor and stage—perfect for a head table—plus the magnificent harbor view. (Delicate cornflower-blue mood lights are suspended from its coiled redwood ceiling—a sweet little touch.) Pod 2 has a grand staircase descending from the restaurant's entry tower, as well as a wine cellar and dining booths. Pod 3, which affords direct access to the patio, has a long bar and an intriguing Art Deco/1950s look.

Still more! Besides a terrific location and singular architectural style, Chart House has another great thing going for it: an experienced kitchen staff that has garnered a devoted clientele over almost three decades. That kitchen is one of the reasons why Chart House attracts dozens of daytime wedding receptions each year. Brides also like having the whole venue to themselves for the day.

From the road, Chart House is almost hidden. You see its signature view before you see its redwood entry tower, and you see the tower before you see the restaurant itself. That slow unfolding of delights is this place's greatest strength and its greatest charm.

CEREMONY CAPACITY: The facility accommodates 200 seated guests outdoors.

EVENT/RECEPTION & MEETING CAPACITY: The site holds 200 seated or standing guests indoors and 80 seated or standing outdoors.

FEES & DEPOSITS: A nonrefundable deposit is required to reserve your date. The reception package is $600 and the ceremony package is $600. Plated entrées range $39–80/person and buffets range $48–60/person. Tax, alcohol and a service charge are additional. Food and beverage minimums may apply to specific times, days, and rooms.

AVAILABILITY: Year-round, daily, 10:30am–4pm.

SERVICES/AMENITIES:

Catering: in-house, no BYO
Kitchen Facilities: n/a
Tables & Chairs: provided
Linens, Silver, etc.: provided
Restrooms: wheelchair accessible
Dance Floor: provided
Bride's & Groom's Dressing Area: no
Meeting Equipment: some provided, BYO
Other: event coordination

Parking: on street, large lot, valet required
Accommodations: no guest rooms
Telephone: emergency use only
Outdoor Night Lighting: CBA
Outdoor Cooking Facilities: no
Cleanup: provided
View: coastline, Dana Point harbor, landscaped grounds

RESTRICTIONS:

Alcohol: in-house, no BYO
Smoking: not allowed
Music: amplified OK with restrictions

Wheelchair Access: yes
Insurance: not required

Laguna Cliffs Marriott Resort & Spa

Resort & Spa

25135 Park Lantern, Dana Point
949/661-5000
www.lagunacliffs.com
weddings@lagunacliffs.com

- Rehearsal Dinners
- Ceremonies
- Wedding Receptions
- Private Parties
- Corporate Events
- Meetings
- Film Shoots
- Accommodations

Just south of Laguna Beach lies a picturesque curve of coastline with white sandy beaches and balmy breezes wafting in from the Pacific. At the tip of this idyllic cove is Dana Point, a historic headland named for 19th-century seafaring adventurer and author Richard Henry Dana, who dubbed it "California's most romantic spot."

If romantic celebrations are on your agenda, then you'll love the Laguna Cliffs Marriott, a AAA Four Diamond luxury retreat perched on the bluffs high above Dana Point. The upscale resort's steeply pitched red-shingled roof and multipaned windows may whisper of Cape Cod, but this fresh interpretation of a New England classic has a decidedly contemporary flair. Both public and private spaces are decked out with dark woods and textured finishes like mosaic tiling and polished granite, and the lobby boasts a lofty water wall. But the star of the scene is the dramatic panorama, encompassing acres of emerald green parks, a bustling marina, and the boundless blue sea.

The Laguna Cliffs takes full advantage of its breathtaking setting by offering three beautiful outdoor locations for wedding ceremonies. The secluded Del Mar Lawn embraces a layered view of mountains, sea, and a section of shore known as "the California Riviera." The Vue Lawn treats guests to a colorful parade of yachts and sailboats against an ocean backdrop. A third enclave, the Laguna Brick, captures glorious sunsets unfurling across the watery horizon. The resort's ceremony packages include the setup of full wedding regalia—arches, urns, and a rose-petal aisle.

Gala receptions are staged in one of two ballrooms, each illuminated by novel pendant fixtures. A color palette that calls to mind the sea and sun-kissed sand, gold Chiavari chairs, and the soft flickering of votive candles contribute to an ambiance of sophisticated coastal elegance. Equally impressive is the award-winning catering that puts a new spin on California cuisine.

The resort staff takes your event as seriously as you do. A dedicated team of Wedding Professionals, along with your Wedding Concierge, ensures that every detail is just the way you envision. Wedding packages come with upgrades such as cake cutting, a luxurious bridal suite, and a "Couple's Spa Massage" to soothe any pre-wedding jitters. Speaking of spa, this one is a favorite in the O.C. and has been named by *Spa Finder* magazine "Best Spa" and "Best Spa for Romance." Your friends and family will appreciate a customized group spa day, and brides, you'll want to indulge in the "6-Week Countdown Package" that includes hair and makeup.

You and your guests will also appreciate the first-class accommodations, updated with the latest amenities. Thoughtful comforts like plush feathertop beds, duvets and spa robes encourage relaxation. With a host of diversions on site—croquet, lighted tennis courts and yoga classes—Laguna Cliffs Marriott is a fun place, too.

The Director of Catering Sales told us, "We strive to create a customized event experience that reflects each couple's personal vision." We think you'll agree that Laguna Cliffs is a most hospitable ambassador for the Southern California lifestyle.

CEREMONY CAPACITY: Indoors, the hotel holds up to 500 seated; outdoors up to 500 seated on the lawn. Smaller spaces are also available.

EVENT/RECEPTION CAPACITY: Indoor spaces accommodate 30–600 seated or 40–900 standing. Outdoors, the site holds 250–500 seated or 350–900 standing.

MEETING CAPACITY: Several rooms accommodate up to 1,000 guests seated theater-style.

FEES & DEPOSITS: 25% of the estimated event total is required to reserve your date; the remaining balance is paid in 3 additional equal installments between reservation and event date. Luncheon plated meals begin at $132/person, dinners at $138/person. This includes butler-passed hors d'oeuvres, 1 hour hosted bar, 3-course meal, custom-designed wedding cake, wine service throughout the meal, champagne toast, gold Chiavari chairs and complimentary oceanview guest room for the bride and groom. Tax, alcohol and a 23% service charge are additional. The ceremony package includes an oceanview location, fresh floral arch or two pedestal arrangements, aisle runners or petals, rehearsal time, bride's and groom's dressing rooms, wedding concierge and a couple's spa massage at Laguna Cliffs' award-winning Spa.

AVAILABILITY: Year-round, daily, until midnight indoors.

SERVICES/AMENITIES:

Catering: in-house or BYO with approval
Kitchen Facilities: service area
Tables & Chairs: provided
Linens, Silver, etc.: provided
Restrooms: wheelchair accessible
Dance Floor: provided
Bride's Dressing Area: yes
Meeting Equipment: AV equipment
Other: on-site wedding concierge

Parking: valet
Accommodations: 378 guest rooms
Telephone: pay phones
Outdoor Night Lighting: yes
Outdoor Cooking Facilities: BBQ and fire pits
Cleanup: provided
View: Pacific Ocean, Dana Point Harbor, mountains, coastline

RESTRICTIONS:

Alcohol: in-house, or BYO wine with corkage
Smoking: outdoors only
Music: amplified OK

Wheelchair Access: yes
Insurance: not required

Overwhelmed? Use the search criteria on www.HereComesTheGuide.com to narrow down your choices.

St. Regis Resort, Monarch Beach

Waterfront Resort & Spa

One Monarch Beach Resort, Dana Point

949/234-3455

www.stregismb.com
amy.botdorf@stregis.com

- Rehearsal Dinners
- Corporate Events
- Ceremonies
- Meetings
- Wedding Receptions
- Film Shoots
- Private Parties
- Accommodations

You don't recall booking any deluxe trips to Tuscany, but suddenly you find yourself surrounded by magnificent Italianate splendor, in a palatial resort looking out on what could be the Mediterranean coast. The calming sound of water tumbling onto itself is everywhere, cascading from multitiered fountains into gem-like pools. All around there's polished European stone and marble, hand-blown glass, inlaid mosaic tile and intricate ironwork. Overlooking a championship golf course and an ocean panorama stretching as far as the eye can see, a grand outdoor stairway leads to an emerald lawn of regal proportions.

You step onto the outdoor terrace and reach into your pocket, searching for lira that might buy you a cool drink as you contemplate the grandeur before you. Finally, a napkin emblazoned "St. Regis, Monarch Beach" tips you off: You're not in Italy at all, but rather in balmy Dana Point at one of only a few properties in California to receive the coveted Forbes Five Star and AAA Five Diamond rating, not to mention other accolades like a listing on *Travel & Leisure's* "500 Best Hotels in the World" and honors from *Conde Nast Traveler* as one of the top 50 U.S. resorts.

With its Tuscan-inspired architecture and décor, one-of-a-kind art collection and breathtaking sights, sounds and service, the St. Regis offers the ultimate in luxury for a wedding or corporate event. You'll be the belle of the hotel ball when you tie the knot under a stately colonnade on the Grand Lawn, fringed by majestic palms that filter views of world-class links and the ocean beyond. More private ceremonies are held on the Pacific Lawn or in the intimate Botanical Garden, the latter an explosion of seasonal color studded with whimsical statuary.

The resort's most opulent reception site is the 12,000-square-foot Pacific Ballroom, an inspired setting with fine architectural detailing, dazzling chandeliers and French doors opening onto an outdoor terrace. The Monarch Ballroom, capped by a lower coffered ceiling, features a separate entrance for more private affairs. Other indoor options include Club 19, offering expansive views of the Monarch Beach Golf Links, and the Wine Cellar, where 17,000 bottles from around the world are housed amidst rich mahogany and custom iron furnishings. Al fresco receptions are held on either of the hotel's spacious lawns or on the Sunset Terrace, which overlooks the Grand Lawn, golf course and ocean beyond.

As you might expect of one of the world's top resorts, the St. Regis is more than an event venue; it's an extraordinary leisure experience for luxury travelers that will tempt you and your guests to stay awhile. Book a poolside cabana, take a complimentary shuttle to a private beach, challenge yourself on the Robert Trent Jones, Jr.-designed golf course, or learn to ride the waves with your own "surf butler." Then let yourself be pampered and beautified at the on-site Spa Gaucin with its own salon. However you spend your time, you'll discover one thing for sure: No place on the Italian Riviera can top this singularly sensational destination hideaway for flawless service, comfort, cuisine and first-class amenities.

CEREMONY CAPACITY: Indoors, the hotel holds up to 750 seated, outdoors up to 750 seated on the Grand Lawn. Smaller spaces are also available.

EVENT/RECEPTION & MEETING CAPACITY: The resort accommodates up to 750 seated or 1,200 standing guests indoors or outdoors. Several smaller spaces are available, call for details.

FEES & DEPOSITS: 35% of the estimated event total is required to reserve your date. A second deposit of 65% is due 120 days prior and the final balance is due 2 weeks prior to the event. Rental fees range $4,500–7,000 depending on the date of the event and space rented. Daytime packages range $85–180/person and evening packages range $180–275/person. Tax and a 23% service charge are additional.

AVAILABILITY: Year-round, daily, anytime.

SERVICES/AMENITIES:

Catering: in-house, no BYO
Kitchen Facilities: n/a
Tables & Chairs: provided
Linens, Silver, etc.: provided
Restrooms: wheelchair accessible
Dance Floor: provided
Bride's Dressing Area: no
Meeting Equipment: AV equipment, more CBA

Parking: valet required
Accommodations: 400 guest rooms
Telephone: house phone
Outdoor Night Lighting: CBA
Outdoor Cooking Facilities: BBQ CBA
Cleanup: provided
View: coastline, ocean, fountain, patio, fairways
Other: wedding cake, spa services, grand piano golf, preferred list of wedding coordinators

RESTRICTIONS:

Alcohol: in-house
Smoking: outdoors only
Music: amplified OK indoors only

Wheelchair Access: yes
Insurance: liability required
Other: an approved wedding coordinator is required for all weddings

Dove Canyon Golf Club

Golf Club

22682 Golf Club Drive, Dove Canyon
949/858-2800

www.pacificlinks.com/dove-canyon-golf-club
facebook.com/dovecanyoncc
bhalbreich@pacificlinks.com

- Rehearsal Dinners
- Ceremonies
- Wedding Receptions
- Private Parties
- Corporate Events
- Meetings
- Film Shoots
- Accommodations

If you have a very private and elegant setting in mind for your special event, the clubhouse at Dove Canyon will exceed your expectations. Its prime location—in a secluded gated community at the edge of a canyon in the hills of southern Orange County—is matched by its design, style and ambiance.

The clubhouse pays homage to the architecture of Frank Lloyd Wright in its soaring wood-beamed cathedral ceiling lit by skylights, earth-tone slate floors, rich Honduran mahogany paneling, and carved plaster columns. When you hold your special event here you have exclusive use of the entire second floor of the facility. Ceremonies are held in the sunken lounge, whose floor-to-cathedral-ceiling window suspends you right over the canyon, or on the picturesque outdoor terrace below.

Nestled against a wooded hillside that's tamed only by the occasional box hedge, the terrace meets a free-form pond, ringed by seasonal flowers and natural rock formations. The pond gives way to a waterfall that flows out of sight into the canyon below. The canyon vista is your backdrop—a panorama that extends as far as the eye can see. After the ceremony, you and your photographer will be whisked away in a limo golf cart for some photos in front of the waterfall, while everyone else gets to know each other over cocktails and hors d'oeuvres. Take your time—your guests will be busy enjoying the splendor of the clubhouse.

The clubhouse lobby and adjacent Ballroom easily accommodate a large event, and they also work well for intimate gatherings. Cozy sitting areas in the lobby are flanked by double-sided fireplaces, and the sunken lounge demonstrates its versatility. Thanks to tinted glass, it stays cool even on the brightest day, making it a great spot not only for a small ceremony, but for dancing or showcasing the cake, too.

The Ballroom itself is a marvelously conceived space. One wall of floor-to-ceiling windows overlooks the 18th fairway and frames that gorgeous canyon view. Fireplaces blaze at both ends, and a skylight in the peaked ceiling adds more natural light. The warm feeling in the room is enhanced even further by abundant wood detailing and a plush, burgundy and brushed-gold carpet. Adjustable lighting allows you to control the mood, and with candles on the tables and fireplace mantels, romance will definitely be in the air.

Three other rooms are available for rehearsal dinners, showers or brunches. Like the rest of the facility, they benefit from the warmth of wood, natural light and terrific canyon views. In addition to a remarkably beautiful clubhouse and setting, Dove Canyon is very flexible: If none of their packages suits you, they'll customize one for you. As we said, this country club will exceed your expectations.

CEREMONY CAPACITY: Indoors, the Sunken Lounge holds up to 175 seated, outdoors up to 250 seated on the Terrace.

EVENT/RECEPTION: The Ballroom accommodates up to 280 seated or 500 standing guests.

MEETING CAPACITY: Meeting spaces seat 250.

FEES & DEPOSITS: A nonrefundable deposit, which is applied to your food and beverage total, is required to reserve your date. The amount of the deposit is equal to 25% of the estimated event total. 50% is due 4 months prior, and 100% of the final estimated balance is due 7 days prior to the event date. There are no rental fees. Packages range $55–150/person. Tax and a 20% service charge are additional.

AVAILABILITY: Year-round. Weekdays, 6am–12:30am; weekends, 11am–4pm; 6pm–11pm. Clients can purchase additional time beyond the 5-hour block given in the packages.

SERVICES/AMENITIES:

Catering: in-house, no BYO
Kitchen Facilities: n/a
Tables & Chairs: provided
Linens, Silver, etc.: provided
Restrooms: wheelchair accessible
Dance Floor: provided
Bride's Dressing Area: yes
Meeting Equipment: some provided

Parking: large lot, valet optional
Accommodations: no guest rooms
Telephone: pay and house phones
Outdoor Night Lighting: yes
Outdoor Cooking Facilities: BBQ
Cleanup: provided
View: fairways, lake, hills, fountain, waterfall
Other: wedding cake, AV equipment, grand piano

RESTRICTIONS:

Alcohol: in-house
Smoking: outdoors only
Music: amplified OK

Wheelchair Access: yes
Insurance: not required

Colette's at the Meridian Club

Private Club

1535 Deerpark Drive, Fullerton
714/447-9190
www.colettesevents.com
info@colettesevents.com

●	Rehearsal Dinners	●	Corporate Events
●	Ceremonies	●	Meetings
●	Wedding Receptions	●	Film Shoots
●	Private Parties		Accommodations

Set in a residential neighborhood in suburban Fullerton, Colette's Catering at the Meridian Club offers one-stop shopping for brides seeking top value in an easily accessed North Orange County venue. A versatile choice for a rehearsal dinner, wedding ceremony or reception of any size, this comfortable facility offers a spacious patio and several private banquet rooms that can be used individually for smaller functions or combined for large affairs. Ample complimentary parking is available for guests.

Before walking down the aisle in one of the site's indoor or outdoor spaces, relax and get ready in the Meridian Club's calming bridal suite. Appointed with classic upholstered furnishings, a full mirror, Italianate lighting fixtures and scented candles, it's a secluded place where you can enjoy your last moments as a single woman in the company of your bridesmaids.

A loggia enclosed by decorative glass paneling makes a protected outdoor spot for tying the knot. With its fountain and slate rock flooring, it's a blank canvas that can be dressed up to showcase the theme and colors of your party. Alternatively, plan an indoor ceremony in the Ara/Virgo Ballroom, where adjustable lighting and wall sconces allow you to set the mood, and a garland-festooned arch might provide a focal point for your exchange of vows.

For larger functions, the handsome Pavo/Draco Ballroom features rich mahogany paneling, and greenhouse windows that bring the outdoors inside while bathing the space in natural light. Receptions and rehearsal dinners also take place in the elegant Vela Ballroom, with its dark wood wainscoting and neutral grasscloth walls. A portable parquet dance floor can be set up in any area of the facility.

Wherever you hold your special occasion at the Meridian Club, the food will be created by *Colette's Catering*, a company known for their fine cuisine, attentive service and stylish presentation. Founded in 1990 by Fullerton native Colette Coffman, the successful firm has established a reputation for specialty wedding cakes, as well as beautifully prepared hors d'oeuvres, catered buffets and sit-down dinners. Colette's offers comprehensive wedding packages that include centerpieces, staging, silverware, linens, tables, chairs, full bar service and cleanup.

With little to worry about, you can fully experience your day: Concentrate on greeting guests, making memories and looking forward to the future with your new spouse. And because hosting an event at the Meridian Club is such a great value, you may have a little something extra to spend on your honeymoon.

CEREMONY CAPACITY: The club holds 130 seated guests indoors or 100 seated outdoors.

EVENT/RECEPTION CAPACITY: The site can accommodate 250 seated or 350 standing guests indoors, and 70 seated or 175 standing outdoors.

MEETING CAPACITY: Meeting spaces hold 250 seated guests.

FEES & DEPOSITS: A $2,000 deposit is required to reserve your date. The balance is due 7 days prior to the event. Packages range $36–63/person. Tax, alcohol and a 20% service charge are additional.

AVAILABILITY: Year-round, daily, 6am–midnight.

SERVICES/AMENITIES:

Catering: in-house
Kitchen Facilities: n/a
Tables & Chairs: provided
Linens, Silver, etc.: provided
Restrooms: wheelchair accessible
Dance Floor: portable provided
Bride's & Groom's Dressing Area: yes
Meeting Equipment: some provided

Parking: on-site structure
Accommodations: no guest rooms
Telephone: emergency use only
Outdoor Night Lighting: access only
Outdoor Cooking Facilities: no
Cleanup: provided
View: garden courtyard
Other: in-house wedding cake, AV equipment, event coordination

RESTRICTIONS:

Alcohol: in-house
Smoking: outdoors only
Music: amplified OK with restrictions

Wheelchair Access: yes
Insurance: liability required

Coyote Hills Golf Course

Golf Club

1440 East Bastanchury Road, Fullerton
888/327-1474

www.coyotehillsgc.com
privateevents@coyotehillsgc.com

- Rehearsal Dinners
- Ceremonies
- Wedding Receptions
- Private Parties
- Corporate Events
- Meetings
- Film Shoots
- Accommodations

Since opening its doors in 1996, Coyote Hills Golf Course has generated considerable public interest. And it's not just the links that have attracted a following—the versatile clubhouse and lovely setting have become popular for all types of events. And even though fundraisers, theme parties, anniversary celebrations and golf tournaments (naturally) are frequently hosted here, weddings are definitely a specialty.

A long walkway leads to their unique ceremony site, which is custom-built and quite beautiful. Guests take their seats beneath a wisteria-draped wooden pergola that frames a two-tiered waterfall at the far end. It's here that the couple exchanges vows, surrounded by a landscape filled with flowers, trees and an abundance of greenery. This area also lends itself to intimate events and, of course, makes a gorgeous backdrop for photos.

Receptions are held on the upper level of the clubhouse in a pair of banquet rooms that can be used individually or combined, depending on the size of your celebration. The Vista Falls Room, tastefully designed with exquisitely styled Japanese lamps and a lofty ceiling paneled in polished maple, has an elegant simplicity. Plenty of floor-to-ceiling windows take advantage of the inspiring landscape spread out below: acres of green hummocks, footbridges, sand traps, and a gently flowing creek. The room also overlooks a lake and two waterfalls. One of them, the amazing two-tiered water cascade at the ceremony site, is especially captivating at night when illuminated. Four sets of double doors open out onto a long terrace that runs the length of the room. Here, you can sit and enjoy the sunshine or sweet evening air and listen to the music of the falls.

Another benefit of the Vista Falls Room is that you have access to the clubhouse bar, located next door in the facility's restaurant. Airy and inviting, the restaurant is a big octagonal space with creamy walls, tropical plants, and sunlight pouring in through an eight-sided skylight. And, like the Vista Falls Room, it features large picture windows that offer a panoramic view of the fairways.

If you're planning a small meeting, reception or indoor ceremony, reserve the Vista Pointe Room, separated from the Vista Falls Room by a movable airwall. Laid out in an interesting octagonal shape like the restaurant, it shares the same patio as the Vista Falls Room as well as the view of the fairways and waterfalls through plenty of windows.

During our visit, we couldn't help but notice the serene, satisfied faces of the venue's patrons, inside the clubhouse or out on the links. Hold your event at Coyote Hills Golf Course and we bet you'll acquire that look of satisfaction, too.

CEREMONY CAPACITY: The Vista Pointe Room holds up to 150 seated guests indoors, and up to 300 guests can be accommodated in the outdoor ceremony site.

EVENT/RECEPTION CAPACITY: The Vista Falls and Vista Pointe Rooms combined hold 300 seated guests with a dance floor, or 340 seated without.

MEETING CAPACITY: The Vista Pointe Room holds 100 seated theater-style or 70 conference-style; the Vista Falls Room holds 220 theater-style or 120 seated conference-style.

FEES & DEPOSITS: A nonrefundable deposit, which is applied to your food and beverage total, is required to reserve your date. The amount of the deposit varies, depending on how far in advance you book. Payment terms for the balance also vary, and may be arranged on an individual basis. Wedding packages start at $55/person. Tax, alcohol and service charge are additional. Menus and packages can be customized to fit your needs and budget. Call for details.

AVAILABILITY: Special events and business functions, year-round, daily, 7am–1am.

SERVICES/AMENITIES:

Catering: in-house, or BYO
Kitchen Facilities: fully equipped
Tables & Chairs: provided
Linens, Silver, etc.: provided
Restrooms: wheelchair accessible
Dance Floor: provided
Bride's & Groom's Dressing Area: yes
Meeting Equipment: CBA, extra charge; WiFi included

Parking: large lot
Accommodations: no guest rooms
Telephone: emergency only
Outdoor Night Lighting: on Terrace
Outdoor Cooking Facilities: provided
Cleanup: provided
View: waterfall, lake and golf course
Other: event coordination

RESTRICTIONS:

Alcohol: in-house, or corkage $20/bottle
Smoking: on Terrace only
Music: amplified OK indoors

Wheelchair Access: yes
Insurance: not required
Other: no rice, confetti, glitter; decorations restricted

The professionals in the back of this book are the best in the business. How do we know? Read page 549.

Muckenthaler Mansion

Historic Mansion

1201 West Malvern, Fullerton
714/447-9190, Colette's Events

www.colettesevents.com
info@colettesevents.com

● Rehearsal Dinners	● Corporate Events
● Ceremonies	● Meetings
● Wedding Receptions	● Film Shoots
● Private Parties	Accommodations

With its broad lawns and period architecture, Fullerton's Muckenthaler Mansion might be the backdrop for one of the fictitious revelries in an F. Scott Fitzgerald novel. On its gracious grounds a bride can easily imagine herself as the dreamy heroine from *The Great Gatsby* as she glides across the velvety green expanse atop a wooded knoll. The fantasy continues inside, where turn-of-the-century photos document life in a gentler era.

Built in 1924 as the dream home of Walter and Adella Muckenthaler, the stunning Italian Renaissance-style structure stands on nine landscaped acres overlooking a quiet residential neighborhood. In 1965, Adella and her son donated the estate to the City of Fullerton for use as a cultural center for touring art exhibits. Thus, whatever artwork is on display at the mansion contributes a unique aesthetic to special events.

Prior to tying the knot, the bride can prepare and unwind in a dressing room featuring its own private entrance and bathroom. Guests await the bride's entrance in the estate's rose garden, and they're sure to "ooh and aah" as she floats into view surrounded by a flurry of colorful blooms. She meets her husband-to-be by the gazebo set amidst a palm-fringed Italian garden.

After the ceremony, many couples serve cocktails inside the mansion, where almost every room is a gallery filled with art from around the globe. Of particular note is the octagonal solarium, warmed by light flowing in through expansive windows. Meanwhile, the wedding party poses in the mansion's foyer, where a wrought-iron spiral staircase imported from Italy makes a perfect photographic centerpiece.

The Muckenthaler has numerous enclaves for receptions. Al fresco options include: the Center Circle Courtyard, lit by necklaces of twinkling lights; the Adella and Northwest Lawns for larger parties; and the charming Palm Court for daytime events. In the evening you can fête your guests in a fancy tent, or let the starlit sky create the ambiance.

For indoor festivities guests enjoy mingling in the wooden-floored atrium with its ornate tiled fireplace. Dinner and dancing often unfold in the main gallery, where a baby grand piano is on hand for musical entertainment. When it's time to toss the bouquet the bride stands on the mansion's front porch and flings her flowers to the bridal hopefuls waiting below on the lawn.

In addition to its extraordinary setting, the two-story mansion offers exclusive catering and full bar services by *Colette's*. Known for fabulous cuisine, magnificent cakes and impeccable service, the Fullerton caterer offers complete dinner packages, customized international menus, and creative reception ideas for 20 to 1,000.

The Muckenthaler Mansion is one of North Orange County's most picturesque event venues, and a great place to "write" the first chapter of your new life together.

CEREMONY CAPACITY: The Italian Garden holds up to 240 seated guests and the Adella Lawn up to 400 seated. Other areas of the property can accommodate up to 600.

EVENT/RECEPTION CAPACITY: Indoor spaces hold up to 130 seated or 200 standing guests. Various outdoor areas hold up to 500 seated or 700 standing guests.

MEETING CAPACITY: Spaces accommodate 8–120 seated guests.

FEES & DEPOSITS: A $2,000 deposit is required to reserve your date. Half the remaining event total is due 6 months prior to the event, and the balance is due 1 month prior. A catering deposit is required at booking, call for details. Site rental fees for weddings and social events range $2,500–4,500 depending on guest count and day of the event. Ceremony fees start at $950. Catering packages range $73–120/person. Wedding cake or a fabulous dessert are included with all packages. Please call for details on options and pricing. Tax and service charge are additional.

Rental rates for smaller events are negotiable; please call for details.

For business functions, the meeting room rental fee starts at $75/hour.

AVAILABILITY: Year-round, daily, 7am–10pm.

SERVICES/AMENITIES:
Catering: in-house, no BYO
Kitchen Facilities: n/a
Tables & Chairs: provided
Linens, Silver, etc.: provided
Restrooms: wheelchair accessible
Dance Floor: CBA
Bride's & Groom's Dressing Area: yes
Meeting Equipment: CBA, extra charge
Other: event coordination

Parking: large lot, valet optional
Accommodations: no guest rooms
Telephone: emergency use only
Outdoor Night Lighting: provided
Outdoor Cooking Facilities: BBQ CBA
Cleanup: provided
View: garden, park, cityscape, landscaped grounds

RESTRICTIONS:
Alcohol: in-house
Smoking: outdoors only
Music: amplified OK

Wheelchair Access: yes
Insurance: not required
Other: no rice, confetti, or birdseed

Summit House

Restaurant

2000 East Bastanchury Road, Fullerton
714/671-3092
www.summithouseweddings.com
carmenkaiser@summithouse.com

● Rehearsal Dinners	● Corporate Events
● Ceremonies	● Meetings
● Wedding Receptions	● Film Shoots
● Private Parties	Accommodations

Perched on one of the highest points in North Orange County and encircled by 12 acres of Fullerton's Vista Park, the Summit House is one of the most romantic wedding locations in Southern California. No matter where you stand on the grounds, a spectacular panorama inspires you: To the north loom the San Gabriel and San Bernardino mountains; to the east are the Santa Anas; to the south and west are the Laguna Hills and the sparkling Pacific. As night falls and the lights begin twinkling in the valley below, you can easily imagine yourself adrift on a sea of stars.

Equally inspiring is the Summit House Restaurant itself. Built in the tradition of an English country manor, its classic Old World architecture has the appearance and appeal of a much older, wiser structure. Lush sycamores shade the manicured lawns and rose gardens surrounding the building, and it all creates a beautiful setting for the ceremony.

The bride and her party can spend the day preparing in the Summit House's newly completed bridal suite. When she's ready, it's just a short stroll to the wedding gazebo, decorated according to her wishes. As she and her groom exchange vows, they can look out over all their guests seated in the open-air amphitheater carved into the hillside.

After the ceremony, guests may wander around the park or sip champagne on the outside patios before they slip into the Grand Summit Ballroom for the reception. With delicate cream-colored walls, coffered ceilings and pewter chandeliers, the spacious ballroom seats a crowd comfortably. Light flows in through enormous bay windows and oversized French doors, and let's not forget the panoramic view! If your guest list requires more room, a movable wall rolls aside, giving you access to the equally attractive Queen's Room and adjoining patio.

To ensure that your big day is glitch-free, the Summit House provides both a catering and a ceremony coordinator. And what amazing food and service! No wonder this facility has such a great reputation. Truth is, the Summit House will go the whole nine yards to accommodate your wildest wish, whether you want to arrive in a roaring cavalcade of Harleys, as one couple did, or simply leave the old-fashioned way in a horse and buggy. And included in every wedding package is an invitation for the newlyweds to return on their first anniversary to celebrate the special occasion all over again and relive their magical memories, compliments of the Summit House.

CEREMONY CAPACITY: The Gazebo Amphitheater in Vista Park holds up to 250 seated or 500 standing guests.

EVENT/RECEPTION & MEETING CAPACITY: The Grand Summit Ballroom holds 250 seated, 300 with the patio, and 300 standing guests.

FEES & DEPOSITS: A deposit is required when you book the facility. 50% of the balance is due 30 days prior to the event, and a guest count guarantee and final balance are due 10 days prior; incidental fees are payable the day of the event. Luncheons run $30–48/person and dinners $32–50/person. Several wedding packages are available in addition to the above menu prices. Bar charges, bottled wine, tax and a 20% service charge are extra. For ceremonies, there is an $875 fee that includes a ceremony coordinator and upgraded chair rentals as well as a $750 park rental fee.

AVAILABILITY: Year-round, daily, 11am–midnight.

SERVICES/AMENITIES:

Catering: in-house, no BYO
Kitchen Facilities: n/a
Tables & Chairs: provided
Linens, Silver, etc.: provided
Restrooms: wheelchair accessible
Dance Floor: provided
Bride's Dressing Area: yes
Meeting Equipment: podium with microphone
Other: event coordination

Parking: large lot, complimentary evening valet
Accommodations: no guest rooms
Telephone: house phone
Outdoor Night Lighting: yes
Outdoor Cooking Facilities: no
Cleanup: provided
View: surrounding valleys; San Gabriel, Santa Ana and San Bernardino Mountains

RESTRICTIONS:

Alcohol: in-house, or WC corkage $20/bottle
Smoking: outside only
Music: amplified OK indoors with volume limits

Wheelchair Access: yes
Insurance: not required
Other: no birdseed, rice or confetti; open flames restricted

The Villa Del Sol

Garden Courtyard

305 North Harbor Boulevard, Suite 303, Fullerton
714/814-9808, Dunlap Property Group

www.thevilladelsol.com
nervebase@earthlink.net

- Rehearsal Dinners
- Ceremonies
- Wedding Receptions
- Private Parties
- Corporate Events
- Meetings
- Film Shoots
- Accommodations

It's always exciting to see a historic property given new life and purpose, especially when it's done with the integrity and charm of The Villa Del Sol, an enticing haven right in the center of Fullerton's Old Town. The original Spanish Colonial-styled California Hotel has been imaginatively revitalized to house a collection of boutiques, restaurants and businesses that surround an alluring center courtyard, making this delightful 1920s landmark a winning choice for an outdoor wedding.

When you enter the massive wrought-iron gates and pass beneath the vintage black chandelier, you immediately leave the bustle and activity of Harbor Boulevard behind. The white stucco building, which still maintains most of its period details—like the red-tiled roof, decorative setbacks and shaded porticos—encloses a beautiful brick courtyard the size of a village square. Taking center stage, a Spanish-tiled fountain adds to the soothing atmosphere of this al fresco oasis. Directly behind the fountain is what was once the main entrance to Fullerton's first luxury inn, and the word "California" is still proudly visible on its façade. Landscaped with islands of palm trees and flowers, the courtyard boasts even more greenery in ivy-covered breezeways that wrap around the entire area and shade the entries to unique shops offering custom floral arrangements, vintage jewelry, designer clothing, photography services, salon/spa treatments and more. Several storefronts are so picturesque that past couples have opted to take their vows in front of one of them, instead of the fountain or hotel archway! And, of course, it's incredibly convenient to utilize the stores' expertise in planning your special day.

Once you've said "I do," you can take advantage of The Villa del Sol's graceful arches, wrought-iron railings and towering turrets as backdrops for your photo album. Invite your guests to enjoy cocktails either in the courtyard or on the upstairs balcony, a sweeping second-floor terrace that provides bird's-eye views of the courtyard below as well as vistas of downtown Fullerton framed by the graceful colonnades.

Although you can customize the flow of your event, dinner is generally served at elegantly appointed tables in the courtyard. As for the food itself, you can savor the specialties prepared expressly for you by one of the four very popular resident restaurants: Café Hidalgo (authentic dishes from Mexico, Spain and Latin America); The Cellar (first-class Continental with an extensive wine list); Brownstone Café (home-style cooking and catering); or Stadium Tavern (casual favorites).

As night falls, lights strung across the courtyard twinkle and lanterns hung from top-floor walkways cast their magical glow over a scene your guests will not soon forget. And when the party ends, friends and family can skip the hassle of driving because the train station is just blocks away, making it easy to catch an Amtrak or Metroliner home.

CEREMONY, EVENT/RECEPTION & MEETING CAPACITY: The facility holds 250 seated or standing guests outdoors.

FEES & DEPOSITS: 50% of the rental fee is required to reserve your date and the balance is due 60 days prior to the event. Rental fees range $3,250–4,750 depending on the day of the event. Meals range $22–65/person. Tax, alcohol and a 20% service charge are additional.

AVAILABILITY: Year-round, daily, 5pm–midnight.

SERVICES/AMENITIES:

Catering: in-house
Kitchen Facilities: n/a
Tables & Chairs: CBA
Linens, Silver, etc.: provided
Restrooms: wheelchair accessible
Dance Floor: CBA
Bride's Dressing Area: yes
Meeting Equipment: CBA
Other: coordination, spa services, in-house florals, photography, invitations, boutique

Parking: limited on street, valet required, garage nearby
Accommodations: no guest rooms
Telephone: guest phone
Outdoor Night Lighting: included
Outdoor Cooking Facilities: BBQ CBA
Cleanup: provided
View: garden courtyard, cityscape, fountain, landscaped grounds

RESTRICTIONS:

Alcohol: in-house
Smoking: designated areas only
Music: amplified OK outdoors with restrictions

Wheelchair Access: yes
Insurance: liability required
Other: exclusive vendor for party rentals

Hyatt Regency Huntington Beach
Resort and Spa

Waterfront Hotel

21500 Pacific Coast Highway, Huntington Beach

714/845-4652

www.hyattregencyhuntingtonbeach.com
nancy.monte-frye@hyatt.com

- Rehearsal Dinners
- Ceremonies
- Wedding Receptions
- Private Parties
- Corporate Events
- Meetings
- Film Shoots
- Accommodations

If castles in the sand were real, they would no doubt look something like the magnificent Hyatt Regency Huntington Beach Resort and Spa. With its towers, fountains, and gardens, it's positively palatial, offering over 100,000 square feet of indoor and outdoor function space sparkling against the blue Pacific.

Special events unfold with grace and elegance in the sumptuously appointed Conference Center, where the dramatic King Triton Fountain and porte-cochère greet guests upon arrival. The Grand Conference Lobby, with its cathedral-high ceiling and second-story balcony surround, has a sweeping inner courtyard feel. Festivities can easily begin here, or guests can proceed to any one of the property's numerous ballrooms, courtyards, and terraces. The Lighthouse Courtyard is particularly enchanting for your outdoor ceremony or event. It's a wide lawn, surrounded by stately palms, that leads from the shimmering Mermaid Fountain to the resort's stunning white Lighthouse Tower and Bridge. The ocean view is spectacular and uninterrupted here, but that's no surprise—this is a world in which unparalleled Pacific vistas abound.

Coast and sea also captivate from the gorgeous Huntington Ballroom Foyer and Terrace—a delightful spot for cocktails and hors d'oeuvres, where delicate ocean breezes and the sound of the surf drift in through the open archways. A sculpted balustrade and handsome wrought-iron sconces give it a romantically Mediterranean feel. Also opening onto the terrace is the Grand Ballroom, which accommodates up to 2,000 and has its own Grand Foyer. Both ballrooms feature beautiful design elements that reflect the resort's breezy Andalusian style, like regal columns, soaring ceilings crossed with artfully carved and scrolled beams, seashell-shaped sconces, and hand-blown glass chandeliers. The effect is an ambiance that's majestic, yet intimate, whether the rooms are divided into smaller sections or used in their splendid entirety. The Mariner's Ballroom downstairs shares the same subtle allure. Whether partitioned by gauzy draperies or open to seat 600, it feels very private, comfortable and secluded.

The Hyatt Regency Huntington Beach Resort and Spa is a venue where you can entertain on an opulent scale and still feel totally at home...it's a setting that's both luxurious and relaxed. You may get lost just exploring the grounds, checking out the ballrooms, courtyards, and galleries, but you probably won't want to leave. Fortunately you won't have to. The resort has 517 spacious guest rooms, 57 plush suites, a 20,000-square-foot spa, shops, a multitude of services, and an experienced and attentive staff. All you and your guests have to do is settle in, celebrate, unwind, and stay for as long as you like.

CEREMONY, EVENT/RECEPTION & MEETING CAPACITY: The site holds 2,000 seated or standing guests indoors, and 400 seated or standing outdoors.

FEES & DEPOSITS: 25% of the total estimated event cost is required at time of booking, an additional 50% is due 3 months prior and the balance is due 10 days prior to the event. Rental fees start at $500 and vary depending on the guest count, season, time and day of the event and the space rented. Wedding packages range $85–114/person. Tax and a 23% service charge are additional.

AVAILABILITY: Year-round, daily.

SERVICES/AMENITIES:

Catering: in-house or BYO
Kitchen Facilities: n/a
Tables & Chairs: provided
Linens, Silver, etc.: provided
Restrooms: wheelchair accessible
Dance Floor: portable provided
Bride's Dressing Area: yes
Meeting Equipment: some provided
Other: spa services, AV equipment, event coordination

Parking: valet required
Accommodations: 517 guest rooms
Telephone: guest phone
Outdoor Night Lighting: yes
Outdoor Cooking Facilities: no
Cleanup: provided
View: fountain, garden, courtyard, landscaped grounds, coastline, ocean/bay

RESTRICTIONS:

Alcohol: in-house
Smoking: designated areas only
Music: amplified OK with restrictions

Wheelchair Access: yes
Insurance: required for vendors

Want to know WHAT TO ASK a potential location or vendor? Check out our Questions to Ask starting on page 19.

SeaCliff Country Club

Country Club

6501 Palm Avenue, Huntington Beach
888/998-9709

www.countryclubreceptions.com
www.seacliffcc.net
directorofevents@seacliffcc.net

- Rehearsal Dinners
- Ceremonies
- Wedding Receptions
- Private Parties
- Corporate Events
- Meetings
- Film Shoots
- Accommodations

Driving along Palm Avenue, just north of Pacific Coast Highway in one of Southern California's most beloved beach towns, you have a feeling you're headed for someplace special as you make your way past majestic palms, towering like giant sentries all along the wide, landscaped boulevard. Turning into SeaCliff Country Club, your hunch proves right as you come face to face with the sleek, horizontal lines of a Frank Lloyd Wright structure flanked by emerald fairways and exuding a quiet, contemporary allure.

Situated less than a mile from the shore, dependably sun-kissed and cooled by ocean breezes, this sophisticated site is the only private club available for nonmember events in Huntington Beach.

Valets will greet your guests as they arrive in SeaCliff's gracious circular driveway. Leading into the club, a sea of colorful foliage and a stream spilling over stones in a rock garden set a serene tone. Beyond an airy lobby with a soaring ceiling, the Pacific Room has a chic supper club feel with a warm mocha and burgundy color scheme, contemporary upholstered and leather furnishings, a granite-topped bar and an ebony grand piano. Offering panoramic views of the club's lake and 18-hole golf course, this is a stylish area for pre- and post-ceremony mingling. While guests await your arrival, you and your attendants will have full use of a bride's room, where you can simultaneously primp and calm jittery nerves with cheese, crackers and a bit of bubbly.

The Oval Terrace overlooking the lake and fairways provides a stunning backdrop for your outdoor ceremony—and for snapping photos afterwards. You'll walk down a petal-strewn aisle stretching 75 feet to an ivory Grecian arch or pillared colonnade adorned with flowers, where you'll exchange vows.

The Club's two reception spaces offer very different atmospheres. If your guest list is long or you prefer a formal ballroom ambiance, the SeaCliff Room is large enough to accommodate a dance floor and DJ. Smaller gatherings are held in the Pacific Room, with clubby lounge areas and a more intimate space for dancing. No matter which one you choose, you can enhance any of five turnkey reception packages with a dramatic ice sculpture, a martini luge, or a chocolate fountain with your choice of dippers.

Complementing the attractions of this upscale venue are those that surround it in mellow Surf City USA. After your festivities wind down, you'll have miles of uninterrupted beach to stroll along, a historic pier to explore and a colorful oceanfront boardwalk to visit.

CEREMONY CAPACITY: The Oval Terrace accommodates up to 250 seated guests. Indoors, banquet rooms hold up to 250 seated.

EVENT/RECEPTION & MEETING CAPACITY: Indoors, rooms hold up to 250 seated or 300 standing guests; outdoors, the Oval Terrace holds up to 250 seated or 300 standing.

FEES & DEPOSITS: A nonrefundable deposit, which is applied to your food and beverage total, is required to reserve your date. The amount of the deposit varies, depending on how far in advance you book. Payment terms for the balance also vary, and may be arranged on an individual basis. Reception packages start at $47/person. Tax, alcohol and service charge are additional. Menus and packages can be customized to fit your needs and budget. Call for details.

AVAILABILITY: Year-round. 6-hour blocks for ceremonies and receptions. 5-hour blocks for receptions only, with the option to purchase overtime until midnight.

SERVICES/AMENITIES:

Catering: in-house, or BYO with restrictions
Kitchen Facilities: n/a
Tables & Chairs: provided
Linens, Silver, etc.: provided
Restrooms: wheelchair accessible
Dance Floor: provided
Bride's Dressing Area: yes
Meeting Equipment: CBA, extra charge
Other: event coordination, grand piano, AV equipment

Parking: valet required for groups of 60 or more
Accommodations: no guest rooms
Telephone: office phone
Outdoor Night Lighting: access only
Outdoor Cooking Facilities: BBQ CBA
Cleanup: provided
View: landscaped grounds, trees, hills

RESTRICTIONS:

Alcohol: in-house
Smoking: outside only
Music: amplified OK with restrictions

Wheelchair Access: yes
Insurance: not required

Shorebreak Hotel

Waterfront Hotel

500 Pacific Coast Highway, Huntington Beach
714/861-4470

www.shorebreakhotel.com
shorebreaksales@jdvhotels.com

- Rehearsal Dinners
- Ceremonies
- Wedding Receptions
- Private Parties
- Corporate Events
- Meetings
- Film Shoots
- Accommodations

If you're looking for the coolest setting for a California coastal wedding in Orange County, you have to check out this uber-awesome new venue in the heart of Surf City USA. It delivers amazing oceanside views with an energetic Huntington Beach downtown surround and 8,000 square feet of terrific indoor/outdoor event space.

Very likely you and your guests will be carried away instantly by the décor—super, beach-themed touches like the vibrant murals (one is actually an enormous quilt made of wet suits), the surfboard-style sculptural elements, and the iconic images of local beach culture by photographer Aaron Chang. The architectural elements will impress everyone, too: The high ceilings, clean lines and large windows are an airy salute to the breezy Southern California lifestyle. But what's most appealing here is the prospect of hosting an event—be it social or corporate—that's free-spirited, easy-going, and sophisticated at the same time.

The 3,000-square-foot Epic Ballroom (divisible into thirds), its adjoining Foyer, and the adjacent Deck—are all truly epic. Polished and beautifully conceived with every imaginable feature, these spaces are also FUN. Creative forces creep into every tiny detail from the lovely sand, sea and sun-inspired colors to the subtle "footprint" textural effects in the walls and the sustainable landscaping in the outdoor function areas. For smaller groups or for breakout sessions, the Peak Room and Terrace offer still more upscale, yet comfortable opportunities for "peak" entertaining.

Zimzala, the hotel's popular restaurant, is great for intimate parties. Outfitted in brilliant marine-blues and sparkly copper tones, it's sleek, yet laid back, with an adjoining terrace that can add another 660 square feet of outdoor space. The kitchen serves up a host of sophisticated beach-inspired hors d'oeuvres, hand-crafted cocktails, and traditional favorites with a contemporary spin, like their grilled sirloin burgers with gruyère cheese, caramelized onions and parmesan-garlic fries or the pan-seared organic Irish salmon with tarragon-scented pearl couscous.

Of course, in addition to the hotel's experience-enhancing design, the best part of staging an event in a Joie de Vivre® boutique hotel like the Shorebreak is the personalized service from the warm, welcoming staff and all of the on-site amenities. And don't forget there are 157 rooms and 39 suites here for anyone who wants to extend their stay. Our guess is that your guests won't want to leave, and why should they? With the comforting sound of waves within earshot and the enticements of Main Street, Huntington Beach at their feet, this is the ultimate destination for anyone wanting to celebrate or play in true Southern California style. Take a hint prompted by the hotel's surf lingo lexicon or "riptionary": Whether you want to hang loose or amp up, this place is the fall line. It's totally alchemy hour.

CEREMONY CAPACITY: The facility holds 150 seated guests, indoors or outdoors.

EVENT/RECEPTION & MEETING CAPACITY: The hotel can accommodate 150 seated or 250 standing indoors and 100 seated or 150 standing outdoors.

FEES & DEPOSITS: A $2,000 nonrefundable, nontransferable deposit is required to reserve your date. Additional nonrefundable, nontransferable deposits are required at 60, 90 and 120 days prior with the estimated balance due 14 days prior to your date. Ceremony fee is $750. A wedding coordinator is required for all on-site ceremonies. Event space rental fees range $250–1,950 with food and beverage minimum. Taxable service charge and sales tax are additional. Fees for business programs vary based on overnight accommodations, services and menus selected.

AVAILABILITY: Year-round, daily. Business functions: 8am–5pm or 6pm–11pm. Weddings: 11am–4pm and 6pm–11pm.

SERVICES/AMENITIES:

Catering: in-house
Kitchen Facilities: n/a
Tables & Chairs: provided
Linens, Silver, etc.: provided
Restrooms: wheelchair accessible
Dance Floor: portable provided
Bride's Dressing Area: no
Meeting Equipment: provided

Parking: valet and self in garage, extra charge
Accommodations: 157 guest rooms
Telephone: house phone
Outdoor Night Lighting: CBA
Outdoor Cooking Facilities: none
Cleanup: provided
View: cityscape, garden patio, ocean
Other: AV equipment, event coordination

RESTRICTIONS:

Alcohol: in-house; beer, wine or champagne only
Smoking: not allowed
Music: amplified OK indoors with restrictions

Wheelchair Access: yes
Insurance: not required

The Waterfront Beach Resort
A Hilton Hotel

21100 Pacific Coast Highway, Huntington Beach
714/845-8420, 714/845-8421 Catering

www.waterfrontresort.com
atthebeach@waterfrontresort.com

Waterfront Hotel

- Rehearsal Dinners
- Ceremonies
- Wedding Receptions
- Private Parties
- Corporate Events
- Meetings
- Film Shoots
- Accommodations

Overlooking an eight-and-a-half-mile stretch of white sand, this Mediterranean-style resort is a knockout addition to beachfront properties. The hotel's lobby is the epitome of casual seaside luxury: Elegant marble floors and graceful curved staircases coexist quite comfortably with the tropical presence of cascading rock waterfalls, palm trees and lush foliage.

The venue's most popular ceremony site is the Driftwood Pavilion & Courtyard, a private area backed by sheltering palms and a view of the ocean. Seated guests can watch the bride walk down a glittering crushed-abalone shell aisle to meet her groom beneath a white gazebo, often decorated with flowers or draped with flowing colored fabric. Just steps away, a large tented pavilion with roll-up sides is a convenient place for staging, gathering the bridal party before the ceremony, or dining and dancing afterwards.

Other sites for exchanging vows are poolside under the blue sky, in an oceanview ballroom or on an intimate outdoor terrace. Following a ceremony in any of these settings, guests may enjoy cocktails and hors d'oeuvres in the spacious foyer of the Waterfront Grand Ballroom while the bridal party poses for pictures around the hotel or on the beach. The Grand Ballroom—the largest event space at the resort—is notable not only for its size, but also for its eye-catching features: a 14-foot ceiling richly trimmed with golden crown molding and six glowing chandeliers that provide romantic mood lighting.

Another reception option is the Pacific Ballroom and adjoining Terrace, located on the hotel's upper level. The Terrace is perfect for pre-reception cocktails: Here, guests mingle amidst refreshing sea breezes, accompanied by the sound of the rolling surf and a view that extends beyond the resort's pool and beautifully landscaped grounds to the vast ocean. Inside the ballroom, floor-to-ceiling windows take in that fabulous view, and contemporary oil paintings in gilded frames depict coastal life at its best. A 14-foot-tall alcove with arched windows on all three sides makes a dramatic backdrop for the wedding cake.

A smaller ballroom, Cielo Mare—Italian for "Heavenly Sea"—treats you to an ocean vista through windows framed by cascading bougainvillea. On one wall an abstract marble sculpture captures the image of rolling waves, and a marble credenza adds a lovely touch. At the rear of the room, a *trompe l'oeil* "sky" with fluffy white clouds on a baby blue background adorns the ceiling. This is where most hostesses prefer to set the dance floor, so guests can kick up their heels under an imaginary firmament. French doors open to a private glass-walled Venetian room with a full Pacific view—a delightful spot for the wedding cake, bar, or buffet.

The Waterfront Beach Resort is a Four Diamond facility offering an abundance of services and amenities: 290 guest rooms, each with a private oceanview balcony; beach activities galore; and tennis courts, a swimming pool and a fitness center on site. With all these inducements, it's easy to understand why guests coming to the resort for an event are enticed to stay on for a mini-vacation.

CEREMONY CAPACITY: Outdoors, the Driftwood Pavilion & Courtyard seats up to 300; the Pool Deck up to 225, and the Pacific Terrace up to 100. Indoors, the Pacific Room holds 200 seated, the Cielo Mare Ballroom 150 seated, and the Waterfront Grand Ballroom up to 400 seated guests.

EVENT/RECEPTION CAPACITY: The Pacific Room holds 180–200 seated, the Cielo Mare Ballroom 150 seated and the Waterfront Grand Ballroom 400 seated guests.

MEETING CAPACITY: Several spaces are available for 12–450 seated guests.

FEES & DEPOSITS: For weddings, 30% of the estimated event total is required as a nonrefundable deposit to reserve your date. Luncheons start at $60/person, dinners at $80/person. Cakes and/or cake-cutting costs run $7/person. The estimated event balance, along with a guaranteed guest count, is due 10 days prior to the function. Beverages, tax and a 22% service charge are additional. Group rates for overnight wedding guests can be arranged.

For business functions, room rental fees vary depending on the season, room(s) selected and services required; call for more specific information.

AVAILABILITY: Year-round, daily. Weddings take place 11am–4pm or 6pm–midnight. Business functions and special events, 8am–midnight.

SERVICES/AMENITIES:
Catering: in-house, or BYO with approval
Kitchen Facilities: moderate
Tables & Chairs: provided
Linens, Silver, etc.: provided
Restrooms: wheelchair accessible
Dance Floor: provided
Bride's Dressing Area: provided with ceremony package
Meeting Equipment: full range

Parking: valet parking $14–28/car
Accommodations: 290 guest rooms
Telephone: emergency use only
Outdoor Night Lighting: yes
Outdoor Cooking Facilities: no
Cleanup: provided
View: ocean and hotel's pool area

RESTRICTIONS:
Alcohol: in-house
Smoking: outside only, designated areas
Music: amplified OK

Wheelchair Access: yes
Insurance: not required
Other: no rice, birdseed or confetti

Good Shepherd Chapel
at Concordia University Irvine

1530 Concordia West, Irvine
949/214-3141
www.cui.edu/aboutcui/conferencing
sam.nordrum@cui.edu

University Chapel

Rehearsal Dinners	● Corporate Events
● Ceremonies	● Meetings
● Wedding Receptions	● Film Shoots
● Private Parties	Accommodations

Situated high on a 70-acre plateau overlooking the Saddleback Valley, and mere minutes from John Wayne Airport, the Pacific coast and Orange County's major attractions, Concordia University's Good Shepherd Chapel is a truly heavenly place for a wedding—and it's just one of many indoor and outdoor event sites on this beautifully tended campus.

Your Christian ceremony might begin in the chapel itself, a sunlit space with floor-to-ceiling windows; gleaming, honey-colored wood floors; a low, well-lit stage and altar; and a wood-beamed ceiling. The large stained-glass window lets in additional light, and chapel seating can be moved to accommodate any chair arrangements.

Two charming patios flanking the church feature breathtaking views of the surrounding mountains and protected parklands, and the romantically landscaped chapel lawn at the rear of the building is a lovely spot for plighting one's troth or enjoying the party that follows amid beds of white roses, fragrant jasmine, and towering eucalyptus trees.

If dining and dancing indoors is your preference, take the celebration to the Grimm Hall Conference Center just a short walk away. You and your attendants may want to unwind pre- and post-ceremony in the Preus Faculty Lounge, before joining the festivities in the adjacent Conference Center and Terrace. The Hall's ground-floor lobby and art gallery make a sophisticated entry to the venue. Take the elevator up to the third floor, where you'll find a generous salon that opens onto a broad covered terrace and more sweeping views. WiFi and AV capability enable relatives to Skype in so that they can participate long distance.

Concordia University's knowledgeable and experienced conferencing staff and caterers—they partner with *Bon Appétit*—will ensure that your meal is delectable and the service topnotch. You'll be able to relax, savor the day, and look radiant when you strike a pose by the fountain, in the garden, or before one of the canyon or mountain panoramas.

Concordia University can easily accommodate events large and small. This is an extremely flexible setting with seemingly infinite possibilities. For example, Concordia's largest chapel, the

Concordia University Center for Worship and Performing Arts, is a magnificent structure that seats up to 400. It offers a professional stage and lighting, amazing acoustics, and both a Steinway concert grand piano and a 3,290-pipe Casavant pipe organ. And how about cocktails or dinner for all the assembled, elegantly served on the long Center Lawn?

No question about it, whether your event is an inspiring concert performance, a fundraiser for a worthy cause, a wedding celebration, or just about any good-spirited gathering, you certainly want to consider having it at this divine venue.

CEREMONY CAPACITY: The chapel accommodates up to 110 seated guests indoors.

EVENT/RECEPTION CAPACITY: The site holds 110 seated or standing guests indoors or outdoors.

MEETING CAPACITY: Meeting spaces accommodate up to 510 seated guests.

FEES & DEPOSITS: 20% of the rental fee is required to reserve your date and the balance is due 30 days prior to the event. Rental fees start at $800 and vary depending on the facilities required. Meals range $12–24/person or market prices for seafood/prime cut selections. Tax, alcohol and a 15% service charge are additional.

AVAILABILITY: Year-round, Saturdays only.

SERVICES/AMENITIES:

Catering: in-house
Kitchen Facilities: n/a
Tables & Chairs: CBA, extra fee
Linens, Silver, etc.: provided
Restrooms: wheelchair accessible
Dance Floor: CBA
Bride's Dressing Area: yes
Meeting Equipment: CBA, extra fee
Other: grand piano, clergy on staff, picnic area, AV equipment, organ

Parking: large lot
Accommodations: no guest rooms
Telephone: emergency use only
Outdoor Night Lighting: access only
Outdoor Cooking Facilities: BBQ CBA
Cleanup: provided
View: garden, landscaped grounds; panorama of hills, canyon and mountains

RESTRICTIONS:

Alcohol: in-house
Smoking: outside only
Music: amplified OK with restrictions

Wheelchair Access: yes
Insurance: liability required

Want to find more venues and services? Check out our informative website, www.HereComesTheGuide.com.

357

Hyatt Regency Irvine

17900 Jamboree Road, Irvine
949/225-6640

www.irvine.hyatt.com
rosana.winarto@hyatt.com

Hotel

- Rehearsal Dinners
- Ceremonies
- Wedding Receptions
- Private Parties
- Corporate Events
- Meetings
- Film Shoots
- Accommodations

The upscale Hyatt Regency Irvine is a place where almost anything is possible. Expecting hundreds of guests and need a full-service hotel that will accommodate them in style? Looking for a catering manager who understands ethnic traditions and can help you personalize your wedding so that it reflects your colorful heritage? Considering a grand entrance on a silk-draped elephant or a high-stepping stallion? This hotel is known for its exceptional hospitality, amenities, and service, making it one of Orange County's top choices for special events.

With the largest grand ballroom in the area—a refined, 14,700-square-foot space with beaded chandeliers and soaring 18-foot ceilings—this is the perfect venue for a gala affair. Equally unique is the hotel's Garden Pavilion, a versatile indoor-outdoor facility.

A lush walkway fringed by tropical foliage leads guests to the facility. In a 2,300-square-foot outdoor courtyard ringed by mature banana trees and birds of paradise, they'll have ample room to socialize before and after your ceremony. You can tie the knot on a beautiful garden terrace next to the pavilion. Afterwards, step inside for a spectacular reception. With dome chandeliers and ivory walls, the spacious tent-like structure provides a chic *tabula rasa* for creating anything from a traditional garden wedding to a Polynesian-themed event. Customize this flexible space any way you like, designing your own floor plan, importing a baby grand piano from the hotel, or adding a photo table to share memorable moments with guests.

However you decide to stage your affair, you can count on outstanding food and attention to detail by *Regency Caterers*. As the Hyatt's exclusive catering arm, *Regency Caterers* also choreographs events off-site, at such prime Orange County locations as the Richard Nixon Library, Marconi Museum and Tanaka Farms, as well as at private homes. Your Regency Catering Manager at the hotel can discuss these alternatives with you, and provide tours of available facilities.

And, of course, whether you host your event at the Hyatt Regency Irvine or at one of the other venues they cater, you'll have years of experience and the "Hyatt touch" backing the success of your party. From a customized menu and personalized cocktails to full facility setup, there are few details that aren't handled for you. No matter what kind of celebration you envision, the hotel's skilled professionals will be there to make it happen.

CEREMONY CAPACITY: The terrace accommodates up to 250 seated guests. Indoors, banquet rooms hold up to 1,300 seated guests.

EVENT/RECEPTION CAPACITY: Indoors, rooms hold up to 1,300 seated or 1,700 standing guests; outdoors, the terrace holds up to 250 seated or 300 standing.

MEETING CAPACITY: Several spaces accommodate 15–1,200 seated guests; smaller rooms are available, call for details.

FEES & DEPOSITS: 25% of the minimum commitment is required to reserve your date. The balance is due 10 business days prior to the event. Rental fees and minimums range $500–30,000 depending on venue selected. If you use the on-site caterer, meals range $70–115/person. Tax, alcohol, and a 24% service charge are additional.

AVAILABILITY: Year-round, daily, anytime.

SERVICES/AMENITIES:

Catering: in-house or select from list
Kitchen Facilities: fully equipped
Tables & Chairs: provided
Linens, Silver, etc.: provided
Restrooms: wheelchair accessible
Dance Floor: provided
Bride's Dressing Area: yes
Meeting Equipment: CBA, extra charge
Other: event coordination, baby grand piano, wedding cakes, AV equipment

Parking: large lot, valet and self-parking available
Accommodations: 536 guest rooms
Telephone: house phone
Outdoor Night Lighting: yes
Outdoor Cooking Facilities: available
Cleanup: provided
View: garden

RESTRICTIONS:

Alcohol: in-house
Smoking: outside only
Music: amplified OK

Wheelchair Access: yes
Insurance: may be required, call for details

La Mirada Golf Course

Golf Club

15501 Alicante Road, La Mirada
888/998-7024

www.countryclubreceptions.com
privateeventmanager@lamiradagc.com

● Rehearsal Dinners	● Corporate Events
● Ceremonies	● Meetings
● Wedding Receptions	Film Shoots
● Private Parties	Accommodations

Tucked away in a quiet neighborhood, this golf course is one of the most popular in Southern California. It may also be one of the Southland's most wedding-friendly venues.

What's the attraction? Affordable prices, no need to be a member (it's a public course), the biggest dance floor in town, and an accommodating staff that knows how to soothe anxieties and keep things flowing smoothly. And even though this is a very popular course, the banquet facility is completely private: Brides never have to worry about curious golfers wandering through their celebration.

Every wedding here is individualized. The bride meets with the private event staff for a food tasting well before the wedding day. Because the city of La Mirada is an ethnic crossroads, the facility has extensive experience dealing with different religious and cultural needs. They're also very flexible about time, and late evening celebrations aren't a problem—they're relatively far from the nearest neighboring houses, meaning no worries about disturbing anyone.

Many couples start with an outdoor ceremony at the beautiful gazebo overlooking the golf course's signature lake. Afterwards, festivities move to the clubhouse's banquet room, terrace, bar and front patio. A white ceiling and windows on three sides keep the room bright, and it boasts an impressively large dance floor. The spacious terrace offers a perfect view of the golf course, a deep-green panorama of grassy slopes. The fairways seem to go on for miles, and are edged with sycamores, beautiful shagbark eucalyptus and pines.

The patio, a small space near the front of the clubhouse, is a quiet spot where people can take a break from the party. The bar, directly accessible from the banquet room, has a charming Tuscan feel with comfortable booths and an upholstered bar. This unique setup makes for a wonderful flow—just the thing to keep guests happily moving and mingling.

Maybe the best way to think of La Mirada is to remember what was going through Goldilocks' mind when she was testing porridge at the Bear residence. Goldie wasn't looking for too big or too cool; she was looking for Just Right. This place has so many "just right" things going for it that it may just be right for you.

CEREMONY CAPACITY: The site accommodates up to 350 seated guests outdoors and 200 indoors.

EVENT/RECEPTION & MEETING CAPACITY: The banquet room accommodates up to 400 seated or 575 standing guests; outdoor areas up to 500 seated or 775 standing.

FEES & DEPOSITS: A nonrefundable deposit, which is applied to your food and beverage total, is required to reserve your date. The amount of the deposit varies, depending on how far in advance you book. Payment terms for the balance also vary, and may be arranged on an individual basis. Meals start at $25/person. Tax, alcohol service charge are additional. Menus and packages can be customized to fit your needs and budget. Call for details.

AVAILABILITY: Year-round, daily.

SERVICES/AMENITIES:

Catering: in-house
Kitchen Facilities: n/a
Tables & Chairs: provided
Linens, Silver, etc.: provided
Restrooms: wheelchair accessible
Dance Floor: provided
Bride's Dressing Area: provided
Meeting Equipment: CBA
Other: event coordination, wedding cake, florals, chair covers, clergy referrals available

Parking: large lot and on street
Accommodations: no guest rooms
Telephone: pay or house phones
Outdoor Night Lighting: yes
Outdoor Cooking Facilities: BBQ
Cleanup: provided
View: fairways, lake, garden, landscaped grounds

RESTRICTIONS:

Alcohol: in-house
Smoking: outside only
Music: amplified OK indoors

Wheelchair Access: yes
Insurance: not required

Cliffs at Laguna Village

577 South Coast Highway, Laguna Beach
866/321-9876, 949/939-7979 Occasions at Laguna Village
www.occasionsatlagunavillage.com
lagunaoccasions@aol.com

Waterfront Special Event Facility

● Rehearsal Dinners	● Corporate Events
● Ceremonies	● Meetings
● Wedding Receptions	● Film Shoots
● Private Parties	Accommodations

Refreshing breezes, a white sand beach, crashing waves and a beautiful sunset accompany your ceremony … you and your guests dine and dance beneath the stars…. It all sounds pretty fabulous, doesn't it! Well, if you've always wanted a seaside celebration but have been daunted by all the effort involved, why not have your event at the Cliffs at Laguna Village? At this unique facility you can enjoy all the things you love about being near the ocean without having to lift a finger!

Of course, the Cliffs' main attraction is its location: set on a bluff with a 180-degree view of Laguna Beach, the adjacent coastline and the Pacific. A staircase leads from the street-level parking lot down to the venue, a spacious outdoor area with a built-in checkerboard dance floor bordered by a well-tended lawn. Though the site is not actually on the beach, if it were any closer, you might consider wearing a bathing suit!

The most popular ceremony spot is a circular platform near the cliff's edge at one end of the lawn. Although the setting doesn't require it, you can put up a wedding arch or a set of faux Roman columns here if you like. Since this site faces due west, your guests can watch the sun sink behind the two of you while you say your vows. Another option is getting married at the other end of the lawn in an airy white gazebo.

Guests are seated on the dance floor during the ceremony; afterwards they stroll over to the lawn to enjoy cocktails and hors d'oeuvres, while tables are set up around the dance floor for the reception. In the evening, street lamps and twinkle lights augment the glow of candlelit tables, as the waves below murmur a soothing accompaniment.

Aside from its stellar location, the thing that makes the Cliffs at Laguna Village so special is the outstanding service you'll get from *Occasions at Laguna Village,* the on-site coordinator. If you're a fan of "one-stop shopping," this is the place for you. Occasions can provide anything and everything else you might desire, including catering, linens, flowers, entertainment, lighting, market umbrellas and potted palms. So if you think that the words "effortless" and "seaside celebration" can't possibly appear in the same sentence, look into the Cliffs at Laguna Village. Here, you'll be able to have the oceanfront party of your dreams without getting sand in your shoes.

CEREMONY CAPACITY: The Cliffs holds up to 175 seated guests outdoors.

EVENT/RECEPTION & MEETING CAPACITY: This location seats up to 175 guests.

FEES & DEPOSITS: A $7,000 nonrefundable deposit is required, which covers a percentage of the anticipated food and beverage total and rental fee. 50% of the estimated event total is due 3 months prior to the event, and the balance is due 60 days prior. Rental fees range $1,500–4,800. Meals start at $50/person. Packages include tax and staffing charges; alcohol is additional.

AVAILABILITY: Year-round, daily, 9am–10pm in 4-hour time blocks; overtime can be arranged at an additional cost.

SERVICES/AMENITIES:

Catering: in-house, no BYO

Kitchen Facilities: n/a

Tables & Chairs: provided

Linens, Silver, etc.: provided

Restrooms: wheelchair accessible

Dance Floor: provided

Bride's Dressing Area: no

Meeting Equipment: CBA, extra charge

Parking: valet and shuttle required

Accommodations: no guest rooms

Telephone: no

Outdoor Night Lighting: yes

Outdoor Cooking Facilities: CBA

Cleanup: provided

View: panorama of ocean and cityscape

Other: event coordination

RESTRICTIONS:

Alcohol: in-house, no BYO

Smoking: outside only

Music: amplified OK with volume limits, 10pm music curfew

Wheelchair Access: yes

Insurance: required for vendors only

Other: no rice, confetti or birdseed

Hotel Laguna

Waterfront Hotel

425 South Coast Highway, Laguna Beach

949/494-1151

www.hotellaguna.com
sarah@hotellaguna.com
facebook.com/hotellaguna, Twitter: @Hotel_Laguna

- Rehearsal Dinners
- Ceremonies
- Wedding Receptions
- Private Parties
- Corporate Events
- Meetings
- Film Shoots
- Accommodations

The first grand hotel to grace Laguna Beach and the getaway of choice for Golden Age of Hollywood movie stars like Errol Flynn, John Barrymore, Humphrey Bogart and Lauren Bacall, iconic Hotel Laguna is viewed with equal reverence by locals and visitors. Situated in the heart of Downtown Laguna Beach, this landmark building's delightful blend of Old World charm and California-casual style has been pleasing guests for decades … and it's still an oceanfront favorite.

The small private beach at the foot of the property is perhaps the most popular spot in the area for an outdoor wedding ceremony. Couples can get married here with the ocean quite literally at their feet and the surf tumbling in a few yards away. Larger outdoor ceremonies are held in the hotel's lovely Rose Garden, with its Victorian gazebo and Spanish-tile fountain. Surrounded by climbing bougainvillea, colorful hibiscus, and—of course—roses, it's also a great place to stage anything from a cocktail reception to a rocking dance party.

But for a party that's practically on the beach, there's no place like the Laguna Room. Outfitted with fresh white curtains and champagne-colored carpeting, it has a built-in dance floor, oak-and-granite bar, private restrooms and a small foyer/lounge. Its ceiling slopes down to sliding glass windows that frame an expansive ocean view and open onto the Laguna Room balcony, situated right over the beach. Revelers can dance here, indoors or out, with ocean breezes to keep them naturally cool—and the acoustics inside are excellent.

But these aren't the only options for entertaining in this vibrant and widely adored venue. Serve up cocktails or bites in the Catalina Room, where a highly polished granite fireplace set on a wide granite platform with built-in granite benches is large enough to act as a small stage. Windows and doors provide access to the OceanView Bar & Grill's terrace, outdoor walkways and panoramic Pacific views. Party often? How about sipping in Claes' Wine Cellar, where the rich Merlot-colored carpet, handcrafted floor-to-ceiling mahogany wine cabinets, and a cherrywood chef's table create a subtly glamorous dining ambiance. The smoked glass vitrine full of the owner's food and wine competition medals speaks to this venue's award-winning culinary expertise. Or gather your small group of guests for a private rehearsal dinner or extra-intimate reception in the handsomely appointed San Clemente Room, located inside the Claes Dining Room. This cozy event space shares décor elements and gorgeous views with the dining room—which, incidentally, can be bought out for private functions.

When the celebration is over, don't make the mistake of leaving right away. The artsy community of Laguna Beach has so much to offer, and this is the perfect home away from home from which to enjoy it. Snag the Bogart or Errol Flynn suite, book an après-party at OceanView Bar & Grill, and ease into a little vacation fun on California's own Riviera.

CEREMONY CAPACITY: The site holds up to 150 seated guests outdoors, and white chairs are provided.

EVENT/RECEPTION CAPACITY: The facility can accommodate 150 seated or 180 standing guests indoors, and 130 seated or 180 standing outdoors

MEETING CAPACITY: Meeting spaces seat up to 180 guests.

FEES & DEPOSITS: A deposit in the amount of the rental fee is required to reserve your date. The estimated event total balance is due 14 days prior to the event. The rental fee for a ceremony and reception is $2,500 with a ceremony in the Victorian Rose Garden or $3,000 with a ceremony on the beach. The fee includes the ceremony and reception sites with full guest seating, an over-night stay with champagne in the Bridal Suite for the couple, and a 2-hour changing room for the groom and groomsmen. The Bridal Suite serves as the bride's dressing room during the day. Room rental fees for a reception only range $200–1,000 depending on the space rented. Meals range $28–75/person. Tax, alcohol and a 20% service charge are additional.

AVAILABILITY: Year-round, daily, 6am–midnight.

SERVICES/AMENITIES:

Catering: in-house
Kitchen Facilities: n/a
Tables & Chairs: provided
Linens, Silver, etc.: provided
Restrooms: wheelchair accessible
Dance Floor: provided, or BYO
Bride's Dressing Area: yes, with ceremony
Meeting Equipment: some provided, or BYO
Other: spa services, AV equipment, event coordination

Parking: valet available; self-parking nearby
Accommodations: 65 guest rooms
Telephone: house or guest phones
Outdoor Night Lighting: yes
Outdoor Cooking Facilities: no
Cleanup: provided
View: fountain, garden, courtyard; panorama of ocean and coastline

RESTRICTIONS:

Alcohol: in-house, no BYO
Smoking: not allowed
Music: amplified OK with restrictions

Wheelchair Access: yes
Insurance: not required

This is important! Tell venues you're reading HERE COMES THE GUIDE and ask if our information is still current.

365

La Casa del Camino

Historic Boutique Hotel

1289 South Coast Highway, Laguna Beach

949/315-2224

www.lacasadelcamino.com
events@casaresortsinc.com

- Rehearsal Dinners
- Ceremonies
- Wedding Receptions
- Private Parties
- Corporate Events
- Meetings
- Film Shoots
- Accommodations

Even in a town as picturesque as Laguna Beach, the utterly charming La Casa del Camino is in a class by itself. With an alluring mix of waterfront location, early Spanish Mediterranean architecture and expansive views of the Pacific Ocean, this landmark boutique hotel is a standout choice for a romantic wedding celebration.

Built in 1929 and distinguished by its red-tiled roof, classic archways and wooden balconies, this beachside gem provides a tantalizing peek at a time when it was a favorite getaway for Hollywood stars and starlets. Combine that historic cachet with what today's La Casa del Camino has to offer—the hip energy of its wildly popular K'ya Bistro Bar and its open-air rooftop retreat with unparalleled ocean vistas—and you get the quintessential Laguna Beach experience.

The first thing that greets you here is the beautiful lobby, a welcoming Spanish-Mediterranean-style space with high plaster ceilings accented with wooden crossbeams. There's a baby grand piano off to the right, while on the left you'll find an adobe-style fireplace topped with a tiled niche displaying flickering candles that cast a warm glow. This large-yet-cozy setting is perfect for hosting friends and family for cocktails, dinner or dancing.

But without doubt, the _pièce de résistance_ at La Casa del Camino is its Rooftop Lounge. The only one like it in Laguna Beach, it serves up a 360-degree panorama with head-on ocean views. This sprawling, wraparound deck and full-service bar is a spectacular wedding site: You can make a dramatic entrance through a tile-roofed private portal and exchange vows in front of an infinite expanse of sparkling blue water. Your nearest and dearest gather around you in semicircular seating, giving everyone a great vantage for watching the ceremony. Afterwards, invite everyone to enjoy an al fresco toast and bask in the cool marine breezes before sitting down at beautifully appointed tables. Then dine in the company of the surrounding sea and sky.

And if one perfect day is just not enough, you might want to consider reserving the entire hotel for a weekend. Their Spanish-style guest rooms are done in rich, warm tones and feature intricately hand-carved wood furnishings, while the ten Surf Suites offer a more contemporary "beach" vibe. Each one-of-a-kind suite has been branded by a different surf company—like Rip Curl, Roxy, Quiksilver, and Billabong—and incorporates design elements and colors selected by that company. Your out-of-town guests will love spending an extra day or two here, so that they can truly savor their time with you at this wonderful home-away-from-home.

CEREMONY & EVENT/RECEPTION CAPACITY: The hotel holds 120 seated or 150 standing guests indoors and 120 seated or standing outdoors.

MEETING CAPACITY: Meeting spaces seat 25 guests indoors.

FEES & DEPOSITS: 30% of the total event cost is required to reserve your date and the balance is due prior to the event. Rental fees range up to $3,500 depending on the guest count and the season rented. Please inquire directly about our all-inclusive buyout packages. Meals range $49–69/person. Tax, alcohol and a 21% service charge are additional.

AVAILABILITY: Year-round, daily, 8am–10pm.

SERVICES/AMENITIES:

Catering: in-house
Kitchen Facilities: n/a
Tables & Chairs: provided
Linens, Silver, etc.: provided
Restrooms: wheelchair accessible
Dance Floor: CBA
Bride's Dressing Area: CBA
Meeting Equipment: CBA
Other: coordination, AV equipment

Parking: on street, valet optional
Accommodations: 40 guest rooms
Telephone: emergency use only
Outdoor Night Lighting: yes
Outdoor Cooking Facilities: none
Cleanup: provided
View: landscaped grounds; panorama of coastline, hills and ocean

RESTRICTIONS:

Alcohol: in-house
Smoking: not allowed
Music: non-percussion acoustic or amplified (recorded only) with volume restrictions

Wheelchair Access: yes
Insurance: not required

[seven-degrees]

891 Laguna Canyon Road, Laguna Beach
949/376-1555
www.seven-degrees.com
dora@seven-degrees.com

Special Events Venue

● Rehearsal Dinners	● Corporate Events
● Ceremonies	● Meetings
● Wedding Receptions	● Film Shoots
● Private Parties	Accommodations

Attracted by the balmy weather, azure ocean, and la dolce vita of a small seaside town, scores of artists settled in Laguna Beach in the early 20th century. In fact, the first art museum in California was founded here in 1918. Since then the city has established itself as a major player in the art world, hosting numerous galleries and summer art festivals, proud and indulgent of its boho-chic artist population.

Perhaps the most remarkable addition to the city's art community is [seven-degrees], a "multi-purpose idea lab for the promotion of artistic endeavor, invention and exhibition." Built in 2001, its mission is not only to showcase original art but to support the efforts of emerging artists through its in-residence programs. And fortunately for you, one of the ways this innovative entity sustains itself financially is to make its unique facilities available for special events.

Nestled in Laguna Canyon a few blocks from the ocean, this uber-modern glass, steel and granite complex is a visual marvel. The all-glass façade, whose asymmetry and angular lines defy conventional architecture, reflects the surrounding canyon walls while revealing the artwork displayed inside.

When you have an event here, you immediately become part of the art scene. Enter through the gallery, where you and your guests can peruse the exhibition du jour. Then pass by the live/work studios of the artists-in-residence, which are often open for viewing works in progress. Before the festivities begin, mingle with family and friends in the courtyard between buildings or ascend to the Hillside Terrace, a tentable rooftop patio with multiple uses. Ceremonies are often held here, but the space is also perfect for an outdoor cocktail reception. In addition to canyon views, there are meandering trails with bamboo railings, leading to a series of overlooks built into the canyon walls. A gentle waterfall and lush plantings among the rocks make this setting an unexpected oasis.

Nature takes a back seat to your own creativity in the Media Lounge. Unadorned, it's a simple, 4,500-square-foot oblong room with gray concrete walls and floors. But with the help of an in-house design team, the latest in lighting technology and a phalanx of on-site audiovisual equipment, you'll be able to transform the space into anything you like. Past metamorphoses include a Rococo-style ballroom with gilded mirrors and jacquard textiles; a midsummer night's dream with a forest's worth of potted plants and flowers; and a postmodern discothèque thumping with sound and light. Live webcasting is available, and you can even project an image of yourselves (or anyone else!) on internal or external surfaces. Your guests will be part of an unforgettable multimedia experience, limited only by your imagination (and your budget). [seven-degrees] is a true original in the world of event venues, a place inspired by and dedicated to art. Whether you're planning a wedding, a corporate party or any other celebration here, you'll enjoy being an honored artist-in-residence for the day.

CEREMONY CAPACITY: The Hillside Terrace holds up to 150 seated or 300 with some standing guests.

EVENT/RECEPTION & MEETING CAPACITY: The Media Lounge holds up to 300 seated or 388 standing guests.

FEES & DEPOSITS: A $5,000 nonrefundable deposit is required to reserve your date. A payment schedule is agreed upon, with the balance paid in full 30 days prior to the event. Dinners start at $57/person. Tax, alcohol and service charge additional. Full-service packages available; call for details.

AVAILABILITY: Year-round, daily, until 1am. Events take place in 5-hour blocks of time.

SERVICES/AMENITIES:

Catering: in-house or BYO with approval
Kitchen Facilities: full commercial kitchen
Tables & Chairs: included with wedding portfolio
Linens, Silver, etc.: included with wedding portfolio
Restrooms: wheelchair accessible
Dance Floor: yes
Bride's Dressing Area: yes
Meeting Equipment: yes

Parking: large lot
Accommodations: no guest rooms
Telephone: house phone
Outdoor Night Lighting: full specialty lighting
Outdoor Cooking Facilities: CBA
Cleanup: provided, extra fee
View: terraced hillside garden
Other: event coordination, florals & décor, off-site catering available

RESTRICTIONS:

Alcohol: in-house, no BYO
Smoking: outdoors only
Music: amplified OK

Wheelchair Access: yes
Insurance: only required for outside vendors

Surf & Sand Resort

Waterfront Resort

1555 South Coast Highway, Laguna Beach
949/497-4477
www.surfandsandresort.com/weddings.html
surfsales@jcresorts.com

- Rehearsal Dinners
- Ceremonies
- Wedding Receptions
- Private Parties
- Corporate Events
- Meetings
- Film Shoots
- Accommodations

Surf & Sand Resort is renowned for both its prime location in Laguna Beach and its proximity to the ocean. The high-rise hotel sits so close to the water that it puts you quite literally—and hypnotically—right above the crashing surf. If you haven't seen it yet, check out the Mediterranean-style Conference Center, a separate event venue that adds to Surf & Sand's reputation as a place where you can have it all—a corporate gala, an executive meeting or a lovely wedding.

"Conference Center" doesn't do justice to the banquet rooms—the Pelican and Sand Dollar—which are decorated in a Mediterranean beach-luxe style that could grace the pages of *Architectural Digest*. Each one is a handsome and tasteful mix of blond hardwoods, airy hues of sand and cream, coffered ceilings, lots of whitewashed wood-shuttered windows, neoclassical appointments and unique works of art.

Ceremonies at Surf & Sand take place on the Catalina Terrace and on the Ocean Terrace, where you'll have a breathtaking view of Catalina Island while the breaking waves resound just below your feet. After the wedding, guests head off to the largest reception space, the Pelican Room, which has a graceful foyer and a terrace with a view of the hotel and the ocean. Perfectly suited for mid-sized groups, the Sand Dollar Room is complemented by a series of archways forming a patio covered with vinery. And just outside the Sand Castle Room, you'll find a babbling fountain and a peek of the ocean below.

After your event, stay a while longer, or better yet, have your honeymoon here. All of Surf & Sand's luxurious accommodations have seaview balconies, all with commanding views of the Pacific Ocean. While there are plenty of nearby places to go sightseeing or shopping (Laguna Beach boutiques and galleries are within walking distance), you may just want to pamper yourself at the resort's AquaTerra Spa or sink back in your poolside deck chair or beach chair on the sand and enjoy the sun's warmth. With its seabreeze air plus ocean and sunset vistas, Surf & Sand is an exhilarating locale for any celebration.

CEREMONY CAPACITY: The Ocean Terrace can accommodate 80 seated, the Catalina Terrace 180 seated, and South Beach can accommodate up to 80 standing guests.

EVENT/RECEPTION CAPACITY: With dance floor, the Pelican Room holds 180 seated, the Sand Dollar Room 80 seated, the Sand Castle Room 60 seated.

MEETING CAPACITY: Please contact the facility for detailed information regarding meetings.

FEES & DEPOSITS: For weddings, deposits vary based on the food and beverage minimums for your event. The ceremony rental and setup fees range $950–4,000, and vary by location and season. Seated luncheons start at $42/person; dinners start at $78/person. Beverages, tax and service charge are additional.

AVAILABILITY: Year-round, daily.

SERVICES/AMENITIES:

Catering: in-house, no BYO
Kitchen Facilities: n/a
Tables & Chairs: provided
Linens, Silver, etc.: provided
Restrooms: wheelchair accessible
Dance Floor: provided
Bride's Dressing Area: yes
Meeting Equipment: full range, including AV

Parking: valet, nominal fee
Accommodations: 167 guest rooms
Telephone: pay phones
Outdoor Night Lighting: access only
Outdoor Cooking Facilities: no
Cleanup: provided
View: Pacific Ocean, coastal hills, Catalina Island, sunsets

RESTRICTIONS:

Alcohol: in-house, no BYO
Smoking: not allowed
Music: amplified OK

Wheelchair Access: limited
Insurance: not required

The Hills Hotel

25205 La Paz Road, Laguna Hills
949/268-9246, 949/586-5000
www.thelagunahillshotel.com
catering@thelagunahillshotel.com

Ballroom & Hotel

- Rehearsal Dinners
- Ceremonies
- Wedding Receptions
- Private Parties
- Corporate Events
- Meetings
- Film Shoots
- Accommodations

If first impressions make a lasting impression, then The Hills Hotel is a place you're definitely going to remember. After a multimillion-dollar transformation, this boutique hotel is now a trendy, upscale venue for special events.

A grand staircase leads up to the Mezzanine level, where you'll find five event spaces that you can use in the way that best suits your wedding or private party. Guests can mingle in any of the four prefunction areas, which flow from one to another. Each has its own ambiance and all are set with cocktail tables that feature large crystal vases filled with white branches. Walls are covered in light gray leather panels, an understated backdrop to the iridescent glass-tile sign that announces the adjoining ballroom.

Embossed, custom-designed doors open to the Crystal Ballroom, which lives up to its name. Formal and elegant, it's outfitted with crown molding, mirror-backed wall sconces and six glittering beaded crystal chandeliers ringed with sparkling "candles." The walls have a subtle shimmer, thanks to ground crystals embedded in the pearl-colored paper. Colored LED lights in the coffered ceiling allow you to create whatever atmosphere you desire: Choose shades of blue or purple for a sultry, nightclub feeling, or use pink or amber tones for something more romantic or festive. Chiavari chairs (available in a selection of colors) add a sophisticated touch.

Ceremonies can take place in the Crystal Ballroom, but they're often held in the Veranda, an atrium-style corridor that runs the length of the ballroom. Light comes from seven crystal chandeliers suspended from the tray ceiling, as well as from a wall of windows overlooking the trees right outside and the mountains in the distance. This area is also well suited for a cocktail reception or a buffet setup during dinner in the ballroom.

The Crystal Lounge is ideal for relaxing on white tufted benches while sipping cocktails, sampling appetizers and perhaps watching the bride and groom's life stories playing on TV monitors. The Patio, which is staged with lounge furniture, provides another comfortable spot. It has a fuel-burning fireplace and TV monitor, and can double as a cigar lounge.

Couples getting married here have two additional ceremony options: the Garnet Gallery and poolside. All ceremonies include the rehearsal and the assistance of an on-staff coordinator.

The hotel's wedding packages offer a long list of amenities: a champagne toast, the meal, wedding cake, linens, lighting, dance floor, and more. And when the wedding comes to a close, the newlyweds can retire to their complimentary room, where a sweet gift of champagne and chocolate-covered strawberries awaits. The next morning, they'll enjoy a complimentary breakfast in bed or in the hotel restaurant.

Close to beaches, art galleries, shopping, fine dining, local attractions and more, The Hills Hotel is a convenient choice for a destination wedding.

CEREMONY CAPACITY: The site holds 300 seated guests indoors and 150 seated outdoors.

EVENT/RECEPTION CAPACITY: The Crystal Ballroom can accommodate 300 seated or 400 standing guests indoors. The poolside area holds 80 seated or 100 standing outdoors.

MEETING CAPACITY: The site holds 400 guests seated theater-style.

FEES & DEPOSITS: A deposit is required to reserve your date. 50% of the estimated balance is due 180 days prior, and the balance is due 14 days prior to the event. Packages start at $55/person. Tax, alcohol and a service charge are additional.

AVAILABILITY: Year-round, daily, anytime.

SERVICES/AMENITIES:

Catering: in-house or BYO with approval
Kitchen Facilities: fully equipped
Tables & Chairs: Chiavari chairs included
Linens, Silver, etc.: floor length satin linens included
Restrooms: wheelchair accessible
Dance Floor: provided
Bride's Dressing Area: yes
Meeting Equipment: provided
Other: event coordination

Parking: complimentary in large lot, or valet service, extra fee
Accommodations: 147 guest rooms
Telephone: emergency use only
Outdoor Night Lighting: no
Outdoor Cooking Facilities: no
Cleanup: provided
View: panorama of hills and mountains

RESTRICTIONS:

Alcohol: in-house or BYO wine with corkage fee
Smoking: outdoor terraces only
Music: amplified OK

Wheelchair Access: yes
Insurance: not required unless providing outside catering

Overwhelmed? Use the search criteria on www.HereComesTheGuide.com to narrow down your choices.

373

Pacific Hills Banquet and Catering

Banquet Facility

23551 Moulton Parkway, Laguna Hills

949/707-1707

www.ocevent.com
info@ocevent.com

Rehearsal Dinners	● Corporate Events
● Ceremonies	● Meetings
● Wedding Receptions	● Film Shoots
● Private Parties	Accommodations

One of the largest privately held venues in Orange County, Pacific Hills has developed an enviable word-of-mouth reputation for its value, sophisticated level of service, flexibility, and a kitchen that is expert at virtually any cuisine. Orange County's cosmopolitan brides have discovered that this facility can accommodate almost any kind of wedding ceremony, reception and menu they can imagine, and there's one more thing they love: knowing that they'll have exclusive use of the facility for their event.

Pacific Hills displays its charms as soon as you arrive. Its entrance, an appealing Mediterranean-style courtyard edged with marigolds and birds of paradise, leads to a formidable arch-shaped wooden door. The door opens to a grand high-ceilinged foyer, lined with urns and crowned with a dramatic iron chandelier. A left turn takes you into a bright reception room, decorated with yet more imposing chandeliers and boasting substantial columns that separate a bar and gathering space from the ballroom lobby. An ensemble of wrought-iron railings angle their way up and down various ramps and stairs, creating a pleasingly energetic and entertaining visual effect.

All this, of course, is a prelude to the ballroom itself, which has crystal-beaded chandeliers, deep carpeting, creamy white wainscoting and eggshell-colored walls. The magnificent 9,000-square-foot space is like a blank canvas—what you do with it can range from simple to sumptuous. Lighting and decorating effects are almost unlimited, enabling you to create a magical setting.

Brides are always the center of attention here, and Pacific Hills pampers them. Up a stairway off the reception area, away from the clamor of happy celebrants, there's a dressing room with its own private entrance. It features a bathroom and shower, as well as plush carpeting and two large mirrors, positioned so that the bride and her entourage can see themselves from all sides.

Actually, the VIP treatment starts even before the wedding day. The on-site event coordinators pride themselves on "going the whole nine yards," which means taking care of everything from planning, photography and entertainment to decorations, the wedding cake and the reception. Before a prospective bride makes any decisions, Pacific Hills plays a short video for her that features various table settings and configurations. With a hauntingly romantic background track by Irish songstress Enya, the video takes a wonderful "show, don't tell" approach that helps a bride see just how many great decorating options are possible.

Pacific Hills says it wants to provide "the luxury of a four-star venue but with much friendlier prices." Judging from the hundreds of couples who choose to celebrate their wedding here, they've been extremely successful in achieving their goal.

CEREMONY CAPACITY: The venue can accommodate 275 seated guests.

EVENT/RECEPTION & MEETING CAPACITY: The site holds up to 600 guests.

FEES & DEPOSITS: A $2,500 deposit is required to reserve your date. 50% of the estimated event total is required 6 months prior to the event, and the remaining balance is due 14 days prior to the event. Meals range $35–55/person. Tax, alcohol and a 19% service charge are additional.

AVAILABILITY: Year-round, daily. Monday–Friday, 6pm–midnight; all day on Saturday and Sunday.

SERVICES/AMENITIES:

Catering: in-house, no BYO
Kitchen Facilities: n/a
Tables & Chairs: provided
Linens, Silver, etc.: provided
Restrooms: wheelchair accessible
Dance Floor: yes
Bride's Dressing Area: yes
Meeting Equipment: CBA, extra charge

Parking: complimentary
Accommodations: no guest rooms
Telephone: pay phone
Outdoor Night Lighting: yes
Outdoor Cooking Facilities: no
Cleanup: provided
View: garden patio
Other: event coordination, full-service planning

RESTRICTIONS:

Alcohol: in-house, no BYO
Smoking: designated area only
Music: amplified OK indoors

Wheelchair Access: yes
Insurance: not required

Balboa Bay Resort

1221 West Coast Highway, Newport Beach

949/630-4125

www.balboabayresort.com
sales@balboabayresort.com

Waterfront Hotel and Resort

- Rehearsal Dinners
- Ceremonies
- Wedding Receptions
- Private Parties
- Corporate Events
- Meetings
- Film Shoots
- Accommodations

Sprawled along 15½ glorious acres of Orange County's picturesque coastline, Balboa Bay Resort invites you to experience the quintessential Southern California lifestyle. This stunning Mediterranean-inspired oasis is part of the exclusive Meritage Collection of luxury resorts, and offers a sophisticated yet relaxed setting, complete with sunshine, fresh sea breezes and marina views. And as the only AAA Four Diamond and waterfront resort in Newport Beach, it shines as a standout destination wedding venue.

If you're a bride who relishes the spotlight, consider making a unique entrance by yacht, disembarking at Balboa Bay Resort's private dock. Say your vows on the magnificent Beach Front Lawn, bordered by palm trees and overlooking the resort's pristine private beach and Newport Bay. For a more intimate ceremony, tie the knot on the secluded Bay Front Lawn, a hidden waterview garden sheltered by tall greenery. With a panaroma that encompasses the sea, sky and multimillion-dollar bayfront homes, both sites epitomize the romance of California's Gold Coast.

Next, as your photographer captures memories by the bay, your guests get better acquainted over cocktails in the stylish Commodore Room and adjoining bayview patio. Or stage a festive social hour out on the Coconut Grove Courtyard, an al fresco terrace where guests mingle amidst giant palms and banana plants. Receptions are simply dazzling in the Grand Ballroom, a magnificent 7,000-square-foot space with arched doorways and rich burgundy and gold fabrics that convey a refined elegance. The lofty 18-foot ceiling boasts five crystal-and-pearl chandeliers that enhance the ballroom's sparkle and drama.

As you would expect at such an upscale resort, considerable attention is paid to the cuisine, and a range of reception packages include everything from show-off displays and exquisite hors d'oeuvres to staffed carving stations. Menus, which can be customized, feature award-winning, artistically presented continental dishes made with the freshest seasonal ingredients. From planning to celebration, you'll be guided by highly trained and innovative professionals dedicated to personalizing your occasion with creative ideas, specialty décor and flawless execution.

The self-contained resort hosts other wedding-related activities with equal aplomb. Launch your festivities with a themed rehearsal dinner—perhaps a poolside barbecue or a casual beach luau. After-parties are a hit at Duke's Place, a harborfront lounge with live musical entertainment and dancing. At evening's end, retire to your spacious, well-appointed guest room or suite, and admire the starscape from your private balcony. Throughout your wedding weekend, you and your guests will receive plenty of So Cal-style pampering, from exceptional personalized service to the resort's deluxe full-service spa and beauty salon. (Ask about the "Brides and Bridesmaids" Spa Package!) Then, after a memorable stay, bid a fond farewell to your family and friends with a delicious brunch at First Cabin Restaurant, and enjoy one last gorgeous view of Newport Harbor and its colorful boats.

For your own grand finale, cruise through scenic Newport Harbor in a gondola and return to the resort for a romantic honeymoon. Indulge in a massage for two, share a repast and a bottle of wine while admiring the sunset, and settle into your plush bayview suite. Everything is, indeed, perfection at Newport's outstanding resort on the bay.

CEREMONY CAPACITY: The facility accommodates 300 seated guests outdoors.

EVENT/RECEPTION CAPACITY: The hotel holds 450 seated or 700 standing guests indoors and 200 seated or 400 standing outdoors.

MEETING CAPACITY: Meeting spaces hold up to 600 seated guests.

FEES & DEPOSITS: A deposit is required to reserve your date and the balance is due 2 weeks prior to the event. Deposit amounts vary depending on cost estimate. Luncheons start at $42/person and dinners start at $64/person. Tax, alcohol and a 22% service charge are additional.

AVAILABILITY: Year-round, daily, 6am–midnight, with some exceptions.

SERVICES/AMENITIES:

Catering: in-house, or BYO ethnic or kosher caterer
Kitchen Facilities: n/a
Tables & Chairs: provided
Linens, Silver, etc.: provided
Restrooms: wheelchair accessible
Dance Floor: portable provided
Bride's Dressing Area: CBA
Meeting Equipment: CBA
Other: grand piano, spa services, AV equipment

Parking: valet required
Accommodations: 159 guest rooms
Telephone: house phone
Outdoor Night Lighting: CBA
Outdoor Cooking Facilities: BBQ CBA
Cleanup: provided
View: garden courtyard, Newport Harbor, landscaped grounds, pool area

RESTRICTIONS:

Alcohol: in-house
Smoking: outdoors only
Music: amplified OK

Wheelchair Access: yes
Insurance: not required

Electra Cruises

Yachts

3439 Via Oporto, Newport Beach
949/723-1069, 800/952-9955
www.electracruises.com
aboardelec@aol.com

- Rehearsal Dinners
- Ceremonies
- Wedding Receptions
- Private Parties
- Corporate Events
- Meetings
- Film Shoots
- Accommodations

In Newport Beach, when people talk about the "prettiest lady" in the harbor, they're not referring to one of Newport's many long-limbed beach beauties, but rather to *Electra*—a 100-foot, classic fantail yacht in her sixties.

Built in 1929 by A.W. Leonard, the president of Puget Sound Power and Light of Seattle, *Electra* (meaning "shining one" in Greek) was given to Leonard's wife as a Valentine's Day present. Since then, this graceful motorized yacht has led a romantic, colorful life. During WWII she was in the Navy's employ, chasing enemy submarines off Washington's coast. Later, she journeyed to Newport Beach, where she was revamped into a "party" boat.

Thankfully, publishing magnate Fred Ruffner rescued *Electra* and spared her further indignities by moving her to Ft. Lauderdale, where she was lovingly restored. Current owner Randy Goodman was a young man growing up in Newport Beach when he first set eyes on *Electra* and fell in love. Years later, still smitten, he tracked her down in Antigua, and sailed her back to Newport Bay—a stormy 42-day voyage which she endured with nary a scratch. Now, *Electra* plies the West Coast waters and is a popular setting for weddings, corporate dinner cruises and private parties.

Love at first sight is a common response to *Electra*. It's easy to see why—with her dazzling white wood hull trimmed in burnished mahogany, and her brightwork winking in the sun, she is no less beautiful now than on that Valentine's Day so many years ago. Tie the knot on the top aft deck, accompanied by a blast of the ship's horn to commemorate the event. Après ceremony, enjoy hors d'oeuvres and spirits with your guests in the main salon, where you can admire the stenciled wood beams overhead. Or, if you wish, take advantage of the sidedecks that run the length of the vessel to wander freely and explore all of *Electra's* vintage features. Creaky but seaworthy stairs lead to the lower deck, where guests can peek at the elegantly decorated staterooms. The technically curious will want to take a look at the navigational instrumentation and the original mahogany-and-brass wheel in the captain's wheelhouse. Others will prefer to relax on the foredeck's cushioned benches and bask in the sun's rays, misted by ocean spray. With its distinctive, old-fashioned charm *Electra* is a novel setting for any event. Here, you can savor "the remembrance of things past," while enjoying the promise of things to come.

The *Electra* is only one of several cruising options. The slightly larger *Athena,* a 110-foot motor yacht with three levels, has a main salon with full bar, baby grand piano and leather lounges. The top deck is covered for comfort, and has large picture windows for watching the coastline go by. It also has a full bar, a music center and a sizeable area for dancing. The lower deck includes a large bridal dressing room with floor length wall-to-wall mirrors. At 83 feet, the New Orleans-style paddlewheeler *Newport Princess* is a charming, Old World Mississippi riverboat with a lot of character. Another addition to the fleet is *Camelot,* a 141-foot ADA approved yacht. As with *Destiny,* a 125-foot vessel, it features an abundance of glass and ultra-modern décor. Electra Cruises' newest and largest yacht is the 140-foot, ADA-approved *Crystal.* Spacious enough for 330 guests and outfitted with an elevator, it's perfect for a large wedding, corporate event, or unique meeting.

CEREMONY CAPACITY: *Electra's* top deck holds 105 seated guests. The *Athena* and *Destiny* each hold 150, the *Newport Princess* up to 250, and the *Crystal* can accommodate 330 guests.

EVENT/RECEPTION & MEETING CAPACITY: The *Electra* holds up to 150 guests, maximum. The *Athena* and *Destiny* each hold 150, the *Newport Princess* 250, and the *Crystal* can accommodate 330 guests.

FEES & DEPOSITS: A $2,000 deposit is required to secure your date; the estimated balance and a $500 refundable security/damage deposit are payable 14 days prior to the event. Electra Cruises offers full wedding packages starting at $72/person. They include the yacht charter, service staff, catering, wedding cake, bar service, rentals, florals, DJ, photographer, event coordinator and a captain to perform the ceremony. Tax is additional. For weddings on the other vessels, packages range $59–94/person based on 100 guests.

AVAILABILITY: Year-round, daily including holidays, anytime.

SERVICES/AMENITIES:

Catering: in-house or BYO with approval
Kitchen Facilities: full galley
Tables & Chairs: provided
Linens, Silver, etc.: provided
Restrooms: wheelchair accessible
Dance Floor: on top deck
Bride's & Groom's Dressing Area: yes
Meeting Equipment: full range CBA
Other: full event coordination

Parking: self-parking or valet, extra charge
Accommodations: no guest rooms
Telephone: ship-to-shore
Outdoor Night Lighting: yes
Outdoor Cooking Facilities: no
Cleanup: provided
View: Pacific Ocean, Newport Harbor and city skyline

RESTRICTIONS:

Alcohol: in-house, no BYO
Smoking: non-carpeted areas
Music: amplified OK

Wheelchair Access: yes
Insurance: not required
Other: no rice or birdseed

Environmental Nature Center

1601 16th Street, Newport Beach

949/645-8489

www.encenter.org
sarah@encenter.org

Community Center

- Rehearsal Dinners
- Ceremonies
- Wedding Receptions
- Private Parties
- Corporate Events
- Meetings
- Film Shoots
- Accommodations

Building a beautiful future together? How about starting it out with a fabulous eco-friendly celebration at the Environmental Nature Center. This award-winning venue has a dreamy 8,500-square-foot facility with halls, patios, and native gardens planted in the midst of its gorgeous 3.5-acre natural setting. The first building in Orange County to achieve Leadership in Energy and Environmental Design (LEED) Platinum Certification, it features energy-conserving climate control, water efficient systems and fixtures, and the imaginative use of recycled and recyclable materials throughout.

Begin your party in the Center's airy Museum, where guests can marvel at the effortless integration of "green" building solutions into stylish contemporary design. The ENC actually produces more energy than it consumes, and a computer monitor in the hallway displays its usage levels. Guests will find plenty of interactive exhibits to explore and discuss, as they meet and greet one another before stepping out though the glass foldaway doors and onto the broad Garden Patio.

Flanked on one side by a catering prep kitchen and patio, library/lounge with private powder room for the bride and her attendants, and a butterfly garden…and on the other side by the pale desert shades and dramatic shapes of its California native gardens, this is a stunning outdoor venue—day or night—for your scrumptious seasonal, earth-friendly reception. It's also great for dancing under sunny skies or beneath a nighttime canopy of stars and the facility's softly luminous solar-powered lanterns. At the foot of the patio, a small amphitheater with built-in bench seating frames a large open fire pit that's ideal for an elegant version of a favorite campfire activity—that's right, how about toasting the good times with champagne and s'mores?

Wondering about indoor options? Follow the paw prints in the sand-textured walkway to the Oak and Sycamore Rooms, two cozy chambers separated by a movable airwall that can be used individually or combined into one large space. Well-equipped for just about any function, the rooms have picture windows, high ceilings, handsome honey-colored cabinets (composed of recycled materials like wheat chaff and sunflower seed), and AV and internet capability. Center staff can help by providing all kinds of exciting biodegradable and reusable decorating options.

For a surprisingly affordable celebration with the tiniest possible carbon footprint, consider a picnic wedding and reception. You can tie the knot in a picturesque way in the little garden amphitheater or at the end of the small garden stream. Then hold your reception amid berries and blossoms on picnic tables under the trees before releasing guests to wander off along the ENC's many enchanting paths. Whether your affair is large or small, you can be sure that you're doing the world a big favor when you have it here. And you're helping the local community, too, since your event fees are also recycled: Most of them go to supporting the Center's operating costs and programs, and a big portion of your bill is tax deductible, too.

CEREMONY, EVENT/RECEPTION & MEETING CAPACITY: The site holds 125 seated or 245 standing guests indoors or outdoors.

FEES & DEPOSITS: 20% of the total event cost plus tax-deductable membership and permit fees are required to reserve your date and the balance is due 4 weeks prior to the event. The rental fee (including membership) ranges $4,000–6,000.

AVAILABILITY: Year round, daily.

SERVICES/AMENITIES:

Catering: BYO
Kitchen Facilities: limited
Tables & Chairs: some provided
Linens, Silver, etc.: CBA
Restrooms: wheelchair accessible
Dance Floor: provided
Bride's & Groom's Dressing Area: CBA
Meeting Equipment: provided

Parking: large lot
Accommodations: no guest rooms
Telephone: emergency use only
Outdoor Night Lighting: yes
Outdoor Cooking Facilities: no
Cleanup: renter or caterer
View: creek, forest, courtyard, waterfall
Other: picnic area, AV equipment, fire ring and wood

RESTRICTIONS:

Alcohol: select from preferred vendor list
Smoking: not allowed
Music: amplified OK with restrictions

Wheelchair Access: yes
Insurance: liability required

The professionals in the back of this book are the best in the business. How do we know? Read page 549.

Fairmont Newport Beach

Resort Hotel

4500 MacArthur Boulevard, Newport Beach
949/476-2001 X4000
www.fairmont.com
tami.spencer@fairmont.com

● Rehearsal Dinners ● Corporate Events
● Ceremonies ● Meetings
● Wedding Receptions ● Film Shoots
● Private Parties ● Accommodations

After a $35 million makeover, the Fairmont Newport Beach is considered by many to be Orange County's finest luxury hotel. From the moment you step into its gleaming lobby, you'll be impressed with its dramatic new look and feel, and throughout your event here you'll experience the high level of hospitality and service the Fairmont name is known for worldwide. You'll also appreciate the hotel's enviable location: Set in one of Southern California's most affluent coastal cities, it's just a stone's throw from John Wayne Airport, world-class shopping, a multitude of recreational activities and many local beaches.

The Garden Gazebo, edged with multihued impatiens, has been designed for ceremonies. Secluded from hotel guests and protected by tall palms and ferns, it's very private and serene. After walking through an evergreen arch, you meet your groom under the ivory gazebo, which can be enhanced with floral garlands. Following the ceremony, the lovely surroundings serve as a picturesque backdrop for photography.

For your reception, choose from among several elegant ballrooms including the spacious Bay Laurel Ballroom, where you can dance the night away under a magnificent chandelier. In the garden-like Orchid Terrace, glass sliders and ceiling fans contribute to the indoor/outdoor feel. For a quintessential Southern California party, entertain your guests in the new Bamboo Garden with its fireplace, fire pit and water feature, or on the glorious Sky Palms pool deck, whose palm trees, umbrellas and cabanas set the stage for a memorable al fresco celebration. The hotel's cozy bambú Cellar Room is ideal for a rehearsal dinner or farewell brunch.

The Fairmont Newport Beach specializes in California cuisine, but they can customize a menu for you. Also, whether you're planning an intimate gathering or a full-scale gala, the hotel's wedding specialist will work with your wedding coordinator to make sure everything runs smoothly.

To take full advantage of all the Fairmont has to offer, you and your wedding party may want to indulge in an array of soothing treatments in the hotel's Amadeus spa. With more than 8,000 square feet of space and an extensive menu of services, this sanctuary for body and soul provides the ultimate in urban pampering.

One of California's most upscale playgrounds, Newport Beach is not only an A-list wedding location, it's a prime choice for a honeymoon or vacation. So why not extend your stay at this exceptional hotel—you'll have the pleasure of prolonging your Fairmont experience and treating yourself to a wonderful getaway.

CEREMONY CAPACITY: The Gazebo accommodates 250 seated and the Bamboo Garden area holds up to 400 seated guests.

EVENT/RECEPTION CAPACITY: The Ballroom/Bamboo Garden hold up to 500 seated guests.

MEETING CAPACITY: Several spaces hold 20–800 seated guests.

FEES & DEPOSITS: For weddings, a $3,000 nonrefundable deposit is payable when you make reservations. 50% of the anticipated event total is due 120 days before the event; the balance is payable 5 business days prior. Wedding packages start at $60/person for luncheons, $100/person for dinners. Packages include: white glove service of hors d'oeuvres, champagne toast, 2 bottles of wine per table and luxurious overnight accommodations for the bride and groom. Tax and a 22% service charge are additional. For ceremonies, the setup fee is $3,000.

For business meetings, room rental fees vary depending on room(s) reserved and services required; call for additional information.

AVAILABILITY: Weddings, year-round, daily, 11am–4pm or 6pm–midnight. Business functions or meetings, year-round, daily, anytime.

SERVICES/AMENITIES:

Catering: in-house
Kitchen Facilities: n/a
Tables & Chairs: provided
Linens, Silver, etc.: provided
Restrooms: wheelchair accessible
Dance Floor: provided
Bride's Dressing Area: yes
Meeting Equipment: full range

Parking: valet
Accommodations: 444 guest rooms and suites
Telephone: guest phones
Outdoor Night Lighting: at Gazebo only
Outdoor Cooking Facilities: no
Cleanup: provided
View: garden

RESTRICTIONS:

Alcohol: in-house, no BYO
Smoking: designated areas
Music: amplified OK

Wheelchair Access: yes
Insurance: liability required

Harborside Restaurant & Grand Ballroom

Waterfront Events Facility

400 Main Street, Newport Beach
949/673-4633
www.harborside-pavilion.com
banquets@harborside-pavilion.com

- Rehearsal Dinners
- Ceremonies
- Wedding Receptions
- Private Parties
- Corporate Events
- Meetings
- Film Shoots
- Accommodations

Few beach towns on the West Coast can rival Balboa, annexed to Newport Beach on a peninsula between the Pacific Ocean and Newport Bay. Everything about this small community is in perfect balance and proportion. The compact downtown is thriving, but not colonized by chain stores. The neighborhoods range from neatly trimmed cottages to the understated houses of the wealthy. The beach is wide, the municipal pier has a great burger shack and there's a classic bayside strand of amusement parlors, harbor tours and quaint shops that evoke all the heady sights and smells of life at the beach.

At the heart of town is the historic Balboa Pavilion, a majestic Victorian structure overlooking Newport Harbor that was built in 1905 at the foot of Main Street. From the water, the distinctive shape of this two-story building's steeply sloped roof has always made the Pavilion an instantly recognizable landmark. It climbs to a flag-tipped cupola that looks like an exclamation point—perhaps a proclamation of how good life is here. Generations of locals danced, fell in love and got married at the pavilion, and then returned years later to see their children do the same.

The Harborside Grand Ballroom, which is on the second floor of the Pavilion, has the best views of the bay in the harbor. Originally designed as an American answer to the palatial dance halls of early 20th-century Europe, the room is about 140 feet wide and has a huge dance floor. Today, almost everything in this great space is new: new granite tops on the two bars, new wallpaper, a new floor, a new ceiling and new carpeting. A glass-protected terrace just outside the larger of the bars—perfect for catching a breath of fresh air—has been freshly paned and painted. The elegant wide staircase that climbs from the front entryway to the ballroom—and makes a beautiful stage for a photogenic entrance—has been completely refurbished. The color palette of warm browns, creams and light greens is both sophisticated and unobtrusive. The ten-foot-high windows that line every inch of the ballroom on three sides are still here, as are the sweeping views out to Newport Bay.

When you reserve the ballroom, the experienced Harborside staff will assist you with every aspect of your event, from customizing your menu to helping you choose the right linens. They're also skilled at creating whatever celebration you have in mind, be it a formal black-tie affair, a Victorian or contemporary beach-themed wedding or a rousing casino night. As the Banquet Manager says, "There isn't anything we can't do."

The Harborside Restaurant & Grand Ballroom is unquestionably one of the best waterfront locations in Newport Beach. But for all its majesty, it never upstages the bride and groom: On their wedding day, when they are the rightful stars upon whom all eyes should fall, this splendid event space quietly serves as a memorable backdrop.

CEREMONY CAPACITY: This location holds up to 250 guests for a ceremony when combined with the reception.

EVENT/RECEPTION & MEETING CAPACITY: Harborside has two adjoining rooms with a capacity of 250 guests each, or used together for a total of 500 guests.

FEES & DEPOSITS: A $1,000 nonrefundable deposit per room is required to reserve your date. A 50% deposit is due 90 days prior and the balance is due 10 days prior to the event, along with the guaranteed guest count. Room rental fees range $500–1,500 per room depending on the day of the week and date of the event. Dinners range $30–60/person. Tax, alcohol and service charge are additional.

AVAILABILITY: Year-round, daily, 8am–11pm.

SERVICES/AMENITIES:

Catering: in-house, or select from list of approved ethnic caterers
Kitchen Facilities: n/a
Tables & Chairs: provided
Linens, Silver, etc.: provided
Restrooms: wheelchair accessible
Dance Floor: yes
Bride's & Groom's Dressing Area: yes
Meeting Equipment: full range CBA

Parking: self-parking or valet, extra charge
Accommodations: no guest rooms
Telephone: house phone
Outdoor Night Lighting: yes
Outdoor Cooking Facilities: no
Cleanup: provided, extra fee
View: Newport Harbor
Other: full event coordination, WiFi available

RESTRICTIONS:

Alcohol: in-house, no BYO
Smoking: outside only
Music: amplified OK indoors

Wheelchair Access: yes
Insurance: not required
Other: no rice, birdseed, fog machines or glitter

Hornblower Cruises & Events

Yachts

3101 West Coast Highway, Newport Beach
949/650-2412
www.hornblowerweddings.com
nb@hornblower.com

● Rehearsal Dinners	● Corporate Events
● Ceremonies	● Meetings
● Wedding Receptions	● Film Shoots
● Private Parties	Accommodations

When your friends ask where you plan to get married, you say you're not sure yet, but you know it will be on a boat. Actually, what you want is more of a yacht—something sleek and classy that glides through the water like a graceful swan.

You see yourself and your beloved on the sun deck, refreshed by the gentle breeze. As the captain pronounces you husband and wife, you gaze out at the glittering sea and feel at one with the world. If this vision speaks to you, we suggest you pay a visit to Hornblower Cruises and Events, an award-winning yacht charter company where making dreams come true is a way of life.

Each vessel in their fleet of luxury yachts has its own style and personality. Among them (they offer the largest selection in Southern California), is the state-of-the-art _Endless Dreams_. Unlike most big event vessels, which are floating party barges, this one offers the true sophistication of a yacht along with a capacity for 450 guests. The interior is custom-designed with high ceilings and lots of warm wood, granite and stainless steel throughout the spacious Grand Salon and Entertainment Deck. Amenities include a built-in dance floor, raised DJ platform and two plasma TVs. There's an outdoor balcony for ceremonies, and a huge bow and Sky Deck for enjoying the fresh air. With features you won't find on any other boat on the West Coast, _Endless Dreams_ makes other vessels this size pale in comparison.

The impressive _Just Dreamin'_ is a 110-foot mega-yacht that's custom-designed for high-style special events. Her three comfortable cabins, open aft deck, built-in dance floor and, of course, air conditioning and heating, will make your guests feel totally pampered. A long list of assets has made her one of Southern California's most sought-after yachts.

Mojo has long been one of the most popular charter vessels in Southern California. An elegant, 100-foot custom-designed Ditmar-Donaldson motor yacht, she's outfitted with an airy enclosed upper deck available for dining; a plush main salon including a full bar; three contemporary staterooms and a generous forward open bow.

Entertainer boasts two large, fully enclosed decks, each with a full bar and dance floor. With a full galley, high-quality sound system, and open-air lounge deck, she can accommodate 400 guests for seated dining or 550 for cocktails and a buffet. The aft deck provides a "back porch," additional deck space for guests who want to take in the sea air or dance under the stars!

Hornblower Cruises and Events, Newport Beach is more than just the sum of its boats. It's also a full-service event company that offers several budget-friendly packages and the personal assistance of a professional event planner. From entertainment to floral design, Hornblower can help you pull it all together without breaking the bank. (The spectacular sunsets and glittering starscapes come with no extra charge!) If you're looking to put a nautical spin on romance, then let Hornblower Cruises and Events show you the way.

CEREMONY & EVENT/RECEPTION CAPACITY: Hornblower Cruises and Events, Newport Beach accommodates up to 400 seated or 550 standing guests.

MEETING CAPACITY: They can accommodate 10–550 people for business functions, seated conference or theater-style.

FEES & DEPOSITS: A $1,000–8,000 deposit (depending on the vessel's size) is required to book a boat; the balance is payable 30 days prior to the event. Hornblower Cruises and Events, Newport Beach offers wedding packages starting at $73/person that include boat rental, food, cake, nonalcoholic beverages and a ceremony by the captain. Hourly boat rental rates and à la carte services can also be arranged.

AVAILABILITY: Year-round, daily, anytime.

SERVICES/AMENITIES:

Catering: in-house, or BYO depending on the vessel
Kitchen Facilities: n/a
Tables & Chairs: provided
Linens, Silver, etc.: provided
Restrooms: wheelchair accessibility varies
Dance Floor: available
Bride's & Groom's Dressing Area: yes
Meeting Equipment: CBA

Parking: self-parking, shuttle or valet
Accommodations: no guest rooms
Telephone: ship-to-shore radio
Outdoor Night Lighting: yes
Outdoor Cooking Facilities: no
Cleanup: provided and/or caterer
View: Pacific Ocean and coastal skyline
Other: full event coordination, licensed officiant

RESTRICTIONS:

Alcohol: in-house; BYO varies per vessel
Smoking: on decks only
Music: multiple entertainment options are available

Wheelchair Access: varies per vessel
Insurance: not required

Hyatt Regency Newport Beach

Resort Hotel

1107 Jamboree Road, Newport Beach
949/729-6201 Catering Department
www.newportbeach.hyatt.com
weddingsnewpo@hyatt.com

- Rehearsal Dinners
- Ceremonies
- Wedding Receptions
- Private Parties
- Corporate Events
- Meetings
- Film Shoots
- Accommodations

What people love most about Hyatt Regency Newport Beach is the beauty of its 26 landscaped acres. The lush plantings, seasonal flowers and abundant palm trees make even a walk around the grounds a profoundly pleasurable experience. If you're planning a wedding here, you'll find that nature is part of almost every event site at the resort.

A white trellis covered with wisteria and jasmine shades the walkway to the Amphitheater, a dramatic setting for a large ceremony. The couple exchanges vows on a trellised platform, while their guests look on from tiered seating above them. Although there are lots of flowers in surrounding bushes, the trellis can be decorated with more florals for heightened effect.

Reception areas all offer indoor and outdoor options. The largest is the newly renovated Plaza Ballroom, which comes with its own private, enclosed patio. Some couples choose to get married on the patio, but most use it for serving champagne and hors d'oeuvres. Sheltered by a high white arbor, this spacious terrace provides a tropical ambiance with a soothing fountain. It's protected from the elements by windowed sides that can be rolled up or down. Dining and dancing take place in the ballroom, where adjustable recessed lighting and wall sconces allow you to set the mood.

The circular Terrace Room works well for smaller groups. Most of its "walls" are glass, providing a peek-a-boo view of Newport's Back Bay, luxuriant foliage and the adjacent Terrace Courtyard and pool. The Arbor, a sunken patio lined with plants and flowers and surrounded by greenery can, like the Plaza Ballroom patio, double as a ceremony site as well as a spot for pre-reception mingling.

For intimate weddings the Garden Rooms are an excellent choice. This trio of spaces, housed in an L-shaped building, is interconnected by French doors and can be reserved individually or together. They all share a wall of multipaned windows that overlook a courtyard, alive with wide-branching olive trees, planters filled with blooms, and a medley of other plants. An oversized fire pit makes a cozy niche for conversation, and overhead lamps keep guests warm during cool months.

As you would expect, there are many fantastic photo opportunities on the property, including the fragrant Rose Garden (also popular for ceremonies of up to 50) and the lovely multitiered terracotta fountain.

Guests staying here for the weekend will have plenty to do thanks to three pools, a golf course, and a fitness room—not to mention the ocean and beaches nearby. Here at Hyatt Regency Newport Beach you'll enjoy the service and comforts of a large hotel in a free-flowing, natural setting.

CEREMONY CAPACITY: The Amphitheater seats 1,000; the Garden seats up to 100 guests; and the Terrace Courtyard holds 250 seated, 400 standing.

EVENT/RECEPTION CAPACITY: The Terrace Room holds 200 (180 with a dance floor) guests seated. The Garden Rooms hold 160 (120 with a dance floor) seated. The Plaza Ballroom seats 450 guests with a dance floor.

MEETING CAPACITY: Several spaces hold 15–800 seated guests.

FEES & DEPOSITS: For weddings, 30% of the food and beverage minimum is due upon booking; a credit card or cashier's check for the balance is due 10 days prior to the function. The ceremony site fee starts at $1,700. Luncheon packages run approximately $88/person; dinner packages start at $120/person. Wedding packages include 1-hour hosted bar, selection of hors d'oeuvres, artisan cheese & fruit display, house wine with dinner, champagne toast and wedding cake. Beverages, tax and service charge are additional.

For business functions, room rates vary; call the hotel for additional information.

AVAILABILITY: Year-round. Summer weddings usually take place in blocks from 11am–5pm or 6:30pm–midnight; other time frames can be arranged.

SERVICES/AMENITIES:

Catering: in-house
Kitchen Facilities: n/a
Tables & Chairs: provided
Linens, Silver, etc.: provided
Restrooms: wheelchair accessible
Dance Floor: hardwood floors, adjustable size
Bride's & Groom's Dressing Area: yes
Meeting Equipment: full range, extra charge

Parking: self-parking or valet
Accommodations: 403 guest rooms
Telephone: emergency only
Outdoor Night Lighting: provided
Outdoor Cooking Facilities: available
Cleanup: provided
View: Back Bay and Garden

RESTRICTIONS:

Alcohol: in-house
Smoking: outside only
Music: amplified OK outdoors until 10pm

Wheelchair Access: yes, except garden
Insurance: may be required, call for details
Other: no rice, birdseed or confetti

Want to know WHAT TO ASK a potential location or vendor? Check out our Questions to Ask starting on page 19.

Island Hotel Newport Beach

690 Newport Center Drive, Newport Beach
949/760-4907
www.islandhotel.com
jcooper@islandhotel.com

Resort Hotel

- Rehearsal Dinners
- Ceremonies
- Wedding Receptions
- Private Parties
- Corporate Events
- Meetings
- Film Shoots
- Accommodations

Overlooking the nearby isles of Balboa and Lido, as well as Catalina and the shining sea, there's a standout wedding venue in swanky Newport Beach. From Island Hotel's jasmine and lily-scented lobby and richly appointed lounge areas to its lushly landscaped grounds spiked with giant birds of paradise, no detail is overlooked in this Tommy Bahama-inspired setting. The moment your guests arrive at this AAA Five Diamond oasis, they'll experience the casual elegance of "The Center of Coastal Luxury."

For weddings, receptions, rehearsal dinners and post-celebration brunches, there's an array of options and amenities. All wedding couples enjoy use of his-and-hers changing suites with roomy closets, private sitting rooms and spectacular views of the urban landscape fronting the ocean. Both brides and grooms will appreciate the chance to get ready in style, while calming pre-wedding jitters in a space other than their honeymoon suite. For additional renewal and relaxation, the hotel's 4,000-square-foot water-themed spa offers a plethora of island-inspired massages, facials and beauty treatments.

Large affairs work well in the beautifully renovated Ballroom. A soft color palette of gold, tan and sage green provides a neutral backdrop, and cascading crystal chandeliers add a touch of glamour. The adjoining private prefunction room is perfect for mingling and passing hors d'oeuvres, while you and your photographer take photos elsewhere on the hotel's verdant grounds.

More intimate receptions are held in the sun-filled Cabana Room, a sophisticated space that feels like a garden conservatory. Plantation-shuttered floor-to-ceiling windows and folding glass panels open onto a wraparound patio lined with potted palms and vibrant flowers, creating a wonderful indoor-outdoor flow. Wedding ceremonies can take place on the adjacent terrace, where luxuriant foliage and a 17-foot fireplace add warmth to the poolside enclave.

At all venues on the property, you'll be treated to superior service and culinary excellence. Out-of-town guests will also enjoy accommodations in spacious rooms or suites—most with coastal views—as well as the heated pool and all the services of the on-site fitness center and The Spa at Island Hotel. For anyone in your party who wants to explore the area, the hotel is close to everything that defines upscale Orange County—sparkling beaches, championship golf courses, maritime recreation in nearby Newport Harbor and world-class shopping at adjacent Fashion Island.

No matter what the occasion, you'll be delighted with Island Hotel's resort-like atmosphere and professional staff.

CEREMONY CAPACITY: The Ballrom seats up to 900 indoors, and the Cabana Terrace seats up to 220 guests outdoors.

EVENT/RECEPTION CAPACITY: The hotel can accommodate up to 550 seated guests with a dance floor.

MEETING CAPACITY: Several flexible meeting rooms hold up to 940 seated guests.

FEES & DEPOSITS: For weddings, 30% of the estimated event total is required as a nonrefundable deposit to reserve your date. The balance is due 14 days prior to the event. Luncheons start at $60/person, dinners at $80/person. The cake and/or cake-cutting fee is $6/person. Tax, alcohol and a 23% service charge are additional.

For business functions, the room rental fee varies depending on the rooms and services selected. Please call for details.

AVAILABILITY: Year-round, daily, 6am–1am.

SERVICES/AMENITIES:

Catering: in-house
Kitchen Facilities: n/a
Tables & Chairs: provided
Linens, Silver, etc.: provided
Restrooms: wheelchair accessible
Dance Floor: provided
Bride's & Groom's Dressing Area: yes
Meeting Equipment: full range, extra fee
Other: grand piano, in-house wedding cake, spa services, AV equipment, resort-style pool, fitness and business centers

Parking: valet required
Accommodations: 295 guest rooms
Telephone: house or guest phone
Outdoor Night Lighting: provided, special lighting at additional charge
Outdoor Cooking Facilities: BBQ CBA
Cleanup: provided
View: landscaped grounds, pool area

RESTRICTIONS:

Alcohol: in-house
Smoking: not permitted
Music: amplified OK indoors

Wheelchair Access: yes
Insurance: not required

Radisson Newport Beach

4545 MacArthur Boulevard, Newport Beach
949/608-1081

www.radisson.com/newportbeachca
nsohrt@radissonnewportbeach.com

Hotel

● Rehearsal Dinners	● Corporate Events
● Ceremonies	● Meetings
● Wedding Receptions	● Film Shoots
● Private Parties	● Accommodations

Possibly the best-kept secret in this sophisticated coastal enclave, the Radisson Hotel Newport Beach offers upscale comfort without pretension or stuffiness. It's one of the top values in town, and it's just minutes from John Wayne Airport (a mere half-mile way), sunny beaches, renowned golf courses, and world-class shopping and culture.

With all its assets, the Radisson is popular for weddings, reunions, bar/bat mitzvahs, quinceañeras and other special events. Brides enjoy the services of a certified wedding coordinator, who helps plan every detail and provides a patient ear for any concerns along the way. Wedding packages also include a tasting session, so couples can sample the cuisine they plan to serve at their reception and make sure it's to their liking. A duo of changing rooms for the bridal party, a complimentary honeymoon suite and free parking for guests are additional benefits that come with all bookings.

The hotel's capacious Garden Pavilion can be transformed into a magical setting for a wedding ceremony or reception, with elegant chiffon swags. A year-round venue with an indoor-outdoor feel, it's protected from the elements yet awash with natural light.

The Pacific Ballroom, one of the few in Orange County with windows, opens to the pool area. With its dark wood paneling and multiple crystal chandeliers and wall sconces on dimmer switches, it's an impressive stage for formal receptions. For smaller affairs, including rehearsal dinners and farewell brunches, the Palm Garden Room is a lovely space with a dance floor in its glassed-in "wine cellar" area.

Another option for a ceremony or reception is the vibrant Palm Court, a bright atrium which adjoins the Radisson's two mid-rise towers and features a bold tropical-themed mural. There's also the Newport Bay Room, a "junior ballroom" that opens to a private patio shielded by ferns and tall ficus trees.

After your guests depart, come "home" to a suite as spacious as many city apartments, outfitted with marble-topped counters, a giant plasma screen TV and a Jacuzzi tub in one of two bathrooms. And while the Radisson can't guarantee sweet dreams, you'll probably have them once you curl up in your king-size Sleep Number® bed, truly the perfect end to a perfect day.

CEREMONY CAPACITY: The site holds 600 seated guests indoors and 400 seated outdoors.

EVENT/RECEPTION CAPACITY: The hotel can accommodate 500 seated or 700 standing guests indoors, and 350 seated or 600 standing outdoors.

MEETING CAPACITY: Meeting spaces hold 600 seated guests.

FEES & DEPOSITS: 30% of the food and beverage minimum is required to reserve your date. A portion is due 90 days prior to the event. The balance is due 10 days prior to the event. Rental fees range $850–2,800 and vary depending on the ceremony location selected. Meals range $40–103/person. Tax and a 22% service charge are additional.

AVAILABILITY: Year-round, daily, 6am–midnight.

SERVICES/AMENITIES:

Catering: in-house, select from list or BYO
Kitchen Facilities: fully equipped
Tables & Chairs: provided
Linens, Silver, etc.: provided
Restrooms: wheelchair accessible
Dance Floor: provided
Bride's & Groom's Dressing Area: yes
Meeting Equipment: provided, CBA
Other: in-house wedding cake, clergy on staff, picnic area, AV equipment, complimentary suite for bride & groom, podium, risers, event coordination

Parking: large complimentary lot
Accommodations: 335 guest rooms & suites
Telephone: house or guest phone
Outdoor Night Lighting: provided
Outdoor Cooking Facilities: BBQ CBA
Cleanup: provided
View: fountain, garden, landscaped grounds, garden courtyard, pool area

RESTRICTIONS:

Alcohol: in-house or BYO wine w/corkage fee
Smoking: designated areas only
Music: amplified OK

Wheelchair Access: yes
Insurance: liability required

Beachcomber Cafe at Crystal Cove

Waterfront Restaurant

15 Crystal Cove, Newport Coast
949/644-8759
www.thebeachcombercafe.com
catering@thebeachcombercafe.com

- Rehearsal Dinners
- Ceremonies
- Wedding Receptions
- Private Parties
- Corporate Events
- Meetings
- Film Shoots
- Accommodations

Want to treat yourself and your guests to a quintessential Southern California "endless summer" experience? Well, raise the martini flag—as well as your expectations of a really great time—and invite them to an event staged right on the beach at historic Crystal Cove Park, one of the Newport coast's most celebrated sites. This is the place for the classic Southern California beach wedding or party at its best. We're talking anything from gowns and tuxedos to bikinis and board shorts—whatever you envision, it will look amazing with the foaming surf and the scintillating sun close at hand.

Run by *Beachcomber Catering,* experts in coastal entertaining, festivities here unfold in with energy and ease. There are adorable and affordable settings for every kind of affair. A host of tiny cottages and event sites dot the property, all offering varying degrees of privacy and communal activity.

The Beaches Cottage, with its sand-strewn terrace and white picket fence a mere 20 yards from the Pacific, is about as picturesque as you can get. This was the set for the Bette Midler movie, *Beaches,* as well as a long list of other films over the decades. Exchange vows on the inviting blanket of sand out front, then pop around the fence for cocktails, dinner, cake, and a big dose of charm.

The park-like Commons has cute and quirky surfside event areas, as well as marvelous ocean and creek views—Trancos Creek meets the sea here. Not far from the Commons, the Beach Promenade provides a gorgeous sandy stretch for a ceremony, cocktail hour and dining. Imagine a clambake…a luau…a fiesta with mariachis or a romantic tiki-lit banquet with the sea murmuring nearby. Wine tasting, food stations, cracked crab and buckets of ice-cold beer, lobster steamed to perfection, sushi platters, margaritas and mini-ahi tacos, surf and turf extravaganzas—your options are practically unlimited. The dedicated *Beachcomber Catering* team will turn your vision into reality by delivering excellent service, incorporating fresh local products, and customizing every aspect of your event.

Of course you might want to hang out above it all. If that's the case, plan to party up at the Cultural Center Cottage with its expansive deck—it's a heavenly perch designed with elegant entertaining in mind and overlooking exhilarating views of the ocean.

Whatever venue you ultimately choose, we're certain that when your celebration is over you (and some of your guests!) may not want to leave this seductive seaside location. No worries. Just slip off your sandals and stay awhile at one of the many cottages at your disposal. Then take a little time to unwind and explore the coast. You'll soon discover what's made Crystal Cove a popular destination since the 1930s, and why people who arrive as visitors soon turn into devoted fans.

CEREMONY & EVENT/RECEPTION CAPACITY: The site can accommodate up to 200 seated or standing guests outdoors.

MEETING CAPACITY: Meetings spaces hold up to 30 seated guests.

FEES & DEPOSITS: A $2,000 deposit is required to reserve your date, with your final guarantee and payment due 7 days prior to the event. The State site permit fees range $750–2,750 depending on which venue location is selected. Meals range $52–95/person. Tax, alcohol and a 22% service charge are additional. Note that off-premise catering is also available.

AVAILABILITY: Year-round, daily, 8am–9pm.

SERVICES/AMENITIES:

Catering: in-house, or BYO ethnic caterer with approval
Kitchen Facilities: fully equipped
Tables & Chairs: provided
Linens, Silver, etc.: provided
Restrooms: wheelchair accessible
Dance Area: provided
Bride's Dressing Area: yes
Meeting Equipment: n/a

Parking: large lot
Accommodations: 24 cottages
Telephone: office phone
Outdoor Night Lighting: CBA
Outdoor Cooking Facilities: BBQ on site
Cleanup: provided
View: Pacific Ocean
Other: in-house florals, off-premise catering

RESTRICTIONS:

Alcohol: full in-house bar
Smoking: designated areas only
Music: amplified OK outdoors with restrictions

Wheelchair Access: yes
Insurance: not required

Wedgewood San Clemente

Banquet Center

150 East Avenida Magdalena, San Clemente
866/966-3009

www.wedgewoodbanquet.com/san-clemente
sales@wedgewoodbanquet.com

- Rehearsal Dinners
- Ceremonies
- Wedding Receptions
- Private Parties
- Corporate Events
- Meetings
- Film Shoots
- Accommodations

Wedgewood San Clemente offers a relaxed, comfortable atmosphere less than a mile from the beach, and its brand new ceremony site boasts fairway vistas, ocean breezes and peeks of the Pacific. The property's California Spanish architecture and inviting reception area will no doubt appeal to brides, but they'll really appreciate all the extras that add value to this golf course venue.

Since the pre-wedding experience often sets the tone for the whole day, you'll be delighted to learn that your "bridal room" is actually an incredibly charming B&B adjacent to the greens. This intimate cottage has plenty of spots for you to primp and pose for photos, with a sitting room, French doors, tiled staircase and balcony at your disposal. Right outside, the award-winning European gardens are an enchanting locale for capturing shots of that "first look" between you and your groom before you tie the knot.

Your guests, meanwhile, await your arrival on the club's ceremony lawn. Designed with both historic and modern touches, it features a curving walkway of traditional San Clemente tile that leads to a raised stage with clean-lined columns and a wood-beam canopy. A waterfall gently spills over rocks below the platform, and three soaring Eucalyptus trees frame the scene. This area is completely wired, so you can amplify any musical accompaniment and add lights in the evening.

From here it's just a short walk to the clubhouse for cocktails on the wide, stone-floored Patio that wraps around the building. In the main section of this space, multiple conversation groupings with comfy seating and shade umbrellas, along with a brick fire pit, encourage mingling. From the rear of the Patio, you can catch nice sunset views off to the west. (Be sure to have your photographer snap some "magic hour" couple shots on the golf course, with the sun setting over the ocean behind you.)

When you're ready for dinner, two sets of French doors open to the Banquet Room. Spacious and airy, it showcases a beamed cathedral ceiling, lovely iron chandeliers and a soft, neutral palette. There's a built-in dance floor, and large windows that let in natural light during the day. If you're hosting a large group, you can double your space by folding back the dividing doors and accessing the adjoining Restaurant and bar. And, of course, the Patio is always available for savoring the cool, night air and starry sky.

At the end of the evening, your out-of-town friends and relatives will be happy to know that they can stay overnight within walking distance of this beautiful setting. Thanks to Wedgewood's affiliation with a local hotel, you and your guests will receive a discount on the guest rooms you book.

The staff at Wedgewood San Clemente go out of their way to make everything easy and convenient, with packages to suit virtually every couple and suggestions on how to personalize your celebration. They can also help you schedule a golf party or San Clemente tour to make your special event even more memorable.

CEREMONY CAPACITY: The site holds 240 seated guests indoors or outdoors.

EVENT/RECEPTION & MEETING CAPACITY: The facility can accommodate 240 seated or standing guests indoors.

FEES & DEPOSITS: 25% of the estimated total event cost is required to reserve your date. An additonal 25% is due 120 days prior to the event and the balance (based on your final guest count) is due 10 days prior. All payments are credited towards your final balance and are nonrefundable and nontransferable. All-inclusive, completely customizable wedding packages start at $33/person. Tax, alcohol and a 21–22% service charge are additional.

AVAILABILITY: Year-round, daily.

SERVICES/AMENITIES:

Catering: In-house
Kitchen Facilities: n/a
Tables & Chairs: provided
Linens, Silver, etc.: provided
Restrooms: wheelchair accessible
Dance Floor: portable provided
Bride's Dressing Area: yes
Meeting Equipment: some provided
Other: in-house wedding cake and florals; clergy on staff; AV equipment; event coordination, extra fee

Parking: large lot
Accommodations: no guest rooms
Telephone: emergency use only
Outdoor Night Lighting: provided
Outdoor Cooking Facilities: none
Cleanup: provided
View: fountain, landscaped grounds; panorama of hills, coastline, ocean and fairways

RESTRICTIONS:

Alcohol: in-house
Smoking: not allowed
Music: amplified OK

Wheelchair Access: yes
Insurance: liability required

Want to find more venues and services? Check out our informative website, www.HereComesTheGuide.com.

Café Mozart

Restaurant

31952 Camino Capistrano, San Juan Capistrano
949/496-0212

www.cafemozart.net
info@cafemozart.net

- Rehearsal Dinners
- Ceremonies
- Wedding Receptions
- Private Parties
- Corporate Events
- Meetings
- Film Shoots

  Accommodations

Romance, nostalgia and the spirit of Early California are entwined in the rich heritage of San Juan Capistrano, the picturesque village where Padre Junipero Serra planted Orange County's earliest roots. Here, brides can step back to a less hurried era at Café Mozart, an ivy-covered gem just blocks from the "Jewel of the Missions" and the train depot where wedding guests might arrive by rail in the centuries-old community.

Strolling down Camino Capistrano, they'll soon come to the twin adobe archways of Mercado Village in the heart of the city's historic downtown. Tucked behind these porticos is the Spanish-style courtyard of Hans Löschl and Carla Ramos' gracious café. Trimmed with lights and lined with languid eucalyptus, blooming oleander trees and a brightly tiled giant mural, the jasmine-scented quad is an enchanting spot for an evening wedding ceremony. To add to the ambiance, some brides opt to float candles or drape greenery in the gurgling tri-tier fountain at its center, which provides a beautiful backdrop.

Once they've exchanged vows, couples have photographs taken in the courtyard, or retreat to numerous more secluded patios on the property—all with Mayan-style fountains. While most sit-down or buffet receptions are held in the courtyard, seated meals can also be served inside the homey, Old World-style restaurant.

For small gatherings, Café Mozart's private dining room has the relaxed charm of a European inn. An eclectic mix of antique furnishings and a baby grand piano contribute to the feeling that you're celebrating in a friend's living room. The dining room looks out on the courtyard, where there's plenty of space for a dance floor and DJ setup. Larger groups can combine restaurant and courtyard seating.

The European flavor of the Café carries over into its cuisine, which is decidedly Continental. Vienna-trained chef Hans Löschl, a former chef at the Westin St. Francis, prepares all dishes fresh and on-site, while his wife, Carla, crafts exquisite custom wedding cakes.

Although Café Mozart is named for Austria's most famous native son, it's a magical setting that truly reflects Orange County's past.

CEREMONY CAPACITY: The Outdoor Courtyard holds up to 200 seated guests. Indoors, the private dining room holds up to 60 seated guests.

EVENT/RECEPTION & MEETING CAPACITY: The Courtyard holds up to 200 seated or 350 standing guests. The indoor spaces accommodate 125 seated or 175 standing guests.

FEES & DEPOSITS: A $750 deposit is required to reserve your date. The balance is due 10 days prior to the event. Package prices range $75–110/person. Tax, alcohol and a 20% service charge are additional.

AVAILABILITY: Year-round, daily, 11am–11pm.

SERVICES/AMENITIES:

Catering: in-house, no BYO
Kitchen Facilities: n/a
Tables & Chairs: provided
Linens, Silver, etc.: provided
Restrooms: wheelchair accessible
Dance Floor: CBA
Bride's Dressing Area: yes
Meeting Equipment: CBA, extra charge

Parking: large lot
Accommodations: no guest rooms
Telephone: emergency use only
Outdoor Night Lighting: yes
Outdoor Cooking Facilities: no
Cleanup: provided
View: garden courtyard and fountain
Other: custom wedding cakes, grand piano

RESTRICTIONS:

Alcohol: in-house or BYO with corkage fee
Smoking: outdoors only
Music: amplified OK indoors and outdoors with volume limits

Wheelchair Access: yes
Insurance: not required

Marbella Country Club

Country Club

30800 Golf Club Drive, San Juan Capistrano
888/995-6224
www.countryclubreceptions.com
events@marbellacc.net

- Rehearsal Dinners
- Ceremonies
- Wedding Receptions
- Private Parties
- Corporate Events
- Meetings
- Film Shoots
- Accommodations

It may be nestled in the pastoral valley between the Pacific Ocean and the Saddleback Mountains, but the elegant Marbella Country Club embodies the spirit of the Mediterranean. Even if you're not jetting off to the coast of Italy for your honeymoon, you'll still get a taste of it when you celebrate your Big Day in this impressive setting.

After driving through the club's gated community, past manicured lawns and a flowerbed blooming with ivory roses, you reach the porte-cochère of the 50,000-square-foot clubhouse where valets await. Glittering like a baronial villa in the San Juan Capistrano sun, the majestic structure offers a genteel welcome with a tri-tier fountain ringed by palms and birds of paradise.

Upon arrival and during the cocktail hour, your guests will mingle in the handsome South Bar and around the fire pit of the spacious Valencia Terrace, enjoying mixed libations and delectable hors d'oeuvres.

Most couples say their vows on the Croquet Lawn, under a lattice garden arch adorned with flowers and greenery that overlooks the championship golf course. Fragrant petals define a colorful aisle, where seating for up to 300 can be arranged. Although the bride and groom garner most of the attention, guests can't help but notice the border of roses and the stunning rock waterfall. Three stairways leading to this area provide numerous ways to choreograph your ceremony for sentimental impact. The club's genial Catering Director will be there to assist with this and other details so you can relax, knowing your important day is in good hands.

After the knot is tied, Marbella's picturesque fairways and beautiful clubhouse architecture make spectacular backdrops for photos. While your photographer is capturing your first pictures as newlyweds, your guests stroll across the lawn to the Pacific Terrace and luxuriously appointed Pacific Grille for the reception. Here, they'll savor creative specialties prepared by the club's Certified Master Chef. If you like, place votive candles on the tables for a romantic touch.

From your sweetheart table you can watch your contented guests as they flow easily between the Pacific Grille and the terrace through five sets of French doors. Après-dinner festivities continue on the dance floor, with a break for tossing your bouquet from one of the sweeping staircases to eager future brides gathered below.

When you have your wedding at the Marbella Country Club, it's the only event scheduled for the entire evening. So take your time and immerse yourself in the celebration, knowing it will be an unforgettable experience for all who attend.

CEREMONY CAPACITY: The Croquet Lawn holds up to 300 seated guests.

EVENT/RECEPTION CAPACITY: The Terrace holds up to 250 seated or 300 standing guests.

MEETING CAPACITY: Indoor spaces hold up to 190 seated guests.

FEES & DEPOSITS: A nonrefundable deposit, which is applied to your food and beverage total, is required to reserve your date. The amount of the deposit varies, depending on how far in advance you book. Payment terms for the balance also vary, and may be arranged on an individual basis. Wedding packages start at $65/person. Tax, alcohol and service charge are additional. Menus and packages can be customized to fit your needs and budget. Call for details.

AVAILABILITY: Year-round, daily, 7am–midnight.

SERVICES/AMENITIES:

Catering: in-house, no BYO
Kitchen Facilities: n/a
Tables & Chairs: provided
Linens, Silver, etc.: provided
Restrooms: wheelchair accessible
Dance Floor: provided
Bride's Dressing Area: yes
Meeting Equipment: provided

Parking: large lot, valet provided
Accommodations: no guest rooms
Telephone: house phones
Outdoor Night Lighting: yes
Outdoor Cooking Facilities: BBQ
Cleanup: provided
View: fairways, garden, landscaped grounds
Other: event coordination, grand piano, ATM

RESTRICTIONS:

Alcohol: in-house or BYO wine with corkage fee
Smoking: outdoors only
Music: amplified OK indoors, and outdoors with restrictions

Wheelchair Access: access limited
Insurance: not required

San Juan Hills Golf Club

Golf Club

32120 San Juan Creek Road, San Juan Capistrano
949/493-1167
www.sanjuanhillsgolf.com
stacey@sanjuanhillsgolf.com

● Rehearsal Dinners	● Corporate Events
● Ceremonies	● Meetings
● Wedding Receptions	● Film Shoots
● Private Parties	○ Accommodations

Cliff swallows have been migrating to San Juan Capistrano to pair up and nest for centuries and we can understand why: One renowned novelist called this sunny southern corner of Orange County "the only romantic spot in California." Well, perhaps this is a bit of an overstatement, but it's definitely a place that inspires romance. Developed around Mission San Juan Capistrano, the area is a charming mixture of old and new worlds, characterized by graceful Spanish architecture, rolling foothills, working ranches, and million-dollar homes in gated communities.

The sun-drenched San Juan Hills Golf Club is built in that welcoming, Early California style. Its hacienda-influenced clubhouse has the easy flow of a structure designed for indoor/outdoor gatherings. The Green View Veranda is a gorgeous setting for an al fresco reception. Framed by fragrant plants like lavender, rosemary, sage and citrus, as well as roses, olive trees, birds of paradise and pampas grasses, it has a pretty half-moon-shaped fire pit and overlooks the 18th hole and the surrounding San Juan Hills. The adjacent lawn has been used for a variety of setups—pavilions, food carts, strolling entertainers, and party games. You can pair terrace and lawn with the Green View Room—the club's lovely banquet space—for cocktails, dinner and dancing. The vaulted, open-beam ceiling, dark walnut accents and Tuscan-style chandeliers give it a warm Mediterranean feel, while glass doors that slide into the walls admit cooling breezes and sweeping golf course views.

A more intimate outdoor reception site is the First T Patio, offering a view of the first tee, green hills and pond. Accented with market lighting, it's perfect for a ceremony or rehearsal dinner as well.

You can also tie the knot on the course's first tee. A cushiony green rise overlooking the club's lake and waterfall, it's both picturesque and musical, the waterfall providing a soft little shower of sound. It's a natural choice for photos, too, though picture-perfect backdrops abound on the beautifully landscaped grounds. A third ceremony option, the Greenside Patio, is nestled between the Veranda and the rolling greens. It features market lighting and a view of the greens and pond.

The bride and groom each have their own retreat. She and her entourage can get ready in a room with softly sueded walls, vanity, full-length mirror and fainting couch. He and his groomsmen can relax in the Board Room off the Pro shop. On request, it converts into the ideal man-lair, outfitted with black leather chairs, a mahogany table, and a big-screen wall TV.

Whatever the function and wherever you decide to host it, the San Juan Hills staff will make sure everything runs smoothly, seeing to everyone's needs and serving up the mouthwatering hors d'oeuvres and entrées for which the club is well known.

All in all, it's an enchanting location for your celebration. When night falls and lights are twinkling, lanterns glow and the music is in full swing, you'll see what makes this venue so special…and why it attracts lovebirds of every kind.

CEREMONY CAPACITY: The site holds 200 seated guests indoors, and 300 seated outdoors.

EVENT/RECEPTION CAPACITY: The facility can accommodate 200 seated (150 with a dance floor) or 250 standing guests indoors, and 300 seated or 400 standing outdoors.

MEETING CAPACITY: Meeting spaces hold 150 seated guests.

FEES & DEPOSITS: A $1,000 deposit is required to reserve your date. 50% of the estimated balance is due 4 months prior to the event, and the balance is due 7 days prior. Ceremony fees range $850–1,250 depending on the ceremony location. Meals range $20–80/person. Tax, alcohol and a 20% service charge are additional.

AVAILABILITY: Year-round, daily, 7am–midnight.

SERVICES/AMENITIES:

Catering: in-house
Kitchen Facilities: n/a
Tables & Chairs: provided
Linens, Silver, etc.: provided
Restrooms: wheelchair accessible
Dance Floor: portable provided
Bride's & Groom's Dressing Area: yes
Meeting Equipment: provided
Other: AV equipment

Parking: two large lots, on street
Accommodations: no guest rooms
Telephone: office phone
Outdoor Night Lighting: provided
Outdoor Cooking Facilities: BBQ on site
Cleanup: provided
View: fairways, hills, pond, landscaped grounds, waterfall

RESTRICTIONS:

Alcohol: in-house
Smoking: designated areas only
Music: amplified OK with restrictions

Wheelchair Access: yes
Insurance: not required

The Hacienda

1725 College Avenue, Santa Ana
714/558-1304
www.the-hacienda.com
weddings@the-hacienda.com

Banquet Facility & Garden

- Rehearsal Dinners
- Ceremonies
- Wedding Receptions
- Private Parties
- Corporate Events
- Meetings
- Film Shoots
- Accommodations

As soon as you walk through the front gates of The Hacienda, you travel back in time to a more peaceful and romantic era. Once part of an orange and avocado ranch from the early 1900s, this whitewashed adobe and its charming courtyard is now one of Orange County's most popular wedding locations.

Two settings are available for both ceremonies and receptions. If you'd like to celebrate outdoors, the flagstone courtyard is ideal. Ivy-covered balconies, an abundance of potted flowers, and a three-tiered fountain in the center give the space an Old World atmosphere. Off to one side is a wooden arbor, hung with stained-glass panels and entwined with vines, that serves as an altar for ceremonies. When a couple exchanges vows here, candelabras provide old-fashioned warmth and sparkle. For courtyard weddings, the bride's dressing room is the old master bedroom in the main hacienda, appointed with antiques and giant mirrors. From here she can step out onto her balcony to survey her guests below.

Indoor events are hosted in the Taos Room, a beautiful ballroom in the building adjacent to the main hacienda. It has a Southwest flavor, with its 200-year-old decorative doors carved from Mexican mesquite wood, oversized fireplace, antiques and original artwork. A 20-foot ceiling with skylights and a row of French doors that open to the courtyard provide natural light. At the far end, a flight of Spanish tile stairs—perfect for making a grand entrance—leads up to the bride's dressing room. Large mirrors, lots of space, and roses stenciled above the doors and windows make brides feel quite comfortable.

The Hacienda, like its sister properties Tivoli Too and Tivoli Terrace, is owned by June Neptune, an experienced wedding maven with a bride-friendly philosophy. "Weddings should be stress-free and fun," she says. Her all-inclusive packages really simplify the planning process, covering everything from floral decorations and live music for the ceremony, to appetizers, drinks, dinner and even the wedding cake. Another built-in benefit is assistance from June's staff of wedding coordinators, who will help you plan your event and make sure it comes off just as you envisioned it.

CEREMONY CAPACITY: The Taos Courtyard holds 220 seated, 300 if combined with the Taos Room. The Inner Courtyard accommodates up to 140 seated guests.

EVENT/RECEPTION CAPACITY: The Hacienda holds 500 guests, maximum.

MEETING CAPACITY: Event spaces accommodate 30–500 seated guests.

FEES & DEPOSITS: For weddings, a nonrefundable deposit of $2,000 is required to reserve your date. The deposit is applied toward the event balance. An additional $500 security deposit is payable 90 days prior to the event. In-house catering is provided. Half the estimated total is payable 90 days prior to the event, and the balance is due 2 weeks prior. Wedding packages include live music, cake, fresh flowers, tables and chairs, linens, food service, passed hors d'oeuvres, unlimited beer, wine and champagne. A 20% service charge and tax are additional. The Brunch Package starts at $60/person. Afternoon/Evening Packages start at $75/person for Fridays, Saturdays and Sundays.

For meetings, a $200 deposit or 10% of the estimated event total is required to reserve your date; the balance is payable 2 weeks prior to the event. Business breakfasts run $15–20/person, luncheons $20–40/person and dinners $28–110/person; tax, beverages and service charges are additional.

AVAILABILITY: Year-round, daily, until midnight.

SERVICES/AMENITIES:

Catering: in-house, no BYO

Kitchen Facilities: n/a

Tables & Chairs: provided

Linens, Silver, etc.: provided

Restrooms: wheelchair accessible

Dance Floor: flagstone patio

Bride's & Groom's Dressing Area: yes

Meeting Equipment: podium, PA system, microphones; other CBA

Parking: several lots nearby

Accommodations: no guest rooms

Telephone: emergency use only

Outdoor Night Lighting: yes

Outdoor Cooking Facilities: no

Cleanup: provided

View: garden, fountains and courtyard

Other: event coordination

RESTRICTIONS:

Alcohol: in-house, no BYO

Smoking: designated areas only

Music: amplified OK

Wheelchair Access: yes

Insurance: not required

Other: no rice, birdseed or confetti; children must be supervised

---

This is important! Tell venues you're reading HERE COMES THE GUIDE and ask if our information is still current.

405

Heritage Museum of Orange County

Museum and Garden

3101 West Harvard Street, Santa Ana
714/540-0404 X223
www.heritagemuseumoc.org
weddings@heritagemuseumoc.org

Rehearsal Dinners	●	Corporate Events
● Ceremonies	●	Meetings
● Wedding Receptions	●	Film Shoots
● Private Parties		Accommodations

The heart of this museum is the old H. Clay Kellogg House, a lovingly restored 1898 Victorian that sits amid ten acres of historic gardens and turn-of-the-century buildings. Created to preserve Orange County's cultural heritage, the museum takes you back to the early 1900s: While you're ambling along its jasmine-covered walkways, or through its orange groves and rose garden, you'll think you've stepped back in time onto a country estate. The great thing about weddings here is that all the local businesses close for the weekend, and you can have a rock 'n' roll band without disturbing a soul.

The Heritage Museum of Orange County has recreated a gracious past, and weddings are often inspired by the setting's peaceful Victorian ambiance. Although you can't host your wedding inside, a stroll around the Kellogg House—outfitted with the utmost in Victoriana—is enough to set the mood. The spacious lawns lend themselves to a number of possibilities for parties and receptions, and the gazebo is popular for ceremonies.

The flexible and experienced Heritage Museum staff are happy to accommodate your special needs in every way they can. All proceeds from weddings and receptions go to support the museum's nonprofit programs, which provide "hands-on" historical enrichment for visitors. A portion of the proceeds are also tax deductible. Not only is the Heritage Museum a lovely place to host your wedding, you'll have the satisfaction of benefiting a wonderful cultural resource.

CEREMONY CAPACITY: The Gazebo Lawn and the front of the Kellogg House hold a maximum of 300 guests.

EVENT/RECEPTION CAPACITY: The Rose Garden Lawn holds 400 seated guests or 600 standing, a shade pavilion holds 150 seated.

MEETING CAPACITY: The shaded pavilion holds 150 seated conference-style or 300 theater-style. Meeting room seats 20 conference-style or 40 theater-style. Audiovisual equipment is not provided by the museum, but can be arranged at an extra charge with advanced notice.

FEES & DEPOSITS: A nonrefundable but tax-deductable $1,500 deposit is required to reserve your date; the estimated event total is due 90 days prior to the event. A portion of the proceeds are also tax-deductable. Rental fees start at $1,400 and vary according to the season and the day of the week. In addition, there is a refundable $1,500 cleaning and damage deposit. Meals (provided exclusively by *Country Garden Caterers*) start at $39/person and include choice of 2 hors d'oeuvres, 1 entrée, accompaniments and salads, choice of any color linens and napkins, china, silverware, glassware, tables and chairs, uniformed servers, coffee station and soft drinks. Tax, alcohol and service charge are additional.

AVAILABILITY: Year-round, Friday and Saturday, 5pm–11pm; Sunday, 4pm–10pm.

SERVICES/AMENITIES:

Catering: provided by *Country Garden Caterers*
Kitchen Facilities: n/a
Tables & Chairs: through exclusive vendor
Linens, Silver, etc.: through caterer
Restrooms: wheelchair accessible
Dance Floor: patio
Bride's Dressing Area: yes
Meeting Equipment: BYO

Parking: ample free
Accommodations: no guest rooms
Telephone: no
Outdoor Night Lighting: yes
Outdoor Cooking Facilities: no
Cleanup: caterer or renter
View: rose garden, fountain, citrus grove, gazebo

RESTRICTIONS:

Alcohol: provided by *Country Garden Caterers*
Music: amplified OK
Smoking: designated areas only

Wheelchair Access: yes
Insurance: certificate required through WedSafe
Other: no rice, birdseed, synthetic rose petals or confetti; no nails, tacks, staples, glue or tape; no sparklers or other pyrotechnics; restrictions on open flames

Old Ranch Country Club

Country Club

3901 Lampson Avenue, Seal Beach
562/594-7202, 714/847-7004
www.oldranchweddings.com
kmesinas@oldranch.com

- Rehearsal Dinners
- Ceremonies
- Wedding Receptions
- Private Parties

- Corporate Events
- Meetings
- Film Shoots
- Accommodations

The Old Ranch Country Club enjoys a reputation for being a place that's easy to get to and easy to work with. With its rambling, comfortable clubhouse, it's also a place where guests feel right at home. Situated at the northern edge of Orange County, Old Ranch is within a short drive to three airports and several major freeways, making it convenient for local or out-of-state travelers en route to your celebration. And once they arrive, they'll be able to stay at the congenial Ayres Suites Hotel located just across the street. The club offers all-inclusive packages, a wide range of menu selections featuring the best of traditional and California cuisine, and special items to make the kids happy. With its dedicated event staff, including an on-site wedding coordinator, the club will ensure that your event is joyous and trouble free.

Although Old Ranch has been a members-only venue since its inception in 1967, their new wing of banquet facilities is available to nonmembers for special events. As you enter the lobby of this recent addition, you're greeted by a huge mural of blue skies, trees and rolling hills—a tableau that mimics the club's pastoral surroundings. Framed by a stone arch, it provides a dramatic backdrop for photos, as well as a conversation piece for guests socializing here before heading into the spacious reception salon.

Once you're in the salon, prepare to be delighted by what you see. A wall of floor-to-ceiling Nana windows open like an accordion to a new outdoor terrace with an expansive view of the redesigned golf course and lake, complete with a fountain that's lit up at night. This modern 6,000-square-foot banquet space is large enough to accommodate both a wedding and reception. However, it's also divisible into four sections that can be used individually or in combination, depending on the size of your event. Coffered ceilings edged with dark wood beams; potted ficus trees at the corners; and an abstract patterned carpet give the room a contemporary ambiance. In the evening, craftsman-style ceiling lamps cast a soft glow. With its casual-yet-refined sensibility, the club atmosphere invites guests to relax with a glass of chilled Chardonnay as they drink in the landscape. Speaking of the landscape, there are a number of photogenic spots overlooking the fairways for some before- or after-ceremony pictures.

Perhaps the club's most popular new area is its gorgeous bridal courtyard, designed especially for outdoor ceremonies. Ringed by flowers, palm trees and other greenery, it has a lush, almost tropical feel. The bride walks down a stone pathway to exchange vows with her groom beneath a lovely Romanesque gazebo. As friends and family look on from their lawn seating, they have a breathtaking view of the lake and golf course in the background.

Old Ranch is not only conveniently located for your special event, it's also only a short drive to the beach for some fun in the California sun. The beach we're referring to is Seal Beach, a haven for those in search of a laid-back, small town atmosphere. Replete with suntanned surfers, a treelined Main Street and a colorful past, the town is packed with seaside delights and history. Between this appealing country club and its friendly coastal neighbor, you'll find all the elements you need for a wonderful weekend wedding.

CEREMONY CAPACITY: Indoors, the club holds up to 300 seated guests. The Bridal Courtyard seats up to 450 guests.

EVENT/RECEPTION & MEETING CAPACITY: The Salon holds up to 400 seated or 500 standing guests. This room can be split into four smaller rooms, each holding 90 seated or 120 standing.

FEES & DEPOSITS: A $4,000 booking fee is required to reserve your date. The balance is due 10 business days prior to the event. All-inclusive wedding packages range $70–165/person. Tax and service charge are extra. An additional ceremony setup fee includes a rehearsal with the wedding coordinator, 1-hour ceremony time and use of a bridal room.

AVAILABILITY: Year-round. Monday–Thursday, 6am–11:30pm, Friday–Sunday, 6am–midnight; extra hours may be available.

SERVICES/AMENITIES:
Catering: in-house
Kitchen Facilities: n/a
Tables & Chairs: provided
Linens, Silver, etc.: provided
Restrooms: wheelchair accessible
Dance Floor: provided
Bride's Dressing Area: yes
Meeting Equipment: CBA, extra charge
Other: on-site event coordination

Parking: large lighted lot
Accommodations: no guest rooms, hotel across the street and local hotels will shuttle
Telephone: house phone
Outdoor Night Lighting: yes, with lighted fountain
Outdoor Cooking Facilities: no
Cleanup: provided
View: golf course, lake, fountain, distant mountains

RESTRICTIONS:
Alcohol: in-house, or BYO wine with corkage fee
Smoking: outside only
Music: amplified OK

Wheelchair Access: yes
Insurance: provided

Silverado

Rancho Las Lomas

19191 Lawrence Canyon, Silverado
949/888-3080

www.rancholaslomas.com
info@rancholaslomas.com

Banquet Facility and Garden

- Rehearsal Dinners   • Corporate Events
- Ceremonies   • Meetings
- Wedding Receptions   • Film Shoots
- Private Parties   Accommodations

Nestled among the rolling hills of South Orange County, the 32-acre Rancho Las Lomas is a testimony to the charms of early California. Surrounded by orange groves and flowering shrubs, the hacienda-style buildings of the ranch sit under the cooling shade of towering oak and sycamore trees, and are connected by terracotta walkways and bridges. Guests can take enchanted strolls through the grounds—redolent of orange blossoms and lush with botanical-garden-quality flora—and peek into the large ornamental bird cages which house a collection of rare tropical birds and exotic animals.

On a plateau at the top of a gentle slope is the Grand Salon, a spacious light-filled room with a big stone fireplace as its stunning centerpiece. The combination of white stucco walls, beamed ceiling, terracotta floor and wood-framed windows makes the Salon ideal for all types of gatherings. The adjoining patio, adorned with a sparkling blue-tile reflecting pool, makes it possible to have an indoor/outdoor reception.

Smaller affairs are often held in Rick's Cafe, a four-level Casablanca-style villa built into the hillside just beyond the Grand Salon patio. An oak bar, rough-hewn beamed ceiling, stone fireplace, and eclectic mix of Victorian antiques in its many inviting conversation nooks create an intimate atmosphere for parties.

Wedding ceremonies at Rancho Las Lomas take place in the Teatro, an open-air theater with a marble stage, stone patio and bubbling fountains. The cozy Casa Bonita next door has full-length mirrors, makeup area and parlor with fireplace, and is one of the loveliest bride's dressing rooms we've seen. Everything at Rancho Las Lomas has been carefully created, from its blossoming foliage to the abundance of hand-painted tile. If you're looking for a simply sensational setting, this is it.

CEREMONY CAPACITY: The Teatro/Chapel seats 325 guests.

EVENT/RECEPTION CAPACITY: The site holds up to 500 guests. Indoors, the facility holds 200 seated guests, 300 for buffets, or 300–500 standing for a cocktail reception.

MEETING CAPACITY: The Grand Salon holds 300 guests seated theater-style.

410

FEES & DEPOSITS: The nonrefundable rental fee ranges $2,500–8,500, and is payable 60 days after booking the site. The fee includes use of both indoor and outdoor facilities for a specific time frame. All-inclusive wedding packages start at $150/person.

Off-season and weekday rates range $2,500–6,000; call for more information.

AVAILABILITY: Year-round, daily, 9am–midnight.

SERVICES/AMENITIES:

Catering: in-house Sat and Sun; optional Mon–Fri with special pricing

Kitchen Facilities: n/a

Tables & Chairs: provided, extra fee

Linens, Silver, etc.: through caterer

Restrooms: wheelchair accessible

Dance Floor: provided, extra fee

Bride's & Groom's Dressing Area: yes

Meeting Equipment: provided, extra fee

Parking: valet required, extra charge

Accommodations: no guest rooms

Telephone: pay phone

Outdoor Night Lighting: provided

Outdoor Cooking Facilities: n/a

Cleanup: caterer

View: garden, Cleveland National Forest

RESTRICTIONS:

Alcohol: in-house, no BYO

Smoking: allowed in designated areas

Music: amplified OK with restrictions; indoors until midnight, outdoors curfew 10pm

Wheelchair Access: yes

Insurance: required for outside caterer

Other: no rice or confetti

Mountain Lakes Area

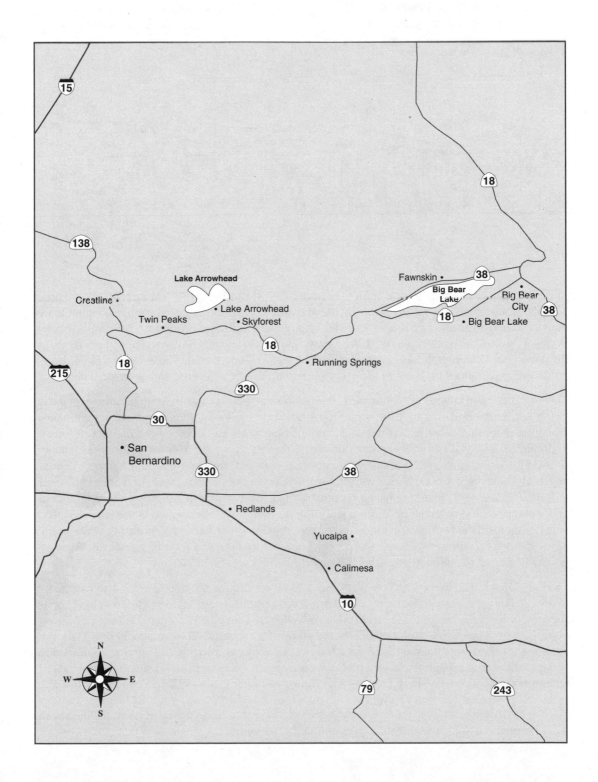

Lake Arrowhead Resort and Spa
An Autograph Collection by Marriott

Resort Hotel

- Rehearsal Dinners
- Ceremonies
- Wedding Receptions
- Private Parties
- Corporate Events
- Meetings
- Film Shoots
- Accommodations

27984 Highway 189, Lake Arrowhead
800/800-6793, 909/744-3061

www.lakearrowheadresort.com
weddings@lakearrowheadresort.com

The picturesque lake region high up in the richly forested San Bernardino Mountains is a favorite Southland destination, attracting skiers, boaters, nature lovers, and engaged couples longing to tie the knot amid unspoiled surroundings. The premier venue for year-round weddings and social events in this scenic landscape is the Lake Arrowhead Resort and Spa. Full-service and pet-friendly, the AAA Four Diamond Resort occupies a prime location along the lakeshore. What's more, it has numerous possibilities for large and small celebrations that showcase the area's seasonal charms.

The wood deck in the resort's Lakeside Lawn is a spectacular spot to exchange vows, especially in the springtime when butterflies, songbirds, and blooming foliage are sweet accompaniments. Towering pines flank each side of the deck, and the blue water and tree-covered mountains form a panoramic backdrop. The adjacent diamond-shaped lawn can be set theater-style for the ceremony or used for receptions. In the summer, why not stage casual festivities right on the resort's private beach, and maybe even say "I do" with the warm sand between your toes? A favorite choice for indoor affairs, especially during winter months, is the Lake Arrowhead Ballroom, whose grandeur and well-appointed detailing make for a stunning reception. Another option is the Lakeview Terrace Room, furnished with warm tones and picture windows that frame a scintillating winterscape or the burnished autumn scenery. Glass doors open out to a terrace, so your guests can enjoy an up-close vista of the shimmering lake and savor the crisp mountain air.

The Lake Arrowhead Resort can host weddings and receptions for 30 to 300 guests, and has plenty of upscale guest accommodations, too: 162 ultra-contemporary, lodge-style rooms and 11 luxurious suites with balconies or patios. Newlyweds can wallow in romance in a spacious Lakeview Suite, outfitted with a fireplace, plush bed linens and an oversize soaking tub (candlelight optional). But what makes the resort unique to the area is its staff's ability to provide full-service coordination and catering for large gatherings. Smaller parties here are no less special: Day-after brunches or rehearsal dinners convene in the resort's fine dining restaurant, BIN189. The refined, yet relaxed, ambiance—replete with water views, a top-flight wine list and acclaimed gourmet menus—ensures a sense of occasion. The Magnum, a cozy private dining room enclosed by glass walls lined with wine bottles, is a sophisticated choice for intimate get-togethers.

Whether you've come to the resort for your wedding, honeymoon, or to relive the memories on your anniversary, be sure to experience the Spa of the Pines. With certified practitioners and nature-inspired treatments, the spa offers supreme nurturing and indulgence.

If you've got a long guest list and a penchant for the pristine alpine environment of Lake Arrowhead, look no further.

CEREMONY CAPACITY: The Lakeside Lawn holds 300 seated. Indoor ceremonies take place in various banquet rooms that can accommodate 30–300 seated.

EVENT/RECEPTION CAPACITY: Indoor areas accommodate 150–300 seated or up to 450 standing. Outdoor seating ranges 80–300.

MEETING CAPACITY: Several spaces seat 16–450 guests.

FEES & DEPOSITS: For weddings, a nonrefundable deposit of 25% of the estimated event total is due with your signed contract; 50% is payable 3 months prior to the event; and the balance is due 14 days prior. Rental fees are discounted on non-holiday Sundays and Fridays. The fee for the Lakeside Lawn area includes white chairs, carpet aisle runner and choice of wedding arch or arbor.

Wedding packages start at $49/person for luncheons or $70/person for dinner and include: champagne and sparkling cider toast, butler-passed hors d'oeuvres (included with dinner package), 3-course meal and wedding cake. Taxes and service charges are additional. A complimentary guest room for the bride and groom is provided with more than 50 guests, and group discounts for overnight wedding guests can be arranged.

For meetings or other business functions, prices vary depending on room, guest count and services selected; call for more specific information. There is an on-site audiovisual company that can accommodate most AV needs.

AVAILABILITY: Year-round, daily.

SERVICES/AMENITIES:

Catering: in-house, no BYO
Kitchen Facilities: n/a
Tables & Chairs: provided
Linens, Silver, etc.: provided
Restrooms: wheelchair accessible
Dance Floor: provided
Bride's Dressing Area: yes
Meeting Equipment: full range

Parking: ample on-site or valet
Accommodations: 173 guest rooms
Telephone: emergency only
Outdoor Night Lighting: some, more CBA
Outdoor Cooking Facilities: BBQs CBA
Cleanup: provided
View: lake, mountains and pine trees
Other: health spa, event coordination on-site restaurant BIN189

RESTRICTIONS:

Alcohol: in-house, no BYO
Smoking: designated areas only
Music: moderately amplified OK indoors until 1am, outdoors until 9pm

Wheelchair Access: yes
Insurance: not required
Other: no rice, birdseed or confetti

Overwhelmed? Use the search criteria on www.HereComesTheGuide.com to narrow down your choices.

415

Pine Rose Weddings and Cabin Resort

Resort

25994 State Highway 189, Lake Arrowhead

909/337-2341

www.pineroseweddings.com
weddings@pinerose.com

- Rehearsal Dinners
- Ceremonies
- Wedding Receptions
- Private Parties
- Corporate Events
- Meetings
- Film Shoots
- Accommodations

Nature lovers and city slickers alike will easily succumb to the charms of Pine Rose Resort. Less than two hours from most So Cal cities, this mile-high country "getaway" near Lake Arrowhead offers six scenic mountain acres with clean, pine-scented air. The woodland setting also provides ceremony and reception sites, lodging for your guests, and a friendly staff—everything you'll need for a wonderful wedding.

While it's pretty hard to improve on Mother Nature, the resort has done exactly that with two magical wedding sites that take full advantage of the property's rustic beauty. The Cedar Creek Pond area, amidst towering evergreens, works well for intimate affairs for up to 70. If you tie the knot here, your guests gather in a cedar-covered area on semicircular rows of smooth log benches. As they await your arrival, you make your entrance via a bridge that crosses a meandering stream, then continue down a flagstone path to the gazebo stage topped with a dramatic, log-and-branch dome. Just beyond the gazebo is a sparkling pond strewn with lily pads and teeming with colorful koi. Enhanced by romantic bridges, boulders and a vintage swing, it's a photographer's delight, presenting lots of choice backdrops.

Your reception takes place on the large decks of two cabins: Storybook and Cedar Creek. The cabins are connected by bridges that span interweaving streams, and their decks overhang Pine Rose Pond. In the middle of the pond, a free-form gazebo made of branches is a unique spot to showcase the cake.

For larger groups, there's the fabulous Hidden Creek Lodge, built by the owners for their daughter's wedding. This multi-tiered site has a stream running down one side and a serene pond at the base. Cut into the natural slope of the land, its amphitheater-like design affords stadium seating with great vistas and even greater acoustics.

At this venue, the ceremony starts with your walk down the aisle under a log trellis, past all your friends and family seated on several levels of decks. You'll exchange vows at the gazebo altar, which is artistically crowned with an organic weaving of branches shed from an old oak tree. Cocktails and dinner follow on three levels of expansive wooden decks adjacent to the lodge. Covered with a wisteria-entwined log arbor, they give everyone unobstructed views of the huge dance floor, festooned with twinkle lights that reflect off the neighboring stream and illuminated waterfall.

Hidden Creek Lodge has five bedrooms, making it perfect for post-wedding family sleepovers as well as pre-wedding preparations with the bridesmaids upstairs and a first-floor game room that's always a hit with the groomsmen. The bride and groom may want to rent the Rustic Romantic Cabin, an ideal honeymoon suite with a stone fireplace and extra-large Jacuzzi tub. Other cabins in the vicinity are also available.

An advantage of hosting a destination wedding at Pine Rose is that they make it so easy for you. With packages created for a range of budgets (and the option of a payment plan), a selection of screened local vendors to choose from, and menu tastings, you'll have a stress-free experience in this fairy-tale place in the woods.

CEREMONY CAPACITY: The site holds 40 seated guests indoors and 175 seated outdoors.

EVENT/RECEPTION CAPACITY: The resort can accommodate 35 seated or 50 standing guests indoors and 175 seated or standing outdoors.

MEETING CAPACITY: Meeting spaces seat up to 40 guests indoors and 175 outdoors.

FEES & DEPOSITS: *Hidden Creek Weddings:* A $1,500 nonrefundable deposit is due at the time of booking, and a monthly payment schedule may be arranged for the balance. All-inclusive and customized packages start at $9,000, and the rate varies depending on guest count (up to 175) and day of the week. All packages include: exclusive use of the wedding site from 1pm on the day of the wedding to 10am the following day; 1-night's lodging for up to 18 wedding guests at Hidden Creek Lodge; ceremony chair placement and takedown; reception table setup and takedown; ceremony coordination; catering, linens, DJ and large dance floor.

Cedar Creek Pond Weddings: A nonrefundable deposit of $1,500 is required to reserve your date, and a monthly payment schedule may be arranged for the balance. For ceremonies, rental fees start at $395 and vary depending on the date and guest count. Site-only rentals start at $995. All-inclusive ceremony and reception packages start at $6,000, and the rate varies depending on the date of the event, guest count, menu, and services requested.

AVAILABILITY: Year-round, daily, call for details.

SERVICES/AMENITIES:

Catering: in-house
Kitchen Facilities: n/a
Tables & Chairs: provided
Linens, Silver, etc.: provided
Restrooms: wheelchair accessible at Hidden Creek
Dance Floor: provided
Bride's Dressing Area: yes
Meeting Equipment: provided
Other: event coordination, WiFi, pool, hot tub

Parking: ample on-site parking
Accommodations: 16 cabins, 4 lodges
Telephone: emergency use only
Outdoor Night Lighting: market lighting
Outdoor Cooking Facilities: BBQs CBA
Cleanup: provided, extra fee
View: creek, forest, pond, meadow, waterfall, log swings, log bridges

RESTRICTIONS:

Alcohol: bar packages available, or BYO with certified bartender
Smoking: designated areas only
Music: OK outdoors, with restrictions

Wheelchair Access: yes
Insurance: liability required

Riverside/Inland Empire

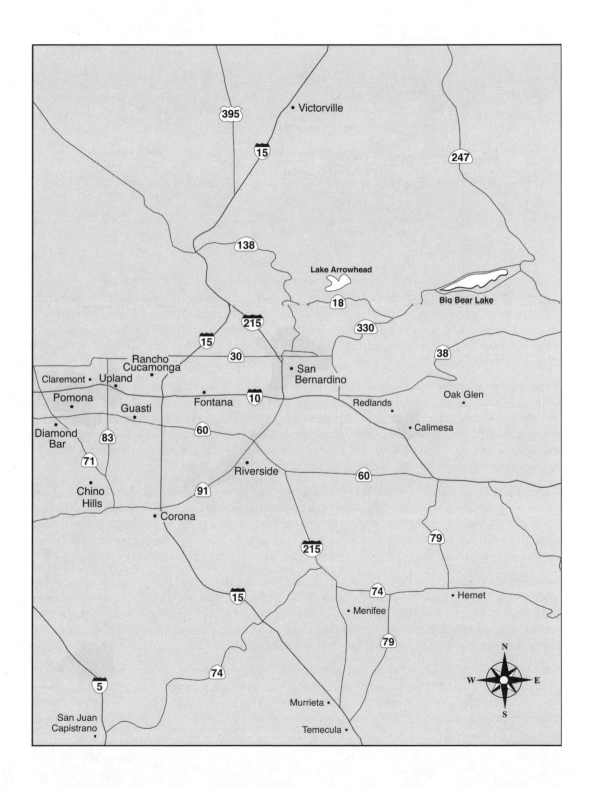

Los Serranos Golf and Country Club

Golf Club

15656 Yorba Avenue, Chino Hills
909/597-1769 x218

www.losserranoscountryclub.com
brent@losserranoscountryclub.com

- Rehearsal Dinners
- Ceremonies
- Wedding Receptions
- Private Parties
- Corporate Events
- Meetings
- Film Shoots
- Accommodations

When you enter Los Serranos Country Club's impressive clubhouse, you may hear the three grand bells in its bell tower ring out the hours. The red-tile roof and adobe-like walls of the Mission-style tower and clubhouse are a reminder of the club's history: It sits on 300 beautiful acres of what was once a Spanish land grant. During California's pioneer days, the ranch that occupied these grounds served as a haven for travelers, and its time-honored tradition of taking care of visitors continues at Los Serranos today.

As expected, wedding couples are exceptionally well taken care of. When brides who've been married here are asked what they like best about Los Serranos, they consistently cite its flexibility and service. For example, while a lot of places have fixed time blocks for weddings, Los Serranos is fine with whatever time of day suits you. You can follow the Inland Empire custom of a late afternoon wedding, when the light and temperature are perfect, but if you'd rather tie the knot in the morning, midday or in the evening, no problem!

Catering is another area where the club is adaptable. Los Serranos' culinary staff does an excellent job catering the hundreds of weddings and golf events that take place every year, but if you have a menu that requires special ethnic dishes, they're happy to let you bring in an outside caterer. "Our willingness to accommodate different needs is based on a core rule," says the course's Events Director. "We're here for the brides. This is their day and we will try to make it the best one possible."

Flexibility also extends to this facility's event spaces, which can handle almost any size group. The heart of Los Serranos' clubhouse is the Montebello Ballroom. By itself it can accommodate up to 300 guests, but when you roll back the oak doors that connect it to the club's restaurant, the two venues combined hold up to 550—with the bonus of a full-service bar at one end. Small party? The ballroom can be sectioned to create a comfortable space for 100.

The Montebello Ballroom is bright and airy thanks to a high, coffered ceiling and three walls of glass that offer a lovely view of the room's veranda, the ceremony garden, and the driving range. The courtyard-like garden is enclosed by the veranda on one side and a long, hedge-lined wall on the other. Guests are seated on the lawn in the center, facing a classic white gazebo. Palms, flowering plants, roses, and other greenery create a photogenic backdrop.

By the way, if your reception is very small, ask about hosting it on the ceremony garden's veranda. On occasion, it's possible to have exclusive use of that area for an al fresco party. Guests enjoy its fresh air, verdant landscaping, and the soothing sounds of a pair of fountains in the background.

The golf club dates back to 1925, and over the years it has become a seasoned event facility known for its attentiveness in serving the needs of brides and grooms. If you have your celebration here, we expect that you, too, will add your voice to the chorus of compliments Los Serranos Country Club receives.

CEREMONY CAPACITY: The site seats 400 guests outside.

EVENT/RECEPTION & MEETING CAPACITY: The club holds 550 seated or standing guests indoors.

FEES & DEPOSITS: A $1,500 deposit is required to reserve your date and the balance is due 14 days prior to the event. Room rental fees start at $500 and vary depending on the type of the event and the day and time rented. Reception packages start at $40/person. Tax, alcohol and a 20% service charge are additional. Call or email for more information or to schedule a tour.

AVAILABILITY: Year-round, daily, anytime.

SERVICES/AMENITIES:

Catering: in-house, or BYO with restrictions
Kitchen Facilities: limited
Tables & Chairs: provided
Linens, Silver, etc.: provided
Restrooms: wheelchair accessible
Dance Floor: portable provided
Bride's Dressing Area: CBA
Meeting Equipment: some provided, more CBA
Other: coordination, in-house wedding cake and florals

Parking: large lot, on street
Accommodations: no guest rooms
Telephone: pay phone
Outdoor Night Lighting: CBA
Outdoor Cooking Facilities: BBQ CBA
Cleanup: provided
View: fountain, garden, fairways, hills, landscaped grounds

RESTRICTIONS:

Alcohol: in-house or BYO with corkage fee
Smoking: outdoors only
Music: amplified OK with restrictions

Wheelchair Access: yes
Insurance: not required

Wedgewood Vellano

2441 Vellano Club Drive, Chino Hills
866/966-3009
www.wedgewoodbanquet.com/vellano
sales@wedgewoodbanquet.com

Event Center

- Rehearsal Dinners
- Ceremonies
- Wedding Receptions
- Private Parties
- Corporate Events
- Meetings
- Film Shoots
- Accommodations

The approach to Vellano Country Club, past a gated entry and into the tree-studded hills of this upscale community, builds an air of anticipation that is justly rewarded when you reach the clubhouse itself. Its Tuscan-inspired design features a red-tile roof, artful use of stonework and stately Italian cypress trees, and its hilltop setting affords wonderful views: looking down over the whole Chino Valley in front, and across the lush, Greg Norman golf course in back.

As guests arrive for your celebration, they can mingle in the Main Lobby, a serene spot with plush seating and modern rugs accenting the terracotta-tiled floor. Or, they can be ushered directly to the ceremony lawn via a curved walkway that passes a profusion of natural landscaping. As it approaches the expansive lawn, fragrant white rosebushes line the path—the same one the bride takes as she makes her grand entrance down the center aisle. Although no decorations are needed, some brides add enhancements like archways made of manzanita branches adorned with crystals that glitter in the sun. At the end of the aisle, the couple says their vows against a tableau of emerald fairways, tree-and-villa-dotted hills, and a vast expanse of sky.

There's ample room to host an al fresco cocktail reception right here, or you can opt for the light-filled second-floor Foyer in the clubhouse. Large, arched windows provide lovely treetop views, and the adjacent outdoor Terrace beckons with spectacular sunset vistas. While guests enjoy libations and hors d'oeuvres, the newlyweds head to the golf course for romantic pictures on the wooden bridge, beside the pond and under the trees. And don't overlook the photo ops indoors: The dramatic, S-shaped staircase leading to the Foyer makes a fun backdrop for bridal party and family photos.

Both the Terrace and the Foyer open to the Grand Venezia Ballroom for the main reception. Modern, gilded chandeliers and gold Chiavari chairs give this venue an understated elegance, while its neutral taupe-and-champagne palette allows you to add any personal touches you wish. Lots of windows provide plenty of natural light as well as evening views, and the central built-in dance floor gives everyone a clear view of the first dance no matter where they're seated. Need to take a quiet moment? Step outside onto the Terrace and relax under the stars.

Since this is a Wedgewood property, you can count on personalized attention to guide you through your choice of menus, décor and preferred vendors, as well as help you customize your event for your specific needs. In addition, your event coordinator can arrange a pre-wedding golf party on the award-winning course or an intimate rehearsal dinner in Vellano's clubby Wine Cellar Room.

CEREMONY CAPACITY: The facility holds 250 seated guests, indoors or outdoors.

EVENT/RECEPTION & MEETING CAPACITY: The site can accommodate 250 seated or standing guests indoors.

FEES & DEPOSITS: 25% of the estimated total event cost is required to reserve your date. An additonal 25% is due 120 days prior to the event and the balance (based on your final guest count) is due 10 days prior. All payments are credited towards your final balance and are nonrefundable and nontransferable. All-inclusive, completely customizable wedding packages start at $33/person. Tax, alcohol and a 21–22% service charge are additional.

AVAILABILITY: Year-round, daily, 7am–midnight.

SERVICES/AMENITIES:

Catering: in-house
Kitchen Facilities: n/a
Tables & Chairs: provided
Linens, Silver, etc.: provided
Restrooms: wheelchair accessible
Dance Floor: provided
Bride's Dressing Area: yes
Meeting Equipment: some provided
Other: in-house wedding cake and florals; clergy on staff; AV equipment; event coordination, extra fee

Parking: large lot
Accommodations: no guest rooms
Telephone: emergency use only
Outdoor Night Lighting: provided
Outdoor Cooking Facilities: none
Cleanup: provided
View: cityscape, fairways, hills, landscaped grounds; panorama of meadow, hills and valley

RESTRICTIONS:

Alcohol: in-house
Smoking: not allowed
Music: amplified OK with restrictions

Wheelchair Access: yes
Insurance: liability required

DoubleTree by Hilton Claremont

Hotel

555 West Foothill Boulevard, Claremont
909/626-2411

www.doubletreeclaremont.com
jgutzwiller@doubletreeclaremont.com

- Rehearsal Dinners
- Ceremonies
- Wedding Receptions
- Private Parties
- Corporate Events
- Meetings
- Film Shoots
- Accommodations

In Claremont, a town many people call "The City of Trees," the DoubleTree stands out as an oasis within an oasis. Its 14-acre grounds, adorned with dozens of different species of flowers and trees as well as some beautiful sculptural elements, are a hub of social life—and weddings—in this westernmost part of the Inland Empire. Besides the earthy and exuberant subtropical feel of its landscaping, the 50-year-old local landmark also has plenty of architectural character. While owners through the years have expanded the facility and remodeled its interior, they've done so carefully, keeping the boutique-hotel vibe intact.

The heart of the DoubleTree is its courtyard, by far the favorite location for weddings. Brides love it both for its look and its privacy (it's closed to everyone but wedding party guests for the duration of the ceremony). The courtyard's focal point is a water feature at one end—a long slate-brick wall set into a high, arched alcove. Water runs gently down the stone, calling to mind the cooling Moorish fountains of old Spain. The water's sparkle and soothing sound are delights to the senses, and add a tranquil element to any gathering. Sometimes, when there's a breeze, swirls of mist dance away from the wall—an entrancing sight. A colorful fringe of ivy, palms and flowers frames the fountain, while overhead, bright cloth streamers span the courtyard and shade people from the afternoon sun.

Just steps from the courtyard, DoubleTree's two neighboring ballrooms are typically used in tandem: one for a cocktail reception and the other for their seated dinner. The hotel also regularly and seamlessly hosts small weddings in its inviting Cedar Room on the second floor. Guests often like to mingle outside on the room's arcaded veranda, where they can enjoy some people-watching in the courtyard below.

An independently operated on-site day spa is a welcome haven for the bride and her entourage to prep for the ceremony or wind down and relax. It's co-ed, so men in the wedding party can step in and have some fun, too. Also on the property, but detached from the main buildings, is "Piano Piano," a lounge that's perfect for bachelor, bachelorette or boy-girl parties. With its dozens of nightclub-style tables and booths, and a stage set with two pianos that professional players often use to engage in some uproarious musical duels, "Piano Piano" is a fine place to get noisy and happy. People can let off steam without worrying about the neighbors.

Getting married at the DoubleTree is like cocooning yourself in a beloved local institution that manages to be hip and traditional, efficient and hang-loose, formal and casual—all at the same time and all to the right degree. When you stand before that glistening slate fountain with your groom, surrounded by greenery, golden light and affectionate well wishers, you'll experience the world at that moment as being just about as right as it can possibly be.

CEREMONY CAPACITY: The hotel holds 400 seated guests indoors and 250 seated outdoors.

EVENT/RECEPTION CAPACITY: The hotel can accommodate 250 seated or 500 standing guests indoors and 100 seated or 370 standing outdoors.

MEETING CAPACITY: Meeting spaces hold up to 400 seated guests.

FEES & DEPOSITS: A 25% deposit is required to reserve your date. The balance is due 7 days prior to event. Rental fees range $0–8,015 depending on the circumstances of the event. Rental fees are normally waived if the food and beverage minimums are met. Meals range $46–70/person. Tax, alcohol and a 21% service charge are additional.

AVAILABILITY: Year-round, daily, anytime.

SERVICES/AMENITIES:

Catering: in-house
Kitchen Facilities: n/a
Tables & Chairs: provided
Linens, Silver, etc.: provided
Restrooms: wheelchair accessible
Dance Floor: provided
Bride's Dressing Area: CBA
Meeting Equipment: CBA

Parking: large lot
Accommodations: 190 guest rooms
Telephone: house phone
Outdoor Night Lighting: CBA
Outdoor Cooking Facilities: BBQ CBA
Cleanup: provided
View: garden patio, waterfall
Other: spa services, AV equipment

RESTRICTIONS:

Alcohol: in-house
Smoking: not allowed
Music: amplified OK indoors

Wheelchair Access: yes
Insurance: not required

The professionals in the back of this book are the best in the business. How do we know? Read page 549.

425

Padua Hills Theatre

4467 Padua Avenue, Claremont
909/624-8628
www.chantrellescatering.com
chantrelles@aol.com

Historic Special Events Facility

- Rehearsal Dinners
- Ceremonies
- Wedding Receptions
- Private Parties
- Corporate Events
- Meetings
- Film Shoots
- Accommodations

Ensconced in the chaparral-covered foothills of the San Gabriel Mountains is the Padua Hills Theatre, a landmark banquet facility with a significant cultural past. The theatre was built in the 1930s as a centerpiece for a community of local artists, and Claremont residents made a tradition of attending dinner theatre in the lovely Spanish-Colonial building. In the early '70s the theatre became a historic site, and by the early '80s it began hosting private special events under the expert direction of *Chantrelles Fine Catering*. Lavishly renovated in 2008, the theatre is more impressive than ever. It's no wonder wedding couples flock here to wed on the tranquil grounds and entertain their friends and family with Old World panache.

Staged against the mountainous silhouette of the Angeles National Forest and overlooking a wilderness preserve, events at the Padua Hills Theatre enjoy a picturesque rural setting. The buildings and landscape capture the simple allure of vintage California, with red-tile roofs, brick and flagstone. As your guests arrive, they walk beneath a long arbor hugged by olive trees and perfumed by jasmine. At the entrance, they're treated to a refreshing glass of iced lemon water and a romantic melody playing in the background.

Three sites offer a variety of ceremony settings. In the Plaza Courtyard, located to the right the arbor, brick and stone paths amble among olive trees, manicured shrubbery and terracotta pots brimming with blooms. Couples say "I do" beneath a unique wrought-iron gazebo. The courtyard is also a versatile option for receptions. You can host an al fresco cocktail hour next to a blazing fireplace, or a sumptuous dinner with linen-draped tables, Chiavari chairs and the sparkle of twinkle lights.

The breathtaking Sunset View Terrace wraps around the banquet hall and provides a spectacular vista. As the sun sets over the densely forested canyon and the city lights begin to shimmer on the horizon, it becomes the perfect backdrop for a ceremony and wedding photos (you'll want to pose next to the terrace's beautiful fountain, too!). If you're lucky, you may even catch a glimpse of a hummingbird or a baby deer, out for a stroll in the fresh mountain air.

From the terrace, French doors open into the Garner Dining Room, where guests mingle over cocktails and delicious hors d'oeuvres. The room's original hardwood floors give off a rich luster, and the ceiling's open beams can be decorated to suit any occasion. A neighboring alcove also has doors to the terrace, as well as a built-in bar covered with painted Spanish-style tiles. On the upper level of the Garner Room is an oversized fireplace that warms the space during the winter months.

Dinner is served in the stunning Theatre Ballroom, with a vaulted ceiling, wrought-iron chandeliers and the original wall sconces. Lining the walls are hand-carved mirrors framed by rich draperies, lending an overall impression of grandeur. The room's design enables each guest to witness everything that takes place: the first dance, cake cutting, bouquet toss, etc.

Your hosts at the Padua Hills Theatre, *Chantrelles Fine Catering,* are renowned for their delectable gourmet fare, themed buffets and elegant presentation. They're also experienced event planners, so relax. In their hands your celebration will unfold as smoothly as a professional theatrical production—but you'll get all the applause.

CEREMONY CAPACITY: The Plaza Courtyard can hold 250+ seated. The Sunset View Terrace area can hold up to 120 seated guests.

EVENT/RECEPTION & MEETING CAPACITY: The Dining Room accommodates up to 270 seated or 300 standing guests; the Courtyard up to 300 seated; and the Garner Room up to 110 guests. Interior spaces combined seat up to 380.

FEES & DEPOSITS: A deposit ranging from $6,500 to one third of the estimated event total (payable to *Chantrelles Fine Catering)* and the full rental fee are required to reserve your date. Rental fees range $3,000–6,500 depending on the day of the week. Buffets start at $49.50/person, and sit-down meals at $50/person. Tax, alcohol and a 20% service charge are additional. Alcohol is provided through *Chantrelles Fine Catering;* call for package pricing. Ceremony-only fees start at $1,750. A security guard fee may apply.

AVAILABILITY: Year-round, daily, anytime.

SERVICES/AMENITIES:

Catering: provided by *Chantrelles Fine Catering*
Kitchen Facilities: n/a
Tables & Chairs: provided
Linens, Silver, etc.: provided, linens extra charge
Restrooms: wheelchair accessible, call for details
Dance Floor: yes
Bride's Dressing Area: provided
Meeting Equipment: CBA or BYO

Parking: large lots or valet CBA
Accommodations: no guest rooms
Telephone: house phone
Outdoor Night Lighting: yes
Outdoor Cooking Facilities: CBA
Cleanup: provided
View: Claremont and Pomona Valley
Other: event coordination and on-site entertainment company available

RESTRICTIONS:

Alcohol: provided by *Chantrelles Fine Catering*
Smoking: outside only in designated areas, call for details
Music: amplified OK indoors, with restrictions

Wheelchair Access: yes
Insurance: required for DJs and bands
Other: no rice, confetti or outdoor flames

Eagle Glen Golf Club

Golf Club

1800 Eagle Glen Parkway, Corona
951/278-2842 x206
www.eagleglengc.com
tbell@eagleglengc.com

- Rehearsal Dinners
- Ceremonies
- Wedding Receptions
- Private Parties
- Corporate Events
- Meetings
- Film Shoots

Accommodations

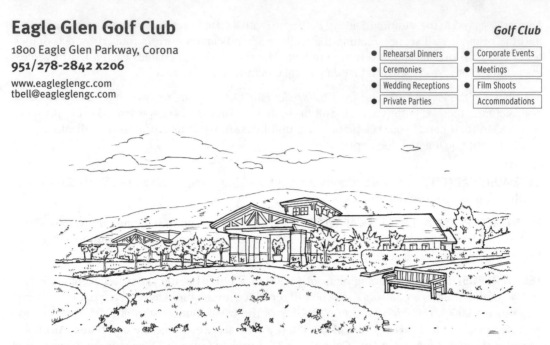

One of the best things in life is pleasant surprises, and Eagle Glen Golf Club on Corona's lofty west side is full of them. The first time you lay eyes on its cupola-topped clubhouse with its impressive entrance of cinnamon-colored wood trusses, you may be amazed to find a place like this up here. The next surprise comes when you step into the soaring light-splashed lobby and see the quality of the architecture and design. But that's just a prelude to the final treat, first glimpsed through the lobby's glass doors and windows: the stunning view of the verdant golf course against a backdrop of chaparral-covered hills.

Eagle Glen ambles along the base of some very steep hills on the eastern edge of Cleveland National Forest. While you're on the golf course, you're in a private, human realm. But once you leave the greens and start heading up the hills, you enter a wild domain of untamed landscapes. Eagle Glen gives you the wonderful sensation of gazing over nature's might from an absolutely civilized vantage.

There are two outdoor ceremony options to choose from. The Lakeside site features a wrought-iron arbor, perched on a small rise above a reed-ringed pond with a fountain playing at its center. Surrounding it are close-cropped greens that flow up to the foot of the hills. A graceful low wooden bridge that spans the pond at its narrowest point is a splendid spot for photos. For a more dramatic setting, take a stroll over to the Mountainside site, which has a mountain vista. Here, you can get married beneath a wrought-iron gazebo, enclosed by a semicircle of sheltering pine trees.

Eagle Glen's spacious ballroom is managed by a seasoned catering staff that handles scores of weddings each year. Floor-to-ceiling windows and glass doors let in lots of natural light, and look out to the veranda and beyond. Here, guests can sit and savor picturesque views of the back nine's grand swath of lawn, as it tumbles toward the clubhouse from the edge of the national forest. In the afterglow of a lovely ceremony and great food, you and your guests will feel a sense of total satisfaction as the sun sets behind the mountains.

Perched just above the treelined streets of the surrounding community, and next to a national forest, Eagle Glen really is one of Corona's best-kept secrets. After experiencing this inviting venue's beautiful location and high-quality services, you and your guests will not be disappointed.

CEREMONY CAPACITY: The Club holds up to 500 seated guests outdoors, and 340 indoors.

EVENT/RECEPTION & MEETING CAPACITY: Indoor spaces accommodate 340 seated or 600 standing guests.

FEES & DEPOSITS: A $1,000 deposit is required to reserve your date. The balance is due 30 days prior to the event. Meals range $10–85/person. Tax, alcohol and a 20% service charge are additional.

AVAILABILITY: Year-round, daily, 6:30am–midnight.

SERVICES/AMENITIES:

Catering: in-house, no BYO
Kitchen Facilities: n/a
Tables & Chairs: provided
Linens, Silver, etc.: provided
Restrooms: wheelchair accessible
Dance Floor: yes
Bride's Dressing Area: yes
Meeting Equipment: CBA
Other: event coordination, wedding cake

Parking: large lot
Accommodations: no guest rooms
Telephone: house or office phones
Outdoor Night Lighting: access only
Outdoor Cooking Facilities: no
Cleanup: provided
View: fairways, mountains, canyon, lake, grounds

RESTRICTIONS:

Alcohol: in-house or BYO with corkage fee
Smoking: outside only
Music: amplified OK

Wheelchair Access: yes
Insurance: liability required

The Veranda at Green River Golf Club

Golf Club

5215 Green River Road, Corona
951/739-5985
www.playgreenriver.com
events@playgreenriver.com

- Rehearsal Dinners
- Ceremonies
- Wedding Receptions
- Private Parties
- Corporate Events
- Meetings
- Film Shoots
- Accommodations

It seems like most of us look forward to getting away from the hustle and bustle of the city, and going to a tranquil setting where we can become one with ourselves and nature. Green River Golf Club, located in the Santa Ana Canyons in Corona, is just such a place. The Santa Ana River wends its way through this 560-acre property, filled with rolling hills, trees and lakes. Over 50 species of birds—including the endangered golden eagle—call Green River home. If this sounds like a picture-perfect location for a wedding or special event, it is.

Because along with this venue's natural beauty, Green River Golf Club will not only ensure that your celebration unfolds effortlessly, but will do it all for a reasonable price.

Against this serene backdrop, The Veranda at Green River Golf Club is a sophisticated venue. Guests stroll into the Spanish Revival-style building under a gabled roof and green awning, and through a doorway flanked on both sides by huge urns. They mingle in the foyer, and enjoy cocktails served in an adjacent peach-hued room, where they can also sit at tables and chat. When it's time for the reception everyone gathers in the banquet room, an inviting space with subtle recessed lighting in a coffered ceiling. The neutral color scheme makes it easy to decorate the room to your taste: Do something simple, or if you really want to pull out all the stops, create an ethereal wonderland with yards of tulle and white fairy lights. Large picture windows frame views of the verdant fairways and ravines beyond.

Those of you who choose to get married here, too, will appreciate the ceremony sites. One of them is a garden, bounded by a trellised fence and located on a sloped area right next to the immaculately groomed fairway. Two stone-edged steps lead to a platform where vows are exchanged. The second option, a recently added gazebo, provides a vista of the Santa Ana mountain range. If you tie the knot here, don't be too surprised if a deer decides to join your party!

Wonderful photo opportunities abound, among them a burbling stone fountain and an arcaded cloister not far from the banquet room. Green River's appealing combination of skilled staff and gorgeous natural surroundings promises an unforgettable celebration.

CEREMONY CAPACITY: The club holds up to 400 seated guests outdoors.

EVENT/RECEPTION & MEETING CAPACITY: There are several indoor spaces that accommodate 60–200 seated guests. The entire club holds up to 450 seated or 600 standing guests.

FEES & DEPOSITS: 25% of the estimated event total is required to reserve your date. Wedding packages start at $31/person and include rental fee, bartenders, outside ceremony setup and cleanup. Tax, alcohol and service charge are additional. Customized packages are also available.

AVAILABILITY: Year-round, daily, anytime.

SERVICES/AMENITIES:

Catering: in-house, or BYO ethnic caterer
Kitchen Facilities: fully equipped
Tables & Chairs: provided
Linens, Silver, etc.: provided
Restrooms: wheelchair accessible
Dance Floor: yes
Bride's Dressing Area: CBA
Meeting Equipment: AV equipment CBA

Parking: ample on site
Accommodations: no guest rooms
Telephone: emergency use only
Outdoor Night Lighting: yes
Outdoor Cooking Facilities: no
Cleanup: provided
View: fairways, mountains
Other: event coordination CBA

RESTRICTIONS:

Alcohol: in-house
Smoking: outside only
Music: amplified OK

Wheelchair Access: yes
Insurance: not required
Other: no open flames

Wedgewood at The Retreat

Event Center

8007 Soft Winds Drive, Corona
866/966-3009

www.wedgewoodbanquet.com/the-retreat
sales@wedgewoodbanquet.com

- Rehearsal Dinners
- Ceremonies
- Wedding Receptions
- Private Parties
- Corporate Events
- Meetings
- Film Shoots
- Accommodations

Wedgewood at The Retreat is a true beauty inside and out. From its enviable location at the top of a hill within a gated community and semiprivate golf and country club, this popular Inland Empire wedding venue does indeed provide a quiet retreat with sweeping views, cooling breezes and a sprawling Tuscan-inspired clubhouse.

The sun-drenched building has covered breezeways along the front, and a fountain courtyard planted with roses and fluttery palm trees. From the courtyard, double doors open to the clubhouse's grand entry, a high-ceilinged "great room" with wood-and-iron crossbeams, a stone fireplace, and casually elegant leather and velvet furnishings. During the evening, this area is available for your guests to sign in and mingle before your event.

Vows are exchanged on the manicured ceremony lawn out back, where friends and family can savor the unobstructed view of the Temescal Valley while awaiting your arrival. You make your grand entrance from a shaded side patio, heading toward the archway at the far edge of the lawn. Since you'll be facing east, if you time it right you'll get to tie the knot during the "magic hour," just as the setting sun casts a romantic pink glow on the mountains in the distance.

While there's more than enough room to have cocktails right here on the lawn, the entire back of the clubhouse—with its flagstone patios—is yours to enjoy for drinks, dinner, and even dancing. Half shaded, half sunny, and decorated with olive trees in large terracotta pots, these expansive patios overlook terraced gardens filled with roses and geraniums, as well as the tree-studded hills beyond. Richly scrolled gold chandelier pendant lights hang from the eaves above the patios, adding a touch of glamour (as well as the flavor of a private Italian villa).

Then, as evening descends, your guests can drift over to the outdoor fireplace, ringed with comfy seating for intimate conversations. Or, you can take the party inside to the dining room, transformed for dancing with your DJ or band setup by the arched glass doorway or in front of the large stone fireplace. (By the way, this area makes an excellent weather-contingency ceremony site.) Just beyond the dining room is a handsomely detailed bar, complete with marble fireplace, soft leather chairs, dark wood and a high, coffered ceiling, where friends and family can cap the evening with a final toast.

In addition, there's an intimate, tucked-away dining room for small gatherings or rehearsal dinners and a glass-enclosed banquet area that offers a climate-controlled, indoor/outdoor event space for year-round celebrations.

Since events are held away from the golf course, there are no distractions and plenty of private areas for photo opportunities, including a great spot to take a bird's-eye group shot of your entire wedding party.

One key to your fête's success is the experienced Wedgewood staff, who'll customize their all-inclusive wedding packages to your exact specifications. Their convenient, value-packed services make for a day that's not only memorable, but virtually effortless as well.

CEREMONY CAPACITY: The site holds up to 150 seated indoors and 250 seated guests outdoors.

EVENT/RECEPTION CAPACITY: The facility can accommodate 150 seated or standing guests indoors, and 250 seated or standing outdoors.

MEETING CAPACITY: Meeting spaces hold 150 seated guests.

FEES & DEPOSITS: 25% of the estimated total event cost is required to reserve your date. An additonal 25% is due 120 days prior to the event and the balance (based on your final guest count) is due 10 days prior. All payments are credited towards your final balance and are nonrefundable and nontransferable. All-inclusive, completely customizable wedding packages start at $33/person. Tax, alcohol and a 21–22% service charge are additional.

AVAILABILITY: Year-round, daily, times may vary.

SERVICES/AMENITIES:

Catering: in-house
Kitchen Facilities: n/a
Tables & Chairs: provided
Linens, Silver, etc.: provided
Restrooms: wheelchair accessible
Dance Floor: provided, CBA
Bride's Dressing Area: yes
Meeting Equipment: CBA
Other: complimentary event coordination

Parking: large lot
Accommodations: no guest rooms
Telephone: emergency use only
Outdoor Night Lighting: CBA
Outdoor Cooking Facilities: BBQ CBA
Cleanup: provided
View: fairways, fountain, courtyard, landscaped grounds; panorama of mountains and valley

RESTRICTIONS:

Alcohol: in-house
Smoking: outside only
Music: amplified OK

Wheelchair Access: yes
Insurance: not required

Want to know **WHAT TO ASK** a potential location or vendor? Check out our Questions to Ask starting on page 19.

Wedgewood Glen Ivy

Event Center

24400 Trilogy Parkway, Corona
866/966-3009

wedgewoodbanquet.com/glen-ivy
sales@wedgewoodbanquet.com

- Rehearsal Dinners
- Ceremonies
- Wedding Receptions
- Private Parties
- Corporate Events
- Meetings
- Film Shoots
- Accommodations

Ever since honeymooners discovered Niagara Falls, brides have felt an affinity for waterfalls. So it's no wonder that Wedgewood Glen Ivy proudly showcases not one, but three impressive cascades, including a spectacular two-tiered beauty. But start to explore this Inland Empire venue and you'll find even more to appreciate.

Located on the same sprawling complex as the Glen Ivy Hot Springs & Spa (pre-wedding bridal party, anyone?), the golf course begins to reveal itself as you climb towards the clubhouse. This modern, low-slung building has a slate façade and is landscaped with thick shrubbery, queen palms and a graceful willow that sways in the breeze.

To the right is the outdoor ceremony site, a lush, wide lawn with a paved bridal aisle leading to a canopied gazebo altar. Framed by colorful blooming hedges and a towering oak tree, you and your beloved tie the knot against a picturesque backdrop of the 9th-hole pond, where water flowing from all the falls merges. In the distance, the verdant mountains of the Cleveland Forest are a nice contrast to the earth tones of Temescal Canyon below.

After vows are exchanged, it's time to raise a glass of champagne at the Canyon Grille, situated at the back of the clubhouse and reachable via a dramatic walkway, marked with stone pillars and a redwood lattice roof. The views from this bright, open restaurant/bar and its adjacent terrace are fantastic. Guests can mingle at the stainless-and-granite bar or step outside to drink in the wide-angle panorama, from the Chino Hills to the manicured fairways and rugged forest beyond. Meanwhile, you and your photographer head off to capture memories: sitting on a sweetheart bench beside a running creek with a bower of trees above; a cinema-worthy kiss in front of the signature 30-foot granite waterfall (equally fabulous taken from the base or a grassy knoll towards the top)…and the "money shot" at the end of a long tunnel with that signature waterfall glistening behind you. In fact, this tunnel is so cool and has such great acoustics, you just might want to serenade your sweetie or bring your attendants inside it for a doo-wop session.

Join your party for dinner and dancing in the reception tent. The draped cathedral ceiling, wall-to-wall windows, and modern chandeliers give this space an airy, indoor/outdoor feel—with the added benefit of year-round climate control. A wooden dance floor in the center and ample room for a band or DJ station keep the party going well after the sun sets, and lights from hillside homes set the night aglow.

The staff at Wedgewood Glen Ivy are experts at making everything easy and convenient, with packages that can be customized to your needs and budget. And of course, they'll help you plan your wedding from start to finish.

CEREMONY CAPACITY: The site holds 220 seated guests, indoors or outdoors.

EVENT/RECEPTION CAPACITY: The facility can accommodate 220 seated or standing indoors.

MEETING CAPACITY: Meeting spaces can seat up to 220.

FEES & DEPOSITS: 25% of the estimated total event cost is required to reserve your date. An additonal 25% is due 120 days prior to the event and the balance (based on your final guest count) is due 10 days prior. All payments are credited towards your final balance and are nonrefundable and nontransferable. All-inclusive, completely customizable wedding packages start at $33/person. Tax, alcohol and a 21–22% service charge are additional.

AVAILABILITY: Year-round, daily, office hours: 9am–6pm, event hours: 6am–11pm.

SERVICES/AMENITIES:

Catering: in-house
Kitchen Facilities: n/a
Tables & Chairs: provided
Linens, Silver, etc.: provided
Restrooms: wheelchair accessible
Dance Floor: portable provided
Bride's Dressing Area: yes
Meeting Equipment: some provided
Other: in-house wedding cake and florals; clergy on staff; event coordination, extra fee

Parking: large lot
Accommodations: no guest rooms
Telephone: emergency use only
Outdoor Night Lighting: provided
Outdoor Cooking Facilities: none
Cleanup: provided
View: creek, garden, fountain, courtyard, waterfall, landscaped grounds; panorama of hills, lake, mountains and fairways

RESTRICTIONS:

Alcohol: full in-house bar
Smoking: not allowed
Music: amplified OK

Wheelchair Access: yes
Insurance: liability required

Diamond Bar Center

Event Center

1600 Grand Avenue, Diamond Bar
909/839-7082

www.diamondbarcenter.com
reservations@diamondbarca.gov

- Rehearsal Dinners
- Ceremonies
- Wedding Receptions
- Private Parties
- Corporate Events
- Meetings
- Film Shoots
- Accommodations

From the moment the Diamond Bar Center opened, it garnered raves and it's easy to see why. Designed to blend into its surroundings, the serenely modern venue is actually quite a standout. Taking a cue from iconic architect Frank Lloyd Wright's work, this city-owned facility incorporates natural materials, clean lines and large expanses of glass to both take advantage of, and become part of, its hilltop setting in Summitridge Park. Atop its lovely perch within the 26-acre recreation area (which abuts 250 additional acres of wild preserve), the center affords sweeping vistas of tranquil gardens, hiking trails and city lights down below, making it feel like a deluxe retreat that's remarkably close to three major counties.

If you have your ceremony here, your day will probably start at the aptly named Wedding Oval. You'll make your entrance down a long, covered walkway, bordered by red carpet and white iceberg roses as well as iris. Your path takes you past the oval to a stream studded with small boulders, beside which you'll exchange vows. Guests are seated just steps away in the Wedding Oval itself, an elliptical lawn ringed by an array of native plants. From this site, you and your guests will be able to see the San Gabriel Valley behind you and, depending upon the time of year, you might even catch a glimpse of snow on the mountains.

Continue to drink in the panoramic views while enjoying cocktails and hors d'oeuvres on the center's wraparound patio, or head inside to mingle in the foyer. Either way, you can keep the ballroom doors closed until you're ready for dinner ... and the big "reveal." The soaring, two-story-high ballroom seems even taller because of the coffered ceiling and expansive windows. Organic stonework in shades of sandstone and dusky adobe adds visual drama to some of the walls. The large room has a raised center stage with a dropdown screen and everything you need to present an audiovisual show. It also features customized zone and accent lighting, which allows you to control the level of light inside so that everyone can see the city sparkle in the distance.

For a more intimate gathering, use just a section of the ballroom, or consider the similarly styled Pine Room or the Sycamore Room, which has its own patio for that indoor/outdoor flow.

Whichever space you choose, the entire facility provides an elegant, minimalist backdrop for you to embellish any way you wish. Flexibility is key here, so you have enormous freedom to bring in whatever catering services, flowers, decorations, etc., that best match your vision and your budget. But remember, the Diamond Bar Center is *very* popular and books up fast, so reserve early!

CEREMONY CAPACITY: The site holds 822 seated guests indoors and 250 seated outdoors.

EVENT/RECEPTION CAPACITY: The facility can accommodate 438 seated banquet-style and 822 seated theater-style.

MEETING CAPACITY: Meeting spaces hold 822 seated indoors.

FEES & DEPOSITS: A $500 refundable deposit is required to reserve your date and the balance is due 60 days prior to the event. Rental fees range $165–600/hour depending on the room requested, and the day and time of the event.

AVAILABILITY: Year-round: Sunday–Thursday, 7:30am–11pm; Friday & Saturday, 7:30am–midnight.

SERVICES/AMENITIES:

Catering: BYO
Kitchen Facilities: prep only
Tables & Chairs: provided
Linens, Silver, etc.: BYO
Restrooms: wheelchair accessible
Dance Floor: CBA, extra fee
Bride's Dressing Area: CBA, extra fee
Meeting Equipment: CBA

Parking: large lot
Accommodations: no guest rooms
Telephone: emergency use only
Outdoor Night Lighting: access only
Outdoor Cooking Facilities: no
Cleanup: renter
View: creek, garden, landscaped grounds; panorama of cityscape, mountains and hills

RESTRICTIONS:

Alcohol: BYO
Smoking: designated areas only
Music: amplified OK indoors

Wheelchair Access: yes
Insurance: liability required

Diamond Bar Golf Course

Golf Club

22751 Golden Springs Drive, Diamond Bar
888/360-9796

www.countryclubreceptions.com
privateevents@diamondbargc.com

● Rehearsal Dinners	● Corporate Events
● Ceremonies	● Meetings
● Wedding Receptions	● Film Shoots
● Private Parties	Accommodations

Diamond Bar is a popular golf course whose vibrant greens, bordered by tall shade trees, seem to run off into infinity. But golfing activities don't interfere with the venue's gem of a wedding site, located around a corner and away from all of the bustle. From the front of the clubhouse there's no hint of this sweet place, but once you come upon it you have one of those pure "ahh" moments. You see a flower-fringed white gazebo nestled under a grove of leafy syca-mores. A paved path curves away from it over luxuriant grass to a terrace that runs the length of the inviting banquet room. The room's tall north and east windows create "walls" that appear to be made of pure glass, and a shady patio at its far end—only steps from the gazebo—features a koi pond.

A hedge of red-tipped photinia sets the lawn, gazebo and banquet room apart from the rest of Diamond Bar. Beyond it you can glimpse the golfing activities, but they all seem to be at a peaceful remove. Inside the hedge's perimeter there's a sheltered world of colorful flowers, lush grass, and the speckled white bark of the sycamores. Standing here, you feel like you're in a protected glade in the woods.

The banquet room is a bright place, its walls finished in a creamy white with pale yellow highlights. Dramatic trusses span the space, and brass chandeliers with tulip-shaped sconces drop gracefully from the cathedral ceiling. Next to the glass wall that runs beside the patio is an impressive wall-to-wall dance floor—this is one serious boogie zone that has probably clinched the deal for many a bride. The lobby outside the banquet room also accesses a bridal changing room, the terrace and the clubhouse bar. Wedding parties often begin the processional from there, walking along the terrace to the gazebo.

Besides the gazebo, Diamond Bar offers several excellent backdrops for wedding photos, including the course's picturesque lake and, in season, a high bank of blazing bougainvillea downslope from the banquet room.

A facility's good looks are important, but there's an equally critical factor: Can the kitchen cook? The answer is yes! The Inland Empire has become such a mosaic of ethnicities that Diamond Bar's banquet staff learned long ago how to prepare almost any cuisine. The accommodating kitchen, which handles scores of weddings every year, is scrupulous about arranging advance tastings so you can be confident of the dishes that will be served at your event.

When you go down the checklist of the things that make for a fine wedding day, Diamond Bar has as good an ensemble as you're likely to find. Saying "I do" here could well be a decision you'll be glad you made for years to come.

CEREMONY, EVENT/RECEPTION & MEETING CAPACITY: The facility holds 250 seated or 400 standing guests, both indoors and outdoors.

FEES & DEPOSITS: A nonrefundable deposit, which is applied to your food and beverage total, is required to reserve your date. The amount of the deposit varies, depending on how far in advance you book. Payment terms for the balance also vary, and may be arranged on an individual basis. Meals start at $34/person. Tax, alcohol and service charge are additional. Menus and packages can be customized to fit your needs and budget. Call for details.

AVAILABILITY: Year-round, daily.

SERVICES/AMENITIES:

Catering: in-house
Kitchen Facilities: n/a
Tables & Chairs: provided
Linens, Silver, etc.: provided
Restrooms: wheelchair accessible
Dance Floor: provided
Bride's Dressing Area: provided
Meeting Equipment: some provided, more CBA

Parking: large lot
Accommodations: no guest rooms
Telephone: emergency use only
Outdoor Night Lighting: CBA
Outdoor Cooking Facilities: BBQ CBA
Cleanup: provided
View: fairways, meadow, garden, koi pond
Other: private event specialist, WiFi

RESTRICTIONS:

Alcohol: in-house
Smoking: outside only
Music: amplified OK

Wheelchair Access: yes
Insurance: not required

Menifee Lakes Country Club

Country Club

29875 Menifee Lakes Drive, Menifee
951/672-4824

www.menifee-lakes.com
angelad@menifee-lakes.com

- Rehearsal Dinners
- Ceremonies
- Wedding Receptions
- Private Parties
- Corporate Events
- Meetings
- Film Shoots
- Accommodations

"Wall of windows." Keep that phrase in mind when you come to this low-key country club to check out the venue. Why? Because the bank of big, tall windows in the main dining room frames a superb golf course view, and will probably be what makes you ask, "Where do I sign?"

You'll be impressed even before you reach the windows. The club's stucco-clad main building has a beautiful entrance: A circular drive is rimmed by pepper trees, Canary Island palms and flowering eucalyptus, and centered by a burbling three-tiered fountain. As you step out of your car beneath the grand columned portico, you immediately notice the imposing pair of front doors capped with a classic lunette window.

The foyer, which many wedding parties use for their dance floor and DJ stand, leads directly to the main dining room and those spectacular windows. On the other side of the glass, soaring ornamental palms flank fairways and winding paths, and Menifee's two manmade lakes glint blue. In the distance are high desert hills, including a dramatic peak of boulders that looks like a giant's rock pile.

The view, however, is not this room's only asset. Painted in creamy earth colors, it also features a large fireplace, a lodge-like ceiling (the rafters are made of rounded timbers with the bark still on), and an eye-catching chandelier shaped like a great metallic hoop skirt. Half-walls help separate the room visually from the foyer. The combination of outdoor panorama and interior features are such strong points that many brides decide the room needs little decoration.

Right next door is a bar that belongs exclusively to wedding parties after 6pm. (The club can also provide a standalone bar.) Folding doors to one side open to a smaller banquet room that can be used independently or in conjunction with the main dining room. All three of these rooms have access to a terrace, shaded in the afternoon, that overlooks the excellent golf course vista.

For smaller weddings, the downstairs grill room and its adjoining terrace are available.

The club also hosts rehearsal dinners, bachelorette parties and post-ceremony brunches. Menifee's obliging kitchen can accommodate almost any budget, and will customize menus. Large wood-paneled changing rooms for both brides and grooms provide abundant sinks, storage and mirrors.

A striking landscape, an attractive interior space, a capable kitchen and lots of experience with weddings…Menifee Lakes has all the virtues you'd expect a good country club to offer.

CEREMONY & EVENT/RECEPTION CAPACITY: The site holds 300 seated or 400 standing guests, indoors or outdoors.

MEETING CAPACITY: Meeting spaces hold 200 seated guests.

FEES & DEPOSITS: A $1,000 deposit is required to reserve your date. The balance is due 10 days prior to the event. Rental fees range $500–1,500 depending on the day of the event and the space rented. Meals range $29–99/person. Tax, alcohol and a 20% service charge are additional.

AVAILABILITY: Year-round, daily, 6am–1am.

SERVICES/AMENITIES:

Catering: in-house
Kitchen Facilities: n/a
Tables & Chairs: provided
Linens, Silver, etc.: provided
Restrooms: wheelchair accessible
Dance Floor: provided
Bride's & Groom's Dressing Area: yes
Meeting Equipment: CBA
Other: complimentary event coordination

Parking: large lot
Accommodations: no guest rooms
Telephone: office phone
Outdoor Night Lighting: provided
Outdoor Cooking Facilities: BBQ on site
Cleanup: provided
View: fountain, fairways, lake, landscaped grounds, mountains

RESTRICTIONS:

Alcohol: in-house
Smoking: not allowed inside
Music: amplified OK

Wheelchair Access: yes
Insurance: liability required

Want to find more venues and services? Check out our informative website, www.HereComesTheGuide.com.

441

Serendipity

Private Estate

12865 Oak Glen Road, Oak Glen
909/754-3134
www.serendipitygardenweddings.com
serendipitygardenweddings@gmail.com

Rehearsal Dinners	● Corporate Events
● Ceremonies	● Meetings
● Wedding Receptions	● Film Shoots
● Private Parties	Accommodations

We're intrigued whenever we hear about a venue that's been specifically designed for weddings. What that usually means is that the owner is serious about them, and has put a lot of effort into making their place extra wedding-friendly. Serendipity certainly fits that description.

Peaceful and secluded, this private estate has a superb location at the edge of a mountain canyon that overlooks an oak-sheltered creek. At 4,200 feet in the San Bernardino Mountains, it's high enough to be 10 or 15 degrees cooler than the flats below, making it popular for July and August weddings—something few outdoor wedding sites in the region can boast.

An array of pleasing elements makes for a nice whole here. First there are the flowers: The path connecting the ceremony and reception areas is flanked by hundreds of dazzling white rosebushes. The ceremony site itself, set halfway down the canyon slope, is a showstopper: Look south and there's a panorama of the Inland Empire's mountains and valleys. Look north, and the soaring granite peak of Mt. San Gorgonio looms imposingly, close enough to seem just a short drive away. Guests seated on a lawn face this inspiring view and the couple, who recite their vows on a simple wooden dais that's easily adorned to taste. Off to one side, a small reed-filled pool teems with little freshwater critters—sweet symbols of the abundance of married life to come.

After the ceremony, guests gather on the new cocktail terrace, where they're served the bride and groom's signature cocktail and hand-passed hors d'oeuvres.

From here they can watch the newlyweds posing for photos below, and take in the expansive view of the valley to the south.

When it's time for the reception, everyone finds their table in Serendipity's spacious and beautifully conceived outdoor dining and dancing area near the top of the property. It's an expansive "patio," made up of large stone-tiled squares separated by bright strips of grass that together form an appealing geometric pattern. Tables are arranged on the squares, there's a permanent dance floor on one side (with the canyon as its dramatic backdrop), and a full bar with a blazing fireplace on the opposite side. The resulting setup encourages a convivial flow of people as they move from music to drink to mingling at tables. Most weddings here are evening affairs, taking advantage of the balmy air, the region's glorious sunset colors, the romance of lights strung across the patio, and the glow of stars under a smog-free sky.

Serendipity's all-inclusive wedding package covers a wide range of items, including catering, cake, flowers, a DJ, a golf cart shuttle for guests, and a horse-drawn carriage ride for the bride and groom to the ceremony site and reception area. Package services are provided by a select group of trusted, seasoned vendors, and there are no hidden charges.

When we asked Serendipity's owner how this unique, weddings-only facility in the highlands has worked out, she clearly enjoyed answering the question: "Each bride tells me, 'This is my little haven, my own piece of the mountain for a day.'"

Note that in 2014, Serendipity will have a wonderful new barn available for indoor receptions.

CEREMONY & EVENT/RECEPTION CAPACITY: The facility holds 200 seated guests outdoors.

MEETING CAPACITY: Meetings spaces hold 200 seated at tables.

FEES & DEPOSITS: A $2,000 deposit is required to reserve your date and the balance is split into 3 payments made prior to the event. Serendipity's all-inclusive wedding packages cover catering, cake, flowers, a DJ, a golf cart shuttle for guests, and a horse-drawn carriage ride for the bride and groom to the ceremony site and reception area. The packages range $11,500–16,500 depending on the guest count and the services selected. Tax is additional.

AVAILABILITY: Year-round, 9am–10pm.

SERVICES/AMENITIES:

Catering: in-house
Kitchen Facilities: n/a
Tables & Chairs: provided
Linens, Silver, etc.: provided
Restrooms: wheelchair accessible
Dance Floor: provided
Bride's Dressing Area: yes
Meeting Equipment: some provided
Other: coordination, grand piano

Parking: large lot
Accommodations: no guest rooms
Telephone: emergency use only
Outdoor Night Lighting: yes
Outdoor Cooking Facilities: BBQ on site
Cleanup: provided
View: garden, waterfall, pond, fountain, landscaped grounds; panorama of mountains, canyon, cityscape, valley, hills and fields

RESTRICTIONS:

Alcohol: BYO
Smoking: designated areas only
Music: amplified OK outdoors

Wheelchair Access: yes
Insurance: liability required

Mountain Meadows Golf Course

Golf Club

1875 Fairplex Drive, Pomona
888/998-2969

www.countryclubreceptions.com
privateeventmanager@mountainmeadowsgc.com

● Rehearsal Dinners	● Corporate Events
● Ceremonies	● Meetings
● Wedding Receptions	● Film Shoots
● Private Parties	Accommodations

A curving boulevard whisks you swiftly up from the valley floor to this popular golf course. Its many jacaranda trees will be ablaze with lilac-colored blooms when you arrive, and if it's a clear day the San Gabriel Mountains will pop up bold and high—one of several pleasing sights that will capture your interest here.

As is the case with all savvy golfing venues, Mountain Meadows has set its banquet room and ceremony site apart from the workaday bustle of the rest of the course. The banquet room lies at the far end of the clubhouse and, because it has a separate entrance, no uninvited guests will inadvertently pass through. Many elements combine to make this room inviting: A wall of tall windows lets in a crystalline northern light and looks out past the adjacent patio to the action of the driving range and first hole. The remaining walls are painted the softest possible cream, which complements the gray-brown rafters. Large supporting beams, including three massive horizontal ones, add a dramatic element to the space. Swags of tulle laced with miniature lights spiral out from the center of ceiling and translucent glass wall sconces add ambient light.

The banquet room opens to a large patio, where waist-high walls lined with boxes of exuberant flowers form a colorful backdrop to outdoor festivities. Right off the patio, a four-sided gazebo stands beside a putting green with grass so smooth it could just as well be the felt covering on a pool table. You can imagine how nice white chairs look, arranged in neat rows on this perfect lawn.

The gazebo is only one of several places that offer wonderful photo ops. There's also the patio and the course's man-made lake. Or you can ride a golf cart up to a scenic overlook with a fantastic view of Mountain Meadows. One special favorite is a small garden close to the banquet room. Bordered by ferns, small shade trees and flowers, it has an appealing three-tier fountain at its center.

Finally, the on-site kitchen knows what it's doing. As is typical in the Inland Empire, with its rich variety of cultures, customs and ethnic groups, the banquet staff—who handle more than 100 weddings per year—are old hands at seamlessly accommodating brides' different tastes and needs.

Mountain Meadows achieves something that looks easy only if you have a lot of experience doing it: balancing privacy and elegance with accessibility and affordability.

CEREMONY CAPACITY: The site holds up to 400 seated guests.

EVENT/RECEPTION CAPACITY: The banquet room accommodates up to 330 seated or 450 standing guests.

MEETING CAPACITY: The banquet room accommodates up to 500 seated guests.

FEES & DEPOSITS: A nonrefundable deposit, which is applied to your food and beverage total, is required to reserve your date. The amount of the deposit varies, depending on how far in advance you book. Payment terms for the balance also vary, and may be arranged on an individual basis. Wedding packages start at $33/person. Tax, alcohol and service charge are additional. Menus and packages can be customized to fit your needs and budget. Call for details.

AVAILABILITY: Year-round, daily, 6am–2am.

SERVICES/AMENITIES:

Catering: in-house
Kitchen Facilities: no
Tables & Chairs: provided
Linens, Silver, etc.: provided
Restrooms: wheelchair accessible
Dance Floor: provided
Bride's Dressing Area: yes
Meeting Equipment: some provided, more CBA

Parking: large lot
Accommodations: no guest rooms
Telephone: emergency use only
Outdoor Night Lighting: CBA
Outdoor Cooking Facilities: no
Cleanup: provided
View: fairways, hills, mountains, grounds
Other: event coordination

RESTRICTIONS:

Alcohol: in-house
Smoking: outside only
Music: amplified OK

Wheelchair Access: yes
Insurance: not required

Christmas House

Historic Victorian Inn

9240 Archibald Avenue, Rancho Cucamonga
909/980-6450

www.christmashouseinn.com
contact@christmashouseinn.com

Rehearsal Dinners	● Corporate Events
● Ceremonies	Meetings
● Wedding Receptions	● Film Shoots
● Private Parties	● Accommodations

All the quaint pleasures we associate with a Victorian Christmas—old-fashioned elegance, warm family gatherings, and a childlike sense of wonder—are available year-round in 21st-century Southern California. Where? At the Christmas House Inn, a historic landmark that received its yuletide moniker because of the extravagant holiday parties hosted by its early owners. Built in 1904, the three-story mansion is a charming example of the Queen Anne-style favored by late Victorian architects. For decades it was the showpiece of an 80-acre citrus ranch, but by the 1970s, it had fallen into neglect. In 1983, Janice Ilsley and her husband came to the rescue, launching a complete renovation that restored the Christmas House to its former glory. The inn boasts all of the original stained-glass windows and gorgeous woodwork—the seven Victorian fireplace mantels are each made of a different wood, and accented with Italian tiles and beveled glass mirrors. The success of this popular bed & breakfast owes as much to the Ilsleys' service-oriented attitude as to the inviting surroundings. "We want couples to feel like the Christmas House is their own home," reveals Janice, "especially on their wedding day."

Brides, you'll definitely feel at home in the Celebration Suite, the spacious upstairs dressing room replete with fireplace, lacy adornments, an abundance of mirrors—and plenty of room for doting bridesmaids. In the cool autumn months or if the weather looks iffy, follow Victorian tradition and say "I do" in front of the parlor's hearth, decked with shimmering candles. As the accompanist plays the processional on the grand piano, glide down the carved, redwood burl staircase and pass among your guests, gathered close enough to hear your vows, even if they're whispered. Indoor reception buffets are served in the formal dining room, another fetching space where details like a gleaming silver coffee urn and antique curios enhance the turn-of-the-century patina. Guests mingle and munch as they soak up the nostalgic ambiance in the library and adjoining salons, which are lavished with comfortable period furnishings and authentic Victoriana.

At the Christmas House, you can also have your ceremony amid the romance of an English Garden behind the home. A lawn cradled in flowering shrubbery features a brick path lined with candle lanterns. This natural wedding aisle culminates at a gazebo swathed in greenery, where bride and groom make a radiant tableau. At the ceremony's conclusion, guests pass under a vine-covered archway to the front of the home, where they savor hors d'oeuvres passed on silver trays in a lovely rose garden, or lounge in the shade of a broad veranda and watch the butterflies flit among the blossoms. When guests return to the rear garden for the reception, they'll find tables and chairs elegantly set with floor-length linens and gleaming glass and cutlery. Guests dine beneath the leafy boughs of magnolia and guava trees strung with twinkle lights. Nearby, a citrus tree draped with gossamer netting shades the wedding cake, poised atop an antique table. Japanese lanterns cast a soft glow on an adjacent courtyard, where the newlyweds share their first dance.

Among the most endearing attractions of the Christmas House are the six distinctive guest rooms. The luxurious bridal suite comes with a fireplace, a private garden courtyard with hot tub, and delicious breakfast the morning after. With affordable packages that include gourmet catering and other extras, this venue is simply irresistible. Many couples create their own Christmas House tradition: They rekindle their fond wedding memories by returning to the inn on their anniversaries!

CEREMONY, EVENT/RECEPTION CAPACITY: The Parlor holds up to 50 seated or 75 standing guests, the garden up to 150 seated guests.

FEES & DEPOSITS: A $500 nonrefundable deposit is required to reserve your date. Another $400 is due 1 month later. 50% of the remaining event total is due 4 months prior to the event, and the balance is due 2 weeks before the event. For indoor events, packages start at $5,800 for up to 50 guests and include exclusive use of the site, all rentals, catering and staff, wedding cake and all setup and cleanup. For each person over 50 guests, pricing starts at $35/person. For garden events, packages range $9,900–13,500 for up to 100 guests and include everything that's in the indoor package plus professional DJ services. For each person over 100 guests, pricing ranges $35–48/person. Tax and service charge are additional on the catering portion of the total. If you serve alcohol, bartending services are required at an additional charge.

AVAILABILITY: Year-round, daily, 9am–10pm.

SERVICES/AMENITIES:

Catering: in-house
Kitchen Facilities: n/a
Tables & Chairs: provided
Linens, Silver, etc.: provided
Restrooms: limited accessibility
Dance Floor: provided for garden receptions
Bride's & Groom's Dressing Area: provided
Meeting Equipment: n/a

Parking: on site and street
Accommodations: 6 guest rooms
Telephone: house phone
Outdoor Night Lighting: yes
Outdoor Cooking Facilities: no
Cleanup: provided
View: landscaped Victorian gardens
Other: event coordination, bar service

RESTRICTIONS:

Alcohol: in-house
Smoking: outside only
Music: amplified OK with volume restrictions until 10pm

Wheelchair Access: limited
Insurance: not required
Other: no rice, birdseed or confetti

Victoria Gardens Cultural Center

Cultural Center

12505 Cultural Center Drive, Rancho Cucamonga
909/477-2773
www.vgculturalcenter.com
annette.mumolo@cityofrc.us

● Rehearsal Dinners	● Corporate Events
● Ceremonies	● Meetings
● Wedding Receptions	● Film Shoots
● Private Parties	Accommodations

The delightfully imaginative Victoria Gardens Cultural Center has a motto: "Where Dreams Come to Life." But it could just as easily be "Let's Put on a Show," because that's what they do so dynamically at this outstanding venue.

The center, known primarily for its Lewis Family Playhouse, one of regional theater's rising stars, is a multifaceted performing arts mecca that includes several unique indoor and outdoor sites for special events. Here, they believe that every wedding is a story, and they love having the same creative wizards who put the magic into dozens of critically acclaimed theatrical productions each year help you tell yours.

The Cultural Center, comprised of the playhouse and Celebration Hall, is an architecturally colorful treat. The curved buildings, sporting hues of pink, desert rose and verdigris, form a semicircle around the Imagination Courtyard, a large, cobble-stoned space that lends itself to outdoor gatherings. Ringed by tall, feathery palms, it's open on one side to the Victoria Gardens shopping and entertainment plaza (a big plus during the holidays when the majestic Christmas tree is visible from here), and anchored on the other by the center's soaring, arched glass entrance. Topped with a backlit, stylized marquee, this façade makes a picturesque backdrop for an al fresco ceremony.

Many brides opt to have cocktails (or even dinner) out here and exchange vows in the more private Lobby, a whimsical stage set of the perfect little street, complete with storefronts and trees—it's like having your very own village! On one end of "town," there's a staircase to use either as a riser for your altar, or as a starting point for your dramatic descent to the main floor where you can say "I do," bathed in light filtering through that gorgeous glass entrance behind you.

The center gives you enormous flexibility in choosing how you want to use its spaces, but it's the way the staff works with a team of art and entertainment professionals to turn your vision into reality that makes this place so special. Want to add an animal to the proceedings? No problem.

They've wrangled camels, horses, an elephant—even albino peacocks—for various events. Unconventional entertainment? They can find everything from acrobats to belly dancers to gospel choirs. And with the help of some of L.A.'s most talented set decorators, lighting designers, seamstresses and hair/makeup artists, they will produce an affair to remember.

Nowhere is their creativity more rewarded than in the Celebration Hall Ballroom. A wonderful blank canvas, this huge space has polished concrete floors, cream-colored walls, windows on two sides and an adjacent Patio hugged by shrubbery. In it's natural state, it's a bright and airy spot for dinner and dancing with an indoor/outdoor flow. But say the word and they can transform it, with elegant draping and dramatic lighting, into a romantic oasis, a sophisticated supper club or an exotic foreign locale. There's no charge for either the consultation or design, making this an incredible value. Plus, they do so much of the work in-house that you can also save on flowers, catering, and more for a one-of-a-kind event that's sure to win rave reviews.

CEREMONY CAPACITY: The site holds up to 400 seated guests indoors or 600 seated outdoors.

EVENT/RECEPTION & MEETING CAPACITY: The facility accommodates 250 seated or 350 standing guests indoors and 500 seated or 600 standing outdoors.

FEES & DEPOSITS: A $1,000 refundable deposit is required to reserve your date and the balance is due 30 days prior to the event. Rental fees range $1,200–3,200 depending on the length of the event, guest count and custom décor options. Meals range $30–60/person. Tax and alcohol are additional.

AVAILABILITY: Year-round, daily until 1am.

SERVICES/AMENITIES:

Catering: in-house
Kitchen Facilities: n/a
Tables & Chairs: provided
Linens, Silver, etc.: provided
Restrooms: wheelchair accessible
Dance Floor: provided
Bride's Dressing Area: CBA
Meeting Equipment: provided

Parking: large lot, valet optional; garage nearby
Accommodations: no guest rooms
Telephone: pay phone
Outdoor Night Lighting: CBA
Outdoor Cooking Facilities: no
Cleanup: provided
View: garden courtyard, landscaped grounds
Other: in-house florals, AV equipment, custom décor services

RESTRICTIONS:

Alcohol: in-house
Smoking: not allowed
Music: amplified OK

Wheelchair Access: yes
Insurance: liability required

This is important! Tell venues you're reading HERE COMES THE GUIDE and ask if our information is still current.

449

The Mitten Building

345 A North Fifth Street, Redlands
909/793-1294
www.mittenbuilding.com
mittenbuilding@gmail.com

Historic Event Facility

● Rehearsal Dinners	● Corporate Events
● Ceremonies	● Meetings
● Wedding Receptions	● Film Shoots
● Private Parties	Accommodations

Redlands is a city that has always had its own, unique character, which derives in part from its distinctive buildings: one of the best-preserved collections of late 19th- and early 20th-century architecture in all of Southern California.

So, a building has to be pretty special to stand out here. And stand out is exactly what the Mitten Building does.

Built in 1890, the brick structure not only has a fine looking exterior, it impresses on the inside as well. With its exposed rafters, beams and joists, and its stairs and banisters flying up and down each floor, the interior is a tumult of wood, an almost giddy exposition of the carpenter's art. It's the kind of place people love, because they're endlessly fascinated by all its nooks, angles and wondrous lines.

And it's perfect for brides who prefer a venue with character and history. The current owners have lovingly restored the Mitten, wisely retaining the things that give the building its wonderful patina of age: the weathered beams, the heavy freight door that opens along an overhead metal track, and the original swaths of paint on some surfaces. They cleaned but did not alter the Mitten's sturdy brick walls, knowing how crucial they are to the building's feel. The bricks vary in color from gray, dusty pink and fiery red to nearly maroon, while their textures range from baby-smooth to worn and rough. If a building can have the equivalent of a beautifully aged human face, these walls are that.

The multilevel interior invites people to move around, explore and mingle. Typically, the downstairs is set up as a reception area. Wrought-iron chandeliers descend from the Mitten's 50-foot ceiling, and garlands entwined with twinkle lights run along every rail and banister, sparking a festive air. Big windows set into the thick north brick wall admit a mellow northern light—the kind artists adore because of the way it complements everything it falls on. The mezzanine above has a beautiful narrow-slat maple floor, and its slender iron support beams are each flanked by two shiny brass lamps. Couples often wed on the upper level, head downstairs for their reception, then come right back up to dance away the evening.

The recently refurbished basement level is now a bar featuring turn-of-the-century dark wood cabinetry with inlaid detailing. Reminiscent of a speakeasy, it fits right in with the 1890s period when the building was constructed. On request, this space also serves as a groom's pre-ceremony getaway.

The Mitten Building's newest addition is the Summerbell Ballroom, which has a decidedly modern feel. Colored LED uplights transform the walls and pinpoint lights overhead showcase each table's centerpiece. There's also a granite-topped bar, a dance floor, and a lounge section with leather couch and bar tables. An adjoining patio, overlooking a lushly landscaped garden, lends itself well to outdoor ceremonies.

Since its restoration the building has become a favorite among locals (and out-of-towners in the know). Everyone who celebrates here owes a debt of gratitude to the visionaries who looked at this building with affectionate eyes, saw its magnificent possibilities, and brought it to life as a splendid event site.

CEREMONY CAPACITY: The Upper Level holds up to 400 seated guests. The new courtyard space seats 100 guests.

EVENT/RECEPTION & MEETING CAPACITY: The location accommodates up to 725 seated or standing guests. The new Summerbell Ballroom and outdoor patio holds 30–225 seated or standing guests.

FEES & DEPOSITS: A $1,000 deposit is required to reserve your date. The balance is due 14 days prior to the event. Rental fees range $500–8,000 depending on guest count, day and time rented and services included. If you choose to use the on-site caterer, meals range $18–40/person. Tax and alcohol are additional.

AVAILABILITY: Year-round, daily, 7am–1am.

SERVICES/AMENITIES:

Catering: in-house, select from list or BYO
Kitchen Facilities: prep only
Tables & Chairs: provided
Linens, Silver, etc.: some provided, more CBA
Restrooms: wheelchair accessible
Dance Floor: CBA, extra fee
Bride's Dressing Area: yes
Meeting Equipment: some provided, more CBA

Parking: large lot and garage nearby
Accommodations: no guest rooms
Telephone: emergency use only
Outdoor Night Lighting: yes
Outdoor Cooking Facilities: BBQ CBA
Cleanup: provided
View: cityscape, garden patio
Other: coordination available for fee, florals

RESTRICTIONS:

Alcohol: in-house
Smoking: outside only
Music: amplified OK

Wheelchair Access: limited
Insurance: liability required

Canyon Crest Country Club

Country Club

975 Country Club Drive, Riverside
951/274-7900
www.canyoncrestcc.com
contactus@canyoncrestcc.com

- Rehearsal Dinners
- Ceremonies
- Wedding Receptions
- Private Parties
- Corporate Events
- Meetings
- Film Shoots
- Accommodations

Everything works just right at Canyon Crest, a country club whose combined outdoor and indoor assets are appealing for all types of events, especially weddings.

A treelined boulevard sweeps its way to the club, making you feel like you've arrived at a capital "D" destination. The golf course, set along the contours of a natural bowl at the foot of desert mountains, has a touch of the exotic, with its subtropical assortment of palms, pines and eucalyptus. A fountain in the middle of a man-made lake jets water 50 feet into the air against a backdrop of nearby peaks.

But perhaps the best feature on the grounds is the ceremony site: A simple white stone arch—which you can decorate any way you like—sits at the edge of a knoll above the course, flanked by a lawn where guests assemble to witness vows. Overlooking the lake and fountain, fairways and scenery, this spot feels set apart from the country club's bustle.

The broad red canopy that shades the steps down from the parking lot to the clubhouse's gleaming glass doors imparts a decidedly upscale feel. Walk inside to the dining room, where an all-glass wall lets you gaze out on the vast and impressive green of the course—in fact, lush green is all you see. Three wide doors open onto an adjoining canopied terrace, which offers a splendid view of the fairways, lake and nearby highlands. Located just above the putting green, the tiled terrace is ideal for hosting pre- and post-wedding gatherings and cocktails, and it serves as an overflow space for dining. At dusk, lights strung along its rails and overhead supports create an enchanting look.

Just off the terrace is a spacious room set aside for the bride and her bridesmaids. The room, which is perfect for hanging out and relaxing, happens to be located so that she and her entourage can discreetly peek out the windows to see who's arrived and what's going on.

The coordinator here takes care of everything—vendor selection, menu planning, setup and takedown. She's there at the rehearsal and on the day of the wedding to make sure all goes well. The flexible kitchen can custom-design menus, offer recommendations based on their experience, and provide almost any style of food. Canyon Crest also accommodates rehearsal dinners, bridal showers and brunches. The club is private, so indoor music can go on forever. (Outdoor music has to shut down by 11pm.)

We think Canyon Crest's good looks and versatile kitchen, as well as its relaxed feel and flow, make it one of the Inland Empire's best contenders for a one-stop, affordable wedding venue.

CEREMONY CAPACITY: The site holds 200 seated guests outdoors.

EVENT/RECEPTION CAPACITY: The club can accommodate 150 seated or 300 standing guests indoors, and 100 seated or 300 standing outdoors.

MEETING CAPACITY: Meeting spaces hold up to 200 seated guests.

FEES & DEPOSITS: A deposit ranging $1,000-1,500 is required to reserve your date. 50% of the estimated event total is due 60 days prior to the event, and the balance is due 10 days prior. Rental fees range $250–500 depending on the day and time of the event. Meals range $35–89/person. Tax, alcohol and a 20% service charge are additional.

AVAILABILITY: Year-round, daily, anytime.

SERVICES/AMENITIES:

Catering: in-house
Kitchen Facilities: n/a
Tables & Chairs: provided
Linens, Silver, etc.: provided
Restrooms: wheelchair accessible
Dance Floor: portable provided
Bride's & Groom's Dressing Area: yes
Meeting Equipment: provided
Other: grand piano, on-site florals, clergy on staff picnic area, AV equipment, event coordination

Parking: large lot, valet required
Accommodations: no guest rooms
Telephone: office phone
Outdoor Night Lighting: provided
Outdoor Cooking Facilities: BBQ on site
Cleanup: provided
View: canyon, fountain, golf course fairways, lake, landscaped grounds, pool area, panorama of mountains

RESTRICTIONS:

Alcohol: in-house or BYO with corkage fee
Smoking: OK in designated areas
Music: amplified OK

Wheelchair Access: yes
Insurance: liability required

The Mission Inn Hotel & Spa

Historic Inn

3649 Mission Inn Avenue, Riverside
800/344-4225

www.missioninn.com
weddings@missioninn.com

- Rehearsal Dinners
- Ceremonies
- Wedding Receptions
- Private Parties
- Corporate Events
- Meetings
- Film Shoots
- Accommodations

Upon arriving at The Mission Inn Hotel & Spa you may wonder, as we did, exactly what kind of missionaries had inhabited this unique and eccentric edifice. The truth is, the Inn was never an actual mission housing actual missionaries; it was the personal, lifelong and quixotic "mission" of Frank Miller, the man who built what some have called an "architectural wonder."

In 1876, Miller purchased a small adobe building known as the Glenwood Inn, added a four-story wing, and the Mission Inn was born. Over the next 30 years, he built three additional wings, each more elaborate than the last. By the 1930s, the Mission Inn had expanded to fill an entire city block and had become Riverside's most visited attraction.

A wondrous, eclectic assemblage of styles, the Mission Inn achieved its national historic landmark status in 1976. Starting with Mission Revival, the hotel now incorporates architectural styles from all over the world: Moorish, Italian Renaissance, Spanish Baroque, Chinese and Japanese. It's a dazzling array of flying buttresses, domes, fountains, statues, carved pillars, towers, gargoyles, balconies, plazas, turrets, spiral staircases, gardens, bells, colorful tile and stained glass, all constructed to display the extensive collection of art and artifacts that Miller gathered on his world travels.

Perhaps the most stunning of these is the Rayas Altar, which Miller bought sight unseen in 1920 and had shipped from Mexico. Hand-carved from cedar and covered in gold-leaf, the size and beauty of the altar inspired Miller to build the Chapel of St. Francis to house it. This ornate non-denominational chapel, with its 30-foot beamed ceiling, Louis C. Tiffany stained-glass windows and enormous carved mahogany doors quickly became one of California's most popular wedding sites. Humphrey Bogart, Bette Davis (twice) and Constance Bennett all recited vows here, as have over 300 other couples each year.

After its heyday in the 1930s and 1940s, a succession of owners and repeated bankruptcies brought the hotel close to demolition, but a seven-year, $55-million renovation during the 1980s restored the Mission Inn's grandeur. The St. Francis of Assisi Chapel is once again luring betrothed couples through its doors in droves, and the Inn's many banquet rooms provide wedding celebrations with timeless artistic environments.

CEREMONY CAPACITY: The St. Francis of Assisi Chapel seats 150 guests, the St. Cecilia Chapel seats 12, the Rotunda seats 90, and Al Fresco Courtyard seats 170.

EVENT/RECEPTION CAPACITY: The Inn can accommodate wedding receptions for 20–296 guests seated or 20–350 guests standing.

MEETING CAPACITY: Indoor meeting facilities accommodate 10–310 guests.

FEES & DEPOSITS: For wedding receptions, a nonrefundable 25% deposit is required to confirm your date; the estimated event balance is payable 2 weeks prior to the event. Reception luncheons start at $52/person, dinners at $72/person, and both include a two-course meal, cheese display, tray passed champagne and cider during the cocktail hour, champagne toast and wedding cake. Alcoholic beverage service, 20% service charge and tax are additional. The Chapel Package ranges $1,000–3,000, and includes an on-site ceremony administrator, wedding night accommodations for the bride and groom, and dressing areas for the bridal party and groomsmen.

Catering menus are available for all corporate and non-wedding social events. Luncheon menus start at $25/person, dinners at $36/person. The Mission Inn Hotel & Spa offers complete meeting and event services; please call for further information.

AVAILABILITY: Year-round, daily, 6am–midnight.

SERVICES/AMENITIES:

Catering: in-house, no BYO
Kitchen Facilities: n/a
Tables & Chairs: provided
Linens, Silver, etc.: provided
Restrooms: wheelchair accessible
Dance Floor: portable parquet provided
Bride's Dressing Area: provided with chapel package
Meeting Equipment: full range, extra charge

Parking: on-site self & valet, additional charge
Accommodations: 238 guest rooms & suites
Telephone: house phones
Outdoor Night Lighting: provided
Outdoor Cooking Facilities: no
Cleanup: provided
View: landscaped courtyards
Other: wedding coordinator, 7,000-sq-foot spa

RESTRICTIONS:

Alcohol: in-house, no BYO
Smoking: outside only
Music: amplified OK indoors

Wheelchair Access: yes
Insurance: liability required
Other: no rice, birdseed or confetti

Wedgewood Indian Hills

Event Center

5700 Club House Drive, Riverside
866/966-3009

www.wedgewoodbanquet.com/indian-hills
riversidesales@wedgewoodbanquet.com

● Rehearsal Dinners	● Corporate Events
● Ceremonies	● Meetings
● Wedding Receptions	● Film Shoots
● Private Parties	Accommodations

Two very good things come together at Wedgewood Indian Hills: a service-oriented venue and a scenic public golf course that envelops the Inland Empire's often dry landscape like a luxuriant green stole.

Wedgewood's forte is its can-do attitude: They're happy to take care of everything for you—flowers, food, cake, photographer and more. Their Indian Hills venue offers five all-inclusive packages designed for "value, service and convenience," and each one can be customized. Wedgewood Indian Hills works with the best event professionals in the area, who will meet with you personally to help create a wedding that fits your style. However, if you prefer to hire your own vendors, you can bring in any that you like—except for caterers. All catering is done in-house, and the kitchen's seasoned chefs can handle almost any cuisine. If a certain dish is outside their repertoire, they still do their best to make sure it gets served: Recently an Eastern European wedding had a special recipe that only the bride's relatives knew how to prepare correctly, so the kitchen invited them to cook it themselves.

Indian Hills' convenient location is only a short drive from San Bernardino, Riverside and Ontario. Its two ballrooms, both with full-service bars, easily accommodate groups large and small. The spacious Sunset Room has picture-window views of the golf course, while the more intimate Scenic Room overlooks the course's ceremony site. Guests often gather in this ballroom to enjoy post-ceremony champagne and hors d'oeuvres, as the new bride and groom pose for photos just outside.

Ceremonies take place on a flower-fringed lawn with a classic white gazebo, flanked on either side by a colonnade of majestic palms. However, it's the dramatic backdrop that really captures people's attention: Behind the gazebo, the ground drops away steeply to the fairway below, which seems to blend into the tree-covered hills in the distance. There are several popular photo op sites, including the gazebo itself, but one of the sweetest has to be a leafy shade tree nearby that forms a cool canopy over the couple, with the vibrant green golf course in the background.

The bride's room comes with creamy white leather couches, mirrors and direct access to a nicely outfitted bathroom with showers. There's even a steamer should the bridal gown or bridesmaid dresses require a little last-minute wrinkle removal.

Couples love Indian Hills' country club feel—especially since it comes without country club prices. From its flexible event spaces and award-winning food to the personal attention its staff gives each bride and groom, Wedgewood Indian Hills puts its stamp of excellence on every celebration that's held here.

CEREMONY & EVENT/RECEPTION CAPACITY: The banquet center holds 350 seated or standing guests, indoors or out.

MEETING CAPACITY: Meeting spaces seat 350 guests.

FEES & DEPOSITS: 25% of the estimated total event cost is required to reserve your date. An additonal 25% is due 120 days prior to the event and the balance (based on your final guest count) is due 10 days prior. All payments are credited towards your final balance and are nonrefundable and nontransferable. All-inclusive, completely customizable wedding packages start at $33/person. Tax, alcohol and a 21–22% service charge are additional.

AVAILABILITY: Year-round, daily, 6am–midnight. Afternoon and evening time slots are available.

SERVICES/AMENITIES:

Catering: in-house
Kitchen Facilities: n/a
Tables & Chairs: provided
Linens, Silver, etc.: provided
Restrooms: wheelchair accessible
Dance Floor: portable provided
Bride's Dressing Area: yes
Meeting Equipment: some provided
Other: coordination, in-house wedding cake and florals, AV equipment

Parking: large lot
Accommodations: no guest rooms
Telephone: house phone
Outdoor Night Lighting: access only
Outdoor Cooking Facilities: no
Cleanup: provided
View: landscaped grounds, garden, fountain, lake; panorama of mountains, forest and hills

RESTRICTIONS:

Alcohol: in-house
Smoking: designated areas only
Music: amplified OK

Wheelchair Access: yes
Insurance: not required

Overwhelmed? Use the search criteria on www.HereComesTheGuide.com to narrow down your choices.

457

Lake Oak Meadows, Weddings and Events

Private Waterfront Estate

36101 Glen Oaks Road, Temecula
951/676-6162

www.LakeOakMeadows.com
info@LakeOakMeadows.com

- Rehearsal Dinners
- Ceremonies
- Wedding Receptions
- Private Parties
- Corporate Events
- Meetings
- Film Shoots
- Accommodations

In the heart of Temecula wine country is a private ten-acre estate, where rose bushes scent the air and a wonderful variety of trees form shady groves around a serene lake, known for its spectacular nighttime display: "Fountains of Fire and Water."

While this serene, almost Eden-like oasis is terrific for concerts, retreats and reunions, it's utterly romantic for weddings. Couples recite their vows under a flower-adorned arch on a grassy peninsula that juts out into the lake. Ornate lamps and fragrant roses edge the ceremony space, and stately pepper trees form a sheltering backdrop. Just across the lake, a picturesque waterfall cascades down large rocks.

Guests enjoy post-ceremony cocktails under a shady arbor and on the adjoining lawn. A dramatic fireplace at one end of the lawn has a broad stone patio that also doubles as a dance floor. Strings of twinkle lights dangle from the arbor and wrap around the trees, and the optional addition of delicate Japanese lanterns enhances the romantic atmosphere. At night, the illumination elicits many "oohs" and "ahhs," which multiply even more when the lake's fountains light up in their fiery dance.

Steps away from the arbor, the reception lawn is a particularly comfortable spot as Temecula's famous late afternoon breeze begins to stir. Caterers enjoy having a prep room close to it, so keeping food coming fast and fresh is a snap. The lawn, which can be canopied, has lines of lights streaming above it and along the low wooden fence that borders it. With a bar and grill tucked in one corner, there's plenty of room for setting up tables and chairs.

Conveniences abound in the bride's room, including air conditioning, full-length mirrors, mirrored makeup seating, kitchenette, refrigerator, plasma TV, fireplace and shower. Outside, her private patio is enclosed by wisteria-clad wood lattice walls. There's a space for serving hors d'oeuvres and wine, as well as a fire pit, grill, and shaded tables and chairs. A popular tradition at Lake Oak Meadows is for the bride to emerge from her dressing room, walk across a small bridge with a rock waterfall, and step into a horse-drawn carriage that takes her to the lakeside ceremony site.

A grassy knoll behind the lake is a favorite spot for photos. Pepper and black gum trees shade this pleasant green rise, which is bordered by a quaint split-rail fence that zigzags between the lawn and flowerbeds.

Lake Oak Meadows has a distinct "ranch feel," but with all the rough edges smoothed away. What remains is a beautiful, amenity-rich place that immediately captures the fancy of almost everybody. Just take a stroll from the parking lot down the terraced stairway to your first dazzling lake view to see why this location is worth considering for any event or social gathering.

CEREMONY CAPACITY: The site can accommodate up to 1,000 seated guests outdoors.

EVENT/RECEPTION & MEETING CAPACITY: The resort holds 500 seated guests.

FEES & DEPOSITS: A $3,500 deposit is required to reserve your date. Contracted balance is due 18 days prior to the event. Rental fees range $2,000–4,000 depending on the day of the event. Meals range $60–90/person. Tax, alcohol and a 20% service charge are additional.

AVAILABILITY: Year-round, daily, anytime.

SERVICES/AMENITIES:

Catering: in-house
Kitchen Facilities: n/a
Tables & Chairs: provided
Linens, Silver, etc.: provided
Restrooms: wheelchair accessible
Dance Floor: provided
Bride's & Groom's Dressing Area: yes
Meeting Equipment: some provided
Other: event coordination provided

Parking: large lot
Accommodations: honeymoon suite
Telephone: emergency use only
Outdoor Night Lighting: provided
Outdoor Cooking Facilities: CBA
Cleanup: provided
View: forest, fountain, garden, hills, lagoon, lake, landscaped grounds, meadow, waterfall, park; panorama of mountains and vineyards

RESTRICTIONS:

Alcohol: in-house
Smoking: designated areas only
Music: amplified OK

Wheelchair Access: yes
Insurance: liability required

Leoness Cellars

Winery

38311 De Portola Road, Temecula
951/302-7601 x114
www.leonesscellars.com
weddings@leonesscellars.com

● Rehearsal Dinners	● Corporate Events
● Ceremonies	● Meetings
● Wedding Receptions	● Film Shoots
● Private Parties	Accommodations

The picturesque drive to your destination passes one well-kept horse farm after another before segueing to gentle hills planted with grapevines. This is "the other" wine trail in Temecula, less traveled and more tranquil than the main tourist route. It's also home to one of the loveliest wineries and wedding venues in the whole valley—Leoness Cellars.

The name "Leoness" is a nod to the mythical village where King Arthur first spotted Guinevere and fell in love, although the owners add that in Scottish it means "village of dreams." Clearly, this is their field of dreams. After decades of growing grapes for other vintners, the two partners decided to open their own winery in 2003. And as pristine as the surroundings may be, there exists a palpable connection, throughout your event, to the romance of the land, or "terroir" as it's known in the wine world.

The first thing you notice when you arrive is the line of stately Italian cypress trees leading up to a European chateau-styled building which houses the very popular tasting room. Just a short distance from there is the serenely beautiful outdoor ceremony site. A rear wall, adorned with a lion's head fountain, creates privacy and heightens the drama of your entrance. As you walk down the long center aisle, to the left are graceful Japanese plum trees interspersed with red and white roses. On the right are neat rows of Cabernet plantings. Straight ahead stands the white wooden arbor where you'll exchange vows, backed by a wide-angle vista of neatly tended vineyards and the Mt. Palomar Observatory perched on a distant mountaintop.

Celebratory cocktails are served on the Lower Lawn. Guests can toast the newlyweds at tables arranged on the grass, or mingle around the bar on the adjoining shaded patio, set right at the edge of the Cabernet vines. As night falls, twinkle lights around the patio bring this spot to life. Afterwards, in a rare treat, you'll all be invited into the vineyard itself for an unforgettable walk down a softly lit pastoral path. It's the perfect way to get up close and personal with the versatile fruit that has engendered so much passion throughout the ages…and a great way to transition to dinner.

The freestanding Barrel Room, site for your reception, comes with a charming country patio that's partly enclosed by the ivy-covered walls of the building and lit by old-fashioned lampposts. Inside, however, it's all industrial chic with soaring ceilings, iron chandeliers, and oak barrels stacked up along every wall (this is, after all, part of the integral workings of the winery, as are the gleaming metal tanks around back, which make a unique photo backdrop).

This towering space has great acoustics and a polished concrete floor for dancing, yet it takes on an elegant intimacy as clusters of votive candles flicker against its dark brown walls. Soft leather club chairs are arranged in a corner for lounging, and there's even a cozy niche where you might want to offer "wine flights" so guests can sample a broad range of Leoness varietals. For the perfect finale, cap off the evening with a glass of their sensual and earthy Cinsaut Port paired with a rich bittersweet truffle. It just might make you fall in love all over again.

CEREMONY CAPACITY: The site can accommodate up to 500 seated guests outdoors.

EVENT/RECEPTION CAPACITY: The site holds 250 seated or 400 standing guests indoors, and 500 seated or 600 standing outdoors.

MEETING CAPACITY: Meeting spaces hold 350 seated guests indoors.

FEES & DEPOSITS: A deposit of $2,900 is required to reserve your date, 50% is due 6 months prior to the event date, and the event total balance is due 15 days prior to the event. Packages range $85–125/person and include facility rental, hors d'oeuvres, meal and more. Tax, alcohol and a 20% service charge are additional.

AVAILABILITY: Year-round, daily, 10am–11pm, excluding major holidays.

SERVICES/AMENITIES:
Catering: in-house
Kitchen Facilities: n/a
Tables & Chairs: provided
Linens, Silver, etc.: provided
Restrooms: wheelchair accessible
Dance Floor: provided
Bride's & Groom's Dressing Area: yes
Meeting Equipment: CBA
Other: picnic area, event coordination

Parking: large lot
Accommodations: no guest rooms
Telephone: emergency use only
Outdoor Night Lighting: provided
Outdoor Cooking Facilities: no
Cleanup: provided
View: garden, courtyard, hills, landscaped grounds, mountains, valley, vineyards

RESTRICTIONS:
Alcohol: in-house
Smoking: designated areas only
Music: amplified OK with restrictions

Wheelchair Access: yes
Insurance: not required

Temecula Creek Inn

Inn

44501 Rainbow Canyon Road, Temecula
951/587-1479
www.temeculacreekinn.com
tciweddings@jcresorts.com

- Rehearsal Dinners
- Ceremonies
- Wedding Receptions
- Private Parties
- Corporate Events
- Meetings
- Film Shoots
- Accommodations

Look up the word "charming" in the dictionary and you might find a picture of the Stone House at Temecula Creek Inn, because whoever first came up with the adjective surely had someplace just like this in mind.

Tucked away in a secluded section of the 350-acre property, this fairy-tale setting with its peak-roofed stone cottage dates back to the 1800s when the area served as a granite quarry. Today, instead of sheltering quarrymen, the stone-and-granite building has found what may be its true calling: an unforgettable site for a romantic wedding.

Your guests are shuttled down the winding path to the Stone House, which is set on a large grassy clearing against a woodland backdrop and enclosed by split-rail fencing. The building's old wood shutters, little porch and neat border of colorful flowers give the scene an enchanted feeling. Across the front lawn there's a wooden footbridge that leads to a sylvan ceremony site where everyone awaits your arrival (by horse-drawn carriage, if you wish). You make your grand entrance over that same bridge and up the aisle to a bentwood arbor, exchanging vows under a canopy of oak trees strung with lights.

Cocktails are served on the side lawn to the left of the house, where oak barrels used as tables add a nice wine country touch. Dinner follows on the main lawn, which affords a direct view of a distant fairway plus a sweet tableau of another wooden bridge and blooming hedges to the right. Create an indoor/outdoor event and take full advantage of the Stone House by adding a buffet or dessert bar inside. Later, turn the quaint interior, with its fireplace and cross-beam ceiling, into an after-hours lounge. Guests can also enjoy cocktails and warm themselves at glowing fire pits on both sides of the house, or play bocce ball and other games on the adjacent activity lawn.

Temecula Creek Inn offers two additional wedding venues. The newest is Stone Meadows, an expansive lawn where you can host your entire celebration. For the ceremony, say "I do" framed by natural foliage and fragrant rosebushes. The reception follows nearby around flickering fire pits. The Yula Ballroom and Waterfall Plaza provide an indoor/outdoor option for your event. Get married next to a cascading rock waterfall, then invite your guests into the adjacent ballroom for a delicious dining experience. Spacious and elegant, the ballroom comes with an outdoor patio, complete with wood-burning fireplace.

Besides being a popular wedding location, this resort has plenty of other assets, including: a championship 27-hole golf course; 130 well-appointed guest rooms, each with its own balcony or terrace; and their restaurant, Farm House Kitchen, with an eclectic menu and lively adjacent bar. Temecula Creek Inn also makes a fabulous home base for visiting the numerous wineries and attractions of the Temecula Valley, so go ahead and extend your stay here—you'll be so glad you did!

CEREMONY CAPACITY: The site can accommodate up to 300 seated guests outdoors.

EVENT/RECEPTION CAPACITY: The site holds 220 seated guests indoors, and 300 seated or standing outdoors.

MEETING CAPACITY: Meeting spaces hold 220 seated guests.

FEES & DEPOSITS: A nonrefundable deposit and a signed contract are required to reserve your date. A nonrefundable deposit of 50% of the total estimated cost is due 30 days prior to the event, with the final estimated balance due 5 business days prior to the scheduled function. Rental fees range $500–4,000 depending on the space rented. Meals start at $56/person. Tax, alcohol and a service charge are additional. Food & beverage minimums apply based on the date of your event and the areas reserved.

AVAILABILITY: Year-round.

SERVICES/AMENITIES:

Catering: in-house
Kitchen Facilities: fully equipped
Tables & Chairs: provided, upgrades available
Linens, Silver, etc.: provided, upgrades available
Restrooms: wheelchair accessible
Dance Floor: provided
Bride's Dressing Area: yes
Meeting Equipment: provided
Other: spa services, AV equipment
event coordination

Parking: large lot, self-parking
Accommodations: 130 guest rooms
Telephone: house or guest phone
Outdoor Night Lighting: provided, upgrades
available
Outdoor Cooking Facilities: no
Cleanup: provided
View: courtyard, fountain, landscaped grounds; golf course fairways; panorama of forest, hills, lake and mountains

RESTRICTIONS:

Alcohol: in-house
Smoking: designated areas only
Music: amplified OK with restrictions in some areas

Wheelchair Access: yes
Insurance: liability required

Wedgewood Upland Hills

Event Center

1231 East 16th Street, Upland
866/966-3009

www.wedgewoodbanquet.com/upland-hills
sales@wedgewoodbanquet.com

- Rehearsal Dinners
- Ceremonies
- Wedding Receptions
- Private Parties

- Corporate Events
- Meetings
- Film Shoots
- Accommodations

Although contemporary in construction, Wedgewood Upland Hills conveys a more Old World character. With its high, hipped roof, veranda, and series of brick columns and French doors, the banquet center's architecture echoes the aesthetic of *fin-de-siècle* colonial buildings found in the West Indies. Indeed, as you lean out over the upstairs terrace, mint julep in hand, the air is so balmy and the fairways so green that visions of Martinique or Antigua come to mind. As you might imagine, this pretty and perennially lush landscape is an appealing backdrop for weddings and receptions.

Wedding ceremonies are held in a white, old-fashioned wedding gazebo just a short distance from the clubhouse. Skirted by red roses and framed by the slate blue silhouette of the San Gabriel Mountains in the distance, it's a lovely, poetic setting. To further the romantic atmosphere, some brides arrive via horse-drawn carriage; others add drama by making a slow entrance on a gently winding path that has been trimmed into the grass.

For a post-ceremony photo safari, newlyweds and their photographer are welcome to take a golf cart out for a spin on the adjacent golf course. Meanwhile guests can enjoy cocktails and happily hobnob on the clubhouse patio.

Small to mid-size receptions are hosted in the Fountain View Room, which spans the length of the clubhouse's upper level. Lined with windows and five sets of French doors, this radiant, light-filled space features a glorious vista of the fairways, lakes and fountains below. For an up-close-and-personal view of the golf greens, have your soirée out on the wraparound covered veranda. Here guests will appreciate the sound of palms rustling in the breeze, and the scent of pines and freshly mowed grass.

Larger gatherings are held in the newly constructed Mountain View Room, a freestanding 4,000-square-foot pavilion with a full wall of floor-to-ceiling windows that capture sweeping views. Highlights of this versatile space include a private bar, dance floor and beautifully draped ceiling.

The venue's easy, breezy ambiance is made even more so thanks to Wedgewood's event professionals. Their all-inclusive and reasonably priced wedding packages are customizable, giving you the choice of leaving everything up to them or selecting which services you'd like to take on yourself. Either way, you'll be in experienced hands so you can enjoy your celebration to the fullest.

If pristine fairways and an elegant, yet relaxed, country club environment appeal to your sensibilities, then Wedgewood Upland Hills is the perfect place for your party!

CEREMONY CAPACITY: The Garden Gazebo Area can accommodate 250 seated or standing. The Event Tent will hold up to 250 guests.

EVENT/RECEPTION & MEETING CAPACITY: The facility holds 250 seated or standing guests indoors.

FEES & DEPOSITS: 25% of the estimated total event cost is required to reserve your date. An additonal 25% is due 120 days prior to the event and the balance (based on your final guest count) is due 10 days prior. All payments are credited towards your final balance and are nonrefundable and nontransferable. All-inclusive, completely customizable wedding packages start at $33/person. Tax, alcohol and a 21–22% service charge are additional.

AVAILABILITY: Year-round, daily, 9am–midnight, including holidays.

SERVICES/AMENITIES:

Catering: in-house, no BYO
Kitchen Facilities: n/a
Tables & Chairs: provided
Linens, Silver, etc.: provided
Restrooms: wheelchair accessible
Dance Floor: provided
Bride's Dressing Area: yes
Meeting Equipment: provided
Other: wedding cake and florals on site, clergy on staff, AV equipment, event coordination

Parking: large lot
Accommodations: no guest rooms
Telephone: house phone
Outdoor Night Lighting: access only
Outdoor Cooking Facilities: BBQ CBA
Cleanup: provided
View: fountain, fairways, lagoon, landscaped grounds

RESTRICTIONS:

Alcohol: in-house
Smoking: designated areas only
Music: amplified OK

Wheelchair Access: yes
Insurance: liability required

The professionals in the back of this book are the best in the business. How do we know? Read page 549.

Spring Valley Lake Country Club

Golf Club

13229 Spring Valley Parkway, Victorville
760/245-5356 x232

www.spring-valley-lake.com
contactus@spring-valley-lake.com

- Rehearsal Dinners
- Ceremonies
- Wedding Receptions
- Private Parties
- Corporate Events
- Meetings
- Film Shoots
- Accommodations

Spring Valley Lake Country Club is a shimmering green mirage: Its lush 18-hole golf course overlooks a deep blue lake ringed by weeping willows.

Coming inside the clubhouse, you leave the desert sun behind and enter a cool, calm sanctuary. The Via Verde Room has a view of the fairways and the San Bernardino Mountains beyond. It also boasts a large, picturesque stone fireplace that dominates one wall. With the ambiance of a cozy drawing room, it's often used for small private parties, intimate cocktail receptions and wedding ceremonies.

The Mirage Room is the club's main reception space. Cantilevered over the lake, it has floor-to-ceiling windows on three sides that look out onto the water, the verdant golf course and the majestic mountains in the distance. Skylights running the length of the wood-beam ceiling fill the room with light. A full-service bar, dance floor and a nook for a DJ or a band allow for a wide range of entertainment, and there's a balcony that wraps around the entire perimeter of the room. Your guests will want to linger here, drinking in the lovely panorama—they may even be regaled by one of those fiery sunsets particular to the desert.

If you're extending your stay through the weekend and you're partial to golf, arrange a tee time on the club's Robert Trent Jr./Sr. championship fairways. Non-golfers will find plenty of other activities within an easy drive of Victorville. Nearby Calico is the site of an Early Man archaeological dig and an Old West ghost town. Even closer, the city of Barstow offers a terrific shopping outlet center and one of the last drive-in movie theaters in California. In the winter, snowboarding and skiing are less than an hour away in Big Bear.

Spring Valley provides a private club experience, with service being their top priority. They'll help you with every aspect of your event, and make sure that you'll have a beautiful celebration at an affordable price.

CEREMONY CAPACITY: Indoors the Via Verde Room seats 80 guests, and the Mirage Room seats up to 180. Outdoors the site holds 200 seated guests.

EVENT/RECEPTION & MEETING CAPACITY: The Via Verde Room holds 80 seated or 150 standing guests. The Mirage Room holds 180 seated or 250 standing. Smaller rooms can be arranged.

FEES & DEPOSITS: A $500 deposit is required to reserve your date. 50% of the estimated event total is due 90 days prior to the event and the balance is due 10 days prior. Rental fees range $400–1,000 depending on the day and time of the event and the space rented. Meals start at $21/person. Packages start at $39/person. Tax, alcohol and a 20% service charge are additional.

AVAILABILITY: Year-round.

SERVICES/AMENITIES:

Catering: in-house

Kitchen Facilities: n/a

Tables & Chairs: provided

Linens, Silver, etc.: provided

Restrooms: wheelchair accessible

Dance Floor: provided

Bride's Dressing Area: yes

Meeting Equipment: screen, podium, microphone, projector

Parking: large lot

Accommodations: no guest rooms

Telephone: emergency use only

Outdoor Night Lighting: yes

Outdoor Cooking Facilities: no

Cleanup: provided

View: lake, golf course, mountains

Other: wedding coordinator

RESTRICTIONS:

Alcohol: in-house, no BYO

Smoking: outdoors only

Music: amplified OK indoors

Wheelchair Access: yes

Insurance: not required

Other: no rice, birdseed or confetti

San Diego Area

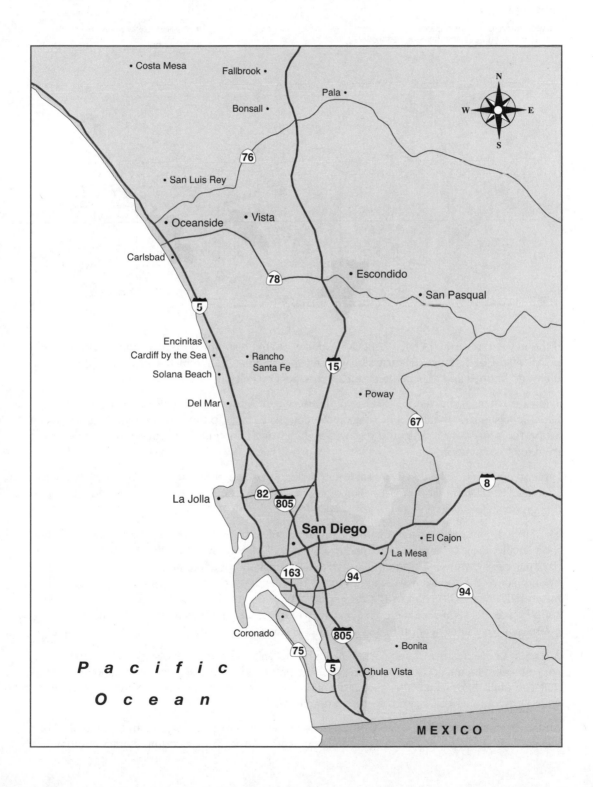

Chula Vista Golf Course

Golf Club

4475 Bonita Road, Bonita
888/292-6120

www.countryclubreceptions.com
privateeventmanager@chulavistagc.com

- Rehearsal Dinners
- Ceremonies
- Wedding Receptions
- Private Parties
- Corporate Events
- Meetings
- Film Shoots
- Accommodations

If the newly refurbished Chula Vista Golf Course had to be summed up in a single word, it would be "distinguished." The clubhouse's beautifully appointed interior, which features rich dark wood, high-end fixtures and fine architectural accents, suggests elegance at every turn.

The care taken in the venue's 2012 remodel is evident from the moment you walk in the door. Little details—from the just-right vase on the entryway hutch to the original paintings and metal art on the walls—are a delight to the eyes and convey the notion that your wedding will benefit from a lot of attention, too.

Larger receptions are held in the Vista Room, a slightly contemporary take on the stately ballroom-style facility. Tasteful two-tone mocha-colored walls and a neutral brown carpet add warmth to this grand space.

The Links Room, which overlooks the manicured hills of the golf course, is a distinctive setting for a smaller crowd. Sunshine streams through a wall of windows, bringing out the luster of the dark mahogany wainscoting and pillars. Historical sepia photos and paintings of San Diego's South County adorn the room's ivory walls. Toward the rear, a set of stairs takes revelers to the Loft, a raised half-enclosed section of the room that is typically used for the DJ and dance floor. Many couples like this semi-separate area because, while the partying is going on full force in the Loft, guests seated at tables can still carry on a conversation.

Attention to detail at the Chula Vista Golf Course doesn't end with its décor. The chef can customize your event menu, and their wedding package provides little extras that come standard—extras that you often have to pay for at other locations. For instance, there's no cake-cutting fee and a wide array of linen colors are offered at no additional charge.

All the effort that the Chula Vista Golf Course has put into creating a stylish and dignified setting has paid off—it now possesses everything you need to make your wedding a gracious affair.

CEREMONY, EVENT/RECEPTION & MEETING CAPACITY: The location holds a maximum of 200 seated guests.

FEES & DEPOSITS: A nonrefundable deposit, which is applied to your food and beverage total, is required to reserve your date. The amount of the deposit varies, depending on how far in advance you book. Payment terms for the balance also vary, and may be arranged on an individual basis. Meals start at $25/person. Tax, alcohol and service charge are additional. Menus and packages can be customized to fit your needs and budget. Call for details.

AVAILABILITY: Year-round, daily.

SERVICES/AMENITIES:

Catering: in-house
Kitchen Facilities: fully equipped
Tables & Chairs: provided
Linens, Silver, etc.: provided
Restrooms: wheelchair accessible
Dance Floor: provided
Bride's Dressing Areas: no
Meeting Equipment: CBA

Parking: large complimentary lot
Accommodations: no guest rooms
Telephone: office phone
Outdoor Night Lighting: provided
Outdoor Cooking Facilities: no
Cleanup: provided
View: golf course, landscaped grounds
Other: event coordination

RESTRICTIONS:

Alcohol: in-house
Smoking: outdoors only
Music: amplified OK indoors only

Wheelchair Access: yes
Insurance: not required

Orfila Vineyards and Winery

Winery & Vineyard

13455 San Pasqual Road, Escondido
760/738-6500 x24

www.orfila.com
steffi@orfila.com

- Rehearsal Dinners
- Ceremonies
- Wedding Receptions
- Private Parties
- Corporate Events
- Meetings
- Film Shoots
- Accommodations

Alejandro Orfila, the man behind lovely Orfila Vineyards and Winery, has led an extraordinary life. Formerly Argentina's ambassador to the United States, and later Secretary General of the Organization of American States, he has hobnobbed with every U.S. president from Truman to Clinton. When he retired from his 39-year diplomatic career, he bought a small winery in sleepy San Pasqual Valley and turned its 70 acres into an unexpectedly world-class operation. Credit also goes to winemaker Justin Mund, who joined Orfila in 2010 and continues to maintain and enhance the winery's high-quality standards.

Orfila's grounds are as spectacular as their wines, and they make a decidedly romantic backdrop for a wedding. Ceremonies are held on an expansive lawn with a classic wine country view: countless well-tended rows of Syrah, Sangiovese, Cabernet Sauvignon and Merlot grapes receding towards unspoiled hills rising in the distance. Only the occasional bird chirping interrupts the quiet of this valley, which becomes your cathedral. Its timeless natural beauty complements any celebration, whether formal, relaxed, or somewhere in between.

It's a short stroll from the lawn to the patio, where your guests gather for cocktails. Surrounded by flowers and lit by charming gas lamp-style fixtures, it's the perfect spot for mingling on a balmy summer evening. Bartenders typically dispense libations under the long, vine-covered grape arbor, as your family and friends sample hors d'oeuvres—you may also be inspired to host a wine and cheese tasting!

There is no shortage of photo opportunities at Orfila: down in the vineyard; in the sprawling, grassy rose park among white, pink, peach, yellow and red roses; and up in the aromatic barrel room (you're sure to recall its intoxicating aroma every time you open your wedding album).

Are you planning to invite a lot of people? They'll all fit under the 6,000-square-foot white pavilion adjacent to the patio, with plenty of room left over for your band or DJ and dancing on a hardwood floor. Heaters and ceiling fans provide comfort in any weather; leave the tent sides tied open to enjoy the breeze and the view of the vineyard when the weather is good (which is most of the time). Dramatic spotlights, uplights and "gobo" lights can be adjusted to create whatever mood you like.

In keeping with its commitment to quality, the winery only works with a handpicked coterie of preferred caterers who can handle the full range of events, from a simple down-home dinner to an elaborate gala. In addition, Orfila will assign an event supervisor to make sure everything runs smoothly.

Finally, what would make a more fitting keepsake of your marriage at the winery than a bottle of your favorite Orfila vintage, customized with your own private, commemorative label? Uncork one bottle per table and let your guests raise their glasses together, or give every adult a bottle to take home to remind them this was a very good year.

CEREMONY & EVENT/RECEPTION CAPACITY: The site holds 100 seated or standing guests indoors, and 350 seated or 400 standing outdoors.

MEETING CAPACITY: Meeting spaces can accommodate 350 seated guests.

FEES & DEPOSITS: One third of the rental fee is required to reserve your date. The balance is due 7 days prior to the event. The rental fee ranges $2,000–3,600.

AVAILABILITY: Year-round, weekdays until 8pm, and weekends until 10pm.

SERVICES/AMENITIES:

Catering: select from list
Kitchen Facilities: prep only
Tables & Chairs: provided
Linens, Silver, etc.: through caterer
Restrooms: wheelchair accessible
Dance Floor: rental available
Bride's Dressing Area: yes
Meeting Equipment: CBA
Other: picnic area, complimentary event coordination

Parking: self-parking or valet
Accommodations: no guest rooms
Telephone: office phone
Outdoor Night Lighting: provided
Outdoor Cooking Facilities: BBQ CBA
Cleanup: provided
View: hills, landscaped grounds; panorama of vineyards, valley and mountains

RESTRICTIONS:

Alcohol: bar service in-house
Smoking: not allowed inside tent
Music: amplified OK outdoors with restrictions

Wheelchair Access: yes
Insurance: not required

San Diego Zoo Safari Park

Wildlife Park

15500 San Pasqual Valley Road, Escondido
619/685-3259

www.sandiegozoo.org/weddings
events@sandiegozoo.org

- Rehearsal Dinners
- Ceremonies
- Wedding Receptions
- Private Parties
- Corporate Events
- Meetings
- Film Shoots
- Accommodations

A herd of gazelles calmly roams the vast plain, while a group of giraffes clusters under a tree. Maternally, one lowers her long neck to groom her youngster. Sound like an exotic scene from Africa? It could be, but it's actually a lot closer to home, and you can have the fun of sharing it with those you love on your wedding day.

The San Diego Zoo Safari Park, an 1,800-acre conservation center, will stir your soul with the wonder of seeing nearly 400 wild and often endangered species like zebras, bison, gorillas and condors. Perhaps the most popular attraction is watching different animals—rhinos, antelopes and yes, those gorgeous giraffes—graze together harmoniously in their natural habitat. So, it's an unexpected treat to use this idyllic tableau as a backdrop for your celebration.

After the public has left for the day and the park takes on a hush, your guests begin their safari with a shuttle ride to the Heart of Africa. This grassland ceremony site, shaded by a grove of trees, is within site of the cheetah habitat, and if you're lucky you might see a couple of these magnificent creatures lazing on the hillside. (By the way, for something your guests will never forget, arrange a close encounter with a cheetah or another exotic critter.) Bronze statues of African tribesmen peek out from the surrounding bush as you take your place at the altar, which frames that distant plain.

The adventure continues with a journey past African landscapes to the edge of Nairobi Village and the Hunte Nairobi Pavilion, a spacious, covered venue-in-the-round, for dinner and dancing. Boasting a 35-foot vaulted ceiling and screened-in sides, it lends a wonderfully airy, indoor/outdoor feel to your reception. Gourmet menus add a touch of elegance to the affair, but the icing on the cake may be ending the evening astride a galloping elephant (or crocodile) when the park opens its unique carousel for everyone to take a private spin.

If, however, you prefer a waterside event (or don't want to wait until after hours), you can host your wedding at the Mombasa Island Pavilion. Begin at the Lagoon Overlook, a short walk from the main entrance that meanders past playful meerkats and sparkling waterfalls. Friends and family gather at the ceremony site, a wide plaza that extends in a semicircle above the lagoon, where you'll arrive via cart down a private pathway. Just beyond the altar are a series of small water islands, home to rare birds and plant life. The entire setting is lushly landscaped with flowering shrubs and tall water grasses.

Just steps away, your reception is held at the Mombasa Island Pavilion, a thatched-roof hut with flagstone flooring, rough-hewn wooden columns and tribal painting designs. This rotunda-style building has virtually no walls, allowing for unobstructed views of the waterfowl preening outside while you dine and dance.

And if all of the amazing assets of Safari Park aren't enough, there's another benefit to having your event here: A portion of the proceeds helps support ongoing conservation and wildlife protection efforts. Imagine, by celebrating your new life, you will also save the lives of animals in danger around the world…how wild is that!

CEREMONY, EVENT/RECEPTION & MEETING CAPACITY: The site holds 250 seated or 400 standing guests indoors or outdoors.

FEES & DEPOSITS: 25% of the total event cost is required to reserve your date. A portion is due 30 days prior to the wedding day and the balance is due 5 days prior. Wedding packages range $84–112/person and include: all-day admission for your guests on your wedding day; complimentary general parking; first hour hosted beer, wine and soft drinks; butler-passed hors d'oeuvres; jungle juice toast; your choice of plated entrées or buffet service; linens; waived cake-cutting fee; complimentary floral centerpieces; and a complimentary 1-year membership to the Zoological Society of San Diego for the bride and groom. Tax and alcohol are additional.

AVAILABILITY: Year-round, daily, 9am–11pm.

SERVICES/AMENITIES:

Catering: in-house
Kitchen Facilities: n/a
Tables & Chairs: provided
Linens, Silver, etc.: some provided
Restrooms: wheelchair accessible
Dance Floor: CBA
Bride's Dressing Area: yes
Meeting Equipment: provided
Other: in-house florals, picnic area, AV equipment, wild animals, event coordination

Parking: large lot, valet required
Accommodations: no guest rooms
Telephone: office phone
Outdoor Night Lighting: CBA
Outdoor Cooking Facilities: BBQ CBA
Cleanup: provided
View: canyon, hills, lagoon, waterfall, landscaped grounds; panorama of fields, mountains, park and valley

RESTRICTIONS:

Alcohol: in-house
Smoking: not allowed
Music: amplified OK with restrictions

Wheelchair Access: yes
Insurance: not required

Want to know WHAT TO ASK a potential location or vendor? Check out our Questions to Ask starting on page 19.

Grand Tradition Estate
Beverly Mansion & Arbor Terrace

220 Grand Tradition Way, Fallbrook
760/728-6466

www.grandtradition.com
info@grandtradition.com

Victorian Mansion & Exotic Gardens

● Rehearsal Dinners	● Corporate Events
● Ceremonies	● Meetings
● Wedding Receptions	● Film Shoots
● Private Parties	Accommodations

For a small country town, Fallbrook happens to have a surprisingly large and lovely wedding facility called the Grand Tradition Estate. Set on 30 acres of gently rolling hills in a secluded valley, the estate includes two distinctive venues for events, each with its own personality.

The first is the Beverly Mansion, a Victorian-style mansion surrounded by magnificent gardens. As you stand on the veranda, inhaling the fragrance of fresh-cut grass and surveying the pastoral scene down below, it's clear why so many couples come here to say "I do." Before you, a vast expanse of lawn slopes down to a serene heart-shaped lake ringed by weeping willows. A forest creates a dense green backdrop that shelters your celebration from the outside world. Couples often take advantage of the site's storybook quality by riding around the lake in a white carriage drawn by two sleek Arabian horses before saying their vows at the gazebo. Afterwards, while the bride and groom pose for photos among the many picturesque settings, guests can also take a carriage ride, or indulge their sweet tooth at a decadent chocolate fountain.

Receptions are held in the mansion's Crystal Ballroom, a nostalgically elegant hall illuminated by glittering Swarovski crystal chandeliers. Opulent furnishings and fruitwood Chiavari dining chairs make a bold statement against the room's rich taupe patina. At one end of the hall, a grand staircase with gleaming banisters awaits the formal entrance of the new Mr. and Mrs. Other event-friendly amenities include a curtained stage for the head table, a hardwood dance floor, a baby grand piano, and an English pub.

An alternate and separate venue is the Arbor Terrace Pavilion, a more informal gathering spot set amidst gorgeously landscaped grounds. Palm trees swaying in the floral-laced breeze and cascading waterfalls evoke the romance of a tropical paradise, an alluring atmosphere for wedding vows. Graceful bridges, water features and expansive lawns adorned with statuary enhance the site's natural splendor.

The Pavilion itself has its own charms, including arched French-style windows, a fabric-draped ceiling canopy and a built-in bar with a stone façade. Designed to offer shelter while embracing the outdoors, the three-sided Pavilion lets guests dine while gazing out at an elevated garden patio, with a waterfall tumbling softly in the background and a fire blazing in a flagstone hearth.

The Grand Tradition Estate was designed for events, and weddings are a specialty. Bridal couples will appreciate the exceptionally attentive, friendly service, which includes customized menus by culinary artists who take pride in serving only the freshest and most flavorful dishes.

With two such distinctly beautiful event areas, the Grand Tradition Estate has done more than its share to put the town of Fallbrook on the map! Not surprisingly, it's been selected as a top venue for the 2013 "The Knot Best of Weddings."

CEREMONY, EVENT/RECEPTION & MEETING CAPACITY: The Beverly Mansion seats up to 300 and the Arbor Terrace holds 220 seated guests.

FEES & DEPOSITS: A $1,500 reservation fee is required to book your date. 25% of the estimated event total is due 9 months prior to your event, and another 25% is due 6 months prior. The final guest count and balance are due 10 days before your event. Wedding ceremony & reception packages range $70–140/person, and include meals and all site fees. Tax and a 20% service charge are extra. Discounted rates are available for events on weekdays, Fridays and Sundays, and may also be offered for short notice or off-season bookings.

AVAILABILITY: Year-round, daily. Times vary depending on season and existing event bookings. Please call to check current date and time availability.

SERVICES/AMENITIES:

Catering: in-house, no BYO
Kitchen Facilities: n/a
Tables & Chairs: provided, Chiavari or white padded
Linens, Silver, etc.: provided
Restrooms: wheelchair accessible
Dance Floor: provided
Bride's & Groom's Dressing Area: yes
Meeting Equipment: podium, easels, DVD projection system, wired & wireless microphones
Other: event coordination, wireless internet audio technician, pianist, horse-drawn carriages, chocolate fountain, kosher & ethnic catering CBA

Parking: complimentary parking included, valet CBA
Accommodations: hotels nearby, shuttle CBA
Telephone: house phone
Outdoor Night Lighting: provided
Outdoor Cooking Facilities: no
Cleanup: provided
View: landscaped grounds, mountains, creek, wooded area, fountain, garden, patio, valley, hills, waterfall, pond, lake

RESTRICTIONS:

Alcohol: in-house, no BYO
Smoking: outdoors only
Music: provided or BYO; amplified OK indoors with volume limits, outdoors until 10pm

Wheelchair Access: yes
Insurance: not required

Wedgewood Fallbrook

Event Center

3742 Flowerwood Lane, Fallbrook
866/966-3009

www.wedgewoodbanquet.com/fallbrook
sales@wedgewoodbanquet.com

- Rehearsal Dinners
- Ceremonies
- Wedding Receptions
- Private Parties
- Corporate Events
- Meetings
- Film Shoots
- Accommodations

From its vantage point on a hill overlooking a pristine golf course, Wedgewood Fallbrook sets the stage for a seamlessly flowing wedding or special event by skillfully integrating romantic outdoor courtyards, big airy indoor spaces, and a variety of tranquil views.

Its classic Mission-style architecture, featuring a smooth white stucco exterior, red-tile roof and shaded arcades, adds to the overall serene atmosphere of the venue. A set of arched double doors beneath a gold Spanish chandelier open to the main foyer, which provides a congenial staging area for your bridal party.

As your guests arrive, they can mingle on the circular Fountain Plaza just to the right of the main doors. This picturesque setting is enhanced by bursts of colorful blooms, tall palms and flowering vines wrapped around the dark wood pillars of the surrounding building. Meanwhile, you and your attendants will enjoy primping in the Bridal Suite, set up in a separate wing with plenty of space and light for capturing those important, pre-ceremony photos.

When you're ready to make your entrance, friends and family will already be seated in a truly lovely, terracotta-tiled courtyard ceremony site that feels sequestered, yet open and airy. This private spot is nestled between the clubhouse and a charming outdoor fireplace flanked by two Moorish-styled wooden doors. A treelined center aisle leads to a tall, curved arch that frames you and your groom against a planted breezeway with the lush fairway beyond. Picture perfect!

While your photographer takes photos of you and the bridal party, cocktails and hors d'oeuvres can be served on the Fountain Plaza or, on Saturday nights only, in the Members Bar. High-ceilinged with crossbeams and a two-sided fireplace, this huge—yet homey—lounge has a granite bar backed by windows framing the putting green, rustic iron chandeliers, cushy leather chairs and big-screen TVs. On the other side of the fireplace are leather sofas and club chairs, arranged for easy conversation. Also on Saturday nights, you can enjoy use of the adjacent stone-tiled side patio, which has a beautiful view of the lake and surrounding trees.

Then it's on to the ballroom for dinner. Filled with light from five sets of double glass doors that look out onto the plaza as well as from a dozen softly glowing chandeliers, this L-shaped banquet space can be set with a sweetheart table against the windows, a buffet or dessert bar in the alcove, or any way you wish. After all, this venue is part of the Wedgewood family of wedding and banquet centers, known for offering a full range of options and services designed to meet your particular needs and budget.

CEREMONY CAPACITY: The facility can accommodate 300 seated indoors and 300 seated outdoors.

EVENT/RECEPTION CAPACITY: The facility can accommodate 300 seated or standing indoors.

MEETING CAPACITY: Meeting spaces hold 300 seated guests.

FEES & DEPOSITS: 25% of the estimated total event cost is required to reserve your date. An additonal 25% is due 120 days prior to the event and the balance (based on your final guest count) is due 10 days prior. All payments are credited towards your final balance and are nonrefundable and nontransferable. All-inclusive, completely customizable wedding packages start at $33/person. Tax, alcohol and a 21–22% service charge are additional.

AVAILABILITY: Year-round, daily, 11am–11pm.

SERVICES/AMENITIES:

Catering: in-house
Kitchen Facilities: n/a
Tables & Chairs: provided
Linens, Silver, etc.: provided
Restrooms: wheelchair accessible
Dance Floor: provided
Bride's Dressing Area: yes
Meeting Equipment: some provided
Other: in-house wedding cake and florals, spa services, clergy on staff, picnic area, AV equipment, complimentary event coordination

Parking: large lot
Accommodations: no guest rooms
Telephone: guest phone
Outdoor Night Lighting: provided
Outdoor Cooking Facilities: BBQ
Cleanup: provided
View: landscaped grounds, courtyard, fairways, lake, hills, mountains

RESTRICTIONS:

Alcohol: in-house
Smoking: designated areas only
Music: amplified OK

Wheelchair Access: yes
Insurance: not required

Estancia La Jolla Hotel & Spa

Hotel and Spa

9700 North Torrey Pines Road, La Jolla
858/550-1000

www.estancialajolla.com
estanciacatering@estancialajolla.com

- Rehearsal Dinners
- Ceremonies
- Wedding Receptions
- Private Parties
- Corporate Events
- Meetings
- Film Shoots
- Accommodations

To truly appreciate the charm of Estancia La Jolla Hotel & Spa, it helps to envision its first incarnation as the 10-acre rancho retreat of two wealthy and prominent San Diego families, both with a reputation for being down-to-earth. Their time at the ranch was spent riding horses, lounging outdoors among citrus and avocado trees, and picnicking on simple grilled foods made even more aromatic by the scent of Mexican sage, carried on the light coastal breezes.

Today, when you come up Estancia La Jolla's driveway, you still have the impression you're approaching someone's personal estate. Nothing about the hotel feels large or impersonal. The venue's early California Rancho architecture—characterized by exposed-beam ceilings, arches, and surfaces of distressed brown brick, plaster and ceramic tile—inspires relaxation, and subtle lighting lends indoor spaces a warm, cozy glow. Taking advantage of Southern California's temperate climate, every room on the property, including the guest rooms, opens to an inviting outdoor area.

With so many assets, it's no surprise that this AAA Four Diamond-rated hotel has become a popular choice for romantic San Diego weddings. The favorite spot for a ceremony is the Garden Courtyard, a manicured lawn bordered with native foliage and magnolia trees flush with creamy blooms in the summer. The courtyard was designed with a bride's grand entrance in mind: Two tiled staircases sweep down from the surrounding buildings and converge at a landing, where the bride makes a dramatic pause before descending the final few steps to the landscaped courtyard. Then she makes her way across an aisle strewn with rose petals, and joins her groom in front of the hotel's signature stone fountain.

The hotel has a variety of distinctive banquet rooms, each with its own special appeal. For smaller receptions, the Grande Room is particularly pleasing, with chandeliers that cast golden light and Frank Lloyd Wright-inspired chairs befitting the dining room of a well-furnished home. The spacious La Jolla Ballroom accommodates larger weddings without feeling cavernous, and a portable bandstand and dance floor will help kick the festivities into high gear. In all of the event spaces, Fili D'oro linens, fine china and custom-designed flatware add sumptuous touches.

The hotel's on-site amenities make it well-suited for multi-event destination weddings. Its rancho-themed restaurants and bars, and the intimate Library are all wonderful options for pre- and post-wedding gatherings; as an added bonus, the bridal party can beautify and unwind in the full-service spa. Estancia La Jolla's prime location on the La Jolla cliffs—just minutes from the beach and world-renowned Torrey Pines Golf Course—is just one more reason weddings here are a standout California experience.

CEREMONY CAPACITY: The Garden Courtyard holds 300 seated and the Olive Lawn holds 130 seated guests.

EVENT/RECEPTION CAPACITY: The La Jolla Ballroom holds up to 350 seated guests, the Grande Room holds up to 130 seated.

MEETING CAPACITY: The facility can comfortably accommodate 10 to 400 guests.

FEES & DEPOSITS: 25% of the estimated event total is required to reserve your date; the balance is due 14 days prior to the event. Ceremony rental fees are $1,000–3,000 depending on the location. Reception pricing is $72–150/person, depending on the menu selected. Tax and a 22% service charge are additional.

AVAILABILITY: Year-round, daily. The gardens are available 10am–9pm, the ballroom 7am–1am. Only 2 ceremonies and receptions take place per day, at separate locations on site. Events occurring on the same day will have staggered start times.

SERVICES/AMENITIES:

Catering: in-house, no BYO
Kitchen Facilities: n/a
Tables & Chairs: provided
Linens, Silver, etc.: provided
Restrooms: wheelchair accessible
Dance Floor: provided
Bride's Dressing Area: yes, complimentary
Meeting Equipment: full range CBA

Parking: valet required
Accommodations: 210 guest rooms
Telephone: house phone and guest phone
Outdoor Night Lighting: CBA
Outdoor Cooking Facilities: CBA
Cleanup: provided
View: fountain, garden, pool, grounds
Other: spa, AV equipment

RESTRICTIONS:

Alcohol: in-house
Smoking: designated areas only
Music: amplified OK indoors until midnight

Wheelchair Access: yes
Insurance: required from vendors

La Jolla Beach & Tennis Club

Beach & Tennis Club

2000 Spindrift Drive, La Jolla
877/828-0856
www.ljbtc.com/weddings
catering@ljbtc.com

- Rehearsal Dinners
- Ceremonies
- Wedding Receptions
- Private Parties
- Corporate Events
- Meetings
- Film Shoots
- Accommodations

Tying the knot on one of the toniest sections of Southern California's coast isn't just for celebrities. You can create a stellar wedding of your own at the exclusive La Jolla Beach & Tennis Club. This landmark resort, stretching magnificently from one end of a picturesque cove to the other, is home to one of the last remaining private beaches along the coastline … and that's only the beginning of its seductive allure.

Sprawling across 14 acres, the historic property encompasses a par-3 golf course, 12 championship tennis courts, a beautifully landscaped pond and a hacienda-style clubhouse with 90 guest rooms and suites—easily turning your romantic affair into a spectacular getaway for family and friends.

The club's oceanfront north wing, which wraps around a lovely esplanade with killer views, becomes your own enclave where out-of-towners and the bridal party can settle in. As the time for the ceremony draws near, your guests are ushered to the impeccably groomed beach, mere steps away and reserved solely for you. Your grand entrance begins down the curved staircase from your bridal suite to the sandy aisle. Then, accompanied by the sound of gentle waves lapping at the shore, you exchange vows against the unforgettable panorama of the big blue Pacific.

This quintessential waterfront locale is so fantastic you might not want to leave it, so why not have cocktails and even your main reception (whether a brunch buffet or a sunset dinner) right here, beside the sea? If, however, you want a change of scenery, there are myriad options.

The bucolic Duck Pond and its large expanse of manicured lawn (as well as a nearby rose garden) is a picture-perfect site for both ceremonies and receptions. Natural stone borders, lush plantings and towering palms complete the look, while graceful swans and playful ducks add charm.

The Poolside Patio, nestled between the clubhouse and the Olympic-sized pool, makes a nice choice for a cocktail and/or dinner reception with the verdant hills of La Jolla as a backdrop. The red-tiled roof of the club provides an interesting architectural detail, and a wonderful old stone hearth in the corner beckons as a cozy conversation area.

There are also two indoor venues: Their largest banquet room, La Sala, features wainscoted walls and impressive amber glass chandeliers. The stately Walnut Lounge has a drawing-room ambiance (with a hint of Downton Abbey), thanks to rich walnut paneling and antique candelabra-style light fixtures hanging from the ornate white plaster ceiling. Tall arched windows overlook the esplanade and ocean, and a fireplace makes this your go-to spot for cool-weather weddings.

Whichever setting you choose, you'll savor the sumptuous cuisine. Under the direction of renowned Chef Bernard Guillas of Marine Room* fame, the emphasis is on fresh ingredients and innovative preparations, and many dishes also incorporate ethnic flavors. The knowledgeable catering staff will happily work with you to customize your menu, too.

There are so many fun activities, both here and in the surrounding area, that we recommend staying over a few days. From tennis lessons and golf clinics to kayaking, wine tasting, a summer kids' club, and even just lazing on the beach, there's something for everyone. Between your fabulous wedding and equally fabulous mini-vacation, you'll have plenty of great memories from your La Jolla Beach & Tennis Club experience.

*Note: The Marine Room is the Four Diamond Award-winning fine-dining restaurant on the property. See the description on page 488.

CEREMONY CAPACITY: The site holds 190 seated indoors and 200 seated outdoors.

EVENT/RECEPTION CAPACITY: The club can accommodate 150 seated or 250 standing guests indoors and 200 seated or 250 standing outdoors.

MEETING CAPACITY: Meeting spaces hold 150 seated guests, or 160 seated theater-style.

FEES & DEPOSITS: 20% of the estimated event total is required to reserve your date and the balance is due 30 days prior to the event. Rental fees range $350–750 depending on the day of the event and the space rented. Meals start at $55/person. Tax, alcohol and an 18% service charge are additional.

Hosting an event at the La Jolla Beach and Tennis Club requires either club membership or sponsorship by a club member. Hotel guests also may host an event subject to approval and based on occupancy. Guest fees apply—please contact Catering for more information.

AVAILABILITY: Year-round, daily, until 10pm.

SERVICES/AMENITIES:

Catering: in-house or select from preferred list
Kitchen Facilities: fully equipped kitchen
Tables & Chairs: provided
Linens, Silver, etc.: provided
Restrooms: wheelchair accessible
Dance Floor: portable provided
Bride's Dressing Area: CBA
Meeting Equipment: provided
Other: AV equipment, grand piano, spa services, in-house florals

Parking: large lot, on street, valet available
Accommodations: 90 guest rooms
Telephone: house phone
Outdoor Night Lighting: CBA
Outdoor Cooking Facilities: BBQ CBA
Cleanup: provided
View: fountain, courtyard, fairways, pool area, landscaped grounds; panorama of ocean and coastline

RESTRICTIONS:

Alcohol: in-house
Smoking: designated areas only
Music: amplified OK indoors

Wheelchair Access: limited
Insurance: not required

Want to find more venues and services? Check out our informative website, www.HereComesTheGuide.com.

483

La Jolla Cove Suites

Waterfront Hotel

1155 Coast Boulevard, La Jolla
858/551-3414
www.lajollacove.com
sales@lajollacove.com

Rehearsal Dinners	● Corporate Events
● Ceremonies	● Meetings
● Wedding Receptions	● Film Shoots
● Private Parties	● Accommodations

The beaches of La Jolla are known all over the world for their stunning beauty. One of the town's most treasured spots is La Jolla Cove, where a manicured greenbelt overlooking the sparkling Pacific gives a panoramic view of San Diego's scenic coastline.

High above this coastal jewel is the Rooftop Terrace of the La Jolla Cove Suites hotel. From this spacious outdoor venue, you experience the unspoiled Southern California coast in a way that delights all the senses: breathtaking vistas, tangy ocean breezes, the sound of waves tumbling onto the shore and the warm kiss of the sun.

The 12,000-square-foot Terrace is like a grand blank canvas on which you can paint your own event. There are very few restrictions, and a dedicated staff is available to help you design the space to suit your needs. Use tents or lattice walls to create intimate "rooms," or take advantage of the openness for a big-party feel. At night built-in lamps resembling old-fashioned streetlights provide soft romantic lighting. Decorating the lampposts and terrace railings with flowers and fabric in the colors of your choice is an excellent way to personalize the site for your event. You're also free to choose your own caterer, cake maker and other service providers.

Guests arrive via the elevator, which opens into the Solarium, a glass-enclosed room that serves as a lobby for rooftop events. This is the perfect place for the guest book and place card tables, and perhaps poster-size photos of the bride and groom displayed on easels.

Couples usually say their vows under an arch or chuppah set in the Terrace's northwest corner, the best vantage point to view the coastal cliffs and picturesque hillsides of San Diego. After the ceremony, guests gather in the Solarium or on the south side of the roof for cocktails and conversation, while reception tables are set up and the bridal party goes downstairs for photos on the beach or on the bluffs overlooking the cove. As day turns to evening, the sun sets in a blaze of color over the Pacific, providing a gorgeous backdrop to the festivities.

A wedding at La Jolla Cove Suites also affords out-of-town guests a chance to visit one of California's vacation hot spots and stay in an oceanview apartment-style suite at a group discount depending on the season. The beachfront hotel is just a short stroll from Downtown La Jolla, a shopping district with galleries and upscale boutiques that's often compared to Rodeo Drive. A wealth of casual and fine-dining options, jazz and piano bars, nightclubs and a comedy club all are within walking distance. For those more interested in the area's natural gifts, the hotel is close to several choice snorkeling points and steps from a beach where seals often congregate. Visitors can also tour the coastal caves just a block away.

Spectacular views, maximum flexibility and plenty of nearby activities to entertain your family and friends…yes, La Jolla Cove Suites definitely has all the makings for a memorable event.

CEREMONY, EVENT/RECEPTION & MEETING CAPACITY: The location holds 225 seated or standing guests on the outdoor Terrace, including indoor seating for up to 75 guests.

FEES & DEPOSITS: A $1,250 deposit is required to reserve your date. The balance is due 60 days prior to the event. Rental fees range $3,000–5,000 depending on the date of event and number of suites booked.

AVAILABILITY: Year-round.

SERVICES/AMENITIES:

Catering: select from list or BYO
Kitchen Facilities: prep only
Tables & Chairs: some provided, more through *Raphael's Party Rentals*
Linens, Silver, etc.: through *Raphael's Party Rentals*
Restrooms: wheelchair accessible
Dance Floor: CBA
Bride's Dressing Area: CBA
Meeting Equipment: full range CBA

Parking: limited on property, garage nearby
Accommodations: 110 guest rooms
Telephone: guest phone
Outdoor Night Lighting: yes
Outdoor Cooking Facilities: yes
Cleanup: caterer or renter
View: ocean, coastline, park
Other: AV equipment, pool, spa, pets OK

RESTRICTIONS:

Alcohol: CBA
Smoking: not allowed
Music: amplified OK outdoors

Wheelchair Access: yes
Insurance: required for vendors only

La Jolla Shores Hotel

Waterfront Hotel

8110 Camino del Oro, La Jolla
888/694-5411

www.ljshoreshotel.com
ljshcatering@ljshoreshotel.com

- Rehearsal Dinners
- Ceremonies
- Wedding Receptions
- Private Parties
- Corporate Events
- Meetings
- Film Shoots
- Accommodations

With some of the most beautiful coastline in the world, it's no wonder California makes so many brides think BEACH WEDDING. The sun sparkling on the water…the sound of the surf…a cool breeze…it's the quintessential SoCal scene for tying the knot. The tricky part is finding a place on the beach that also takes care of all the details, offers several reception options, serves up a menu to die for, and is located in a town oozing with charm. Well, we've found it for you: the La Jolla Shores Hotel.

Located on two acres of beachfront property, this rambling hacienda-style resort is one of the very few in San Diego County that's allowed to host weddings directly on the sand. Before every event, they groom the shoreline and, as if waves lapping ashore right next to you wasn't heavenly enough, they can even add a bamboo structure along the aisle or an altar of tropical flowers.

With a setting like this, you may want to continue your celebration seaside, or you can head to the private, second-floor Acapulco Deck for cocktails and killer coastal views. When you're ready for dinner, move inside to the Acapulco Room, where floor-to-ceiling windows showcase dazzling sunset vistas.

If you prefer to see and hear the ocean but not necessarily have your ceremony on the sand, the three-story hotel's central Garden Courtyard is a perfect alternative. Shaded with lattice and paved with terracotta tiles, this festive open-air space affords a long center aisle for a dramatic walk to the altar. Lushly planted borders—abloom with birds of paradise, hibiscus, azaleas and various palms—set the stage, framed by the red-tiled-roof overhangs of the surrounding guest rooms. Afterwards, guests can mingle over cocktails on the adjacent Fountain Patio, featuring a tall, arched breezeway with the beach just steps away.

Then, host your dinner reception on the Shores Patio, directly facing the beach. In fact, many couples choose to say "I do" on the patio in front of that magnificent ocean, which is equally captivating at night when the surf is illuminated by spotlights. If you get married here, you can join your family and friends for a glass of bubbly, and segue to dinner and dancing in the La Jolla Room. This romantic space has a vaulted ceiling, graceful arched windows and glass doors so it feels airy and open—plus it's the best spot in the hotel to kick up your heels with music and dancing.

Beach hotels rarely win raves for their food, but the award-winning culinary team at the La Jolla Shores Hotel will customize a delectable menu for you with ingredients so fresh you'll swear they were just plucked from the sea or farm. The entire staff is also incredibly accommodating, and can arrange everything from in-room massages to tennis games to shopping trips in the chic town of La Jolla for guests who want to stay over and make a weekend of it.

CEREMONY CAPACITY: The hotel can accommodate 100 seated guests indoors and 200 seated outdoors.

EVENT/RECEPTION CAPACITY: The site holds 100 seated or 120 standing guests indoors, and 200 seated or 250 standing outdoors.

MEETING CAPACITY: Meeting spaces hold 80–100 seated guests.

FEES & DEPOSITS: 20% of the event total plus the signed contract is required to reserve your date and the balance is due 30 days prior to the event. Rental fees range $500–2,500 and vary depending on the room rented. Meal packages start at $85/person. Tax, alcohol and an 18% service charge are additional.

AVAILABILITY: Year-round, daily, indoors. Beach wedding services not available in July or August.

SERVICES/AMENITIES:

Catering: in-house
Kitchen Facilities: n/a
Tables & Chairs: provided
Linens, Silver, etc.: provided
Restrooms: wheelchair accessible
Dance Floor: portable provided
Bride's Dressing Area: yes
Meeting Equipment: provided
Other: spa services, picnic area, AV equipment, free WiFi, beach and poolside amenities

Parking: on street, valet required, garage nearby
Accommodations: 128 guest rooms
Telephone: house phone
Outdoor Night Lighting: yes
Outdoor Cooking Facilities: BBQ CBA
Cleanup: provided
View: fountain, courtyard, landscaped grounds; panorama of coastline and ocean

RESTRICTIONS:

Alcohol: in-house
Smoking: not allowed
Music: amplified OK with restrictions

Wheelchair Access: yes
Insurance: required from vendors

The Marine Room

2000 Spindrift Drive, La Jolla
888/339-2483

www.marineroom.com/weddings
mrcatering@marineroom.com

Waterfront Restaurant

- Rehearsal Dinners
- Ceremonies
- Wedding Receptions
- Private Parties
- Corporate Events
- Meetings
- Film Shoots
- Accommodations

Admit it, you know what you want: breathtaking ocean views, a relaxed and elegant ambiance, service fit for an A-lister and 4-star cuisine that's a feast for your senses. Worried that you might be asking for too much? Don't be—The Marine Room has it all!

This La Jolla Shores treasure sits right on one of the prettiest stretches of beach in San Diego. Consistently showered with superlatives like "most romantic," "most scenic," "best fine dining" and "overall favorite," it's been a celebration touchstone for decades, the place where VIPs, tourists and locals commemorate the special moments of their lives.

You enter through a sleek Mezzanine Lounge that seems to float above the open, airy dining room below. A dramatic staircase leads downstairs where the décor is timeless, like the interior of a great beach house that's posh, yet comfortable. The color scheme is neutral with lots of cream and white, and the high-peaked ceiling is inset with skylights that bathe the space in natural light. From every corner, your eye is drawn to the amazing view just outside the windows: a vast tableau of white sand, craggy hills and the big blue Pacific. Boats, seagulls and kayakers provide an interesting show that's reflected in the mirrored walls along the back of the restaurant. And as fabulous as tangerine sunsets over the horizon can be, stormy skies are just as awesome (the High Tide Dinners, where waves lap against the windows, are always quickly sold out).

For the ultimate Marine Room wedding experience, reserve the entire venue and go from ceremony and cocktails to dining and dancing. The restaurant can be configured into four separate sections, so it's easy to create a wonderful flow throughout your event. This flexibility is also great if you just want to reserve one or two areas for a small reception, rehearsal dinner, or other more intimate gathering: The Seahorse Lounge affords total privacy, the South End comes with it's own bar, and the Terrace (an elevated indoor space) treats diners to a coastline panorama.

As mesmerizing as the vistas are, the food is equally compelling. Renowned Executive Chef Bernard Guillas and Chef de Cuisine Ron Oliver repeatedly earn kudos from critics, including a Four Diamond rating from AAA. Chef Bernard, who grew up in Brittany, France, says he was influenced by Monet and it shows in the French-inspired menu where flavors are layered subtly, like the colors in an impressionistic painting. The focus is on fresh, local ingredients with an affinity for seafood, but there are numerous beef, fowl and wild game selections as well. Particular standouts are the blue crab cake, sesame crusted tuna and savory appetizer "cones" filled with velvety tuna tartare, crab or scallops. Plus, the presentations are edible art!—diners often whip out their phones to photograph the magnificently plated meals as they arrive. Completing your gustatory adventure is an impressive wine list that has won praise from *Wine Spectator* magazine, and service that's both attentive and discreet.

After dinner, you can take a moonlit stroll along the beach and, like countless couples before you, make plans to come back here for all your future anniversary celebrations.

Note: The La Jolla Beach & Tennis Club next to the Marine Room is available for overnight accommodations as well as special events. See their profile on page 482.

CEREMONY CAPACITY: The site holds 80 seated or 100 standing guests indoors.

EVENT/RECEPTION CAPACITY: The restaurant can accommodate 230 seated or 275 standing guests indoors.

MEETING CAPACITY: Meeting spaces hold 100 seated guests.

FEES & DEPOSITS: There is no rental fee, but food and beverage minimums apply and vary depending on date and time of the event and the space reserved. Meals range $29–95/person. Tax, beverages and an 18% service charge are additional.

AVAILABILITY: Year-round, daily, 10am–4pm or 5pm–midnight.

SERVICES/AMENITIES:

Catering: in-house
Kitchen Facilities: fully equipped
Tables & Chairs: provided
Linens, Silver, etc.: provided
Restrooms: wheelchair accessible
Dance Floor: CBA
Bride's Dressing Area: CBA
Meeting Equipment: CBA
Other: AV equipment, in-house wedding cake

Parking: valet available
Accommodations: CBA at La Jolla Beach & Tennis Club
Telephone: house phone
Outdoor Night Lighting: provided
Outdoor Cooking Facilities: none
Cleanup: provided
View: panorama of ocean and coastline

RESTRICTIONS:

Alcohol: full in-house bar
Smoking: designated areas only
Music: amplified OK indoors with restrictions

Wheelchair Access: yes
Insurance: not required

El Camino Country Club

Country Club

3202 Vista Way, Oceanside
888/643-3516

www.countryclubreceptions.com
eventdirector@elcaminoclub.com

● Rehearsal Dinners	● Corporate Events
● Ceremonies	● Meetings
● Wedding Receptions	● Film Shoots
● Private Parties	Accommodations

El Camino Country Club is both relaxed and elegant. The clubhouse's classic décor is timeless, and its meticulous upkeep is evident throughout, from the manicured lawns to the orchids thriving in the foyer.

Ceremonies typically take place outdoors, with the couple exchanging vows in a beautiful white gazebo. Guests seated on the lawn are treated to sweeping views of the lush greens and treelined fairways in the background.

After the ceremony, family and friends enter the charming, sunny Garden Room just off the patio for cocktails and conversation. Meanwhile, the bride and groom are chauffeured in a cart around the golf course for photos in several picturesque spots, including a bi-level lake framed by a graceful weeping willow.

Later, the party moves to the more formal Main Dining Room for the reception. This spacious venue is decorated in neutral colors, and a series of multipaned windows overlook the expansive 18th fairway.

With white linens and chair covers, the room becomes a storybook wedding vision. Silver and crystal gleam in the soft, romantic glow of the chandeliers. When the best man is ready to make his toast or the couple takes to the floor for their first dance, the recessed lights in the ceiling can be turned up to create a theatrical effect.

The club's friendly and accommodating private events office offers a broad array of wedding packages, from a simple and quite affordable afternoon affair to a decadent evening gala with a hosted bar and surf-and-turf dinner.

Regardless of your budget, your wedding at the El Camino Country Club is certain to reflect the class and attention to detail that makes this facility such an enchanting place.

CEREMONY CAPACITY: The lawn holds up to 200 seated guests

EVENT/RECEPTION & MEETING CAPACITY: The Main Dining Room accommodates up to 200 seated or 250 standing guests; the Patio up to 200 seated or 250 standing; and the Garden Room up to 70 seated or 89 standing. The Cabana can be used by a bride and her bridal party for pre-wedding preparation (up to 15 total).

FEES & DEPOSITS: A nonrefundable deposit, which is applied to your food and beverage total, is required to reserve your date. The amount of the deposit varies, depending on how far in advance you book. Payment terms for the balance also vary, and may be arranged on an individual basis. Luncheons start at $14/person, dinners at $29/person and buffets at $30/person. Tax, alcohol and service charge are additional. Menus and packages can be customized to fit your needs and budget. Call for details.

AVAILABILITY: Year-round, daily.

SERVICES/AMENITIES:

Catering: in-house
Kitchen Facilities: n/a
Tables & Chairs: provided
Linens, Silver, etc.: provided
Restrooms: wheelchair accessible
Dance Floor: provided
Bride's Dressing Area: yes
Meeting Equipment: some provided, more CBA

Parking: large lot
Accommodations: no guest rooms
Telephone: office phone
Outdoor Night Lighting: CBA
Outdoor Cooking Facilities: BBQ CBA
Cleanup: provided
View: garden, pond, hills, grounds, fairways
Other: event coordination

RESTRICTIONS:

Alcohol: in-house
Smoking: outdoors only
Music: amplified OK indoors with restrictions

Wheelchair Access: yes
Insurance: not required

This is important! Tell venues you're reading HERE COMES THE GUIDE and ask if our information is still current.

Morgan Run Club & Resort

5690 Cancha de Golf, Rancho Santa Fe
858/759-5468

www.morganrun.com
contactus@morganrun.com

Private Country Club & Ballroom

- Rehearsal Dinners
- Ceremonies
- Wedding Receptions
- Private Parties
- Corporate Events
- Meetings
- Film Shoots
- Accommodations

Rancho Santa Fe, one of the most desirable communities in California, is the kind of discreetly luxurious place that many aspire to but few actually reach unless, of course, you're a business mogul, Hollywood star or … if you're having your wedding at Morgan Run Club & Resort.

Located just three miles from the Pacific Ocean and a half hour from Downtown San Diego, this private country club and resort is, fortuitously, available to the public for special events. As you drive up, you catch sight of the 27-hole golf course on your right and, straight ahead, the gray-and-white clubhouse with its cupola, clock tower and flags—all a bit reminiscent of the great horse ranches back East (not surprising considering the area's love of horses and the resort's proximity to the beautiful Del Mar race track).

Behind the clubhouse, a vast sea of green spreads before you, encompassing acres of manicured fairways. The Morgan Lawn, a large grassy swath near the putting green, is a premier ceremony site with panoramic views that include stands of oak, palm and pepper trees. In fact, two tall, slender palms, their trunks nearly touching as they rise to the sky, form a distinctive backdrop to the altar as you exchange vows.

The adjacent, raised Morgan Patio is the scene for congratulatory toasts. Family and friends can mingle over cocktails and hors d'oeuvres, while you and your photographer hop into a golf cart to take pictures out on the golf course. Then, as night falls, tiki torches are lit along with the fire pit, and the twinkle lights wrapped around nearby trees begin to sparkle.

Dinner and dancing follow in the large ballroom, which overlooks the patio on one side and the club's front entry on the other. Elegant, milk-glass chandeliers hang from the vaulted ceiling, and decorative white molding adds a nice contrast to the muted earth tones of the carpet. There are several alcoves off the main room that can be set up for beverage service or dessert tables, creating nice little conversation areas. And, once your party begins to wind down, if you just don't want the evening to end you're welcome to head on over to the Members Bar for an after-hours nightcap.

If you're in the mood for a more pastoral affair, consider holding your ceremony and/or reception outdoors on the Glenbriar Lawn, which is often used as a VIP area during major golf tournaments. Nestled between the guest buildings, this pretty site has borders of colorful flowers and wide-open views of the 18th hole and distant hills.

The resort can also arrange a casual rehearsal dinner or bridal shower at the outdoor pool, adding a touch of fun by serving finger food. And while the bride is spending some quality time at the spa, the groom can enjoy a little down time with his buddies by hosting his own outing. Out-of-town guests who choose to stay overnight in one of the 68 rooms or suites will no doubt appreciate their member-for-a-day privileges, which allow access to the full spa and fitness center (complete with a Pilates studio), turning your celebration into an indulgent getaway.

CEREMONY CAPACITY: The club holds 150 seated guests indoors and 300 seated outdoors.

EVENT/RECEPTION CAPACITY: The site can accommodate 180 seated or 250 standing indoors and 300 seated or 350 standing outdoors.

MEETING CAPACITY: Meeting spaces hold 180 seated guests.

FEES & DEPOSITS: A $2,000 nonrefundable deposit is required to reserve your date. 50% of the estimated event total is due 60 days prior to the event and the balance is due 10 days prior. All-inclusive wedding packages range $85–140/person. Tax, alcohol and a 20% service charge are additional.

AVAILABILITY: Year-round, daily, including holidays.

SERVICES/AMENITIES:

Catering: in-house
Kitchen Facilities: n/a
Tables & Chairs: provided
Linens, Silver, etc.: provided
Restrooms: wheelchair accessible
Dance Floor: provided
Bride's Dressing Area: CBA
Meeting Equipment: full range
Other: spa services, event coordination, golf course, tennis courts

Parking: complimentary guest lot; valet available, extra charge
Accommodations: 68 guest rooms
Telephone: guest phone
Outdoor Night Lighting: yes
Outdoor Cooking Facilities: no
Cleanup: provided
View: garden, courtyard, landscaped grounds, pool area; panorama of fairways, hills and mountains

RESTRICTIONS:

Alcohol: in-house, or BYO with corkage fee
Smoking: outdoors only
Music: amplified OK with restrictions

Wheelchair Access: yes
Insurance: not required

The Abbey on Fifth Avenue

2825 Fifth Avenue, San Diego
619/686-8700

www.abbeyweddings.com
sd@hornblower.com

When people step into the Abbey, they're often so awestruck they just stand there with their mouths open. They can't believe what a stunning building it is, and that they can actually have their wedding or special event here.

This striking embodiment of Spanish Colonial Revival architecture boasts two enormous domed stained-glass skylights that bathe the interior in a pale yellow glow, while 12 luminous stained-glass windows cast their own heavenly light. Standing in the middle of this former church, you feel as if you're in a Renaissance cathedral: Dark, polished redwood molding and woodwork is everywhere—framing doors, railings, walls and in curved balconies. Exquisite fixtures made of hand-blown orange-yellow glass are suspended from 50-foot ceilings. No longer a church, the Abbey is a nondenominational venue open to couples of all faiths.

This century-old landmark has undergone several incarnations, and in 1984 an award-winning renovation transformed it into a popular restaurant christened "The Abbey." The statue of Gabriel that crowns the roof was coated in gleaming gold leaf, but with the exception of a little wood refinishing and the replacement of some light fixtures and stained glass, nothing was done to alter the facility's vintage beauty.

Today, The Abbey is a private special event facility managed by Hornblower Cruises & Events, two-time recipients of the prestigious "Finest Service Award." They invite you to stage your party, wedding or corporate function in this unique setting, where both traditional and themed events feel equally at home.

Wedding ceremonies take place where the pulpit used to be, and no matter where guests are seated—on the ground floor or up on the mezzanine—they can easily see the goings-on. Add a few candelabras and you have the perfect place for a classic black-tie affair or a Renaissance-themed party (one wedding couple and their entourage actually wore tights!).

When it's time for the reception, guests are treated to an elegant meal featuring gourmet cuisine prepared on site and overseen by Christopher Schlerf, the Food & Beverage Director here for 25 years. Wedding and reception packages are available, but if you prefer, Hornblower's professional planners can custom-design your celebration.

With their expert staff and full services, Hornblower will ensure that your event makes the most of this historic and romantic location.

CEREMONY & EVENT/RECEPTION CAPACITY: Indoors, the site holds 300 seated guests or 475 standing for a cocktail reception.

MEETING CAPACITY: Meeting spaces accommodate 300 seated guests.

FEES & DEPOSITS: A nonrefundable deposit is required to reserve your date. The on-site executive chef provides meals starting at $61/person. Four hours of room rental fees are waived with a food minimum: $5,500 for daytime events before 4pm; $7,000 for evening events after 6pm. Additional hours can be arranged at $750/hour.

AVAILABILITY: Year-round, daily, anytime.

SERVICES/AMENITIES:

Catering: in-house
Kitchen Facilities: n/a
Tables & Chairs: Chiavari chairs provided
Linens, Silver, etc.: provided
Restrooms: wheelchair accessible
Dance Floor: portable provided
Bride's & Groom's Dressing Area: yes
Meeting Equipment: CBA

Parking: on street
Accommodations: no guest rooms
Telephone: emergency use only
Outdoor Night Lighting: provided
Outdoor Cooking Facilities: no
Cleanup: provided
View: no
Other: piano (CBA), complimentary event coordination

RESTRICTIONS:

Alcohol: in-house, or BYO with corkage fee
Smoking: not allowed
Music: amplified OK indoors

Wheelchair Access: limited
Insurance: not required

Hornblower Cruises & Events

Yachts

970 North Harbor Drive, San Diego
619/686-8700

www.hornblower.com
sd@hornblower.com

● Rehearsal Dinners	● Corporate Events
● Ceremonies	● Meetings
● Wedding Receptions	● Film Shoots
● Private Parties	Accommodations

One of our acquaintances was married on a yacht, and we can personally attest to the fact that it was a memorable experience for everyone aboard. We enjoyed it all—the glorious day, the light breezes, and the joy that comes with being on the bay. If a wedding on the water sounds like a great idea to you, Hornblower Cruises & Events has a fleet of 32 yachts in five California ports that can accommodate almost any type of celebration you can think of. Each of Hornblower's vessels has its own individual style.

High Spirits, easily the most romantic yacht in the San Diego fleet, is perfect for groups of 80 to 120. Designed by world-renowned yachtsman John Trumpy, this teak-and-mahogany sloop was built in 1929 and features exquisite antique furniture and detailing, including some classic appointments from the Prohibition Era. *High Spirits* was originally constructed as a sister ship to the *USS Sequoia,* President Franklin D. Roosevelt's presidential yacht, and now is one of the finest historic yachts available for entertaining on the West Coast.

Emerald Hornblower is a sleek 85-foot Skipper liner, popular for private weddings and reception charters for groups up to 72. The boat's state-of-the-art convertible sunroof lets guests enjoy San Diego's sunshine and fresh sea air at the push of a button. There's also a spacious main dining salon that boasts giant windows, a bar and a full-service galley. Guests can take in San Diego Harbor's stunning views as they eat, then ascend to the Starlight deck for outdoor dancing on the 460-square-foot parquet floor. For those who simply wish to relax after their meal, the plush and contemporary Admiral's Cabin is available for a little luxury at sea. Any Hornblower yacht will also pick up guests at any waterfront hotel guest dock.

For a more intimate celebration of up to 40, *Renown* is an excellent choice. While the ship was constructed mostly out of mahogany, the interior is done in warm dark cherrywood. The roomy and handsome main salon also includes a solid teak bar and touches of hand-rubbed natural walnut throughout. Both the main salon and dining deck provide panoramic views, complemented by a walkway encircling the entire yacht. Topping off *Renown's* extensive list of amenities are three private staterooms, a bar, dance area, stereo system, and an on-board full-service galley.

Hornblower's traditional table service includes white linens, fine china and glassware, and service by an award-winning, nautically attired crew. Whether you're planning an elaborate formal affair or a more casual one, you can be sure this seasoned staff will customize your event to suite your personal tastes.

CEREMONY, EVENT/RECEPTION & MEETING CAPACITY: Seven yachts are regularly available. They differ in size and capacity, accommodating up to 1,000 guests. Other yachts can be arranged. Ceremonies are performed on deck.

FEES & DEPOSITS: A $1,500–25,000 deposit, depending on yacht size, is due when the reservation is made, with the balance payable 5 days prior to the event. Hornblower offers $89–155/person wedding packages, which include boat rental, food, unlimited champagne, and a ceremony performed by the captain. Hourly rates and à la carte services can also be arranged.

AVAILABILITY: Year-round, daily, anytime.

SERVICES/AMENITIES:

Catering: in-house, no BYO
Kitchen Facilities: n/a
Tables & Chairs: provided
Linens, Silver, etc.: provided
Restrooms: inquire for wheelchair access
Dance Floor: provided
Bride's & Groom's Dressing Area: limited
Meeting Equipment: CBA

Parking: fee lots near dock
Accommodations: no guest rooms
Telephone: ship-to-shore
Outdoor Night Lighting: yes
Outdoor Cooking Facilities: n/a
Cleanup: provided
View: San Diego Bay, city skyline
Other: complimentary event coordination

RESTRICTIONS:

Alcohol: in-house, no BYO
Smoking: outer decks only
Music: amplified OK

Wheelchair Access: limited
Insurance: not required

Karl Strauss Brewery Gardens

Restaurant & Gardens

9675 Scranton Road, San Diego
858/581-7324

www.karlstrauss.com
catering@karlstrauss.com

●	Rehearsal Dinners	●	Corporate Events
●	Ceremonies	●	Meetings
●	Wedding Receptions		Film Shoots
●	Private Parties		Accommodations

Okay, so you've read the word "Brewery" in the name and you're ready to turn the page. Don't do it!—you'll miss one of San Diego's surprise special event locations. This place may have a microbrewery somewhere on site, but we never saw it— we were too busy admiring the five and a half acres of beautiful Oriental gardens.

Who would have thought that in the midst of the ultra-modern San Diego Tech Center, with its gleaming glass highrises, you'd find such a lush oasis? It was quite a shock—albeit a delightful one—to step into this private world, literally hidden behind dense stands of bamboo and tall hedges. A restaurant with a two-tiered deck at both ends sits right at the edge of an emerald-green pond. Clusters of lily pads float on the still surface, while multicolored koi swim below. The entire site is ringed by a profusion of trees, bushes and grasses; an arched wooden bridge, stone lanterns perched on rocks and a cascading waterfall complete the picture.

The restaurant, designed like the one in Munich's famous Chinese Pagoda Beer Garden, is filled with natural light from a wall of windows that wrap around three sides. Natural pine beams span the high peaked ceiling, and wooden planters overflowing with greenery bring the garden inside. While most receptions or parties are held in here, ceremonies usually take place on the largest deck. The bride and groom say their vows at the end of the deck, with the gardens as a backdrop. Both decks—shaded by plenty of umbrellas and an occasional tree growing up through the flooring—are also just as popular for outdoor celebrations. A white canopy protects the lower tier of the main deck, and heaters can be turned on if the temperature drops a bit.

Noisy signs of civilization? You won't find any of them at Karl Strauss' Gardens. Peace and tranquility reign here, so you might as well just sit down, sip something cool, and watch the koi gently ripple the still surface of the pond.

CEREMONY CAPACITY: The outdoor garden patio can accommodate 125 seated guests.

EVENT/RECEPTION CAPACITY: Using both indoor and outdoor spaces, the site holds up to 325 seated or 400 standing; indoors only, 170 seated guests. The private Bonsai Room holds 50 seated or 70 standing.

MEETING CAPACITY: Meeting spaces accommodate 15–325 seated guests.

FEES & DEPOSITS: For weddings, a $1,500 nonrefundable deposit is required to book the site, and the balance is payable 3 days prior to the event. Meals start at $79/person for weddings. In addition to the meal, this pricing includes the wedding cake, colored linens, and disc jockey. Alcohol, tax, setup, security and service charges are additional. For ceremonies, there is a $650 setup fee.

For business functions, a goodwill deposit is required to secure your date. Menus can be customized and start at $25/person for dinners, or $15/person for hors d'oeuvres. Alcohol, tax and service charges are additional. A room rental fee may apply; call for more information.

AVAILABILITY: Year-round, daily, until midnight.

SERVICES/AMENITIES:
Catering: in-house, no BYO
Kitchen Facilities: n/a
Tables & Chairs: provided
Linens, Silver, etc.: provided
Restrooms: wheelchair accessible
Dance Floor: front deck
Bride's & Groom's Dressing Area: CBA
Meeting Equipment: CBA, extra charge

Parking: large lots, self-parking
Accommodations: no guest rooms
Telephone: emergency use only
Outdoor Night Lighting: yes
Outdoor Cooking Facilities: no
Cleanup: provided
View: Japanese gardens, koi ponds & waterfall
Other: event coordination

RESTRICTIONS:
Alcohol: BW provided, no BYO
Smoking: outside only
Music: amplified OK

Wheelchair Access: yes
Insurance: not required
Other: no rice, confetti or birdseed

Overwhelmed? Use the search criteria on www.HereComesTheGuide.com to narrow down your choices.

499

The Prado at Balboa Park

1549 El Prado, San Diego
619/557-9441 X501
www.balboaparkweddings.com
info@pradobalboa.com

Historic Restaurant & Banquet Room

● Rehearsal Dinners	● Corporate Events
● Ceremonies	● Meetings
● Wedding Receptions	● Film Shoots
● Private Parties	Accommodations

What would you build if you wanted to wow the world?

For the organizers of the 1915–16 Panama-California Exposition in Balboa Park, it was a flamboyant group of Spanish Renaissance-style structures, whose elaborate design captured the fancy of cosmopolitan travelers. The centerpiece is the magnificent House of Hospitality, with intricate scrollwork that trims its sand-colored walls, tower and arched windows and doors just like frosting on a wedding cake.

Now a National Historic Landmark, the House of Hospitality was carefully rebuilt in 1997. Hand-stenciled doors, ceilings, and beams in Spanish motif were scrupulously restored or reproduced. In fact, each room had more than 4,000 historical features, and the love and attention that went into preserving and replicating them seems to radiate in every direction. But although the building looks the way it did a century ago, it meets modern building standards and is 100% handicapped accessible.

A new chapter in the House of Hospitality's history was written in 2000, when it became the home of The Prado, a gourmet restaurant from San Diego's best-known and perhaps most decorated family of restaurateurs, the Cohn Restaurant Group. The Cohns have been named Restaurateurs of the Year both city- and statewide.

There's no more picturesque setting for a ceremony than the Casa del Rey Moro Gardens, a reproduction of the grounds of a Moorish king's home in southern Spain. Exchange vows by the wishing well with a lush canyon behind you, a reflecting pool before you, and as many as 300 smiling faces looking on from semicircular terraces around you.

After cocktails in an elegant courtyard centered around "Women of Tehuantepec," a famous limestone sculpture and tiled fountain, larger parties meet in the Grand Ballroom. Skylights set in 27-foot hand-stenciled ceilings warm the space. Custom bronze chandeliers provide night lighting, and optional "pin spotlights" highlight table centerpieces. The band plays your song from the theatrical stage, as you and your new spouse glide across the gleaming hardwood floor for your first dance.

After cocktails on adjoining rooftop terraces, medium-sized parties often dine in the Loggia, a charming second-floor space featuring vaulted ceilings, colorful beams, French doors, and many windows. More intimate gatherings can celebrate on the covered balcony overlooking Casa del Rey Moro Gardens, before settling in the cozy Alhambra room for lunch or dinner.

The award-winning food is stylishly presented with synchronized service: All the guests at a table are served simultaneously, making for a "voila!" moment that not only delights diners, but prevents food from going cold as everyone waits for that last plate to arrive.

As it has for decades, a wedding at The Prado will surely wow everyone in your world.

CEREMONY CAPACITY: The site holds 300 seated outdoors in the Casa del Rey Moro Gardens.

EVENT/RECEPTION CAPACITY: The Grand Ballroom accommodates up to 300 seated or 500 standing (with dance floor); the Loggia Room up to 100 seated or 140 standing; and the Alhambra Room up to 80 seated or 120 standing.

MEETING CAPACITY: The venue accommodates 10–400 seated theater-style, or over 1,000 guests with a facility buyout.

FEES & DEPOSITS: A signed contract and a deposit (based on the space reserved) are required to secure your date. A second nonrefundable deposit in the amount of 50% of the estimated event total will be due when stipulated by the contract. The remaining balance is due 3 business days prior to the event. Wedding packages start at $105 per person and include 1 hour of hosted bar, tray-passed hors d'oeuvres with White Glove Service, luncheon or dinner menu designed by The Prado's award-winning culinary team, wedding cake provided by *Flour Power,* formal champagne toast, professional staff-synchronized service, full-length table linens, porcelain china and gold Chiavari chairs.

A ceremony package is available for $1,250 in conjunction with a reception booked at The Prado. It includes the use of the venue's Casa del Rey Moro Gardens (which seats up to 300 guests), white outdoor chairs, gift and guest book tables, bridal changing room, scheduled rehearsal time and outdoor sound system for the officiant.

AVAILABILITY: Year-round, daily.

SERVICES/AMENITIES:

Catering: in-house
Kitchen Facilities: n/a
Tables & Chairs: provided
Linens, Silver, etc.: provided
Restrooms: wheelchair accessible
Dance Floor: portable provided
Bride's & Groom's Dressing Area: yes
Meeting Equipment: some provided
Other: gold Chiavari chairs and wedding cake provided

Parking: large lot, valet available
Accommodations: no guest rooms
Telephone: pay phone
Outdoor Night Lighting: available
Outdoor Cooking Facilities: no
Cleanup: provided
View: canyon, cityscape, fountain, garden patio, landscaped grounds, park

RESTRICTIONS:

Alcohol: in-house
Smoking: not allowed
Music: amplified OK

Wheelchair Access: yes
Insurance: liability required

Rancho Bernardo Inn

Resort Hotel

17550 Bernardo Oaks Drive, San Diego
858/675-8420

www.ranchobernardoinn.com
rbiweddings@jcresorts.com

- Rehearsal Dinners
- Ceremonies
- Wedding Receptions
- Private Parties
- Corporate Events
- Meetings
- Film Shoots
- Accommodations

Rancho Bernardo Inn has so many spectacular sites for ceremonies, receptions and photo ops that even the most ardent romantics among us could renew their vows yearly and still find unique spots they hadn't seen before. This 200-acre resort melds its California Rancho history with modern amenities to create a four-star retreat without a hint of stuffiness. So whether you want a wedding that's posh and sophisticated or one that's casual and relaxed, you can host it here and feel pampered in the process.

A beautiful place to start is Aragon Lawn, an expansive, fairy-tale garden lushly bordered by white roses and trees. The long center aisle leads to a trellised arbor where you'll exchange vows beneath a canopy of grape leaves. Afterwards, serve cocktails and dinner on the adjacent Aragon Terrace, replete with more signature white roses. The terrace wraps around to reveal another grape arbor that's lovely for a sun-dappled reception—there's also an outdoor fireplace to provide a warm glow in the evening. If you prefer a more formal affair, start with cocktails in the Aragon Foyer where arched glass doors open to the terrace, then follow with dinner and dancing in the stately Aragon Ballroom, which boasts honey-toned walls, a high ceiling and gorgeous pendant chandeliers.

There are several other intimate ceremony sites, including the North and Valencia Lawns, that feature arbors, white roses, or even a dramatic stone backdrop. But if you want sweeping views of the 18-hole golf course, check out The Promenade, a brick courtyard with 180-degree fairway panoramas.

Santiago Courtyard is a must-see, partly because of its graceful olive trees and hacienda feel, but mainly because of its magnificent Italian fountain, a centerpiece that truly says "amore": A pair of stone-carved lovers, gazing adoringly at each other, stand above a stunning mosaic waterfall gently cascading into a sculpted pool. This courtyard has an adjacent ballroom, making it easy to flow right into your reception. However, flexibility is top priority here, so you can use spaces that are next to each other or mix and match options to suit your event—including the inn's completely re-imagined restaurant.

AVANT is Rancho Bernardo's sophisticated step forward in dining. Recently opened to great fanfare, the restaurant's new menu focuses on local, sustainable and fresh ingredients. (In fact, one can often see the chef harvesting bounty from the inn's garden for that night's dishes.) Taking a wine country approach, the offerings—from artisan cocktails to charcuterie, small plates and seasonal specialties—showcase unpretentious food that will please your most discriminating guests. And the cuisine is not the only thing that's changed. The Main Dining Room's clean-lined, contemporary décor includes dark wood floors, soft leather seating, a rich granite bar and a vaulted, beamed ceiling. Along one wall, picture windows frame manicured fairway vistas, and at the far end a shaded patio is a cool setting for al fresco gatherings. For an exceptional rehearsal dinner, reserve one of the chic private dining rooms or AVANT Kitchen's "chef's table."

Frankly, there's so much to love at Rancho Bernardo Inn that we suggest taking a tour. And while you're here, why not stop by their spa—it's never too early for a little pre-wedding indulgence!

CEREMONY CAPACITY: The hotel holds 1,000 seated guests indoors and 750 seated outdoors.

EVENT/RECEPTION & MEETING CAPACITY: The site accommodates 840 guests seated or 1,150 standing indoors and 200 seated or 300 standing outdoors.

FEES & DEPOSITS: 25% of the food and beverage minimum, service charge, location fee, and taxes are required to reserve your date. An additional 50% deposit is due 3 months prior to the event and the balance is due 5 days prior. Location fees range $1,800–3,500 depending on the day and time of the event, guest count and the space rented. Meals range $48–130/person. Tax, alcohol and a 22% service charge are additional.

AVAILABILITY: Year-round.

SERVICES/AMENITIES:

Catering: in-house, or BYO ethnic caterer with approval
Kitchen Facilities: n/a
Tables & Chairs: provided
Linens, Silver, etc.: provided
Restrooms: wheelchair accessible
Dance Floor: portable provided
Bride's Dressing Area: CBA
Meeting Equipment: CBA
Other: spa, in-house florals, AV equipment, event coordination

Parking: large lot, valet available
Accommodations: 287 guest rooms
Telephone: guest phone
Outdoor Night Lighting: CBA
Outdoor Cooking Facilities: BBQ CBA
Cleanup: provided
View: fountain, garden, hills, lake, landscaped grounds, mountains, pool area, waterfall

RESTRICTIONS:

Alcohol: full in-house bar
Smoking: designated areas only
Music: amplified OK

Wheelchair Access: yes
Insurance: not required

Sheraton San Diego Hotel & Marina

Waterfront Hotel

1380 Harbor Island Drive, San Diego
619/692-2761

www.sheraton.com/sandiego
stacey.levasseur@sheraton.com

- Rehearsal Dinners
- Ceremonies
- Wedding Receptions
- Private Parties
- Corporate Events
- Meetings
- Film Shoots
- Accommodations

Commanding an enviable location on the pristine shores of Harbor Island, the Sheraton San Diego Hotel & Marina combines the refreshing ambiance of a seaside refuge with the deluxe amenities of the finest hostelries, including sophisticated dining, a state-of-the-art Spa and Fitness Center and plush accommodations with spacious private balconies. Recreation options also abound (tennis, anyone? bike riding or scuba diving?). Yet the most spectacular feature of this two-towered establishment has got to be its unmatched panoramic views. The West Tower faces the action at the harbor and marina where sleek pleasure craft either bob in their moorings or wend their way out to sea. To the east, twinkling city lights fill the million-dollar vista with the nighttime energy of a dynamic metropolis.

Recently favored with a $35-million renovation, this urban resort also boasts an astonishing 120,000 square feet of award-winning event space, including some of the prettiest ceremony sites we've seen: On the marina side, the Garden Terrace bursts with multihued flowers and bushes. Fragrant white tea roses, lavender, gardenia, jasmine, box hedges and magnolia trees line a latticed arbor walkway, winding to a fountain created solely to soothe the spirits of brides as they prepare to take those momentous steps down the aisle. Beyond an arched, white lattice gate, friends and family assemble, taking their seats on an always-perfect lawn alongside the water. Another site, the Bayview Lawn, is nestled under shade trees near the East Tower and offers southerly views of passing ships.

If you prefer a ceremony at sea, board a private yacht and have the captain officiate your wedding. Participate in the tradition of scattering rose petals to the wind, and watch the waves carry them to the horizon.

During the cocktail hour, numerous patios, terraces, and lounges allow guests to mingle in the glow of the setting sun, perhaps taking in the customary evening regatta or departing ocean liners. Clear glass panels surrounding some patios allow unobstructed views comfortably protected from ocean breezes. Then it's off to one of the Sheraton's half-dozen versatile ballrooms for dinner and dancing. Whether you choose an intimate room for 10 or the 100,000-square-foot tented Bayshore Pavilion for 1,500 of your closest friends, the hotel can accommodate any size reception.

The Bel Aire Ballroom, for example, is a popular choice, with marble walls complemented by understated striped wallpaper and navy carpet, and an immense mirrored chandelier that evokes icicles dangling in a winter castle. Like the Bel Aire, most of the venue's reception spaces boast spectacular floor-to-ceiling views of the water or city skyline. Seated on custom-made blue-striped parlor chairs, your guests will savor their gourmet food served on fine English white porcelain china and drink from posh stemware. Named "Best Caterer" by *San Diego Magazine* 15 years running, the Sheraton's team of culinary all-stars are sure to impress.

In fact, everything is impressive about this world-class resort. Just minutes from all of San Diego's attractions, the Sheraton San Diego Hotel & Marina provides you and your guests with a luxurious San Diego experience, served up with warmth and flair.

CEREMONY CAPACITY: The site holds 1,000 seated guests, indoors or outdoors.

EVENT/RECEPTION CAPACITY: The hotel can accommodate 2,000 seated or 3,000 standing guests indoors, and 1,000 seated or 3,000 standing outdoors.

MEETING CAPACITY: Meeting rooms hold 3,000 seated guests.

FEES & DEPOSITS: A deposit is required to reserve your date. The estimated event total is due 10 days before the event and final payment is due 72 business hours prior. Complete wedding packages start at $50/person. Tax, alcohol and a 24% service charge are additional.

AVAILABILITY: Year-round, daily, anytime.

SERVICES/AMENITIES:

Catering: in-house
Kitchen Facilities: fully equipped kitchen
Tables & Chairs: provided
Linens, Silver, etc.: provided
Restrooms: wheelchair accessible
Dance Floor: provided
Bride's & Groom's Dressing Area: CBA
Meeting Equipment: provided, CBA

Parking: large lot
Accommodations: 1,044 guest rooms
Telephone: pay or house phone
Outdoor Night Lighting: CBA
Outdoor Cooking Facilities: BBQ CBA
Cleanup: provided
View: panorama of bay and ocean; garden
Other: grand piano, spa services, picnic area, AV equipment

RESTRICTIONS:

Alcohol: in-house
Smoking: not allowed
Music: amplified OK

Wheelchair Access: yes
Insurance: liability required

Star of the Sea Event Center

Waterfront Event Center

1360 N. Harbor Drive, San Diego
619/232-7408

www.starofthesea.com
jcepeda@starofthesea.com

● Rehearsal Dinners		● Corporate Events	
● Ceremonies		● Meetings	
● Wedding Receptions		● Film Shoots	
● Private Parties		Accommodations	

For more than four decades, Anthony's Star of the Sea restaurant was San Diego's "go-to" place for celebrating life's special occasions. Located at the north end of the Embarcadero between Anthony's Fish Grotto (owned by the same family) and the Maritime Museum, its combination of unbeatable bay views, fine dining and impeccable service made for a most memorable evening. Now, the beautifully renovated and renamed Star of the Sea Event Center offers all that plus exclusivity: You have the entire facility for just you and your guests. That's great news for brides looking for a chic venue with a unique waterfront setting.

And, by the way, when we say "waterfront" we don't mean *by* the water. We mean *on* the water—literally. Built atop pilings, Star of the Sea juts out into the bay itself, giving you the feeling that you're aboard a combination luxury yacht/supper club.

Behind a private, decorative iron fence, a set of double glass entry doors opens to a foyer, where a sandblasted mural of a fantasy mermaid beckons you into her domain. Straight ahead is a sophisticated, black granite bar adorned with sparkling blown-glass pendant lights and a row of sleek chrome chairs with circular backs resembling the inside of a conch shell and seat cushions evocative of waves. To the left is the Lounge, featuring floor-to-ceiling glass panels—sandblasted along the bottom like undulating dunes—that provide a glimpse of the Embarcadero. But the *pièce de résistance* is the large Dining Room to the right, occupying the lion's share of the center.

Bathed in sunlight flowing in through wraparound picture windows that frame superlative views of the water, boats, Harbor Island and the Point Loma hills in the distance, this main event space is mesmerizing. Although it's hard to take your eyes off the tableau outside, the interior incorporates some visually pleasing features, too, such as a curving cornice running the length of the room, a slightly domed barrel ceiling with pinpoint lights, and thick-cushioned, comfy chairs.

Many couples hold their ceremony in the Dining Room against that gorgeous aquatic backdrop. Then, while the room is being reset for dinner, guests can enjoy cocktails in the Bar and Lounge, or outdoors on the private wooden deck that wraps around two sides of the venue. From here, (or inside the Dining Room for that matter) they'll be treated to a dynamic show: historic ships such as the neighboring Star of India, pirate ships taking tourists out to sea, a private catamaran tacking into the wind, or even a Navy training session with dolphins or seals.

As night falls and the harbor lights twinkle, your guests can dance to your favorite band or DJ. You can even program your own music by syncing your iPod through Star of the Sea's sound system. In fact, each event is completely customized. The center provides a wide array of preferred vendors who will create the celebration you envision.

CEREMONY CAPACITY: The site holds 175 seated guests indoors.

EVENT/RECEPTION CAPACITY: The venue can accommodate 120 seated or 200 standing guests indoors.

MEETING CAPACITY: Meeting spaces hold 80 seated guests.

FEES & DEPOSITS: 50% of the total event cost is required to reserve your date and the balance is due 7 days prior to the event. Rental fees range $750–1,500 depending on the day and time of the event. Meals range $35–50/person. Tax, alcohol and a 20% service charge are additional.

AVAILABILITY: Year-round, daily.

SERVICES/AMENITIES:

Catering: in-house or select from preferred list
Kitchen Facilities: fully equipped
Tables & Chairs: provided
Linens, Silver, etc.: CBA
Restrooms: wheelchair accessible
Dance Floor: CBA
Bride's Dressing Area: no
Meeting Equipment: CBA

Parking: on street; valet, extra charge
Accommodations: no guest rooms
Telephone: emergency use only
Outdoor Night Lighting: yes
Outdoor Cooking Facilities: no
Cleanup: provided
View: panorama of bay and ocean
Other: bar glassware, patio furniture, belly bars, complimentary event coordination

RESTRICTIONS:

Alcohol: in-house
Smoking: outdoors only
Music: amplified OK indoors

Wheelchair Access: yes
Insurance: not required

The professionals in the back of this book are the best in the business. How do we know? Read page 549.

507

The University Club Atop Symphony Towers

Private Club

750 B Street 34th Floor, San Diego
619/702-1987
www.uc-sandiego.com
contactus@uc-sandiego.com

- Rehearsal Dinners
- Ceremonies
- Wedding Receptions
- Private Parties
- Corporate Events
- Meetings
- Film Shoots
- Accommodations

As a famous ad line once said, "Membership has its privileges," so it's quite exciting to find that one of San Diego's most exclusive urban retreats, The University Club Atop Symphony Towers, will extend their VIP treatment to nonmembers when they host a wedding or special event here.

This super-chic, downtown penthouse exudes understated elegance, not to mention jaw-dropping, panoramic views of the entire city. Originally founded in 1909 to promote education, literature and art, the club now counts many of San Diego's elite business and cultural luminaries among its members. But toss out any preconceived images you might have of stuffy rooms and a stodgy atmosphere, because with its recent expansion and renovation, this 34th-floor aerie is *au courant* and stunning.

The elevator whisks you to the white-marble entry where a receptionist greets you. Straight ahead is the expansive main section, where dark ceramic floors and a striking color palette of crisp white and black get a vibrant pop with splashes of lime green on high-backed sofas and modern club chairs. Huge floor-to-ceiling picture windows frame the spectacular vistas that showcase San Diego Bay (including the Embarcadero, harbor and Coronado Bridge), the convention center and surrounding skyline, as well as Tijuana to the south and the hills to the east. A large alcove even provides binoculars on each of the tables so you can get a bird's-eye peek of the Padres in action down at Petco Park.

Speaking of action, to your left is the Media Room, featuring a 103″ flat screen TV and an array of signed baseball bats hanging in Lucite boxes, which have been donated by an owner of the hometown team. Since the University Club likes to highlight its local connections, there are Taylor Guitars displayed on one wall and a John Bishop-designed longboard-cum-table in the hip and casual Apollo Room Lounge. Glittering chrome chandeliers spiral from the ceiling like tiered sculptures and art is everywhere, from classic oils to a changing display of mixed media pieces that you pass en route to the Laureate Ballroom.

This grand space is the hub for your private event. The rich, muted colors of the room make the sensational views of lush Balboa Park through walls of glass even more dramatic. Opulent French doors allow you to divide the ballroom and have your ceremony on one side and your reception on the other. (On Sundays, you can have use of the entire club so you might want to start by exchanging vows in the Boardroom, which looks out onto the eastern edge of the city.)

Live music is welcome—they've had everything from jazz piano to rock to mariachi bands and even the USC marching band. And, of course, your dining experience will be as impeccable as the venue: The chef and culinary team are used to catering to a discerning clientele, and use only the freshest ingredients, putting a contemporary spin on classic favorites.

This place is truly special, but be forewarned: The University Club opens its doors to only 16 nonmember events per year. For those who love going where few have gone before, this is the perfect place—just remember to book your date early!

CEREMONY CAPACITY: The club holds 200 seated guests indoors.

EVENT/RECEPTION & MEETING CAPACITY: The club can accommodate 204 seated or 350 standing guests indoors.

FEES & DEPOSITS: A $1,500 deposit is required to reserve your date. 50% of the estimated event total is due 60 days prior to the event and the balance is due 10 days prior. Food and beverage minimums range $3,500–15,000 depending on the day and time of the event and the guest count. Meals range $45–95/person. Tax and a 22% service charge are additional.

AVAILABILITY: Year-round, daily.

SERVICES/AMENITIES:
Catering: in-house
Kitchen Facilities: n/a
Tables & Chairs: provided
Linens, Silver, etc.: provided
Restrooms: wheelchair accessible
Dance Floor: provided
Bride's Dressing Area: CBA
Meeting Equipment: provided
Other: grand piano, in-house wedding cake and florals, AV equipment, event coordination

Parking: self and valet available
Accommodations: no guest rooms, hotel nearby
Telephone: guest phone
Outdoor Night Lighting: yes
Outdoor Cooking Facilities: no
Cleanup: provided
View: panorama of city, coastline, park and ocean

RESTRICTIONS:
Alcohol: in-house
Smoking: outdoors only
Music: amplified OK indoors

Wheelchair Access: yes
Insurance: not required

Lomas Santa Fe Country Club

Country Club

1505 Lomas Santa Fe Drive, Solana Beach
888/994-5447

www.countryclubreceptions.com
eventdirector@lomassantafecc.com

- Rehearsal Dinners
- Ceremonies
- Wedding Receptions
- Private Parties
- Corporate Events
- Meetings
- Film Shoots
- Accommodations

Can't decide between a reception at a secluded country club or an oceanview location? Have the best of both worlds at the Lomas Santa Fe Country Club in Solana Beach, just north of San Diego. Perched on a hill a few miles from the dazzling blue Pacific, the club's landscaped grounds are an open-air delight, while the indoor spaces capture the cozy appeal of a ranch retreat.

On the day of a wedding, the public areas of the club are given over entirely to your event. Heavy oak doors open to the lobby, where the pine-beamed, vaulted ceiling, comfortable furnishings and soft lighting welcome guests to a casual, homey atmosphere. The lobby's desk, hutch and sideboard can be dressed up with flowers, candles, and framed photos of the couple.

Ceremonies are typically held outdoors to take advantage of the stunning ocean vista and almost year-round gorgeous weather. The verdant, tree-dotted surroundings and watery horizon create a peaceful and scenic environment for tying the knot.

After the ceremony, the wedding party can have photos taken in any number of idyllic locations, such as a tranquil pond or cluster of cypress trees. Meanwhile, guests head up to the ballroom, which overlooks the manicured golf course. Certainly one of the room's best features is its spacious veranda, partly enclosed by windows so that the captivating scenery can be enjoyed throughout the evening and in all seasons.

The ballroom has other charms as well. A warm color scheme plus a fireplace adorned with flowers and candles give the space an intimate ambiance. The room's décor and architectural details, paired with that lovely panorama through the wall of windows, provide enough visual satisfaction that the flower-and-votive centerpieces included in the club's wedding packages are all the table decoration you need. A dance floor placed in the center of the room is visible from every spot—even the veranda—so guests are sure to feel like part of the festivities no matter where they're seated.

Three wedding packages and a tempting selection of hors d'oeuvres and entrées ensure that couples can customize their celebration to their taste and budget. A dignified yet unpretentious venue, Lomas Santa Fe Country Club is a winning combination of picturesque setting and relaxed hospitality.

CEREMONY CAPACITY: The ceremony site holds up to 250 seated guests.

EVENT/RECEPTION CAPACITY: The ballroom accommodates up to 230 seated or 350 standing guests.

MEETING CAPACITY: The club seats 300 guests.

FEES & DEPOSITS: A nonrefundable deposit, which is applied to your food and beverage total, is required to reserve your date. The amount of the deposit varies, depending on how far in advance you book. Payment terms for the balance also vary, and may be arranged on an individual basis. Meals start at $65/person. Tax, alcohol and service charge are additional. Menus and packages can be customized to fit your needs and budget.

AVAILABILITY: Year-round.

SERVICES/AMENITIES:

Catering: in-house
Kitchen Facilities: fully equipped, extra fee
Tables & Chairs: provided
Linens, Silver, etc.: provided
Restrooms: wheelchair accessible
Dance Floor: provided
Bride's Dressing Area: yes
Meeting Equipment: some provided

Parking: large complimentary lot
Accommodations: no guest rooms
Telephone: office phone
Outdoor Night Lighting: CBA
Outdoor Cooking Facilities: BBQ CBA
Cleanup: renter
View: fairways, pond, ocean, grounds
Other: event coordination, florals, spa services

RESTRICTIONS:

Alcohol: in-house, no BYO
Smoking: outside only
Music: amplified

Wheelchair Access: yes
Insurance: not required

Shadowridge Country Club

Golf Course

1980 Gateway Drive, Vista
760/727-7700

www.shadowridgecc.com
contactus@shadowridgecc.com

- Rehearsal Dinners
- Ceremonies
- Wedding Receptions
- Private Parties

- Corporate Events
- Meetings
- Film Shoots

Accommodations

Enveloped by flowering shrubs and bougainvillea, Shadowridge Country Club's hilltop ceremony site provides the sheltered privacy of a secret garden. Tall hedges embrace the intimate spot, where a classic gazebo at the far end overlooks the Vista hills. As perfect as this setting is, you're welcome to add your own unique touches, from lanterns and draping to a rose petal aisle or even crystals. Sculptural boulders, trees and sweeping hillsides around the perimeter serve as ideal backdrops for wedding photos and a post-ceremony champagne toast.

Once vows are exchanged, you and your guests will be shuttled aboard luxury buses to the modern, Mediterranean-style clubhouse with its wide circular drive, white-washed exterior and red-tiled roof. A graceful staircase leads up past feathery palms to your exclusive entrance and a small "welcome" patio overlooking the immaculate golf course.

Double French doors open to the newly renovated reception wing, whose rooms can be used in whatever combination best suits your event. The light-filled Turnberry Room has wraparound picture windows, offering magnificent views of the verdant fairways and distant hills dotted with upscale homes. A raised white ceiling and contemporary cylindrical chandeliers lend an open, airy feel, while seagrass-covered walls add texture to the neutral palette.

You can expand the space (and the view) by opening the retractable doors to the adjacent and identically decorated Ridge Room, providing ample room for a large hardwood dance floor and dropdown screen for home movies. Want to increase your square footage even more? The Gleneagles Room just across the hall can be utilized for a separate cocktail reception. When all three spaces are used together, they give your party a great flow.

The Sanders Social House, otherwise known as the members' private dining room, is now available at certain times for special events. The comfy, chic décor features sleek banquettes, artsy club chairs and a cool teardrop chandelier over the U-shaped, granite bar. Foldaway glass doors open to a huge patio with overhead fans, a fire pit and wide-open vistas of manicured fairways and starlit nights, making this indoor/outdoor venue a sweet choice for late-night dancing and cocktails.

Flexibility is Shadowridge's specialty. No matter which spaces or package you choose, the highly trained staff will work with you every step of the way to make sure your celebration matches your style and budget so that you get the best possible value. The club's accomplished chefs can also help design the right menu for your affair—with popular selections like Almond Crusted Halibut, Char-Grilled Filet Mignon and Chicken Fontina—or plan a buffet with fun options like a Potato Martini Bar.

Thanks to service like this, it's no wonder Shadowridge hosts so many special events, including Sweet 16s, bar/bat mitzvahs and quinceañeras. But with one of the prettiest ceremony sites to grace a golf club, it's easy to see why weddings top the list.

CEREMONY CAPACITY: The facility accommodates 300 seated guests indoors and 250 seated outdoors.

EVENT/RECEPTION CAPACITY: The site holds 300 seated or 350 standing guests indoors and 600 seated or 1,000 standing outdoors.

MEETING CAPACITY: Meeting spaces hold 300 seated guests indoors.

FEES & DEPOSITS: A $1,000 minimum deposit is required to reserve your date. 50% of the estimated event total is due 60 days prior to the event and the balance is due 10 days prior. Rental fees range $100–1,000 depending on the day and time of the event, guest count and the space rented. Meals range $22–100/person. Tax, alcohol and a 20% service charge are additional.

AVAILABILITY: Year-round, daily, 6am–midnight.

SERVICES/AMENITIES:

Catering: in-house
Kitchen Facilities: n/a
Tables & Chairs: provided
Linens, Silver, etc.: provided
Restrooms: wheelchair accessible
Dance Floor: portable provided
Bride's Dressing Area: yes
Meeting Equipment: provided
Other: AV equipment, event coordination

Parking: large lot, valet available
Accommodations: no guest rooms
Telephone: guest phone
Outdoor Night Lighting: CBA
Outdoor Cooking Facilities: BBQ on site
Cleanup: provided
View: garden, lagoon; panorama of landscaped grounds, fairways and mountains

RESTRICTIONS:

Alcohol: in-house
Smoking: designated areas only
Music: amplified OK

Wheelchair Access: yes
Insurance: not required

Greater Palm Springs

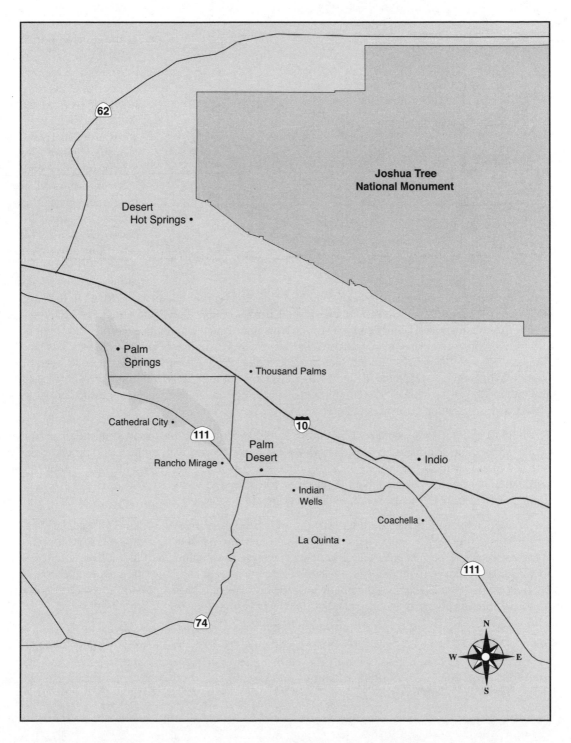

Indian Wells Country Club

Country Club

46-000 Club Drive, Indian Wells
760/834-6018
www.indianwellsclub.com
contactus@indianwells.com

- Rehearsal Dinners
- Ceremonies
- Wedding Receptions
- Private Parties
- Corporate Events
- Meetings
- Film Shoots
- Accommodations

A short drive out of Palm Springs leads to one of the region's most prestigious communities—Indian Wells. The pretty town with the unusual name was originally a Native American village with a hand-built well at its center. From this humble beginning Indian Wells has grown into California's second-wealthiest community, a miraculous transformation that owes a debt to both dates and golf. Among the settlers who arrived in the early 1900s was pioneer Caleb E. Cook, who established a series of successful date ranches. As the town prospered, the unspoiled beauty and year-round sunshine attracted the notice of influential golfers, and in 1955 construction began on Indian Wells Country Club. Among the original owners was Desi Arnaz, who invited celebrity buddies like Arnold Palmer, Bing Crosby and Bob Hope to become members. In 1960 Bob Hope made the Indian Wells Golf Course part of his famous Desert Classic, and Indian Wells was dubbed "The Fun Club." Today, the club still reflects its distinguished heritage, as well as its reputation for first-class entertaining.

You might expect a venue with such a renowned pedigree to be a bit snooty, but the exact opposite is true. The banquet staff at Indian Wells will embrace you with enthusiastic professionalism and treat you to the same exceptional service that has made the Club a favorite of four U.S. presidents. It was the club members themselves who decided to welcome outsiders for special events, expressing a particular fondness for weddings.

No wonder, since ceremonies on the lovely grounds fill observers with romantic nostalgia. Wedding guests gather on the grassy plain of the 18th hole, where the surrounding Santa Rosa foothills convey a sense of permanence and grandeur. Towering date palms and lush foliage encircle a sparkling lake, fed by fountains and a waterfall flowing over rocky outcroppings. As the couple say their vows, cattails lean into the balmy breeze and seasonal flowers provide splashes of color. A more intimate ceremony site is located at the 9th hole alongside another waterfall pond.

Afterwards, everyone adjourns to the striking clubhouse, a contemporary version of Southwest style that incorporates wood, glass and stone in an angular design. The interior artfully combines the rich palette of a desert sunset with the earth tones of dark woods and imported marble. Luxurious carpeting, abstract stone sculptures and tapestries embody both sophistication and a subtle Native American motif.

Cocktail receptions for smaller events are held in the Main Lounge, a split-level area with a crescent-shaped bar and a distinctive wooden ceiling. Relax in the comfy armchairs and watch the ducks cavorting in a pair of ponds, just beyond the floor-to-ceiling windows. Receptions feel right at home in the Main Dining Room, a sunken banquet space with lofty windows overlooking manicured fairways. An imposing mantel of smooth stone frames a fireplace, and ornate chandeliers with matching sconces adorn the cut-stone walls—details that impart both classic formality and convivial warmth.

Your most lavish gala will come alive in the expansive Bob and Delores Hope Ballroom. Crystal prisms dangle from the extravagant lighting elements, and an entire wall of windows lets in the view of that gorgeous 18th hole. An adjoining veranda invites guests outside to enjoy the stunning starscape of a desert night. The staff at Indian Wells knows how to bring out the Ballroom's elegance, and they'll help you merge the best of their delicious menu and the finest vendors to create an event worthy of their sterling reputation.

CEREMONY CAPACITY: Outdoors, the Pointe holds 130 seated, the Cove Course View up to 300 seated, and the 18th Fairway 300 seated. Indoors, the Foyer holds 56 seated, the Ballroom 400, and the Main Dining Room 100 seated guests.

EVENT/RECEPTION CAPACITY: The facility holds 400 seated or 700 standing in the Grand Ballroom, and various rooms seat 30–200 or accommodate 50–400 for a standing reception. Complete outdoor receptions are also possible on the 1st or 18th fairways of the Classic Golf Course.

MEETING CAPACITY: Several rooms hold 22–600 seated guests.

FEES & DEPOSITS: A nonrefundable deposit is required to confirm your date. Half the event total is payable 90 days prior to the event, and the balance is due 10 days prior. The ceremony setup fee ranges $1,000–4,000 depending on space rented. Wedding packages start at $65/person. Packages vary and may include: hors d'oeuvres, champagne toast, meal, open bar and beverages, as well as valet service, linens and room fees. Tax and a 22% service charge are additional. For business functions or other special events, room fees range $300–1,000, depending on the room(s) selected. Food service is provided; call for specific meal rates.

AVAILABILITY: Year-round, daily, 6am–midnight.

SERVICES/AMENITIES:

Catering: in-house
Kitchen Facilities: n/a
Tables & Chairs: provided
Linens, Silver, etc.: provided
Restrooms: wheelchair accessible
Dance Floor: provided
Bride's & Groom's Dressing Area: yes
Meeting Equipment: full range, extra fee
Other: coordination, grand piano

Parking: large lot, valet available
Accommodations: no guest rooms, hotel partnership
Telephone: house phone with credit card
Outdoor Night Lighting: yes
Outdoor Cooking Facilities: BBQs
Cleanup: provided, extra fee
View: fairways, mountains, lake and waterfall

RESTRICTIONS:

Alcohol: in-house, or wine corkage $15/bottle
Smoking: outdoors only
Music: amplified OK indoors, outdoors OK with volume limits

Wheelchair Access: yes
Insurance: not required

Want to know WHAT TO ASK a potential location or vendor? Check out our Questions to Ask starting on page 19.

Miramonte Resort & Spa

Resort & Spa

45-000 Indian Wells Lane, Indian Wells
760/837-1645
www.miramonteresort.com
miramonteweddings@destinationhotels.com

- Rehearsal Dinners
- Ceremonies
- Wedding Receptions
- Private Parties
- Corporate Events
- Meetings
- Film Shoots
- Accommodations

At the Miramonte Resort & Spa, the natural beauty of the desert eloquently merges with the sensual allure of Northern Italy in 11 acres of flowering pathways, tiled fountains and mountain vistas. Styled after a luxurious Tuscan village, this Mediterranean-inspired oasis is reminiscent of classic Italian living, and every thoughtful amenity puts you in the mood for romance.

Just a stroll from the lobby to your room can be a transcendent experience—the splashing of the fountain, a whiff of rosemary, and suddenly you're transported to a sunny piazza in Siena. This flight of fancy is encouraged by the resort's Italianate architecture, a tasteful blend of high ceilings and soaring archways accented with sleek marble, stone and rich wood. Throughout the resort, a distinctly European decorative flair turns ordinary objects like a bowl of fruit into works of art. Guest rooms are discreetly spread out among gently downlit garden lanes, lending a feeling of seclusion and calm. The Miramonte embodies *la dolce vita,* making it a sublime getaway for all of life's celebrations.

Wedding ceremonies are *bellisimo* in any of Miramonte's outdoor sites. The Olive Grove is a meticulously groomed grassy courtyard ringed by mature olive trees. Strawberry-colored bougainvillea sprawls theatrically over balconies that overlook the Grove, and a magnificent fountain plays a trickling melody. In another part of the resort, weddings blossom on the Miramonte Green, a manicured lawn bordered by flowers in a spectrum of vibrant ball-gown hues. For intimate ceremonies, couples share their vows in the Herb Garden, where a small fountain bubbles amidst fragrant sage and lavender.

To keep the rest of the festivities outdoors, venture upstairs from the lobby to the Piazza, a broad, colonnaded patio with a spectacular view of the resort, the Santa Rosa Mountains and the ever-changing desert horizon. Guests savor fine wines and Tuscan-influenced cuisine, while basking in the glow from an outdoor fireplace fashioned of creamy stone. Terracotta floors and rustic fixtures contribute to the Piazza's convivial, Old World ambiance. Next door to the Piazza is the Terrace, a fabulous outdoor option for a cocktail hour, especially in combination with the Miramonte's four ballrooms and their foyers. The rich, earthy palette of desert sunsets and vineyard mornings reflected in the resort's color scheme are especially beautiful in the ballrooms. Spacious and flexible, any of these grand indoor spaces makes a glamorous setting for a sit-down affair.

The Grove Artisan Kitchen, Miramonte's on-site restaurant and patio, provides a gourmet experience for a congenial rehearsal dinner or distinctive brunch—or reserve any of the other event areas for these customary wedding gatherings. Miramonte's catering experts offer many delicious culinary themes, from *Toscano* to Caribbean, and pride themselves on both exquisite taste and service. A member of Destination Hotels & Resorts, this property features gracious accommodations, a state-of-the-art spa, and an uplifting atmosphere—all of which will make it hard for you to leave its serene embrace. You might as well plan on spending at least part of your honeymoon right here!

CEREMONY CAPACITY: The Mediterranean Lawn holds up to 250 seated, the Olive Grove up to 120 seated, the Miramonte Green up to 200 seated, the Piazza holds up to 120 seated, and the Herb Garden holds up to 50 seated. Indoors, the resort can accommodate 350 seated guests.

EVENT/RECEPTION & MEETING CAPACITY: Several venues hold up to 350 seated guests, including the new Mediterranean Ballroom.

FEES & DEPOSITS: Wedding packages are customized for each event. The catering contract along with payment of the site fee is the deposit to confirm your date. The balance is due a minimum of 1 week (7 business days) prior to the event. The site fee, which starts at $20/person, varies depending on the guest count and whether you plan to host the ceremony along with the reception at the resort. Meals start at $65/person. Beverage service, service charge and sales tax are additional. For business functions or other special events, room rental fees are applicable. The resort provides all food and beverage services; contact them for current banquet menus and rates.

AVAILABILITY: Year-round.

SERVICES/AMENITIES:

Catering: in-house, no BYO

Kitchen Facilities: n/a

Tables & Chairs: provided

Linens, Silver, etc.: provided

Restrooms: wheelchair accessible

Dance Floor: provided

Bride's & Groom's Dressing Area: yes

Meeting Equipment: full range, extra fee

Parking: valet and self-parking

Accommodations: 215 guest rooms

Telephone: emergency use only

Outdoor Night Lighting: some, call for details

Outdoor Cooking Facilities: CBA

Cleanup: provided

View: mountains, gardens and fountains

RESTRICTIONS:

Alcohol: in-house; 21 years and older

Smoking: outdoors only

Music: amplified OK

Wheelchair Access: yes

Insurance: not required

Heritage Palms

Golf Club

44291 South Heritage Palms Drive, Indio
760/534-8695

www.heritagepalmsindio.com
garras@heritagepalms.org

● Rehearsal Dinners	● Corporate Events
● Ceremonies	● Meetings
● Wedding Receptions	● Film Shoots
● Private Parties	Accommodations

Many venues say that they offer flexibility, but at Heritage Palms Golf Club they take the concept so seriously they don't even have a standard wedding brochure. That's because everything can be customized here. Why so many options? Very simple: The accommodating staff wants you to feel that it's your club for your unique event.

The entry to the clubhouse is an impressive, three-story-high rotunda Lobby lined with classic columns around the periphery. Light streams in through clerestory windows just below the coved ceiling, as well as through a wall of windows showcasing the golf course. Glass pendant chandeliers and a gleaming grand piano add touches of elegance to what is already a beautiful spot for an indoor ceremony. However, if you'd like to get married outdoors, exchange vows overlooking the verdant greens next to the clubhouse, then come back inside the Lobby for a swanky cocktail hour.

Either way, the adjacent Library, with its curved wall of windows and dramatic chandelier, serves as your very spacious bridal party lounge. Down the hallway, the Pool Room with billiard and card tables is a perfect hangout for the groom and his attendants.

The smartly decorated, modern San Jacinto Room and Terrace is a great choice for an indoor/outdoor reception. Normally a members-only dining room, it's yours to enjoy exclusively during your celebration. The comfortable space features plush seating, soft lighting, a soothing water wall and a low bar that runs the length of the room. Picture windows frame a lovely view of the terrace, fairways and jagged San Jacinto Mountains in the distance.

A short walk from the main clubhouse is the Heritage Room, which is not just a room but a separate building and grounds that offer a completely different setting for your festivities. Say "I do" beneath a pyramid-topped pavilion facing your guests seated on tiers of grass, then proceed inside for cocktails in the cool, marble-floored foyer. The dining room, visible beyond an etched-glass wall, treats everyone to a glorious vista of the fairways and mountains, enhanced here by two shimmering ponds edged with palm trees right outside the door. There's even an attached dance studio that can double as a club/lounge.

For brides who want to pull out all the stops, check out the ballroom. In this large, neutral-toned banquet space you can unlock your creativity: It's easy to transform the look of the room with uplighting, draping, and any décor that strikes your fancy. The full-sized, raised stage (including dressing rooms) is ideal for a band, humorous toasts or producing your own YouTube video sensation. A sound control booth helps your DJ rock the house, and a drop-down HD screen by the dance floor lets you share home movies.

Heritage Palms hosts a wide range of social and business events with equal finesse, including more intimate gatherings like meetings, welcome brunches or rehearsal dinners. Remember, at this golf club you can mix and match the spaces and configure them however you like. After all, it's your wedding, your way.

CEREMONY & EVENT/RECEPTION CAPACITY: The facility holds 250 seated or standing guests indoors and 500 seated or 1,000 standing outdoors.

MEETING CAPACITY: Meeting spaces can seat up to 300 guests.

FEES & DEPOSITS: 20% of the total event cost is required to reserve your date and the balance is due 30 days prior to the event. Rental fees range $800–2,000 depending on the season. Meals range $28–60/person. Tax, alcohol and a 20% service charge are additional.

AVAILABILITY: Year-round, daily, 10am–3pm for lunches; 7am–midnight for meetings; and 3pm–midnight for weddings.

SERVICES/AMENITIES:

Catering: in-house, or choose from preferred list
Kitchen Facilities: fully equipped
Tables & Chairs: provided
Linens, Silver, etc.: provided
Restrooms: wheelchair accessible
Dance Area: provided
Bride's Dressing Area: yes
Meeting Equipment: provided
Other: grand piano, picnic area, AV equipment

Parking: large lot, valet required
Accommodations: no guest rooms
Telephone: house phone
Outdoor Night Lighting: CBA
Outdoor Cooking Facilities: BBQ CBA
Cleanup: provided
View: landscaped grounds; panorama of mountains, fairways, hills and lake

RESTRICTIONS:

Alcohol: full in-house bar; or BYO wine with corkage fee
Smoking: not allowed
Music: amplified OK

Wheelchair Access: yes
Insurance: not required

Desert Falls Country Club

Golf Club

1111 Desert Falls Parkway, Palm Desert

760/340-5646 x224

www.desert-falls.com
contactus@desert-falls.com

- Rehearsal Dinners
- Ceremonies
- Wedding Receptions
- Private Parties
- Corporate Events
- Meetings
- Film Shoots
- Accommodations

Beyond the gate to Desert Falls Country Club, a long drive lined with stately palms hugs the golf course as it leads you up the gentle hill. At the top, you arrive at your destination: the sprawling clubhouse set against a panorama of distant mountains.

To the right of the building, mere steps away, is the Lakeside Ceremony site. Here, in the midst of green fairways, your guests will be seated on a wide swath of lawn landscaped with beautiful trees to await your entrance. As you make your way past a petite rose garden and down the aisle, you'll join your groom beneath the wedding arch and exchange vows with a sparkling lake behind you.

After this picturesque beginning, it's time to celebrate with a glass of champagne. The clubhouse Grand Foyer, a large central space with a grand piano, is just one of several settings for a cocktail hour—and it's also a terrific alternative for an indoor ceremony. The building's distinctive three-tiered roofline creates a "stepped" ceiling with multiple skylights that soars more than 30 feet high, giving the room a sense of drama.

If you prefer cocktails al fresco, serve them on the Lakeview Terrace along the back of the clubhouse. The view from here is glorious and encompasses the lake as well as a pond and rock-strewn brook. At sunset, tiki torches and outdoor heaters are lit so you can enjoy the Terrace in comfort throughout the evening.

Your reception takes place in the Lakeview Room, a two-level dining room featuring white walls with dark wood accents and floor-to-ceiling windows. Seating on the main floor as well as up a few stairs on the "balcony," affords everyone an unobstructed view of the action (think first dance…). Also, consider expanding the festivities into the adjacent Grill Room. Decorated with soft leather banquettes, a long black granite bar and a more sophisticated, clubby ambiance, it's just right for cocktails or after-dinner drinks.

Rehearsal dinners and other more intimate gatherings are held in the Private Dining Room just off the Grand Foyer. Like many of the spaces here, it has a high ceiling with an intricate design of carved wood and lots of natural light streaming in through a wall of windows. It comes with its own private patio, too.

Desert Falls offers enormous flexibility and the staff will work with you to create the best package and value for your specific needs. For example, in addition to the popular and varied catering menu, the chef is not only happy to add ethnic dishes but will even recreate one of your cherished, family recipes. Now that's customizing!

CEREMONY CAPACITY: The site holds 250 seated indoors and 300 seated outdoors.

EVENT/RECEPTION CAPACITY: The facility can accommodate 250 seated or 300 standing indoors.

MEETING CAPACITY: The site holds 250 seated guests.

FEES & DEPOSITS: A nonrefundable deposit is required to confirm your date. 50% of the estimated event total is due 60 days prior to the event, and the balance is due 10 days prior. Ceremony and Clubhouse rental fees range $400–600 depending on the space rented. Wedding packages start at $32/person. Packages vary and may include: hors d'oeuvres, champagne toast, meal, open bar and beverages, as well as valet service, linens and room fees. Tax and a 20% service charge are additional.

AVAILABILITY: Year-round, daily, 6am–midnight.

SERVICES/AMENITIES:

Catering: in-house, or BYO ethnic
caterer with approval
Kitchen Facilities: fully equipped
Tables & Chairs: provided
Linens, Silver, etc.: provided
Restrooms: wheelchair accessible
Dance Floor: portable provided
Bride's Dressing Area: yes
Meeting Equipment: provided

Parking: large lot, valet optional
Accommodations: no guest rooms
Telephone: emergency use only
Outdoor Night Lighting: CBA
Outdoor Cooking Facilities: BBQ CBA
Cleanup: provided
View: fairways, lake, landscaped grounds,
mountains
Other: grand piano, AV equipment,
event coordination

RESTRICTIONS:

Alcohol: in-house
Smoking: outdoors only
Music: amplified OK

Wheelchair Access: yes
Insurance: not required

Desert Willow Golf Resort

Golf Club

38-995 Desert Willow Drive, Palm Desert
760/346-7060 x103

www.desertwillow.com
catering@desertwillow.com

- Rehearsal Dinners
- Ceremonies
- Wedding Receptions
- Private Parties

- Corporate Events
- Meetings
- Film Shoots
- Accommodations

Your Desert Willow experience begins with a mile-long drive through a serene landscape, where the resort's deep green fairways are interspersed with the subtle hues of regional flora: silvery sage, golden-tipped brittlebush, and tiny lavender blooms of the namesake desert willow. A flicker of white is a cottontail rabbit scampering through the fields, and tawny roadrunners take respite beneath the shade of a yucca. Leaving the well-planned town behind, visitors get the sense they're embarking on a desert safari. However, upon spying the award-winning clubhouse in the distance, any expectation of "roughing it" is instantly dispelled and replaced by the blissful anticipation of luxury.

Desert Willow's sleek contemporary clubhouse sports a bold portico, yet is warmed by the generous use of flagstone and wood that harmonize with the earthy surroundings. Honored for its environmentally sensitive design that includes the skillful integration of native plants, Desert Willow has even graced the cover of *Smithsonian* magazine. Environmental awareness extends to aesthetic elements as well; the club is active in Palm Desert's acclaimed Art in Public Places program, and commissioned special sculptural fences around their golf courses to ensure unobstructed views. Inside, the lobby offers a stunning example of their cultural sensibility: Suspended from the high ceiling is artist Dale Chihuly's flamboyant blown-glass sculpture, whose gumdrop colors and whimsical curlicues are a treat for the eyes.

However, the most eye-catching element at Desert Willow is its scenic panorama, captured through an entire side of double-tall glass walls. Celebrations in the Firecliff Ballroom look out across beautiful terraces and landscaped walkways to the mountain-rimmed links dotted with trees and lakes. Large enough for a picturesque reception for 250 guests, the ballroom can easily be divided into separate salons. The nearby Lobby Bar with a stacked-slate fireplace accommodates your cocktail hour, and hi-tech built-ins make audiovisual entertainment a snap. At the farthest end of the ballroom, frosted-glass doors open to the Palm Desert Room, used for Asian tea ceremonies, ketubah signings, a kids' room, or even to showcase the wedding cake.

Wedding ceremonies are simply divine outside on the Palm Desert Terrace, which overlooks the scenic Firecliff Golf Course. The lake and oasis below, along with the sun-drenched Chocolate Mountains as a backdrop, make wedding photos look like picture postcards. Another wonderful setting is the Event Lawn, a sweep of grass that faces the 18th fairway and the shimmery lake.

Where cuisine is concerned, Desert Willow surpasses expectations. Their award-winning chef creates meals that rival those served in the finest restaurants.

As classy and exacting as many exclusive venues, Desert Willow is actually a public facility that welcomes residents and resort visitors alike. Once you take a tour, you'll no doubt have the same thought we had: "I can't believe it's not private!"

CEREMONY CAPACITY: Outdoors, the site accommodates over 400 seated guests; indoors, the ballroom holds up to 300 seated guests.

EVENT/RECEPTION CAPACITY: Indoors, the Firecliff Ballroom accommodates 250 seated or 750 standing guests. Outdoors, the Event Lawn holds over 200 seated or 600 standing guests, and the Terraces accommodate up to 600 seated or 1,300 standing guests.

MEETING CAPACITY: The club holds up to 400 seated guests.

FEES & DEPOSITS: 30% of your event total is required to reserve your date. The balance is due 7 days prior to the event. Rental fees range $150–1,400 depending on the day and time of the event. Meals start at $30/person. Tax, alcohol, and a 22% service charge are additional.

AVAILABILITY: Year-round, daily, 6:30am–1:30am.

SERVICES/AMENITIES:

Catering: in-house
Kitchen Facilities: n/a
Tables & Chairs: provided
Linens, Silver, etc.: provided
Restrooms: wheelchair accessible
Dance Floor: provided
Bride's Dressing Area: yes
Meeting Equipment: full range

Parking: large lot
Accommodations: no guest rooms
Telephone: house phones
Outdoor Night Lighting: yes
Outdoor Cooking Facilities: BBQ CBA
Cleanup: provided
View: mountains, fairways, lake, pond, garden
Other: event coordination, AV equipment, WiFi

RESTRICTIONS:

Alcohol: in-house or BYO with corkage fee
Smoking: outdoors only
Music: amplified OK

Wheelchair Access: yes
Insurance: not required

Want to find more venues and services? Check out our informative website, www.HereComesTheGuide.com.

525

Monterey Country Club

Country Club

41500 Monterey Avenue, Palm Desert
888/995-7732

www.countryclubreceptions.com
events@montereycc.com

- Rehearsal Dinners
- Ceremonies
- Wedding Receptions
- Private Parties
- Corporate Events
- Meetings
- Film Shoots
- Accommodations

With the congenial ambiance of a lively social center and the endearing appeal of historic California architecture, the Monterey Country Club both welcomes and charms its visitors. The seduction begins at the clubhouse entrance, where tidy hedges and multicolored florals adorn a pretty plaza. As you admire the building's Old World façade and traditional red-tile roof, you're soothed by the sound of water cascading down a triple-tiered fountain inlaid with Spanish tiles. Arched front doors of sturdy oak gracefully invite you to enter.

The Monterey Lobby could pass for the tasteful drawing room of an Early California land baron. You'll be particularly impressed by the immense wrought-iron candelabra-style chandelier hanging from the wood-beamed cathedral ceiling. Chairs face a soaring cut-stone fireplace that's ablaze in wintertime, scenting the air with a piquant, woodsy aroma. Rich oriental carpets and plush furnishings infuse a classic elegance here and in all the public spaces. On Saturday evenings the clubhouse is reserved for private functions, allowing you to make this glorious entrance hall an integral part of your event. For example, its mezzanine with a carved wood balustrade is an inspired spot for tossing the wedding bouquet!

An open floor plan has the Lobby flowing into the spacious Main Dining Room. Though Spanish-style décor usually tends to be dark and heavy, the Monterey interiors are awash in soft and creamy hues. Yet it's the view through a series of arched windows that really makes your reception sparkle: Acres of grass spread before you into the distance, where a crystal-blue lake glints in the sunlight; further in the background, the snow-capped San Jacinto Mountains make an enduring statement. The Sunrise Room next door looks out to the same breathtaking vista. Double doors between the two banquet rooms allow you to use them together for a lavish gala, or individually; perhaps stage your entertainment and dancing in the Sunrise, or reserve it for a view-filled ceremony in inclement weather. At the other end of the Main Dining Room, the club's Lounge also has a fireplace, as well as a long granite-topped bar for your cocktail hour; a shaded outdoor patio means guests are free to meander outside to enjoy their champagne in the open air.

It's usually the great outdoors that brings bridal couples to the desert, dreaming of a sun-kissed ceremony that unfolds in the lap of nature. Monterey's two enchanting ceremony sites don't disappoint. On Nine West and One West, sweeps of manicured lawn stretch to the opposite shores of the lake, accented with a spraying fountain. Giant palms, luxuriant foliage and mature trees gather lakeside, and ducks play hide-and-seek among languid willow branches. Songbirds come to drink at the water's edge before taking flight into the clear blue sky. Then, as the rosy hues of sunset begin to bloom on the horizon, you'll feel as if the desert were speaking to you in a timeless whisper.

At the Monterey Country Club the service is courteous and professional, and the event packages are easy on the wallet—which makes the beguiling scenery all the more amazing!

CEREMONY CAPACITY: Indoors, the club holds 170 seated guests, outdoors up to 210 seated guests.

EVENT/RECEPTION & MEETING CAPACITY: The club accommodates up to 210 seated or 250 standing guests.

FEES & DEPOSITS: A nonrefundable deposit, which is applied to your food and beverage total, is required to reserve your date. The amount of the deposit varies, depending on how far in advance you book. Payment terms for the balance also vary, and may be arranged on an individual basis. Meals start at $35/person. Tax, alcohol and service charge are additional. Menus and packages can be customized to fit your needs and budget. Call for details.

AVAILABILITY: Year-round, daily, anytime.

SERVICES/AMENITIES:
Catering: in-house, no BYO
Kitchen Facilities: n/a
Tables & Chairs: provided
Linens, Silver, etc.: provided
Restrooms: wheelchair accessible
Dance Floor: provided
Bride's Dressing Area: yes
Meeting Equipment: CBA

Parking: large lot
Accommodations: no guest rooms
Telephone: office phone
Outdoor Night Lighting: access only
Outdoor Cooking Facilities: BBQ CBA
Cleanup: provided
View: mountains, fountain, fairways

RESTRICTIONS:
Alcohol: in-house or BYO with corkage fee
Smoking: outdoors only
Music: amplified OK indoors with restrictions

Wheelchair Access: limited
Insurance: not required

Palm Valley Country Club

Country Club

39205 Palm Valley Drive, Palm Desert
888/998-3043

www.countryclubreceptions.com
directorofsales@palmvalley-cc.com

- ● Rehearsal Dinners
- ● Ceremonies
- ● Wedding Receptions
- ● Private Parties
- ● Corporate Events
- ● Meetings
- ● Film Shoots
- Accommodations

There's a friendly competition amongst the many fine country clubs in Greater Palm Springs, each one laying claim to the prettiest mountain view, best banquet room, or superior chef. That sense of pride and desire for excellence is good news for anyone planning a wedding or special event in the desert. At Palm Valley Country Club, the good news is even better—not only does the club boast great views, banquet space and food, but it's also one of the best regional values for weddings and hosted events.

To reach the country club, visitors first pass through a private gated community of luxury condos that flank Palm Valley's two picturesque golf courses. A long curving avenue lined with robust palms culminates at a rectangular fountain pool and waterfall, a refreshing introduction to the large clubhouse. Though its design is decidedly contemporary, the building's use of geometric shapes and natural materials like stone, wood, and tinted concrete recalls those fantastic Meso-American temples that so amazed European *conquistadores*.

A bright, inviting interior continues the congenial welcome, courtesy of double-high ceilings, skylights, and generous use of glass accents. The lobby flows right into the Main Dining Room, a favorite space for receptions—and gazing out the wall of windows it's easy to see why! Guests are treated to a panorama of the club's palm-lined fairways, with flowing brooks and waterfalls embraced by a mountainous skyline. Opposite the windows, a long built-in bar affords effortless drink and buffet service for your event. Muted earth tones combined with abstract art convey a modern and convivial aesthetic. A double-sided hearth on one wall is framed by a marble mantel. Next door, the cocktail lounge has an extra wall of view-filled windows opening to a small outdoor patio. At the other end of the Dining Room are two adjoining salons dubbed Palm and Valley, where indoor ceremonies enjoy an up-close view of the waterfalls. These spaces can even be opened up to the Dining Room to hold a super-sized gala.

Whatever the length of your guest list, everyone can be accommodated on the club's outdoor ceremony site—an expanse of manicured lawn spreading out like a sea of green velvet. White lawn chairs are set facing a lush grove, and a white arch between two majestic trees awaits your florist's talents. Above the treetops the jagged silhouette of the San Andreas Mountains is a dynamic counterpoint to the clear blue sky.

Palm Valley offers attractively priced wedding packages, including spa and salon options at their on-site facilities. Customized menus are provided with a smile, and the attentive staff will happily arrange add-ons like chair covers and eye-catching ice sculptures. With scenery, service and savings all at one location, Palm Valley is sure to keep their rivals on their toes!

CEREMONY CAPACITY: Outdoors, the lawn holds 250 seated guests; indoors, the Main Dining Room holds up to 250 seated.

EVENT/RECEPTION & MEETING CAPACITY: The club accommodates 250 seated guests.

FEES & DEPOSITS: A nonrefundable deposit, which is applied to your food and beverage total, is required to reserve your date. The amount of the deposit varies, depending on how far in advance you book. Payment terms for the balance also vary, and may be arranged on an individual basis. Meals start at $16/person. Tax, alcohol and service charge are additional. Menus and packages can be customized to fit your needs and budget. Call for details.

AVAILABILITY: Year-round, daily, 6:30am–midnight.

SERVICES/AMENITIES:

Catering: in-house, no BYO
Kitchen Facilities: n/a
Tables & Chairs: provided
Linens, Silver, etc.: provided
Restrooms: wheelchair accessible
Dance Floor: provided
Bride's Dressing Area: yes
Meeting Equipment: some provided, more CBA
Other: coordination, spa services, grand piano, golf

Parking: large lot, valet optional
Accommodations: no guest rooms, condo rentals available
Telephone: pay and house phones
Outdoor Night Lighting: CBA
Outdoor Cooking Facilities: BBQ
Cleanup: provided
View: fairways, pool, mountains, lake, grounds, fountains

RESTRICTIONS:

Alcohol: in-house, no BYO
Smoking: outdoors only
Music: amplified OK

Wheelchair Access: yes
Insurance: not required

Colony Palms Hotel

Hotel

572 North Indian Canyon Drive, Palm Springs
760/969-1814

www.colonypalmshotel.com
echuryan@colonypalmshotel.com

- Rehearsal Dinners
- Ceremonies
- Wedding Receptions
- Private Parties
- Corporate Events
- Meetings
- Film Shoots
- Accommodations

Just below the surface of the newly revamped and fashionably chic Colony Palms Hotel lies a hint to its colorful past. A slightly risqué Art Deco mural, recently unearthed in a hidden room beneath the restaurant, was once part of the notorious underground speakeasy, casino and brothel established here in 1936 by Detroit mobster and Purple Gang leader Al Wertheimer. His then-named Colonial House, with its unique lure of desert beauty, proximity to Los Angeles and frisky debauchery, was catnip to Hollywood celebs like Bogie, Gable and Lombard.

Today, although the gambling—and brothel—are gone, the allure is definitely back after the new owners' two-year, $17 million renovation spearheaded by Martyn Lawrence-Bullard, designer to such stars as Cher, Elton John, Vidal Sassoon, Kid Rock and Christina Aguilera. Combining a Moroccan-Mediterranean aesthetic with rich exotic textiles, old Hollywood glamour and cutting-edge amenities has resulted in a sophisticated mosaic with just the right balance between trendy and serene.

The property, hailed by *Condé Nast Traveler, In Style, Travel+Leisure, The New York Times, Town & Country* and virtually every style-conscious publication, lends itself beautifully to memorable weddings. For the ultimate in privacy and flexibility, you can buy out the 56-room, two-story hotel with its brand new spa facilities and acclaimed gourmet restaurant, or if you have a smaller group—or budget—you can pick and choose from a variety of lovely spots for your ceremony and celebration.

The main entrance to Colony Palms is through a wrought-iron gate to a tile-floored breezeway with a tropical ceiling fan and large Buddha statue (the first of many Zen-like statues you'll see on the grounds). A curved archway frames the centerpiece pool area straight ahead. A walkway to the right will take your guests to the quiet Garden Area for your ceremony, while you and your bridal party are getting ready in the 900-square-foot Winner's Circle Suite. As your guests await your arrival, they'll enjoy majestic mountain views and garden lawns punctuated by feathery palms, colorful hibiscus and purple-bloomed "sweet memory" shrubs. You can also have your cocktail reception here, or move your party to the fabulous Pool Courtyard.

The huge pool is truly the focal point of the hotel. It's anchored on one end by an enormous sofa lounge (long enough and deep enough for major cuddling or group conversation) and on the other by striped cabanas, which can be used for private tables or even a cozy rehearsal dinner. Off to the side is an intimate fire pit, surrounded by greenery, for quiet talks or to use as a cigar lounge. And behind the pool is the signature Purple Palm Restaurant, a "wink" to the hotel's infamous beginnings. With deep purple walls, Moroccan tiled floors, Mediterranean-colored chairs and tufted banquettes accented with oversized lampshade chandeliers, the restaurant's setting, like its menu, revels in sensory satisfaction. For anything other than small groups, dinner is usually served outside around the pool, and the romantic restaurant becomes a hip lounge and dance club.

As to that secret room with the deco mural…well, someday, that will be the setting for a modern-day speakeasy.

CEREMONY CAPACITY: The site holds 250 seated guests outdoors.

EVENT/RECEPTION CAPACITY: The site can accommodate 80 seated or 150 standing guests indoors, and 250 seated or 400 standing outdoors.

MEETING CAPACITY: The hotel holds 200 seated classroom-style.

FEES & DEPOSITS: 25% of the food and beverage minimum is required to reserve your date and the balance is due on the day of the event. Rental fees range $1,000–3,000 depending on the season, event design and the number of guests. Meals range $65–100/person. Tax, alcohol, a 5% administration fee and a 15% service charge are additional. Pricing for rooms and wedding packages vary significantly based on season.

AVAILABILITY: Year-round, daily, contact for details.

SERVICES/AMENITIES:

Catering: in-house
Kitchen Facilities: n/a
Tables & Chairs: some provided
Linens, Silver, etc.: provided
Restrooms: wheelchair accessible
Dance Floor: CBA
Bride's Dressing Area: yes
Meeting Equipment: CBA
Other: spa services, AV equipment CBA

Parking: valet or self-park
Accommodations: 56 guest rooms
Telephone: guest phone
Outdoor Night Lighting: CBA
Outdoor Cooking Facilities: no
Cleanup: provided
View: panorama of hills, mountains and canyon; garden patio, pool area, fountain, landscaped grounds

RESTRICTIONS:

Alcohol: in-house
Smoking: designated areas only
Music: amplified OK until midnight

Wheelchair Access: yes
Insurance: not required

Historic Cree Estate

Private Estate

Address withheld to ensure privacy. Palm Springs
760/772-8313 Locations Unlimited

www.creeestate.com
sylvia@locationsunlimited.com

- Rehearsal Dinners
- Ceremonies
- Wedding Receptions
- Private Parties
- Corporate Events
- Meetings
- Film Shoots
- Accommodations

Many Palm Springs residents know of pioneer Raymond Cree only because a local school is named after him. In fact, Cree was one of the area's most important developers who recognized early on the exciting potential of the Coachella Valley's wide open spaces and captivating beauty. One of Cree's spectacular contributions is the lavish hacienda he built back in the 1930s as his own private hideaway. Sprawled over two and a half acres of lush landscaping, the Cree Estate captures the simplicity and warmth of old-fashioned Mexican architecture, while artfully incorporating modern amenities in a way that makes them seem as apropos as the Spanish red-tile roof. For your most important celebration, this embodiment of Old World charm can become your personal desert paradise.

A grand Spanish fountain greets guests as they approach the large driveway that circles around a grassy island. Orange and lemon trees filter the sunlight alongside a cluster of lofty palms—an impressive 78 of those graceful emblems of the desert are scattered over the grounds. The hacienda is a genuine all-adobe home, and the front wall has cunning miniature alcoves that showcase antique statuary. A wrought-iron gate leads to a wide lawn just right for a wedding ceremony, and a vine-covered arbor along one side makes a picturesque aisle. Whitewashed adobe walls decked with autumn-hued lantana enclose the grass, and include two old wooden doors, delightfully weathered and worn, that evoke a sense of timelessness and tradition.

Delicate tree branches form a natural archway from the ceremony site to an attractive poolside plaza, adorned with several patches of emerald lawn. A black-bottomed swimming pool, one of two on the estate, features a tiled border reminiscent of an intricately embroidered ribbon. In the first rays of twilight guests savor their glasses of bubbly amidst stone benches and classical statuary, accompanied perhaps by the stirring strains of a Spanish guitar.

Stepping-stones lead to the gently rolling greens of the reception area, highlighted by the dramatic main swimming pool. One of the largest and most beautiful pools in all of Palm Springs, it is elaborately tiled in Catalina blue, and has both a spa and waterfall. It has the look of a tropical lagoon, enhanced by its curving shape, a swim-up bar, and birdcages and lanterns strung from surrounding trees. Twinkle lights on the trees, candles and floral displays afloat in the water, and a lifelike statue resembling Michelangelo's David further heighten the exotic ambiance. Near the pool a built-in dance pavilion inspires guests to tango in the moonlight. If anyone is feeling sporting, a lighted tennis court is also at hand, and some brides add astroturf and a tent in order to hold their reception courtside.

The best way to appreciate all of the Cree Estate's attractions is to book the entire place for a wedding weekend. With six bedrooms, three kitchens and a formal dining room, the Cree can effortlessly take you from rehearsal dinner to post-wedding brunch. The estate's interior décor has an authentic Mission quality, and the living room's rustic wood-beam ceiling, whitewashed brick walls, and hearth all create a mood of intimacy. Romance is in the air in the Bridal Suite, where a skylight invites the newlyweds to "wish upon a star," and the scent of burning logs in the fireplace kindles earthy desires.

At the Cree you and your guests can party in style and then unwind, enveloped by the estate's romantic atmosphere. Why not take your cue from the many Hollywood couples who've stayed here and make the Cree Estate your *own* love nest?

CEREMONY CAPACITY: The Wishing Well Lawn holds up to 200 seated guests.

EVENT/RECEPTION & MEETING CAPACITY: The location accommodates up to 200 guests.

FEES & DEPOSITS: A $2,000 deposit is required to reserve your date. The estimated total balance is due 60 days prior to the event. The rental fee starts at $4,500 for a wedding and reception, and includes one night's stay for up to 16 people. Each additional night is $1,500–2,000, with a 2-night minimum.

AVAILABILITY: Year-round, daily, 8am–11pm.

SERVICES/AMENITIES:

Catering: BYO

Kitchen Facilities: for house guests only

Tables & Chairs: BYO

Linens, Silver, etc.: BYO

Restrooms: not wheelchair accessible

Dance Floor: provided

Bride's & Groom's Dressing Area: provided

Meeting Equipment: BYO

Parking: some on site, shuttle or valet suggested

Accommodations: for up to 16 guests

Telephone: emergency only

Outdoor Night Lighting: CBA

Outdoor Cooking Facilities: BBQs

Cleanup: provided, extra fee

View: San Jacinto Mountains

RESTRICTIONS:

Alcohol: BYO, licensed server

Smoking: outdoors only

Music: amplified OK with volume restrictions

Wheelchair Access: yes

Insurance: not required

Other: no rice or confetti

This is important! Tell venues you're reading HERE COMES THE GUIDE and ask if our information is still current.

533

The O'Donnell House at The Willows Historic Inn

Historic Inn

412 West Tahquitz Canyon Way, Palm Springs
800/525-7634

www.thewillowspalmsprings.com
laurie@eventsdepartment.com

- Rehearsal Dinners
- Ceremonies
- Wedding Receptions
- Private Parties
- Corporate Events
- Meetings
- Film Shoots
- Accommodations

Imagine: You arrive at your private mountainside hideaway, where you have exclusive use of two distinctive venues that radiate Old World charm: The Willows Historic Inn and The O'Donnell House. The estate's wrought-iron gates open, admitting only you and your privileged guests. Under the shade of towering palms, you leisurely make your way up flagstone steps, past trailing magenta bougainvillea and creekside cactus bowers to the inn itself. Stepping into this enchanting villa, you'll want to cozy up by the Great Room's fireplace, surrounded by relics from bygone decades. You begin to sense what it was like back when The Willows hosted movie stars, powerful politicos, world-class intellectuals … and now, you.

The Inn specializes in intimate gatherings, but if you have a larger bash in mind you'll be captivated by The O'Donnell House. Your scenic shuttle ride to this hilltop home ascends past picturesque rocks and greenery to wrought-iron gates bearing the sign "Ojo del Desierto"—Eye of the Desert. Surveying the sweeping valley vistas from on high, you certainly feel that all the desert's delights are yours to command. A spacious cliffside stone terrace seems to float above the world, making receptions here both dramatic and exhilarating. Behind the two-story Spanish Revival hacienda, rock archways lead to green meadows dotted with colorful native blooms, a supremely romantic milieu for wedding ceremonies. Whether sealing your vows with a kiss amid the mountain wilderness or dancing cheek to cheek on the terrace, you'll savor being close to nature and yet so very pampered.

The O'Donnell is available on its own for your event, but why not splurge on a buyout of The Willows' eight stunning guest rooms, too? That way, you and your bridal party will be treated to unparalleled accommodations, and you'll also have the option to hold a rehearsal dinner or small celebration at this elite haven. The Willows' Great Room, with its high, open-beam ceiling, wrought-iron embellishments and grand piano, lends an air of refined luxury to any gathering. French doors lead to the Veranda, a divine spot to sip cocktails. Wedding ceremonies are held in the adjacent Dining Room, which features a striking frescoed ceiling and antique chandeliers. A cut-stone floor and tiled hearth enhance the rustic Mediterranean ambiance. Friends and family are seated facing glass doors left open to a patio, where a waterfall cascading into a garden pool offers a dreamy backdrop for exchanging vows.

The Willows' seductive guest rooms each have their own character: The Art Deco-style Marion Davies Room is tempting, with sumptuous pearl-white bedding, and a satin chaise lounge alongside a clawfoot tub big enough for two. A balcony overlooks the pool, and comfy loveseats are perfect for curling up by the fireplace. Clark Gable and Carole Lombard spent part of their honeymoon in the Library, which boasts rich mahogany furniture, an elaborate coffered ceiling, and French doors that open onto a private garden courtyard. Or cuddle up to the Loft's serene mountain views, and be lulled to sleep by the sound of the waterfall...

Originally built in 1925, The O'Donnell House and The Willows have been lovingly restored to their former magnificence and, judging by the awards and raves they've received, the project was a smashing success. Steeped in vintage glamour, these unique venues pay homage to a storied past and inspire couples to create lasting memories of their own.

CEREMONY CAPACITY: The Willows accommodates 40 seated guests indoors and O'Donnell House seats 125 outdoors.

EVENT/RECEPTION & MEETING CAPACITY: The Willows holds up to 50 seated or standing guests indoors and O'Donnell House holds 140 seated or standing outdoors.

FEES & DEPOSITS: A deposit of 50% of the total is required to reserve your date and the balance is due 30 days prior to the event. The basic rental fee for The O'Donnell House is $8,250–9,000 depending on the expected guest count. Deluxe Event Packages that include additional services and amenities are also available, and provide a greater overall value. Please inquire for details.

AVAILABILITY: September–June, daily, 11am–10pm.

SERVICES/AMENITIES:

Catering: preferred caterer or BYO, extra charge
Kitchen Facilities: no
Tables & Chairs: provided (limited number)
Linens, Silver, etc.: BYO
Restrooms: not wheelchair accessible
Dance Floor: yes
Bride's & Groom's Dressing Area: provided
Meeting Equipment: BYO

Parking: valet and/or shuttle service required
Accommodations: 8 guest rooms in The Willows, 4 guest rooms in The O'Donnell
Telephone: in guest rooms
Outdoor Night Lighting: yes, extra CBA
Outdoor Cooking Facilities: no
Cleanup: through caterer
View: San Jacinto Mountains, waterfall, garden; cityscape from The O'Donnell House

RESTRICTIONS:

Alcohol: in-house or BYO, licensed server
Smoking: no
Music: amplified OK until 10pm

Wheelchair Access: limited
Insurance: liability required
Other: no rice, birdseed or confetti

Smoke Tree Ranch

1850 Smoke Tree Lane, Palm Springs
800/525-7634

www.smoketreeranch.com
laurie@eventsdepartment.com

Ranch Resort

● Rehearsal Dinners	● Corporate Events
● Ceremonies	● Meetings
● Wedding Receptions	Film Shoots
● Private Parties	● Accommodations

Walt Disney loved Smoke Tree Ranch so much it became his home away from home. Since 1925, this exclusive 375-acre gated western-style resort in historic Palm Springs has been a favorite of celebrities, heads of state and anyone lucky enough to discover it—and savvy enough to spend time on its scenic grounds. If you're looking for gold in the desert, you might as well stop right here.

Strangers to the area probably won't find Smoke Tree Ranch, which accounts for the privacy that those who own and rent its handsome ranch-style houses and guest cottages enjoy. This versatile getaway is not only a unique choice for an elegant indoor/outdoor wedding, it's also a great place for a dynamic corporate function, a relaxing retreat, or an exuberant family reunion. And while you're at the ranch you'll have your very own playground, including an Olympic-size pool, world-class tennis courts, a three-hole golf course, bowling green, and miles of trails for birding, hiking, jogging, and horseback riding.

Quail, squirrels, roadrunners and jackrabbits, peering from behind the barrel cactus, towering saguaro, and feathery smoke trees might note your progress along the private drive that leads into this captivating hideaway. You'll park in the spacious lot near the old-style Ranch House, where guest registration, greetings and smaller meetings and gatherings take place. Its gracefully rustic interior is replete with a wood-beamed ceiling, stone floors and fireplaces, hand-carved chairs and suede-soft couches in rich chocolate browns.

Just a short walk away, the Kiva Room and Disney Hall offer poolside entertaining possibilities. The ocean blue-tiled Kiva Room, with its three walls of sliding glass windows and ample bar, is ideal for pre-dinner appetizers and passed hors d'oeuvres. An adjacent living room has a fireplace and a piano for even more socializing. Disney Hall, named after the celebrated animator, features spot lighting in its vaulted ceiling, sand-colored carpets, and an entire wall of windowed sliders that lead to patio and pool. Dine or dance inside, or allow your celebration to flow into the great outdoors.

The sun shines year-round in this desert oasis, so why not let the bright blue sky or the dusky night sky tent your event? There's plenty of room for a band under the loggia or on the patio next to the pool. There's even a children's play area complete with treehouse close at hand. If your wedding dreams are cast in green, you might want to take over the entire three-hole golf course for your ceremony and, after a cocktail break, for a fabulous dinner al fresco. Imagine your guests on the perfect lawn framed by regal trees and a 360-degree surround of soaring mountain ranges.

Visiting family, friends and colleagues who want to make your event the trip of a lifetime should definitely book one of the charming cottages and sally forth to enjoy the fine restaurants, shows, casinos, shopping and parklands that make Palm Springs a five-star destination. It's a California dreamscape like no other: naturally inspiring and wildly beautiful. If you hear coyotes howling or owls hooting at midnight it might just be your happy guests.

CEREMONY & EVENT/RECEPTION CAPACITY: The ranch holds 125 seated or 300 standing guests indoors and 500 seated or 750 standing outdoors.

MEETING CAPACITY: Meeting spaces accommodate 100 seated guests.

FEES & DEPOSITS: 50% of the total event cost is required to reserve your date and the balance is due 30 days prior to the event. Site fees range $0–5,000 depending on the total guest count and rooms secured. Event catering starts at $65/person, including service charge. Tax and alcohol are additional.

AVAILABILITY: November–April, daily, 8am–midnight.

SERVICES/AMENITIES:

Catering: in-house
Kitchen Facilities: n/a
Tables & Chairs: some provided
Linens, Silver, etc.: some provided
Restrooms: wheelchair accessible
Dance Floor: CBA
Bride's Dressing Area: CBA
Meeting Equipment: CBA, extra charge
Other: tennis courts, bowling lawn, horseback riding, croquet lawn, hiking trails, Olympic-size pool

Parking: large lot
Accommodations: 49 guest cottages
Telephone: emergency use only
Outdoor Night Lighting: CBA
Outdoor Cooking Facilities: no
Cleanup: provided
View: panorama of mountains, garden, hills and fairways; pool area, landscaped grounds

RESTRICTIONS:

Alcohol: in-house
Smoking: in designated areas only
Music: amplified OK with restrictions

Wheelchair Access: yes
Insurance: liability required

Spencer's Restaurant
and the Bougainvillea Room

701 West Baristo Road, Palm Springs
760/327-3446

www.spencersrestaurant.com
info@spencersrestaurant.com

Restaurant & Banquet Facility

- Rehearsal Dinners
- Ceremonies
- Wedding Receptions
- Private Parties
- Corporate Events
- Meetings
- Film Shoots
- Accommodations

There are so many good reasons to celebrate your next special event at Spencer's Bougainvillea Room, but we're going to give you just three: The Location (ideal), The Setting (beautifully novel), and The Cuisine (awesome).

Within easy walking distance of fabled Palm Canyon Drive in downtown Palm Springs lies a gateway to an unspoiled wilderness: San Jacinto Mountain, whose waterfalls and treelined canyons are held sacred by the Cahuilla tribe. Ensconced at the base of this imposing natural monument is Spencer's Restaurant, a local hotspot with an award-winning wine list, picturesque grounds and a hip private event space, the Bougainvilla Room. The buildings are a tasteful interpretation of '50s modernism, and picture windows, patios and outdoor event lawns make the most of the scenic desert terrain. Spencer's shares its historic facilities with the venerable Palm Springs Tennis Club, which has been an exclusive gathering place for celebrities since its launch in the late 1940s. The Bougainvillea Room was the site of many a star-studded soirée during Hollywood's Golden Age. (Make sure to tell your guests that they're sipping martinis where Sinatra once partied!)

Spencer's has recently renovated the spacious Bougainvillea Room so that contemporary hipsters, including your own entourage of glitterati, have a fresh place to party. Located on the Tennis Club's second floor, the room is wrapped with two walls of picture windows. One side overlooks the treetops, a turquoise swimming pool, and the town just beyond. Its windows are lined with planters filled with bromeliads, ferns and other tropical foliage. The other wall of double-tall windows frames a spectacular mountainside waterfall that cascades down weathered, rocky outcroppings—a pleasant habitat for sundry birds, desert flowers, and butterflies—before flowing inside to the room's own rock pool. When decked with luminarias, the waterfall becomes the breathtaking centerpiece of your celebration.

If all this proximity to nature has you yearning for more, then step outside to the adjacent grassy bluffs. Two expansive, terraced lawns surrounded by colorful gardens let you drink in a sweeping panorama of Palm Springs: behind you, the dramatic face of the mountain burnished by the rays of the setting sun; before you, the evening lights of the city, just beginning to sparkle. What a magnificent spot for saying "I do"!

If you have a rehearsal dinner, brunch or other intimate gathering in mind, then celebrate on one of the restaurant's pretty outdoor patios. Casually elegant affairs are lovely poolside under the dappled shade of towering palms.

Not convinced yet? Then you haven't tried the food! Spencer's is a four-star dining establishment that has garnered a string of awards and raves from regional press as well as the hard to impress food editors at the *San Francisco Chronicle* and *The New York Times*. Led by award-winning Executive Chef/Author Eric Wadlund, Spencer's offers stylish presentations of American cuisine with a French and Pacific Rim influence. Wadlund's banquet menus are imaginative, yet approachable. As one reviewer gushed, "Spencer's is Palm Springs' 'it' place for any occasion."

CEREMONY CAPACITY: Indoors the ballroom holds 200 seated or 250 standing, outdoors up to 150 seated or 200 standing guests.

EVENT/RECEPTION & MEETING CAPACITY: The lawn accommodates up to 200 seated or 300 standing guests; the Bougainvillea Room up to 200 seated or 250 standing.

FEES & DEPOSITS: A $1,000 deposit is required to reserve your date and the balance is due 14 days prior to the event. Meals start at $79/person. Tax, alcohol and a 22% service charge are additional.

AVAILABILITY: Year-round, daily, anytime.

SERVICES/AMENITIES:

Catering: in-house
Kitchen Facilities: n/a
Tables & Chairs: provided
Linens, Silver, etc.: provided
Restrooms: wheelchair accessible
Dance Floor: provided
Bride's & Groom's Dressing Area: no
Meeting Equipment: provided
Other: event coordination, grand piano, wedding cake

Parking: valet and self-parking
Accommodations: no guest rooms
Telephone: emergency use only
Outdoor Night Lighting: yes
Outdoor Cooking Facilities: no
Cleanup: provided
View: garden, pool, waterfall; panorama of mountains

RESTRICTIONS:

Alcohol: in-house
Smoking: outdoors only
Music: amplified OK

Wheelchair Access: yes
Insurance: not required

Las Casuelas Nuevas

Restaurant

70-050 Highway 111, Rancho Mirage
760/328-8844

www.lascasuelasnuevas.com
lcnuevas@aol.com

● Rehearsal Dinners	● Corporate Events
● Ceremonies	● Meetings
● Wedding Receptions	● Film Shoots
● Private Parties	Accommodations

One of the most popular dining destinations in Greater Palm Springs is Las Casuelas Nuevas, which boasts a long tradition of hearty food and warm hospitality. It's also considered the showcase venue of the Delgado family, whose Coachella Valley restaurants have made significant contributions to the local culinary scene. In 1958, inspired by recipes passed down from his grandmother, Florencio Delgado launched the very first Mexican restaurant in Palm Springs. By popular demand, other eateries followed and in 1973 the opening of Las Casuelas Nuevas paved the way for "restaurant row" in posh Rancho Mirage. Today, Nuevas, as it's sometimes known, is run by 4th-generation Delgado restaurateurs who are enthusiastic about sharing their rich heritage with their patrons.

Las Casuelas' eye-catching design has a tropical Mexican flair that echoes the family's roots in coastal Mazatlan. The butterscotch façade is topped with a red-tiled roof and graced with slender palms. An Old World-style fountain offers a refreshing welcome, and imposing carved wood doors open to a quaint hacienda-inspired layout. Versatile and spacious, Nuevas' private dining rooms and terracotta-tiled patios invite festive gatherings both large and small.

It's hard to resist holding at least part of your celebration on the sprawling bi-level courtyard. Mature ficus trees provide a leafy canopy overhead, and splashing fountains, potted plants and wrought-iron details convey the relaxed vibe of a balmy South-of-the-Border hideaway. As the sun sets, antique lamps and market lights lend a fairy-tale ambiance, enticing some couples to hold an intimate ceremony in a secluded corner patio, accompanied by the soothing strains of flowing water.

Afterwards, guests toast the newlyweds with frosty margaritas on the neighboring patio that surrounds the huge Three Ladies fountain. Convene for dinner and dancing on the lush adjoining *terrazas,* where dining tables are set up family-style. Buffet tables come decorated with colorful serapes and floral arrangements, so little additional embellishment is needed.

Our favorite indoor banquet space is the Cantera Room, named after its four archways fashioned of fine cantera stone. The room is shaped like a rotunda whose high ceiling holds a huge wrought-iron chandelier reminiscent of a renaissance castle. Pale yellow walls display antique plates, and the room is well-suited to classically elegant styling of white linens and candlelight. But if you want to embrace *la vida Mexicana,* why not have the restaurant's strolling Mariachis serenade your guests? After all, as one reviewer put it, "Everything is better when there's a mariachi band." The archways connect to a broad windowed breezeway, so there's plenty of room for dancing.

Your hosts Andres and Tajah Delgado are some of the nicest folks around, and they've put together wedding packages for a range of budgets. In addition to Mexican fare, dishes include carved prime rib, pasta and fresh fish, and they're happy to customize your menu. One more thing—if you want to extend the revels until midnight, that can be arranged, too.

Thinking beyond the reception, Las Casuelas is a wonderful choice for rehearsal dinners, bridal showers and bachelorette parties, and their award-winning Sunday Brunch is perfect for your day-after get-together. After experiencing this enchanting venue firsthand, we wholeheartedly agree with Las Casuelas Nuevas' motto: "Why have a party when you can have a fiesta?"

CEREMONY CAPACITY: The site can accommodate 85 seated guests outdoors.

EVENT/RECEPTION CAPACITY: The site holds 110 seated or 160 standing guests indoors, and 200 seated or 250 standing outdoors.

MEETING CAPACITY: Meeting spaces hold 100 seated guests.

FEES & DEPOSITS: A $200–500 deposit is required to reserve your date and the balance is due at the conclusion of the event. Wedding packages start at $35/person. Tax, alcohol and an 18% service charge are additional.

AVAILABILITY: Year-round, 10am–10pm.

SERVICES/AMENITIES:

Catering: in-house
Kitchen Facilities: n/a
Tables & Chairs: provided, CBA
Linens, Silver, etc.: provided, CBA
Restrooms: wheelchair accessible
Dance Floor: CBA
Bride's Dressing Area: CBA
Meeting Equipment: some provided, CBA
Other: AV equipment, event coordination

Parking: large lot
Accommodations: no guest rooms
Telephone: emergency use only
Outdoor Night Lighting: yes
Outdoor Cooking Facilities: CBA
Cleanup: provided
View: fountain, garden patio, mountains

RESTRICTIONS:

Alcohol: in-house
Smoking: not allowed
Music: amplified OK with restrictions

Wheelchair Access: yes
Insurance: not required

Overwhelmed? Use the search criteria on www.HereComesTheGuide.com to narrow down your choices.

541

Mission Hills Country Club

Golf Club

34-600 Mission Hills Drive, Rancho Mirage
760/324-9400

www.missionhills.com
contactus@missionhills.com

● Rehearsal Dinners	● Corporate Events
● Ceremonies	● Meetings
● Wedding Receptions	● Film Shoots
● Private Parties	● Accommodations

For more than 20 years at Mission Hills Country Club, it's been a tradition for the winner of one of the LPGA's most prestigious championships to jump into the lake surrounding the celebrated 18th green. So far, to the relief of friends and family, no bride or groom has decided to "take the plunge" in quite that way, preferring instead to soak up the sights, sounds and splendor of this desert oasis while staying picture-perfect dry.

With the jagged Santa Rosa Mountains reaching skyward in the background, you drive through the wrought-iron gates and truly feel that you've left the world behind as you arrive at those famous jade-green fairways studded with enormous rustling palms. For your ceremony, you have a choice of two stunning locations—The Lakefront or The Grove.

At the Lakefront, your family and friends will be seated overlooking the renowned 18th green, an island reachable by a footbridge anchored by a bronze statue of Dinah Shore (who first created the women's tournament here in 1974). As your guests take their seats facing the lake, everyone has a perfect line of sight to watch you make your entrance down the stairs from the clubhouse.

The Grove is an equally spectacular setting. Guests are welcomed into a secluded orchard of young citrus trees, whose fragrant blossoms offer a seasonal surprise. Lush green hedges and bright splashes of colorful flowers surround a carpet of manicured lawn where seated guests face an elevated altar. Then you and your fiancé say "I do" against a majestic backdrop of Mount San Jacinto and mature palms gently swaying in the breeze.

Afterwards, celebrate the moment with cocktails and hors d'oeuvres, served either on the spacious clubhouse veranda overlooking the golf course or inside the air-conditioned lounge with floor-to-ceiling, wraparound windows that seem to bring the outside in.

The clubhouse offers an understated elegance with a modern take on mid-century themes. There's a subtle interplay between soft and hard, like the placement of plush carpets and a red velvet settee around a marble fireplace ... and an inventive use of natural materials, like panels of polished picture quartz, backlit and set into the textured stone wall behind the bar. Directly over the bar, dramatic circular teak chandeliers descend from the coffered ceiling while a gleaming player piano sits prominently at the hallway entrance, ready to entertain you. The entire lounge area is large, bright and inviting, with a mixture of traditional tables and chairs in the center and more intimate, curved banquettes around the perimeter.

The adjoining banquet rooms continue the same design themes, and have the flexibility to be opened fully to accommodate 350 people or reconfigured for smaller gatherings. As with the lounge area, the full-length windows allow the tall, exterior columns and vibrant pinks, yellows and greens of the outside landscaping to become part of the room.

And if one day is just not enough to contain your bliss, Mission Hills Country Club offers a full spa on the property for pre-wedding pampering, plus a separate compound of four villas ranging in size from 1,700 to 3,200 square feet. With a combined total of 13 bedrooms to house you and your out-of-town guests, this very private, gated area includes a party-sized barbecue grill, putting green, and hot tub and pool, where everyone will most definitely enjoy each other and the relaxing ambiance.

CEREMONY CAPACITY: The site can accommodate 200 seated guest indoors or 350 seated outdoors.

EVENT/RECEPTION CAPACITY: The site holds 300 seated or 500 standing indoors

MEETING CAPACITY: The site accommodates 200 seated guests.

FEES & DEPOSITS: A nonrefundable deposit is required to confirm your date. Half the event total is payable 90 days prior to the event, and the balance is due 7 days prior. Ceremony and Clubhouse rental fees range $500–2,000 depending on the space rented. Wedding packages start at $50/person. Packages vary and may include: hors d'oeuvres, champagne toast, meal, open bar and beverages, as well as valet service, linens and room fees. Tax and a 22% service charge are additional. For business functions and other special events, room fees range $200–1,000 depending on the room(s) selected. Food service is provided; call or email for specific meal rates.

AVAILABILITY: Year-round, daily.

SERVICES/AMENITIES:

Catering: in-house
Kitchen Facilities: n/a
Tables & Chairs: provided
Linens, Silver, etc.: provided
Restrooms: wheelchair accessible
Dance Floor: provided
Bride's & Groom's Dressing Area: yes
Meeting Equipment: some provided
Other: grand piano, spa services, AV equipment, golf, tennis

Parking: large lot, valet provided
Accommodations: 4 villas
Telephone: house phone
Outdoor Night Lighting: yes
Outdoor Cooking Facilities: BBQ on site
Cleanup: provided
View: panorama of mountains and fairways, lake

RESTRICTIONS:

Alcohol: in-house, or wine corkage $15/bottle
Smoking: outdoors only
Music: amplified OK with restrictions

Wheelchair Access: yes
Insurance: not required

The Westin Mission Hills Golf Resort and Spa

Resort Hotel & Spa

71-333 Dinah Shore Drive, Rancho Mirage
760/770-8252

westinmissionhills.com
wmh.weddings@westin.com

- Rehearsal Dinners
- Ceremonies
- Wedding Receptions
- Private Parties
- Corporate Events
- Meetings
- Film Shoots
- Accommodations

The Westin Mission Hills is no ordinary resort, but an exclusive Mediterranean-inspired retreat that evokes the romance and natural elegance of the desert. Highlighted with cobalt blue domes and tile insets, the resort's graceful pale-blush façade stands out against a backdrop of silvery hillsides. Arched breezeways and curved walls throughout please the eye, while 360 acres of waterways and lush landscaping harmonize with the picturesque surroundings.

Even a brief visit here entices you to surrender to the desert's rhythm: Swim in cool pools resembling tropical lagoons. Sip a glass of frosty champagne after your afternoon massage, and admire the snow-topped mountain peaks bathed in the rosy glow of sunset. At night, celebrate in exquisite ballrooms and impeccably designed outdoor locations beneath a star-studded sky. Under the accomplished direction of Westin's event professionals, your special event will be customized for your budget, taste and unique style, from bridal shower to day-after brunch.

Many couples stage a "welcome reception" for their guests in the Oasis Den, a fun game lounge and social media hub. With a pool table, shuffleboard, full arcade, and its own bar, the Den's interactive atmosphere is a perfect place for everyone to get to know each other before the festivities begin.

The resort's most popular ceremony site is quintessential Palm Springs: a generous swath of manicured lawn sheltered by a towering palm canopy at one end and sweet-scented citrus trees at the other. Vows are exchanged in front of a modern fountain, whose water cascades into a trio of sparkling aqua pools. Just beyond, a sweeping arcade leads to a dramatic rock waterfall fringed with tropical foliage—couples come from miles around just to be photographed at this gorgeous spot.

Near the waterfall, the bi-level Masters Plaza is large enough to accommodate all phases of your event outdoors. Exchange vows under a grand pergola facing the adjacent golf greens, and then dine amidst rows of stately palm trees.

Each of the resort's two luxurious ballrooms comes with a stunning foyer and private view-filled patio. The lavish Celebrity Ballroom features opulent beaded chandeliers that glitter overhead, lending a contemporary glamour to any celebration. True to its name, this magnificent space has hosted celebrity-studded galas for up to 1,200 guests to rave reviews. The cuisine at your reception will also receive raves. Event menus are overseen by a James Beard Foundation-honored chef who'll personalize your culinary presentation to your specific vision.

Friends and family will be delighted that you've chosen Westin Mission Hills for your wedding weekend—there's so much to do! Two world-class golf courses, seven tennis courts and three swimming pools provide plenty of recreation options. Then relax and renew at the tranquil spa, which offers an extensive treatment menu as well as a full-service hair and nail salon. Dining choices range from a poolside bar to the resort's signature restaurant, Pinzimini. Boasting sophisticated modern Italian fare, Pinzimini can also host rehearsal dinners and parties in their private atrium dining room or outdoor fire pit patio. At the end of the day, a dream-filled sleep is virtually guaranteed in Westin's ultra-plush "Heavenly Bed."

And "heavenly" is how you'll describe your total experience at the enchanting Westin Mission Hills Resort—your oasis in the desert.

CEREMONY CAPACITY: The site holds 1,000 seated guests indoors and 500 seated outdoors.

EVENT/RECEPTION CAPACITY: The resort can accommodate 1,100 seated or 1,500 standing guests indoors, and 1,500 seated or 2,000 standing outdoors.

MEETING CAPACITY: Meeting spaces hold 1,800 seated guests.

FEES & DEPOSITS: 25% of the total estimated event cost is required at contract signing to reserve your date. The balance is due 14 business days prior to the event. Rental fees range $500–2,000 depending on the season. Meals range $83–103/person. Tax, alcohol and a 22% service charge are additional.

AVAILABILITY: Year-round, daily, anytime.

SERVICES/AMENITIES:

Catering: in-house
Kitchen Facilities: n/a
Tables & Chairs: provided
Linens, Silver, etc.: provided
Restrooms: wheelchair accessible
Dance Floor: provided
Bride's & Groom's Dressing Area: yes
Meeting Equipment: on-site AV company
Other: spa services, event coordination, group golf packages

Parking: valet and self-parking available
Accommodations: 512 guest rooms
Telephone: house or guest phones
Outdoor Night Lighting: provided
Outdoor Cooking Facilities: BBQ
Cleanup: provided
View: fountain, garden patio, fairways, landscaped grounds, waterfall; panorama of hills, canyon and mountains

RESTRICTIONS:

Alcohol: in-house
Smoking: designated areas only
Music: amplified OK

Wheelchair Access: yes
Insurance: liability required

Part Two: Event Services

All our Event Services have been

1.
We only represent the best professionals in the biz.

The professionals featured in our Service Directory aren't plucked from the *Yellow Pages* or a random Google search. They're a carefully selected group of vendors who we'd recommend to our friends and business associates without hesitation.

2.
Because we're picky, you don't have to worry about who to hire for your event.

We've thoroughly checked the professional track record of our event pros so you can be as confident about their abilities as we are. The companies we highlight have passed our reference check with flying colors, and we're honored to represent each of them. They've all been *Certified By The Guide*. To see all of our prescreened vendors, go to HereComesTheGuide.com.

3.
Getting into Here Comes The Guide is tough.

The service providers we represent are topnotch. We put each one through a rigorous reference check, which involves interviewing up to 30 other event professionals and brides. We contact every single reference and ask about the professionalism, technical competency and service orientation of the advertiser in question.

When you invest 7–10 hours talking to that many brides and professionals, you get a crystal clear picture of who's doing a superb job and who isn't. Those candidates who received consistent, rave reviews made it into *The Guide*. Those who didn't were (nicely) turned down.

Working With Event Professionals

Hiring a Caterer: Get References and Look for Professionalism

If you're selecting your own caterer, get references from friends and acquaintances or, better yet, contact any of the the caterers featured in *Here Comes The Guide*. For a full list, see HereComesTheGuide.com. We've thoroughly screened these companies and can assure you that they're in the top 5% of the industry in terms of quality and service. We keep all of their references on file, so you can contact us and ask questions about them.

Every caterer is different. Some offer only pre-set menus while others will help you create your own. Menus and prices vary enormously, so try to have a good idea of what you want and what you can spend before interviewing prospective caterers. After you've talked to several caterers and have decided which ones to seriously consider, request references from each one and call them. Ask not only about the quality of the food, but about the ease of working with a given caterer. You'll want to know if the caterer is professional—fully prepared and equipped, punctual and organized. You may also want to know if the caterer is licensed, prepares food in a kitchen approved by the Department of Health, or carries workmen's compensation and liability insurance. Although this level of inquiry may seem unnecessary, responses to these questions will give you a more complete picture of how a caterer runs his or her business, and will help you determine which one is best suited for your event.

Facility Requirements for Caterers

Facilities often have specific requirements regarding caterers—they may have to be licensed and bonded, out by 11pm or fastidiously clean. Before you hire a caterer, make sure that he or she is compatible with your site. In fact, even if the facility does not require it, it's a good idea to have your caterer visit the place in advance to become familiar with any special circumstances or problems that might come up. You'll notice throughout *Here Comes The Guide* the words "in-house" or "select from list" after the word *Catering*. Sites that have an exclusive caterer or only permit you to select from a preferred list do so because each wants to eliminate most of the risks involved in having a caterer on the premises who is not accustomed to working in that environment. Exclusive or preferred caterers have achieved their exalted status because they either provide consistently good services or they won the catering contract when it went out to bid. Whether you're working with one of your facility's choices or your own, make sure that your contract includes everything you have agreed on before you sign it.

Working with an Event Planner or Wedding Coordinator

Opting to hire a professional planner may be a wise choice. A good consultant will ask you all the right questions, determine exactly what you need, and take care of as much or as little of your affair as you want. If you'd like to feel like a guest at your own event, have the consultant manage everything, including orchestrating the day of the event. If you only want some advice and structure, hire a planner on a meeting-by-meeting basis.

Most of the principles used in selecting a caterer apply to hiring an event coordinator. Try to get suggestions from friends or facilities, follow up on references the coordinators give you, compare service fees and make sure you and the coordinator are compatible. The range of professionalism and experience varies greatly, so it really is to your advantage to investigate each coordinator's track record. You can save a lot of time by starting with the coordinators featured in the *Here Comes The Guide* book or on HereComesTheGuide.com.

Again, once you've found someone who can accommodate you, get everything in writing so that there won't be any misunderstandings down the road. Although engaging a professional to "manage" your event can be a godsend, it can also be problematic if you turn the entire decision-making process over to them. Don't forget that it's your party, and no one else should decide what's right for you.

For a list of questions to ask potential wedding venues and vendors, go to page 19 in this book. You can also find them on HereComesTheGuide.com.

Event Services by Category

Caterers

Contemporary Catering & Event Production 554
New York Food Company 556

Coordinators

Bob Gail Special Events 558

Disc Jockeys

Mobile Disc Music 560

Entertainment

Fifth Avenue Orchestras & Entertainment 562

Party Rentals and Linens

A1 Party... 566
Premiere Party Rents 564

Photographers

B&G Photography 568
Epic Imagery... 570

Contemporary Catering & Event Production

Classically trained chefs, wildly creative cuisine, a commitment to service, and charisma—that's how folks characterize Contemporary Catering. From gala fundraiser dinners for over 1,000 to an intimate proposal dinner for two on a sunset beach (romance-inducing dishes like raw oysters, truffles, chocolate and champagne were on the menu), they know just how to individualize every event to suit the client's expectations. Contemporary Catering's team of professionals are experts in buying, preparing and serving the freshest ingredients. They are specialists in food, from the farm to the table and everything in between.

Since he came onto the scene, owner Nathaniel Neubauer has become a major contender in the Los Angeles catering industry. From overseeing production and operations management to designing a nine-course tasting menu with five-star service, Nathaniel's dedication to his clients and his company is unparalleled. Yet he still manages to be a down-to-earth, personable guy. "We loved just hanging out with him," said one groom. "Seeing my dad or grandma chatting away with Nathaniel—and him even making time to listen to their concerns—was a true bonus."

Neubauer and his team know how to deliver the best while respecting their clients' budgets. The variety and volume of business they do make it possible to get incredible prices and treatment from their many suppliers, which ultimately benefits the client's pocketbook. "They bring exciting and fresh ideas to their clients," reports an associate. "And they also have a willingness and ability to provide several visions for a party—Nathaniel and his staff are as smooth with buffet as they are with sit-down." Another vendor adds, "Nathaniel's very helpful and offers expert information in spite of the fact that we are competitors. He really knows his stuff."

This knowledge, plus a reputation for excellent food and outstanding presentation, has contributed to the company's popularity with a wide range of clients. They do everything from record release parties to corporate luncheons, and from a $500/person cocktail reception to a $15/person barbecue in the park. A typical weekend of events for Contemporary Catering proceeds in an atypical fashion: On Saturday they might be serving a high-end seafood extravaganza with dishes like Lobster Grilled with Saffron Butter; a Caviar Bar; oysters on a half-shell; crab legs and scallop cakes. Sunday might be a multicultural affair with Latin and Asian buffets consisting of fried plantains, coconut rice and a sumptuous beef, garlic and ancho chili combination known as Ropa Vieja, as well as dishes like Ahi Tuna Tartar Tacos topped with a Napa Cabbage Slaw; Smoked Duck Quesadillas topped with Avocado Crème Fraîche and Cilantro Jalapeño Oil; and Grilled Garlicky Laughing Bird Shrimp in a Tasting Spoon with Pink Grapefruit and Yellow Pepper Purée.

At Contemporary Catering they won't settle for less than the best. They get the job done, and they know how to get creative when dollars are short. Take the word of a client who says, "They didn't make me feel 'less-than,' just because my budget was limited," or the bride who confesses, "I was not an easy client. I had numerous questions and made lots of last-minute changes, but Contemporary Catering accommodated me. I didn't have to worry about a thing. They are simply superb."

310/558-8190
nathaniel@contemporarycatering.com
www.contemporarycatering.com

New York Food Company

From seasoned foodies to culinary newbies, New York Food Company's clients are crazy about them. This amazing group of food professionals is known for delivering mouth-watering menus and incredible service, and each person on their expert staff—which includes talented chefs, special events designers, venue managers and customer service personnel—plays a starring role in the way this company operates.

But the real star of the show is you. "It's not about us; it's about providing the quality and style that our clients require," say the founders. And they've succeeded at providing exactly what their clients want for over three decades. Since their humble beginnings as a storefront deli in 1979, their ability to perfectly match up a menu with a client's tastes and to execute that menu superlatively has made them one of the most sought-after caterers around.

The NYFC experience revolves, of course, around the food. It's locally sourced, nothing is pre-made or frozen, and every menu is customized to your desires. From food stations featuring Kobe beef sliders, salmon blini and pulled pork biscuits to colossal shrimp kabobs or petite potato pancakes topped with homemade applesauce and crème fraîche, the dishes are delectable. NYFC's creativity shines in palate-pleasing mouthfuls like balsamic marinated lamb lollipops served with green apple mint chutney, tiramisu votives, and cheesecake and chocolate macaroons served croquembouche-style. Or how about gold-dusted raw oysters with caviar pearls? Their range is international. If you request Indian food, they'll ask, "Northern or Southern? Lots of heat or just a little? How does your mom make it?" There's virtually nothing beyond your reach when you work with NYFC. They want to replicate your best food memories and make them even better.

These are constantly inventive people with a food passion so profound that they not only follow trends, they lead them. New clients who want to know how good they are can sample some of their fabulous fare at one of their mini-events, which are designed to showcase not only the scrumptiousness of the food, but how perfectly it's set up and served.

"The NYFC staff always anticipates," reports a delighted customer. "It's really great when things are taken care of without you having to ask. I loved the overall beauty of the service—the tables, the chairs, the buffet line, the traveling waiters plus the excellent food selections."

"NYFC not only paid attention to our needs and requests, they accommodated our budget too," declares another.

"What a terrific team," raves yet one more. "I'm so happy NYFC was a part of my event. I was truly a guest at my own party!"

310/643-6151
jim.wharton@newyorkfood.com
www.CelebrationsbyNYFC.com

Bob Gail Special Events

It's always a celebration at Bob Gail Special Events. This popular event design company is also one of the largest talent and booking agencies in the nation. Their extraordinarily experienced and creative staff can arrange and produce all styles of weddings from simple and elegant to over-the-top extravagant—not to mention just about every other type of event you can imagine, from a Rose Bowl pep rally for 20,000 to an exquisitely nuanced evening for two, staged on a bed of roses beneath a flowing canopy.

Corporate event, fundraising gala, formal ball, entertainment industry extravaganza, bar or bat mitzvah, proposal dinner—whatever the occasion, they have the knowledge, the resources and skills to execute it with proficiency and style. "Everything they do is simply amazing," raves a colleague. "Their beautiful events always come off without a hitch."

It really doesn't matter what you're planning; the Bob Gail Events team is going to make it phenomenal. They've decorated TV show sets, styled commercials, produced mini-musicals and added the polish and imagination that has made literally thousands of parties and special events shine. "We are a full-production company," says Bob Levine, founder—along with wife Gail Levine—of this A-list establishment. "Our services include award-winning designers, one of the busiest event flower sources in L.A., and the largest theme prop inventory in California." Event planning, design, coordination, décor, lighting, lounge furniture and fabric draping are among their many services. In addition, they're renowned experts in the field of music and entertainment and they bring all of this talent and experience to every event, large or small.

According to Bob, one key to their success is their ability to handle the majority of the services they provide in-house. The company's 50,000 square feet of space allows them to conveniently keep things under one roof. "We are dedicated to versatility and customization," he explains. "Our clients are demanding, and we love that about them. They push us. As artists we always want to evolve."

It's that philosophy that leads many to insist that Bob Gail Special Events is the best in the business. "They're family run and they're a great team," declares a wedding professional who has worked with them for years. "They also have great taste. They take care of their clients at a personal and professional level that's hard to beat." "They offered so many wonderful services that we ended up going with them for everything," recollects a delighted bride. "They were a one-stop shop," adds another. "They made all my dreams come true."

310/202-5200
esales@bobgail.com
www.bobgail.com

bob gail

SPECIAL EVENTS

FULL-SERVICE WEDDING PLANNING, DESIGN AND PRODUCTION
MUSIC, FLORALS, DÉCOR, LIGHTING, RENTALS, AND PROPS

LOS ANGELES 310.202.5200   LAS VEGAS 702.380.8140   WWW.BOBGAIL.COM

Mobile Disc Music

He's DJ'd some very high-profile celebrations and it's no wonder: Damon Tedesco has the reputation, the credentials and the talent to take any event and turn up the quality. A professional recording engineer and the son of a studio musician, he grew up in the music business, tagging along to recording sessions since age ten. In high school he was a guitarist and saxophonist, and contemplated a career as an instrumentalist until he was distracted by music technology.

He went on to get a degree in Recording Arts from Loyola Marymount University, where he also taught audio editing for a while. "My first job out of college was sound engineer at Warner Brothers Studios," he recalls. In that environment the talents he'd developed deejaying in high school and college were not easy to keep under wraps. "They started hiring me for corporate film and TV wrap parties," remembers Damon. Naturally, word spread. "Whether it be a wedding, or corporate or private party, our first call is to Damon," says a production company executive who greatly admires his work. "Through the years he has always shown nothing but professionalism in every aspect of the job."

Today, in addition to wrap parties, Damon deejays weddings, reunions, corporate events, fundraising galas and more. He still works on film scores with composers like Maria Newman and Don Davis—recording and mixing music that builds emotional context, frames key events, heightens drama, and orchestrates the ebb and flow of energy on the Big Screen—but he really loves the feeling of doing all of this in real time. "I enjoy mixing and recording concerts and live performances," admits Damon, "and special events fall into that category, too. I get excited about the interaction between the music and the gear."

All of his equipment is state-of-the-art, and he has a museum-quality music library. Clients have access to the entire collection, which is divided up by era and alphabetized within those divisions for easy reference. "I've collected music since I was a kid," reports Damon. "I still have every CD and piece of vinyl I ever bought." In addition he's always searching for new songs and new versions of old standards, and he welcomes a challenge from clients. He's not a ham; he's an artist and that's what you'll find this professional focusing on: artistry, musicality, subtle shifts in emotion, elegant transitions, and flow. He is so NOT the guy in the giant foam cowboy hat.

"Mobile Disc Music stands out from other companies because Damon is not a 'cheesy' DJ," reports an event coordinator. "He knows how to put on a classy party. He's amazing at getting even truly shy people up and dancing without making them feel pressured. He can read a crowd well and is constantly adapting to the mood of the event."

"Music transports people; it carries the energy," declares Damon, whose low-key yet high-energy style has a large fan base. "Brides and grooms have enough on their minds. It's the music that helps them relax and enjoy the party."

Damon is also a professional recording engineer for film and television and has worked with such composers as Danny Elfman (*Spiderman*), Tom Newman (*American Beauty*), Don Davis (*The Matrix*), and Randy Newman (*Seabiscuit*) to name a few.

310/670-6155
damon@mobilediscmusic.com
www.mobilediscmusic.com

Fifth Avenue Orchestras & Entertainment

Elegant, tasteful, exquisite. . . AND the greatest party ever—those are the wedding wishes that Fifth Avenue Orchestras & Entertainment fulfills again and again.

"Our daughter's wedding took place in April, and a month later we're still getting calls including wonderful praise for the orchestra," exclaims an exhilarated pair of clients. "They set up early, stayed late and sounded great. The dance floor was packed all evening."

Headed by award-winning musician George Banfalvi and recommended by many of Southern California's most prestigious venues, Fifth Avenue Orchestras & Entertainment offers an elite roster of cutting-edge musicians who play in what *Los Angeles Magazine* has called "Southern California's premier party bands."

"Having come from the recording industry, our musicians and singers are driven to continually update and expand their repertoire," says Banfalvi. "Music is the single most important element in a wedding, but in order to be successful, it's got to be incredibly diversified and above all—relevant. While American standards like Sinatra and great Swing music are perennial crowd pleasers, bridal couples also want to hear the music that's vital to their generation: everything from the classic ' 80s to current hits by performers like Maroon 5 and Bruno Mars, and their favorite contemporary dance songs. In the end, we want everyone to be totally exhausted because they just can't stop dancing," laughs George.

Fifth Avenue, which has orchestrated performances for heads of state and Fortune 500 corporations throughout the U.S., along with their extensive wedding clientele, does not do assembly-line presentations. The challenge, as Banfalvi sees it, is to respect clients' wishes and budgetary constraints while treating the music for each aspect of the wedding as a specialization.

It begins with the ceremony. Music sets the tone. Classical chamber ensembles connote elegance; keyboard or guitar ensembles underscore romance or theme; gospel choirs—like the one they used for the film, *Leap of Faith*—inspire hallelujahs and ethnic instrumentations celebrate diversity. All of these evoke feelings of family, spirituality and friendship. Then comes the cocktail hour, the prelude to partying. Although many clients favor light jazz, Fifth Avenue offers a plethora of musical combinations including small reggae bands, digital jazz, island calypso groups, passionate Gypsy Kings-style ensembles and a variety of cool vocal groups. And finally, there's the reception. "Wedding reception music should reflect the bride and groom's musical souls," explains George. Whether it's a front line of four singers who've been with Earth, Wind & Fire, a guitar player who sounds like Dave Matthews, a vocal/horn combo that conjures up the best of Tony Bennett or Nat King Cole, or any kind of groove music that creates the desire to get up and party, Fifth Avenue is pleased to provide it.

"George and his staff are the ultimate professionals," says an admiring associate. "I've been in the entertainment business for 25 years and have worked with bands, orchestras and entertainment companies throughout the U.S. Fifth Avenue's musicians are the best I have ever had the pleasure of working with. Their skill, talent and class are unsurpassed."

"Wedding clients place the fate of their affair in our hands, and we're grateful for that trust," concludes George. "Seeing the look on a bride's face as she watches her family and friends dancing, partying and being utterly joyous with each other—there's nothing like it."

818/368-3299
info@fifthavenuemusic.com
www.fifthavenuemusic.com

Premiere Party Rents

Tables, chairs, china, linens, lights, tents … whatever your needs for a grand celebration, Premiere Party Rents is ready to fulfill them. "They keep their promises and everything is perfect," says a client who uses them for most events, including a recent sit-down dinner party for 2,000 guests. "They're an excellent, reliable resource with a vast selection of inventory and a terrific service track record." Another customer declares, "They get the job done, and it's done right."

Add advice and a generous helping hand to the list of services rendered. Owner Sandy Radicevic is devoted to making sure her clients' every wish is granted. She's been in the business for nearly 30 years, and she is passionate about her profession. "I love parties," she admits. "I love making peoples' dreams come true, and I love seeing the smile on their faces." Known for her creativity and quick response, Sandy is also applauded for her industry knowledge and her research. "If Premiere Party Rents doesn't have the product in inventory, Sandy will go to the ends of the earth to find it," reports one event planner. "She's very service-oriented and wants to take care of the client, getting them whatever they ask for." Another attests, "If you have an idea, no matter how simple or complex, Sandy will find a way to make it happen. She always comes from a place of 'Yes!' I don't know how she does it."

Take, for example, the time Sandy handled a company's holiday party and turned a Southern California backyard into a Winter Wonderland, complete with a little train, ice rink, snow machine (it snowed the entire time), and hundreds of Christmas trees. When the party was over, the grass went back to green and all the Christmas trees went to children who wouldn't ordinarily have them. Or how about the elegant tailgate party that PPR tented and furnished with sofas, bars, plasma TVs, and video games? "I think

Premiere Party Rents is the best-kept secret in town," confides a caterer who has worked with them for many years. "They provide everything: lower prices, quality rentals, timely quotes, pleasant office staff, and efficient, on-time deliveries and installations."

Wedding clients agree. "Frankly, planning my wedding was the most stressful task of my life," confesses a bride, "but Sandy made it so tolerable. My wedding was also a very do-it-yourself type affair, and I was on a tight budget. I'm so happy to say that the day was a huge success, and I am so impressed at how it turned out. Without Sandy's help and attention I don't think it would have turned out nearly as well as it did."

"Because of her I only had to hire a day-of coordinator," announces a bride-to-be. "Sandy helped me find the venue and put together my vendor team. That's the great thing about working with Sandy—you don't just get a rental contact, you really get a wedding planner. She comes up with great ideas and tips, and she always has a plan B. She really goes above and beyond. My wedding is three months away and it's been such a stress-free process. I owe that all to Sandy!"

310/670-3400
info@premierepartyrents.com
www.premierepartyrents.com

A1 Party

A1 Party is a flexible, all-inclusive shop with expertise in everything you need to produce a spectacular event: layouts, logistics, permits, construction, installation and design. They have a carefully maintained collection of unique event items, and their experienced team has an eye for interior design—they can transform any space into an unforgettable setting.

Trends in the event industry are constantly evolving, and A1's inventory keeps up with the changes. Their 40,000-square-foot warehouse is fully stocked with decorative chairs, specialty linens, elegant tableware, theatrical lighting, chandeliers, elegant wood-finished tables, fine china, crystal stemware, and so much more.

A1's event specialists will work closely with you to ensure no detail is overlooked, and that you have all the equipment and support you need for a stress-free affair. They'll help you select just the right elements so that your event looks exactly as you envisioned it and reflects your unique personality.

One of the remarkable things about A1 is that if you want something that's not in their warehouse or readily available elsewhere, there's a good chance they can manufacture it for you. They regularly produce custom items including light-up bars, lounge furniture, special tent designs, and props.

Another benefit of hiring A1 Party is that they've produced events at venues all over Southern California and know the ins and outs of working at each of them. Their experienced coordinators and field crew are familiar with the strict rules, regulations, and time constraints involved, which enables them to set up and take down your event in a smooth and efficient manner.

Clients agree: A1 Party does much more than provide the window dressings for parties—they literally 'make' the celebration. "I truly enjoy working with this company," says a client. "They've always gone above and beyond. I would recommend them to my sister and best friend—and I have. They are reliable, easy to work with, respectful, and their customer service is excellent!! They really try to get to know you as a person."

One father of the bride recollects, "Our event coordinator said that in 18 years she had never seen the venue look so beautiful. My daughter was ecstatic." A bride who selected them after a great deal of research into other vendors also couldn't be happier, saying, "They were accommodating and friendly and their prices were reasonable. It was a great experience. They totally transformed the space and made our budget wedding look posh and magical."

You're invited to visit their warehouse and show-room to gather ideas and information.

866/217-2789
theguide@a1partyrental.com
www.a1partyrental.com

B&G Photography

Jen Berggren started B&G Photography to explore a non-formulaic approach to wedding photography. "When I'm documenting a wedding, I don't go in with a preconceived notion of what I'm going to shoot," she says. "I draw my inspiration from the venue, the décor, and especially the couple—I want to capture what's unique about them and the day they've created."

A graduate of Santa Monica College's photography department, Jen's able to harness her innate artistic sensibility and her professional training to deliver candid, humorous, and soulful shots. There's no such thing as a typical wedding image. She's developed a more open-ended and fluid way of working that allows events to unfold naturally. Invariably, this method yields images that reflect the essence of each person, the atmosphere of the setting, and the immediacy of what she sees through her lens. And from the sweet, wordless looks couples give each other to the tender inscription inside a wedding band, there's not much Jen doesn't see.

She traffics in laughs, smiles, sideways glances, and the festive nature of every ceremony and reception; stiff or extremely posed pictures are nowhere to be found. "I prefer to be a fly on the wall, recording moments as they happen instead of creating them," says Jen.

Her fun-loving personality also offers a counterpoint to the intensity of the special day. "She just has a way with people," says a bride. "She's great at working with everyone." Jen feels that the couple should be the center of attention, adding, "My ego always takes a back seat—this day is about them, not about me."

Whatever she's doing, it's turning her clients into a legion of fans. "Jen's simply a blast to be around," attests one very happy bride. "I felt like she became our friend."

310/441-1581
hello@bandgphotography.com
www.bandgphotography.com

 **PHOTOGRAPHY**

BANDGPHOTOGRAPHY.COM
310-441-1581

Epic Imagery

Take one look at the wedding photos from Epic Imagery and you will certainly be swept off your feet. Photographer Danny Baker's passion is people, and he's clearly a master at capturing the energy and emotion that connects every one of us.

It's no wonder clients are head over heels for this talented professional and his team. Inspired early on by his mother's artistry, he explains that, even though his focus was sports, he always had an eye for art, architecture, fashion and beauty. Later on, a master-apprentice relationship with a photographer turned a natural affinity into a well-developed craft. "Photography is what I'm meant to do," says Danny. I'm carried away by the work. I pour everything into finding the beauty of an event and providing a commentary on joy and celebration."

And it shows—not just in his photos, which draw torrents of praise from clients, but in the graceful and generous way Danny handles every task. "Everybody loves him, just everyone," says a colleague. "His images are fabulous. We've been working on an upcoming wedding and every time he calls, I'm happy all day long—he just leaves a big old smile on your face!" Brides agree. "I've been a bridesmaid in six weddings and part of numerous others," recollects one of his client-fans. "I've never encountered a photographer that was as personable, attentive and fun as Danny. My wedding party felt like they were Hollywood movie stars, because we were having so much fun doing the photo shoots. Time flies when you're with him. After our engagement session with Danny, my now-husband and I both walked away saying it was one of the most fun days we've ever had."

High praise, but the ultimate proof is in the photos. Danny's extraordinary and unexpected magazine-quality images sparkle with vitality.

"Every photo reflects my clients," he explains. "It's all about them. The creative process is not formulaic. It's complex and riddled with excitement. I'm building stories about life, and life is amazing—it's epic!" His brilliance at documenting cherished moments and relationships may be why Danny's clients stick with him from engagement to wedding to family photos, and why they're eager to share him with family and friends.

"He's a gem," declares one of the many brides he's photographed. "You can't afford not to hire him!"

"I cannot say enough about how wonderful Danny is both personally and professionally," adds another. "He is an amazing photographer, so creative, so personable and just so great to work with! He really takes the time to get to know you and what you want. Each of my bridesmaids has said that they've made it their goal to hire Danny when they get married—now all they need are the fiancés!"

818/832-2700
info@epicimagery.com
www.epicimagery.com

EPICIMAGERY.COM | 818.832.2700

Indexes

Event Venues

a

The Abbey on Fifth Avenue 494
Agoura Hills/Calabasas Community Center 126
Aliso Viejo Conference Center 306
Aliso Viejo Country Club 308
Altadena Town & Country Club 226
Anaheim Hills Golf Course Clubhouse 314
Aquarium of the Pacific 256
Ayres Hotel & Suites Costa Mesa/Newport Beach 320

b

Balboa Bay Resort 376
Beachcomber Cafe at Crystal Cove 394
Bluewater Grill 290
Braemar Country Club 144
Brookside Golf Club 234

c

Ca' Del Sole Ristorante 136
Café Mozart 398
Calabasas Country Club 128
Calamigos Equestrian 122
Calamigos Ranch Malibu 194
California Yacht Club 206
Cambria Pines Lodge 54
Canary Hotel Santa Barbara 64
Canyon Crest Country Club 452
Casa del Mar 212
Casino Ballroom
     A Santa Catalina Island Company Wedding Venue 152
Castle Green 236
Cellar360 Paso Robles 56
Center Club 322
Chart House Dana Point 330
Chart House Redondo Beach 292
Chester Washington Golf Course 164
Christmas House 446
Chula Vista Golf Course 470
City Club Los Angeles 166
Cliffs at Laguna Village 362
Colette's at the Meridian Club 338

Colony Palms Hotel 530

Coto de Caza Golf & Racquet Club 326

Coyote Hills Golf Course 340

Crowne Plaza Redondo Beach
and Marina Hotel 294

Crowne Plaza Ventura Beach Hotel 108

Cypress Sea Cove 196

d

Descanso Beach Club
A Santa Catalina Island Company Wedding Venue 154

Descanso Gardens 230

Desert Falls Country Club 522

Desert Willow Golf Resort 524

Diamond Bar Center 436

Diamond Bar Golf Course 438

DoubleTree by Hilton Claremont 424

DoubleTree by Hilton Los Angeles Downtown 168

Dove Canyon Golf Club 336

Duke's Malibu 198

e

Eagle Glen Golf Club 428

Eagle's Nest Restaurant & Banquets 328

Earl Burns Miller Japanese Garden
California State University, Long Beach 258

The Ebell of Los Angeles 170

Eden Gardens Weddings 86

El Camino Country Club 490

El Dorado Park Golf Course 260

Electra Cruises 378

Elings Park 66

Environmental Nature Center 380

Estancia La Jolla Hotel & Spa 480

f

Fairmont Newport Beach 382

Five Crowns Restaurant 318

Friendly Hills Country Club 222

g

Gainey Vineyard 74

Good Shepherd Chapel
at Concordia University Irvine 356

The Grand Ballroom & Civic Auditorium
at the Pasadena Convention Center 238

Grand Tradition Estate
Beverly Mansion & Arbor Terrace 476

h

The Hacienda.. 404
Happy Trails Garden 240
Harborside Restaurant & Grand Ballroom 384
Hartley Botanica...102
Heritage Museum of Orange County.................................... 406
Heritage Palms.. 520
The Hills Hotel... 372
Hilton Los Angeles Airport 172
Historic Cree Estate 532
The Historic Park Ballroom and Park Place........................... 58
Hollywood Hotel® 160
Hornblower Cruises & Events, Marina del Rey..................... 208
Hornblower Cruises & Events, Newport Beach.................... 386
Hornblower Cruises & Events, San Diego............................ 496
Hotel Laguna... 364
Hotel Ménage...310
Hummingbird Nest... 140
Hyatt Regency Huntington Beach
Resort and Spa.. 348
Hyatt Regency Irvine 358
Hyatt Regency Newport Beach.. 388
Hyatt Santa Barbara... 68
Hyatt The Pike 262
Hyatt Westlake Plaza in Thousand Oaks 114

i

Indian Wells Country Club..516
InterContinental Los Angeles Century City...........................174
Island Hotel Newport Beach.. 390

j

June Mountain Resort... 48

k

Karl Strauss Brewery Gardens 498
Knollwood Golf Course 132

l

La Cañada Flintridge Country Club 232
La Casa del Camino.. 366
La Jolla Beach & Tennis Club 482

La Jolla Cove Suites 484

La Jolla Shores Hotel 486

La Mirada Golf Course 360

La Venta Inn.. 278

Laguna Cliffs Marriott Resort & Spa 332

Lake Arrowhead Resort and Spa
    An Autograph Collection by Marriott 414

Lake Oak Meadows, Weddings and Events 458

Lakewood Country Club 254

Las Casuelas Nuevas... 540

Lawry's The Prime Rib 158

The Legendary Park Plaza....................................... 176

Le Méridien Delfina Santa Monica............................ 216

Leoness Cellars 460

Limoneira Ranch.. 96

Lindley-Scott House and Gardens 228

Loews Santa Monica Beach Hotel 214

Lomas Santa Fe Country Club................................. 510

The Los Angeles Athletic Club.............................. 178

Los Angeles Union Station 180

Los Coyotes Country Club...................................... 316

Los Serranos Golf and Country Club 420

Los Verdes Golf Course 284

Luxe Sunset Boulevard Hotel................................. 182

m

Malibou Lake Mountain Club.................................. 120

Malibu West Beach Club 200

Mammoth Mountain Resort..................................... 50

Manhattan Beach Marriott....................................... 272

Marbella Country Club 400

The Marine Room.. 488

Matteo's Restaurant 184

McCormick Home Ranch 78

Menifee Lakes Country Club.................................... 440

Michael's Tuscany Room.. 300

Middle Ranch 134

Miramonte Resort & Spa 518

Mission Hills Country Club 542

The Mission Inn Hotel & Spa................................... 454

The Mitten Building.. 450

Monterey Country Club... 526

Morgan Run Club & Resort 492

Mountain Meadows Golf Course 444

MountainGate Country Club 186

Muckenthaler Mansion 342

n

Newhall Mansion 94

Noor 242

o

The O'Donnell House at The Willows Historic Inn 534

Old Ranch Country Club 408

Orfila Vineyards and Winery 472

Oviatt Penthouse 188

p

Pacific Hills Banquet and Catering 374

Padua Hills Theatre 426

Palm Garden Hotel 104

Palm Valley Country Club 528

Palos Verdes Golf Club 280

Petersen Automotive Museum
    and Rooftop Penthouse 190

Pickwick Gardens 124

Pine Rose Weddings and Cabin Resort 416

Porter Valley Country Club 138

The Portofino Hotel & Marina 296

The Prado at Balboa Park 500

Puddingstone Resort 248

q

Queen Mary 264

r

Radisson Newport Beach 392

The Ranch House 92

Rancho Bernardo Inn 502

Rancho de las Palmas 88

Rancho Las Lomas 410

Recreation Park 18 Golf Course 266

The Redondo Beach Historic Library 298

Renaissance Long Beach Hotel 268

Rincon Beach Club 62

The Riviera Country Club 210

s

Saddle Peak Lodge 130

Saddlerock Ranch and Vineyard.. 202

San Diego Zoo Safari Park 474

San Dimas Canyon Golf Course 250

San Juan Hills Golf Club 402

Santa Barbara Zoological Gardens 70

SeaCliff Country Club.. 350

Serendipity 442

Serra Center 80

Serra Cross Park..110

[seven-degrees] 368

Shade Hotel..274

Shadowridge Country Club...512

Sheraton Anaheim Hotel 312

Sheraton Pasadena.. 244

Sheraton San Diego Hotel & Marina................................. 504

Sheraton Universal.. 146

Shorebreak Hotel..352

Shutters on the Beach 218

Skylinks at Long Beach 270

Smoke Tree Ranch... 536

South Coast Botanic Garden.. 282

Spencer's Restaurant
    and the Bougainvillea Room... 538

Sportsmen's Lodge Events Center.....................................142

Spring Valley Lake Country Club....................................... 466

St. Regis Resort, Monarch Beach 334

Star of the Sea Event Center 506

Summit House 344

Sunset Hills Country Club... 106

The Sunset Restaurant... 204

Surf & Sand Resort... 370

t

Taglyan Cultural Complex..162

Temecula Creek Inn 462

Torrance Cultural Arts Center.. 302

Tropical Paradise Camarillo 82

Trump National Golf Club, Los Angeles................................ 286

u

Unitarian Society of Santa Barbara 72

The University Club Atop Symphony Towers 508

v

The Veranda at Green River Golf Club 430

Verandas Beach House 276

Vibiana 192

Victoria Gardens Cultural Center 448

The Victorian 220

The Villa Del Sol 346

Vintage Weddings
    at the Ventura County Agriculture Museum 98

w

The Walnut Grove at Tierra Rejada Farms 90

The Waterfront Beach Resort
    A Hilton Hotel 354

Wayfarers Chapel 288

Wedgewood at The Retreat 432

Wedgewood Buenaventura 112

Wedgewood Fallbrook 478

Wedgewood Glen Ivy 434

Wedgewood Indian Hills 456

Wedgewood San Clemente 396

Wedgewood Sterling Hills 84

Wedgewood Upland Hills 464

Wedgewood Vellano 422

The Westin Mission Hills Golf Resort and Spa 544

Westin South Coast Plaza 324

Westlake Village Inn 116

Westminster Presbyterian Church 246

Wood Ranch Golf Club 100

Woodland Hills Country Club 148

Event Venues by Region

Eastern Sierras

June Lake   June Mountain Resort 48
Mammoth Lakes   Mammoth Mountain Resort 50

Central Coast

Cambria   Cambria Pines Lodge.. 54
Paso Robles   Cellar360 Paso Robles.. 56
                       The Historic Park Ballroom and Park Place 58

Santa Barbara Area

Carpinteria   Rincon Beach Club 62
Santa Barbara   Canary Hotel Santa Barbara 64
                       Elings Park.. 66
                       Hyatt Santa Barbara 68
                       Santa Barbara Zoological Gardens 70
                       Unitarian Society of Santa Barbara 72
Santa Ynez   Gainey Vineyard 74

Ventura Area

Camarillo   McCormick Home Ranch.. 78
                       Serra Center.. 80
                       Tropical Paradise Camarillo...................................... 82
                       Wedgewood Sterling Hills 84
Moorpark   Eden Gardens Weddings 86
                       Rancho de las Palmas 88
                       The Walnut Grove at Tierra Rejada Farms 90
Ojai   The Ranch House.. 92
Piru   Newhall Mansion 94
Santa Paula   Limoneira Ranch 96

Santa Paula	Vintage Weddings at the Ventura County Agriculture Museum	98
Simi Valley	Wood Ranch Golf Club	100
Somis	Hartley Botanica	102
Thousand Oaks	Palm Garden Hotel	104
	Sunset Hills Country Club	106
Ventura	Crowne Plaza Ventura Beach Hotel	108
	Serra Cross Park	110
Ventura	Wedgewood Buenaventura	112
Westlake Village	Hyatt Westlake Plaza in Thousand Oaks	114
	Westlake Village Inn	116

San Fernando Valley

Agoura	Malibou Lake Mountain Club	120
Burbank	Calamigos Equestrian	122
	Pickwick Gardens	124
Calabasas	Agoura Hills/Calabasas Community Center	126
	Calabasas Country Club	128
	Saddle Peak Lodge	130
Granada Hills	Knollwood Golf Course	132
Lake View Terrace	Middle Ranch	134
North Hollywood	Ca' Del Sole Ristorante	136
Porter Ranch	Porter Valley Country Club	138
Santa Susana	Hummingbird Nest	140
Studio City	Sportsmen's Lodge Events Center	142
Tarzana	Braemar Country Club	144
Universal City	Sheraton Universal	146
Woodland Hills	Woodland Hills Country Club	148

Santa Catalina Island

Avalon	Casino Ballroom, A Santa Catalina Island Company Wedding Venue	152
	Descanso Beach Club, A Santa Catalina Island Company Wedding Venue	154

Los Angeles Area

Beverly Hills   Lawry's The Prime Rib 158

Hollywood   Hollywood Hotel® 160

Taglyan Cultural Complex 162

Los Angeles   Chester Washington Golf Course........................... 164

City Club Los Angeles... 166

DoubleTree by Hilton Los Angeles Downtown...... 168

The Ebell of Los Angeles..170

Hilton Los Angeles Airport.......................................172

InterContinental Los Angeles Century City 174

The Legendary Park Plaza..176

The Los Angeles Athletic Club 178

Los Angeles Union Station...................................... 180

Luxe Sunset Boulevard Hotel 182

Matteo's Restaurant 184

MountainGate Country Club 186

Oviatt Penthouse.. 188

Petersen Automotive Museum
   and Rooftop Penthouse 190

Vibiana..192

Malibu   Calamigos Ranch Malibu 194

Cypress Sea Cove... 196

Duke's Malibu 198

Malibu West Beach Club.. 200

Saddlerock Ranch and Vineyard............................. 202

The Sunset Restaurant 204

Marina del Rey   California Yacht Club.. 206

Hornblower Cruises & Events, Marina del Rey...... 208

Pacific Palisades The Riviera Country Club...210

Santa Monica   Casa del Mar.. 212

Loews Santa Monica Beach Hotel...........................214

Le Méridien Delfina Santa Monica...........................216

Shutters on the Beach..218

The Victorian.. 220

Whittier   Friendly Hills Country Club 222

San Gabriel Valley

Altadena	Altadena Town & Country Club	226
Azusa	Lindley-Scott House and Gardens	228
La Cañada Flintridge	Descanso Gardens	230
	La Cañada Flintridge Country Club	232
Pasadena	Brookside Golf Club	234
	Castle Green	236
	The Grand Ballroom & Civic Auditorium at the Pasadena Convention Center	238
	Happy Trails Garden	240
	Noor	242
	Sheraton Pasadena	244
	Westminster Presbyterian Church	246
San Dimas	Puddingstone Resort	248
	San Dimas Canyon Golf Course	250

South Bay

Lakewood	Lakewood Country Club	254
Long Beach	Aquarium of the Pacific	256
	Earl Burns Miller Japanese Garden	258
	El Dorado Park Golf Course	260
	Hyatt The Pike	262
	Queen Mary	264
	Recreation Park 18 Golf Course	266
	Renaissance Long Beach Hotel	268
	Skylinks at Long Beach	270
Manhattan Beach	Manhattan Beach Marriott	272
	Shade Hotel	274
	Verandas Beach House	276
Palos Verdes Estates	La Venta Inn	278
	Palos Verdes Golf Club	280
Palos Verdes Peninsula	South Coast Botanic Garden	282
Rancho Palos Verdes	Los Verdes Golf Course	284
	Trump National Golf Club, Los Angeles	286
	Wayfarers Chapel	288

Redondo Beach	Bluewater Grill	290
	Chart House Redondo Beach	292
	Crowne Plaza Redondo Beach and Marina Hotel	294
	The Portofino Hotel & Marina	296
	The Redondo Beach Historic Library	298
San Pedro	Michael's Tuscany Room	300
Torrance	Torrance Cultural Arts Center	302

Orange County

Aliso Viejo	Aliso Viejo Conference Center	306
	Aliso Viejo Country Club	308
Anaheim	Hotel Ménage	310
	Sheraton Anaheim Hotel	312
Anaheim Hills	Anaheim Hills Golf Course Clubhouse	314
Buena Park	Los Coyotes Country Club	316
Corona del Mar	Five Crowns Restaurant	318
Costa Mesa	Ayres Hotel & Suites Costa Mesa/Newport Beach	320
	Center Club	322
	Westin South Coast Plaza	324
Coto de Caza	Coto de Caza Golf & Racquet Club	326
Cypress	Eagle's Nest Restaurant & Banquets	328
Dana Point	Chart House Dana Point	330
	Laguna Cliffs Marriott Resort & Spa	332
	St. Regis Resort, Monarch Beach	334
Dove Canyon	Dove Canyon Golf Club	336
Fullerton	Colette's at the Meridian Club	338
	Coyote Hills Golf Course	340
	Muckenthaler Mansion	342
	Summit House	344
	The Villa Del Sol	346
Huntington Beach	Hyatt Regency Huntington Beach Resort and Spa	348
	SeaCliff Country Club	350
	Shorebreak Hotel	352
	The Waterfront Beach Resort A Hilton Hotel	354

Irvine	Good Shepherd Chapel at Concordia University Irvine	356
Irvine	Hyatt Regency Irvine	358
La Mirada	La Mirada Golf Course	360
Laguna Beach	Cliffs at Laguna Village	362
	Hotel Laguna	364
	La Casa del Camino	366
	[seven-degrees]	368
	Surf & Sand Resort	370
Laguna Hills	The Hills Hotel	372
	Pacific Hills Banquet and Catering	374
Newport Beach	Balboa Bay Resort	376
	Electra Cruises	378
	Environmental Nature Center	380
	Fairmont Newport Beach	382
	Harborside Restaurant & Grand Ballroom	384
	Hornblower Cruises & Events, Newport Beach	386
	Hyatt Regency Newport Beach	388
	Island Hotel Newport Beach	390
	Radisson Newport Beach	392
Newport Coast	Beachcomber Cafe at Crystal Cove	394
San Clemente	Wedgewood San Clemente	396
San Juan Capistrano	Café Mozart	398
	Marbella Country Club	400
	San Juan Hills Golf Club	402
Santa Ana	The Hacienda	404
	Heritage Museum of Orange County	406
Seal Beach	Old Ranch Country Club	408
Silverado	Rancho Las Lomas	410

Mountain Lakes Area

Lake Arrowhead	Lake Arrowhead Resort and Spa An Autograph Collection by Marriott	414
	Pine Rose Weddings and Cabin Resort	416

Riverside/Inland Empire

Chino Hills   Los Serranos Golf and Country Club...................... 420

Wedgewood Vellano.. 422

Claremont   DoubleTree by Hilton Claremont 424

Padua Hills Theatre 426

Corona   Eagle Glen Golf Club.. 428

The Veranda at Green River Golf Club................... 430

Wedgewood at The Retreat 432

Wedgewood Glen Ivy.. 434

Diamond Bar   Diamond Bar Center.. 436

Diamond Bar Golf Course....................................... 438

Menifee   Menifee Lakes Country Club 440

Oak Glen   Serendipity... 442

Pomona   Mountain Meadows Golf Course 444

Rancho Cucamonga   Christmas House.. 446

Victoria Gardens Cultural Center........................... 448

Redlands   The Mitten Building.. 450

Riverside   Canyon Crest Country Club....................................452

The Mission Inn Hotel & Spa 454

Wedgewood Indian Hills.. 456

Temecula   Lake Oak Meadows, Weddings and Events............ 458

Leoness Cellars... 460

Temecula Creek Inn.. 462

Upland   Wedgewood Upland Hills 464

Victorville   Spring Valley Lake Country Club............................ 466

San Diego Area

Bonita   Chula Vista Golf Course 470

Escondido   Orfila Vineyards and Winery 472

San Diego Zoo Safari Park 474

Fallbrook   Grand Tradition Estate
Beverly Mansion & Arbor Terrace........................476

Wedgewood Fallbrook.. 478

La Jolla	Estancia La Jolla Hotel & Spa	480
	La Jolla Beach & Tennis Club	482
	La Jolla Cove Suites	484
	La Jolla Shores Hotel	486
	The Marine Room	488
Oceanside	El Camino Country Club	490
Rancho Santa Fe	Morgan Run Club & Resort	492
San Diego	The Abbey on Fifth Avenue	494
	Hornblower Cruises & Events, San Diego	496
	Karl Strauss Brewery Gardens	498
	The Prado at Balboa Park	500
	Rancho Bernardo Inn	502
	Sheraton San Diego Hotel & Marina	504
	Star of the Sea Event Center	506
	The University Club Atop Symphony Towers	508
Solana Beach	Lomas Santa Fe Country Club	510
Vista	Shadowridge Country Club	512

Greater Palm Springs

Indian Wells	Indian Wells Country Club	516
	Miramonte Resort & Spa	518
Indio	Heritage Palms	520
Palm Desert	Desert Falls Country Club	522
	Desert Willow Golf Resort	524
	Monterey Country Club	526
	Palm Valley Country Club	528
Palm Springs	Colony Palms Hotel	530
	Historic Cree Estate	532
	The O'Donnell House at The Willows Historic Inn	534
	Smoke Tree Ranch	536
	Spencer's Restaurant and the Bougainvillea Room	538
Rancho Mirage	Las Casuelas Nuevas	540
	Mission Hills Country Club	542
	The Westin Mission Hills Golf Resort and Spa	544

Event Services

a

A1 Party...566

b

B&G Photography...568
Bob Gail Special Events...558

c

Contemporary Catering & Event Production 554

e

Epic Imagery..570

f

Fifth Avenue Orchestras & Entertainment............562

m

Mobile Disc Music...560

n

New York Food Company......................................556

p

Premiere Party Rents...564

About the Authors

Jan Brenner has co-authored and edited all of Hopscotch Press' books. Although she received a BA in English from UC Berkeley, she backed into writing only after spending ten years in social work and four in publishing. Along the way she got a couple of other degrees that have never been put to official use. A lifelong dilettante, she's quasi-conversant in 3.1 languages, dabbles in domestic pursuits and travels whenever she gets the chance.

Jolene Rae Harrington has been with Hopscotch Press since she first fell in love with their groundbreaking publications while planning her own beach wedding in 1995. In addition to co-authoring and editing the *Here Comes The Guide* books, she serves as Director of Creative Content for HereComesTheGuide.com and is a frequently quoted expert on the bridal industry. Beyond her work at Here Comes The Guide, Jolene's writing credits range from an award-winning television script to a best-selling children's computer game. She lives in her native Southern California with her husband and various animal children.

About the Founder

Lynn Broadwell is an author, publisher and former marketing professional for the special events industry. Her company, Hopscotch Press, provides a website and publications designed to meet the needs of the general public and special event professional. Ms. Broadwell has been featured in many articles and has appeared on radio and TV.

Ms. Broadwell is a graduate of UC Berkeley, with both an undergraduate degree in landscape architecture and a masters degree in business.

Virtual tours let you visit event venues without leaving home!

Use your computer to visit hundreds of sites without ever leaving home. Each tour gives you a 360-degree view of a venue's event spaces—it's like standing in the middle of the room and turning in a complete circle so you can see everything. By taking a "tour" online, you can quickly decide if the location you're viewing is a good fit for you.

See a variety of spaces

360-degree moving images

Virtual tours at www.HereComesTheGuide.com

Dresses by Designer Loft, New York; Photo by Judy Pak

HereComesTheGuide.com also lists Designer Wedding Dress Trunk Shows and Sample Sales!

Trunk shows offer you a chance to shop a designer's entire collection during a personal consultation with style experts—it's free, and frankly, it feels fabulous to be the center of attention. Many of these events also offer sales incentives.

Sample sales feature deep discounts on in-stock bridal gowns. Though sizes and styles are more limited, it's a fantastic way to get a dreamy designer look for less.

And don't forget: There are also Trunk Shows and Sample Sales for fashion accessories, bridesmaid dresses, cocktail dresses and formalwear for Moms, too!

Notes

Notes